To See Paris and Die

To See Paris and Die

THE SOVIET LIVES OF
WESTERN CULTURE

Eleonory Gilburd

THE BELKNAP PRESS OF
HARVARD UNIVERSITY PRESS

Cambridge, Massachusetts
London, England
2018

Library of Congress Cataloging-in-Publication Data

Names: Gilburd, Eleonory, author.
Title: To see Paris and die : the Soviet lives of Western culture / Eleonory Gilburd.
Description: Cambridge, Massachusetts : The Belknap Press of Harvard University Press, 2018. |
Includes bibliographical references and index.
Identifiers: LCCN 2018009238 | ISBN 9780674980716 (cloth)
Subjects: LCSH: Soviet Union—Civilization—Western influences. | Soviet Union—
History—1953–1985. | Western countries—Foreign public opinion, Soviet. |
Public opinion—Soviet Union. | Soviets (People)—Attitudes.
Classification: LCC DK276 .G55 2018 | DDC 303.48 / 247018210904—dc23
LC record available at https://lccn.loc.gov/2018009238

For Anthony
For my parents
In memory of my grandfather

Contents

Note on Transliteration

I have followed the Library of Congress system for transliterating Russian words, with the exception of names standard in English. Thus, I have written Ilya (not Il'ia), Ehrenburg (not Erenburg), Mayakovsky (not Maiakovskii), Intourist (not Inturist), Gogol (not Gogol'), and so on.

To See Paris and Die

Introduction

In the mid-1950s, hundreds of Western books, films, paintings, and sounds arrived in the Soviet Union. They arrived during its remarkable opening to the world after Stalin's death and the xenophobia of his last decade. And they came to stay, becoming a defining feature of late Soviet life. For the next thirty years, cityscapes, pastimes, and relationships would be shaped by an obsession with things Western.

This book follows the Soviet lives of Western novels, films, and paintings primarily during the 1950s and 1960s. Known as the Thaw, this period was pivotal in the centuries-long process of Russia's Westernization. In the quantity of Western images and artifacts, in their enduring presence, the Thaw-era opening to the West can only be compared to that initiated by Peter the Great. Unlike the Petrine revolution, however, this was a nonviolent moment of Westernization. Until then, access to Western cultures had been largely a privileged domain, whether in imperial Russia or in the Soviet Union. But during the Thaw, social and intellectual exclusivity gave way to widespread dissemination. The 1950s also marked the Soviet Union's entry into the international networks of film festivals, exhibitions, and soundscapes. In all these ways, the Thaw turned around the story of Russian Westernization.

Extraordinary at first, Western imports became an intimate part of Soviet cities and biographies. Western texts, sounds, and images entered countless apartments as hard-to-find books, postcards of film stars, tunes on the radio, and late-night television shows. Pop songs and instrumental music hailing from the West framed popular Soviet programs, while the love theme from *The Godfather* filled the pauses. Every evening, the TV weather forecast played André Popp's "Manchester et Liverpool" against the background of Soviet landscapes. To understand how the Soviets made sense of what they read and saw, I rely on the notion of translation—as a mechanism of transfer, a process of domestication, and a metaphor for the

1

ways cultures interact.[1] Meanings emerged at the confluence of a translated text and Soviet context. To a large degree, then, the Soviet pleasures
in things Western were "the pleasures of recognition."[2]

However, this story ends in a pervasive sense of loss, as Soviet citizens
themselves became foreigners. "To see Paris and die," the Soviet version
of "Vedi Napoli e poi muori," was a dream and a death wish. The idiom
meant that Paris was the ultimate fulfillment of life's aspirations, with
nothing else left to experience. And the idiom also intimated the willing-
ness to pay with one's life: death was the ultimate price for seeing Paris.
Soviet translation culture, as well as restrictions on information and cross-
border mobility, generated and maintained the Western utopia. That
Atlantis, the Soviet West, sank together with the Soviet Union. After the
disintegration of the USSR, the cherished illusion of familiarity deteriorated into a profound sense of dispossession. The Western books, names,
and images that had become Soviet household belongings turned out to
have been somebody else's cultural property all along.

For three centuries, Russian politicians and intellectuals have defined the
country's future vis-à-vis the West. Both in imperial and Soviet societies,
the West had been alternatively a tool for self-examination, an exemplar,
or a bogeyman in discussions of domestic concerns. Russians measured
their position on the historical timeline against European notions of progress and found their country lacking. Most of Russia's reformist attempts
aimed to align the nation with European developments and with European political and social thought. The West has been a mirage, a temptation, a supranational location of the all-human, and a savior.[3] At the same
time, images of the materialistic and philistine West, the West of the
Antichrist, the West in crisis, have been similarly enduring.[4] The West has
been Russia's "to be or not to be."

Westernization had always been the work of the Russian state and also
the modern state's progenitor.[5] The reforms of the archetypical Western-
izer Peter the Great established Russia's awkward place in the world: a great
military power on the one hand, and on the other, Europe's dependency—
at least in the eyes of educated Russians. Russia's rise to great power status
relied on Western learning, tools, experts, dress, and vocabulary in fields
as diverse as shipbuilding, medicine, administration, and architecture.[6]
Peter the Great set in motion a characteristic feature of Russian reformism:
the compression of centuries of Western technological, aesthetic, and

political advancements into the Russian here and now. Henceforth, as Russian reformers looked to European models, reforms entailed information diversity, travel, and other cross-border contacts.[7] During the Great Reforms of the 1860s, legislation proposals typically began with a memo on the historical evolution of an issue in Russia *and* in Europe. This comparative ethos pervaded debates in scholarly societies and literary journals. Henceforth, counterreforms, too, implied not only modifications of earlier reforms, but also cultural isolationism and xenophobia.[8]

Peter the Great foisted Western dress and learning upon an unwilling population.[9] The iconic image of Westernization as a bodily and spiritual violation remains the order to cut the boyars' beards. Adversaries of the Petrine reforms—and of Western imports generally—came to voice their opposition in a moral language. Believers resisted Westernization by evasion, escape, and exorcising the devil; conservative elites turned their pens against European vices.[10] "The corruption of morals" endured as a persistent theme in writings about Western imports and their Russian consumers.[11] The figures of a provincial fashionista and a well-traveled, bored fop became a staple in Russian literature. From the late eighteenth century onward, writers satirized Westernization as trivial, limited to material goods and trendy ideas, a surface concealing boorishness, brutality, and servility.[12] Russian classical literature pioneered the view of superficial Westernization, which did not alter the autocratic political foundations and did not touch the serf majority of the population.

Europe was loved as passionately as it was hated. Different European countries appealed to different Russians: Britain to masons, imperialists, liberals, industrialists, and dandies; Germany to philosophers, natural scientists, poets, bureaucrats, and officers; France to courtiers, literati, salonnières, revolutionaries, and enlightened monarchs; Italy to artists, Silver Age poets, and pilgrims to European antiquities. Notwithstanding these distinctions, Russians tended to speak of undifferentiated "Europe" in the singular.[13] As the postrevolutionary émigré philosopher Georgii Fedotov wrote, "a unified Europe had more reality on the banks of the Neva or the Moscow River than on the banks of the Seine, Thames, or Spree." By Europe's reality on the banks of the Neva, Fedotov meant Russian Europeans, a distinct cultural type and a product of Westernization.[14] Strangers at home and rootless moderns amid the traditional countryside: alienation between the Westernized elite and the rest of the population has been a dominant theme of Russian intellectual history.[15] The distinction between high and low cultures was the distinction between European and Russian. It was also a watershed question for Russian intellectuals. In the nineteenth century, Russia's relation to the West became the overarching concern of literary, political, and philosophical minds. During the 1830s and 1840s, universities, periodicals, and salons were divided between Westernizers, who sought progress in Europe, and Slavophiles, who found Russia's unique destiny in Orthodoxy. According to the Slavophiles, hypocritical, formalistic, and decrepit Europe had lost the natural harmony between man and society. Russia, meanwhile, retained communalism, unaffectedness, and virtue, and would deliver Europe from its plight.[16]

In the nineteenth century, Russian Europeans imported major intellectual and aesthetic trends from Europe. In the twentieth century, Russia would reexport one of them, socialism, to Europe and the world.

The Bolsheviks envisioned their Revolution as the beginning of a pan-European and ultimately worldwide conflagration. Their messianic ambitions married the Westernizing and Slavophilic strands of Russian thought. Increasingly, they came to see a redeeming role for Russia as leading the world to socialism. During the Civil War, they imagined their territorially shrinking country as the hub of international communism and a home to all progressives. Even before resolutely establishing themselves in power, they gave this vision an institutional form: the Communist International, dedicated to exporting the revolution abroad. In the 1920s, they began to develop a complex bureaucracy devoted to supporting this vision.[17] The conservative turn of the mid-1930s undermined the expansive conception of proletarian internationalism. In its place resurfaced the Russian empire of old: the glorification of Russian historical figures, the celebration of Russian classics, and patriotic education.[18]

Yet the West (still in the singular) was formative for the Stalinist order, not only as socialism's legitimizing capitalist other, but also as Russia's old identity problem and cultural ideal.[19] Indeed, challenging the picture of isolationism, recent scholarship has highlighted the centrality of transnational interactions to Stalinist culture. The 1930s were the heyday of Western intellectual engagement with the Soviet experiment, when thousands of Europeans and Americans traveled to the USSR to learn how to make progressive schools, a society free of racism, or socialist revolution.[20] For their part, Soviet intellectuals were steeped in the European world. The West was a set of great texts (written, musical, architectural), to which the Bolsheviks ascribed universal significance.[21] In the 1930s, they sponsored translation of Western prose ranging from the Renaissance to select modernists. The journal *International Literature* was a conduit of new Western writing: Thomas and Heinrich Mann, Dos Passos, Feuchtwanger, Malraux, and Hemingway. Soviet directors studied Hollywood productions intensely, recreating the dynamics of American musical comedies at the Moscow Film Studio.[22]

In the 1930s, the Soviet Union rivaled Nazi Germany as the location of "true culture."[23] In the face of Nazi book burning, Soviet intellectuals forged Moscow's guardianship over "world culture"—and their colleagues throughout Europe accepted this custody. The Soviet Union championed international congresses, theater and film festivals, and literary journals in multiple languages, so that a pan-European cultural formation based in Moscow was not as far-fetched in 1935 as it appears in retrospect.[24] The Popular Front's broad alliance of antifascist intellectuals was a moment when culture was called to arms and writers were politically relevant. During the Spanish Civil War, some of them fought two battles: against fascism and, as the Great Terror (1936–1938) raged in the Soviet Union, for their waning faith in Soviet socialism.[25] All the while, the menace of foreignness was invoked during the Terror. The press, fiction, cinema, and political rituals linked internal and external enemies. Border guards were glorified as new Stalinist heroes, while the borders, depicted as "locked" and sacred, separated good from evil.[26] Spy mania permeated public culture, and vigilance emerged as the order of the day. Accusations of espionage figured prominently during the Moscow show trials of 1936–1938. Contact with foreigners could be lethal. Western tourism to the Soviet Union collapsed.[27] Knowledge of foreign languages became a dangerous liability. In the dark of night, foreign books were going up in flames.[28] But the paradox was that the international romance of the Spanish Civil War and the xenophobia of the Great Terror happened at the same time. Western visitors and transnational interactions were lauded in the same newspapers that also stoked the pervasive fear of foreigners. The expansive culture of the Popular Front coincided with the establishment of restrictive socialist realism, the mandatory aesthetic for all the arts.[29]

The precarious balance between openness and security concerns, between internationalism and fear of foreigners remained a structural feature of the Soviet system until nearly the end. Even as books, films, music, and objects from across the world crowded late Soviet life, travel restrictions and closed borders persisted. What is more, cultural exchange projects, including such epochal events as the 1957 Moscow International Youth Festival, were punctuated by espionage panics. In the 1950s, friendship societies, travel agencies, and other institutions of cultural exchange were direct successors to the ones that had enjoyed a high point in the mid-1930s. In the late 1950s and early 1960s, the conceptual justifications for "peaceful coexistence" recalled and romanticized the 1930s antifascist international community: the periodicals, congresses, voyages across embattled Europe, and the times when intellectuals commanded military detachments. The critics and translators from the *International Literature* journal of the 1930s revitalized the publication of Western prose in the 1950s and 1960s.

While mindful of long-standing questions about how intellectuals promoted the Soviet cause abroad, how the USSR retained or lost its worldwide appeal, and how Soviet developments paralleled those in other countries, the following pages address different concerns. This history explores what Western cultural imports meant for Soviet audiences in the context of the Thaw. Continuities notwithstanding, the Thaw was not simply a reprise of the 1930s.[30] The scope and diversity of imports were striking. Their ubiquity and visibility were unprecedented, and so were the political and cultural concerns that came to the foreground. A newly prosperous Europe and Cold War America differed from what they had been in the interwar years. Engaging them was a different Soviet Union, where people no longer were executed for knowing a foreign language.

Executions for any reason declined precipitously after Stalin's death in 1953, as his successors abandoned governance by mass terror. The move from mass violence in the Stalin years to the sporadic episodes of political repression thereafter represented a sea change. The Thaw fundamentally reconfigured the relationship between the Soviet state and the population. Not only was terror as a mechanism of governance abandoned, but in 1956, the party initiated a society-wide reevaluation of the Stalinist past. In February of that year, at the Twentieth Party Congress, Nikita Khrushchev delivered his Secret Speech, in which he held Stalin's warped sense of self-importance and paranoia responsible for the Terror.[31] The speech captured the human dimension of spiraling arrests, fear, and despair. It presented the Terror as a moral crisis.[32]

The Terror defined conversations about the Stalinist past until the end of the 1960s, and beyond.[33] Audiences also read the Terror into Western texts unrelated to the Soviet context. At exhibitions of modernist Western paintings, viewers repeatedly confounded aesthetic preferences with political attitudes. The enthusiasts of modernism applied the label of Stalinist henchmen to the devotees of realism. Editors and critics spoke about "rehabilitation" of Western books withdrawn from circulation in the 1930s, or simply out of print. Rehabilitation was a key term in the political and moral vocabulary of the Thaw. Between 1953 and 1957, the term assumed a stable meaning: a recognition of innocence and restoration of a good name for the wrongly accused during a particular time—Stalin's time.[34] In the mid-1950s, Soviet filmmakers and critics saw Italian neorealist aesthetics as a deliverance from Stalinist cinema. In the process, they invented a critical perspective on late Stalinist film as theatrical. The opening to the West produced a sense of rupture with the most immediate memory of Stalin's final eight years, when ideological campaigns "against kowtowing before the West," "servility before foreigners," and "cosmopolitanism" had afflicted all intellectual pursuits.[35]

This account relies on the metaphor of the Thaw, rather than de-Stalinization. Of Western origin, the notion of de-Stalinization emerged in the American popular and scholarly press after the Twentieth Party Congress. Even early commentators were not very comfortable with "de-Stalinization," because it implied "the fault of one man."[36] In reducing a complex terrain to Stalin's single-handed creation, the term unwittingly follows the "cult of personality" logic. Of course, Stalin's legacy looms large, but "de-Stalinization" obscures the possibility that the Soviet order, as well as attempts to reform or conserve it, originated beyond Stalin's or Khrushchev's personalities.[37] By contrast, the Thaw metaphor, which appeared in Soviet print in mid-1954, represented abstract politics in an immediate physiological sense.[38] Depicting nature in a transitional stage, the metaphor suggested a world in the making, a cultural system open to chance and change. It conveyed a condition of possibilities.[39]

The Thaw was an open-ended phenomenon that defined the entire second half of the Soviet period. That is why this book does not stop in October 1964, when Khrushchev was ousted from power, or in August 1968, when Warsaw Pact troops invaded Czechoslovakia. Important as they were, neither event terminated or even fundamentally altered the story of Western imports in the Soviet Union. Novels continued to be published; exhibitions continued to be hosted; viewers continued to expect, and find, erotic and aesthetic revelations in Italian and French films. The process, as well as the institutional and intellectual channels established in the 1950s and 1960s, would remain practically unchanged in the subsequent two decades—only the field of imports would grow more catholic, and the visual and literary languages available for translation would grow more daring. On occasion, this book ventures into the 1970s when translations halted in the 1950s were finally printed, into the 1980s when Olympian fantasies were restaged once more, and even into the present, since some texts and institutions created in the late 1950s and early 1960s retain their importance to this day. A rigid periodization with identifiable breaks does not work for the last thirty-plus years of Soviet history.[40]

During the Thaw, cultural exchanges with Western countries were part of the Soviet Union's global opening.[41] The USSR assumed the mantle of patron of decolonization. What had been a trickle of African-American visitors in the 1930s became a wave of African students in the 1960s. The Soviet government sponsored festivals of emerging cinemas. Each year brought a new exchange of films with Korea, India, Egypt. If there was one place in the world that would celebrate and pay royalties for public self-expression of, say, a young Congolese poet, then the Soviet Union was it. The Soviet cultural establishment promoted Cuban poetry and Mexican lithographs, Indian films and Egyptian prose. In the 1970s and 1980s, Progress Publishing House ran a series, Select Works of Asian and African Writers, with an encyclopedic range from Cameroon to Nepal.

Yet the Soviet Union remained profoundly West-centric. The West had been Russia's most important interlocutor for centuries and remained so for the Soviet Union.[42] Amid the Cold War competition, the capitalist West was the standard of development and a challenge to be overtaken. The West was a Soviet utopian construction, an expansive idea that included Argentina and Greece. Opening to the West represented the most visible rupture with Stalin's last decade and, for those who remembered, with the late 1930s. That is why Western literature, film, and art were such a suitable repository of ethical and political readings. And of course, a permanent orientation toward the West (e.g., "the common European home") determined not only the life, but also the death, of the Soviet Union.[43]

Soviet exposure to the West is a European story, rather than one centered solely on the United States. American culture takes pride of place in scholarship on Western fashions and fandom in the Soviet Union. The focus typically is on Hollywood, jeans, and jazz (later on Anglo-American rock). This is an important account, populated by colorful personages

whose memoirs and novels chronicled the nylon and neon America of Soviet fantasies.[44] But significantly, nylon and neon were also the Europe of
Soviet fantasies. Pop music in the Soviet Union was inspired by European
as much as American examples. Foreign cinema, whether elite or popular,
was primarily French and Italian. Moreover, in Europe and the United
States, the 1950s and 1960s were remarkable for the extraordinary scope of
cultural exchange, irreducible to "Americanization."[45] In the Americanization scenario, Europe rarely exported songs, films, books, or paintings;
American consumer goods and popular culture swept away small groceries,
town markets, and national cinemas.[46] But in the Soviet Union, American
presence coexisted with imports from other countries and was only one
among many.[47] What is more, American and European texts recombined
in a novel constellation of meanings.

For in translation, these texts accumulated new connotations and intonations. Translation is at the heart of this book. Translation highlights the
channels of cultural transfer and the ways in which imports and their recipients change in the process. And it underscores the agency of the recipient,
frequently lost in the usual schematic vocabulary of model and imitation.
The book's first chapter outlines the cultural exchange policies that made
possible the arrival of Western imports. The second chapter, on the Moscow
International Youth Festival, emphasizes literary, cinematic, painterly, and
travel experiences at the festival and serves as the springboard for the pages
that follow. Subsequent chapters on literature, film, and art exhibitions
proceed from literary to visual imports, from texts that Soviet audiences
came to claim as their own to those that they aggressively rejected—
from translatability to the limits of translation, to inscrutable visions and
ineffable experiences.[48] In each chapter, the narrative ranges across three
interconnected levels: cultural diplomacy and channels of import; translation and mediation; and reception. High-stakes diplomacy created spaces
for the cultural effervescence of the Thaw and determined what would be
available to the audiences. Translation installed Western imports in Soviet
homes and streets. Reception is formative for translations in general, since
they act in the interfaces of text and context; and in turn, Western translations were formative for late Soviet audiences.[49]

Appropriation was fundamental to the Russian, and then Soviet, translation culture.[50] A history of exoticisms in Russia and the Soviet Union
is a history of domestication, not estrangement.[51] In Russian, the words

for "self" and "other" designate not only identity, as in English, but possession—or identities through possession. "Self," *svoe*, suggests ownership: of the self, to the self. Signaling difference, danger, and distance, "other," *chuzhoe*, is at root about belonging to another.[52] Even at the lexical level, the relationship between Russian and foreign is expressed as a claim to ownership or a disavowal.

Translation shaped Russian language, literature, and statehood.[53] In the seventeenth century, translations from Latin and Polish had changed the Russian lexicon. Under Peter I, translation acquired high state priority: the new scientific, administrative, economic, and naval vocabulary accompanied the transfer of institutions and practices. Translators faced texts and terms that had no analogues in the Russian language and material reality—new words and things arrived simultaneously. This absence of words for conveying new knowledge propelled the translator to the status of author. Indeed, in Russia, the distinction between translation and original emerged only in the nineteenth century. Grounded in the eighteenth-century classicist heritage, Russian translations had been traditionally domesticating. But, unlike other producers of domesticating translations, most of whom hid behind effortless native prose, Russian translators, whose fealty to their readers often exceeded their fidelity to the texts, were highly visible.[54] They were among the makers of the literary canon and political lexicon. During the 1820s–1830s, when Russian Romantic culture was at its height, and again at the turn of the twentieth century, during the symbolist moment, "foreignizing" translations did seek to capture the strangeness of the original.[55] However, these challenges to the principle of domesticating translation did not upend the foreign protagonists who had merged with Russian literary life. We thus have the phenomena of Russian Hamlet, Russian Faust, Russian Don Juan, Russian Don Quixote. Each was emblematic of a disposition, a way of life, and the domestication of Western characters as Russian cultural scripts.[56]

The Soviet context inherited this literary situation, but also endowed translations with exceptional status and significance. Translation helped to provide evidence for Soviet claims to cultural ascendancy. The USSR was depicted as a country open to "the best" of "world literature" and promoting literary interactions among its many nationalities.[57] In the first decade of the Bolsheviks' rule, translation was at the heart of their attempts to deliver all artistic and intellectual creations to the proletariat. During the 1930s, translation became a way to announce the Soviet project to the

world and to censor unwelcome information about the world.[58] In conditions of closed borders and information scarcity, translation played an
amplified role in social life. Information hunger persisted throughout the
Soviet decades, and translated artifacts offered precious tidbits on topics
ranging from alternative political systems to sexual relations. From the 1930s
on, translation was a survival strategy, a creative niche and financial shelter
for some of the country's greatest authors at a time when their own works
were censored and went unpublished. Personae non gratae, from Acmeist
poets to Gulag returnees to dissidents, earned their living by translating.[59]
Emerging in the early 1950s to define the subsequent approach to cultural
exchange, Soviet translation theory postulated the absolute translatability
of all cultures.[60]

And then came the watershed of the mid-1950s, when Soviet society
parted with the extreme xenophobia of the late Stalin years. Translation
became a utopian urge to bridge not only linguistic but also ideological
divides, a fundamental tenet of official exchanges, and a key mechanism
for purifying capitalist imports. At epistemological crossroads, such as the
Thaw, translated texts gain centrality: they step into a cultural vacuum to
advance new languages, role models, and behaviors.[61] Cultural mediation
during the Thaw overlapped with concerted reforms and vocal debates on
the ills of Soviet society, acquiring particular potency in this context. Translated texts were packed with Soviet political and cultural connotations.

The following pages uncover what the Soviets found in translation. Thaw
culture fused together incompatible forms of aesthetic expression, as well
as artists who are traditionally seen as poles apart. Pablo Picasso and Rockwell Kent, Ernest Hemingway and Erich Maria Remarque—they are rarely
placed in the same aesthetic context in the West, but in the Soviet Union
they coexisted and became interdependent. Western imports did not constitute a stable set of rarefied texts. Picasso, Hemingway, and the Western
modernist canon were not at all canonical for Soviet audiences, but became so in the process of translation, during politically charged circumstances. Transfer and translation fashioned a distinctive canon, eclectic
stylistically and chronologically.[62] The interpretive context of the Thaw
stressed an ethical reading: for Soviet audiences, Hemingway and Remarque held similar connotations of stoical machismo, and in both,
readers searched for models of human relationships. Of course, texts
crossing borders also lost some of their earlier context. In interwar Europe,
Remarque's novels were a bitter pacifist statement. In Soviet readings of

the late 1950s, this meaning was overshadowed by other concerns: the plight of the lone individual against impersonal forces, the saving grace of love and male friendship. Across Europe, Italian neorealist films were celebrated for leftist politics, social themes, and documentary aesthetics. But in neorealism's impoverished neighborhoods and street urchins, Soviet critics discerned a material accuracy they found inspirational, and spectators detected exposed, beautiful, or indecent bodies. Italian neorealism and French "cinema of quality" (historical drama, adaptations of literature) could not have been more different. Yet moviegoers discovered passion and intimacy in French and Italian films alike. It is easy to interpret Pablo Picasso's landmark exhibition of 1956 in Moscow and Leningrad as an aesthetic revolution. But first and foremost, the Picasso exhibition was a political event. By contrast, Rockwell Kent's paintings were an aesthetic experience. Practically unknown at home, in the Soviet Union, Kent came to represent something quintessentially American. Translation thus helps us to understand how works and figures marginal in the native culture move to the center of the recipient culture.[63]

The main conduit of Western imports was the Russian language, the Soviet Union's lingua franca. Non-Russian speakers had diverse but also fewer and less predictable opportunities to access Western imports. Polish books circulated in Western Ukraine. In Estonia and Soviet Karelia, people could tune into radio and eventually television broadcasts from Finland. Cross-border traffic had long been an important channel, but it grew even more vital with the influx of tourists and the expansion of radio and television in the late Soviet decades.[64] Important as this channel was, however, it was also local and sporadic. Cultural products from the West were the work of central agencies, which drafted exchange agreements, made selections, and paid in convertible currency.

Most Western imports physically moved through Moscow, where they began to accrue meaning. Films were dubbed first and, for the most part solely, into Russian.[65] Over decades, Russian dubs would create habits of viewing, listening, and enjoyment. And they would acquire associations with Western cinema and with a media culture of "quality." For these reasons, Russian dubs continue to structure consumption practices today, even in those linguistic communities that had resisted russification successfully.[66] The Thaw saw a dramatic increase in translations. A counterpart to this boom in some republics was an attempt to revise long-standing translation practices. Russian—as a language of original prose and as an intermediary language of translation—structured republican translation efforts.[67] In the early 1950s, translators working in the ethnic languages of the Soviet republics could get in trouble for translating from originals, rather than from Russian translations. Fidelity to foreign languages was suspect during those xenophobic years, while Russian-language translations were equated with originals in quality.[68] During the Thaw, dislodging Russian translations from this canonical status became a determined project, especially in the Baltic republics.[69] Even so, republican literati did not ignore Russian translations, but engaged with them, if only to disagree, and thus entered their force field.[70]

Finally, Russian was the only language that could ensure countrywide dissemination. Important and interesting as local projects in republican languages were, they could not promise broad circulation. A *Russian* translation was a prerequisite for a pan-*Soviet* conversation.[71] This book, therefore, concentrates on Russian-language channels and the Russian-speaking population. Significantly, the geography of dissemination was broader than either Russia itself or ethnic Russians. Many viewers and readers who engaged with Western films, paintings, and books lived in the republics and multilingual autonomous regions of the RSFSR. Local linguistic regimes varied considerably, with some languages reserved for home and others for work, some for the courtyard and others for the May Day parade. But when it came to Western imports, people operated within the field of Russian culture.

Central to the domestication of Western imports were cultural mediators. This cosmopolitan elite included writers Ilya Ehrenburg (1891–1967) and Viktor Nekrasov (1911–1987), translator Ivan Kashkin (1899–1963), filmmaker Sergei Yutkevich (1904–1985), and a host of less-prominent translators and critics. Some of them did not know foreign languages well, but toured Europe, the United States, and the world extensively. Others had never traveled abroad, but lived in an intimate communion with foreign words and literary protagonists. What these people held in common were a culture and a mission. Many of them belonged to the same cohort; their childhood or adolescence coincided with the fin-de-siècle, and they began their careers in the exciting atmosphere of the 1920s. Perhaps ironically for people who so profoundly shaped Thaw culture, they had been Stalin's men.[72] They had published their best-known books, received their own theaters, film workshops, and professorial positions in the late 1930s. They had won Stalin Prizes in the 1940s. By the 1950s, they had become authoritative figures at the apex of Soviet culture, its makers and beneficiaries.[73]

Cultural mediators held positions of eminence that gave them access to mass media—and they could not have adopted their role without it. They went abroad on state missions (conferences, tours, festivals) and publicized Western cultural products through state channels. And it was the state's monopoly on radio, print, and cinema that assured them a countrywide audience. The general Soviet condition of restricted information and closed borders created opportunities for a few commanding voices to have a profound impact. The paucity of other information, as well as the subterranean nature of nonofficial channels, highlighted *their* travel stories, the paintings and novels *they* endorsed, and the names *they* mentioned. Their lengthy apprenticeship (and survival) in the Soviet cultural system taught them how to use it: how to draw on patronage networks, to spot opportunities, and to provide the press, airwaves, or museum halls with texts, ideas, sounds, and images unthinkable a week or a month earlier. They could afford to be mavericks, and they were, redefining what was thinkable in their day.

They pursued a self-delegated mission. Cultural mediators spoke about paintings and trips to choice audiences in elite enclaves and in radio programs for millions. They published articles and travel drawings in the popular press, edited documentary films, and told stories into a microphone. Sharing is not a retrospective metaphor, but a basic practice of cross-cultural mediation. They cared deeply about the reception of their efforts, reading fan mail with a pencil in hand and marking in the margins the passages they liked or disliked. They, or their secretaries, responded to letters from audience members and sent copies of travelogues or foreign postcards to their correspondents from engineering bureaus and student clubs. Sharing, however, did not mean an exchange between equals. Intellectuals approached their audiences with a good deal of patronizing. They often saw viewers and readers as uncultivated, unappreciative, and naive. Cultural mediation was a Soviet enlightenment project.

Their audiences, the subjects of this book, were a diverse and geographically dispersed population. Western imports circulated far beyond the intellectual elite and beyond Moscow and Leningrad. The audiences overwhelmingly consisted of teachers, librarians, doctors, engineers, and students (studying to become teachers, librarians, doctors, and engineers). They were geologists stationed in the South Siberian mountains at Sorsk, Khakassia, and in Trans-Ili Alatau, the Northern Tian Shan ranges of

Kazakhstan. They were engineers in design bureaus of the Leningrad electronics and the Riga railcar plants, at the heavy machinery factories in Stalino (today's Donetsk) and in Stavropol'. They were dentists, pediatricians in district clinics, and surgeons in town hospitals. They taught in music schools and in rural schools, where they organized art history and foreign language study groups for peasant children. In our own society, engineers and teachers would be called the professional middle class. In Soviet social classification, they were called the "people's intelligentsia" or "industrial-technical intelligentsia." Brought to life during the industrialization of the 1930s, the white-collar professional workforce was trained in ever greater numbers after the war.[74] They would remain demographically prominent in the late Soviet decades: educated professionals were a fast-expanding social group, growing by a factor of five between 1939 and 1970 and almost doubling between 1959 and 1970.[75]

Cultural activities were integral to their daily lives. The usual distinction between "high" and "low" cultural forms, neatly overlaying social divisions, did not apply in the mid-1950s.[76] Rather than the domain of highbrow intellectuals, reading serious literature and going to museums were the daily pursuits of educated professionals. According to Soviet sociologists of leisure, more engineers than other professionals read newspapers, journals, and books, listened to the radio, and attended the theater. In going to the movies and visiting museums, they were second only to students.[77] Culture happened in district libraries and neighborhood theaters. Books and films were sources of common pleasure and information unavailable elsewhere, about fashion, for example, or love.[78]

Educated professionals invested so much effort in cultural pursuits in part because of the Soviet ambition to make culture broadly accessible. The Bolsheviks had aspired to bridge that impermeable divide between the Europeanized elite and the illiterate masses, between high and low cultures. Along with buildings and factories, the Revolution had expropriated high culture for the benefit of the working classes. Universal literacy had been one of the Bolsheviks' earliest, most prized, enduring, and intrusive projects.[79] Museologists sought to turn museums—often the aristocracy's and the bourgeoisie's former dwellings—into workers' cultural homes, to "open and make accessible for all working people the treasures of art."[80] Cinema offered great hopes for education-as-indoctrination, and the pronouncements of Soviet leaders about moving images would decorate theater walls for many decades. The government struggled to create a radio network that would encompass impassable places, connect the city and the village, and build a unified cultural community across great distances.[81] In the 1950s and 1960s, radio and film would become vital conduits of Western imports across the USSR. Radically democratized high culture was the essence of Soviet enlightenment.

Many Soviet citizens identified with this goal and strove for cultural self-improvement.[82] Accessibility of culture was their right, but too often, it was not their reality. Journal volumes, books, and tickets to concerts and film screenings were governed by the economy of shortages. Standing in queues for scarce clothes or food and mobilizing various connections to procure it absorbed much of Soviet citizens' time, effort, and ingenuity.[83] At least from the mid-1950s on, a good deal of that resourcefulness went into cultural aspirations. Like everything else in short supply, access to exhibitions, high-demand books, and rare music albums was an important part of the informal economy.

The story of shortages is less surprising, however, than the remarkable reach of Western imports. They came to the village Bystri in the Vichuga district of the Ivanovo region and the settlement Mishelevka, standing amid the taiga, of the Usol'e district in the Irkutsk region. To places such as the northernmost city in the world, Noril'sk, enveloped in a month-long polar night, and Ukhta, in the Republic of Komi, both of which had started out as Gulag sites. To places such as Sterlitamak in Bashkiriia and Kovylkino in Mordoviia. The Thaw extended far from Moscow.[84] For even as the capital was best supplied with everything from consumer goods to cultural fare, radio, cinema, and print infrastructures expanded dramatically during the Thaw.[85] Locales that would never see an art exhibition benefited from the arrival of the printed word—translated books and travelogues. In turn, radio and cinema affected people and places unreachable by print. And Soviets carried Western imports in their suitcases as they moved from home and in their bags as they made the trek from district hubs to villages. The technical intelligentsia was educated in republican and regional centers. Afterward, their institutes and universities assigned them to jobs, often in inhospitable and isolated places, according to requests of central economic planners.[86] We find these graduates in remote villages, at construction sites, in new settlements amid the steppe, in places often unmarked on the map. To these places, they brought big-city experiences and that Soviet aspiration to cultural accessibility.[87]

They, the audiences, were the co-creators of Soviet translations and the ultimate interpreters. They chased after books, standing in line through the night at retail kiosks. They elbowed their way through museum halls. They collected reproductions of paintings and preserved postcards of Western films stars. They dropped house chores and homework to tune in to radio lectures. And they paid highly inflated prices on the black market for the pleasure of holding and keeping the fragments of a world they thought they would never see. Their intense feelings—surges of anger, tears of joy, revulsion, humiliation, pleasure, longing—transformed distant Western stories and images into Soviet possessions.

1

Soviet Internationalism

A round the corner from Nikitskii Boulevard, on Vozdvizhenka, stands one of the strangest buildings in Moscow. An ornamented castle with heavy arched portals, lacy balcony rails, shell-shaped stucco molding, two round towers, twisted columns of sandstone, and an entrance in the shape of a lucky horseshoe, this building transports visitors to the Lisbon of Vasco da Gama and the Age of Discovery, to the Salamanca of Isabella and Ferdinand, of Rodrigo Arias Maldonado, an ambassador of the Catholic king and a knight of the Santiago Order.

If the building's central ensemble and decorative grapevines bear uncanny similarity to the Pena Palace in Sintra, and if the shell-embossed facade calls to mind the Casa de las Conchas in Salamanca, it is because the building also belongs to another context—the Moscow eclecticism of the Russian fin-de-siècle.[1] Together with late Gothic, Renaissance, and Mudéjar architectural elements, these symbols were imported to Moscow in the 1890s, after a tour of Europe by Arsenii Morozov, a dandy, prankster, and scion of the Morozov dynasty of merchants and philanthropists. The building and its interior embodied a fusion of all things and times, serving as a meeting ground of East and West in the heart of Moscow, only a short distance from the Kremlin. After the Revolution, the building was home to an avant-garde theater and then to Proletkul't, an early Soviet organization of writers and artists who wanted to create a distinctly proletarian culture. Following the eclipse of Proletkul't, the house lost its cultural liveliness and became solemn and unapproachable: for the next thirty years, until the late 1950s, it would accommodate diplomatic missions.

But there was another context to the life of this building and another incarnation of universalist yearnings within its walls—when Vozdvizhenka was the street's unofficial name, when only old-timers knew who had built this castle, when Moscow guidebooks offered this listing: Kalinin Street,

16, The House of Friendship. In 1958, ownership of the castle was transferred to the recently founded Union of Soviet Friendship Societies (SSOD), and the building regained its associations with both culture and internationalism. It became an unambiguously public structure. The reorganization of the interior served to highlight the building's new status. Partitions, columns, and entire walls were demolished in an effort to enlarge the foyer, cinema, coatrooms, and theater, to make room for potential visitors. SSOD plans and reports were crammed with ideas for events.[2]

The House of Friendship, like the SSOD itself, epitomized Soviet international efforts of the mid-1950s, which combined exuberant populism with informational hierarchy, conspicuous new openness with gnawing old suspicions. The House had long-standing associations with exclusivity, so its open doors symbolized the difference between the mid-to-late 1950s and the xenophobia of the late 1940s. Offering a European landscape steps away from the Kremlin, the House again became a meeting ground of all things and places.

Cultural Diplomacy

The arts have long been set pieces of diplomatic interactions. Artists often journeyed in ambassadorial entourages as guides, raconteurs, and spies. Men of letters doubled as representatives especially prized for their oratorical gifts. Polyglot Peter Paul Rubens traveled to London to negotiate an end to the Anglo-Spanish War (1625–1630). Charles Le Brun guided Siamese envoys to the court of Louis XIV and also drew the bowing emissaries, their hands folded, before the king. Nicolas Poussin informally advised French diplomats in Rome, where he served as a mediator between Italian artists and merchants, on the one hand, and illustrious French buyers, on the other. Voltaire was every bit a diplomat at the court of Frederick the Great. During the Renaissance, paintings functioned as subtle instruments of diplomacy. Ambassadors commissioned artworks for their personal collections or those of their masters. Diplomats negotiated not only princely alliances, but also artistic gifts. In turn, objets d'art underpinned political and military pacts. Artists painted allegorical figures and included symbolic objects meaningful for contemporaries, while ambassadors interpreted the pictures for monarchs, introducing images into diplomatic dialogues.[3] In the second half of the seventeenth century, particularly in France, language, learning, and the arts came to symbolize national grandeur.

The politicization of culture in the context of interstate relations and the projection of national glory through artworks were not unique to the twentieth century. And yet, in the twentieth century, the nexus between culture and diplomacy took unprecedented forms, practices, and meanings. Cultural diplomacy between states now operated within a system of international organizations. The arts were increasingly institutionalized in both governmental and nongovernmental structures. France installed cultural programs as part of the diplomatic corps. The Soviet Union pioneered the use of overtly civic organizations for the operations of the state. Nazi Germany and fascist Italy established international associations around high culture and nationalist values, or hijacked the existing liberal ones. The United States oscillated between private foundations and state bureaucracies, until cultural initiatives became part and parcel of foreign policy.

Instrumentalization of the arts took a quantum leap in the age of ideologies. Images, texts, and sounds embodied competing political and social discourses: egalitarianism and accessibility (the Soviet Union), racial purity and national transcendence (Nazi Germany and fascist Italy), or freedom, democracy, and individualism (the United States). Now artworks exemplified the totality of culture, which, in turn, represented a way of life.[4] And each regime promoted itself as the most propitious order for creating cultural artifacts of lasting value.[5]

New international events and institutions emerged in mid-nineteenth-century Europe as a collective celebration of reason, science, and progress. At world fairs, Europeans delighted in crafts, machines, and specimens attesting to a soaring industrious spirit. At the turn of the twentieth century, international scientific, professional, and religious societies and periodicals burgeoned in response to the rising threat of nationalism and militarism. This time, the mood was anxious. Yet, the Paris Universal Exposition (1900), the Union of International Associations in Brussels (1910), Ludwik Zamenhof's Esperanto textbook (1887), the International Congress of Arts and Science in St. Louis (1904), and the Carnegie Endowment for International Peace in New York (1910) offered a hopeful vision of international relations, based on culture and intellectual life. None of these forestalled the Great War, but all of them left a resilient faith in the power of the arts to unite people beyond state boundaries.

The 1920s saw no end to visionary proposals for "a single world community" and "world government": a United States of Europe, the League of Nations, the International Institute for Intellectual Cooperation in Paris. During those years, the writings on war and peace imagined a future in which internationalist forms of association would replace the nation-state. If, with the hindsight of World War II, these writings on world community appear to traffic in fantasy, in the 1920s their authors saw them as realistic measures for securing peace. After all, as Leon Trotsky argued, total war showed "the indissoluble tie between the fate of the individual and the fate of all mankind." He called this new sensitivity to the world beyond oneself "the feeling of 'universality.'"[6]

Among the most universal of doctrines was socialist internationalism. And among the most steadfast believers in the saving grace of culture were the Russian revolutionaries. They and their successors proclaimed the Soviet Union a cultural dreamland. To demonstrate its wonders to foreign, mainly Western observers, in 1925 the Soviet government created the All-Union Society for Cultural Ties with Foreign Countries (VOKS). The society's mission was to cultivate relations with foreign intellectuals and coordinate the activities of various "Friends of New Russia." Beginning in the early 1920s, Soviet sympathizers had assembled in associations, where they read lectures and staged exhibitions, both of their own making and under the auspices of VOKS. Like the "Friends of New Russia," VOKS was an ostensibly civic association.[7] It represented the separation of cultural affairs from the diplomatic corps. At the time VOKS was founded, France offered another model of cultural diplomacy. In 1923, the French Ministry of Foreign Affairs established the office of Cultural Relations, the first of its kind in diplomatic practice, for "the intellectual expansion of France abroad." In the interwar years, the handsomely funded office and its growing staff kept busy financing French schools, institutes, and language classes abroad.[8] VOKS, however, maintained professed independence from the Commissariat of Foreign Affairs. It could speak to foreign peoples above the heads of state and distinguish itself from "red propaganda," so suspect in Western countries. In reality, however, VOKS was a veiled branch of the government bureaucracy, entwined with the censorship apparatus and the secret police.[9]

Whereas the Quai d'Orsay's office of Cultural Relations staked French "intellectual expansion" upon language, VOKS had a different use for culture. VOKS translators, analysts, and intellectuals threw their (and the state's) resources into enticing foreign visitors to communism. The trips of Western tourists and dignitaries were elaborately staged and carefully managed: travelers were escorted to model socialist sites and surrounded by the best of conversations.[10] Soviet cultural diplomacy of the late 1920s and 1930s was not about exchange and reciprocity. It was about forthright, if sometimes subtle, ideological recruitment. Travelers not only discovered Soviet accomplishments, they also learned a socialist realist optics that portrayed a Soviet world in the making, the future amid the imperfect present.[11] VOKS instrumentalized creative texts and cultural figures to a previously unparalleled degree, embedding the pursuit of favorable opinions in a web of publications, translations, and public performances. Even as translators and guides courted foreigners, they also harbored a deep-seated suspicion of their guests and remained vigilant. Anxiety and distrust were at the heart of Soviet cultural diplomacy no less than polished photographs in multilingual journals.[12]

Two other models of cultural diplomacy emerged in the 1930s: the German-Italian and the American. Germans and Italians established new pan-European associations and forged bilateral cultural agreements that promoted nationalism as the foundation of interstate relations.[13] The Nazis withdrew Germany from international institutions and established rival organizations of writers, composers, filmmakers, and scholars.[14] The Italian government remained a participant in international organizations until the late 1930s. While remaining a participant, Italy managed to transform, subvert, or branch out from international cultural platforms. Fascist events and institutions that gained distinction in Europe, such as the International Film Festival in Venice or the International Institute for Educational Cinematography, originated in nonfascist structures, the Biennale and the League of Nations.[15] The Nazis and fascists saw the road to European domination through their exploitation of international networks, which they seeded with racial ideology and corporatism.[16] At events in Berlin, Munich, Rome, and Venice, the Nazi and fascist regimes recreated a dazzling cosmopolitan atmosphere, with thousands of foreign guests, multiple languages, a forest of national flags, and international symbols and rhetoric.[17] Incidentally, such symbols of the 1935 International Film Congress in Berlin as a film reel encircling the globe would become a staple of international film festivals after World War II. Internationalism on the right, appealing to conservative elites disenchanted with aesthetic modernism and political democratization, was as convincing and potent as its socialist counterpart.

The Axis countries came to coordinate their actions, signing a comprehensive cultural exchange agreement in 1938. In the late 1930s, artworks, orchestras, films, and people traveled between Italy and Germany—all amid remilitarization, occupation, and war.[18] The German-Italian Cultural Accord of 1938, and other agreements that Italy had pioneered in the mid-1930s, redefined cultural exchange. If, earlier, exchanges had been instituted in multilateral international organizations, now they were specifically bilateral. And if earlier the philosophy behind cross-cultural relations had assumed that intellectual and artistic life was universal, the makers of the Italian-German Accord envisioned discrete and bounded national cultures. Cultures expressed the national spirit; nations showcased their cultures to celebrate uniqueness and cultivate an appreciation of their own distinction rather than a sense of commonality.[19] Long after the logic of racial purity would be discredited, the structure developed by the Axis in the 1930s—bilateral exchange agreements reflecting national cultures—would remain.

Elsewhere in the world, Nazi Germany gamely exploited preexisting institutions such as German language institutes and émigré communities. The Axis cultural presence in Latin America spurred the United States government to engage in cultural diplomacy.[20]

The United States enjoyed a tradition of philanthropic cultural activities. Congress generally resisted the conflation of private initiative and public office.[21] For conservative lawmakers, bringing cultural diplomacy under State Department control amounted to a loathed expansion of federal bureaucracy, while for liberals, cultural programs in the hands of the government raised the dreaded specter of propaganda. Among members of Congress and the staffs of philanthropic foundations, universities, and scholarly associations, and across the political spectrum, faith in private initiative was nearly absolute.[22] So, even when cultural diplomacy came to be integrated with foreign policy, philanthropic foundations continued to shape its practices.

American cultural diplomacy first began to take shape in the context of inter-American relations and President Franklin D. Roosevelt's "good neighbor" policy to reverse US interventionism in the affairs of its neighbors. At the Inter-American Conference in Buenos Aires in 1936, Roosevelt connected cross-cultural relations with democracy and security in the context of the impending war in Europe. The result of the conference was a multilateral agreement for an annual exchange of students. The critical fine print of the agreement was the idea of reciprocity, which would become paramount in American-Soviet relations two decades later. This was a very modest beginning of the global cultural expansion of the United States.[23]

World War II decisively altered the practice and structure of American cultural outreach. In 1938, the State Department created the Division of Cultural Relations amid fears that the United States was "missing the bus" and losing Latin America to "Axis penetration." As the war loomed, the State Department discovered that there was no shame in propaganda. In August 1940, Roosevelt established the Office of the Coordination of Commercial and Cultural Relations between the American Republics to project American culture to its neighbors via print, radio, and cinema.[24] In 1942, Roosevelt launched the Office of War Information, with press offices around the world, and a radio station—soon to be called the Voice of America.[25] A year later, the State Department created the position of cultural attaché. And thus were cultural programs incorporated into foreign policy.

The entanglement of culture and foreign affairs—a wartime emergency—would remain a permanent feature of American politics. This turn was motivated by fear of communism. In 1947, several congressmen toured Europe and learned from American diplomats about the omnipresence of the Soviet Union. In London, Paris, Warsaw, communism was on the offensive. In London, Paris, Warsaw, Soviet cultural presence—associations of friends, exhibitions, publications—surpassed that of the United States. In London, Paris, Warsaw, American diplomats begged congressmen to untie the purse strings for cultural programs. Again, the United States appeared to have missed the bus. To catch that bus, in 1948 Congress authorized the State Department to engage all cultural means in promoting the United States, supporting its foreign policy, and countering Soviet propaganda. The wartime offices of information and cultural and commercial relations became the foundation of the United States Information Agency (USIA)—the center of American cultural programs for the duration of the Cold War.[26] This new cultural diplomacy was not about language, national influence, or genuine reciprocity. Rather, it was about an unsubtle ideological recruitment for "the free world."

To the congressmen touring Europe, the Soviet Union seemed everywhere, because European, especially the French and Italian, communist parties experienced their star moment after the war.[27] The Soviet Union itself, however, was nowhere: it adopted an increasingly isolationist stance in the late 1940s.[28] Only in 1955 did the Soviets try to break out of isolation. This was the year of far-reaching change in Soviet-Western cultural relations, when the Central Committee resolved to end artistic autarky and join a growing international exchange, now mediated by mainstream diplomacy. But why abandon traditional strongholds and friends who styled themselves in the Soviet likeness, promoted various leftist causes, and engaged in extensive propaganda on behalf of the USSR?

First came the realization that nobody in the West read Soviet books, watched Soviet movies, or had the slightest idea about Soviet art, dance, theater, and music. Nobody, that is, besides "our friends," and this meant that Soviet propagandists had been preaching to the converted. Many were communists, all were supporters, and their associations were close-knit, exclusive organizations on the margins of capitalist society, even when they could boast prominent writers, artists, or politicians. Such, for instance, was the France-USSR association. France-USSR was as anticollaborationist as it was pro-Soviet; a good deal of its original spirit came from the experiences of occupation, resistance, and liberation, and so, too, did its orthodoxy and rigidity. Its proclamations spoke about the darkness of Nazism, the holy flame of the Resistance, and human dignity recovered at Stalingrad. Its postwar politics were shaped by these memories and by boundless respect for Stalin.[29] Such associations worked closely with VOKS, and their activities seemed to please Soviet cultural bosses—until 1954–1956. That was when Soviet journalists and academics began to travel to the West and write reports for the Central Committee. They visited the premises of friendly associations and were dismayed to see that Soviet books and magazines were catastrophically undersold, while membership rolls were catastrophically low. Yesterday's best friends were now criticized for inflexibility, sectarianism, and leftism.[30]

Just as the possibility of Soviet influence in Europe had galvanized American cultural diplomacy in the late 1940s, the results of new American initiatives now frightened the Soviets. Upon inspection, VOKS propaganda abroad looked unimpressive, compared to American efforts in Europe. Soviet observers were shocked. Consisting of encyclopedic lists, the reports that they wrote for the Central Committee conveyed both admiration and exasperation. "The USA has special, well-managed information services in England, . . . maintaining contact with the government, officials, publishing houses, writers, union leaders, and other public figures" and producing info-bulletins three times per day. Thousands of these brochures were sent to all corners of Britain, and thousands of films were lent free of charge to British schools. There were also exhibitions and a library, not to mention America's most feared weapon—popular music. To Soviet eyes, all this looked like a colossal attempt to "infiltrate" the hearts and minds of Europeans.[31]

Their eyes did not mislead them. While the anticosmopolitan campaign had raged in the Soviet Union in the late 1940s and early 1950s, the United States had dramatically expanded its cultural programs in Europe. The Marshall Plan underwrote distribution of American films and books. In 1951–1952, the renewed agreements specified that films and books exported to Europe should "reflect the best elements of American life and shall not be such as to bring discredit upon the United States." Besides commercial entertainment, the United States also disseminated dozens of propagandistic pictures produced by the Office of International Information and Cultural Affairs and later by the USIA. To reach potential viewers, USIA posts around the world boasted thousands of projectors and hundreds of mobile units, and could always count on Hollywood's help.[32] American libraries that the Soviets observed in Europe dated to the 1920s and 1930s. During the war, the State Department had taken over selection of books for outposts abroad from the American Library Association. At the same time, the Office of War Information had developed a network of overseas libraries that were incorporated into the work of US embassies. By 1956, the USIA had organized 160 libraries around the world.[33] At its founding, a number of voices within the USIA had advocated greater efforts to present to Europeans a cultured America. The first steps were a series of concerts, titled "American Cultural Weeks." In 1955, the State Department intervened to mount prodigious and sustained artistic programs. The department assembled *Highlights of American Paintings* for a global tour. Performances soon followed: a "Salute to France" music season and George Gershwin's *Porgy and Bess* (with a stopover in the Soviet Union).[34] The importance of the American presence in Europe for the Soviet understanding of artistic and intellectual exchanges cannot be overstated. The American factor was a prerequisite for Soviet bilateral cultural agreements with other countries.

In 1955, talk of "cultural agreements" and "cultural exchange" resonated across Europe, the United States, and the Soviet Union, thanks to the Geneva Summit held that July. Geneva hosted Soviet, American, French, and British delegations, represented by their heads of state: Nikita Khrushchev, Dwight Eisenhower, Edgar Faure, and Anthony Eden. The purpose of this summit—the only such event during the Cold War—was to ease East-West tensions. Participants expected to discuss the status of divided Germany and the terms of its reunification and integration into the West. As it happened, nothing about the German question, disarmament, or even trade was decided there. Geneva's significance was largely symbolic: the Soviet Union asserted parity with the West; France and Britain were able to claim great power status in a bipolar world; and the United States projected a peacemaking image.[35] But the long-term, if underappreciated, outcome of the summit was institutionalized and regularized East-West cultural exchanges. As practices of cultural exchange took shape in the second half of the 1950s, they incorporated various models pioneered in the interwar years: front organizations, separation or merger of culture and foreign policy, bilateral reciprocity, and agreements highlighting national cultures. Cultural exchange was not merely the soft underbelly of conventional diplomacy. It emerged as a constitutive element of the Cold War international system.[36]

Ideological Shift

Cultural exchange came to occupy a central place in the Soviet conception of foreign relations between the Twentieth Party Congress in 1956, when peaceful coexistence became an explicit policy, and the Twenty-second Party Congress in 1961, when the policy entered the Third Program of the Communist Party.[37]

It did not have to be so. Peaceful coexistence could have been limited to disarmament, neutrality treaties, trade, technical cooperation, even travel. It did not have to include paintings, books, films, musicians, and performing troupes. In 1952, Stalin had spoken about "peaceful coexistence of capitalism and communism" on the occasion of the International Economic Conference, whose purpose had been to reestablish economic relations between socialist bloc countries and the West. A catchphrase of the time, "peaceful cooperation," had then referred exclusively to trade and resolution of urgent crises.[38] To read press accounts published between 1951 and 1954 is to watch how, slowly and hesitantly, "cultural relations" emerged as a distinct and legitimate concept, sometimes mentioned once, sometimes making up a subordinate clause. At first, the concept was attached to a decolonizing country—India, for example—then to neighbors like Finland, until the expression shed geopolitical qualifiers altogether.[39]

Soviet commentators did not take peaceful coexistence for granted. They tried to explain on what grounds socialist and capitalist cultures would interact. The people who invested much effort into explicating the principles of cultural exchange often had firsthand international experience and a professional stake in the matter. One such person, for example, was Gennadii Mozhaev, a young World War II veteran and a graduate of Moscow University's international law department, who went to work for the Soviet Commission at UNESCO in 1956. He would remain with the commission almost until the end of the Soviet Union, eventually as the first assistant to the commission's secretary, Sergei Romanovskii, and as a diplomat in the rank of first counselor. While Mozhaev was learning the ropes at UNESCO, in 1956–1957, Romanovskii, a secretary of the Komsomol Central Committee, was organizing the Moscow International Youth Festival. A career diplomat, Romanovskii would go on to chair the Council of Ministers' State Committee for Cultural Relations with Foreign Countries—the same committee that coordinated cultural exchange in the 1960s. People like Mozhaev did not make foreign policy, but they stood close to the apex of power where policy was made and were part of the diplomatic corps that implemented it.

Mozhaev's public statements reflected the changing ideological principles behind the Central Committee's decision to engage in mainstream cultural diplomacy. In the late 1950s and early 1960s, Mozhaev provided some of the more comprehensive and consistent justifications for cultural coexistence. Socialist and capitalist cultures might be incompatible and incomparable, but some capitalist creations had enduring and universal value.[40] Mozhaev wrote about "all-human (*obshchechelovecheskaia*) culture," about "a preeminent creation of an artist or a sculptor, a cinematic masterpiece, a moving musical symphony" understood by all people, irrespective of their ideology.[41] Such arguments derived from Lenin's theory of two cultures, progressive and reactionary, corresponding to two classes in every historical epoch.[42] Just as classes rise and fall, so also do their cultures. While the culture of late capitalism was degenerate, that of nascent capitalism had been progressive and had left a lasting heritage. Lenin's theory came to mean, in Mozhaev's words, that "the culture of any bourgeois nation is not monolithic or homogenous," and that there was something called "democratic culture," which capitalist countries could offer Soviet audiences.[43] On these grounds, Soviet theoreticians argued that "spiritual culture" had classless "components."[44]

These intellectual endeavors were underpinned by two assumptions about culture: that it was a transparent medium of communication, and that the reason for its transparency was its universality (when a work of art was not intelligible, it was not "true" art). Culture spoke a shared language.[45] Journalists and filmmakers were delighted to snatch common features—a sound, an image, a gesture, a body movement—from the cultural conglomerate. Foreign stories in the Soviet press were about love and labor, fundamental, all too human, and hence universal. Universality became a key principle (*printsip universal'nosti*) of cultural exchange, an invitation to "all nations, all peoples, and all countries of the globe" to "make a contribution to the common treasury of world culture" on "an equal footing." The "treasury" was a metaphor for a common stock of classic books, paintings, and music scores available to each according to his needs.[46]

Already in 1955, the Soviet Academy of Sciences resolved to participate in a multivolume, internationally authored, UNESCO-sponsored *History of Mankind: Cultural and Scientific Development.* The Soviet archaeologists and historians invited to consult on the project imagined a *History* that would show how, over centuries, mutually enriching interactions had created a common "world culture" and "the unity of human society." People had traded goods from time immemorial, and, traveling with goods, they had spread their technologies and alphabets along the way. Isolated civilizations, whose development was doomed to repetition, à la Arnold J. Toynbee, were unpalatable to Soviet historians.[47] For five years, the Soviet Group for the Study of World Culture argued for its version of human development, but ultimately broke away from the UNESCO project and, in the early 1960s, proceeded to work on a counteraccount. As its guiding principle, the Soviet version took "the idea of the original and permanent unity of mankind."[48] The Academy of Science's early decision to participate in this project brought to the fore a language of universalism and impelled the creation of a journal, *The Messenger of the History of World Culture,* devoted to all countries and centuries.[49]

The Group for the Study of World Culture and its *Messenger* were only the first in a series of institutions that would be established in the next fifteen years to study the world. These would include the Institute of World Economy and International Relations, the Institute of the Economy of the World Socialist System, the Institute of Africa, the Institute for the US and Canadian Studies, the Novosibirsk Institute of Economics and Industrial Organization, and other think tanks. They published their own journals and admitted eager PhD students, who would praise their alma maters for an incredible variety of information, for lively debates, analytical rigor, and open horizons—if not borders quite yet. The graduates would go on to shape the Soviet Union in important ways, covering international affairs for Soviet news agencies, devising opinion polls, advising the Central Committee's international and ideology departments as instructors, and, eventually, orchestrating perestroika. Some of them would abandon coexistence for convergence, becoming the country's first globalists. In the 1950s and 1960s, the students' inspired readings, overcrowded lecture halls, and endless discussions were suffused with a keen sense of belonging to a wider, multilingual "scientific space" that knew no ideological boundaries. They spoke about "the oneness of humanity," "the formation of one international community," and "world civilization."[50]

In the Soviet language, "civilization" (*tsivilizatsiia*) carried unifying rather than divisive implications. It did not connote a particular way of life; there were socialist and capitalist "socioeconomic formations," but there was no such term as socialist civilization in the Soviet vocabulary. There were no civilized and uncivilized countries, only developed and un(der) developed (*razvitye/slaborazvitye*) ones.[51] In Western thought, "civilization" denoted both a quality (first personal, then national) and the process of acquiring that quality, of becoming clean, private, well-behaved, and cultivated. This notion recalls the Soviet "culturedness" (*kul'turnost'*)— from hygienic habits to polite and politically correct speech, from self-discipline to rationalized production, from literacy to literature.[52] Tsivilizatsiia represented these as well, but also meant something else: civilization was accumulated, not acquired. In the Soviet context, it retained a static, even permanent, quality. From the turn of the nineteenth century, when "the ethnographic concept of civilization"—in the plural—first emerged, to the twentieth century, when the idea of multiple civilizations gained power and was translated into politics, the challenge to the vision of a single human civilization has been considered a major intellectual breakthrough.[53] Soviet philosophy did not recognize this breakthrough. Even the word itself, tsivilizatsiia, with its meta-historical and global connotations, was used sparingly, primarily in conjunction with antiquity, modernity, the West, and the world.[54] Civilization meant cultural capital and generational continuity, history and heritage. There was only one "civilization," shared by all.[55]

The vision of common humanity so prominent in the mid-1950s had first emerged in the mid-1930s, in the context of approaching war. Between 1933 and 1939, the Soviet journal *International Literature*, a voice of the transnational literary left, had developed the language of "world culture" and "civilization" most articulately and passionately.[56] After the war, the victory over Germany was discussed not only as evidence of socialism's superiority and durability, but also as the triumph of books over flames, buildings over bombs, "civilization" over "the plague."[57] Countless articles pronounced the Red Army the savior of "civilization." But would the Red Army be able to do so again?

The idea that the Third World War might not have a winner slowly and inconclusively took hold among the Soviet leadership between 1953 and 1956. Already in the summer of 1953, the Council of Ministers chairman Georgii Malenkov, addressing the Supreme Soviet, rejected the inevitability of a Soviet-American confrontation on "objective grounds." Eight months later, in March 1954, Malenkov spoke before voters in Moscow's Leningrad district about universal destruction (and implicitly, the possibility of salvation), about "the end of world civilization" in a nuclear war—only to be berated by Khrushchev and Minister of Foreign Affairs Viacheslav Molotov, who were more comfortable with the language of class.[58] Turned against Malenkov in the subsequent power struggle, the (in)famous speech was not solely a plea for salvation. It was also a declaration of a vastly exaggerated Soviet capacity to retaliate and an affirmation of faith in nuclear security. Indeed, "the objective ground" that could avert a Soviet-American confrontation was the Soviet testing of the hydrogen bomb in the summer of 1953.[59] Yet the phrasing—suggesting that the world was one and war was preventable—rang outlandish in 1954–1955. War was central to the Soviet cosmos, to the Marxist-Leninist understanding of both international relations and "the objective laws" of history. One of the most indisputable of such laws was capitalism's propensity to start wars. In turn, war would be a cataclysm that would destroy capitalism. Much in Soviet public life, from industrialization to spy mania, had been inspired, explained, or justified by the specter of war.[60] In the spring of 1954 and at the January 1955 Central Committee plenum, Malenkov admitted his theoretical mistakes and lost his job as chairman of the Council of Ministers. (Molotov, who never stopped speaking the language of class, also lost to Khrushchev shortly thereafter.) In March 1955, the party press denounced civilizational language as a ruse of capitalist warmongers and a "thoroughly falsified" threat designed to sow despair among the laboring masses and colonial peoples.[61] It took the bomb to alter the meaning of war in the Soviet political imagination, but even the bomb had not conclusively settled the matter.[62] As late as 1961, a foremost Soviet scholar of international law (known as "Mister Peaceful Co-Existence" among his Western colleagues) could argue that a "world war in our days spells the annihilation of imperialism," and, in the same breath, talk about war as "catastrophic" for humanity in general.[63]

Still, in the course of 1955–1956, Khrushchev appropriated the language of universal threat, elevated peaceful coexistence to a policy, and spoke about it more consistently than anybody else. He advanced "peaceful competition" as a new doctrine of foreign relations at the Twentieth Party Congress in 1956, where he presented an uncompromising choice: "either peaceful coexistence or the most destructive war in history." There was, he assured Congress deputies, "no third way."[64] The doctrine still envisioned a divided world, a global class struggle, and the ultimate disappearance of capitalism. In his own person, Khrushchev managed to combine international coexistence and the Communist International.[65] He remained apprehensive of Western politicians and wounded by Western prosperity, even as he enjoyed trips abroad and admired American productivity. In the annals of the Cold War, Khrushchev is as infamous for nuclear brinkmanship as he is famous for peaceful coexistence. Moreover, despite a substantial reduction of armed forces, the doctrine of peaceful coexistence had a negligible effect on Soviet foreign policy. The profundity of its impact lay elsewhere: in cultural policy, where summit diplomacy opened spaces for translation, exhibition, and creativity.[66]

Once the general secretary embraced peaceful coexistence as a policy, the imperative for journalists, international law experts, and philosophers was to prove the very possibility of peace. After all, Khrushchev himself announced at the Twentieth Party Congress that war was not inevitable.[67] Hence the proliferation of new legal treatises on international organizations and international law, whose potential to preserve peace had been dismissed or derided for decades.[68] Hence, too, the invocations of thinkers unconventional in the Marxist-Leninist canon: Russian translations of Thomas More and Tommaso Campanella, Erasmus and Hugo Grotius, abbé de Saint-Pierre and Fichte, William Penn and Wilhelm Weitling aided in the search for the legitimate origins of peaceful coexistence.[69] Immanuel Kant long had been on the margins of official philosophy, but in the late 1950s, his essay on *Perpetual Peace* proved useful. Harboring few illusions about the harmonious state of nature, Kant accepted the antagonism of states and admitted an obligation to go to war under certain circumstances. Peace, nonetheless, was possible, but not by way of a supranational state, a merging of states, or a world government (the anathema of cosmopolitanism in Soviet discourse), for Kant resolutely defended sovereignty.[70] If states were to retain their sovereignty, then, Kant maintained, the only way of ensuring peace was with a "union of nations." As Kant envisioned it, the union of nations would be held together by three linchpins: mutual commercial interests, increased communications, and a shared world culture. All three were also the main goals, practices, and slogans of "peaceful coexistence."[71] The new Soviet readings of such texts as Kant's *Perpetual Peace* or, for another example, Grotius's *On the Law of War and Peace* devoted much space to the development of the idea of "perpetual peace" in its socioeconomic context. The emergence of the idea was linked to the transition from feudalism to capitalism, and peace was declared productive of other historic shifts, including the one from capitalism to socialism.[72]

In 1961, the Third Party Program decisively reconceptualized the place of war in history—and practically in the same terms as scholars and journalists writing about world culture, one mankind, and *Perpetual Peace*.[73] This was the only time between 1919 and 1986 that the Communist Party changed its strategic document. The program declared "war and peace" to be the pivotal question of modern times. War, no longer the engine of revolutionary change, "could bring unspeakable destruction of entire countries, could annihilate entire peoples." Peace was not only possible, the program emphatically declared, "perpetual peace" was also "the historical mission of communism." Capitalism and socialism were still locked in a "class struggle," there were still the rich and the poor, the imperialists and the colonized. But "thermonuclear war" was class-blind, and so the party program spoke of "entire mankind" in the singular. Its internationalist visions were addressed not only to Soviet citizens, but to foreign peoples, movements, and "bourgeois circles," to anybody who would embrace peaceful coexistence. And for all those willing to read it, the program explicated the principles of peaceful coexistence: a rejection of war in favor of diplomacy, parity, sovereignty, and economic and cultural cooperation. The culture that the program predicted—the culture of communism and of the future—would be "classless" and "common to all mankind."[74] But if Soviet society was as close to communism as the party program promised (only twenty years away), then did this not mean that "there [we]re elements" already in the present that "took on universal character"?[75]

The ideological shift was gradual but permanent: books, paintings, and images held universal value and spoke to indivisible humanity.

People-to-People, Soviet Style

Soviet cultural efforts abroad thus pivoted to the "bourgeois" public: to bourgeois writers, intellectuals, artists, and the press.[76] It turned out that most people living in foreign countries were not wrongdoers, and this was true not only of "ordinary" people, who were "peace-loving" by definition, but also of bourgeois elites, intellectuals, well-known figures, and even businessmen. Yes, they were confused, but they were also curious about the Soviet Union. Yes, they wavered, but they were not enemies. With the brief exception of the late 1940s and early 1950s, winning the sympathies of foreign intellectuals had always been an important—and often successful— Soviet project.[77] It returned to the spotlight in 1955.

In one respect, however, this project was unlike the efforts of the 1930s. Now it was envisioned as a dramatically democratized undertaking, and policy makers insisted on setting it apart from its predecessors. Cultural exchange of the mid-1950s was suffused with a new-fangled populism. Populism emerged at home in 1954, when Khrushchev struck at state institutions, invoking the old threat of bureaucracy that revolutionaries had feared in the 1920s and 1930s: bureaucratization eviscerated party initiative, fostered complacency, and muffled principled communist stance.[78] In the mid-1950s, campaigners against bureaucracy sought to restructure state institutions, champion accountability, inspire initiative from below, and promote popular (self-)supervision. The more immediate goal was to endow public organizations—the party, the unions, various soviets, committees, and societies—with greater powers by transferring to their jurisdiction a host of functions that previously had belonged to state agencies. In the course of Khrushchev's administrative reforms, numerous ministerial departments and government offices were abolished and replaced by public organizations.[79] Among them was VOKS, disbanded in 1957–1958. Although nominally a civic association, in fact, "boasting a network of representatives in Soviet embassies abroad and complete integration into the branches of the bureaucracy," VOKS "most resembled a regular state agency."[80] Historians and memoirists expose VOKS as a facade: a public organization providing cover for police networks and state control.[81] VOKS was abolished for its bureaucracy, secrecy, hypocrisy, and exclusivity.

The Union of Soviet Friendship Societies (SSOD), which came to replace VOKS in 1958, was conceived as its opposite on all these counts. The rationale behind SSOD was two-pronged. SSOD would consist of distinct friendship societies devoted to various countries. These societies would help to deflect accusations of inequality in relations between VOKS and Soviet sympathizers abroad. Clubs of friends and fellow travelers displayed pictures and books from VOKS, but there were no counterparts in the Soviet Union to showcase materials they might wish to send. Pressure from Western (mostly French) friends was customary, and socialist bloc fraternal clubs (mostly Polish) occasionally muttered complaints about unilateral Soviet propaganda. But VOKS continued to stage touring photo exhibits of Soviet achievements, send books and magazines, and ignore the grumbling, at least until late October 1956, when the Hungarian Revolution broke out. During the uprising, the Hungarian-Soviet Society, along with other communist and Soviet organizations, became a target of the insurgents' attacks. The society's offices across Hungary were looted, and its activists were evicted from their apartments and beaten. VOKS-sponsored photo exhibits and books were burned.[82] The offices were a symbol that brought to the fore the problem of Soviet cultural conceit. This was true not only of socialist countries. In Western Europe, especially in France and Britain, where the left had a long tradition of mobilization on behalf of the Soviet Union, the absence of analogous *civic* organizations in the USSR "triggered misunderstanding and bewilderment."[83] SSOD, then, was about reciprocity and exchange at a time when these became key words in the new international vocabulary.

SSOD was envisioned as a magnet for popular participation. The Central Committee faulted VOKS for its inability "to draw upon the Soviet public (*obshchestvennost'*)."[84] Whereas VOKS aimed its outreach at foreigners, the SSOD leadership harbored enlightenment ambitions for domestic audiences. Shortly, its work would include exhibits and lectures about foreign countries for Soviet visitors to the House of Friendship. SSOD's House of Friendship became a place where one could see photographs of Parisian sights, watercolors Soviet artists painted in Florence, and drawings sketched in New York. Reflecting on the union's first year, SSOD officials patted themselves on the back: "We have found the right, all-inclusive form of *direct* participation of the Soviet public in strengthening friendship and cultural relations . . . work has become mass-scale, go[ing] beyond the framework of a certain elitism that afflicted VOKS's activities."[85] With pride they underscored "new forms" of work, which they credited with attracting thousands of people. Drawing on Soviet mobilization practices (mass holidays, parades, meetings, propaganda trains), SSOD created participatory spectacle: "friendship evenings" in parks, with music, dancing, and games; rallies with songs, flowers, and handshakes at "trains of peace and friendship" and "peace cruises"; meetings with foreign tourists in large factories, and more handshakes, as well as pins, stamps, and souvenirs.[86] In 1958–1959, many of SSOD's internal deliberations were about the evils of speechifying and paper pushing; the remedy was direct action and personal involvement by large numbers of people.[87]

Assembling these people, several hundred to several thousand participants per event, was made possible by another innovation central to the institution's self-image. Like VOKS, friendship societies were membership-based; unlike VOKS, whose associates were prominent writers and scholars, friendship societies boasted a broad membership of ordinary people. There was a catch, however. In 1958, the new societies and the publicity campaign that accompanied the SSOD's founding conference attracted very real enthusiasm and much curiosity. In some towns and places of employment, people began to form friendship "circles" without permission or guidance.[88] Membership in a friendship society brought no tangible benefits. People who volunteered their efforts expected a cultural experience: they would learn new things and partake of another world vicariously. Petitioning SSOD for membership, they wrote about closeness, about making distant places intimate. M. V. Sinoiskii, a bank employee in Moscow, tried never to miss a French film or art exhibition, read novels in Russian translation, and savored stories about French history. Nonetheless, he felt himself inadequate, because he did not know the language. Membership in the Soviet-French society would be the culmination of a lifetime of gathering information or a compensation for linguistic inaccessibility.[89] Dmitrii Mikhailovich Popov, a retiree and old revolutionary from Moscow, devoted thirty years—he underlined and repeated this for rhetorical clout—to collecting cultural knowledge about France. He did know the language: "For *thirty years*, I have been teaching myself French."

He, too, saw all the performances of the 1954 tour of the Comédie-Française and every picture screened at the 1955 French film festival. His letter was filled with the names of poets he memorized, novelists he admired, painters he loved, and composers whose music he heard in his mind's ear. He felt himself a cultural insider and wanted to join the friendship society so he could share, "selflessly, gratuitously," his knowledge with everyone: to "propagandize everything French."[90] Danila Ivanovich Muts, a worker from a coal mining settlement, Belitskaia, in Donetsk, boasted no special knowledge and made no emotional claims. His letter was an "application," an understatement in Soviet administrative vocabulary. If admitted to the Soviet-French friendship society, he promised to discharge his responsibilities "honestly and conscientiously."[91]

Alas, as many letter writers petitioning for membership in the societies would discover, in those early years it was collective, not individual. The "wide circles of the Soviet public" entered the picture as entire factories, institutes, libraries, collective farms, and unions. There was some individual membership, but, like associates of the old VOKS, this was reserved for prominent scientists, writers, scholars, artists, musicians, plus some model peasants and workers.[92] As SSOD president Nina Popova explained, "We cannot leave things to themselves, that is why each society can permit individual members [only] with the approval of the Board of Directors. But who [should get individual membership]? . . . These must be people who have already proved themselves . . . who are prepared for this work."[93] SSOD's prominent affiliates held differing opinions, too: "it's a pity we don't allow individual membership in societies."[94] Meanwhile, greeted by silence or bureaucratic formulas, letter writers were beginning to suspect that, in the words of one such person from Kuibyshev, "membership in the societ[ies] was a privilege of famous writers and performers, inhabitants of the capital."[95] SSOD was created in the spirit of activism and participation, but its founders sought supervised participation and controlled activism. The numbers of people who volunteered individual commitment threatened to overwhelm the institution; but such numbers were the least of the problems Soviet officials would face should they leave communication with foreigners to the discretion of "*random* people."[96]

Yet "random people" was precisely the point. One of the more remarkable aspects of the new diplomatic course was the idea of public and personal diplomacy. It was a literal reading of an old motto: the people, "the masses"—not diplomats and governments—make history, including

38

international history.[97] What made for novelty was the attempt to put this reading into practice. At the SSOD founding conference in February 1958, hardly a speaker missed the most prominent theme of the campaign for public activism in international affairs—personal relations (*lichnye sviazi, lichnye kontakty*) with foreigners.[98] This idea departed from the usual propaganda methods that centered on demonstrating superiority and embodying it in images of success: photographs, posters, and sketches. These same photographs and success stories were still important, but now they were to be distributed by ordinary people rather than state-sponsored magazines. And they were to come with a personal touch, by word-of-mouth, first (good) impressions, and letters from Soviet citizens to pen pals abroad. International personal correspondence seemed especially promising: "For people abroad personal contact starts with mutual sympathy," and "it would be interesting," argued Popova, "to have a comrade send a letter in which he would speak his mind extensively. We need documents that will awaken sympathies."[99]

This was the Soviet version of President Eisenhower's People-to-People program, born of the same Geneva moment and launched in 1956, two years before the SSOD idea. At the heart of the American project were ordinary people, informal contacts, and goodwill initiatives—all camouflaging a government-sponsored information campaign. Americans banded in ostensibly independent committees (created by the State Department's Office of Private Cooperation) according to their professional and personal interests. Citizens organized book drives and donated magazines that were shipped to communities abroad. Some hosted exchange students. Others dispatched rose bushes to gardening enthusiasts across the world. And most participants, from pet owners to gardeners to camping pros, wrote letters, thousands of them, with personal stories and photographs of the good American life. These documents were meant to "awaken sympathies," because they came from ordinary people rather than from the State Department and the US Information Agency. Even the most idealistic moments were underwritten, on both sides, by counterpropaganda campaigns, government funds, and psychological warfare schemes. (Eisenhower himself saw People-to-People as total mobilization along wartime lines, and some of the letters were sponsored by the CIA.)[100] But this should not detract from very real excitement, among Soviet citizens no less than among Americans.

In the Soviet context, the idea of exchanging letters with people abroad was unprecedented, and, like the friendship societies, it elicited a surge of enthusiasm. Soon enough, the press was talking about personal contacts and foreign pen pals. The effect was a "flood" of mail, from both Soviet and foreign citizens, requesting addresses and help in finding correspondents.[101] Toma Osotrova from Vladivostok, Valya Kobzeva from Azerbaijan, Lida Ivanova from Magadan, Natasha Balakshina from Tomsk, K. M. Volkov from the fast-growing town of Rudnyi, in Kazakhstan, and many others thought that Soviet bureaucracies maintained addresses of foreigners with whom they could correspond.[102] The pen pals they sought were generic "youth" or "friends." Other people were devoted to particular countries or dedicated to specific cultural pursuits. Mining technician Ermolaev, from the settlement of Krasnogvardeisk (Lugansk, Ukraine), was a music buff and especially fond of Italy. His quest was to find an Italian counterpart with whom he could share his interests and exchange music records. By his third letter, Ermolaev had grown exasperated: the Soviet-Italian friendship society and SSOD would not help, and he was beginning to wonder whether "such cultural exchange" was "politically" acceptable.[103] Letters were sent to every conceivable institution, where officials were taken by surprise. They conceived of yet another campaign, but discovered that people's interest in relations with an invisible, unreachable, faraway somebody was genuine and massive. They had no idea what to do with these requests, booting letter writers like Ermolaev from one agency to another.

The main problem was control. Until the requests started arriving, nobody had thought through the regulatory mechanisms—how correspondence would be supervised and the correct content assured. Ordinarily, people could write letters to friends and relatives in the socialist bloc, while famous scientists, writers, and filmmakers carried on both professional and personal correspondence with friends in capitalist countries. Interception and inspection of letters by the authorities was an open secret. The question of private correspondence between "ordinary" Soviets and citizens of capitalist countries initially emerged in the context of expanded travel.[104] In predeparture lectures and en route instructions, tourists were forbidden to give their home addresses to "strangers."[105] The injunction worked until the summer of 1957, when, during the Moscow International Youth Festival, Soviet citizens were suddenly encouraged to exchange addresses with foreigners. Thousands of addresses were jotted on scraps of paper and passed from hand to hand, filling entire address books of hosts and guests. The press published numerous stories about long-lasting international friendships formed in Moscow and cemented through an exchange of addresses.[106]

That was how affairs stood in 1957–1958, when, in the wake of the festival, officials were blindsided by hundreds of requests to exchange addresses. While they scratched their heads and wrote reports, letters continued to pile up, and no bureaucracy wanted to take responsibility for them. In desperation, SSOD officials turned to their Presidium: "the SOD departments want to know how to respond to such requests . . . The main question has not been settled—is it allowed to give Soviet citizens' addresses to foreigners and foreigners' addresses to Soviet citizens? . . . The question of correspondence has outgrown the institutional framework . . . and has become a political matter."[107] "Contacts with ordinary people" was one of SSOD's chief projects and a prominent theme in the press discourse of peaceful coexistence. Vacillations and inconsistencies "produce[d] unhealthy moods in Germany," "made a bad impression in England," and led "to undesirable consequences, to assertions that Soviet citizens are supposedly forbidden to have personal correspondence with foreigners."[108] At home, confusion reigned:

> Some people are convinced that they can't write anything at all. Some people think that writing is allowed only through institutions. Some people think that everybody who so wishes can write whatever they want. There are no such people here among us, right?
>
> Some people are afraid to respond, and that is why there are so many nonresponding people, a very large number, inversely proportional to the number of promises—there are many promises and no letters.
>
> The question of personal contacts through various channels is very important because personal contacts are so significant. Why, what's the matter? It is very serious: An eye should match an eye, a hand should match a hand, a letter should match a letter.[109]

SSOD officials proposed several solutions. One was to establish a special department that would maintain a database of addresses, translate letters, and "be responsible for international correspondence from the point of view of state secrets" (read: exercise censorial supervision). Another was to channel correspondence through local party and trade union cells, which would review individual candidates, issue permissions, and "help with letter writing" (read: exercise censorial supervision).[110] Not much came of either, and communication with foreigners remained mostly and legitimately collective. That both solutions included a provision for censorship underlined the problem of trust, which was at the heart of the campaign against bureaucracy and for public activism. Despite all the talk about personal relations, the decision against individual membership in friendship societies and direct correspondence with foreigners had the upper hand. Perhaps this was to be expected. But the fact that the other option was considered seriously is indicative of the 1950s moment when it became possible to envision a less partitioned world.

Public diplomacy was quickly reverted to diplomacy personalized by the cultural elite.

Cultural Exchange Agreements

Whereas popular diplomacy flashed across newspapers, the idea of peaceful coexistence and the ideological shift toward universalism had an enduring impact on Soviet culture. For the second, and more lasting, innovation of the 1950s moment were bilateral cultural exchange agreements. These accords became the primary transmission channel of Western cultural imports for the next three decades.

After the Soviet delegation returned home with renewed confidence from the Geneva Summit in the summer of 1955, the Central Committee passed a series of nearly identical resolutions on the "expansion of cultural ties" with various countries.[111] In late 1955 and early 1956, the Ministry of Culture welcomed contractual relations with "private firms" from the capitalist world. At the end of 1955, when the agenda for 1956 was in the works but before formal cultural agreements were signed, exchanges with capitalist countries expanded dramatically. Earlier, only cultural relations with the socialist bloc had been subject to planning; now, the practice was extended to capitalist countries—with important implications.[112] The new policy crucially erased the formal distinction between approaches to socialist and capitalist cultures. Placing exchange with the West on the books assured regularity. However carefully measured and censored, capitalist imports would be an accepted and recurrent presence in Soviet theaters, libraries, and museums. The concept of "peaceful coexistence" was

embodied in real people, images, and sounds. These were its most significant aspects at the time and its most significant legacy thereafter. Diplomatic
conferences and summits not only produced official communiqués, they
also were surrounded by first-time-ever cultural events—foreign exhibitions,
film festivals, tourist delegations, and radio concerts.

The initial move toward regularized exchanges and broader cooperation
between the USSR and Western countries was the Soviet-French rapprochement. Following Geneva and in an effort to improve relations, the
Soviet government invited French prime minister Guy Mollet and minister of foreign affairs Christian Pineau to visit the USSR in May 1956. (The
invitation had been extended earlier to Mollet's predecessor, Edgar Faure.)[113]
This state visit, the first in over a decade, focused on security in Europe,
disarmament, and economic assistance to the developing world. These
issues had comprised Faure's "Memorandum on Disarmament," which
he had announced at Geneva a year earlier. The Europe that Faure had
imagined stretched "from the Atlantic to the Urals," undivided by curtains
and indivisible. It included the Soviet Union. This Europe would be connected by the circulation of people, texts, artworks, discoveries, and goods.[114]
In his own pronouncements, Mollet rebuffed concerns about the Soviet
military threat and called for negotiating with the USSR "always and
everywhere." For his part, Pineau made a plea for East-West cultural
exchanges at a March 1956 press conference.[115] And according to the assessment of the Soviet Ministry of Foreign Affairs earlier that year, mutual
trade was the key that would unlock French domestic politics for Soviet
influence.[116]

Commerce and culture, therefore, were the lubricants of the talks in
Moscow that spring as well as the linchpins of security as it was understood
in 1956. Mollet and Pineau's trip to the Soviet Union was framed by two
exhibitions of French art in Moscow and Leningrad. Drawn from Soviet
museums, the first exhibition in late 1955 was an embarrassment of riches:
antique furniture, enamel, porcelain, tapestries, medals, ivory daggers,
miniatures, drawings, prayer books of parchment and gold, popular prints
from the French Revolution, sculptures, and hundreds of paintings in ornate
frames. The French ambassador was enraptured, and the Soviet Ministry
of Culture smug.[117] The exhibition was promoted as "proof of long-term
and fruitful cultural ties, . . . of our people's constant interest in French
artistic life."[118] The ministry saw the exhibition as the first step in fulfilling
the Central Committee and the Council of Ministers' July 1955 resolution

"On the Expansion of Cultural Relations between the Soviet Union and France." In 1956, the French government sent to Moscow an exhibition of its own—as evidence of the new rapprochement.[119]

In the mid-1950s, France was celebrated in the Soviet Union unequivocally and passionately. In late summer of 1955, hundreds of French tourists arrived at the Leningrad port as crowds flocked to the Neva embankment, waving and chanting greetings. Marseille and Odessa became sister cities, the first French film festival sparked the Soviet love affair with Gérard Philipe, and the first USSR-France soccer match drew 80,000 thrilled fans and ended diplomatically, in a draw. In the spring of 1956, the Soviet Radio Administration gave airtime to French music, intending the broadcasts to coincide with Mollet and Pineau's visit. The month was May, the windows were open, and "the sounds of Paris" filled Soviet courtyards.[120] On May 19, 1956, Soviet and French statesmen signed two documents. The first was "A Statement on Negotiations between the USSR and France," composed in the language of "peaceful coexistence." This announcement acknowledged unresolved disagreements on the vital question of European security and frankly lamented the persistent "absence of necessary [mutual] trust." The building blocks of trust were "commercial relations" and "cultural intercourse." Both were to be regulated by a "long-term agreement." The second document signaled a special place for the idea of exchange and a special role for the arts: "A Joint Statement by the USSR and France Concerning Cultural Intercourse" announced agreement on a reciprocal publication of periodicals, promised an exchange of films, athletes, students, educational materials, and mass media programs, and revealed preparations for a "Convention on Cultural Cooperation." The "joint statement" meant that the music would remain after the politicians left.[121]

During the same post-Geneva summer of 1955, the Central Committee resolved to expand Soviet-British cultural relations.[122] Under the resolution's mandate, the Ministry of Culture directed a comprehensive effort at introducing British culture to Soviet audiences. "Cultural measures" to be carried out efficiently, "in operational order," applied to all media, so in the spring of 1956, Soviet information space was inundated with everything English. Items from Britain were included in newsreels, and British films from the early 1940s reappeared in Soviet theaters. In Moscow, sixty theaters, clubs, and houses of culture screened the films, and more than a million people rushed to see them during the first week. The Lenin Library showcased English literature published in the Soviet Union; and the

Ministry of Culture made sure to invite the British ambassador to the exhibit of English porcelain, glazed pottery, and precious stones from "unique [Soviet] collections." Moscow was awash in lectures and programs: the All-Union conference "Shakespeare on the Soviet Stage" and the festival of Shakespearean film adaptations, the evening on "English Literature and Art" at the Central House for Artistic Workers, and yet another at the House of Cinema. These performances were limited to the capital, but radio broadcasts and newspapers reached the rest of the country with classical and contemporary music, recitations of English fiction, literary reviews, and cultural overviews commissioned by the Central Committee.[123] For its part, the British Council invited the Soviet Minister of Culture to London in the summer of 1955. Several limited agreements on exhibitions and performing troupes were settled during this visit, and reciprocal film festivals were decided upon the following spring.[124]

These efforts surrounded preparations for Nikita Khrushchev's and Chairman of the Council of Ministers Nikolai Bulganin's trip to London in April 1956. Soviet statesmen had been invited by Prime Minister Anthony Eden at the Geneva Summit the year before. British politicians wished to use the occasion of Khrushchev's trip for casting Britain as a mediator of East-West relations amid the Cold War. Eden harbored ambitions for high-stakes negotiations on the key priorities of the mid-century (divided Germany and the Middle East). But both the British and the Soviets proved inflexible, and no diplomatic breakthrough came from the trip. The occasion's importance lay in a shift in British public opinion toward negotiating with the Soviets and in a commitment to cultural and trade accords. A cultural exchange agreement had been prepared by the British and accepted by the Soviets even before the trip. The Soviet delegation arrived enthusiastic about exchanges and ready to purchase a billion pounds worth of goods. But disputes plagued even that conversation on culture and trade, as Eden tied the exchange agreement to his negotiation priorities on Germany and the Middle East. As Khrushchev and Bulganin departed, the agreement remained unfinished.[125] By the end of 1956, the goodwill and exchanges discussed throughout the year lay in waste, among the many casualties of the Soviet invasion of Hungary and the British-French-Israeli invasion of Egypt.[126]

In the Soviet Union, the British and French culture campaigns of 1955–1956 were orchestrated, but no less significant for that. Nor does orchestration necessarily imply disingenuousness. The Soviet government was eager to sign cultural exchange agreements, and throughout 1956, negotiations with all Western (and non-Western) powers proceeded in earnest. What the Soviets wanted was to break out of leftist enclaves, stop preaching to the converted, and enter mainstream theaters, concert halls, and museums. They saw cultural exchange as an opportunity to appeal to the middle class and to Main Street. During the Cold War, cultural exchange was highly visible—and a highly visible opportunity to proclaim Soviet parity with the capitalist world. In all transactions, Soviet negotiators insisted on reciprocity. They were certain that they had something to be proud of: cultural exchange offered an occasion to display Soviet strengths in realist drama and painting, classical music and ballet.[127] Moreover, as Soviet diplomats and their Western counterparts knew, the Soviet government had a vast apparatus of censorship and propaganda to excise, alter, hush up, and reinterpret the images and texts they found unacceptable. The government was willing to take the risk entailed with exchanges.

In the fall of 1957, the French and Soviets came to negotiations in Moscow with a vision of broad "cultural intercourse." The meetings were not easy, however. The French made a cultural convention conditional on the lifting of Soviet travel restrictions and the distribution of foreign publications, particularly through a French reading room in Moscow.[128] During Stalin's last decade, obtaining a Soviet visa had been next to impossible, but even for the few who had visited the USSR, about half of the country had been forbidden territory. In the summer of 1953, the map of forbidden places was redrawn to allow greater mobility, but as of early 1955, 30 percent of the Soviet Union was still off limits to foreigners.[129] The cultural convention— which would have assured the stability of exchange, while keeping the door open to extemporized changes and to nongovernmental organizations like friendship societies—had been the key negotiation priority for the Soviets. They had envisioned a broad and general document stipulating such principles of cultural exchange as parity, fixed for five years and renewable automatically, unless expressly terminated.[130] Instead, the talks yielded only a short-term, but still comprehensive, program of exchanges for 1958, to be evaluated and renegotiated annually.[131]

The French-Soviet program of exchanges became the prototype for the initial conversations with the Americans that same fall of 1957.[132] Ad hoc trips of American and Soviet professionals, scientists, and handpicked students had made astonishing news since 1955, and the performing arts were the muses that kept the cannons silent that year.[133] In late 1957, the talks aimed to put the muses in the plan: to normalize and quantify artistic ex-changes and to fold them into broader bilateral relations. But the Amer-ican negotiators, like the French before them and the British after, staked the whole project on the exchange of uncensored information, including the press, radio, and television programs. In fact, both sides hampered the flow of information. Individual subscription to noncommunist foreign periodicals was unthinkable for Soviet citizens, and even newspaper editors whose job was counterpropaganda struggled for access to Western publi-cations. Meanwhile, the Post Office Department would not deliver Soviet newspapers to American politicians and research institutions.[134] Soviet jam-ming of Western radio broadcasts was a focal grievance for Americans (as for the French and the British). Unless the Soviets lifted restrictions on mass media, President Eisenhower's special assistant on East-West exchanges, William Lacy, seemed to imply, the State Department would not be able to convince businessmen and interest groups to uphold the American side of the bargain. The famous US-Soviet agreement, signed by Lacy and the Soviet ambassador to the United States Georgii Zarubin on Jan-uary 27, 1958, after three months of talks and almost three years of false starts, papered over these divisions and left Soviet officials to negotiate many clauses directly with the relevant US agencies.[135] Despite the gaps, the Lacy-Zarubin agreement was a milestone—for its scope, and for the totality of life and knowledge that it embraced through mass media, print, and travel. In a symbolic touchstone, the agreement provided for direct flights, as if a straight line in the sky signified open communication.[136]

In the summer of 1957, as the exchange of notes with the French and the Americans began, Bulganin also sent a letter to Prime Minister Harold Macmillan, inviting the British government to continue the exchange proj-ects of 1955–1956.[137] The same story, with yet more mistrust and tension, was repeated. The Soviets wanted to put cultural exchange on "a sound and permanent basis." But the British called for open travel and corre-spondence, uncensored distribution of foreign press, and a halt to radio jamming.[138] By the time negotiations finally started in 1959, there was no mention of a permanent convention, and only a limited program for the next year was signed.[139]

At first, it seemed the Italian story would be different. Regularized cul-tural exchange with the Soviet Union had a sympathetic ally in President Giovanni Gronchi, who had been carried to the Quirinal Palace by com-munist and socialist votes and who had worked to bring both parties into the government. Between 1958 and 1960, the Soviet Union and Italy concluded a series of trade agreements, thus more than doubling their commercial transactions.[140] In February 1960, Gronchi came to Moscow, and cultural programs—specifically, an exchange agreement between Italy and the USSR—were again to accompany the state visit. Although the diplomats negotiated a generous convention, conversations between the heads of state did not go quite as well. This, according to eyewitnesses, was largely on account of Khrushchev's impromptu jokes, toasts, threats, and invitations to Gronchi to join the Communist Party. The personal disconnect between Gronchi and Khrushchev poisoned whatever common ground the two may have shared. At the last minute, the Italian delegates postponed the ratification of the convention until the spring of 1961, and in the meantime, the Soviets had to be content with "a temporary program of cultural exchange."[141]

The Lacy-Zarubin agreement is the best known, but the Soviet Union negotiated similar agreements with many other countries. These agreements meticulously quantified cultural programs: everything was itemized, and the numbers (of people, performances, films) carefully noted. Although the specifics varied, these documents were nearly identical from year to year. It was these stultifying inventories that assured the richness and regularity of cultural imports.

There were two major moments of peril, when the shaky structure of cultural exchange was on the brink of collapse. The first was the Hungarian Revolution in October 1956; the second was the domestic ideological panic of late 1962–1963.

In 1956, Khrushchev's Secret Speech, which Radio Free Europe obligingly broadcast across Eastern Europe, excited hopes for economic, cultural, and political reforms. Between October 23 and 30, Hungarian students and writers, soon joined by thousands of people, rose against the Soviet regime, toppled statues of Stalin, attacked Communist Party buildings, executed communists, occupied communication points, and declared the country's withdrawal from the Warsaw Pact. Soviet troops invaded Hungary on November 1 and entered Budapest three days later. All talks about art exhibitions and films collapsed as Western cultural diplomats swiftly abandoned negotiations.[142] Soviet officials tried to keep exchange projects on the books, arguing that the crisis was temporary.[143] Indeed, already in the summer of 1957, the French were willing to discuss exchanges, and by fall, diplomats were back at the negotiating table. The Soviets saw the cultural agreement with the French as "the first major breakthrough" in "the boycott against us by capitalist countries."[144] Behind the scenes, American negotiators assured their Soviet counterparts that talks were merely postponed until public outcry subsided. The American approach was pragmatic, based on potential propagandistic dividends in the psychological war against the Soviet Union.[145] In Britain, Hungary left a more permanent trace, and for another two years the British Council refused to formalize cultural relations with the Soviet Union. Nor was this attitude unique to the post-Hungarian moment: mutual suspicion had a long history in both countries.[146] Yet, even in Britain, let alone in the United States and France, Hungary did not have a permanent effect on Soviet-Western relations. Ad hoc and unstable as the framework for cultural interactions was, it weathered the Hungarian crisis—and it would survive international emergencies in the future.[147]

The suppression of the Hungarian Revolution boomeranged at home. In the Soviet Union, 1956 was a year of unplanned collective action: public discussions and demonstrations for any and all reasons. Crowds seized public spaces, orators took turns to speak with polemical pathos, participants refused to disperse.[148] In an attempt to reestablish control, on December 19, 1956, the Central Committee sent a secret circular to party organizations across the country, identifying the offenders—ex-convicts and Gulag returnees, nefarious bourgeois agents, and wavering intellectuals of dubious political commitments. Erratic arrests and convictions for anti-Soviet propaganda followed in 1957.[149] Western cultural imports were implicated in the circular and in some of the collective actions. However—and this bears emphasis—there was no disavowal of new cultural exchange policies in 1957.

Nor was there any such disavowal during the ideological campaign of 1962–1963. The two moments, Hungary and the ideological panic, were directly related. In 1958, reacting to the intellectual ferment of 1956–1957, the Central Committee established a series of ad hoc ideological commissions. Their task was to oversee ideological orthodoxy in a new cultural landscape—which remained fundamentally unchanged after Hungary and in which Western imports abounded, while mass terror was no more. In the late 1950s and early 1960s, similar commissions were reproduced throughout the party hierarchy, at municipal, district, and institutional levels, all with the same objective: to struggle against "the infiltration of bourgeois ideology." We know what movies played at which theaters and what books were checked out from district libraries, because commission inspectors investigated these venues. Inspectors went to neighborhood parks and could not believe their eyes at how young people danced. They stopped at used bookstores and were mortified to find books that had been long banned. In Moscow, ideological commissions surveyed drama theaters and learned that, in 1962–1963, no fewer than eleven plays drew from "contemporary Western repertory." Reviews of movie theaters in Khar'kov, Ukraine, presented similar results: there were hardly any Soviet films in release. Commissions examined universities and institutes, too, because the new cultural exchange agreements meant that foreign students now shared dormitories with Soviet youngsters and dozed off during lectures on dialectical materialism. In the early 1960s, reports from these commissions rushed up the party hierarchy, creating a tense atmosphere. The reason for the frenzy was the massive presence of "bourgeois" novels, films, paintings, persons, and sounds—at every turn, on every corner. The commissions' internal documents were full of observations on the novelty of this situation: "our enemies are fortifying the ideological struggle." Nobody mentioned that the flood of Western imports was the result of Central Committee cultural exchange policies.[150]

The people who directed the Central Committee's Ideological Commission, the overseer of all commissions, finally had enough. Its chairman, Leonid Il'ichev, and his staff masterminded an ideological attack. Il'ichev was a skilled practitioner of such campaigns: he had served on the editorial board of the chief party journal in the late 1930s, edited the main government newspaper in the late 1940s and the leading party newspaper in the early 1950s, in times when such campaigns had been deadly. On December 1, 1962, Khrushchev visited the Soviet art pavilion at the Manezh Central Exhibition Hall. It was a frame-up: past socialist realist classics, Il'ichev directed his boss to a hall with nonfigurative paintings.[151] Khrushchev's profanities are still the stuff of memoirs. Between late December 1962 and the first half of 1963, stern people from the Ideological Commission staged a series of meetings with the recalcitrant cultural elite to drive home the message that there would be no compromises with "bourgeois ideology," or, in the idiom of the time, "no peaceful coexistence" on "ideological questions." The meetings left intellectuals deeply shaken: in this moment of truth, they realized that the general secretary was a boor and that the regime remained brutal.[152] But the archives reveal aspects of the campaign that the hysterical press and bitter recollections do not illuminate. The stringent pitch of campaign spokesmen only incited anger in the audiences. People wrote to defend their favorite cultural figures and the very idea of artistic plurality. And they wrote with uncommon aggression, throwing cusswords at high authorities. Moreover, once the dust settled, cultural exchange policies remained unaltered: on translations, exhibitions, music albums, film screenings there would be no retreat.

Historians and memoirists sometimes consider these moments, late 1956–1957 and late 1962–1963, as retrenchment from reforms. However, the early 1960s saw not only an ideological campaign against modernism in poetry, painting, and cinema, but also the most vigorous public conversations on the Terror before perestroika. Even as Khrushchev berated intellectuals, the party allowed publication of key texts about Soviet labor camps and the atmosphere of fear in the late 1930s.[153] This culture was multifaceted and fragmentary, defined by countervailing tendencies and disrupted by scandals, rather than counterreforms. As for "bourgeois infiltration," under attack in 1956–1957 and 1962–1963, neither Hungary nor the ideological campaigns of the early 1960s had a permanent effect on Western cultural presence in the Soviet Union.

In fact, within a few months of the Hungarian Revolution, in March 1957, the Central Committee established the Committee for Cultural Relations with Foreign Countries (GKKS). This committee coordinated propaganda outreach abroad and crafted integrated annual plans of cultural exchange across Soviet ministries, institutions, and republics. The GKKS was so important that it was conceived as an almighty department of the Central Committee, subject only to its Secretariat. GKKS's affiliation with the Council of Ministers would be a "conspiratorial" cover for party work under the guise of a state institution. SSOD, meanwhile, maintained the fiction of an independent civic association.[154] Almost immediately, however, the GKKS became the arm of cultural diplomacy. It received recommendations from Soviet embassies and missions about tailoring propaganda for targeted audiences abroad, and its representatives participated in negotiations of cultural exchange agreements.[155] Concluded for a term of just a year or two, none of the agreements was particularly binding. There were no juridical mechanisms for enforcing them. Everything hinged on goodwill, interpersonal relations, and mutual propagandistic benefits. The structure of bilateral agreements allowed for flexibility, while also imparting fragility to the system: one partner could send it spiraling down. The exchange agreements were highly responsive to the big and small fluctuations in conventional diplomacy, and those with France, Britain, and the United States did not stipulate the conditions for renewal.[156] Even so, by the mid-1960s, there was already a measure of predictability to the procedures and regularity to the plans. In 1967, GKKS was dissolved. Cultural diplomacy came to occupy a normal office at the Ministry of Foreign Affairs.[157] Remarkably, this system of cultural exchange between the USSR and Western countries proved durable, lasting as long as the Soviet Union itself.

What went on inside the strange house on Vozdvizhenka during the late 1950s was a good match for its exterior: cultural exchange was one of the strangest things the new Soviet leadership undertook. The reason for this strangeness lies in the events of the late 1940s. The 1950s looked and felt very different from the xenophobia of Stalin's last decade, when the Soviet Union seemed to have conclusively abandoned its early internationalism—a process that had begun in the second half of the 1930s, if not earlier.[158] Nonetheless, internationalist thinking persisted throughout the late 1930s and even in the late 1940s, when cultural exchange within the socialist bloc was both thinkable and commonly practiced.[159] As a political project, Soviet internationalism had incredible staying power, despite varying degrees of public prominence. By the time it took the limelight in the mid-1950s, a well-developed vocabulary and Soviet precedents had already existed, the most important of which was engagement with the Popular Front. In the 1950s, we find behaviors and conceptual categories borrowed from the mid-1930s.

The Soviet Union in the mid-1950s represented a case of governmental internationalism, which sought to reformulate foreign relations as cross-national cooperation and to extend foreign affairs beyond the Ministry of Foreign Affairs.[160] The government initiated an unprecedented campaign for public, popular diplomacy. In principle, the new policy was to be based on trust in the Soviet people. In practice, officials could not give up controlling and censoring the population. The idea of public diplomacy flared briefly and died down by the early 1960s, but the impulse behind it remained, sustaining continued Soviet participation in international cultural traffic.

That impulse was the notion of a shared language called culture. Between the mid-1950s and the early 1960s, a group of Soviet philosophers postulated a set of values they declared to be "universal": fundamental behavioral norms, scientific discoveries, a great "world culture," and the desire to avert war. Class understanding of social life, class analysis of culture, and class morality were by no means abandoned, but the language of common humanity helped to legitimate the new policy of cultural exchange with capitalist countries. "Peaceful coexistence," as the Soviet press never tired of saying, was a long-term policy that would last until it would no longer be necessary—that is, until capitalism would disintegrate under the weight of its internal contradictions. Until then, the policy would ensure peace. Afterward, peace would become eternal and natural, since the reasons for waging war would disappear. In fact, Soviet thinkers spoke of permanent peace right then and there.[161] There was no convincing Marxist justification for these provisions, so Soviet authors situated "peaceful coexistence" within the classics of European political philosophy, drawing a genealogy from the treatises on "perpetual peace."

The Soviet Union's great power status made it possible to conceive of cultural exchange as a way of creating an international audience, gaining recognition in the West, and reinforcing political supremacy. The USSR was a latecomer to the circulation of cultural and consumer goods in postwar Europe, the process usually termed Americanization. American things, symbols, movies, and music made it to many places first, and this was not only the result of US military presence. Another reason was lack of interest on the part of the Soviet government. In the late 1940s, at a time when American policy makers, designers, entertainers, and entrepreneurs were striving to gain mass appeal in Europe, the Soviet leadership had opted for rigorous adherence to the party line and restricted associations of loyal followers. Consequently, by the mid-1950s, the Soviets had to reclaim substantial cultural ground. They sought to break out of the confines of friendship societies and appeal to a broader, nonleftist, "bourgeois" public.

Once the Soviet government started on this path, it remained committed to cultural exchange. During negotiations with their Western counterparts, Soviet representatives would haggle about the minutest articles, stall talks, and slam doors, but they would return to renew the agreements. The most important result was a constant presence—controlled, censored, distorted but nonetheless constant—of Western books, paintings, films, and songs in the Soviet Union.

In the mid-to-late 1950s, when cultural exchange was a novel project, there was one building in Moscow that symbolized foreignness: the House of Friendship. By the mid-1960s, this exotic building would lose its exclusive significance. In the process of cross-cultural transfer that began in the mid-1950s, the foreign became a stable, diffused, and, through translation, intimate presence in Soviet cities. Western imports filled Soviet public places: movie theaters, museums, dancing grounds, university dormitories, and libraries. And they also filled many homes—eventually so seamlessly and imperceptibly that, by the late Soviet decades, people had forgotten about the House of Friendship.

2

The Tower of Babel

Cultural universalism and popular diplomacy were eccentric ideas in the mid-1950s, concentrated in enclaves such as the House of Friendship. But the most prominent manifestation and perhaps the most fitting embodiment of these ideas was not a building. It was an event—ephemeral, unpredictable, and conspicuous. That event was the Sixth International Youth Festival, which brought to Moscow 34,000 foreigners for two weeks in August 1957. In the plans for several years, the festival was meant to clinch the new diplomatic course: the openness and publicity of bilateral exchanges and personal contacts. Ideas elaborated in backstage negotiations—behind ornate doors of exclusive buildings—now came alive in festival streets. Unlike the attempts at exchanges of the previous two years, the festival was not about any particular country or relationship, the capitalist West or the socialist bloc. It was about discovering the world. A utopian endeavor and a voyage (for Soviet and foreign participants alike), the festival belongs to the centuries-long quest for a universal language.[1] In classical utopias and fantasy fiction, a common language is a set piece for a perfect society. In the Soviet Union of the mid-1950s, the perfect language that promised unity across geopolitical borders was the "language" of culture—of literary archetypes, painting and cinema, music, dance and gestures. It was this language that the festival embraced and promoted, as its creators fixated on the story of Babel.

The festival was a signature event, a landmark moment in the mythology of the Thaw, and a watershed in the lives of numerous participants. It was unparalleled in scale, scope, investment, excitement, and impact on the lives of participants and on the city of Moscow itself. The festival launched artistic styles, cultural institutions, and the careers of countless musicians, singers, actors and actresses, artists, comedians, and athletes; it was "a ticket to life" of the Thaw years. It was also a logistical tour de force, whose traces are still evident in Moscow: in the names of streets and metro stations, in neighborhoods, parks, buildings, and in Luzhniki Stadium. Above all, for the majority of Soviet citizens, it was the most concentrated exposure to foreigners they had ever experienced.

Memoirists and interviewees recall "the atmosphere" of "something special, new, and inexplicable."[2] The novelty struck people even when it was encountered secondhand; for one such memoirist, who was not in Moscow that summer, the festival still marked the beginning of "a new life, *vita nova*."[3] For another memoirist, who was in Moscow and who had experienced the jostling crowds, the festival as a popular fête was almost comparable to the spontaneous celebrations in May 1945. There was something of the same communal elation when, on the festival's opening day, July 28, 1957, people poured onto the streets, throwing flowers and holding out their hands. They, participants and onlookers, were the principal makers of the event and its meanings. Underpinning recollections of the festival is a strong sense of empowerment: "Completely spontaneously, without any preparation, Moscow demonstrated—with hundreds of thousands of handshakes, hugs, and kisses—what it supported and what it wanted."[4] So strong was this sense that, remembering the feeling years later, some people consider the festival to have been one of the Soviet government's fatal mistakes for opening the country to the world.[5]

Given this impression, it is ironic that the festival was meticulously scripted, including the crowds in the streets, the flowers, even the hugs. This fact does not mean that participants were naive, complicit, or disingenuous: without those enraptured crowds, the festival and its impact would have been very different. It does, however, reveal the festival as a literary enterprise, a spectacular invention on paper, before it became real. It is astounding to see just how closely the festival matched the scripts, sketches, and preparatory plans. The thousands of textual pages do not portray what really happened during that summer of 1957. Rather, they betray the meanings and imaginings invested in the festival. A Tower of Babel completed, the festival highlighted cross-cultural communication as an intellectual problem and a source of creative expression.

How the Festival Became a Cultural Event

The festival as a cultural celebration was not made entirely in the Soviet Union. The massive publicity effort and the dividends that Soviet propagandists expected to reap, as well as fears on the other side of the ideological divide about communist seduction, have obscured the international contribution to the festival's conception. The festival program that left so significant a mark in late Soviet culture would have been very different had it been crafted by the Komsomol alone.

After World War II, biannual international youth festivals were among the most prominent leftist events in the world. By 1957, they had had only a decade-long history, but each event had taken place at turning points in the Cold War—from the Prague festival of 1947, the year Czechoslovakia joined the Cominform, to the Bucharest festival staged days after the ceasefire in Korea, to the Warsaw festival of 1955, held less than two weeks after the Geneva Summit, by way of the 1951 festival in divided Berlin.[6] The festivals were organized by the World Federation of Democratic Youth (WFDY) and the International Union of Students (IUS). Both are typically treated as communist front organizations, and indeed, they were. But in the immediate postwar period, their leaders strove for a broadly leftist alliance. This changed in 1948, when the federation and the IUS were Sovietized and their political basis narrowed substantially, while the tone of their meetings and publications turned shrill. As a result of backstage maneuvers, communists emerged in key positions of both organizations.[7]

In 1956, however, Sovietization became irksome to the top leadership of the WFDY and the IUS. That summer, the IUS convened a meeting of communist youth unions in Prague, and the WFDY Council held its session in Sofia. The key issue in those discussions was autonomy, or, in communist parlance, "democratic centralism": as the Chinese, British, and Italian representatives complained, there was too much centralization and not enough democracy. This was an intra-communist affair, but even tried and tested comrades resented Soviet interference. The Sofia and Prague meetings spurred decentralization proposals, some so extreme as to advocate disbanding the WFDY. Alarmed by these "abolitionist moods," Komsomol first secretary Aleksandr Shelepin endorsed a closed meeting, where leaders of the communist youth movement were to reformulate the WFDY Charter on new principles: autonomy for national unions and admission for youth organizations regardless of politics—in the spirit of peaceful coexistence. The meeting was set for October 1956 at the WFDY headquarters in Budapest.[8]

The meeting did not take place. What did take place in Budapest that October was the Hungarian Revolution. The festival began to take shape in its immediate aftermath. In mid-November, the Council of Ministers passed a resolution on the festival, defining its purpose defensively: to demonstrate "the historic accomplishments of the Soviet people in the building of socialism during the forty years of Soviet power." Socialism in its Soviet version, and only such.[9] This defensive language, however, is not as surprising as the staunch commitment to the festival. The commitment may have even intensified after Hungary, as national preparatory committees throughout Europe faced the disintegration of the festival. Pope Pius XII denounced the festival and announced an alternative celebration of Catholic youth for August 1957. The British Council's Soviet Relations Committee proposed a festival of young people from around the United Kingdom, and the NATO Council considered convening its own youth festival in Paris. On numerous occasions, the U.S. Department of State and the British Foreign Office delayed processing the passports of people traveling to Moscow.[10] Countless articles denounced the festival in ever-stronger language, and noncommunist youth organizations that had enlisted began to withdraw.[11] The festival was truly in danger from October to December of 1956, when activities on its behalf—singing, dancing, painting, competing in sports, collecting money, forming delegations—were suspended in Europe.[12]

In an attempt to pick up the festival's broken pieces, the European organizers staked their propaganda efforts on the cultural program—because it was entertaining, innocent, and held out a promise of broad appeal. In the Netherlands, recruitment for the festival was particularly successful among students and various "cultural organizations," which volunteered ballet performers, orchestras, acrobats, magicians, a pantomime troupe, a documentary film, four sports teams, and a band of concert whistlers. In West Germany, which had not participated in earlier festivals, much of the organizational work passed to artists and academics. Even in Britain, where the Hungarian events resonated strongly and where the government had suspended cultural relations with the Soviet Union, many cultural and athletic organizations still joined the festival preparations.[13]

The Soviet planners' heightened sense of circumstances and the recognition that they had to reclaim moral ground proved to be Hungary's most consequential impact on the festival. That was how the festival became *conceivable* as an expressly cultural event.[14] And that, partly, was how the festival did indeed become a cultural event, one of the most spectacular in Soviet history. To be sure, previous festivals mixed political rallies and national concerts.[15] But nowhere else was the sheer variety of cultural offerings, from folk dancing to rock 'n' roll, from academic realism to abstract expressionism, so disorienting yet electrifying; nowhere else was the multitude and simultaneity of performances so overwhelming; and nowhere else was the cultural program so pivotal for legitimizing the festival as a whole.

The same quest for legitimacy, together with plummeting prestige and international pressures, compelled the planners to broaden the festival's politics in word and in deed. This was where the International Preparatory Committee had some real bearing, beyond the consultative and consenting functions it had performed until then. A three-part structure oversaw the arrangements of youth festivals: the International Preparatory Committee, consisting of WFDY and IUS leaders as well as representatives of international youth organizations; the national preparatory committees, which raised funds and assembled delegations; and the preparatory committee of the host country, which handled logistics. The Soviet Preparatory Committee was a member of the International Committee, in principle no different from its other national counterparts. In practice, the Soviet Committee did not answer to anybody but the Komsomol (and ultimately, the CPSU). Festival programs originated in host countries and were submitted to the International Committee, which circulated them among participant countries. Revisions to the programs took into account the interests, events, and wishes favored by national committees.[16] In early January 1957, as soon as the crisis in Hungary had subsided, the International Committee's decision makers met for three days to discuss the new situation and its ramifications for the festival.[17] European members of the committee seized the moment to urge Shelepin toward a more inclusive festival: "open to all movements, to all organizations."[18]

Their advocacy was surprisingly effective. The Komsomol and the Soviet Preparatory Committee had a limited role in choosing delegates. Selected as part of professional groups or performing troupes, delegates often came representing nobody but themselves, simply because they had applied. Some applied because they excelled at basketball; some were musicians, avid stamp collectors, amateur photographers, or professional filmmakers; some loved the outdoors; some were writing a thesis on Russian literature or on Soviet peace aims. Others applied because their parents were Russian or Ukrainian or Jewish émigrés; still others applied because they were workers in the nth generation or intellectuals; and yet others because they were anti-Soviet or anti-American or pan-Arabic or communist. And while some attended as pilgrims to the Promised Land, many others came out of curiosity, for here was an opportunity to travel cheaply to a "great mysterious country," an unfathomable place "behind the iron curtain," "an entirely different world."[19] The unbelievable stories that many claimed to have read about the USSR had only confirmed their decision to see Moscow for themselves. Not even rumors of danger—that foreigners would be shipped immediately to Siberian camps, or trained to be Soviet spies, or murdered—could deter the adventure seekers.[20]

Whatever their motives for attending, they were all permitted to enter the country—and with everything they chose to bring. The Ministry of Foreign Trade repealed customs regulations and lifted the mandatory luggage examination, in effect equating festival participants with invitees of the Communist Party (who, since 1953, had not been subject to border searches). For its part, the Main Censorship Administration revoked the inspection of musical recordings and printed material, although there was a good chance that foreigners would bring "unwelcome books, recordings, postcards."[21] So, when festival guests crossed the Soviet borders, nobody checked their bags, counted their money, or held them responsible for importing foreign currency, contraband gold watches and silk stockings, pornography, rock 'n' roll records, "I Like Ike" buttons, and anti-Soviet pamphlets. And if they left the USSR with more banknotes than they brought (from selling contraband gold watches and silk stockings), nobody stopped them: inventories, declarations, and other slips of paper were discarded, too.[22]

Among these discarded papers were visa applications and registration stamps. The entry permit was a special festival card, rather than the customary visa. The cards were issued by Soviet embassies, consulates, and missions upon receipt of the lists of delegates from the national preparatory committees.[23] Even when foreign "friends" tipped off embassy officials about suspected moles and provocateurs, and even when the Soviet Preparatory Committee rejected such people, there was little that the Ministry of Foreign Affairs could do.[24] Only at the request of an individual delegation could potential participants be denied the festival card and, with it, admission to the country.[25] And so it was that festival planners were able to maintain, almost by default, the appearance of an open society. Indeed, the delegates were quite a sight in Moscow: socialists from France and Christian Democrats from Italy, falangistas from Spain and empire loyalists from Britain, as well as committed Zionists from around the world.[26]

The festival was the first public event held in the Soviet Union that was made in part elsewhere—abroad, by capitalist entrepreneurs, modernist artists, sultry dancers, folk singers, political skeptics, religious believers, socialist parliamentarians, embittered people's democrats, disobedient communists, decolonizing natives, sleek teenagers, and intelligence agents. The result was not exactly the festival that the Komsomol bosses wanted, but it was the festival that they got: a fantastic (in both senses of the word) cultural celebration.

Theatrical Moscow

The conflict between the political and cultural conceptions of the festival was at the heart of competing visions of celebratory Moscow. The city and the event were designed by Moscow's decorator Mikhail Ladur (1903–1976), the stage artist Boris Knoblok (1903–1984), and the directors of mass spectacles Iosif Tumanov (1909–1981) and Betti Glan (1903–1992), all members of the Soviet Preparatory Committee.

The festival broke new aesthetic ground, but its creators did not belong to a new generation. Coming of age in the 1920s, they had choreographed Soviet public events throughout the 1930s: physical culture parades, mass celebrations, and central streets—a glossy socialist realist life. It was to the celebratory culture of these decades that they looked for inspiration in designing the festival. They were the surviving enthusiasts of the early Soviet theater that had aimed at dissolving the boundaries between stage and auditorium, leaving the buildings, and taking to the streets. After the Revolution, mass festivals had appealed to many people, from reformers of conventional theater to literacy campaign advocates, for unifying the audience and actors, the arts and the senses. In the immediate postrevolutionary years, directors of mass spectacles had mixed and matched medieval mystery plays and effigy burnings, religious processions, court ceremonies, circus and gymnastics, commedia dell'arte and Russian fairground amusements.[27] While some of the more unconventional plans and their creators had disappeared in successive attacks on "formalism," the theater of the masses lived on in park carnivals, physical culture parades, and street festivities of the 1930s.[28]

Mass theater persisted in the 1930s, not least because the people who had created these carnivals, parades, and festivities—the poster images of merry

Soviet life—had been educated in the art studios and theaters of the Soviet avant-garde as well as in the Komsomol clubs of the 1920s. Take the story of Betti Glan, for instance. A provincial girl, Glan had come to Moscow in 1920 to study foreign languages. There, she began the hungry but happy student life of a Komsomol enthusiast. Glan loved organizing revolutionary anniversaries, theatrical productions, music circles, and people in general. In 1929, she was appointed the director of the Central Park of Culture and Rest, soon named after Gorky. She invited stage artists, assembled a team of young architects, commissioned famous sculptors, repainted all structures in blue and lemon hues, planted bird cherry, lilacs, jasmine, barberry, tulips, peonies, and forget-me-nots, and so established the Gorky Park that became a favorite setting for popular pastimes and a recurring subject of journalistic coverage. Glan set out to create an enchanted place of her imagination. She dreamed epic dreams: of classical tragedies in open-air amphitheaters, of medieval mystery plays and French Revolutionary festivals, and also of the Soviet mass spectacles from the immediate postrevolutionary years. Like those avant-garde celebrations, the park's theatrical productions often dispensed with the conventional stage and used the natural environment instead. In Glan's descriptions, the park was a fairyland. The summer carnivals were spectacles of illuminated miracles: mirrors, fake fruits hanging from trees, exotic fish and flowers floating in a pond, and pyrotechnic pictures. During the winter, a huge electric panel made of thousands of light bulbs stood in the center.[29]

Glan's fantastic world—magic amid terror—intersected with the biographies of other festival designers.[30] In 1933, another young provincial, Mikhail Ladur, arrived in the park with bold sketches and models of sideshows designed to "shock the viewer." Glan and Ladur had similar temperaments—energetic, excitable, easily carried away—and she hired the young man on the spot. For the next four years, Ladur designed the Gorky Park exhibitions, ballets and other dramatic productions, and the first carnival in 1935. He worked with Glan until 1938, when she was arrested. Ladur left the park, and his subsequent rise was meteoric: the ornamental pavilions of the All-Union Agricultural Exhibition and the perfectly synchronous physical culture parades of the late 1930s were his handiwork.[31] His goal was to turn the vacant spaces of the city's squares and parks into "a festive state of being." Soon, that vacant space would become the whole of Moscow: Ladur was the chief choreographer of festivities in the capital until the 1960s.

The Festival Preparatory Committee brought Ladur and Glan, now released from the Gulag, together again. In designing the festival, their first and singularly influential references were the mass celebrations of the 1920s *and* the carnivals and gymnastics parades of the 1930s. From the 1920s, these people had preserved their zeal for the avant-garde art of the squares. But in the meantime, they also had acquired a love of symmetry and order, as well as a fondness for the plush curtains, papier-mâché, telling details, and historical accuracy of the realist stage. Many attractions, special effects, and carnival tricks came to the festival from the Gorky Park of the 1930s. Gorky Park had been an oasis, where "the miracles" had been confined.[32] Festival Moscow would be a citywide Gorky Park. The artists conceived of the city as a stage, the buildings and boulevards, parks and ponds as stairs, aprons, proscenia, curtains, and cycloramas. They designed their events to match the theatrical Moscow of their sketches.[33]

But the city itself posed a challenge. As the head of the Preparatory Committee's program department explained, there was "a danger that the festival would be lost in such a huge city as Moscow. That is why we must give Moscow a feel for the festival." How to make the city *feel*?[34] One way of assimilating the festival in Moscow was to disperse it, and this was exactly what Ladur proposed. "Scatter the spectacle all around Moscow. Explain to the people that interesting things are not to be seen in one [specific] place, one square, but all around Moscow."[35] The thinking behind Ladur's suggestion was that Soviet holidays were centripetal: for the most part, they took place in city centers, with a parade down the main street toward the seat of power, or, in Moscow, down the streets converging at Red Square. By contrast, the festival sprawled, radiating out to the train stations, to the outskirts beyond the nascent Moscow Automobile Ring Road, then to Khimki. The festival's opening motorcade was linear, circumventing the center and connecting the opposite ends of the city, the northeast and the southwest. The procession and foreign presence spotlighted these two neighborhoods within the capital's order of places. The delegates were housed in the environs of the All-Union Agricultural Exhibition and the Botanic Gardens in the northeast; their final destination was the new Luzhniki Stadium located in a new neighborhood, the South-West, whose construction had begun in 1952 and whose landscape was still pierced by lifting cranes.[36] Before the festival, foreigners had been consigned to specific places, enclaves invisible to much of the population and coded as dangerous (as well as privileged) in the Soviet press, fiction, film, and popular imagination. The festival recast the place of foreigners in Moscow. They could be found anywhere, even beyond city limits.

Iosif Tumanov and Boris Knoblok invented an even more "radical" way to domesticate the festival—by bringing it to people's homes, in the form of manufactured decorative kits, complete with ribbons, vinyl flowers, little flags, triangular streamers, and stickers depicting the festival emblems, the daisy and the dove. A month or two before the event, the population busied itself with cutting out paper lanterns and carving plywood daisies. Crimped paper, cardboard and gauze for sturdiness, ropes and wires for hanging, paper streamers and fabrics, even white towels in place of canvas: people glued together and painted whatever they wanted and thus made the event their own. They transformed a state holiday into something of a personal celebration, much like New Year's Eve, when the long-standing practice of devising ornamental birds, snowmen, snowflakes, and paper lanterns doubled the festive anticipation and familial togetherness. Not only the skills but even the patterns came in handy for the festival: the summer season notwithstanding, paper snowflakes embellished some windows.[37]

The Soviet system of festivities provided the practical know-how, but the influence ended there. If there were any Soviet celebratory rituals in the event, they slipped in by habit or mistake. Festival planners repeatedly urged each other to pay attention to foreign audiences and were mindful of avoiding overtly Soviet themes. Instead, they sought universal symbols: dove, torch, fire, water, white and blue.[38] At the opening ceremony, the "festival flag" was to be carried before national and Soviet banners. The flag was a white silk field with a daisy of five colorful petals standing for the five continents. The daisy was designed in Moscow specifically for this event, and its red, blue, green, yellow, and purple petals recalled a different ceremonial order. Its closest visual and symbolic kin were the five intertwined Olympic rings.[39] When the Olympic Games finally took place in Moscow in 1980, some of the same people who had staged the festival, notably Iosif Tumanov, would design the opening and closing ceremonies.[40]

Torches were among the most prominent "Olympic" elements in the festival ceremonies. Thousands lit torches at the "rally against nuclear warfare" and carried them through the streets. The grand ball in the Kremlin ended in a farewell ritual that involved torches. At midnight, Soviet hosts, torches in hand, lined up at the Spasskii Gates as foreigners disbanded. Cardboard and real torches were also part of city décor, and the torch became a second symbol of the festival: a hand raising a torch appears on festival keepsakes, on everything from glass holders to flashlights.[41] All this, including the release of doves and the flame, had more to do with the Olympics—or with Olympian dreams—than with the structure and symbolism of Soviet celebrations.

Fire was ubiquitous in the festival theater. Invested with significance at all times and in all cultures, fire has represented passions, enlightenment, transformation, and purification. It seemed a perfect element for an event whose makers so self-consciously wished to stir lofty feelings, impart knowledge, and transform participants. At "the rally against warfare," fire meant passion and pathos. A hand holding a torch was a declaration of activism, while rows of such hands were a statement of strength and unity.[42] Fire was the centerpiece of "the evening of solidarity with colonial youth" in Ostankinskii Park. This production drew on another staple of fire references: elemental, primordial, sacred. A motionless pond—the counterpoint to fire—added a touch of mystery to the performance. Canoes carrying torchbearers glided gently toward the center of the pond, where participants set afire a daisy-shaped raft, fusing flame and water.[43] Back on the shore, a bonfire soon transformed the grounds into a place of bonding and magic. People began to move into the fire circle—to move round and round, to sing and dance and beat the djembes deep into the night. Blazing flames, rising smoke, drum rolls, "bodies and faces flushed" with excitement: years later, Knoblok recalled the scene as spellbinding, practically shamanistic.[44]

And then there was the question of how to represent Russia while striking universal recognition. Bygone Russia mattered to the artists' conception of the festival, and it left its traces on postcards and in street ornaments, whose distinctive curly floral patterns were inspired by traditional wood paintings in black and gold. Bygone Russia also made an appearance in folk costumes and repertoire, and in celebratory sequences, which extensively relied for mise-en-scène on old Russian street fairs. The circus cavalcade was stylized as a Russian outdoor fête.[45] Festival artists brought out show booths, market tents, street vendors hawking trifles, dancing bears, fluffy pancakes, gingerbread, and mead, and so mixed the recognizable ingredients of the Shrovetide into a mid-twentieth-century international mega-event.[46] But "the image of Russia and her bears" was precisely what the head of the Komsomol Aleksandr Shelepin wanted the festival to dispel. Show booths, popular fêtes, and "antediluvian costumes" "à la russe" were no longer the essence of the Russian "national character." They were a joke. The serious content was this: "We must show [Russia] as an advanced, mighty power with one of the greatest cultures that any country could envy."[47]

Preparatory Committee discussions about city décor were tense, coming close to a showdown between Shelepin and Ladur. Shelepin did not like the sketches that Ladur presented in the spring of 1957 for two reasons: the projects were too costly and too avant-garde. The artists envisioned a sensuous festival that would overwhelm people's eyes and ears, even their noses, and thus reach their hearts. Think about it, Tumanov urged the Committee, and let us paint poppies and daisies on the ground, turning roads into flower fields.[48] Shelepin, however, never tired of repeating that the festival was a very serious political matter, and Committee meetings often were disturbed by his accusations that the artists were brazenly indifferent to politics.[49]

The artists were offering a city of excess, a city-theater, a festival-carnival. To turn Moscow into a celebratory city, Tumanov and Knoblok even resolved to repaint streetcars, buses, taxis, as well as vans, cars, and pickup trucks carrying the foreigners. For the artists, this was essential, because, in Knoblok's words, everything bore "military color." It was the pervasive olive and brown that ultimately broke the Preparatory Committee's resistance to the idea of portable color. As Knoblok reported, "No argument or reason worked until the very day, or more precisely, the very morning of the motorcade rehearsal." That morning was damp and dull; the ground was shiny black; it had rained. Hundreds of cars and trucks covered in khaki began their slow journey through the rain, as if straight from a battleground. "The sight was so dismal that no other proof was needed: everybody at once started saying how necessary repainting was!" To paint trucks and vans—from olive green to orange, blue, yellow, lilac; to paint them twice over—with exotic flowers, birds and butterflies, with wavy azure stripes.[50] To this day, in interviews and memoirs, mention of the festival triggers recollections in color and of color: "Before, we had known no other but camouflaged trucks in Moscow, as if they all were ready for sudden mobilization, for transfer to the army regime. But at the Moscow festival there appeared trucks of different, sometimes unthinkable colors."[51] There was something wild about purple cars. Aesthetic and emotional abandon replaced homogeneity and solemnity.

The most elaborate transformations, such as the scenography for Kropotkin Square and Gogol Boulevard, often were not realized. On the boulevard, plans called for every few steps to disclose a different act in the story of "literary characters at the festival." A multilevel installation would turn

Figure 2.1. Carnival procession in Okhotnyi riad. VI International Festival of Youth and Students, 1957. Photographer unknown.

Photo provided by the Central State Archive of the City of Moscow, Archival negative no. 1-18392.

Kropotkin Square into a wharf, with a street in the immediate foreground, followed by the sea, mooring ships, and disembarking travelers—literary protagonists arriving in Moscow. The wind would blow the pink and yellow sails, and the festival daisy would hold the mooring lines. This composition would blend seamlessly with the natural landscape, the river, and the embankment sweeping before the square, the shaded Gogol Boulevard sloping behind it. The blue band depicted in the sketch may have been the real Moscow River; it certainly cast Moscow as the proverbial port of five seas. And the characters—courtiers in puffed trousers and ruffed collars, gentlemen in long overcoats and tall cylinder hats, from sixteenth-century Spain to Victorian Britain—would at last fulfill the wishful prophecy of Peter the Great in Pushkin's rendition: "Ay, ships of every flag shall come." Farther along the boulevard, on the ground, disrupting all scale and proportion, a gigantic Gulliver was meant to dwarf passersby. As the sketches envisioned it, his bent legs, stretched across the alley, were to form a gate, and the pocket of his blue jacket was to house a book kiosk.[52]

Figure 2.2. F. Sevartian, Decoration for Kropotkin Square, "Literary characters at the International Festival of Youth and Students in Moscow," Sketch, 1957.
Reproduced from *Sovetskoe dekorativnoe iskusstvo, 1945–1957: Ocherki* (Moscow: Iskusstvo, 1989).

Although this particular composition did not take shape during the festival, the main ideas—literary themes triggering universal recognition, the arrival of ships of every flag, the re-creation of foreign vistas in Moscow—did come to fruition in one form or another. Tverskoi Boulevard was transformed into an encyclopedia of fairy tales and legends. A "magical village" mixed and matched different cityscapes. Here, a caliph's palace stood side by side with a Chinese pagoda, palm trees doubled as partitions between curling eaves and domes crowning octagonal arcades, and real tree leaves embraced all this strangeness. Throughout Moscow, trucks carried models of Paris, London, and Venice on rooftops, and any street could open onto surprising vistas.[53]

The idea of the "ships of every flag" coming to Moscow was most explicit in the festival water show, when all the world's ships did indeed reach Moscow. Varangian carved boats and Greek biremes appeared. Columbus's caravel and Afanasii Nikitin's vessel arrived. Chinese junks carried the sounds of dizi flutes, bells, cymbals, and lutes; gondolas, sentimental barcarolles. Every kind of ship imaginable, staffed with sailors and passengers in historical and national costumes, was here: galleys, frigates, clippers, corvettes, barges, schooners, sloops, launches, karbasses, canoes, pirogues, feluccas, and even an Inca wooden raft Kon-Tiki, under the likeness of the

Figure 2.3. L. Egorkina, I. Lavrov, and others. Decoration for Tverskoi Boulevard, "Fairytales around the world." VI International Festival of Youth and Students, 1957. Photographer unknown.

Reproduced from *Sovetskoe dekorativnoe iskusstvo, 1945–1957: Ocherki* (Moscow: Iskusstvo, 1989).

sun god Viracocha. The ships were accompanied by real and fantastic creatures of the seas: mermaids crowned with flower-wreaths and monsters covered with seaweed; whales turned into fountains; crocodiles and dragonflies; and the lord of the show, Neptune, whose trident was now a conductor's baton, now a magic wand igniting "oceans of lights."[54] Some of these creatures and boats had appeared before, at Gorky Park carnivals in the late 1930s.[55] The vision of the "ships of every flag" was the guiding concept for the creators of the water show; Pushkin's verse was on the very first page of their script.[56]

Even events with solemn political purposes were embellished by stage props and a theatrical conception of enclosed space. At Manezh Square, for the "rally against nuclear warfare," Knoblok devised a multistoried stage, a vertical installation of the kind that constructivist theater in the 1920s had invented to allow for simultaneous action.[57] Here, however, the structure was static, meant to convey gravity, tragedy, and unbending will. The vertical design of the stage repeated in hundreds of raised torches, brought by participants and twinkling in mid-air to the sounds of Beethoven's

Fifth Symphony. The seriousness of the occasion and the tragedy it marked were also conveyed by patches of white in the darkness—the white shirts of the torchbearers, the white blouse of a Japanese girl from Hiroshima, and a white dove flapping its wings in the loop of crisscrossing projector lights.[58] The dramatic action hinged on the stark contrasts of silence and symphony, stillness and flight, white and black, fragility and determination.

The Preparatory Committee's report to the Central Committee of the Communist Party could find no better term than "modernism" to describe these carnivalesque and theatrical designs.[59] The charge was not entirely erroneous. The projects to paint flowers on the ground echoed the November 1918 celebrations, when avant-gardist Natan Al'tman had spray-painted trees and grass. At the "evening of solidarity with colonial youth," the felucca-shaped stage cut deeply into the water, its movement and direction recalling the experimental stages of the 1920s.[60] Yet the festival also marked a professional turning point for urban designers. Festival blueprints were distinguished from earlier decorative practices by a new conception of city décor as three-dimensional and interlinked with the surrounding architecture. Previously, posters, portraits, and banners, as well as any flat surfaces mounted on building facades, had had no special—spatial—relationship to the streets, or even to the facades they covered. For the festival, however, stage artists and architects worked together to create entire narrative settings.[61] The decorative sets, like the festival itself, were a fantasy world on the verge of coming true and upsetting the familiar pattern of celebrations, from colors to routes to performances to the structure of public feeling.

Socialist Moscow

The politicians on the Preparatory Committee had a different city in mind: clear lines, smooth facades, wide avenues—the first socialist metropolis. They wanted the itinerary of the opening motorcade to show the new Moscow. At the beginning and end of the route, the highways had been widened and paved, ramshackle wooden houses had been leveled, and multistoried symmetrical apartment buildings faced the road.[62] These were a source of pride, while small, old, or one-storied structures, usually described (decried) as homely, were cause for embarrassment. One of the biggest fears during festival preparations was that malevolent foreigners would seek out and photograph small, dilapidated buildings, so as to put the Soviets to shame.[63] Breadth, space, distance—these were the photogenic qualities depicted in dozens of lavishly colored pictorial albums, in thousands of postcards produced as keepsakes for festival guests, in retouched photographs with sharply drawn contours.[64] Shot at a wide angle, such photographs offered a dramatic perspective and created a sense of expandable space. The avenues impressed at least some festival participants, who noted with mixed feelings of admiration and disbelief: "It looked beautiful, with wide streets and green trees, and a sensation of space that I had never felt in a city of such size."[65]

Although Moscow's size was a problem for the artists, it was also a cause for satisfaction and spirited propaganda. In Festive Moscow, a documentary film prepared for foreign guests and for distribution abroad, portrayed the capital as so vast that the sun shines and the rain pours at the same time on opposite ends of the city.[66] Here was a metropolis that touched the heavens with the steeples of the "Palace of Knowledge," the Moscow University skyscraper, and reached into the depth of the earth with its "underground palace," the Moscow metro.[67] A regal city, then, the symbolic center of the world: Moscow was a port of five seas, announced the film's narrator, and via the waterways of the Black or Baltic seas, the delegates could reach their native shores.[68] The vision of Moscow as a palatial city and center of maritime networks had emerged in the 1930s, when the creators of the metro had erected neoclassical columns and domes underground, while the Moscow-Volga Canal connected the two rivers and led, via other canals, to the Baltic, Black, Caspian, White, and Azov seas.[69] The festival brought to life (and turned into a carnival) the monumental symbols of the 1930s.

But if Moscow was to become a meeting point of the five continents, as it was so insistently portrayed during the festival, then it would first have to become a modern megalopolis, where communications were swift, conveniences abundant, and services convenient. In other words, Moscow would have to become a Western megalopolis. According to the assumptions of Soviet officials, pace and commerce were probably the most important features of capitalist cities. There, information traveled at the speed of light, newspapers covered kiosk counters, telephone wires enveloped neighborhoods, and cars sped about while neon lights flickered madly. Such images came from several decades of Soviet travel writing and also from firsthand experiences, as many members of the Soviet Preparatory Committee traveled abroad frequently. Soviet athletes had just returned from the Olympic Games in Melbourne, and the director of Luzhniki Stadium joined the December 1956 deliberations of the Preparatory Committee, offering his personal impressions. Little lights hidden in trees illuminated Melbourne, each street with a different color—"there are streets that are entirely green, entirely yellow, and this creates a very unusual impression." The main decorations were colors and lights, rather than texts, the customary practice in the Soviet Union.[70]

Political prejudice (these were capitalist cities, after all) intertwined with visual extravaganza, confusing, outrageous, enticing, or everything at once. For Soviet travelers, one of the most memorable experiences was found in the shopping and entertainment districts. The encounter proved instrumental in attempts to upgrade Moscow to a world-class megalopolis. In its earliest and most adamant demands on the municipal authorities, the Preparatory Committee called for big advertisement boards and neon signs above store entrances and movie theaters.[71] These would suggest the bustle of Moscow's commerce, the kind of vibrant scene that astonished Soviet visitors to the West. The advertisements were not meant to market specific products. What the instructions stipulated was simply "raise advertisement boards"—just like in Western cities, where banners and billboards punctuated cityscapes.[72] Or perhaps unlike in Western cities. This was another opinion within the Committee: "We must have billboards, but they should be special, befitting our way of life. They should have nothing in common with advertisement boards in Paris, New York, London."[73]

Festival planners also made a concerted attempt to narrow the gap between Soviet stores and capitalist service standards. At Preparatory Committee meetings, people who had traveled to the West bore witness: yes, smiling saleswomen, hotel towels changed daily, hot water around the clock, clean public bathrooms.[74] In the West, there were clever little things that made life easier. Experts from the Ministry of Trade observed how consumer services were organized at the Melbourne Olympic Games. They brought back samples of curiosities, plastic straws and small water bottles, and the Preparatory Committee asked the Ministry of Light Industry to make the same for the festival.[75] In Melbourne, Ministry of Trade envoys also saw plastic tableware and foldable cafeteria furnishings. Their sketches of saltshakers and tables went to the Preparatory Committee, along with their recommendation: "For serving the festival delegates, adopt the same forms and procedures as in Melbourne" and "construct summer cafeterias on the model of the Olympic ones."[76] The politicians and financial managers pursued their own vision of the Olympian city.

Much of the preparatory effort focused on architectural renovation and infrastructural modernization. Along Yaroslavskoe Highway, in the vicinity of the Agricultural Exhibition, new, multicompound hotels with five stories and broad facades were a natural choice for housing delegates.[77] Some of the hotels had sprung up in the mid-1950s (Zolotoi kolos, Turist, Vostok); others (Ostankino, Altai) were under construction and completed just in time for the festival. In the process, several neighborhoods in the north of Moscow (Ostankinskii district, the settlements of Marfino and Vladykino) were colonized. The sparse apartment buildings and whatever wooden houses that remained were razed, ditches and ravines were filled, and the ground cleared.[78] The festival became the impetus for paving, construction, and the installation of radio networks and telephony, thus accelerating the integration of the northwest and northeast settlements within city limits. Present-day Moscow has long outgrown the boundaries established by the festival, but the northeast still recalls the festival in street names. Even the outlying suburban settlements (Lobnia, Akulovo, and Shchelkovo on the east) have Festival streets, often running next to Peace and Friendship streets.

Advances in communications technologies encompassed the entire city. Until then, the Soviet Union had been rather marginal to the network of nascent global communications. In Moscow, there was just one public telephone location, amounting to three booths, where people could place international calls—something that was exceptional to desire, dangerous to try, and nearly impossible to accomplish. The forty cables stretching from Moscow to Khar'kov, Minsk, Kaliningrad, Tallinn, and then abroad ended mostly in socialist Europe. But Moscow's newly imagined role as the crossroads of the world required a network of lines radiating the world over. In 1956, the Council of Ministers and the Ministry of Communications were determined to set up just such a network for the festival. Within a year, three new telephone substations carried the buzzes from Moscow across Europe and beyond over eighty-four cables, half of them brand new. Thanks to the first transatlantic telephone cable, TAT-1, new networks also connected Moscow to Washington and New York, and through New York with twenty-one more countries.[79] Festival participants could call home from their hotels practically at any time, and in the evenings, "shouts rang down the hall, as well as across the Atlantic: 'Please, Mom, be reasonable!'"[80] Before TAT-1, a joint American, British, and Canadian project completed in September 1956, radio waves and telegraph cables had been the only connection that the Soviet Union, and Europe, had had with the United States. TAT-1 generally is considered an inaugural moment in the system of modern global communications; the Soviet Union was part of this system almost from the start.

The sites, sporting grounds, and parks slated to host festival events were transformed, often beyond recognition, and the transformation proved permanent.[81] The most important such site, the biggest sporting ground ("the Palace of Sports"), and the general pride of the city was Luzhniki Stadium, completed in 1956 and shimmering in the sun. The stadium and the festival were related in several ways. The government resolutions that initiated both were passed in the same year, 1954, and the same internationally minded logic of a Soviet Union ascendant underlay the two projects. They reinforced each other: the festival demanded a stadium big enough to seat a hundred thousand people and may have spurred its speedy construction; in turn, the pace of construction set 1957 as the festival year.[82] The stadium stimulated transportation networks and road development in an area that had had a limited connection to the center. An underground tunnel led to the new metro station; terraces, staircases, and moorages led to the river. The Moscow River was encased in a sloping gray embankment with a pedestrian lane and cast-iron railings. The 1930s constellation of central bridges and embankments—the aesthetic linchpins of socialist Moscow, built to support the Moscow-Volga Canal—was completed here, in Luzhniki, in time for the festival. Aspirations for turning this area into an athletic campus dated back to the early 1920s, to the first plans for a "new," "red" Moscow.[83] According to the city's 1935 Reconstruction Plan, the blueprint for a stately and rational ideal metropolis, this was one of the last sections of the Moscow River to be developed. And according to festival plans, this was the last stretch of showcase Moscow that foreigners would see before the festival officially began—the last stretch of the first impression.[84]

The four main parks in the city and all the smaller district parks, public gardens, and boulevards, even the little plots within courtyards, in short, every last corner, were cleaned, trimmed, mended, and planted anew.[85] For the festival, Moscow would be a garden city. Sokol'niki Park created a rosarium for summertime and a dance hall for year-round use; Izmailovskii Park built an open-air movie theater and a variété stage; and all parks received the latest thrills of the roller-coaster industry.[86] Movie theaters renovated not only facades, seats, curtains, and staircases, but also, and more radically, technology. Here was a development that profoundly affected the senses: stereophonic sound, wide screen, and circarama.[87] For the festival, a dozen old cinemas were fitted with updated projectors, amplifiers, and perforated aluminum screens, but still they could not play foreign Cinemascope-format pictures.[88] New movie theaters were clearly in order, and in 1956, the Moscow municipal Administration of Culture sponsored an All-Union architectural contest. The initial models and calculations were worked out with an eye to such European cinemas as the Gaumont-Palace, Odeon, Rex, and Palais des Festivals in Cannes.[89]

Although the socialist metropolis differed from the carnival city, the politicians and bureaucrats controlling the purse strings shared one fundamental aspiration with the recalcitrant artists. They all imagined Festival Moscow as an Olympian center of international mega-events.

Cosmopolitan Lessons

When the festival was first announced, surveillance reports found Muscovites unenthusiastic and apprehensive. The event was audaciously novel, and nobody knew what to expect. So people expected the worst. Rumors circulated in Moscow, with new festival-related content developing the old themes of famine and repression. One rumor held that food would disappear from stores, another that all young people would be deported from Moscow, while still another prophesied an epidemic.[90] The rumors made symbolic sense. Where the press told of young foreigners arriving, the rumors told of Soviet youth driven out. If the press described popular festivities, strongly associated with abundance, then the rumors warned of shortages.

The rumors inverted the official line, but they were grounded in precedent and reality. Various categories of people were periodically expelled from Moscow, and the festival became an occasion for massive round-up police operations intended to cleanse the city of tramps, thieves, prostitutes, and illegal traders.[91] The criterion for scrutiny was the existence of a criminal record: more than 25,000 people with previous convictions were investigated; some 8 percent were rearrested and sentenced again (while almost 40 percent were co-opted into the network of police informers).[92] People without stable employment or Moscow registration also fell into the net.[93] Whether or not they had committed a crime, such people were apprehended because their presence was an ideological anomaly. Prostitution and pauperism were among the social ills of capitalism, whereas socialist society had no social ills. Although these operations were not reported in the press, Muscovites could not help noticing that familiar beggars kept disappearing from street corners and metro stations. The rumor about the deportation of young people thus took the city's cleanup to a logical (or absurd?) conclusion in a mockery of the festival project. The second rumor likewise had foundations in lived experiences. In an economy of shortages, provisions were always of concern. Add to this some stories in the press about exporting food to help fraternal peoples, or about lavish receptions held in the Kremlin for foreign dignitaries (a frequent news tidbit in the early Khrushchev period), and resentment toward both such reportage and the export of food rose.[94] Now, at the festival, not figurative and unspecified foreigners but real ones—many thousands of them—would have to be fed.[95]

Rumors were hardly unusual for the police and the Komsomol. What was extraordinary was that ordinary people spreading rumors and otherwise grumbling today would tomorrow speak to foreigners spontaneously, in situations where anybody could be an ambassador or a traitor. Since the planners expected ordinary Muscovites to mingle with foreigners, much of their preparatory propaganda concerned mundane comportment, communication, and body language. Komsomol chiefs wanted young Soviets to be worldly and easygoing, modeling calm confidence for foreigners. The key ingredients of winning comportment were pride (in Soviet accomplishments) and respect (for foreign cultures) in equal measure: too much pride could easily become chauvinism; too much respect could easily become groveling.[96]

Festival planners geared instructions according to the degree of proximity to foreigners. Translators were mentally outfitted for closeness. One feature set their lessons apart from the drab lectures of ordinary propagandists. These lessons were structured as answers to foreigners' provocative questions, so the questions, "cunning" and even outright hostile, had to be asked first.[97] Service personnel in restaurants, stores, and especially hotels, where the Soviet staff had the keys to foreigners' rooms and shared intimate space with them, were screened vigilantly.[98] As part of their training, they were introduced to new foreign objects, textures, and sounds. Employees working at dry cleaners were taught how to handle nylon and other synthetic fabrics, while hairdressers had to learn "not only our styles, but also the best foreign ones."[99] Foreign language tutoring was de rigueur for all service personnel.[100] Some 120,000 delegates from the Soviet republics were another category of people slated for special instruction. They would be the ones participating in cultural contests and staged debates; their relationship with foreigners was meant to be visible but not particularly close. They listened to surveys of current events and were trained to answer confrontational questions about Soviet life.[101]

But the delegates learned something else as well. For example, three months before the festival, a crash course in foreign cinema, with screenings, began for film students scheduled to participate in an international colloquium. A month and a half later, a parallel program on Soviet cinema was added. Besides cramming the resolutions of the party plenums, students spent many hours on a journey through world cinema.[102] The purpose of the lessons was to create an image of sophisticated Soviet youth. In the process, thousands of people were exposed to what previously had been restricted, privileged knowledge.

Indeed, festival preparations democratized elite knowledge of foreign places, languages, and cultures. Schools, institutes, clubs, factories, entire neighborhoods, young and old, took up foreign languages as the latest fad, which, for once, was widely endorsed in the press. In 1956, the Twelfth Moscow Komsomol conference pronounced on how important it was to know foreign languages—at least two, an "international language (English, French, Spanish, German, Hindu, Chinese)" and "any other language" of one's choosing.[103] The Moscow Komsomol and festival newspapers started running columns of foreign terms and expressions. A little later, Central Television began broadcasting language lessons in English, German, French, Spanish, and Chinese.[104] Language courses were set up in every conceivable setting, from libraries to factories. Courses were sometimes formal and sometimes a private initiative where a few people taught each other small-talk expressions as best they could. Dictionaries and phrase books became bestsellers.[105] Even so, resources and experience in non-institutionalized language study were meager—ten years earlier one could have been arrested for doing that. So people used newspaper clippings to assemble makeshift "pocket phrase-books"; Moscow library no. 94, for example, maintained a folder of such clippings.[106]

Before long, the publishing industry, which had reoriented toward the festival, exploded with information about exotic places and sites: medieval castles, crooked side streets, palm trees, tropical forests, skyscrapers, piazzas and arcades, ice-lined expanses, and many more. The Distributing Center for Scientific Libraries compiled a bibliographic reference about the 131 countries represented at the festival. With this guide at hand, librarians could readily recommend books and articles, as well as brief readers on basic facts about any country.[107] Another bibliography, also for librarians, covered foreign literature, visual art, music, song, dance, and theater.[108] Such encyclopedic bibliographies—all countries from A to Z—epitomized a remarkable expansion of the geographic imagination.

The frequency with which maps were mentioned during festival preparations reflected this new disposition. Or, rather, it was the map in the singular—the map of the whole world, the proof that encompassing everything on a single sheet of paper was possible. The map was a concept on the order of the festival itself, whose planners were trying to embrace the world in one city. A month before the festival, four movie theaters in Moscow ran a series of documentaries, "The Countries of the World."[109] The activists of the "Torch" club in Moscow's Kuibyshev district called their "spoken journal" "At the Map of the World." Meanwhile, a similar spoken journal in the Sokol'niki district took the audience "Around the World" in a series of lectures.[110] "Maps of the world" covered ordinary newspaper stands in Moscow parks and spread across the walls of neighborhood libraries, where bookcases showcased artifacts, postcards, fact sheets, and novels from different countries.[111] Nooks of all kinds—library corners, theater foyers, billboard displays at park entrances—often unexpectedly revealed a foreign site in a collage of images or a montage of articles and salutations. "The map" was a vocabulary as well. It functioned as an indicator of curiosity and knowledge, and it filled Soviet spaces with foreign appellations, which were pronounced with gusto.

Clubs and Houses of Culture were keen on inviting people who had traveled abroad.[112] They could give color, voice, and substance to abstract facts from brochures and to contours on maps. In 1956, a group of writers and journalists traveled around Europe on the steamship *Victory* in a much-publicized voyage. Afterward, they helped to produce a documentary about the trip and wrote travelogues. Among the earliest audiences for their manuscripts were the inhabitants of Moscow's working-class Stalin district, who came one cold evening to their local library no. 72. For hours, they listened to the writers speak of Europe.[113] Another local library invited a journalist who recently had visited Brazil to "share his impressions about

[that] country's culture and political life." In addition to his impressions, he shared a record, and the evening ended with the assembly tapping toes to Brazilian songs.[114] Gossip and frenzy surrounded recordings purchased abroad. They became objects of devotion, advantageous exchanges, and underground business, and to this day memoirists write about them with considerable emotion.[115] In 1957, these coveted but inaccessible albums were spinning at neighborhood libraries and clubs throughout the city.

When local activists could not enlist such speakers, they tried to recreate foreign experiences on their own. Sokol'niki Park set up lectures about French music and lessons in Latin American songs, which people could learn and rehearse with instructors.[116] As administrators of dance establishments and directors of the houses of culture quickly realized, preparing for the festival was a lucrative undertaking. The Palace of Culture at the Likhachev Automobile Factory had cover charges for its "dance parties," as did the Constructors' House of Culture and Izmailovskii Park; the music was almost exclusively foreign, "tango, rumba, foxtrot," and jazz—that was what people paid for. These venues were usually sold out, and queues of fashionably dressed people lined the streets around 11 pm, waiting for admission and creating something of a nightclub atmosphere.[117] The Moscow University club, which did not charge for its "balls" and "festival evenings," was more crowded. On any given evening, nearly 4,000 people would overtake its audience halls, lobby, even corridors and back rooms. They danced on every square inch of ground.[118] A "student evening" equaled a "dance party" equaled foreign music equaled festival preparations.

Fascination with Latin American music may be traced to the tangos and rumbas of the 1930s, but its sources probably had a more recent provenance—the Argentine film *The Age of Love* (1954). Purchased in 1955 and shown to enraptured audiences for the next few years, the film had one scene in particular that begged to be reproduced: Lolita Torres dancing and singing "Coimbra Divina." The song was rendered into Russian and replicated endlessly through radio broadcasts and recordings. People transcribed the words both in Russian and in the original language, sometimes mangled by the unaccustomed ear, and sang the lyrics whenever they could, even at work. In Aleksandr Iakovlev's famed aircraft design bureau, a twenty-three-year-old engineer named Maya sang "Coimbra Divina" during lunch breaks. Without understanding a word, she had written down the original lyrics, memorized them, and thus entertained her coworkers amid drafting boards and slide rules. A decade later, in a survey of television viewers, Maya Kristalinskaia, by then a star performer, would be singled out as "the best singer of the year," and forty years later, she would be called "the lyrical voice of a generation."[119]

One of the most important inspirations for a Western accent in Soviet performances was Yves Montand. His songs were aired on the radio in 1954–1955, acquiring Russian lyrics and Russian admirers in the farthest reaches of the country, and his figure assumed cult-like proportions following landmark concerts in Moscow, Leningrad, and Kiev (1956). The streets around the concert venue in Kiev were crowded with girls waiting in the brutal winter cold to catch a glimpse of their darling and to get his autograph.[120] In the provinces, in Molotov (today's Perm'), Irkutsk, Novocherkassk, Vladimir, or Derbent (Dagestan), students organized their own Montand concerts in a perfectly Soviet manner: peace slogans, amateur performers memorizing the lyrics in French, exhibits of photographs and newspaper clippings, and a gramophone playing "C'est si bon."[121] In addition to authentic ballads and stylized ditties, festival songbooks also printed Montand's "Les Grands Boulevards." The song was enormously popular in various versions, thanks to the catchy melody and to the people who engaged with it. The handsome and sweet-voiced Gleb Romanov, whose popularity peaked in the mid-1950s, sang it in French. Leonid Utesov, probably the most influential entertainment artist, sang the Russian translation. And Mark Bernes, who had personified manliness and courage in the films of the late 1930s, crooned about what happens "when a faraway friend sings." "Huge distances shorten," "the smile of Paris" illuminates Moscow, and "les Grands Boulevards" join Garden Ring. Bernes's song was dedicated to Montand, the "faraway friend" who effected such physical transformations. The lyrics to both Bernes's and Montand's songs were published, along with "The Anthem of Democratic Youth," under the rubric "What we will sing at the festival."[122]

The best Moscow amateur bands—a trio from the Plekhanov Institute, a guitar quartet from the Second Medical Institute, and a band from the Energy Institute—all emerged from their rehearsals to offer Montand and the "Mexican-Brazilian repertory."[123] In Leningrad, an undisputed success and a student favorite, the pop band "Friendship," created a program consisting mainly of foreign songs: "Czerwony Autobus," "Guitare d'amour," "When the Saints Go Marching In," "Kasztany," "Twenty Tiny Fingers," "Mademoiselle de Paris." The foreign repertory made better sense in this case than in others, since some of the vocalists were students from socialist-bloc countries studying in Leningrad. This Sovietized foreignness and the slight Franco-Polish accent of the lead singer Edita P'ekha provided their distinctive charm. (P'ekha, the daughter of a French father and Polish mother, had been born in France and lived there for the first ten years of her life, until her mother moved to Poland.)[124] During concerts, P'ekha took the microphone off its stationary stand, walked around the stage, and spoke to the audience directly, thus bringing a minor revolution to Soviet performance culture. The band's very existence, their multilingualism, and the role of song as a shared communication mode symbolized the festival.[125]

Such performances were filled with countless moments of creative appropriation: Russian lyrics invented for foreign melodies, popular Soviet theme songs rearranged with foreign inflections, dance steps learned from imported movies and retraced from memory. A new band established at the Central House of the Arts Workers (TsDRI) in 1957 offered an irreverent remix of Isaak Dunaevskii's classic songs, including "Broad Is My Native Land," which, over the years, had become an unofficial anthem.[126] Now, just two years after Dunaevskii's death, the rhythms of this and other songs had changed dramatically: "A . . . song in a Russian melodious style is rendered in *style moderne*, in the style of American jazz. From the aesthetic point of view, this is a distortion."[127] The person who railed so categorically against this composition, titled "Duniada," was Aleksandr Tsfasman, an old jazzman, one of the Soviet Union's most celebrated and versatile. What jarred him was the contamination of the Soviet with the Western. The Western was not necessarily bad, but it was somebody else's, while the Soviet melodies in question were the lyrical songs and spirited marches of "the happy-go-lucky guys" from the beloved musical comedies of the 1930s. Tsfasman wished to maintain distinctions of country and genre: "If you want to show our friends [at the festival] that we understand what American jazz is, then just play Gershwin."[128] A "jazz mania" overtook "almost all institutions of higher learning [and] upper divisions of high schools" in Moscow, Leningrad, Kazan', Sverdlovsk, Tbilisi, Kiev, and other urban centers.[129]

By the time the Preparatory Committee caught up with the action and began to issue one warning after another, it was already too late. Jazz quartets and girls doing the *Cachucha pas de basque* were everywhere. In Moscow, over 150 variety bands and instrumental orchestras of jazz devotees sprang up during festival preparations.[130] "A grave mistake is being committed," complained Komsomol secretary (and career diplomat) Sergei Romanovskii at the end of 1956. "We are learning Spanish dances, Portuguese songs, Chinese dances, various other dances and songs, but nobody knows Russian Soviet songs. This is an unacceptable thing."[131] In mid-June 1957, just over a month before the festival was to begin, the Moscow municipal Komsomol conference ordered city district committees to monitor amateur bands.[132]

To no avail. The process assumed a momentum of its own—and *even before the presence of real foreigners*. Conventional wisdom, based on memoirs, suggests that foreigners, bringing to the festival unthinkable sounds, dance steps, and images, set in motion a stylistic revolution. Indeed, they did. But the aesthetic mobilization had begun before their arrival. It hinged on the anticipation of foreigners and developed in an expectant atmosphere.

Before Babel

On the morning of July 28, anticipation filled the air. Only a day or two earlier, the weather forecast had predicted rain, but now the sky was clear and promised a hot Sunday ahead. Except for a few pedestrians, Garden Ring was empty. Traffic had been blocked from all side streets, so it seemed emptier still to the young men lining the road.

They were the voluntary—or rather, the involuntary—patrols, whose members had no desire to be there, but who were partly coerced and partly seduced by their Komsomol secretary's tales of difficult work ahead.[133] These nineteen-year-old students from the Moscow University law department were among the 30,000 or so Komsomols enlisted to police the streets, parks, and hotel grounds during the festival. The Komsomol patrols were the Preparatory Committee's best hope for law and order, because festival planners wanted to minimize the presence of uniformed men on the streets, lest the foreigners perceive Soviet society as militarized or regimented.[134] That morning, the Komsomols' job was to stand guard every few steps along the sidewalks while the opening motorcade advanced along Garden Ring. They would assure efficiency, discipline, and decorum during the first, most important hours.[135]

Around eleven o'clock, when the motorcade was scheduled to leave the hotels, the streets began to fill with spectators. In photographs of the opening procession, the most salient feature is an infinite sea of people, nearly bursting out of the frame in the foreground and stretching toward the horizon as far as the eye can see. The dominant plane is diagonal, capturing the sheer scale of the throng and extending the movement of outstretched hands. The frame could not accommodate these multitudes; neither could the streets. People leaned out of windows and hung from or sat atop fences. They were jammed on balconies, squeezed tightly together and standing on tiptoes to catch a glimpse from behind the backs of others. They climbed on the roofs of smaller buildings, causing much consternation among the police, and with good reason: the pressure of the crowd brought down a grocery store at the corner of Kolkhoz Square.[136] Windows, balconies, and roofs were perhaps the best seats—the dress circle and the gallery—for the grand theater about to commence.[137]

That morning, Knoblok and Tumanov were at the square by the Agricultural Exhibition, attending to final details. Then they set off: the camera crews, the sentry cars, the directors of the spectacle, the motorcyclists, their chrome-covered bikes sparkling in the sun, the flag bearers carrying an enormous white silk banner and a forest of smaller blue ones, the gigantic daisy, and the somersaulting gymnasts. At the other end of the course, in Luzhniki, the stands filled quickly. Just past noon, journalists, foreign dignitaries, leaders of youth organizations, high-ranking members of fraternal parties, and Soviet government officials began to arrive.[138] The Komsomol patrols and the militia took their posts, the law students at Smolenskaia Square.

There they waited for "an incredibly long time." For over two hours, the Central Committee waited. The foreign dignitaries and journalists and the thousands of people in Luzhniki waited; millions more waited on the sidewalks. The minutes dragged on. For Knoblok, who had already arrived at the stadium, "time had split into two": "Nervousness gave way to intense vexation. . . . The hands of the clock implacably move[d] toward the scheduled hour. And suddenly—information from the route: at Mayakovsky Square the procession was stalled."[139]

When the painted trucks and buses carrying the delegates came in sight, the crowd nudged the first row and, as if whirled by a mighty wave, burst onto the road. In a split second, the human cordon gave way and disappeared. Nobody, especially not the participants, understood what happened next. The disciplined patrols of law students turned back into nineteen-year-old boys. They jumped onto footboards, climbed into trucks, broke into dance, stuffed bouquets into bus windows. They screamed and

Figure 2.4. Opening procession, Zubov square. VI International Festival of Youth and Students, 1957. Photographer unknown.

Photo provided by the Central State Archive of the City of Moscow, Archival negative no. 0-6488.

sang. And everybody else seemed to have turned back into nineteen-year-olds. Leaping into trucks, Soviet citizens pulled foreigners onto the ground to embrace them. People stretched out hands not only to wave or salute — to touch, to partake of another world physically. This was the "enchanted feeling" of belonging to humankind, "of being a tiny particle, a grain of sand in an immense celebration," as one student in the Komsomol patrol experienced it.[140] Mothers offered their toddlers to the foreigners to hold, thousands of hands picking children up, passing them to the trucks and back to the women. And more gifts: ribbons, pins, even earrings poured into bus windows.[141] The motorcade stopped completely. Buses and trucks drowned in flowers. In turn, the impulse entranced the foreigners. They began to jump over the truck rails, uniting with the crowd, or to lift people from the sidewalks onto the trucks, chairing them in the air. The next day, translators reported, some delegates' voices turned hoarse from all the shouting and singing.[142]

The sounds were multifarious: the squawking loudspeakers, the clanging orchestras, the blaring trumpets that delegates were playing en route, the blustering radios and gramophones that Muscovites had placed in their windows, and the crowds—rumbling, rolling, roaring. Sound itself went out; word snatches, song snatches—everything sank. The noise had reached so high a pitch that it became literally deafening. The scene went surreally mute, like something out of a silent film.[143] That is why the unused cinematic sequences *without* a score are, in some way, the most accurate imprints of the opening procession. The filming crews were nonplussed as they rushed about in their open ZILs, took bird's-eye shots from the roofs, and watched each day's reels at night. They were awed, proud, and lucky to have captured it all. Shortly after the festival, with a touch of retrospection but without losing immediacy, the documentary filmmaker Vasilii Katanian described the scene: "I will probably never forget the first day. Until then, I had not seen anything of the kind. . . . Nobody had expected it, we were blown away." In the trucks, in the crowds, people cried, and his camera caught their tears.[144]

The opening motorcade became one of the best propaganda feats, but the first minutes after the procession had finally extricated itself from the throngs and passed on were embarrassing. The crowds dispersed, and Garden Ring rapidly emptied, leaving the lone Komsomol patrols and militiamen to sober up. In those first moments, it seemed that the festival was ruined.[145] What happened was part of the script—and yet it was not. Yes, people were supposed to stand on the sidewalks, applaud, wave flags and flowers. No, they were not supposed to fling themselves before buses, climb atop trucks, dance with foreigners, stop the movement, and lose restraint.

In its physical expressiveness, in the noise and mute moments, the opening procession epitomized the festival's central quest: the search for a universal language with which to confirm and proclaim common humanity, the search for ways to speak beyond not only geopolitical and ideological borders but linguistic ones as well. Even before the festival began, journalists and documentary filmmakers had referred to a special "festival language" that would allow people to communicate across linguistic barriers. The festival dreamers, who had choreographed the sequences and scripted the city, envisioned an event that would undo God's punishment and reverse our post-Babelian condition. An early draft of the documentary film *Above Us Is One Sky* bound the festival to the story of the origin of languages, thereby imparting world-historical and prophetic significance to this event: "Once upon a time, as legend has it, God confounded the tongues of nations, which had dared to build the Tower of Babel reaching the skies; then people speaking different languages ceased to understand each other, and the Tower remained unfinished." Would festival participants, "so different, so unlike each other," "build their own tower of Friendship and Peace"? The question was rhetorical. The rest of the film—and the entire festival—would answer in the affirmative.[146]

It was no accident that the festival revived Esperanto, which had been effectively banned in the Soviet Union since the mid-1930s.[147] But during the festival, the search for a universal tongue went beyond synthetic international language, linguistic fluency, or language at all. The phrase books and courses notwithstanding, there was a sustained discourse on the superfluity of dictionaries, of grammatical forms and verbal coherence in general. The festival was a quest beyond verbal languages. In fact, polyglot fluency was suspect unless the speakers were appointed translators. Foreigners with Russian facility were singled out for extra surveillance.[148] Rather than celebrating linguistic fluency, the press, as well as postfestival fiction and eyewitness accounts, relished the moments of inarticulateness. Such accounts were filled with dialogues in multiple languages, grammatically misconstrued Russian sentences, transliterated foreign words and expressions inserted right into the Russian text, and awkward, good-natured laughter. And the worse the mistakes, the more good-natured the laughter.[149]

Inarticulateness was compensated for by gestures, songs, dance, art, and objects. The songs worked as a greeting. In a delightful Soviet circus act, a Russian clown ridiculed a pile of dictionaries when a foreigner attempted a phrase-book conversation. Words only caused confusion, so the clown traded dictionaries for an accordion and presented his guest with recognizable choices: "Krakowiak," no; "Csárdás," no; "pas d'Espagne," no. And thus the accordion played until the clown stumbled upon the waltz from René Clair's old film, *Under the Roofs of Paris*, and was immediately rewarded with applause and a cheerful "Yes, I am a Parisian!" from the foreigner. The two departed, no longer strangers.[150] In the words of the Bolshoi Theater stage director, "there is no other language in the world . . . that gives such opportunities for conversations as the language of art"; and in the words of the documentary *Above Us Is One Sky*, "song, music, and dance" were "the best" translators.[151] Nothing else could solve the language problem in all circumstances with the same efficacy. Journalistic accounts of the festival abound in moments when rendering a conversation between two languages took several interpreters and a chain of translations.

Gestures and performances had the benefit of immediacy. Professional entertainers and mere passersby exchanged performances in the streets, bursting into dance and song with an abandon seldom seen in modern urban settings.[152] A couple would dance in a circle while somebody else would play an accordion, guitar, drums, or banjo. The conclusion of one dance was an invitation to the next. Volunteers (not Soviet instructors, but anyone who wanted to) gave dancing lessons right in the streets, showing a few simple moves and letting followers repeat as best they could. The music could be anything danceable, and this, too, was the point of the exchange. In a scene that became famous thanks to photographs, drawings, documentaries, and stories, an American boy played the banjo, while two American girls, one having kicked off her shoes, danced hand-in-hand an improvised mélange of steps. The song to which they timed their movements was the Russian "Katiusha." The documentary *The Art of Our Friends* showed a similarly emblematic episode of cultural unity: an all-embracing round dance. A Russian folkloric melody flowed from two musicians, an ethnically clad Russian playing the accordion and a sombrero-wearing Mexican beating the drums.[153]

Much of the dancing consisted of jumping in circles—a way to express the overwhelming emotions that, participants often said, they could not convey verbally, not even in their mother tongue. During a dance of Russian and Hungarian passersby in the Alexander Garden, "we join[ed] hands, hop[ped] around in circles, and [sang] together: 'Rich-rach, riblebum, riblebum, riblebum! / Rich-rach, riblebum, riblebum, bum!'" Here was a breakdown of language; the Russians had no idea what these sounds meant, and as far as they were concerned, it did not matter. The gibberish only proved that gestures were truer than words, and surely more meaningful. Dance was an escape from the verbal order. It disrupted dialogues: often, an invitation to dance promptly followed a reciprocal introduction, an exchange of names. Or so noted the journalists, whose professional being depended on verbal communication but who repeatedly announced the lexicon's inability to do justice to the festival.[154] Romping in circles or lines was emotionally bonding in a direct and physical way, for to synchronize one's steps with the bodies and sounds of others was to become immediately and manifestly absorbed into a community.[155]

In keeping with its mission to find a fully realized Tower of Babel, *Above Us Is One Sky* arrayed shots from gala concerts, open-air performances, untutored and impulsive street dancing into a story of universal harmony and interchangeability. The story unfolded through a montage of sequences from a Japanese lion dance, the Mexican courtship dance *jarabe tapatío*, a fast-paced Russian character dance, a Scottish jig, and the Cueca. Focusing on the moving feet, the camera sought a common step to relate one dance to the next in an associative chain of cultural universality. The shot began with the plodding feet of dancers hidden under the lion costume and ended as the camera zoomed in on the same stomping feet, then glided up to show the Mexican dance.[156] In another documentary, *The Art of Our Friends*, a traditional Korean dance became a classic Indian dance became a Japanese flower dance became an Egyptian belly dance. Lest the common routines be interpreted as "Eastern," the segment itself was framed by an Italian love song. The editing techniques elaborated the notion of a common cultural lineage through analogous gestures, steps, turns, and whirls, with a half-spin of the body or a turn of the head revealing an entirely different world.[157]

Out in the streets, gifts nearly replaced speech. People bartered pins, pens, stamps, signatures, addresses, plush toys, and anything else that could serve as a keepsake. Festival souvenirs were sold every few steps, so even those who had brought nothing could still exchange gifts, purchased but a moment earlier.[158] The meaning of these gifts derived from the very situation of exchange. That situation, as photographs attest, involved excited polyglot groups, people in widely different attire and headgear, sharing *this* literal incomprehension, *this* immediate sense of surrounding others, *this* moment—of which the gifts were now tokens. In lieu of a common language, pins told stories. Flags and other country symbols did the honor of introduction. Professional and political badges revealed life choices. Pins from previous festivals spoke of journeys. Hats and shirts became portable museums of these identity markers. What they meant in the festival context is best illustrated by immaterial exchanges: addresses and autographs. Photographs show highly public, crowded, and indiscriminate interactions around the address book. Multiple hands hold out address books for signatures; people scribble their addresses on one pad after another; several signatories are writing at once, as if in an assembly line. Such exchanges were about accumulation. Address books were collections that served as witnesses to foreignness and as tokens of presence—not only in the sense of having been at the festival, but also in the sense of otherness, of another person, perhaps from a remote or romanticized country, who stood nearby in the crowd and whose only trace was a hurried handwriting.[159]

Figure 2.5. Signing address books at the festival. Photographer: L. Mechetovich, "Let's be friends!"

Reproduced from *Sovetskoe foto* no. 7, 1958, p. 3, published by the Union of Journalists of the USSR.

Foreign Bodies

The smudged scribbles in address books were the beginning of epistolary friendships that lasted for years to come. One such address book was carried by an exuberant American participant, Sally Belfrage. A curious twenty-one-year-old from a family of leftist American expatriates in Britain, a self-styled rebel not averse to defying the orders of the State Department, Sally was determined to prolong her Moscow visit after the festival. She stayed in Moscow through the winter. She hoped to see "what [Moscow] was really like," as she later explained in an interview, to make friends, reach out to people "on a human level," and to forget the "big ideas that everyone was throwing back and forth."[160] And she wanted to write about an ordinary Moscow, perhaps just for herself, perhaps for the travelogue that she would publish later. In her address book, Sally recorded stories that Soviets told her, scraps of jokes and toasts, things at once strange, frustrating, and endearing. The notebook served as a little dictionary, in which she kept handy commonplace Russian words that she might need: "repeat," "slowly," "wait," "danger," "vegetables," "milk," "meat."[161] Her festival notepad was the first draft of her future book, one of the warmest Cold War accounts of the Soviet Union, vehemently denounced by American critics as the "cleverest piece . . . of pro-communist propaganda," and by Soviet officials as "libelous concoctions" besmirching Soviet reality.[162]

Sally's festival address book was a registry of mundane relationships. It listed her friends, usually students, journalists, artists, some of them apolitical and some regime critics, people who, in several years' time, would grow up to become Soviet professionals or dissidents: Slava (Rostislav) Rybkin from Zhdanov Street (building 23/5, room 10), another Slava (Viacheslav) Repnikov, from 3rd Tverskaia-Yamskaia Street (building 44/7, apartment 13), Faina from the Frunzenskaia Embankment, and Kostia from Bol'shaia Polianka in Moscow, the Leningrader Andrei Mikov, who fell for Sally's beauty and wit, and the trusted friend Mira, who refused to answer when called in by the KGB for questioning about Sally.[163] These were the people with whom Sally spent evenings and weekends, traveled and talked, danced and drank.

Apparently, she meant very much to them—to the characters of her published book and to the real people in her address book. As she recognized, "I wasn't me, I was a symbol." Her friends or dates, she felt, "had their prestige soar to unprecedented heights" thanks to her company; "almost everyone in the place came up to them and asked them where they had found the American girl."[164] Sally's persona was symbolic twice over, as an authentic foreigner and an existential statement: "Joe said I represented something magnificent to him & his friends—now they can never re[turn?] to their old standards of people & Soviet women in partic[ular]. We are sick; you are healthy. You know how to live." The people from the address book felt responsible for her well-being. They taught her a modicum of Russian and tried speaking English to her. They helped her to navigate a cold and crowded Moscow, saved her from the faux pas of mistranslations, and shared with her their secrets or suspicions. And they did all this even as they feared that they would jeopardize their own well-being for consorting with foreigners. Constantly on tenterhooks, Andrei dreaded the moment of her departure, dreaded the relationship too, yet could not pull himself away decisively. He could only walk out, despite wanting "to stay the night," "because the doorman & floor desk man haunted us as we entered."[165] Their relationship took place in the winter; they often met in the darkness, and descriptions of their encounters feature dusk and snow, creating an emotional atmosphere of doom. Their sad affair was shot through with anxiety and awareness of impossibility.[166] Several years later, Andrei's letter to Sally still registered, despite the clumsy English, the double bind of this relationship: "Dear Sal—I was very glad to receive some news from you. For so a long time we have no contact that I was sure that I went clean out of your mind. It grieves me to think so cause I know now for sure that you'll stay a girl of my dream for all my life. I am always thinking with pleasure about you and a nice time we have together. It's a pity that I can't see you now or have any chance to see you later."[167]

The amorous relationships formed at the festival usually ended in failure, in heartbreak and missed opportunities. They were frustrating and dangerous. The documents of two international (Soviet-American and Soviet-Swedish) couples seriously contemplating marriage and subsequent emigration landed in the KGB offices. Thence their paper trails disappear, but it is unlikely that T. Strel'nikova got her passport in time to procure a marriage certificate and emigration papers. And it is also improbable that Svetlana Karas', a theater student from Kiev, was able to introduce her American boyfriend Fred to her hometown, let alone register their marriage and depart for the United States.[168] If the festival was about unity, then romantic relationships held out the promise of the ultimate, most intimate communion. Although there were very few such relationships between foreigners and Soviets, love affairs were an apt metaphor for the allure and repulsion of foreignness as such.[169] The failure of festival romances—and most, if not all, were abortive, impossible logistically and emotionally—reflects a larger theme in Soviet-Western cultural relations.

Foreign threat and foreign temptation had been sexualized from the start, with the result that curiosity about foreigners was tainted with—or mistaken for—sexual advances. One interviewee, an English teacher and a graduate of the Foreign Languages Institute, recalls the precautions she took to avoid a tarnished reputation. She was determined never to remain alone with a foreign man. She was not worried about possible political charges of consorting with foreigners; what scared her was common talk and sidelong glances. Where did this fear come from? In her case, from the late 1940s, when, as a student, she had sat among a sizable audience watching another student tried for having an affair with a foreigner. Being privy in public, against her will, to something so intimate had been terribly embarrassing, and the brand of shame chilling. At the festival, she was drawn to groups of foreigners in the streets: they were interesting, and she wanted to hear authentic English speech, as well as try out her own English. But wherever she went and whatever group she joined, she brought her brother along as a mute escort. When a friend fell for a foreign boy and asked her to interpret, she refused to enter his room; the declaration of love would have to take place in the hotel lobby, or she would not translate. And when she took a liking to a Briton named Peter, she would not admit it even to herself. But she did come to the train station to say goodbye to him and trade addresses, as was the festival custom. She also preserved a photograph of Peter and other delegates boarding a train. For several years afterward, they corresponded in letters that were irreproachable in every way. Then she married another man, and he put an end to this epistolary friendship.[170] Despite its importance to her, the photograph that she preserved for almost six decades is entirely undistinguished. Dozens and dozens of photographs just like this—girls and boys with flowers standing on platforms, leaning out of train windows and waving—appeared in numerous postfestival journalistic accounts. Before long, such pictures became hackneyed, but who could vouch that there were no similar stories, wistful and deeply personal, behind the visual clichés.

Hotel settings were perfect for suggestive encounters, flirtation, flaunted physicality, and rival glances. Between 10 pm and 4 am, these grounds swarmed with young men and women, Soviet and foreign.[171] The police and delegation supervisors were helpless, unable to break up these gatherings and hardly better at keeping track, for later investigation, of who came and went. "At the moment," one horrified chaperone reported, "nobody controls the settlement of Vladykino [where the delegates were staying], the entry for unauthorized persons is unlimited. In the evenings, crowds assemble at the hotel and in the environs. People are making their way into the rooms, they are interacting with the delegates."[172] Some men and women may have met up and departed for the bushes, as rumors had it; over four dozen girls were caught in "intimate intercourse with foreigners" and taken to a police station for "explanatory work."[173] But what most people actually did was dance. Neighborhood residents brought out gramophones; foreigners brought musical instruments. Bands improvised on the spot, and the area turned into an open-air dance ground, while the proximity of foreigners' private quarters created a sexually charged environment.[174] In the milling crowds, in the heat of the moment, legitimate ways of interacting could swiftly become indecent. The journalist Nikolai Eremchenko remembers how a stolen dance ended in a brawl:

> There was a scene at the hotel "Tourist," where the Americans were staying. . . . There was a factory in the vicinity, and such was this neighborhood. . . . In the evening there was dancing, of course rock 'n' roll, the Americans had everything blasting, and the girls [were there]. A [Soviet] fellow [was there] with a girl. And one American—he was so dashing—asked the girl to a dance, and started to fling and toss her, and she was very lively and supple. And, as the fellow thought, [these were] very immodest poses. So he came up . . . [saying] let's go, but the American raised his hand against him, [the Soviet fellow] hit him, and a fight broke out.[175]

Did the American want to hit the Russian, or did his hand gesture mean something else, and the Russian responded with violence to the dance itself? After all, the festival exposed Soviet citizens to a variety of postures, gestures, and body movements, of which the most unsettling was "rocking and rolling." The British concert included a professional rock 'n' roll performance that was hissed down by "Soviet youth," or, rather, by people planted in the audience for this purpose. Rock 'n' roll, however, broke out in random places like an epidemic (to borrow the Soviet lingo used to describe it). Anybody who wanted to try could rock: the British rocked in Ostankino Park, a Swiss boy with a Russian girl at a meeting of railroad workers, a German couple at the Agricultural Exhibition, and the French were invited to the Gorky Film Studio to perform the dance.[176] Rock 'n' roll was nightlife in Moscow.

The dancing at the festival overturned the comfortable perspective on the body. Watching those movements, whether British students leaping to rock 'n' roll or Egyptian belly dancers, proved an awkward and disturbing experience, even for professionals. Soviet spectators had to adjust their senses at the sight of agile bodies twisting and bending in unimaginable ways, at the dissonant sounds of drums, rattles, tambourines, and high-pitched bamboo flutes.[177] Consider, for instance, the challenge of Naïma Akef, the Egyptian actress and legendary belly dancer. Scantily clad in a low hip scarf and glistening top, her body appeared to make music of its own volition, so perfectly were its movements synchronized with every lilt. You could *hear* her body: when she glided across the stage, it played the flute, and when she thrust her hips forward, it struck the doumbek drums. She hypnotized. No Soviet newsreel or documentary film about the festival bypassed Akef dancing. Filmmakers could not take their eyes or cameras off her.[178] Members of the international jury evaluating festival concerts agreed that she was incredible, and that much of the hypnotism was surely erotic.[179] What to do with a dance like this, virtuoso and sensuous? The only way to rescue it was to announce it as ancient and ethnic, and this was a fiercely debated point at the jury deliberations. To jury members from Bulgaria and Korea, the dance was quite the opposite of traditional "Eastern" performances, addressed to the gods and about the godly. This one spoke to men about the sensual; it belonged in an oriental "cabaret" for the Western rich.[180] But Akef had one unexpected and commanding supporter, Igor' Moiseev, the Soviet Union's most prominent choreographer and director of the USSR Folk Dance Ensemble. Maybe there was something of the "cabaret" in her outfit, but if so, then the "cabaret" was to blame, not the dance. His sheer authority and insistence earned Akef a gold medal at the festival.[181]

For decades, sexual depravity had seemed to come from the West via popular music and dance. Entire cultural institutions (cabaret, music hall), musical genres (jazz), and dance styles (the shimmy, foxtrot, rumba, and from the late 1940s on, the tango) had been methodically eliminated in periodic campaigns to cleanse Soviet popular culture of Western inspirations. By the late 1940s, the range of acceptable dance moves on the professional stage had narrowed tremendously, even in comparison with the 1930s. As for popular pastimes, dance floors in parks, and school formals, there were pas de grâce and pas de trois, half-antiquated, half-invented routines. Statements like Moiseev's were a first stride toward reconsidering the relationship between foreignness and cultural forms, as well as the place of sensuality in the performing arts.

The festival did not dispel the fear of cabaret, and there would be no belly dancing on the Soviet stage. But the festival did have long-term effects on the cultures of dance and entertainment. When, a few days after the festival, dance critics gathered at a Ministry of Culture conference to compare notes about foreign concerts, they discovered that, despite great ballet and folk dancing, there seemed to be something wrong with the bodies of Soviet performers—or with their attitude toward their bodies. They did not move with the same ease, the same playfulness and abandon as foreign performers. Soviet participants failed in ballroom and pantomime contests at the festival and had little idea of how to comport themselves on stage.[182] After the foreign extravaganza, the Soviet variété, as well as the entire entertainment industry, appeared dull and outdated. Even the traditional forte and the citadel of Soviet dance culture, the Bolshoi Theater, was now deemed "a gigantic antiquarian shop."[183] At the conference, Moiseev pleaded for tolerance, this time on behalf of ballroom dancing, generally considered one of the chief cultural threats from the West.[184] Three years after the festival, the music hall was reestablished in Moscow (and within a decade, in Leningrad and Kiev), and the outfits of girls dancing the cancan there ranged from slick pants and tuxedoes to transparent tunics to flouncing, ruffled petticoats, feathered hats, and glistening corsets. In the 1960s, professional dancers on stage and young people at parties gyrated to the mambo, the Brazilian tico-tico no fubá, and boogie-woogie.[185] Not only did the festival introduce routines and costumes hitherto unimaginable, it also revealed that human bodies could do much more than choreographers had previously allowed.

The emancipation of bodies began with jazz, which the festival made commonplace and then disseminated far and wide. One could catch a refrain from "Maple Leaf Rag" or "Memphis Blues" just by standing on the sidewalk if the Italian Dixieland band "Roman New Orleans" happened to pass by. The musicians, dressed in classy striped suits, rode sitting atop the folded roof of a convertible and played their instruments en route.[186]

Nearly all Western—and aspiring Western—delegations arrived with jazz bands. The Czechs came with several, all under the euphemism of variété, and they agreed to play at dances in addition to daily concerts. The Poles brought a jazz band without the cover of euphemisms. The British jammed eleven times on makeshift stages in squares and parks, presenting a gamut of jazz, including the unfathomable skiffle and the renowned blues singer Bertice Reading.[187] The Swedes, Danes, Norwegians, Austrians, and Belgians also had jazz bands.[188] The French delegation introduced Michel Legrand, just at the start of his international fame as a jazz pianist and composer of scores for the iconic films of the New Wave. By the mid-1960s, when the musical *The Umbrellas of Cherbourg* overtook Soviet screens, and its theme melody "I Will Wait for You" became synonymous with ill-fated romance, Legrand was already familiar to Soviet audiences. Everything about these bands, from the beats to their behavior on stage, struck Soviet observers as uninhibited and improvised. The culture of performance—the gestures and movements of the musicians, their stage interactions and easy-going manners—was as influential as the music itself. To Soviet spectators, Legrand looked spontaneous and debonair:

> The jazz was led by the composer . . . hm . . . hm . . . later . . . a French composer, very fashionable nowadays. . . . *The Umbrellas of Cherbourg* . . . Legrand, yes, Michel Legrand. He was maybe eighteen years old, nineteen. Yes, so. A curly haired boy. The band sits in a baffling way. Our orchestras sat at attention. And his somehow lounges about. . . . And he walks around. He played every single instrument that was there. Then appears Juliette Gréco, with her thin arms, wearing a black dress. She sang, and he played. Of course, there were various performers. But I noticed this one because, for us, this was too defiant.[189]

What was so defiant about Legrand? Something as elusive as the fluency of movement.

The demeanor of performers and fans—and Soviet audiences were beginning to behave like swooning and screaming fans—irked the authorities as much as the music did. Variété critics who witnessed the performances had little to say about the music apart from the psychological effects it seemed to have on participants. Keenly attentive to body movements and facial expressions, their reports described the musicians and audiences as overcome by "rabid, almost pathological agitation." "During the performance, the musicians, in their entire appearance, their manners, their facial expressions, looked like people possessed by some maniacal fit, some feverish jolting."[190] The frenzy began at theater entrances. Tickets or no tickets, people were determined to overtake the theater by sheer force, crumpling police patrols in the process. Special reserve forces were summoned to contain the crowd and to make way for the musicians and the jury. Leonid Utesov, a member of the jury caught in the screaming and jostling mob, recalled the experience as hair-raising: "Something frightening! . . . It was an absolutely frightening phenomenon . . . All told, the situation was tragic."[191] By the time viewers got inside the theater, they were already aflame. A few more degrees, one Soviet expert thought, and the audience at the concert of "Roman New Orleans Jazz" would have broken into "a mass choreographical orgy."[192] Jazz concerts seemed to turn every festival slogan on its head: the joy of "peace and friendship" into untamed exaltation; "Russian hospitality" into indiscriminate adoration of foreignness; the universality of music into cryptic beats and a closed community of fans; the transparency of body language into gestures that escaped interpretation; the communitas of brotherhood into an orgy. As the foreign musicians departed, they left behind an audience of Soviet boys and girls rocking to and fro, whooping, clapping wildly, and stamping their feet, "the walls . . . practically collapsing from the howls of our youths."[193] It was the Soviet bodies that were now out of control. Jazz at the festival precipitated a widespread moral panic.[194]

That is why the festival also precipitated the most serious and consequential discussion of jazz yet. Within days of the festival, in several closed conferences at the Ministry of Culture, choreographers, variété critics, and the patriarchs of Soviet jazz, Utesov and Tsfasman, debated how not to lose entirely those whooping, clamping, stamping boys and girls. While none of the speakers accepted the American or "Americanized" jazz that they had seen at the festival, neither did they seek to banish jazz altogether. Here was a fundamental shift in perspective: they would not mind Soviet boys and girls cheering for jazz, provided it was Soviet. But there was no such thing, they all agreed.[195] The yearning for a Soviet jazz reflected a new opinion on the nature of the genre: there was nothing wrong with jazz itself, only with how the music was arranged and performed in the West. This, in turn, meant that Soviet jazz was neither a misnomer nor a political impossibility. Rather, Soviet jazz was desirable as a unique incarnation of the polyphonous experience, cultural democratization, and jarring pace of the twentieth century.[196] These arguments helped to legitimize the notion of Soviet jazz among Ministry of Culture officials. Now, all that was left was to create it. This, perhaps, was the last act of the festival Preparatory Committee.[197] With the Komsomol's powerful patronage, jazz cafes, clubs, and contests would shortly sprout around the country and flourish.[198]

There was another outcome of the moral panic surrounding jazz, body culture, and foreign relationships. For the next several years, offenses ranging from prostitution to illegal trade in foreign goods to high treason would be traced to the festival. A strong repressive underside characterized the moral campaigns and spy tales in the wake of the festival: the police trailed after people who had established close friendships with foreigners. The names from Sally Belfrage's address book turned into caricatures of evil in the Soviet press. In 1959, Slava Rybkin from Zhdanov Street and Slava Repnikov from 3rd Tverskaia-Yamskaia were arrested, and in January 1960, both were tried and convicted of anti-Soviet propaganda and treason.[199] In several newspaper installments narrating the CIA's cunning steps, a gory picture emerged of Repnikov's transformation from sloth to spy. His entire life foreshadowed the fall. Repnikov did not work anywhere and "had no big dream," according to the journalist who led the press campaign of vilification.

But actually he did: Repnikov was obsessed with Western things and acquaintances, and his dream was to emigrate from the Soviet Union. This much he would acknowledge in a mid-1970s petition to end administrative exile: "I admit to interacting with foreign journalists and private persons from various countries, speaking with them about my wish to unlawfully depart from the USSR."[200] It appears he had harbored the wish since the early 1950s, when he had begun to seek the company of Americans stationed in Moscow, and until 1980, when, as a member of the Moscow Helsinki group, he would finally emigrate from the USSR to the United States. But aside from long-term plans and ideological convictions, foreignness was simply great fun. In the mid-1950s, Repnikov, in telltale "narrow jeans," joined a coterie of youths (*stiliagi*) obsessed with Western clothing and jazz. The other Slava, Rostislav Rybkin, possessed a literary mind and a gift for languages: a polyglot whose skills ranged from Italian to Indonesian, he later became a professional translator after his release from confinement. In the 1950s, he loved to read foreign authors and browse through *Time*, *Life*, and *Look*.

The festival was the turning point on the road from collecting foreignness as a hipster to collecting intelligence as a spy. That was when the American delegate Richard Lane (in the words of the Soviet press, "according to the documents, a University of California student but in reality a very different bird") recruited Repnikov into CIA service. It happened in a typical festival encounter, at the Mayakovskaya metro station, right in the center of the city and in broad daylight. Lane also introduced Repnikov to Rybkin, as the two were to work together, gave them a secret code, recordings of Western music, "anti-Soviet literature," and whisky, and later sent them a book with a double binding. Inside the binding was a cache with instructions and carbon paper for cryptography. But they did not have a chance to use it: their game was up.[201] Sally read a summary of the story in the *Daily Express* and felt "pretty defeated by the whole business."[202]

It was a dirty story, designed to effect revulsion and issue a warning: "American agents hope to stupefy, to pervert [Soviet] youth with pornographic magazines, bubble gum, portraits of Hollywood stars and jazz kings, with smuggled whisky." During the festival, hundreds of thousands of encounters like those between Repnikov and Lane had taken place at the Mayakovskaya metro station, and this detective story suggested that a nefarious trap may have lurked behind any of them. The story cast foreignness as black magic: its seduction was irresistible, its influence thoroughly corrupting, and the descent infernal. The journalistic exposé was titled "The Ones Who Have Sold Their Souls"—presumably, to the devil.[203]

The festival was over.

But not entirely. The Repnikov-Rybkin case is too bleak a conclusion for an event created and remembered with such fancy. The artists called their masterpiece "a time of miracles," when fairy tales came alive in the streets, and people who witnessed the festival found it unforgettable.

Was festival Moscow a Potemkin village? In a sense, yes, because it was a showcase city that took two years to create and into which billions of rubles were invested. Yes, because the resolutions and reports were overwhelmingly about the central streets and their facades. Yes, because it was all done on the occasion of a major "review"—the arrival of foreigners, Russia's ultimate inspector general. But there was more to it. Theatricalization of the streets conferred symbolic value on the city, and all of it was done for real, some in brick and stone, some meant to become permanent. Much of it did, indeed, stay, not least in the city toponymy. New stores, new swimming pools, new theaters, and new communications lines became permanent structures, and the flowers planted for the event were perennials. Like mega-events everywhere, the festival represented a key moment of concerted infrastructural change.[204] Melbourne was only the most immediate exemplar for the modeling of Moscow into a modern Western city, but the choice of an Olympic host for an exemplar is revealing. Likewise, architects and the municipal Administration of Culture looked to grand European cinemas, such as the Palais des Festivals, the venue of the Cannes Film Festival, when designing new movie theaters. The youth festival transformed Moscow from a beacon of communist, socialist, and various "progressive" causes into a center of international mega-events: film festivals, exhibitions, Olympic games.

The festival's two weeks were a concerted experience of elation, though they were nonetheless permeated by a repressive streak. At the time, foreigners suspected police presence in the hotels, at the colloquia, on the buses—and they were right. Surveillance, manipulation, and the detailed training of thousands of Soviet participants did take place; on this, the written record is overwhelming. And yet, those who worked as translators would be hard-pressed to remember any instruction or intrusion whatsoever.[205] Nothing in these lectures was unfamiliar to young people from the capitals. The instructions were merely a reminder of truths many held self-evident—for example, that the Soviet Union had a pioneering welfare system with excellent and free education, as well as free healthcare; that the Soviet Union was home to some of the world's greatest classical music and ballet; that the Soviet people were avid readers; or that the Moscow Art Theater, the Bolshoi, the Conservatory, and the Hermitage were simply the best. When translators, girls in their twenties, proudly enumerated these facts to visiting foreigners, they did so with confidence.[206] The correct answers and invisible boundaries were unquestionable, and the presence of Komsomol overseers was part of the normal order of things. It was easy not to notice. Even so discerning a memoirist as the jazzman Alexei Kozlov did not. In his recollections, he contrasts the "crowded, joyous" festival with the 1980 Olympics, "devoid of people, all prearranged, cheerless." Kozlov remembers how beggars, tramps, prostitutes, and ex-prisoners were expelled from Moscow for the duration of the games; how the police made apartment rounds looking for people without Moscow registration; how cordons blocked approaches to the city. Of course, the same thing, and on a mass scale, had occurred in 1957, but it had not affected the festival or its domestic reception.[207] What was so out of the ordinary, so beyond the conceivable in 1957, was the opportunity to stand surrounded by foreigners on a street corner or to sit in their company on a park bench, to exchange whispers with them in dimly lit theaters, invite them home for tea, walk them back to the hotels, and speak to them firsthand.[208] And this is what became singularly memorable.

The festival existed outside the boundaries of the habitual—both customary events and imaginings. It wreaked havoc on familiar time and routine and implanted miniature foreign cities in Moscow parks and squares. The festival reveals how the outlandish became intimate. The songs, dance moves, accents, and festival projections were based on new cultural knowledge. Lolita Torres and Yves Montand had only recently appeared on the screens, radio waves, and in the press—and were immediately recycled and reinterpreted in festival scripts. They were the models for film titles, the characters in documentaries, the exemplars of deportment on the stage and in the street. New imports did not displace old ones; they coexisted and interacted, with one song, one film triggering recollections of the next. The festival thus illustrates the process by which foreign cultural products, embraced and domesticated, became the interpretive context for the reception of later imports. Translations begot translations. Ultimately, the chain of Western inflections in Soviet culture would become endless.

Fundamental to the festival was the idea that the arts spoke surer than words. And indeed, literature, film, and painting were everywhere at the festival.

The festival was a literary endeavor, initially taking shape and place in hundreds of pages of scripts. Before the decorations were drawn and painted, they were narrated; before the documentaries were filmed, they were written. It was no accident that fairy tales, literary characters, poetic verses, fantastic creatures, and enchanted vistas made frequent appearances in these scripts and on the streets. The festival asked its creators and participants alike to suspend disbelief and become children. In return, it delivered magic that rarely, if ever, touches our everyday lives. This was a long-standing Soviet trope: art into life, fairy tale into reality. Literary realism, meanwhile, was debated at a seminar on "tradition and innovation" for future writers and critics.[209] Celebrity invitees for this seminar represented the roll call of Soviet publishing during the Thaw: Ernest Hemingway, Graham Greene, Arthur Miller, Miguel Ángel Asturias, Vasco Pratolini, Heinrich Böll.[210]

Centered on action, the festival was filmed nonstop; its sequences were distinctly cinematic. What is more, the festival offered the occasion for the first international film event in the Soviet Union in over two decades. Initially, cinema entered festival plans as another form of propaganda to teach Soviet citizens about the socialist motherland and to show foreigners Soviet life. But during the wearisome discussions about what to show and what to shoot, film increasingly became a crucial part of the Soviet (self)-image.[211] Film and festival: Why not a film festival? Cannes and Venice served as exemplars for the rules and procedures of the new Moscow project. Conveying just how ambitious the project was, the wish lists of potential jurors included Claude Autant-Lara, René Clair, Marcel Carné, Laurence Olivier, Luchino Visconti, Roberto Rossellini, Pier Paolo Pasolini, Jean Cocteau, Bette Davis, Paul Strand, Nicholas Ray, and Charlie Chaplin.[212] These names would lend international legitimacy to this inexpert undertaking, which admitted to the contest even amateur movies and student theses.[213] The youth festival was the first step toward the biannual Moscow International Film Festival, which opened two years later and which today remains a central cinematic event in Russia.[214]

Color was the festival's second name: it was a singularly vivid spectacle. Painting and repainting were among the main preparations, and artists were its main creators. Everything in festival streets was a show, a display, an exhibition. And Gorky Park indeed staged the Exhibition of Fine and Applied Arts. Scheduled for those two weeks, it attracted, on average, 45,000 people a day, and its success was so phenomenal that the Ministry of Culture and the park administration extended it for ten days.[215] The exhibition's 5,000 paintings were hung alphabetically by country, rather than by stylistic movements, and the result was a dizzying sense of diversity. In Soviet aesthetic discourse, painting was an entirely accessible medium. The festival exhibition did not overturn this notion, but by presenting expressionist and abstract paintings alongside verisimilitude, it was among the first events to insert a big question mark next to the idea.[216] In the next decade and a half, the question mark would reappear incessantly at Western art shows.

For all its singularity, the festival reflected the themes that came to structure the Soviet-Western cultural encounter for the rest of the Soviet era: the possibilities and limits of translation, and the role of emotional intensity in transforming Western cultural figures and texts into Soviet scenarios.

3

Books about Us

The Youth Festival briefly turned fiction into reality. Although its planners created the festival according to the idea of cultural transparency, they had little choice but to rely on translation. In turn, Soviet translation theory and practice were based on ideas strikingly similar to those animating the festival itself: the universality of literature and the superfluity of words as units of meaning.

There was perhaps no experience more celebrated and mythologized in late Soviet autobiographical prose than reading Western literature during the Thaw. Between the mid-1950s and the early 1960s, thousands of Western books arrived in the Soviet Union, some to acquire lives of their own and to challenge fundamental principles of class-based morality. Readers modeled their lives and loves on Western novels, which blended seamlessly into literature-centric Soviet civilization. After all, people were encouraged to shape their lives according to fictional exemplars—a key dictum of socialist realism and a time-honored practice since the nineteenth century, when readers had indeed lived and loved as creative literature dictated. But even for Russia, where the distinction between fiction and life had long been blurred, the relationship between Soviet readers and Western books during the Thaw was unusually intense. Readers approached them as paradigms of manners, language, and friendships. Many Western volumes published at this time belonged to an entirely different epoch. They arrived in the Soviet Union two decades too late, yet passed for contemporary works and were read as such.[1] The books themselves became objects of affection and remain so—though now as nostalgic mementos—long after the end of the Soviet Union.

It was translation that transformed Western texts into an intimate page of Soviet biographies, into "books about us."

Translation efforts were keenly responsive to the political context of the Thaw. Western books coincided with a polarized exchange on language, which involved central newspapers, literary journals, and educational establishments, and which concerned the power and powerlessness of words.[2] According to participants in the debate, in Stalin's time, the languages of propaganda, literature, and cinema had become ossified and ritualized. Words had lost moral authority.[3] One retrospective scholarly explanation contends that Stalin was the creator of Soviet discourse, and so upon the death of the language master, party leaders opted for de-individualized and repetitive texts.[4] This interpretation, however, leaves unexplained one of the main themes in the history of Soviet language: the regular campaigns against the ossification of language on the one hand and for linguistic purity on the other. Calls to rescue language from ideological clichés first had appeared amid the linguistic experimentation of the 1920s, before a singular author of discourse emerged. In 1918–1922, linguists had turned to the languages of the revolution, the Civil War, and the factory, placing emphasis on oral narration and fiery oratory.[5] In 1926–1927, avant-garde linguists and writers had dreamed about "the living word" and sought authenticity and cultural renewal in the vernacular.[6] In the early 1950s, the press discussion of language paralysis commenced while the master was still in a position to legislate meaning. During the Thaw, instead of producing an anonymous and invariable ideological script, the press called for diversifying and thus reanimating language.[7]

Even as many old arguments from the 1920s were rehashed, the late 1950s debate on the ossification of language had a different spirit and its participants, a different aim. They pursued not only a "resurrection of the word"; they sought individual and communal resurrection through the word.[8] Their search was shot through with moral urgency. Words brought dread. The press had been deeply implicated in repressive campaigns, and sloganeering had run amok. Kornei Chukovskii, a grand old man of Soviet belles-lettres who helped to set the terms of the language debate, saw clichés as a moral malady. They masked indifference—worse, crimes—behind a facade of exalted promises.[9] Chukovskii's 1962 book on language was not so much about grammar rules as about a "pathological deafness," a "verbal gangrene," a terrible disease of the heart—at the very heart of society.[10] Yet cleansing Soviet culture of clichés and bureaucratic speak was no easy task.[11] Bureaucratese seemed a pervasive and active foe: it "penetrated" and "perverted," "nestled" and "ate away," "eroded," "burst into," "gushed in," and "invaded" dictionaries, newspapers, radio broadcasts, novels, schools, and homes.[12] Linguists perused the press and created lists of bureaucratic expressions. Satirists misplaced and mispronounced newspeak and bureau-cratese for comic effect.[13] Writers tried to reanimate language by inserting conversational speech or subverting high style through irony. Literary critics denounced stilted characters, while literary characters rejected "verbal fetishes" or vowed to "purify lofty words." All saw recovery in "sincerity."

In winter of 1953, Vladimir Pomerantsev's article on "Sincerity in Liter-ature" detonated the smooth socialist realist narrative by documenting *insincerity*: literary clichés, wooden characters, and politically correct nar-ratives—a "varnishing of reality."[14] Pomerantsev did not advocate a private truth or unique authorial vision. Sincerity for him was a political mission of allying "belief, text, and the greater [Soviet] cause." More than utopian ethics, however, sincerity in Thaw culture meant an intimate bond between readers and writers, an emotional fellowship that implied proximity.[15] Truth resided in gesture, voice, and intonation. On the written page and beyond, on the radio, on the screen, sincerity had an audible texture, sometimes quiet or reedy, sometimes strained and raspy, but always unprofessional, even inarticulate. The writer, actor, or performer appeared as "one of us," and the audience took him for a friend.[16] Sincerity could not be known, only implied—a shared secret, forever in the eyes or ears of the beholder, rather than in the text, a behavioral code, which had to be recognized by others.[17] "Sincerity" during the Thaw was a deliberate aesthetic that recy-cled Romantic tropes.[18] Its synonyms were immediacy and instinctiveness.[19] This culture venerated unmediated "first" experiences: "unvarnished" sights and "natural" voices, free of political or technological editing.

In "books about us" by Ernest Hemingway, Erich Maria Remarque, and J. D. Salinger, translators and readers discovered the "sincerity" apparently missing in Soviet literature. Russian translations of Hemingway's brevity, Remarque's unabashed emotionality, and Salinger's colloquialisms were among the earliest texts to break with polished, normative speech.[20] Hemingway was read not so much for his modernism as for his stoical morality, bitter merriment, and lonely courage. Largely overlooking Re-marque's pacifism, readers saw saving grace in love and friendship, the leit-motif of his novels. To Soviet audiences, Salinger's Holden Caulfield was not merely an adolescent in search of himself, but a figure of universal tragedy. Phrases from Western novels became idiomatic expressions that subtly populated Soviet prose and post-Soviet memoirs.

This love affair with Western books began in a prosaic way. In 1954, the country's main newspaper on cultural affairs, *Literary Gazette*, decried the inadequate and sluggish publication of foreign prose in Russian translation.[21] The Central Committee's Science and Culture Department responded with a memo proposing increased print runs and an expanded range of "bourgeois writers" who exposed the existential dilemmas of life under capitalism. Central Committee Secretary Petr Pospelov studied the memo twice, endorsed it, and sanctioned a meeting of officials from the Agitation and Propaganda Department, the Science and Culture Department, the Ministry of Culture, VOKS, the Writers' Union, the Gorky Institute of World Literature, the literary press, and directors and editors of publishing houses. The meeting launched the journal *Foreign Literature* (*Inostrannaia literatura*) and a wide-ranging plan for publishing foreign classics and contemporary prose.[22] This conference thus set in motion a publishing apparatus that would produce some of the most desired "cult" books (*kul'tovye knigi*) in late Soviet culture, including texts that negated the very tenets of Soviet ethics. Of all the cultural artifacts imported to the Soviet Union in the 1950s, foreign literature was hardest to control, because, as physical objects, books and journal volumes were durable and portable. They were shelved in home libraries for decades and passed from generation to generation.

The Foreign Literature Project

"Foreign literature" was a concerted endeavor and a series of interlinked institutions. There was the journal *Foreign Literature*; there was the publishing house of the same name; there were divisions and departments within republican presses that reprinted texts translated into Russian and published first in Moscow; and there were dozens of literary series and monthlies that brought out an occasional Western novel. The Thaw is famous for new books and new names, for first-time events and encounters. In the mid-to-late 1950s, however, the most voluminous output consisted of republications—the collected works of nineteenth- and twentieth-century classics. These were the preserve of the Foreign Literature Publishing and State Publishing Houses. Readers sought books by writers who were long familiar and published conspicuously throughout the 1930s: Honoré de Balzac, Gustave Flaubert, George Sand, Sir Walter Scott, Victor Hugo, Alexandre Dumas, Charles Dickens, Lord Byron, Mark Twain, Émile Zola, Guy de Maupassant, Stendhal, John Galsworthy, Theodore Dreiser, Lion

Feuchtwanger, and Anatole France, to name the most frequently requested authors. Demand for their novels was enormous. While "boring" socialist realist classics gathered dust "for months and even years," multiple reprints of Galsworthy's *The Forsyte Saga* sold out instantly. Long queues for books wreaked havoc: at the Leningrad House of Book, for example, glass counters were cracked and smashed, unable to withstand the onslaught of a crowd standing in line for Dumas.[23] Readers besieged publishing houses with requests. These letters shared overlapping wish lists of books and recollections of earlier editions—a keen awareness of reading as a déjà vu experience and of publication as a recurrence.[24] By the late 1950s, books published in the 1930s had become bibliographic rarities.[25] Their fate mirrored that of people: volume after volume had perished in successive cataclysms. They had been confiscated and sealed away during arrests, burned as fuel in wartime cities or appropriated by new owners, purged from libraries, withdrawn from public circulation, and hidden in storage.[26] To literary critics and translators advocating comprehensive republication in the 1950s, the effort meant, in the words of German literature specialist Ilya Fradkin, "a repayment of debts," a rehabilitation akin to political exoneration of Stalin's victims: "Reinstated in their rights were Stefan Zweig, L[eonhard] Frank, Fallada . . . reinstated was Remarque, the Remarque of precisely those fifteen years when there had been a certain hiatus in publishing German literature."[27] In the late 1950s and early 1960s, republications filled empty spaces on library and home bookshelves. They also filled generation gaps, for during those fifteen years, a new cohort of readers had emerged.

Meanwhile, *Foreign Literature* appeared in 1955 to become the most important outlet for contemporary foreign (not only Western) prose and poetry in the last thirty years of the Soviet regime.[28] The journal cultivated a reputation for innovative prose, and the vibrant abstract designs, patterned mosaics, and angular outlines of lithographs on its cover signaled its vanguard role. It was forever in short supply. After the war, the government had imposed subscription quotas for all periodicals across the Soviet Union.[29] This meant, for example, that the Latvian town of Jelgava, with 75,000 inhabitants, received ten copies of *Foreign Literature*, three of which were reserved for institutional use and seven for individual subscription.[30] The journal's inaccessibility triggered a frenzy. In the Urals town of Nizhnii Tagil, for example, people "hunted" for its volumes "as one hunts for an animal in the taiga." They scurried across town, stood all night in line at retail kiosks, and did their best to curry the favor of salespeople.[31] Readers shared and sometimes stole the journal. One subscriber from Leningrad asked the editors to send an extra volume, because "some swine had stolen" his own right from his mailbox.[32]

Foreign Literature inherited the prestige, as well translators, critics, and even authors, of a similar journal of the 1930s, *International Literature*.[33] But *Foreign Literature*'s calling was different. No longer a platform for the leftist Republic of Letters united in the antifascist cause, *Foreign Literature* spoke to a domestic readership in the language of accessibility, education, and expanding geographical imagination. Its editors claimed an aesthetic mission: to enlighten readers about the world and to inculcate what they understood as "good taste."[34]

Two further principles underlay the journal's work: balancing coverage of different themes and regions of the world, and exposing the sins of capitalism. Halfway through its founding year, 1955, the editors evaluated the journal's contents in this way: "Published foreign authors are distributed as follows: writers from the countries of people's democracy—%, writers from the capitalist world ideologically connected to the communist movement—%, bourgeois writers—%."[35] Percentages could change depending on political circumstances, but not the idea of proportionality. The journal was obliged to publish fiction from the socialist bloc, from the decolonizing world, from "progressive" bourgeois authors.[36] The editors even tried to maintain emotional equilibrium, with despair, optimism, innocence, and darkness in equal measure. A "terribly gloomy" text, like Erskine Caldwell's story "Masses of Men," in which a mother sold her daughter for a quarter (to buy some food for her other children), could not follow Jean-Paul Sartre's play about racial injustice, "The Respectable Prostitute."[37] Such literature appeared in the first place because it did the ideological labor of exposing the capitalist order more convincingly than anything Soviet authors could write. And it did this work even when texts were not about poverty or racism. Increasingly faced with evidence of Western prosperity, the Soviet press promoted a more subtle anticapitalist message. Where money reigned supreme, relationships between men and women, fathers and sons were distorted. Ennui, demoralization, angst, and loneliness: this was life under capitalism. As Soviet critics often said, the worldview of bourgeois writers was "limited," for they did not find salvation in social struggle. Nevertheless, they did capture existential malaise.[38]

There was nothing surprising about the editors' high-handed treatment of the domestic audience; it was part and parcel of Soviet enlightenment. Nor was there anything unexpected about the selection logic—a moral critique of capitalist society through the words of its intellectuals. But the consequences of this careful calculus were momentous: a much broader and more diverse space for publication than at any time in Soviet living memory. Moreover, the principle of balance allowed imagery and themes that editors found vexing to be published, provided more palatable works diffused the impact. The idea of geographical equilibrium, meanwhile, meant that publication of collective farm novels from the socialist bloc also made room for Western fiction. And the embrace of moral critique meant that various stylistic devices—grotesque, stream of consciousness, and non-normative speech—could now be printed. Those unsurprising foundations resulted in a remarkably elastic field for translated prose.

This field was created neither by ideological bosses nor by censors, but by editors, translators, and critics, who established publication priorities and thus shaped the choices available to Soviet readers. In 1959, translators and critics gathered to discuss American prose and offer new and old names for publication. The people attending this meeting had published and interpreted American literature for decades: literary critics Aleksandr Anikst, Raisa Orlova, Tamara Motyleva, Lev Kopelev, Abel' Startsev, and translators Boris Izakov and Evgeniia Kalashnikova. Each of them had a favorite author, privileged access to books in original languages, and a personal literary calling. Despite their ideological orthodoxy, they proposed for publication controversial works, whose artistic merits seemed to outweigh politics. Their opinions mattered: they advised publishers on what to select, compiled and prefaced anthologies, and translated prose.[39]

Translators played a defining, if underappreciated, role.[40] The initiative for publishing Italian novelist Alberto Moravia's *The Time of Indifference*, for example, came from translators Zlata Potapova and Grigorii Breitburd. Breitburd convinced the director of the State Publishing House to include the book in the plan for 1957.[41] This was how titles began to move horizontally through editorial portfolios and vertically from editorial offices to Central Committee departments. Unless there was a special prohibition, translators could usually secure publication. In the case of *The Time of Indifference*, however, there was a special prohibition from the Central Committee, whose instructors did not mind Moravia himself but did object to this particular novel as "decadent."[42] It would take almost twenty years for *The Time of Indifference* to appear in Russian. But such failed Thaw-era projects were important, because banned books never really disappeared. Once in the plans, they remained there for decades, resurfacing now and then. The title of Moravia's novel began to live apart from the text; or, to put it differently, *The Time of Indifference* amounted to a title, regularly mentioned in critical articles and prefaces to his other books. There were numerous such catch-phrase titles in circulation. Many books published in the late 1960s and throughout the 1970s originated in ventures from the mid-to-late 1950s. In turn, publishing efforts in the 1970s relied on translations created during the Thaw. The intellectual and cultural tasks unfinished in the 1950s were completed, rather than reversed, in the 1970s.

The "decadence" of *The Time of Indifference* is emblematic of the challenge that nearly all Western prose presented to the puritanical culture of socialist realism. Moravia was only the most consistent and forthright in treating sex, which for him was something of an aesthetic credo and a philosophical statement. He rejected metaphors of "idealized" love, sought to represent "the sexual act . . . directly, explicitly, realistically and poetically," and detached it from both morality and love.[43] How to translate this aesthetic project into Russian was puzzling, because after the 1920s, Soviet literature had lost the language of sex. What remained in officially published prose were the very euphemisms for lofty love that Moravia had discarded.[44] Generally, editors and translators removed explicit episodes, while preserving deviant sexuality and psychological violence as long as it was linked to politics or implicated capitalists and fascists. This was the case with Wolfgang Köppen's *Death in Rome*, narrated by an unrepentant SS officer who was also a homosexual; Moravia's *Two Women*, which enlisted a rape scene as a metaphor for Italy ravished by war; and Salinger's *The Catcher in the Rye* with its suggestions of pedophilia. These texts were extremely disturbing and occasioned protracted editorial debates at *Foreign Literature*. In such cases, actual descriptions were omitted or toned down, while suggestiveness was retained for political reasons.[45] In *Two Women*, translators preserved the objectionable scene as an intimation, but removed the account of the women's struggle with a soldier and the description of a violated body. Russian translations conveyed allusions but not actions, traces but not depictions.

Soviet literary criticism related sexuality to "naturalism," a term that encompassed physiological functions and distortions: the bodily effects of illness or poverty, psychic derangement, ugliness in nature and in people.[46]

The leftist Pierre Gascar's autobiographical novella *The Seed*, about an unloved boy growing up in poverty, was exactly the kind of book that the Soviet literary establishment loved to publish. Although ideologically faultless, it presented a distressing scene of the boy raking through refuse in search of pear seeds.[47] Robert Merle's *Death Is My Trade*, based on the life of Rudolf Höss, condemned Nazi death camps in ways that were both haunting and graphic. The pages depicting the destruction of corpses in Auschwitz made for such agonizing reading that the novel was almost not published, despite the politics.[48] Vomit, urine, entrails, corpses, open wounds, dumpsters, and degradation were warily modified in translation.[49]

The changes were subtle, on the order of single words, rather than paragraphs or pages. Sexual or "naturalistic" language was easier to alter in translation, political themes less so. Politically motivated excisions were not so much related to hostile ideas (such works would not be selected in the first place) as to sentences, analogies, and uninvited allusions.[50] Some were reworked in Russian, but just as often, dialogues (even between bad guys) that, say, ridiculed communism or compared the Soviet Union to Nazi Germany were dropped altogether.[51]

In thus tampering with texts, Soviet editors faced a very real political problem, which they did not take for granted. They feared international scandals over the slightest of changes. According to a long-standing view, Soviet editors were pirates who altered foreign works at will. But in fact, they introduced censorial deletions with utmost caution and persistently sought permission from foreign authors. With rare exceptions, foreign authors conceded.[52] One reason for seeking cuts, Soviet editors argued disingenuously, was space. While they may have conserved space, they also highlighted some narrative threads at the expense of others. With Miguel Ángel Asturias's permission, *Foreign Literature* condensed *The Green Pope*, but "carefully preserv[ed] the anticolonial, anti-American line"—which became the only line in the Russian translation.[53] Communists and sympathizers understood the politics behind excisions, yet they not only approved the requested changes, they gave carte blanche for any alterations the Soviets saw fit.[54] Other writers, Alan Sillitoe for instance, had initiated the relationship with Soviet editors and volunteered authorization for cuts even before the Soviets decided to publish his novel *Key to the Door*.[55] Wolfgang Köppen resisted demands for excisions, upholding the aesthetic integrity of *Death in Rome*, its depictions of homosexuality included: "It stands to reason," he noted defensively, "that my hero is endowed with certain homo-erotic traits not accidentally and not for the sake of some outward effect, but from much deeper considerations." Ultimately, Köppen gave in: "I don't want to be obstinate."[56] Graham Greene wanted to be obstinate to the end, unconditionally rejecting excisions to A Burnt-Out Case.[57]

Censorship in translation was enabling, rather than prohibitive. How easily a text lent itself to infinitesimal cutting and stitching determined its suitability for publication.[58] Conversely, the novels that resisted omissions, largely because cuts threatened to destroy narrative unity and thus political efficacy, went unpublished.

Since the Soviet Union did not adhere to international copyright conventions, on the surface of it, literary officials virtually had a free hand at all stages, from selection and translation to publication, distribution, and interpretation.[59] But matters were not that simple. Literary imports were entangled in a web of transnational institutions and commitments. Soviet publishers and editors were not bound by the letter of copyright law, but they were nonetheless constrained by its spirit. And while shunning institutional charters and obligations, they painstakingly cultivated individual authors, one by one. All relations with foreign intellectuals were personal, all dispensations were patronage.

The Central Committee was against the kinds of international arrangements that conferred duties in addition to privileges. Its instructors consistently opposed membership in copyright conventions—they saw no benefits there, only liabilities. To be sure, the Soviet legal code had well-established copyright provisions and procedural norms.[60] But until 1973, when the Soviet Union joined the Universal Copyright Convention, this legislation protected only those creative works of foreign citizens that were first published, or present in manuscript form, in the USSR.

Originals initially printed abroad were excluded from legal safeguards. In principle, Soviet presses could publish foreign works without permission or compensation. In practice, they did so with great circumspection. But the principle itself greatly irritated foreign writers and publishers, and complaints were endless.[61] Intermittently, the Central Committee reviewed the legislation. In 1961–1962, and again in 1965, ad hoc commissions considered the matter seriously, only to deem the liabilities too numerous to risk membership even in the less restrictive and less costly Universal Copyright Convention, let alone its Berne counterpart.[62] The most frequently cited reason for not participating was financial: royalties were expensive, and the money in question was precious hard currency. Then, there was the risk of sustaining ideological losses. On the one hand, distribution of Soviet literature would pass to capitalist publishers, who could refuse to purchase books with obvious ideological content. This also meant possible damage to leftist presses and friendship societies, and thus a potential loss of existing propaganda channels. On the other hand, Soviet publishers would have to forgo abridged or even imperceptibly altered translations.[63] The Central Committee preferred unwritten rules and personal dependencies to formalized arrangements.

In the absence of binding norms and clear procedures, relations with foreign authors were governed by patronage.[64] The process was entirely personal. Soviet bureaucracies dealt with foreigners directly, tolerating no formal mediators, whether publishers or heirs.[65] Royalties were granted in exchange for loyalty. Payments were not the writers' entitlements but favors bestowed upon them. Sometimes, in fact, books were published just so the Soviets would have an opportunity to show largesse and establish dependencies.[66] There were other rewards, too: vacations at choice Soviet resorts, specialty medical treatment, banquets at the famed Georgian restaurant Aragvi and the Central Writers' House in Moscow, and, not least, comfortable travel around the Soviet Union.[67]

All monetary payments were exceptions—this was the one identifiable rule of remuneration. The Cultural Department of the Central Committee made such financial decisions on a case-by-case basis. The chiefs of the Foreign Commission of the Writers' Union acted as "brokers," couching their petitions in the customary, and therefore compelling, language of help and support: this or that writer was impoverished, "indigent to the extreme"; wronged by capitalist publishers, he barely made ends meet ("it was wintertime, but he did not even have the most necessary clothes"); such was the price he paid for his progressive views. Money came as compensation for progressive views rather than literature, as well as a credit that would bind recipients to Soviet benefactors. Moreover, whatever they thought of the literature, Soviet editors had little choice but to publish the people who shared their progressive views. As *Foreign Literature* editors concluded: "friends who do not spare their life for the sake of friendship [with us] should not be treated with such indifference; at the least, their works must be published, they must be supported."[68] Money came not only to the faithful, but also and perhaps especially to those whose faith was in crisis; it came in moments of doubt and ideological distress.[69] These personal relationships were more successful than Soviet institutional obligations, and for this reason, they were more important for the process of textual transference.

For the Love of the Word

Among participants in these personal relationships, translators were the most consequential for Soviet culture, largely because, in the mid-1950s and early 1960s, their meetings, classes, workshops, and theoretical articles shared one principle: "Every translation of a foreign work must become a phenomenon of Russian literature."[70]

The principle had emerged in the mid-1930s and coalesced into a coherent system in the early 1950s. In the 1930s, writers, linguists, and censors had standardized Russian literary language. Literature had been purged of colloquialisms on the one hand and of experimental word play on the other: accessibility was socialist realism's creed. In the late 1930s, critics had carped about translations that retained foreign elements, branding them as elitist for their unusual syntax and exotic vocabulary. The patriotic crusade of the early 1950s added another charge to accusations of social snobbery. Not only were foreignizing translations "difficult," they were also "cosmopolitan." They elevated foreign originals at the expense of the Russian language, and they contaminated Russian with loanwords and neologisms. In 1951–1952, a series of articles attacked the creators of unpatriotic translations and the idea of fidelity to the original. The author of most (although not all) of these articles was Ivan Kashkin (1899–1963), a translator from English and an influential theorist. As the anticosmopolitan campaign raged, Kashkin and his opponents drew upon its perilous political terminology.[71] His attack on foreignizing translations came on the heels of Stalin's "Marxism and the Problem of Linguistics," which asserted that when languages mixed, one inevitably prevailed (as Russian had done).[72] And so Kashkin's argument carried the day. Within a few years, the dangerous political accusations were gone, but the principle of domesticating translations remained.

By the late 1950s, the practice and theory of Soviet translation had become increasingly, even definitively, dominated by people who argued for the translatability of all literary texts and rejected out of hand the possibility of inaccessible cultural experiences.[73] No text was difficult enough, no cultural experience was unique enough to prevent "believable" translation—not necessarily precise but convincing, in the same sense that a performance on stage can be lifelike. Indeed, acting was a frequently cited analogy for translating, which was conceptualized as reincarnation (*perevoploshchenie*), a key word in the writings of the 1950s. If this calls to mind the Stanislavsky method, known for its "believable truth" and permitted liberties with the script, that is because Stanislavsky's theater was the established model of Soviet performance in general and the source of inspiration for some translators.[74] Like an actor, a translator embodied other people, the author of the original as well as the characters, enacting their lives in his own one-man theater.[75] "Be sure to check," veteran translator Rita Rait-Kovaleva (1898–1988) advised beginners, "do you *see* the hero, do you *hear* his voice, even its timbre?"[76]

Despite his ability to take on other identities, the ideal Soviet translator would not disappear in the original; instead, he would remain himself and bring his individuality to bear on the translation.[77] As Kashkin stated at a 1960 meeting of the Writers' Union Secretariat, "one cannot recreate the images, emotions, and thoughts of someone else without absorbing them into the mix of one's own feelings, thoughts, and observations."[78] Kashkin made no secret of the fact that his translations were personal interpretations and offered no apology for his subjectivity: "I am deeply convinced that you should translate only the authors and works that you feel you absolutely must translate, as your intuition and inclination impel you." For him, translation was an act of appropriation, entitling the translator to ownership: "my Chaucer," "my Hemingway," "my Sandburg."[79]

Translators like Kashkin and Rait-Kovaleva understood their task as recreating not only the text but, above all, the experience of the original. They wished to compel Soviet readers to have the same feelings, envisage the same images, that is, to undergo the same reading experiences as readers of the original.[80] In the early 1960s, the experiential aspect of translation acquired a special term, "functional correspondence": "translation as the transfer of a work from one space of reading reception to another, when, in the process of redirecting the original, . . . the translator takes into account the associations, historical and cultural traditions, and aesthetic habits specific to new readers."[81] When translators paused to consider what this aspiration would do to the original, they felt no remorse, only pride: a translation would become an autonomous work of Russian literature, "a new cultural jewel in new circumstances."[82] For the beloved children's writer, poet, and translator Samuil Marshak, translations made by Aleksandr

Pushkin, Mikhail Lermontov, Vasilii Zhukovskii, or Ivan Bunin belonged "to the treasure house of Russian poetry. Indeed, it is impossible to consider them English or German!"[83] The same was usually said about Marshak's own translations, because his renditions of English nursery rhymes and of Robert Burns's ballads became indispensable sounds of Soviet childhood. There had been earlier Russian translators of Robert Burns, but Marshak's Burns "seems to us the only possible Burns in Russian—as if there were no other." Moreover, "after Marshak, there is no need to translate Shakespeare's sonnets and Burns's poems into Russian again. [For these translations] are poetry in the highest sense of the word."[84] In the commending words of poet Aleksandr Tvardovskii, "having preserved a Scotsman in Burns," Marshak "has made Burns a Russian."[85]

Translation as original creation was an act of love. The translators' expository writings about the process itself, their memoirs, even their theoretical pieces were confessions of affection. For Marshak, "falling in love" with an author and his style was a precondition for translating. It was Marshak's Burns that prompted the renowned critic and translator from English (himself a favorite children's poet) Kornei Chukovskii to opine that translators should choose "only the author with whom you are passionately in love, whose heart beats close to yours."[86] The product of that love was "a new life," what translators themselves called "the miracle" of creation.[87] "The miracle" was where analysis stopped, giving way to the admiration of the marvelous and inexplicable—"the opening" of foreign books when they become one's own, "cherished, intimate, a part of your very soul."[88] Translators pictured their work as "a friendship, an understanding, a conversation in half-words," and themselves as interpreters of texts.[89] The translator was not a linguist, because he studied not words but "half-words"—that is, cultures, and for many, this was not merely an injunction or wishful thinking but a matter of self-identification.

In the mid-1950s, Soviet translation theory abandoned an exclusively linguistic understanding of translation for a broadly cultural interpretation.[90] In 1954, the Second Writers' Congress pronounced the primacy of images over linguistic relationships. A translator of French poetry and himself a celebrated poet, Pavel Antokol'skii declared, to applause from his audience: "the genre of literary translation rightfully stands next to original genres. We assert that the translator is an author," "an active creator of the literary process," a progenitor who "breathes his own poetic spirit" into the Russian text.[91] The Congress and especially the post-Congress theoretical writings (1955–1956) vigorously stated a normative case for translation as a product of its own cultural context, an "indigenous" literary text.[92] In 1956, during a translators' meeting about a new volume of translation theory, one participant announced in the heat of the polemical moment: "We are members of the Writers' Union, we are writers."[93] That same year, a conference of Moscow translators resolved to petition the Main Publishing Administration to include translators' names on the title page, along with authors' names.[94] Upon the encouragement of the translators' section in the Moscow Writers' Union, the Gorky Literature Institute established a translation department and introduced "The General Theory of Literary Translation" into its curriculum. By the early 1960s, philology departments at other universities had added similar courses. There, students learned the definition of translation as "an especially active form of reader *co-authorship*."[95]

If translators were the equals of writers, what was it that they expressed in translation? Or, to put it differently, if literature reflected reality, as Marxism and socialist realism held, then what did translation reflect?

One answer, which increasingly prevailed in the mid-to-late 1950s, was that translation reflected some reality behind the original, "beyond the text."[96] Kashkin dismissed the text as nothing more than a "conventional verbal sign," even a "screen" that obscured "the initial freshness of the author's immediate perception of reality." The translator's job, then, was to "break through" the screen of language, rendering the images behind linguistic signs.[97] That is to say, the word as a unit of meaning was subordinate to the paragraph, because images emerged from the arrangement of words and marks. In effect, the translator, like the writer, worked with raw reality—except that his task was to interpret foreign reality in a way that made sense to Soviet readers, emphasizing analogies and themes resonant in Russo-Soviet culture.[98] Kashkin called his idea "realist translation," a corollary to the realism so dominant in Soviet aesthetic theory, and the terminology stuck.

Another answer, increasingly on the defensive since the early 1950s, was that the original, the text itself, was the sole reality for the translator. Kashkin's most sophisticated opponent in the late 1950s and early 1960s, the philologist Efim Etkind, could not separate the image from "the verbal form" that contained and conveyed it: "But let us ask: how can reality be knowable if not through that same 'verbal sign'? And further: if one can imagine that a translator, breaking through the verbal 'screen' of a realist work, could perceive reality, what, then, should a translator of Romantic or symbolist works do?" For Etkind, "beyond the text" was an absurdity. It presupposed that "beyond the text" was knowable in a radically different culture, across the world and across time; and moreover, that all texts were fundamentally realist. He defended the original: in his model of translation, there was not much room for license.[99]

This approach tethered the translator perilously to the original, which, as Antokol'skii warned his colleagues at a professional congress, was seductive and treacherous: "For each of us translators, there is a certain danger in a foreign language . . . it possesses a truly hypnotic power over many of our brothers-in-arms."[100] The work of translators was hazardous: they "risk[ed] being taken into captivity by a foreign language." Antokol'skii suggested "striking right and left," Chukovskii called Marshak a "conquistador," but the commander-in-chief in this war was Ivan Kashkin, for whom translation was, indeed, a battle with the original, to be won by "victorious storm" after a "siege," and thus made one's own.[101] There was nothing unique about metaphors of love and warfare; these had been the dominant ways of describing translation in Western culture for centuries.[102] What was noteworthy was the insistence on the absolute translatability of all literature, and on the capacity of the Russian language to assimilate it.

The warriors in this battle were not new blood. Born at the turn of the century, they belonged to the same cohort, had matured in the 1920s and embarked on literary careers in the 1930s.[103] Rita Rait-Kovaleva had arrived in Moscow from the provinces in the early 1920s with a degree in medicine, knowledge of French and German, and a lively interest in the literary world. Plunging into that world with a German translation of Vladimir Mayakovsky's *Mystery-Bouffe* for the Third Congress of the Comintern, she spent those exhilarating years in the Mayakovsky orbit. She learned English later, and it was as a translator from English that she would earn acclaim in the 1960s and 1970s. Her life connected the late Soviet years—the kitchen-table conversations about eternal things, the home jam-packed bookshelves, the domesticity of friendship—with the early Soviet avant-garde and internationalism.[104] Kashkin had studied English language and literature at the Second Moscow State University (today's Pedagogical Institute) and, as a graduate student, at the State Academy of Arts. While a student in the 1920s, he also had taught English and translation.[105] Along the way, American literature became the love of his life. In the early 1930s, he had founded a translation workshop, a gathering of like-minded youths passionate about both foreign literature and Russian language. The Word was at the center of their professional lives, personal friendships, and pas-times. Puns and epigrams lent an element of play and intimacy to transla-tion work, which was often done (or at least completed) collectively, with several people—in cramped communal apartments, in cramped and cold editorial offices—brainstorming tricky turns of phrase.[106] The alumni of Kashkin's "collective," as well as their peers, who had begun translating in the 1930s, went on to create translations unrivaled to this day—unrivaled because they proved formative for countless readers and provided syntax, vocabulary, and images that became normative for subsequent translations. The Thaw was the final triumph of accessible—socialist realist—translation that had emerged in the late 1930s. But this triumph transpired in very dif-ferent cultural circumstances, as the field of translation was expanding rap-idly to vast new terrains.

Hemingway's Code

In this expanding field, Hemingway was among the best-loved and best-known writers. Readers relentlessly tried to procure his address.[107] Amateur authors from the factory bench considered him their "teacher."[108] Admirers traveled outside Moscow, where, word had it, the "legendary" two-volume set of his prose, published in 1959, could be found for sale. The day of this lucky purchase would be remembered for life.[109] No home library seemed complete without these volumes, bound in black with a silver trim. Journal issues with his novellas were eagerly awaited, each becoming an event. But unlike other much-loved authors, Hemingway was more than a writer. He was an oracle. He was a measure of all things, written, spoken, and done. He was a paragon of machismo and manhood, conscience and courage, nobility and knighthood, sincerity and heroism. His titles, descrip-tions, and sentences became idiomatic expressions in Russian. He was the subject of poetry, graphics, parodies, rumors, jokes, and conversations; his name served as an epithet.[110] He was a trendsetter, not only in writing style, but also in dress, dialogue, and demeanor.[111]

The most astonishing thing about Hemingway's enormous popularity is that his signature novels, the ones best loved during the Thaw, were re-publications. A *Farewell to Arms*, *The Sun Also Rises*, *To Have and Have Not*, as well as stories, speeches, a play, and a film script, had been pub-lished repeatedly throughout the 1930s. Indeed, it was in the 1930s when, "for the first time, Hemingway spoke in Russian." The future translator Nora Gal', then a Moscow Pedagogical Institute student with a passionate commitment to literature and a literary gift of her own, would later recall: "it was the most striking, the most memorable event . . . Yes, for people who read, for people who wrote—not to mention us students—this was a huge discovery, I dare say, a shock."[112] The year of Hemingway's sweeping advent in Soviet literary circles was 1934, when several stories were printed in journals and anthologies in rough carton bindings.[113] The following year, Kashkin's disciple Vera Toper translated *The Sun Also Rises* (*Fiesta* is both the Russian and British title), in which the literary elite found "a mirthless smirk, reserved solicitude, concern, compassion, and dreary emptiness." The novel's dialogues "were famous half a century ago. . . . This was it: Hemingway's style, a discovery, a revelation!" For Gal', some lines proved "unforgettable and were not forgotten in dozens of years."[114]

The discoveries ceased around 1939. The most likely, although hypothetical, explanation is political expediency. By this time, as a result of articles on Hemingway's heroism in Spain, his play *The Fifth Column*, and his script for Joris Ivens's film *The Spanish Earth*, the writer's image had merged with the Spanish Civil War.[115] After the Republican defeat and the Molotov-Ribbentrop Pact, cultural antifascism briefly faded from the propagandistic spotlight.[116] In the immediate postwar years, the silence around Hemingway persisted, and libraries no longer lent his books. But he continued to be read and admired nonetheless. Students at the Gorky Literature Institute would try their hand at stylistic imitation, or so thought the institute's director.[117] Two winners of the Stalin Prize in Literature, Viktor Nekrasov's *Front-line Stalingrad* in 1947 and Yuri Trifonov's *The Students* in 1951, were written self-consciously in Hemingway's shadow.[118]

Since Hemingway already had been discovered—translated, published, read, and absorbed—in the 1930s, why so much hubbub in the late 1950s and 1960s? Why did reading Hemingway become a first-time event and a revelatory experience during the Thaw?

It was not exactly a first reading, but a collective rereading instead.[119] Rereading gains poignancy from expectations, and perhaps Hemingway owed his special status in Thaw culture in part to the readings of the 1930s. But the second reading did not necessarily conform to the first, or even to its memory. While Hemingway's books were shared across generations from the 1930s to the 1970s, it was during the Thaw that people singled out reading and, importantly, talking about Hemingway as a defining generational experience.[120] His presence in the late 1950s and 1960s was not only more ubiquitous than in the 1930s, it was also remarkable and fateful, or, at least, that is how readers saw it. Recollections of the 1930s rarely mentioned Hemingway: he may have been present on bookshelves, but he did not constitute a memoiristic presence. By contrast, reminiscences about the 1950s and 1960s frequently spoke of reading Hemingway as a biographical milestone and an emblem of the times. Even the self-consciously ironic chroniclers, those least inclined to romanticize their youthful predilections, mentioned Hemingway, as did those who did not like his books or who later professed aversion.[121] Regardless of reading preferences, most memoirists found his name worthy of space in their recollections.

There was another difference between the 1930s and 1950s readings. Second readings tend to confuse chronological distinctions, repositioning books in another age.[122] As readers returned to Hemingway in the 1950s, the novels written three decades earlier seemed contemporary again. Literature specialists were perplexed: prominent Americanist critic and translator Abel' Startsev argued that Hemingway was "not the present day of American or world literature. He [was] a passing day at best."[123] But such discrepancies did not bother nonprofessional readers or even professionals, to whom Startsev addressed his reproach. Then and later, writings on Hemingway insisted that he belonged to the readers' Soviet world—not just a favorite author but uniquely their own (*nash, svoi, rodnoi*). The fashioning of lives, loves, and literature according to Hemingway was not specific to the Soviet 1950s and 1960s. Hemingway's mystique (in the words of the American critic Edmund Wilson, "gallantry in heartbreak, grim and nonchalant banter, and heroic dissipation") was much the same everywhere, and he devoted considerable efforts to creating a public persona in the likeness of his literary protagonists.[124] But nobody tried as hard to incorporate Hemingway into domestic context as Soviet readers of the 1950s and 1960s.

"Rereading" was prominent in the semantic culture of the mid-to-late 1950s. In 1956, Ivan Kashkin invited readers to do just that—"Rereading Hemingway," published in the *Foreign Literature* journal, was the title of the first article about the writer in over a decade.[125] The Soviet Union's principal authority on Hemingway, Kashkin had studied his works since the late 1920s, written about Hemingway prolifically in the 1930s, corresponded with the subject of his studies, edited several anthologies, and, in the last months of his life, hastened to finish an analytical biography of Hemingway, published posthumously for both of them. Kashkin himself translated very little of Hemingway, but his articles served as interpretive manuals for other translators (most of whom were his followers) and thus for readers as well. He maintained a near-monopoly on translations of Hemingway, only rarely and reluctantly ceding the job to "outsiders" who had not been trained in his 1930s workshop. The Russian-Soviet Hemingway was "his," Kashkin's, creation, and any contrary "legend" irritated him tremendously.[126]

Kashkin saw Hemingway through the prism of "tragedy." Back in 1934, Kashkin had introduced Soviet audiences to the Hemingway myth.[127] He had tried to expose and dispel "the legendary image . . . of a buoyant, strong, somewhat clumsy athlete, an excellent tennis player, a first-rate boxer, an inveterate skier, fisherman and hunter, a fearless amateur matador, an honored front-line soldier, and, incidentally, a world-renowned writer." Kashkin had countered "the legendary" with "the real" Hemingway: sad, rather than buoyant; awkwardly tender, rather than clumsily athletic; a man of "desperate stoic skepticism," rather than fearlessness. But "the legendary" and "the real" Hemingways were not too different: awkward tenderness reinforced clumsy athleticism, and the "sad" and "stoic" author was no less compelling a character. In 1935, Kashkin's article about the tragic Hemingway was published in English. Hemingway read it with bemusement and admiration. In writing about his mirthless smile and wretched disharmony, Kashkin guessed his secrets and thus earned his respect.[128] Kashkin spoke of a mask covering the true face of the writer who was "morbidly reticent, always restrained and discreet, very intent, very tired, driven to utter despair."[129]

The tragic Hemingway was the prevailing interpretation during the 1930s, when other critics also wrote about his dark universe.[130] The writer Yuri Olesha read Hemingway in the terrible 1936 and thought only drinking and death were left to the people of *Fiesta*. The lives of Brett Ashley, Jake Barnes, Mike Campbell, Bill Gorton, and Robert Cohn had an illusionary quality, which was reflected in narrative form: "[Hemingway] describes events sequentially, as they happen. There are no colors, there are no metaphors, there are no allegories. . . . The inner light of language is absent, the center is absent."[131] The missing center, the loss of inner light captivated and frightened critics: "How terrifying is this dead telegraphic world! Hammered out on a telegraph machine, how terrifying is 'Cat in the Rain.'"[132] Rain in this story meant unspeakable despair, while words uttered aloud communicated nothing of consequence.[133] In *A Farewell to Arms*, rain portended disaster, accompanying separations and foreboding death. Soviet lecturers never missed a chance to draw the audience's attention to the transparent symbolism of Hemingway's rain.[134]

With his invitation to a rereading in 1956, Kashkin brought back the lyrical and tragic hero. He intertwined literary history, biography, and stylistic analysis to speak of real men without women, of lone heroes and lost generations, of first war and first love, and of winners who take nothing but their moral victories.[135] In other words, the 1956 article discerned (or shaped, perhaps) the key themes—the value of words and stoical ethics—that made Hemingway especially relevant to Soviet readers during the Thaw.

Kashkin shifted the focus from Hemingway's poetics or politics to his moral code, from text to subtext. To be sure, Kashkin did refer to internal monologues, repetition, irony, stream of consciousness, and telegraphic laconicism. But stylistic discoveries were not the most important thing about Hemingway that he communicated to readers. Kashkin was preoccupied not with Hemingway's language but with his attempts to will words out of existence, replace them with silence, or find some other, truer ones. Kashkin returned obsessively to the problem of words: as in Hemingway, in Kashkin's critical prose, "lofty slogans," "pompous phrases about valor and sacrifice" lie. At war, they kill; at home, they hide "the duplicity of human relationships"; "the big lie" is everywhere. This devaluation of language "generates constraints on speech." Kashkin described Hemingway's early protagonists as "deceived" and therefore "reserved" people, "convulsively" trying "to keep their words in check." Of course, Kashkin developed the context of predatory, imperialist war and told his readers that the lies marked somebody else's life under capitalism and fascism. But his choice of words revealed the Soviet context for reading pompous phrases and constrained speech. Even as Hemingway's heroes desperately tried to keep their words in check, they continued to speak "in half-words." "Half-words" implied particular intimacy, a community of hints, a circle of like-minded people. The term belonged in the repertoire of the Soviet intelligentsia, not Parisian bohemia.[136] Kashkin used the concept of "half-words" to explain "the famous poetics of subtext." He was not the first person in the Soviet Union to analyze Hemingway's "subtext." In the 1930s, writers and critics had been infatuated with this elliptical style. But at no point before the mid-1950s did style become an ethical problem concerning the value and devaluation of language.

Kashkin accentuated the "code of ethics" to unlock Hemingway specifically in the 1950s reading context. He saw Hemingway's "ethics" as grounded in "abstract truth" and "objective impartiality"—that is, in universal, rather than class-based, morality. Kashkin did not like universalist precepts, but he never opposed them with anything else. Instead, he anchored Hemingway's nebulous code in specific situations: "to speak about friends with detachment and with a grin—they would tolerate it all—and to treat enemies with underscored courtliness," "everything that is unnatural is unattractive—unwomanliness for a woman, unmanliness for a man, timidity, cowardliness, evasiveness, dishonesty . . . It is the beauty of good, old moral values: simplicity, honesty, courage, fidelity, love, the work and duty of an artist."[137] The code's centerpiece was courage of the variety that Hemingway himself called "grace under pressure." Perhaps no other passage in Hemingway was so frequently cited in Soviet critical articles, biographical sketches, and poems, as Frederic Henry's sudden premonition of death amid thoughts of love in A *Farewell to Arms*:

> If people bring so much courage to this world the world has to kill them to break them, so of course it kills them. The world breaks every one and afterward many are strong at the broken places. But those that will not break it kills. It kills the very good and the very gentle and the very brave impartially. If you are none of these you can be sure it will kill you too but there will be no special hurry.[138]

These lines struck Soviet readers (including critics and writers) because of the arresting connection between courage and death. In the Russian translation, the connection was keener and the causality more explicit: "*When* people bring so much courage to this world, the world has to kill them *in order* to break them, and *that is why* it kills them."[139] The zero conditional "if" became the unambiguous "when"; inferences were spelled out with "in order to" and "that is why"; and an added coordinating conjunction filled a logical gap.[140] The translation foregrounded "courage" at the beginning of the segment and imperceptibly intensified the defiance and the hardening of character in the second sentence ("many are *yet* stron*ger* at the broken places"). A meditation on the inexorability of death thus became a verification of bravery as well; the world kills as if in retaliation for too much courage.[141]

Excerpted or paraphrased, this passage was reprinted countless times as an obsession and an aphorism. Literary critics applied the moral notion of excessive courage to Hemingway's characters and to the author himself, using this very formulation to explain his popularity:

> Hemingway's heroes bring so much courage to this world, so boldly, silently, and staunchly do they defend themselves [in this world], so ardently do they long for light and sun, that when reading Hemingway's books, one invariably feels energized, even if the subject is most tragic. The stern courage of the heroes is, perhaps, the most attractive feature of this writer's work. It corresponds to the spirit of our stern century, and that is precisely why Hemingway's prose makes such a [strong] impression on readers.[142]

The same notion migrated into depictions of markedly Russian protagonists and topics. In an intellectual bestseller of the mid-1960s, a biography of the outcast nineteenth-century philosopher Petr Chaadaev, Hemingway's passage served as the epigraph to a chapter on the thinker's demise and afterlife.[143] Among other things, the book connected Chaadaev's views and the poetry of Mikhail Lermontov. With Lermontov's story, Hemingway's sentences relating violent death to an excess of courage assumed another literary incarnation. For Thaw poet Vladimir Kornilov, Hemingway was "a teacher of life," who had lived through two centuries of combat and a thousand-year sorrow but remained undefeated.[144] In an early verse about a boyish Lermontov, the twenty-year-old Kornilov explained death to boy poets:

> When you bring
> So much courage,
> Such anger
> And such pain—
> You will be killed.[145]

The analogy between Lermontov and Hemingway was poetic license, but not entirely spurious. Both were romantics, whose lives were routinely and seamlessly conflated, à la Byron, with the lives of their literary creations. Lermontov's Byronism was a famous and culturally profitable case of the tremendous influence that Lord Byron had had on the elite youth of nineteenth-century Russia. In Russian Byronism, American literature scholar Raisa Orlova found the best analogy for conveying Hemingway's significance in the 1960s.[146]

Kashkin's elaboration of stoical ethics and plain words overlapped with a fundamental Thaw project: the widespread discussion of the Stalin terror after the Twentieth and Twenty-Second Party Congresses. *Foreign Literature*'s editorial board met to consider Kashkin's "Rereading Hemingway" in February 1956, right after the Twentieth Party Congress, when board members were still coming to grips with the Secret Speech denouncing Stalin. Thinking about the significance of "Rereading Hemingway," the critic and foremost Shakespeare scholar Aleksandr Anikst spoke of resilience—that quiet courage. But he projected onto Hemingway an entirely different setting, the Soviet 1930s:

> [The] mistake is imagin[ing] that [Stalin's] cult of personality has killed literally everything inside us. [The] gravest mistake is . . . not understand[ing] that even in the harshest and cruelest conditions of the personality cult, Soviet people have survived, Soviet thoughts have survived.
> We cannot agree that everything is dead here.[147]

Most directly, Hemingway and the Thaw preoccupation with the repressive past were entwined in the publication saga of *For Whom the Bell Tolls*. The novel grappled with the tension between necessity and choice, individual and community, impulse and planning, innocence and terror in revolution. *For Whom the Bell Tolls* was treated as a transparent allusion to the Soviet 1930s—because the Spanish Civil War had been romanticized in Soviet public culture during that decade; because the book embraced the leftist cause and proclaimed high ideals, while foregrounding cruel and zealous communists; and because it focused on a reflexive intellectual and raised questions about the morality of killing for a cause. Precisely for these reasons, the novel was difficult to publish. Its Russian translation had existed since 1941. Although the novel was slated for publication with the Foreign Literature Publishing House in that same 1956, and circulated in samizdat thereafter, it did not appear in print until 1968.[148] For all those years, the book remained an open secret, in part because critical articles discussed and cited it, sometimes disclosing the existence of a Russian translation ("quotations are taken from the translation by N. Volzhina and E. Kalashnikova").[149] Beginning in 1955, newspapers and literary journals repeatedly announced the forthcoming publication of the novel.[150] In 1955–1956, the Foreign Commission of the Writers' Union enthusiastically supported the project.[151] But Soviet international commitments prevented these promises from realization. Throughout the 1950s and 1960s, Spanish and French communists adamantly protested publication of the novel (in long, fiery letters to the Central Committee), and Soviet publishers had to oblige.[152] The novel cast doubt on customary communist heroes and real participants. More than anybody else he had met in Spain, Hemingway hated the political commissar of the International Brigades, André Marty. Almost as much he loathed the communist leader Dolores Ibárruri, who had found refuge in the Soviet Union after the fall of Republican Spain.

Through these false starts, For Whom the Bell Tolls was read as an analogy to, and a salvation from, the repressive 1930s. In 1956, Kashkin wrote with regret about devaluation of lofty words. In For Whom the Bell Tolls, he was relieved to find Hemingway "reconsider[ing] words that once upon a time had seemed 'indecent.'" In Kashkin's evocation of Thaw political vocabulary, the Spanish Civil War "rehabilitated" speech: "convulsive intensity disappears, speech flows freely, . . . everything becomes more spontaneous and humane." Kashkin delighted in purification of words, in lofty slogans becoming usable again: "About the heroic one must speak in full voice, and one needs lofty words for truly lofty deeds."[153] The Foreign Literature editor-in-chief Aleksandr Chakovskii, who approached the Central Committee in 1961 requesting approval to publish For Whom the Bell Tolls, argued that the novel would expediently support the work of the Twenty-Second Party Congress. The Congress again had denounced Stalin's "cult of personality" and mandated removal of his body from Lenin's Mausoleum in Red Square. Chakovskii singled out chapter 42 for its anti-Stalinist charge. This chapter recounted a sideline story, in which Soviet journalist Karkov confronted and prevailed over André Marty, a man with "watery eyes," a moustache, and "a look of decay" in his "gray face," a man who sent people to death by firing squads "for political things." The expedient new meaning was the analogy between Marty and Stalin, as well as the implication that "the cult of personality" could be overcome. After all, in the novel, Karkov did prevail, although his real-life prototype, the journalist Mikhail Kol'tsov, executed in Moscow in 1940, did not.[154] This post–Twenty-Second Party Congress interpretation prefigured analogical readings that the novel would receive when it finally was published. But, by 1968, Soviet readers had outgrown analogical thinking. In 1961, when Aleksandr Solzhenitsyn read Hemingway in a samizdat version—while waiting to learn whether his One Day in the Life of Ivan Denisovich would be published—For Whom the Bell Tolls would have been at home in the literary output that followed the Twenty-Second Party Congress. Seven years later, however, people already had read Solzhenitsyn's novella and other texts about their own, rather than somebody else's, repressive past.[155]

The ethical readings of Hemingway rested on the conflation of his life and art: on the notion that his experiences provided the material for his stories and that his stories reflected his experiences. The confusion of fact and fiction in Hemingway's biography was by no means unique to Soviet readers. In the United States, audiences also took his protagonists for the author himself. Hemingway was one of the twentieth-century's greatest literary myths, and Soviet readers availed themselves of his international celebrity.[156] Kashkin not only accepted this myth, he also developed it. Fearing that alternative readings would prompt authorities to ban the novelist altogether, Kashkin wished for a prim and proper Hemingway. In the 1950s and early 1960s, his lectures, particularly to groups of students, attacked "various hipsters [stiliagi] and snobs," who proffered their own Hemingway "legend": "indispensable skeptical stoicism, growling with clenched teeth, macho 'brutality,' 'let's have a drink,' 'the lost generation.'"[157] "I neither want to be, nor can be a passive observer of what the snobs are trying to do to Hemingway," so Kashkin showed photographs to imprint an acceptable portrait upon the imaginations of his listeners. In 1960, displaying a photograph of Hemingway with smooth gray hair, trimmed beard, vest, and tie, Kashkin explained to his audience: "The whole look is a retort [to those who think] that Hemingway is an appropriate object for snobs to worship."[158] Neither drunk nor lost, Kashkin's Hemingway was a man cast in a simple mold, a man who "writes as he lives," "a hunter, soldier, traveler, boxer, fisherman, newspaperman, frontline soldier."[159] Years later, Raisa Orlova, who had edited Kashkin's "Rereading" article and written several essays on Hemingway, repeated this formula almost word for word, only now as part of her own life:

> For us, he was not only a beloved writer, but also a person who lived as he wrote. Reserved, a stranger to exalted talk, a fearless soldier, hunter, fisherman, matador, fighter for the Spanish Republic, comrade-in-arms of the French maquis, in our imagination he was a knight beyond reproach.[160]

So much were the lives of his heroes identified with Hemingway's own life that the journalist Yuri Paporov could not conceal his disappointment upon discovering a different Hemingway—helpless, fearful, easily hurt, even weak. "Truth be told, in our understanding Hemingway is incapable of fear," the journalist noted; "I simply could not accept on faith" Hemingway's vulnerability.[161] Hemingway's writing style was so closely identified with his life that essayists Aleksandr Genis and Petr Vail' explained his Soviet popularity as a matter of lifestyle. It included, in the Russian rendition, a chunky-knit sweater, a beard, dramatized toughness, feigned cynicism, the cult of male friendship, and lots of drinking, plus an olive in a martini—this, among people who most likely had never tasted a martini.[162]

After Hemingway's death in 1961, Soviet commentators were determined to preserve the equivalence between the writer and his protagonists, for the image of the reserved, courageous, and down-to-earth author had become part of Soviet biographies. Raisa Orlova wrote a rebuttal to Western "literary snobs," who tried to keep Hemingway's life and literature apart: "the writer was first the hero and then the author of his books; he hunted and fished, loved and fought first, and only then did he write about hunting and fishing, about battles and love." The Hemingway "we know and admire" lived by and taught "that tough ethical code" of "courageous honesty . . . the authenticity of feelings, fidelity to one's own self, honesty with oneself."[163] The Soviet press in that summer of 1961 was filled with obituaries mourning the loss of a national hero, a treatment afforded Hemingway in the United States and Cuba, but nowhere else. Hemingway had become an official classic, and, with the 1970 publication of his biography in the "Lives of Remarkable People" series, he would enter the Soviet canon.[164]

What few accounts exist suggest that Kashkin was a surly man, but in the beginning of July 1961, he appeared before audiences in particularly low spirits. "I was asked to say a few words about Ernest Hemingway," he began one of his talks, probably on July 4 or 5:

> I just found out about his death from a newspaper and I have no such words. I have no thoughts either; they have been swallowed up by a bitter realization that a great writer is no more; an honest, courageous, and probably good man, whom I had not had a chance to meet, is no more.
>
> A writer, a man has left us. . . . The books remain, the manuscripts remain like his posthumous voice, and the conviction that the writer Ernest Hemingway will not die remains, [too].[165]

The writer Vasilii Aksenov heard the news on the radio and wished that there were neither radios nor telegraphs: "the news would have traveled by sailing vessels and mail coaches for at least three months, and for these extra three months we would have thought that Hemingway was alive."[166] For one extra day, the writer Vladimir Lidin thought that Hemingway was still alive. In a rush that morning, Lidin skipped the newspapers.[167] The *Pravda* headline "Hemingway's Death" was the first thing that screenwriter Gennadii Shpalikov (or his fictional alter ego) saw that same morning as Lidin was rushing about. Before Shpalikov had a chance to reflect on rifles and fatal accidents, he ran into an acquaintance who played up the Hemingway pose and for whom Hemingway's death was an excuse for sad carousing: "He even said, Let us drink to the old man." Shpalikov responded with disgust to the image of "all the scum with doleful faces, and how right now they are on their way to Natsional' [restaurant] to drink to the old man—what a nightmare." He would have nothing to do with this tragedy turned farce. Preferring to live out a scenario from Russian literature, he met a woman and prepared for "an idyll à la Turgenev."

But the idyll "did not transpire." What transpired instead was a reenactment of *Fiesta*. True to form, the woman introduced him to several male friends, and together they set off for a restaurant. Appropriately, one of them had a beard, and "all of them wore old pants . . . and simple shirts, with sleeves rolled up." They ate, and Shpalikov scrupulously, like Hemingway, described just how they did it: they "drank vodka with tomatoes and cucumbers . . . and fresh spring onions dipped into salt." The vodka was cold; they drank it quickly, but left some for the main course.[168]

When Hemingway died, Kashkin called his life "a manuscript." The day Soviet newspapers announced Hemingway's death, almost too true to form, it rained in Moscow.[169]

Remarque's Sanctuary

Shpalikov was able to reenact *Fiesta* because that day he had earned some money by selling his old books. He spared Hemingway on principle, as a "literary act," but did sell "a fat, green" tome—perhaps the biggest hit of the era, the 1959 collection of Erich Maria Remarque's novels, *All Quiet on the Western Front, The Road Back,* and *Three Comrades.*[170] The first two had appeared in Russian in the late 1920s and 1930s but made little impression. In the mid-1950s, these translations occasionally were cited as an example of failure to unlock foreign books.[171] Now translators and literary

critics were determined to save *Three Comrades* from the same fate. And
they did: even before the "fat, green" anthology was published, a separate
1958 edition of the novel had immediately gained enormous popularity.
Another hit from another era, the half-nostalgic, half-triumphant film
Moscow Does Not Believe in Tears (1980), a storehouse of endearing clichés,
did not miss this one: a girl reads the poignantly recognizable *Three Comrades* in a subway car. The art historian Mikhail German, who was then a
twenty-five-year-old reader, calls it "the novel of a generation" or a generation's love affair (*roman pokoleniia*).[172]

Likewise, in his post-Soviet memoirs, the writer Andrei Bitov links the
publication of *Three Comrades* to a figurative appearance on Leningrad's
Nevsky Prospect, where people were waiting in long lines for the "fat,
green" anthology, of another "three comrades," three Soviet young men.
In Bitov's analogy, they represent the generation that emerged from this
book.[173] It was not the book, however, that created this generation, but the
generation that created its book. *The Three Musketeers* for the twentieth
century, *Three Comrades* was about male friendship and love on the brink
of a catastrophe. Robert, Otto, and Gottfried were comrades whose bitter,
self-sacrificial friendship was cemented by irrepressible memories of World
War I, frontline brotherhood, abundant drink, and a cherished auto. The
general catastrophe of Germany's inflation, unemployment, homelessness,
and fascist street violence merged with a personal catastrophe when the
friends discovered that nothing would save Robert's love, the tubercular
Patrice, from death. The end was predictably tragic: Gottfried was killed
by a Nazi stormtrooper, the auto shop the friends ran together went bankrupt, and Patrice died in a Swiss sanatorium, but not before Robert and
Otto rushed to bid her a last goodbye. Andrei Bitov tries to analyze this
novel, but finds himself unable to do so, because there is no novel—there
is nothing except an aftertaste: "Rather than reflecting life, thanks to its
unwrittenness, the novel mirrored our emotions and vision of life."[174] If
readers thus invested the novel with their own personalities and life stories, then the only possible analysis for Bitov and other Russian commentators is self-analysis, the only viable study is a memoir—an indulgent, exuberant, or condescending scrutiny of one's youthful infatuations.

And yet, the book was written—and not only by Remarque. The novel
appeared on the agenda of the State Publishing House in 1955, and it
took almost three years to produce the particular *Three Comrades* that
would become the stuff of memoirs. In addition to Isaak Shraiber, who would

soon establish himself as the principal translator of Remarque's prose, another translator, Lev Kopelev, participated, and the manuscript passed through several hands. There were four directions the final product could have taken, each with a different outcome for reader reception. A critic specializing in German literature, Kopelev translated only a few chapters, but his verbatim rendition, meticulously faithful even to the syntax of the original, was decidedly out of place in 1957. In a review for the press, Boris Suchkov, a leading Germanist, refined polyglot, and deputy editor of the State Publishing House, complained about Kopelev's foreignizing translation. "Many phrases," he wrote, "are strange to the Russian ear—you catch yourself thinking that this is not Russian. In Kopelev's rendition, the novel does not have the feel of a stylistically integrated work; rather, it is a *translation* with no independent literary life." Kopelev's own language intruded throughout, leading Remarque's characters to speak in sophisticated Russian. "The dialogues have lost their liveliness, word usage has lost vigor," and Kopelev lost the translator's job, though he remained on the project as author of the critical introduction.[175]

Shraiber's translation, by contrast, was an organically Russian text, interesting for its interpretation of the novel rather than for stylistic discrepancies. What he captured was that special camaraderie of the novel's title; best of all, his translation conveyed masculinity, "fortitude, [and] stoicism." Kopelev appeared to have shared this interpretation, because the original draft of his introduction highlighted "the poetics of courageous/masculine kindness" as the book's valuable lesson. But upon the insistence of his friend, the critic Tamara Motyleva, who reviewed the introduction for the press, this lesson was scrapped and replaced by another: "a truthful portrayal of the agonies and deformities that capitalism brings."[176] Still, the final text of the introduction retained something of Shraiber's interpretation: Remarque's "spiritually bankrupt" heroes, wrote Kopelev, "followed their simple, stern principles; cynical, crude, they remained faithful to those few truths that they still cherished—the friendship of men, the camaraderie of soldiers, basic humanity."[177] Having served as frontline translators during World War II, Shraiber, Kopelev, and Suchkov also knew these few cherished truths and simple, stern principles. For Kopelev and Suchkov, both former inmates of the postwar Gulag, Remarque's world may have held special undertones.

In the meantime, the editor who worked on the Kopelev-Shraiber translation produced a text of her own, replacing "nonclichéd, unfamiliar" images with "faceless" stock phrases, which, already worn out in Soviet books, "have lost all emotional expressiveness in Russian." Along the way, she added clarifying statements, "simplify[ing] the text, chewing it for readers."[178] Whatever reception this particular version may have met, it left little room for the kind of inspired investment of readers' life stories that Bitov and others would later describe.

The final product retained few traces of this Sovietized version or of Kopelev's intellectualism, but there also was more to it than the machismo of Shraiber's translation. A fourth, defining reading came from Boris Suchkov, who appraised the translation for the press. He conceded male friendships and feigned cynicism, but found the simplicity of the story and style deceptive. For him, the novel's most important feature was "the atmosphere enveloping the narrative, the mood that permeates it." That mood was one of unbounded sadness. It did not originate in unemployment, displacement, and other "vices of capitalist society"—or at least Suchkov did not mention these conventions of Soviet criticism. Rather, it was about "the infantilism, defenselessness, [and] helplessness of [Remarque's] heroes crushed by the evils of life" in general, without qualifiers. This interpretation hinged on "a lyrical subtext," which Suchkov discovered in Remarque, by analogy with Hemingway: "Remarque 'builds' his prose on a profound subtext, on the play and alteration of moods, on lyrical stress, on precise and economically expressed, restrained emotionality." According to Suchkov, Shraiber's translation missed "the poetic element." The subtext was "virtually elusive," but meaningful silences would have to be communicated in Russian if the novel were not to be "received as a banal account of misfortunes."[179] The translation was adjusted to Suchkov's interpretation; marrying lyricism and manliness, it became a Hemingway novel. From then on, the names of these authors would be linked in Soviet culture.[180]

These publication efforts were carried out in good faith, and hardly anybody anticipated what happened next. To be sure, there were people who had warned about Remarque all along: about the "profound pessimism," "the meaninglessness of all political parties," and the special art of drinking, "of consuming daily an unbelievable number of bottles of 60 percent rum" in *Three Comrades*.[181] By this time, however, *Foreign Literature* had serialized, to critical acclaim, Remarque's most recent novel, *A Time to Love and a Time to Die*, and, in 1957, it had published excerpts from *The Black Obelisk*. *A Time to Love* had struck critics as a significant departure from Remarque's earlier works. His heroes were perpetually "unable to sort out the surrounding chaos," life was still "a tragic waste," and the author remained a fatalist. Critics usually explained Remarque's aesthetic universe in terms of indiscriminate pacifism and political passivity.[182] But *A Time to Love* did not feature frontline brotherhood that had motivated Remarque's earlier plots. Instead, hatred and atrocity were all around, at the rear and at the front, not only between soldiers and officers, but also among soldiers.[183] One way to read the book, then, was as a bildungsroman in reverse—a novel of unlearning.[184] After a favorable critical reception, *A Time to Love* was printed in mass editions across the Soviet Union.

Three Comrades followed in 1958 and fared well in the press. Although the novel was chastised for the "limitations" of its "bourgeois humanism" (that is, the absence of a political outlet for the misplaced energies of its protagonists, who dissipated their lives in alcohol), catalogues of recommended titles listed *Three Comrades* among the "outstanding novels" in several categories: "books about love and friendship," "youth in foreign countries," and "paths of the intelligentsia in twentieth-century bourgeois society." A manual for librarians endorsed the novel for the "moving lyricism and warm humor" with which Remarque portrayed "deeply humane, decent, selfless young heroes . . . their strong friendship, their fairness, [and] hatred of hypocrisy and immorality."[185] But librarians did not have to advertise the novel: the life of the book outpaced the manual. "Hundreds of thousands of copies would be sold out in a couple of days, even hours. Those who did not manage to buy [a copy] signed up on waiting lists in libraries and waited sometimes for months . . . Libraries, clubs, institutes, and schools organized readers' conferences devoted to Remarque."[186] Passed from hand to hand, *Foreign Literature* volumes with his novels were worn out to the extreme.[187] While awaiting book reprints, readers also wrote to the journal with inquiries about future publications.[188]

Contrary to Suchkov's fears, *Three Comrades* was not received as a banal account of misfortunes. It was received as a revelation about manhood, pity, dejection, and love—not someone else's manhood, pity, dejection, and love, but "ours." "We read *ourselves* in Remarque": the novel was "about us."[189] According to an enthusiastic letter from several Muscovites to the State Publishing House, *Three Comrades* was a most useful book, "because it teaches camaraderie and delicacy of feelings . . . The very intimate feelings of the heroes, their relationships are depicted beautifully and sensitively."[190] "But who told us, young Soviet men and women, about these feelings," about love "eternal, singular, and unique, the kind that does not exist,"

Andrei Bitov would ask later: "That same Remarque."[191] Bella Ezerskaia, a librarian in Odessa and a contributor to the local press in the 1950s and 1960s, would recall: "We were so moved by friendship and love [in *Three Comrades*] that [reading it gave us] lumps in our throats."[192] Readers did acknowledge the importance of politics in literature, but forgave Remarque his political shortsightedness, "mesmerized," as one of them wrote in 1959, "by humane relationships between these people scarred by war."[193] They celebrated Remarque for "cultivating the senses":

> Want to try buying Remarque in Moscow? You won't find [him]. Young people read *Arch of Triumph* like the first Christians had read *The New Testament*. And this is not because of the depiction of fatal passions, as some tend to think, but because all things human are uneasy, intricate, and difficult in [the book], [and] because the writer CULTIVATES KIND FEELINGS in the reader . . . Much thought and much heart have been invested in this book.[194]

Discussions of Remarque, published and unpublished, invariably referred to relationships and feelings. Just at this time, as Remarque's books were read with twinges and tears, "relationships" and "feelings" were exceptionally prominent in the Komsomol moral vocabulary. In the late 1950s, "love" was printed on bulletin boards and posters; it was the subject of lectures at local clubs, disputes in dormitories, manuals on manners, novels, films, and countless articles in the Komsomol press. In one common newspaper scenario, heartless adults destroyed a fragile first love out of sanctimony, indifference, or insensitivity. In another scenario, love and trust were shattered by cynical womanizers.[195] These stories conceptualized love as an acquired—from great books—and socially meaningful behavior.[196]

Translations of Remarque arrived in this context of heightened attention to emotions and were, in part, responsible for turning "love" into a headline in youth newspapers and dormitory bulletins. His sensational popularity among students urged teachers, librarians, writers, and various experts on "youth" questions to think about the treatment of love in domestic literature and pedagogy: "What largely explains this popularity . . . is that Remarque talks about topics that we so often evade. For example, to this day, in novels and novellas for young people the very word 'love' is mentioned somehow in passing, shyly and vaguely."[197] There were Soviet love novels, of course, but, according to the playwright Viktor Rozov, it was an "idealistic, saintly" love, irrelevant to students' relationships and concerns. In Remarque they saw a "realistic portrayal of love" that was sometimes unseemly, sometimes tragic.[198] Students looked for the same love—carnal, tormented, impassioned—that Rozov could not find in Soviet novels. One such student spoke at a readers' conference:

> When I closed the book [*Arch of Triumph*], I was sad for our literature: Why can't we [write] like that? Different people read Remarque, the snobs [read him] and simple working fellows, too . . . In his books we find something that even the best of our books don't have . . . Our critics bashfully avoid problems of love, of the woman. Remarque writes about intimate life.[199]

There was a perception that domestic public culture ignored certain kinds of questions, ethical and sexual, leaving readers to seek answers in Western literature. The result was a compensatory devotion to Remarque.[200]

Remarque also figured in statements about a love that was neither tragic nor eternal, only dissolute. Readers even suspected that his portrayal of dissipated love was the cause of abridged and excerpted novels in *Foreign Literature*. A reader named Tarnov turned caustic against the "highly moral citizen," the journal's editor-in-chief Chakovskii, the guardian of readers' innocence.[201] In literary and pedagogical discussions, Remarque's books followed in the same train of thought as out-of-wedlock pregnancies, high heels, and rock 'n' roll records.[202] Such associations reveal Soviet phobias of capitalist love and suggest why Remarque's books triggered pleas for the education of the heart. Teachers argued that talking about love was necessary, because students read Remarque—and read him erroneously.[203] Literary critics, meanwhile, were reaching the same conclusion: they should talk about Remarque "with passion [and] infectiousness" matching his own "emotional contagion."[204] Explaining and debunking Remarque, as they did with other Western writers, was not enough. It was the *obsession* with Remarque that they wished to understand, demystify, and discredit.

What was it about *Three Comrades*, a maudlin story set in Berlin in 1928, that was so contagious in the Soviet Union of 1958? "Was it the deliberately raw pathos of Robert and Pat's love that so effortlessly had corresponded to our hearts yearning for compassion?" wonder people nowadays as they reflect on Remarque's place in their lives.[205] The pathos, yes—but had the book been little more than sentimental, it would hardly have stood out among numerous maudlin books. This one, however, was unabashedly, self-consciously, and wryly sentimental; the pathos was both deliberate and veiled behind insouciance. The novel's protagonists, Robert, Otto, and Gottfried, proved infinitely attractive, largely because readers mistook them for real people. Young Mikhail German interpreted the novel's archetypical depictions of male friendship and Romantic—that is, doomed—love as a flesh-and-blood reality:

> stern, ironic, courageous people, ashamed of sentimentality but not of earthly pleasures, people who knew how to drink and eat, who knew the value of a destitute and proud life, who placed friendship and love above all else, and who shrugged off politics—oh how unlike our civic-minded, ruddy, and sexless heroes![206]

In no time, Remarque's protagonists began to lounge about in the recently opened Soviet cafes and scuffle in Soviet streets. As readers took to modeling their actions, conversations, and relationships on this book, it acquired the "independent literary life" that its translators had sought. To many readers, all girls looked like Patrice from *Three Comrades*, and all drinks tasted like Calvados, the beverage of choice in another of Remarque's novels, *Arch of Triumph*.[207] "We sipped the[se] words"—Patrice, Calvados: words in the absence of things, in an effort to recreate, by naming, some elusive foreignness amid Soviet daily life.[208] Shpalikov stole his copy of *Three Comrades* from a credulous friend, who lived by the book, "drink[ing] like those dashing motorcar enthusiasts and wandering in the fog along the Frunzenskaia Embankment with a girlfriend who also took everything as if it were for real." To complete the image, they would need "tuberculosis, a sanatorium in the mountains," and "a sports car, so he could race at high speed through the night along a dark highway to [see] her."[209] Readers styled their loves on those of Remarque's characters:

> After Remarque, we were no longer embarrassed to give [girls] flowers, especially stolen ones. I met my future wife as I was picking lilacs at night in a garden—white lilacs during a white night. . . . We picked lilacs, hopped into somebody's else car, and raced out of the city. An auto, lilacs[—]but it is Remarque who married us![210]

The author does not tell us where and how two Soviet youngsters got a car in Leningrad in 1958; this is not important. What matters is that

Remarque's name was synonymous with the thrill of speed and romance; what matters as well is that some people remembered their love as an incarnation of the book.

In Remarque's novels, love and friendship constituted a philosophical principle, which was not lost on critics or readers. In *A Time to Love*, physical love alone offered shelter from a hostile world and afforded a possibility of salvation. In the words of a sympathetic Soviet critic, love worked "miracle[s]," transforming a "destroyed, ghostly, charred, dead town" "into a kingdom from a romantic dream." All it took was "affixing a colorful groundsheet to the remaining bit of ceiling and blackened timbers."[211] Likewise, in *Three Comrades*, "love acquired a special meaning, love as oblivion, as an elegy . . . Many of Remarque's heroes dreamed of respite— an island of hope where they could take cover from the evils of life. And they considered love to be the best thing possible on this island."[212] Both statements appeared in the Soviet press in 1957; but more than half a century later, love and friendship as a shield and saving grace remain essential to deeply personal recollections of reading Remarque in the late 1960s and 1970s. Translator Aleksandra Borisenko remembers how she read this book: "[In *Three Comrades*], love and friendship are equally important and inseparable. In essence, it is one and the same thing—the only weapon in the face of loneliness and chaos is turning to another person. Turning not to humanity in general, no; any abstract idea is empty. Turning to precisely this, unique, precious person, who is so defenseless before both life and death."[213]

The Remarque novels published in the Soviet Union told stories set during the interwar years or World War II and offered political cautionary tales about fascism. But for readers, Remarque offered an exploration of the universal apolitical. His brand of humanism advanced fundamental, universally applicable ethics and separated private virtue from civic duty. Class morality aside, a lie in Remarque was a lie, and war was war. This ethical position was surprising: in the Soviet philosophical tradition, moral principles were the terrain of political expediency and the purview of a dominant class. In Tamara Motyleva's article about Remarque and his Soviet fans, the idea of abstract good and evil was disconcerting.[214] The discussion of that article at an editorial meeting of the newspaper *Literary Gazette* returned incessantly to "elementary human virtues" and "universal values." In the words of the film critic Yuri Khaniutin:

One student says: "[Reading the novel *Three Comrades*], I felt as if I were living among decent people." The crux of the matter is that Remarque speaks about those simple, even elementary human virtues, which, at some point, our literature expressed insufficiently and continues [to express insufficiently]. Perhaps then it was normal, but [now] it is time to understand: these elementary human virtues that we sometimes push aside, the universal values that we talk about with a disdain of sorts . . . [are] necessary condition[s] for solving big social problems, . . . a person cannot be a real communist without moral cleanliness and such.[215]

Remarque distinguished the private world of elemental human bonds among a lone hero, his best friend(s), and his beloved woman from the public domain, with its official slogans and rituals. To be sure, poverty, unemployment, inflation, fascism, arrests, charred corpses, and concentration camps repeatedly intruded into, and ultimately destroyed, the protagonists' haven. But Remarque retained, or at least entertained, a miraculous possibility of driving away at incredible speed, hanging a groundsheet, drawing a curtain, making the world invisible, and thus becoming invisible to the world. What Soviet readers rarely noticed was that time—private time for private happiness—was sparingly measured; no haven in Remarque's novels was permanent, no heaven was eternal.

Establishing a private sanctuary did not necessarily require a curtain or car. The most basic partition was language, and Remarque's protagonists used a special vocabulary to mark the boundaries of their brotherhood. Remarque, too, was about words. The critic Ilya Fradkin, who welcomed Remarque's "rehabilitation," listened to the sounds of Remarque's world and heard their echo in his own world. "The grandiloquent lie of bourgeois politics" was "stentoriously announced" "from rostrums, tribunes, and pulpits." If tradition, conveyed here with images of church service, and modernity, captured in references to mass politics, were both implicated in the lie, then where could one look for truth? In a surprisingly transparent allusion to the Soviet Union, Fradkin described Remarque as a spokesman for a "deceived generation," rather than the idiomatic "lost generation." Remarque's characters did not "trust high phrases and abstract ideas" any more than did Hemingway's. Truth, explained Fradkin, resided in "'the sky, tobacco, trees, bread, and land, which never deceive,' and also, perhaps, in a loyal friend and a loving woman." Lest anyone miss the Soviet analogy, Fradkin made it explicit:

> Remarque's heroes are disgusted by any posture, [by] pathetic blare . . . the writer begins with the idea that a word quietly and clearly pronounced reaches the heart better than a scream, that the poetry of kind feelings requires a courageously restrained expression . . . Remarque's heroes project their fear of being deceived, their leery skepticism upon humanity's high ideals and goals. This way of thinking, of course, is alien to the Soviet people, but they can understand its origins and reasons with full compassion. They understand the bitterness of critical awakening that overflows the hearts of Remarque's heroes, they understand the distrust of falsely magnificent phrases.

If Soviet readers understood the bitterness of critical awakening, it was perhaps because Remarque—or his Russian translators—still spoke to them in those "half-words, without pretense and without pompous phrases."[216] According to another attempt to decipher Remarque's secret, what mattered was not only what Remarque said but also how he said it: "Everything is important here, everything demands attention: a barely detectable gesture that betrays a movement of the soul, a sudden change of tone, an accidental word. Remarque knows how imperceptibly to 'impose' a certain mood upon the reader." That mood was "an acute, aching sadness enveloping us from the first pages of *Three Comrades*, when nothing bad happens yet"—a sadness that, Suchkov had insisted when the novel was being translated, must be rendered if the book were to find Russian readers.[217]

For some of those readers, Remarque became "a consoler" of "lost, devastated souls" (in the words of students from a transportation institute). Others felt an affinity for his characters.[218] So persuasive was the sadness of his protagonists that readers singled out Remarque for possessing a special psychological acumen: he seemed uniquely capable of understanding the depth of loss and despair. One letter writer, L. A. Shiian, sought his counsel and his portrait:

> In his works, I encounter my thoughts . . . For me, he is a kindred soul . . . His life is probably sad. Maybe I cannot understand a merry, happy life that is like a fairy tale. Remarque writes the

truth, attractive or not, but the truth . . . I am a particle of Remarque . . . The best of epochs cannot give my girls happiness. I am a hopeless case. An unpunished criminal! Remarque would have understood me.[219]

Counselor and confidant, Remarque was also a companion. For Yuri Plashchevskii, who read *All Quiet on the Western Front* at age twelve, Remarque became "an eternal companion." In turn, the boy would grow up to become Remarque's translator.[220] Readers wished to touch or hold a token of Remarque's life; they longed for a relationship, however ephemeral, with their favorite author. They wrote to journals that had published his novels, asking for his address, so they could send a few lines in the only language they knew, that of Soviet clichés. In his letter, reader Platonov would thank Remarque. Third-year college students, having discussed Remarque in a reading circle, would ask him a question. Koprov would send an apocalyptic poem he composed about Remarque the "Fighter for Peace." The poem described the horrors of war and extolled the writer as "a [valorous] hero of the quill."[221] Hardly anything was known about Remarque, and readers chased after every scrap of information. Lia Chavchavadze, a student, was curious where he lived. Shiian, the reader in despair, did not "even know whether he was dead or alive."[222] Igor' Mikhailov took time off work on his thesis at the Moscow Engineering-Physics Institute to study critical reviews, but found little that would explain Remarque's "sincere and powerful" genius for conveying "sadness and death." Mikhailov, too, thought Remarque's life must have been gloomy and wanted to read his intimate biography.[223] People scoured critical articles and cultural news for mention of their writer, wishing to hear his political views in his own words, rather than those of fictional characters.[224] If they could only hold his photograph![225] In *Foreign Literature*'s mail, entreaties for Remarque's picture were the most frequent requests on any single topic.

Three Comrades traveled around the country: from Nevsky Prospect in Leningrad and Gorky Street in Moscow to Kiev, Minsk, Saratov, Ashkhabad, Tashkent, Batumi, and Riga. Between 1958 and 1960, republican publishers printed Remarque's books sixteen times in 3,500,000 copies. And this number excluded excerpts from his novels in the *Literary Gazette*, *Komsomol Pravda*, even *Soviet Sport*, which did not ordinarily publish fiction. Yet more Remarque was in the plans for 1959.[226] But even as *Three Comrades* traveled around the country, translators negotiated future contracts, and readers lined up at bookstores or wrote letters soliciting Remarque's address, officials in the Writers' Union, the Ministry of Culture, and the Cultural Department of the Central Committee were becoming increasingly apprehensive. They were taken aback by Remarque's extraordinary popularity, which, they felt, was incompatible with his literary standing and inappropriate for Soviet youths. In confusion, they "spoke of a Remarquesque flood, deluge, mass psychosis."[227]

In late fall of 1959, the critic Vladimir Kirpotin shaped the public face of the debate. "Remarquism," he argued in a signature article, was not an innocent enthusiasm, but "a certain Weltanschauung that smothers activism and breeds passivity, transforming righteous anger into stupefied, alcoholic despair." Kirpotin's article presented a synopsis of everything unacceptable about Remarque, above all, a universal morality grounded in "the only true constants" of "friendship, love, beauty, pleasures." Kirpotin connected profligate love, universal morality, and apolitical stance. Love in Remarque, he harangued, was a drug that numbed political consciousness, hence the disregard for class-based convictions and descent into universalism.[228] For the next several years, everyone writing about Remarque had to reckon with Kirpotin. Remarqueian love gained ever more noxious connotations: debauchery, vulgarity, sickness, the "fumes and smells" of "the Parisian abyss." It turned out that Remarque's prose was not lyrical, but cheaply sentimental, not manly, but crude, not "critical realism," but banality through and through. Kirpotin's was not yet the official position, but it was fast snowballing into an anti-Remarque campaign. A month after Kirpotin's piece, in December 1959, the Secretariat of the Writers' Union formulated its own judgment:

> We've had enough of Remarque, really. Why should we allow such things, or bypass such things, as [the journal] *Friendship of the Peoples* announcing Remarque. That is the last thing we need!
>
> . . .
>
> Recently, I've visited many young audiences and saw that this journal [*Foreign Literature*] has turned into rags; it has been read to shreds, all because of this *Arch of Triumph*! By the way, had *Foreign Literature* thought this through, it would not have published this novel, with its repulsive ideology. Enough already!

> *Foreign Literature* must take this into account, and I would have
> our Foreign Commission, and all of us together, follow up thor-
> oughly so that our youth gets less of this trash.[229]

Even Aleksandr Chakovskii, who had initiated the publication of Remarque with *A Time to Love* in *Foreign Literature*, was caught off guard.
He was alarmed by the autonomous life that the novels, including those
published in *Foreign Literature*, had assumed. In two letters to Minister of
Culture Ekaterina Furtseva, Chakovskii tried to justify his publishing
policy, retain the prerogative of translating Remarque, and absolve his
journal from associations with Calvados, dissolute love, and universal
ethics.[230] But by writing to the minister, he triggered a process that led to
an implicit ban on Remarque.

The Cultural Department of the Central Committee had all these
materials at hand: Chakovskii's letters, various critical articles, and reports
from the Writers' Union. Finally, in March 1960, the Central Committee
circulated to all republican party organizations a memo, "On the deficiencies and mistakes in publishing and reviewing foreign literature." Remarque
was not the only focus of this document, but he was in the spotlight: there
were too many editions in too many copies, misleading reviews (excessively admiring or excessively censuring), "unnecessary commotion," and
"sensationalism" bound to disorient readers about an author who blatantly
challenged class morality.[231]

With disapproval of the controversial works mounting, the Remarque affair was almost over. Publishing his prose became a risky venture. In
1960–1961, the Foreign Literature Publishing House printed *Heaven Has
No Favorites* and *The Black Obelisk*, and earned the director a reprimand
from the Central Committee.[232] In 1964, the same publisher's attempt to
bring out *Flotsam* was unsuccessful, so this chronicle of exilic wanderings,
ordeals, and sorrows (but also of friendship and love) moved to peripheral
journals.[233] So did his other novels: between the early 1960s and the early
1970s, Remarque was no longer printed in the capitals.[234]

Remarque had been something of a problematic author from the start,
but hardly anybody saw trouble until readers began to live by his books.
The crusading articles and proscriptive resolutions were a rejoinder,
mainly to Soviet readers and only secondarily to Remarque. And it was for
this reason—for the way he was read, rather than the way he wrote—that

the 1958 editions of *Three Comrades* have joined other prominent symbols of the Thaw.

Salinger's Loneliness

Few people in the West would connect Hemingway's and Remarque's names in the same sentence. For Soviet readers, however, they addressed similar issues and held much the same significance. One of the most relevant and resonant concerns that readers discovered in their novels was the problem of words—unspoiled words, terse perhaps, but all the more "sincere," words that matched deeds and meant what they signified. Hemingway and Remarque (re)appeared in the Soviet Union during intense debates on the bureaucratization of language.

What would replace bureaucratese was "the living word"—a prevalent concept in the late 1950s and early 1960s. As in the 1920s, during the Thaw, "the living word" meant the vernacular. Colloquial speech invaded literature, undermining one of the cornerstones of socialist realism: "the cultured language."[235] Many participants in the language debate insisted that realist literature could sidestep linguistic norms and that language was "a living, developing organism." These assumptions had far-reaching implications in late Soviet culture. Here was a separation of a normative literary language from the language of literature: writers no longer had to use grammatically polished Russian if it was not authentic to their characters.[236] Here was a redefinition of literary realism as a reflection of what is—"dialects and slang are part of *real life*"—rather than what should be. In the 1950s and early 1960s, the literary and educational press considered slang the exclusive property of "gamblers, thieves, and criminals," a way to hide "their dark deeds," "thoughts, intentions, and aims."[237] As a social phenomenon, slang seemed impossible in the Soviet Union, for there was no ground for it, like there was no ground for crime. But there it was, used not only by criminals, but also by stiliagi, "style-chasers" obsessed with Western clothes and music. The political establishment found stiliagi offensive on several counts, not least of which was their language. Their jargon coded the essentials of their lives: music, dance, money, drinking, courting, soirees, clothing, men, and women.[238] A closed linguistic system was too suggestive of a secret society, especially for an ideology that attempted to maintain a monopoly on meaning and that espoused accessible language.[239]

Because of their esoteric vocabulary, stiliagi were depicted in the press of the late 1950s as existential strangers, incomprehensible and alone.[240]

But in the 1960s, sociologists and linguists came to see language usage as generationally conditioned. Whereas earlier, argot had been identified as a devious, secretive system, by the end of the decade, professionals had dispensed with conspiracy theories. They began to consider expressive and emotional, rather than criminal and corrupting, functions of slang.[241]

Meanwhile, some educators and Komsomol propagandists increasingly saw the stiliagi jargon as emblematic of youth subcultures more generally and gradually accepted the fact of linguistic fragmentation—young people spoke differently. In the early 1960s, colloquialisms and slang (with several words from the stiliagi lexicon) appeared in "youth prose," authored by youthful bohemians and depicting the lives of restless young people. The incorporation of slang into mainstream literature could be construed as a battle lost by the guardians of uniformity. Or, it could be interpreted as a victory for the Komsomol journalists and officials who feared a secret language: the secret was out, people across the country were reading youth prose.

The sacrosanct literary norms were easiest to challenge in translation; the sacrilege could be blamed on the original. Translators now claimed exemption from "the cultured speech" of socialist realism.[242] Youth slang was not introduced into print by the cultural figures who tended to get credit for it—young men grouped around the journal *Youth*, writers with stiliagi friends and sympathies.

Instead, it was introduced by a sixty-two-year-old woman, Rita Rait-Kovaleva, who, reputedly, studied the stiliagi lexicon as she prepared the literary smash hit of the 1960s, the Russian translation of J. D. Salinger's *The Catcher in the Rye*.[243] Throughout the 1960s, *The Catcher in the Rye* was published several times in large print runs, but demand far outstripped supply, and the book's value on the black market was almost thirty times its official price.[244] Although the novella had been known among Soviet translators and editors for several years, few people wanted to take on the translation. Some interpreted the book as "empty chatter from a failure of a boy," while others considered the language "unthinkable, untranslatable slang."[245] Rait-Kovaleva's translation created a lasting shock wave, which continues to resonate in recollections forty years later: "unprecedented, entirely revolutionary Russian language."[246] The translation was steeped in Russian slang, which merged organically with a foreign character and a foreign storyline.

The novella initially was published at the end of 1960 in *Foreign Literature*, with the editorial board deeply divided. The first concern was Holden Caulfield, his travels, adventures, and encounters. A member of the editorial board and a specialist in European realism, the critic Ivan Anisimov judged the book "very poisonous . . . very cynical . . ." and Holden himself "a cry baby capable of strangling or knifing somebody to death." Other editors were more sympathetic to Holden (or were deceived "by his tears," Anisimov claimed). They read the novella as a "symbolic" "confession of an innocent youth lost in the maze of a capitalist city." Interpreting Holden as "a good boy," an "honest" and "unsullied youth," was politically advantageous: the boy's innocence—out of the mouth of babes—enhanced the novella's propagandistic value. Anisimov's reading ("But where did you get this innocent boy? Where do you see this innocent boy?") was rejected with these words: "You can unmask America, but you cannot unmask this boy." For Holden was "sickened by the American way of life and protest[ed] [against it] in his own way."[247]

The second concern was the harmful appeal that Holden and his freewheeling lifestyle might hold for Soviet youth. "This work can be contagious," Anisimov fretted. "Here is a rich boy, who has extra pocket money, who does God knows what, and anybody may want to do something similar." Editorial board member Evgenii Trushchenko, representing the Central Committee's Cultural Department, thought it was not Holden himself who was so dangerous, but "a vulgar, debauched atmosphere." There were bars, cafes, restaurants, cabs, hotels, prostitutes, and crowded Broadway streets. Chakovskii, the editor-in-chief, dismissed these fears by comparing Salinger to Remarque. Perhaps, he conceded, there was something attractive about Remarqueian "night clubs, Calvados, and so on" for "the young generation, which knows nothing of the active struggle against fascism, which has no understanding of what it means to be homeless." But Chakovskii could think of nothing appealing about "the nasty world in which [Holden] lives": "Is there a single situation, fact, or episode that would inspire our youth to say: I would like to be in his place? What would one wish to copy here?"[248]

Chakovskii, though, overlooked something one might wish to copy: Holden's language. After the journal publication appeared, some of Holden's favorite words, such as the oft-repeated characterization "bastards," became trendy—or, rather, what became trendy were Rait-Kovaleva's oft-repeated words, *gady* and *podonki*.[249] Even more troubling was the legitimization of youth slang in literature, a recovery of urban substandard speech in print. When the paradigmatic "youth" novel, Vasilii Aksenov's *A Starry Ticket*, came out in 1961, the parallels were unmistakable, prompting people to read Aksenov's novella through the prism of Salinger's. A reader who admired the two books as an eighteen-year-old girl in 1960–1961 later compiled an inventory of biographical similarities between Holden and Dimka, *A Starry Ticket*'s main character. Both challenged their surroundings; escapees from home, they grew up in major cities that were frightening and boring, yet full of childhood memories; both had older brothers, were marked by a special sensitivity, envisioned a future of purity, lacked concrete goals, feared "phony" words (hence the (in)famous slang), and indulged their audiences in self-irony.[250] But this reader overlooked a notable difference. To be sure, Aksenov did send his Dimka to Tallinn in Estonia, a European setting with bars and cafes, jazz tunes and dancing couples, sleepless nights of revelry—a fantastic world on the outskirts of the Soviet world. In Aksenov's Hemingwayesque (*Fiesta*) scenario, three friends and a girl traveled around in search of festivities, along the way making complimentary references to the "guys from Remarque" and other assorted Westernisms then in currency. But whereas Holden ended up on a psychoanalyst's couch in a California clinic, Dimka found himself toiling in a remote fishery and battling sea storms on a ship. Unlike Salinger's story, Aksenov's novella was Romantic and, in the final analysis, social realist: sails, storms, pirate-like adventures, tough captains, enduring friendships, and love reconquered.[251] It is unclear whether Holden was saved by psychoanalysis, but it is certain that Dimka was saved by labor and love.

Many readers missed this difference. Letter after letter noted, in disapproval or with admiration, that Aksenov's novella bore striking similarities to "a Western novel," to Salinger's prose, to that of Remarque or Hemingway.[252] At readers' conferences, the inevitable question for Aksenov was: "Did Salinger's *The Catcher in the Rye* influence you?" Aksenov consistently rejected not only the possibility of influence (he had finished writing his novella before the Russian translation appeared), but even the validity of the comparison.[253] Readers were not convinced, however. They continued to compare the runaway boys, their restlessness, trips, and, above all, slang. What was important about such evaluations was not the resemblance between the books, but their covalence in the reading culture of the early 1960s and beyond. The two titles offered a mutually constitutive interpretive framework; they were read in terms of each other, and, in part, it was this cross-referencing that made Holden a natural(ized) inhabitant of Soviet youth prose.

Aksenov's novella and Rait-Kovaleva's translation intersected in the language debate. Defenders of linguistic propriety blamed the stiliagi, youth prose (especially *A Starry Ticket*), and Western literature (especially *The Catcher in the Rye*) for widely disseminating substandard speech.[254] Holden's curses provided a model for the language that Dimka and his friends spoke: "Their actions are a 'fashion' imported from Western countries, drawn from foreign, bourgeois literature. This behavior is alien to the Soviet way of life. . . . Has not Aksenov 'over-Salingered' (*pereselindzheril*) our reality?"[255] The slang baffled Kornei Chukovskii, a prominent contributor to the language debate: he could not understand or accept the "rudimentary and limited" "intonations" in place of "complex, diverse modulations of voice." But he saw youth slang as a response to, even a "salvation" from, "varnished, cloying, and fake speech," which had not "a single sign of sincere feelings." In his reading, the young protagonists of Aksenov's novella remained "good, steadfast, perhaps inspired lads," uncorrupted by slang; their "words were vulgar, but [their] feelings were lofty."[256] Similarly, Chukovskii deciphered Holden's "romantically pure feelings" and "aspir[ation] to humanity and truth," "hidden somewhere in the secret depths of the soul." Indeed, "the coarse but lively jargon" may have conveyed Holden's purity better than a proper literary language would. Chukovskii's private notes show that he treated jargon as Salinger's (and Rait-Kovaleva's) achievement: "And how it is written!! The whole complexity of [Holden's] soul, all the conflicting, heart-rending desires— tenderness and crudeness at once."[257]

Readers understood slang as a stance, a confrontation, rather than a language in its own right that young people spoke ingenuously: in print, this speech read as an act of defiance. On the language issue, readers' letters operated with a set of opposites: fresh versus clichéd, young versus old, insatiable versus complacent, debauchery versus moral exemplars, "life itself" versus "window-dressing." Some people were scandalized and urged writers "to guard the purity of our language." For V. Novikova from Glazov in Udmurtia, slang was not a passing trend or a matter of flawed vocabulary that required schooling. It was a surface corrosion that exposed a deeper corruption. Behind the unseemly words were immoral deeds; "everywhere [there was] vulgarity, some sort of rubbish, . . . practically wantonness":

Where did the author find material of this kind? True, we still
have such youths who imitate the West and pollute our dear Russian language with the type of words spoken in the novella. But
we are struggling with this. For the most part, whether we are
watching movies or reading a novel, novella, or story, we try to
adopt all that is good and we want to resemble positive heroes.
[But] what can our young people adopt from this novella?

Incensed protestations followed a logic of their own: positive heroes, exem-
plary behaviors, literature as a model for life (rather than its reflection). If
fiction had a civilizing mission, then Aksenov's "good-for-nothing" novella
crept into print "illegally." The bizarre argot was bad enough in real life,
but for V. Novikova, its incursion into print threatened to undercut the edi-
fying purpose of literature.[258] In everyday life, slang was furtive; print
exposed it. In everyday life, slang was ephemeral; print authorized it. In
everyday life, slang was diffused; printed jargon dramatized community
boundaries.

Other readers loved seeing these unusual words and thought both books
were "about us (o nas)," precisely because of effortless slang heard in courtyards and at parties. Teachers found slang even in school essays, according
to a participant at a readers' conference about A Starry Ticket. At the conference, everyone agreed on the authenticity of the novella's language; as
a student put it, "Many say that to write about students and to assert that
they speak this language is wrong. But we live in this environment and
sometimes use even rougher expressions."[259] "No matter how much they
talk about jargon, we read Aksenov anyway. He is our author. He understands us," avowed a high school senior from Krivoi Rog in Ukraine.[260] To
demonstrate the relevance and reality of this language, a group of students
composed an entire letter to a publishing house in slang; the letter "had to
be translated, because it was completely incomprehensible."[261] Twenty-
year-old readers resorted to offhand colloquial speech, oaths (dammit!),
and jargon to establish rapport with Aksenov and to show he was one of
them.[262] Their letters sounded moral alarm, too, portraying a world of opposites: "the new" (to be defended) and "old junk" (to be challenged). Slang
played an active part in "the struggle with old junk," which included
language—"a banal, complacent tone," an indifferent or phony voice
announcing "from tribunes" "clichéd . . . speeches about labor, speeches
about duty and honor."[263] Salinger's Russian slang made the novella

"especially real, convincing, and accessible" to a young engineer, Vladimir Tuturin, who had not been "so impressed" by a book since reading Nikolai Chernyshevsky in secondary school. Holden the American teenager was not exactly "about us," but almost: "Although the way of life over there [in America] is very different from ours, of course, young people of all countries have so much in common in terms of psychology and behavior."[264] "Which one of us, Russian readers, did not think of school as 'stupid' (*duratskaia*), of classmates as 'bastards' (*kretiny*), of lessons as 'phony' (*pokazukha*)? . . . If even Holden thinks of life as 'phony' (*lipa*), then what can be said about us?"[265] The language—these were Rait-Kovaleva's words—was crucial to transforming Holden's account into a story "about us."[266]

Aleksandr Chakovskii assumed that this language worked against itself, as an example of how not to speak. Fellow translators praised Rait-Kovaleva for "resolv[ing] an urgent problem": she "clearly and saliently demonstrated to readers the ugliness and poverty of the stiliagi jargon that pollutes Russian speech."[267] But it was neither stiliagi jargon nor even youth slang proper that Rait-Kovaleva employed. The stiliagi used distinctive terms primarily for things and activities; by contrast, slang conveyed Holden's dispositions and sentiments. Rait-Kovaleva retained the standard words for dancing (a favorite activity of both Holden and the stiliagi), walking, playing music, and for wardrobe items, money, parties, cars, and girls—all of which the stiliagi rendered in their own vocabulary.[268] Her text contained several curses, plus two instances of the same near-obscenity. The rest of dozens and dozens of words unconventional in Soviet print were expletives and low colloquialisms. Most of them could be found in normative dictionaries, which were confined to "the literary language" and which were commended for excluding "words that [we]re anachronistic, regional, [or] vulgar."[269]

Rait-Kovaleva did not "unmask" any particular jargon; instead, she created a special expressive universe on the basis of mainstream colloquial Russian. The difficulties that she faced and the solution that she invented were not unique to the Soviet Union. In Europe, Salinger's book tested the conventions of literary language, with two outcomes: either the status quo was maintained, as in West Germany and Portugal, thanks to deletions, or the literary norm was unsettled, as in Finland, thanks to "an artificial vernacular" derived from street idiom.[270] Like many European translations, Rait-Kovaleva's text was more timid than the original when it came to coarse speech. But it was also richer, more expressive, and emotionally charged. Maintaining Salinger's rhythm, she diversified some of Holden's most stable and repetitive words ("terrific" or "goddam") with multiple synonyms and idioms. "Goddam," to take one example, was alternatively translated as *chertov, trekliatyi, idiotskii, duratskii, prokliatyi, poganyi, podlyi,* and *nelepyi.*[271] In the original, repetitions were largely responsible for humorous effects, powerful invectives, "looseness of thought," and "the perpetual insistence" in Holden's voice.[272] Rait-Kovaleva's Holden had a more expansive, precise, and surprising vocabulary than his American prototype; he was also more sensitive, affectionate, and vulnerable.

The Russian translation was so little indebted to the stiliagi jargon precisely because Holden was sensitive, affectionate, and vulnerable. Rait-Kovaleva did not see her hero as "cynical," "sly," a stiliaga, a future assassin, or, for that matter, a fighter against "the American way of life." For her, Holden was "kind and gentle," "restless, unable to adjust, to adapt to life," "selflessly read[y] to help others, especially children, to save them from falling into the abyss." He was "an agitated, tender, and chaste soul," awaiting a translator who would "hear this lovely, pure voice" and, "in trepidation, start looking for Russian words." Holden was awaiting her.[273]

This reading underpinned her work on the text: the abyss and the voice were the foundational concepts of the Russian translation. Consider the crucial moment in *The Catcher*: Holden's confession to Phoebe. He would like to stand on "the edge of some crazy cliff" and guard children playing in the rye so they do not fall off—he would like to be the catcher in the rye. Rait-Kovaleva redoubled the emotional charge of this pivotal image by stringing together increasingly dramatic synonyms. In the Russian translation, the original "And I am standing on the edge of some crazy cliff" reads: "And I am standing on the *very* edge of a cliff, *above an abyss . . .*" In the original, Holden elaborated his task as "the catcher in the rye" ("I'd just be the catcher in the rye"); in the translation, he fancied himself "guarding children *above an abyss,* in the rye."[274] The latter—above an abyss, in the rye—was then carried into the Russian title, *Nad propast'iu vo rzhi.*[275] The titles of translations published in other languages highlighted the person of "the catcher" ("rescuer," "man") or the problem of adolescence ("dangerous time," "outcast youth," "puberty," "the young Holden").[276] Rait-Kovaleva's abyss, by contrast, accentuated a general condition, specifically social or altogether universal, at the expense of a singular "catcher."

Her translation created the *image* of an existential book, and this philosophical reading had staying power.

The Russian translation was self-consciously attentive to the source of Holden's rye-field vision. Salinger's "catcher in the rye" derived from Robert Burns's poem "Comin' Thro' the Rye." Rait-Kovaleva knew the Scottish poet comprehensively and intimately. She had studied Burns since 1953, translating his diaries and letters and writing commentaries and articles; at about the time she began working on *The Catcher*, she published the first Soviet biography of Robert Burns.[277] Despite her profound knowledge of his hymns and ballads, Rait-Kovaleva did not borrow the phrase "in the evening rye field" from "Comin' Thro' the Rye," because it was not there. What Robert Burns had been to Salinger in terms of the dominant image, the poet Samuil Marshak was to Rait-Kovaleva. Marshak was Rait-Kovaleva's "friend and teacher," as well as "the best translator [she] had ever known," and it was to him that she dedicated her biography of Burns.[278] For Marshak was also the most influential interpreter of Burns's poetry in Russian, or, in the words of Rait-Kovaleva's dedication, he "made a gift of Robert Burns to the Russian reader." In fact, Rait-Kovaleva's first studies were prefaces to Marshak's translations; all of the poems cited in her book were Marshak's translations; and all of Burns's poems published in the Soviet Union were Marshak's translations, too.[279]

"Comin' Thro' the Rye" was no exception. Translating the poem, Marshak introduced an entirely new stanza: "If a body calls a body . . . In the evening rye field."[280] Burns's song told about "poor body" Jenny, her bedraggled petticoat and tears, and the cause of this mess—kisses in the glen. Jenny was a somewhat reluctant (if complacent) participant, but in Burns's poem nobody called out to anybody. Rait-Kovaleva's Holden was doubly mistaken. In the original, Holden's version of the verse ("if a body catch a body") turned out to be a memory slip (the correct line was "if a body meet a body / coming through the rye"). In the Russian version, "if a body calls a body," the line that Phoebe offered Holden as the correct one, was itself a translator's poetic forgery. But if in the original, Holden's mistake exposed his frantic rush between innocence (catch a body) and initiation (meet a body), then the Russian translation obscured this nuance.[281] In Rait-Kovaleva's text, the correct version (call a body) explained and validated the incorrect one (catch a body). There was no seduction in the Russian translation—only a possibility of salvation.

Marshak's invention thus underlay Rait-Kovaleva's conception of *The Catcher in the Rye*. To be sure, the problem of communication loomed over Salinger's book. A confessional narrative, it started and ended as a conversation with readers. Salinger's Holden roamed about in search of somebody to talk to, and once his search failed, he fantasized about the pleasures of losing speech and living a simple life as a deaf-mute recluse. The story of Holden's attempts to call out—a lone voice lost in the big, bad city—was pivotal for the Russian version. This was the story the translation highlighted at the expense of other subplots and readings, for, as Rait-Kovaleva put it, she was the translator who "heard" Holden's "voice." The most obvious way to read the novella was through a generational lens. And there was every reason to treat it as a coming-of-age chronicle, especially since the translation coincided with the peak of youth prose and with the debate on language. But the story of an adolescent coming of age was not the dominant reading. On the contrary, several critics deciphered a crafty "substitution of a child's world by a sufficiently mature adult [worldview]," "a stunningly well-imitated ingenuousness" by a "very experienced and very tired man."[282] Holden may have been an adolescent, but his conflict with society was permanent and universalized.

This, then, was an American story, or rather, a story of America, where everything was for sale. Soviet reviewers emphasized Holden's disgust with the world of "phonies," which was also the world of "American civilization," full of things but marked by a "spiritual void."[283] The people who inhabited this world were as calculating and indifferent as they were proper and respectable.[284] Much of Soviet publishing policy was predicated on the assumption that Western "critical realism" offered the most persuasive condemnation of capitalist society. Salinger's novella was doubly convincing, because it had that aura of truth out of the mouths of babes. Missing from *The Catcher* were the favorite Soviet themes of unemployment, hunger, and racism in America. Missing, too, were positive action and social consciousness; several critics saw this as a liability, for Holden's protest was "abstract" and not particularly warranted (there were worse things in America than bad movies, bad grades, and boarding schools).[285] But others found in the novella a priceless cultural critique, conveying "spiritual dissatisfaction" with "a society, [that] 'gives short shrift' to something very important, vital, something that cannot be replaced with comforts—a collective, rather than egoistical, goal, a true, rather than ersatz, culture."[286]

An altogether different opinion existed as well: "There is nothing specifically American in the novella, nothing specifically contemporary; three days in Holden's life . . . could have happened at any time, in any country."[287] In other words, it was everybody's story, a universal tale of loneliness and despair. It was the story of a big, cold, empty city, where Holden, the child in Everyman, was lost. It was a "story of misfortune."[288] It would have been easy to call Holden's tragedy "capitalism" or "bourgeois society" or "the American way of life," but, according to writer Georgii Vladimov, "there is no name in general for Holden's misery." On second thought, Vladimov did find a name for it: "If a body calls a body . . . In the evening rye field."[289]

The émigré journalist and critic Maya Kaganskaia ridiculed the favorite readings of the 1960s, especially Hemingway, with an image of a relationship both illicit and impermanent—"an extramarital affair," "a one-night stand." "Involved in the affair were text and subtext, [the tip of] the iceberg, a little bit of irony and a little bit of erotica . . . Individualism on loan, tragedy on the installment plan, spiced up with scraps and rags of homebred romanticism." Hers was a nativist critique of secondhand cultural goods: "they did not belong to you, they were translations, on loan."[290] The question, then, is about the significance of translations: Was there anything lasting in this literary promiscuity with foreigners? There is reason, however, to resist taking Kaganskaia's nativism at face value. Her ridicule was not a note of detachment, the "you" was self-directed, and the bitter acknowledgment of dispossession (*ne tvoi*) revealed just how much she or her friends wished to claim Hemingway as their own.

Written elsewhere, these books were made in the Soviet Union. Editors, literary critics, and especially translators (sometimes these were one and the same person) had far more power than earlier scholarship has allowed. Traditionally, translation had been just as important in the evolution of the Russian literary system as censorship had been. And like original Russian literature, translation had been implicated in politics. Moreover, in Soviet times, translation assumed an added political dimension, becoming a factor in transnational personal relations and cultural diplomacy. Unlike their counterparts in other times and places, Soviet translators were not marginal or liminal figures.[291] They were resolutely implanted in the Russian literary tradition by personal choice and by historical default. Attempts to dislodge them from authorship failed, as translators claimed a parentage that went all the way to the national poet Aleksandr Pushkin. On a par with originals, translations, Marshak's for example, shaped subsequent translations, supplying set expressions, images, and syntax.[292] Ordinarily, a translator's work "belongs to oblivion," for each generation translates anew.[293] In the Soviet Union, however, some translated texts became extraordinarily authoritative and established normative literary and lexical models as only canonical originals do. The post-Soviet generation has not retranslated much: Hemingway appears in the same translations, with excised sentences reinstated; Remarque appears in the same translations, while several new renditions proved to have been plagiarized; scores of other writers appear in Soviet translations. The only effort to retranslate Salinger—an iconoclastic attempt to challenge Rait-Kovaleva's very conception of the book, beginning with the title—failed. The project was received as an attack on the translator's lifework, on the Russian language, and above all, on the literary canon. For Rait-Kovaleva's translations have become canonical, and so have translations created by Vera Toper, Evgeniia Kalashnikova, Ivan Kashkin, Isaak Schreiber, not to mention Samuil Marshak. Their texts have profoundly affected the language and content of late Soviet culture. They gradually helped to lift taboos on intimate love in literature, to reintroduce substandard speech in print, and thereby to break out of the "paralysis of language," in which "words go dead under the weight of sanctified usage."[294]

Their texts also have had a profound effect on the place and representations of the West in Soviet culture. These translators did not straddle two worlds or inhabit linguistic borderlands. One of the more unusual features of Soviet translators was their near-total immobility.[295] Some of them (Marshak, Antokol'skii) had traveled and studied abroad in the 1910s and 1920s, but many (Kashkin, for instance) had never visited the countries whose literature they translated, or had first traveled only after creating their most influential texts (Rait-Kovaleva, Kalashnikova). In this, they shared the experience of their readers. Until the very end of the Soviet Union, there were practically no opportunities to see foreign places. But travel restrictions and closed borders are two of the reasons why translators had such an important role to play. As they translated foreign texts, they also created images—of a particular book, a writer, an epoch; of an entire national literature or culture.[296] Soviet society was plagued by information deficit. Readers had very few images to choose from; those fashioned by translators were therefore all the more authoritative and persuasive.

But translators were not the only ones who made foreign books Soviet. Readers ultimately transformed translations into "books about us."

Sometimes they created books quite literally, with scissors, glue, and needle. They would unfasten the pages of serialized novels from journals, sew them together, and affix a makeshift cover, or have them bound by a professional trying to earn a little money on the side. Readers who knew a foreign language occasionally could obtain the original at universities or at the Foreign Literature Library in Moscow. They would compare the original with the translation, record missing words and sentences in the margins of translated books, meticulously transcribe omitted passages on blank sheets, and carefully glue their handwritten notes between the pages. The result—typographically published books with handwritten inserts—was a hybrid that muddled the usual distinction between official print and samizdat. Such readers may have forgotten the content, but they remember the excitement and anticipation of discovering a secret, of recovering the whole, of making books.[297] But texts did not have to undergo physical transformations to become valuable and cherished. There was enough excitement and anticipation in the very process of procuring these books to make them memorable: the hunt around town, the rumors and covert deals, the long-awaited subscriptions, and the friendships cemented or broken by these books. Translations carried an emotional charge even before actual reading began.

Reading was a pivotal experience during the Thaw. Memoirs and interviews treat the appearance of each new book as an autobiographical milestone, but without doubting that it was also a milestone in the country's biography. Thus elevated into biographical facts, books provided common experiences and emotional affinities for a generation. And indeed, memoirists have identified themselves as a generational "we" by book titles. That some books published in the 1930s were received as a revelation shows how much the xenophobic years between 1947 and 1953 felt as a caesura. The new (re)publication policies of the mid-1950s may have contributed to an awareness of generational cohesion cultivated by books. The appearance of very different authors, from different countries and decades in a short time span, replaced the diachronic sense of translation with a reading experience in which all books were "contemporary." "Contemporary," however, did not mean domestication, and readers certainly did not claim all books, however great, as their own.

There is no single, neat explanation as to why some books, but not others, at certain times and not at other times, become books "about us." But this transformation seldom occurs without a particular kind of reading—reading as a transaction between text and context. The books that readers claimed as their own intersected with domestic polemics, which have been long forgotten but which commanded considerable attention at the time. Hemingway, Remarque, and Salinger were read in the context of debates on love and relationships, language, morality, and the purification of words. For ethical concerns colored the readings of the 1950s and 1960s: camaraderie and loneliness, love under threat, and grace under pressure were particularly meaningful themes. Foreign books "about us" interacted with—spoke to or against but never past—Soviet literature and journalism. The readings, therefore, were analogical (with Soviet problems) and compensatory (for Soviet prose): they endowed foreign texts with intimacy.

Kaganskaia's image of a dissolute relationship was the converse of this intimacy; it was a mockery of despoiled love, an attempt to reverse the transformation, to turn "books about us" into books that "do not belong to you." But her very choice of the metaphor confirmed the special closeness with Western literature that readers had enjoyed in the 1950s and 1960s. Indeed, people described their readings of these books in the language of romance: "Everybody was infatuated with Hemingway. His rival was Remarque." "Ah, how quickly we then cheated on Remarque!" With Hemingway: "For a long time Hemingway remained my main love, if not the only one." But lately, "I have cooled off" toward Hemingway. While some people abandoned him altogether—frequently for Salinger—others settled into a monotonous relationship with Hemingway: "I love him even now. For the most part, out of habit. Out of sentimental habit." Long after the initial romance, the memory lingered and the books remained: "Even now, accidentally opening a volume of Hemingway, I get a jolt in my heart. The same feeling you get when suddenly, in a crowd, you see the aged face of a woman who was your first love."[298] As first loves go, this book-centered affair was tempestuous yet timid, risqué yet exalted, and altogether impressionable.

4

Cinema without an Accent

Western films were never "about us." On the contrary, movie theaters were places where the fashionable and the mundane, the Soviet and the foreign collided. Literary and cinematic translations were inspired by similar ideas. Both translation communities proclaimed themselves "schools" and believed, albeit for different reasons, that the unit of translation was the image, not the word. The Kashkin school argued for thinking in images, meaning sentences and paragraphs, rather than discrete words. For dubbers, discrete words did not matter as much as facial and bodily movements: the picture on the screen set the parameters of translation. The results of these assumptions differed, however. For all of Ivan Kashkin's statements on images, prose translators worked with lexicons and, unlike dubbers, did not worry about performability and movement. They aimed to hide the operation of transfer and create a Russian original in its own right. Not so the dubbers, who recognized foreignness. To the sounds of flawless Russian speech, Western films foregrounded another reality. Dubbed Western pictures created a sensory forgery: foreign songs, objects, and interiors mixed with Russian voices and scraps of written texts to confound the viewers' sense of reality. Sensory forgeries were disorienting and precluded identification: the material and kinetic aspects left little imaginative space for the kind of relationship readers enjoyed with beloved books. But sensory forgeries also inspired analogical thinking and impersonation. Viewers tried to look like the people on the screen and decorated their dorm rooms or apartments with postcards and cutouts from journals. From the 1950s on, foreign films—billboards, titles running across marquees, schedule stands—brought color, glamor, and otherness to Soviet city centers and fast-developing outskirts. Experienced in public and collectively, these sensory forgeries reconfigured the intimacy of translation.

International Film Circuit: Business

While personal relations defined the transmission and translation of literature, foreign films screened in regular movie theaters for regular audiences arrived through institutional channels. To be sure, famous Soviet directors traveled to festivals and conferences, where they saw the latest films. They could, and did, suggest pictures that they loved and deemed aesthetically significant, but personal relationships rarely intersected with commercial politics. The individuals who made decisions on purchase, translation, and screening acted on behalf of institutions and within diplomatic constraints. Books did not enter into international treaties, but films were an item in biannual exchange agreements, subject to diplomatic negotiations and marketplace logic.

The All-Union Association for the Export and Import of Films, Sovexportfilm, held a monopoly on sales and purchases, and represented the first juncture through which reels passed along their road to local theaters. The organization combined aesthetics and commerce and retained a split personality, passing back and forth between the auspices of the Ministry of Foreign Trade (1953–1963) and the Council of Ministers' more politicized Cinematography Committee (before 1953, then again from 1963 until the late 1980s). The Ministry of Foreign Trade pushed Sovexportfilm officials to worry about profits and, according to critics in the Council of Ministers, to neglect politics. Commercial import and export were mutually dependent activities, as Sovexportfilm reinvested its revenues from the release of Soviet movies abroad into purchasing foreign pictures.[1] The Council of Ministers examined and approved Sovexportfilm's acquisition plans and allocated hard currency in the budget of the Ministry of Foreign Trade.[2] The chairman of the Council held the purse strings, but the Council's Cinematography Committee nonetheless scorned Sovexportfilm as "a purely commercial organization."[3] During the ideological campaign of 1962–1963, the Moscow municipal ideological commission examined movie theaters (along with libraries, dance grounds, and bookstores).[4] What it found were Western films in great abundance, filling all show times, attracting enormous crowds, supplying the urban rumor mill, and competing with Soviet pictures for viewers. The hysteria of 1962–1963 was the broader context for the transfer of Sovexportfilm to the Cinematography

Committee. However, even as the ideological commissions turned shrill, the actual acquisition policies did not change in 1963, and throughout the 1960s and 1970s, the number of Western films in release grew exponentially.

Sovexportfilm operated through a network of representatives, usually housed in Soviet trade missions and embassies. They negotiated the terms of transactions, the matters of how many and how much. And they worked closely with colleagues in neighboring offices—embassy staff, who were often present during Sovexportfilm's negotiations. In 1959, Minister of Culture Nikolai Mikhailov and Minister of Foreign Affairs Andrei Gromyko instructed Soviet embassies to take an active part in the selection process. Embassy officials had to assess the film market and advise Sovexportfilm representatives, while ambassadors were to watch each production before the reels were sealed in canisters destined for Moscow.[5] Sometimes, when it came to famous pictures, ambassadors initiated the process. On other occasions, the Ministry of Culture sought their approval to buttress its advocacy for particular films before the Central Committee. Sovexportfilm representatives conducted the first round of selection and sent their recommendations, along with reel cans, to Moscow.

Dozens of reels arriving in Moscow required a special "commission for the selection of films from capitalist countries" to spend hundreds of hours watching movies in the most exclusive of screenings. The commission, instituted by a November 20, 1958, resolution of the Central Committee, consisted of filmmakers, writers, journalists, critics, and high-ranking cinema bureaucrats. They made the penultimate recommendations to the Central Committee. The minister or deputy minister of culture countersigned memoranda in approval and proposed purchases to the Central Committee.[6] Instructors from the Committee's Cultural Department decided on the recommendations. Their verdict, scrawled on the bottom of memos, went to higher-ups in the Secretariat, who approved the films.[7] That decision, however, was not set in stone. Frequently, movies rejected by the Cultural Department—Billy Wilder's *The Apartment*, for instance, *The Miracle of Father Malachia* (dir. Bernhard Wicki), *Rosemary* (dir. Rolf Thiele), or *The Nights of Cabiria* (dir. Federico Fellini)—appeared in Soviet theaters several years later. In fact, the Cultural Department had dismissed nearly all of the best-loved French and Italian pictures in commercial release in the mid-to-late 1950s.[8] The more important decisions seem to have belonged to the commission; when its members felt strongly enough about a film, they resubmitted their recommendations, time and again—until the right time. Once a movie was approved, Sovexportfilm received permission to negotiate with distributors. This was a complicated chain of command that neither paintings nor books had to navigate. Every film that appeared in the Soviet Union involved ministers, ambassadors, chairmen of artistic unions, instructors from the Central Committee, and other high officials.

The realities of exchange forced the Soviets to share the selection process with their foreign counterparts. Sovexportfilm officials and members of that special commission were keenly attentive to the quid pro quo. This, indeed, was their governing logic: they purchased films when they wished to sell their own and favored the distributors that acquired Soviet pictures, United Artists, Carlton Film Export (UniFrance), or Pegasus Film (FRG). The French Filmsonor, for instance, bought and exhibited *Ballad of a Soldier* (dir. Grigorii Chukhrai) and *Fate of a Man* (dir. Sergei Bondar-chuk), and—in hopes of "selling several new Soviet films"—the commission argued for purchasing a Filmsonor picture.[9] From British Lion Films, the Ministry of Culture recommended buying two movies in 1960–1961, at the very moment when Sovexportfilm was negotiating a Soviet sale.[10] To "maintain good business relations" with foreign distributors, Ministry of Cultural officials even bought films they found disappointing.[11]

Since Soviet purchases depended on sales, foreign markets made a difference—sometimes definitive—for the selection of films destined for Soviet audiences. The British market, still regulated by the protectionist logic of the interwar years, proved one of the most impenetrable. British distributors discriminated not only against features from the socialist bloc, as did American companies, but also against foreign pictures in general, including American ones. Faced with Hollywood and, by the 1960s, with television, British producers protected their national industry. British films were also some of the most expensive on the market. Italian ones, by contrast, offered political engagement, social activism, and lower prices.[12] A generation of Soviets grew up watching neorealist classics and comedies Italian-style, whereas only a handful of the socially charged British "kitchen sink" dramas made it into commercial release.

The Soviet notion of quid pro quo assumed a defensive tone in the aftermath of the Hungarian Revolution. Amid the international crisis, foreign markets for Soviet cinema shrank dramatically. In early 1957, distributors across Europe, the United States, and Latin America halted the release of pictures that already had been purchased. Some, like the Swiss, severed earlier contracts with the Soviet Union. But most did not—according to Sovexportfilm officials, the collapse of these markets would be temporary, "until a change in the general political situation."[13] That change came in the summer/fall of 1957, when negotiations of bilateral film festivals, sales, and exchanges resumed. However, with the optimism of "the spirit of Geneva" fading, exchange emerged as a disputed term. It meant reciprocity, but what, in turn, did reciprocity mean?

The Soviets understood reciprocity as strict parity and symmetry: selling the same number of films as they would buy, for roughly the same amount of money. In 1958, Sovexportfilm chief Aleksandr Davydov and his officials brought this interpretation to the contentious and symbolically momentous negotiations with the United States. Soviet-American media diplomacy was not representative of cinematic transactions between the Soviet Union and other countries. But precisely because they were unique, Soviet-American negotiations offer a magnification of the grand principles and small contingencies that determined what movies would reach Soviet audiences. The first round of talks began in Washington, DC, in late March 1958, following the signing of the Lacy-Zarubin agreement on wide-ranging cultural and scientific exchanges.[14] The agreement's Article 7 formulated media exchanges in broad terms, leaving the details for subsequent conversations among film industry specialists.[15] When Sovexportfilm's Davydov and A. A. Slavnov, representing the Ministry of Culture, Eric Johnston, president of the Motion Picture Association of America (MPAA), and Turner Shelton, chief of the United States Information Agency Motion Picture Service, met that March and April to settle the number of films, the talks were difficult and verged on a breaking-point.

The Americans had a very different understanding of exchange, specifically rejecting one-to-one parity. Davydov and Slavnov saw each transaction as distinct, removed from prior context, and suggestive of a partnership. Johnston and Shelton decoupled sales from purchases, contextualized transactions in the longer history of postwar cinematic relations, and felt uncomfortable about allusions to a partnership of equals.

Since the earliest strides in 1955–1956 toward cultural exchange, the U.S. Department of State "strongly opposed and actively discouraged," to use its own words, any public demonstration of a reciprocal relationship with socialist bloc countries, including coproductions, bilateral sales, and delegations of actors. In those years, American entrepreneurs were captivated by the possibility of exchange with the Soviet Union, besieging the State

Department and the Soviet embassy in Washington with proposals.[16] All, however, ran afoul of the State Department, and none materialized.[17] Similarly, the Department rejected bilateral film festivals with the Soviet Union and ruled against American participation even in Western European events where "East Germans or Red Chinese may be present."[18] At the 1958 negotiations, the Americans' understanding of parity stemmed from the State Department's proscription against reciprocity.

In thinking about parity, the Americans kept in mind film distribution practices from the preceding decade. Johnston defined reciprocity as correcting historical imbalance. According to the MPAA statistics, American distributors had purchased as many as forty-five Soviet motion pictures after the war. No American production, however, had been acquired by the USSR since 1948, at least not officially. To achieve something like historical parity, beyond the immediate moment and over the course of the postwar period, the Americans would have had to sell more films than they purchased.[19] There was some truth to Johnston's calculations: Soviet movies had been screened in the United States for a good decade. But there was also a caveat. The films had not earned the Production Code Seal, required for release in movie theaters under the Motion Pictures Association, and those were the majority, as well as the biggest and best, of theaters.[20] Soviet movies could only be screened by independent exhibitors on the margins of the entertainment industry—in "third rate" theaters, as offended Soviet officials put it.[21] Or primarily in one theater, the Cameo in Midtown Manhattan, owned by Artkino Pictures. Artkino had organized screenings of Soviet pictures in the United States (and in the Western hemisphere) before the cultural agreement was signed.[22] Artkino was perhaps the most stable in the Soviet Union's international network of "progressive" distributors. That network included Tabajara Filmes in Brazil, Dan-Ina Film in Denmark, and Libertas Film in Italy; the France-USSR society promoted Soviet films in France. Listed as joint stock companies, they had only one shareholder: the Communist Party.[23] Throughout the 1950s, these companies fared poorly: Sovexportfilm found their debt "hopeless" and forgave it, year after year.[24]

Artkino held out the longest. Before Cameo would rise to fame in the 1970s as a haven for hardcore pornography, the theater had been a haven for Soviet cinema, from the avant-garde of Eisenstein's variety to Stalinist musicals and filmed ballet.[25] Artkino (registered as an agent of the Soviet Union in the 1940s–1950s) and its movie theater were marginal in American culture. That is what Soviet negotiators meant when they talked about third-rate theaters.[26] Indeed, for them the purpose of cinematic trade with leading distributors was precisely to bring Soviet films out of the shadows of communist networks, working-class neighborhoods, and leftist groups, and into main-street, first-run venues.[27]

Johnston found it difficult to imagine the grounds for one-to-one parity. The difference in the economic organization of the two societies complicated the task of "equalizing" agreements. The United States produced many more films, but the Soviet Union had many more viewers. Moreover, an equal number of films and screening days did not amount to equal control of the exhibition process: the Soviet government regulated movie theaters, printing and distribution organizations, and much else besides— oversight that the American government could not match. Theaters, showtimes, publicity—all would be decided by private owners and commercial interest.[28]

This, then, was the background that shaped the Americans' dismissal of parity during negotiations in the spring of 1958. According to the account of the Soviet delegation to Washington, a tense month of discussion resulted in a proposed compromise: ten American and seven Soviet pictures over the next two years. At the eleventh hour, however, the State Department authorized the purchase of only two Soviet films. Word came the evening before the Soviet negotiators were scheduled to return home. It left them feeling bitter and exasperated.[29] In September 1958, Johnston and Shelton arrived in Moscow, still determined to sell ten American films and purchase half as many Soviet ones. All the while, Soviet officials held dear "the principle of total reciprocity"—the first point in Sovexportfilm's "instructions" to its representatives.[30] As Johnston tried to modify this ratio, the negotiators became embroiled in a prolonged argument.[31]

One significant, albeit implicit, sticking point of these negotiations, which spun endlessly around the same terms, was an acknowledgment of a cooperative relationship. The Americans scoffed at Soviet language trumpeting "the principles of equality and mutual provisions": "we are talking about buying and selling in free conditions," nothing more. But what of "cultural relations," so important to the Soviets?[32] Only at the end of 1959 did Johnston and Davydov work out a joint communique.[33]

And then there was the selection of the ten and seven films. Negotiators spent many days watching films to choose the least ideologically harmful in a vetting process that revealed the two antagonists as a mirror reflection of each other.[34] American officials were as deeply concerned about the ideological impact of motion pictures as their Soviet counterparts were. The State Department tried to achieve control over sales comparable to that exercised by Sovexportfilm. To the delight of department officials ("seems like real progress!" reads a scribble in the margins of a memo on centralization of film commerce), in 1955–1956 the Motion Picture Export Association (MPEA) assumed the role of trade representative. Henceforth, the MPEA would transact business on behalf of production companies. A committee, consisting of representatives from each company, would screen American films designated for sale and create a short list. The short list "would then *informally* be shown to USIA," and, "I believe," assistant secretary Jean Jerolaman noted parenthetically, it "should also be shown to the Department."[35] Production companies would abide by the committee's decision, "refus[ing] to sell any pictures which from overall national interests would seem unsuitable for showing behind the Iron Curtain." To be suitable for sale to the socialist bloc, films would have to convey "our moral . . . values" and a picture of "American well-being." The USIA articulated the same vision. The Agency's Turner Shelton was "violently opposed to the full and fair concept of America" and believed in showing exclusively "the best side," as "a contribution to U.S. foreign policy objectives."[36] This selection process approximated the Soviet one to a remarkable degree.

Among the seven Soviet films that the Americans purchased, two were ballet or circus performances, and four were adaptations of literary classics, only one of which was Soviet (*Othello* by Sergei Yutkevich, *Don Quixote* by Grigorii Kozintsev, Ivan Pyr'ev's *The Idiot*, after Dostoevsky, and Sergei Gerasimov's *Quiet Flows the Don*, after Mikhail Sholokhov). The last was the most famous Thaw film, *The Cranes Are Flying* (dir. Mikhail Kalatozov). Davydov's choices were more heterogeneous: two biopics, *The Great Caruso* (dir. Richard Thorpe) and *Man of a Thousand Faces* (dir. Joseph Pevney), two musicals, Charles Vidor's *Rhapsody* and Fred Zinnemann's Western *Oklahoma!* in TODD-A-O format, fantastic *The Seventh Voyage of Sinbad* (dir. Nathan Juran), William Wyler's romantic comedy *Roman Holiday*, a quiet love drama *Marty* by Delbert Mann, a Hemingwayan tragedy *The Old Man and the Sea* (dir. John Sturges), and Cinemascope *Beneath the 12-Mile Reef.* These films introduced Gregory Peck, Elizabeth Taylor, and Audrey Hepburn to Soviet screens, posters, and illustrated magazines. *Marty* and *The Cranes* premiered in Moscow and

New York during a bilateral film festival that became part of the all-encompassing project of cultural exchanges.[37]

The compromise of 1959 was temporary, subject to changing international pressures. The very next year, the arrangement crumbled following the U-2 incident, when an American reconnaissance plane was shot down over Soviet air space, and both parties returned to the dispute over reciprocity.[38] When, at the end of 1961, in the wake of the Berlin crisis, Soviet representatives arrived in Washington for a meeting of the Permanent Soviet-American Committee on Questions of Cinema, their nerves—and those of their American counterparts—were strained to the extreme. As hostilities intensified in 1960–1961, reciprocity and commerce appeared outdated notions from another age: American companies boycotted Soviet films.[39] Year after year, the whole edifice of media diplomacy teetered on the brink of disintegration. Year after year, the Soviets felt disadvantaged; complaints about American nonfulfillment of the agreement and disregard for reciprocity became clichés in technical reports and diplomatic instructions.[40] Sovexportfilm's annual purchasing plans for American films often went unfulfilled. And for these reasons, the Soviet import-export balance tipped toward France and Italy, disfavoring the United States.[41] In the late Soviet decades, screens and showtimes were overwhelmingly filled with Italian and French films.

International Film Circuit: Pleasure

Italian and French pictures first arrived in the Soviet Union in the mid-1950s, amid a flurry of bilateral film festivals. Earlier, such festivals had been organized only for socialist bloc countries. In 1955–1956, the Italian and French "film weeks," as they were called, were exceptional—for the optimism and jocularity with which the press presented these events, and for screening movies whose drama, suspense, and situational humor were eye-opening. The events snowballed on Soviet audiences, overtaking visual and aural spaces, movie screens, radio waves, central squares, and parks. The 1955 French festival was surrounded by a vast propaganda campaign: press coverage, "special concerts of French music and song" on the radio, billboards and posters numbering in the thousands (5,000 "special" ones and 2,000 more for each film).[42] The concerted propagandistic effort signaled to viewers that it was no longer a lone picture, fortuitously appearing at a local theater but rather something new altogether. Christian-Jaque's *The Charterhouse of Parma* and *Fanfan the Tulip*, Claude Autant-Lara's *The Red and the Black*, all three starring Gérard Philipe, Henri-Georges Clouzot's *The Wages of Fear* with Yves Montand, Marcel Carné's contemporized *Thérèse Raquin* featuring Simone Signoret in the lead role, *Julietta* (dir. Marc Allégret) and *Papa, Mama, the Maid, and I* (dir. Jean-Paul Le Chanois) now were united in a single program.[43] The festival introduced names and faces that would become a mainstay of extra-cinematic life for the next two decades.

Perhaps as important an attraction as the films themselves was the delegation of French filmmakers and actors. Nicole Courcel, Danielle Darrieux, Jean Gabin, and above all, Gérard Philipe were featured in that year's iconic photographs. In one, Philipe, wearing a light, unbuttoned coat, amid a crowd of men dressed in dark, fastened ones, gave a sweet-faced look of surprise. In another, he playfully hit a ball at Dynamo Stadium while a lineup of photographers snapped their shutters. Martians from another planet, French stars stepped out of the screen to mingle—in photographs—with Soviet crowds in the streets, walk in Red Square, or glance down from Sparrow Hills.[44] A certain normalcy about their presence in Moscow and a light-heartedness in their manners—their unbuttoned coats—were a signpost of the festival. Another French film festival, in 1956, served as a set piece for Prime Minister Guy Mollet's visit that May. Few would remember Mollet, and his name disappeared from the Soviet press as soon as he resigned from office, but old people still recall Gérard Philipe with dreamy relish.[45]

At the same time, seven Soviet films, both recent ones and revolutionary avant-garde, were screened in France.[46] This was probably the first time officials consciously used the avant-garde to claim Soviet cinematic ascendancy in the international film circuit—not to propagandize the Revolution, but to announce primacy in modern art. As in no other artistic endeavor, Soviet cinema of the 1920s would become a prominent export item and a declaration of aesthetic legitimacy. At the conclusion of the mutual film festivals, both parties purchased the movies they had screened, a gesture accompanied, again, by much publicity.[47] Thus began systematic Soviet engagement in cinematic trade and international film networks. Throughout the 1950s, the roster of prize winners, nominees, and jurors at Venice, Berlin, and Cannes was a who's who of European cinema: Roberto Rossellini, Luchino Visconti, Giuseppe De Santis, Luigi

Comencini, Pietro Germi, Marcel Carné, Christian-Jaque, Claude Autant-Lara, Max Ophüls, Laurence Olivier. These names also dominated Soviet screens and the press in the 1950s and 1960s.

Soviet presence on the international film circuit was a departure from the prewar and immediate postwar years. The Soviet Union's relationship with the oldest international cinema event, the Venice festival, had been convoluted. After bringing to Venice four pictures in 1934, Soviet film-makers returned home humiliated. It was irksome enough that the films were nominated for a prize bearing Mussolini's name, but that the prize went to another picture was double the insult. After losing the Mussolini Cup, Moscow established a festival of its own in 1935, where it could award ideologically correct prizes to ideologically correct films.[48] That year was the first and also the last of the Moscow event, presumably on account of a conservative and isolationist turn in the second half of the 1930s. The Venice festival, meanwhile, took the same conservative turn under the dominating influence of fascist politics and aesthetics. Beginning in 1936, when Leni Riefenstahl received the Mussolini Cup for *Olympia*, the festival became an Italian-German affair.[49] After the war, Venice rebuilt its reputation by embracing a neorealist aesthetic and a broadly international engagement. In 1946 and 1947, the Soviet Union participated unremarkably and disappeared from this node on the film circuit for the next six years.

Berlin's film festival would not be open to Soviet movies for over twenty years. It was created in 1951 as an expressly Cold War venture, with substantial funding from American authorities and the Federal Foreign Office. The festival's founding moment was unambiguously political and entirely symbolic. It was an outpost of the "free world" in the heart of divided Berlin, it recalled Berlin's vibrancy as a cinematic capital of the 1920s, and through culture it cultivated the sovereignty of the Federal Republic.[50] In the late 1950s, the Foreign Office at long last invited Soviet participation. But the Soviet Union demurred, for, by establishing the festival in West Berlin, the Bonn Republic laid claims to the city, whereas Soviet diplomacy did not recognize its exclusive mandate.[51] The first Soviet picture would be screened in Berlin in 1974, after the commencement of Ostpolitik.[52] Besides its opposition to the communist nemesis, the Berlin film festival derived its identity negatively in another way. With the imprint of destruction and division, Berlin posited itself as a "serious" intellectual endeavor—against the paparazzi, beaches, topless starlets, and cocktail receptions of

Cannes.[53] Because Berlin excluded the Soviet Union, it was not a reference point when the Moscow International Film Festival was in the planning stages. Yet the Moscow event was a manifestly political counterfestival as well, and, like Berlin, it distinguished itself from Cannes. A similar discourse of antiglitter, antitourism, and antiprivilege became defining for Moscow—only with greater consistency than in Berlin.

Ironically, it was Cannes that was the most commanding model for the Soviets, and it was at Cannes that they had their biggest breakthroughs since the 1920s. The Soviet Union had been taking films to Cannes since the immediate postwar years. Founded on the eve of the war, suspended in wartime, and reestablished in 1946 as a hopeful emblem of European revival, the Cannes festival was open to all, including the socialist bloc.[54] By the late 1950s, it had become the most important film event in Europe. Cannes introduced an international audience to a host of aesthetic movements, from neorealism to the new wave, and created an international community of "auteurs." It also represented the new European affluence, a glossy postcard world of transnational wealth, tourism to sunny places, glamorous women, elegant men, and carefree hedonism. As the largest marketplace for film, the festival created a global cinematic network of coproductions and exchanges that contested Hollywood's unilateral domination.[55] Festival posters symbolized this community by depicting a globe, a film reel consisting of different flags, or a female figure robed in flowing national banners—the world united by cinema.

The Soviet Union had been part of this community beginning in the late 1930s and maintained a steady presence at Cannes after the war. Since 1955, Soviet films had garnered prizes, including a special award for "humanism and high poetry," presented to Grigorii Chukhrai's *Forty-First*. The film was the talk of serious critics, and its leading actress, Izol'da Izvitskaia, made the tabloid press.[56] But the biggest triumph came in 1958, when Mikhail Kalatozov's iconic *The Cranes Are Flying* received the first (and only) Soviet Palme d'Or. With *The Cranes*, Cannes launched Thaw cinema as an international phenomenon. *The Cranes* became one of the Soviet Union's more exportable commodities; it would remain a staple of art-house theaters in Europe and the United States for nearly two decades. For international audiences forty and fifty years ago, the lead actress, Tatyana Samoilova, was the most recognizable face of Soviet cinema.

In the mid-1950s, Soviet crews began to accompany their films to Cannes. In 1957 and 1958, amazed and electrified, the directors, cameramen, and lead actors of *Forty-First* and *The Cranes* returned home with a sense of rightful belonging in that transnational cinematic community. At the time of the Palme d'Or, Samoilova was a twenty-four-year-old student at the Shchukin Theater Institute. Fêted and photographed, she shot to stardom. Gérard Philipe and Pablo Picasso, Soviet idols of the time, embraced her, presented her with gifts, and invited her to their homes or movie sets. Both predicted for her an extraordinary life. Her popularity was such that Procinex Production would buy anything, "even a mediocre film," starring Samoilova.[57] At the award ceremony in Moscow, all she could say was that the trip "was the best thing in her life." The film's cameraman Sergei Urusevsky searched in vain for words to convey "rapture": "This is my first trip abroad, and I am literally smitten by everything I saw. I walked in Paris along the Seine ecstatic." It was not something to be described; it was like a painting, to be seen.[58] Urusevsky, too, had met Picasso, who, upon watching *The Cranes*, recognized a fellow painter in him and gestured that each frame was an "independent work of art." During the film screening, Picasso was frozen, taut, stiff. "He did not move," Urusevsky related in his diary, nervously awaiting Picasso's judgment. And then he did move, bursting into kisses and handshakes.[59] Physical reactions and spontaneous emotionality—a conversation in gestures—proved that art traversed borders.

Anxiety and triumph dominated memories of Cannes. There, some Soviet filmmakers encountered "real capitalists," as depicted in caricatures and literature.[60] Chukhrai's accounts of Cannes began with his own sense of penury. To "a fashionable journalist," Chukhrai, "wearing beige sandals and checkered socks," called to mind a worker from the Renault factory— at least according to his proud memoirs, in which art prevailed over class disdain. Izvitskaia arrived in Cannes in 1957 wearing an "inexpensive" floral calico dress, of which the tabloid press made great fun: "she, too, has put on her Sunday best." Fernand Léger's wife bought Izvitskaia "a beautiful dress." Then, newspapers, half-mockingly, called her "the Russian Marilyn Monroe."[61] As Chukhrai explained upon return, "We had to be very vigilant, very attentive [for] very many wanted to photograph us looking improper, to make a joke [at our expense], to laugh [at us]."[62]

A wounded sensitivity to material differences permeated Soviet reports and would mark even Chukhrai's post-Soviet recollections. Speaking in 1957 at the Central House of Cinema, a professional club and an art-house theater in Moscow, Chukhrai described the Cannes festival as "a huge trade fair." His words expressed an artist's axiomatic contempt for commerce: "We witnessed how they trade, create advertisement, sell leading actors and actresses."[63] Everything Soviet directors and critics wrote about Cannes disparaged the commercialization of art.[64] The triumph of *Forty-First* without advertisement and prescreening publicity was a special point of pride for Chukhrai, not only a Soviet achievement, but a victory of art over money. He portrayed the extravagant and overindulged audience at Cannes, who, he feared, could not care less for *Ballad of a Soldier*, his second film and his second nominee for the Palme d'Or.[65] Why would "these perfumed and bedecked gentlemen care about the grief of a Russian mother who lost her son in the war"? For a moment, he regretted bringing the film to Cannes in 1960.[66]

But what Chukhrai discovered there was common humanity. The perfumed and bedecked gentlemen laughed and cried, applauded and fell silent exactly at the same moments as audiences in Riazan'. Laughing and crying, vigorously shaking the hands of Soviet filmmakers, the snobs appeared to lose their affectation. And as they did so, Soviet delegates lost their misgivings, both about themselves and about the people whom they had seen as enemies. The esteem accorded to Soviet delegations by elite society came as something of a surprise.[67] Recognition at Cannes, repeated and noisy, was pivotal to the Soviets' sense of themselves as an aesthetically legitimate presence on the international scene.[68] The contrast between embarrassment and triumph was a Soviet self-perception, but the celebration of Soviet cinema at Cannes was both new and real.[69]

Cannes in 1956–1958 was a moment of mutual discovery and a crucial source of information. Izvitskaia, Chukhrai, and Urusevsky did not make policy, of course. Still, shaken by the experience of the place and the films they had watched there, at home they made emotive statements that contributed aesthetic and affective impetus to diplomatic and commercial transactions. While evidence of exactly how filmmakers influenced purchasing policy is scant, the fact is that the films they found disturbing or politically shortsighted, such as Charles Chauvel's *Jedda*, Elia Kazan's adaptation of Steinbeck's *East of Eden*, or Edward Dmytryk's *The End of the Affair*, remained unknown in the Soviet Union. (Dmytryk's and Kazan's testimonies before the House Un-American Activities Committee greatly contributed to complete erasure of their films from the Soviet public domain.) The pictures that Soviet filmmakers had liked at Cannes—Carol Reed's *A Kid for Two Farthings*, for instance, and Vittorio De Sica's *The*

Gold of Naples—appeared in theaters within a few years and in acquisition plans yet earlier.[70] The 1955 festival introduced Soviet participants to Pietro Germi's *The Railroad Man*, Vittorio De Sica's *The Roof*, Nunnally Johnson's *The Man in the Gray Flannel Suit*, and Roland Verhavert's *Seagulls Die in the Harbor*, all of which Sovexportfilm would purchase shortly.[71] At Cannes, too, Soviet filmmakers watched Ingmar Bergman, Alfred Hitchcock, and Albert Lamorisse; once back home, their lectures about these directors were sensitive, nonjudgmental, and nonpoliticized.[72]

The wonder, recognition, and shared aesthetic the Soviets experienced at Cannes laid the foundation for the Moscow International Film Festival, established in 1959 and still running today. Buoyed by a series of awards culminating with the Palme d'Or for *The Cranes*, the Union of Cinematographers staged a historical retrospective of Soviet pictures from the 1920s and 1930s during the first Moscow festival. This retrospective showed early avant-garde eccentricity, documentary style, and poetic realism as proof of Soviet cinematic importance and as a heritage that the Thaw claimed for itself.[73] But Moscow also spoke in the international language of Cannes. The Moscow logo was the globe in rotation, seen from above, and an overlapping film frame, or a screen, with a bar of frame lines, the year 1959 in the middle, and "Moscow" printed underneath.[74] The festival attempted to live up to the internationalism of this emblem in its extensive invitation roster and in the commanding jury that the Organizing Committee had imagined initially (Claude Autant-Lara, Laurence Olivier, Akira Kurosawa, Giuseppe de Santis). Its daily bulletin ran in English and French, in addition to Russian, a multilingual fantasy of cinema that had begun at the 1957 Youth Festival. For a moment in August 1959, the center of Moscow looked as if the Youth Festival had been restaged. Garlands of flags stretched across central avenues. Country standards flew over buildings, and more banners framed screens inside movie theaters. Enormous tripod stands supporting stills from Soviet and foreign films lined Manezh Square, recalling the three-dimensional scenery and colossal cardboard figures of the Youth Festival.[75] Indeed, the Youth Festival had been the first Soviet foray into the film festival circuit.[76]

The Moscow film festival wanted to be Cannes without beaches, bathing beauties, and monokinis, without social snobbery, commerce, and yellow press. Soviet tropical resorts in Sochi and Yalta were briefly considered as potential festival locations and rejected as unsuitable for thoughtful artistic exploration. Both offered too many opportunities for undressing. Instead,

Figure 4.1. First Moscow International Film Festival, installations in Manezh Square, 1959.

Published by permission of Vitalii Gumeniuk.

Moscow became the festival site because of its symbolic value as a sacred center: in-competition films were screened in the Kremlin.[77] Planners from the Union of Cinematographers defined their project against everything they had learned about Cannes. And they studied Cannes attentively, with the aim of "us[ing] the experience [of other festivals], without imitating them." After the first experiment in 1959, the Organizing Committee prided itself on the uniqueness of the Soviet event as "a mass popular celebration of the art of cinema." Moscow's "popular" and "democratic" character "distinguished it from Cannes, Venice, and other festivals."[78] Here, "popular" and "democratic" meant mass participation in cultural pursuits. The festival program included "meetings" between foreign luminaries and Soviet "collectives." "The Day of Cinema" reportedly brought 120,000 people to Gorky Park, where portable film projectors screened motion pictures, the French communist author Georges Sadoul spoke to crowds about film history, and ordinary people chanced upon famous actors. Another meaning of "democratic" was the inclusion of countries with emerging film industries.[79]

The regularity of the film festival recast Moscow as a site of recurrent mega-events. Moscow planners entered a well-entrenched, hierarchical system of festivals, the most influential of which took place in Europe. Cannes, Venice, Locarno, Edinburgh, Berlin, and Rotterdam represented nodes on a circuit, which elevated certain kinds of productions—art-house, auteur—thereby challenging Hollywood. Hollywood typically has been understood (by scholars and, in their reading, by European filmmakers and festival administrators) as a cinema of entertainment, the box office, and world domination. Indeed, the main framework for analyzing continental film festivals is the opposition between European art cinema and Hollywood.[80] What, then, was the place of Moscow in this circuit, and how did Moscow affect this framework?

Moscow elided the familiar division between European festivals and Hollywood. Soviet anticommercial ethos painted—tainted—both American and European industries as capitalist escapism and profit making. It did not matter whether the pictures were made amid studio props in Hollywood or shot in Parisian and Roman streets. The fault line in Moscow did not demarcate Europe from Hollywood, nor auteur film from entertainment. Rather, it counterpoised "progressive" and "humanistic" filmmaking to everything else. Soviet critics refused to distinguish between intellectual and commercial cinema. They maligned both for perpetuating cultural exclusivity: supercilious refinement for the elite, cheap diversions for the masses.[81] The critics' ideal viewer was "ordinary," but, nonetheless, someone who understood "serious" cinema—meaning movies motivated by social commentary, rather than the singularity of authorial vision. Unlike other "A-list" festivals, Moscow had a political slogan: "For humanism in film, for peace and friendship among peoples!" The Moscow festival showcased a critical cinema that took a searching stance toward life under capitalism. Whereas other festivals could launch a movie into the global market and were crucial to its economic viability, Moscow was a commercial dead-end, even for prizewinners.[82] And perhaps that was its attraction for people like Stanley Kramer or Federico Fellini. In Moscow, celebrated directors could adopt the humanizing role of the artist-missionary.

In 1961, the Moscow festival gained legitimacy, attracting distinguished pictures.[83] Grigorii Chukhrai's *Clear Skies* shared the Grand Prix with Kaneto Shindo's *The Naked Island*, while movies of different genres and without much politics were recognized by special awards. Celebrities like Elizabeth Taylor posed for photographs in Red Square, as elderly Soviet women in floral dresses and boys in plaited shirts and wide trousers halted to stare. In 1963, the festival came into its own. The jury included respected authorities such as Stanley Kramer, Sergio Amidei, and Satyajit Ray, Chukhrai, still basking in the triple glory of his prizewinning films, and Jean Marais, French cinema's symbol of gallantry. Beginning with the earliest ideas about a film festival, the Moscow planners had wanted a work of timeless significance, a discovery. Finally, in 1963, they got such a film. And they hated it.

Fellini's 8½ received the Grand Prix, despite pressure from the Central Committee and amid the collapse of a diplomatic consensus that nearly destroyed the festival.[84] There is a famous story of Khrushchev falling asleep during the screening. The deputy head of the Central Committee's Ideological Department spelled out the implications of this nap to Chukhrai, chair of the jury: since ordinary people could not empathize with the main character Guido's creative impotence, the film could not receive the Grand Prix. According to Chukhrai's memoirs, his job was to sway other jurors toward a Soviet film, or else he would lose his Communist Party membership. All the while, the chief of the Cinematography Committee threatened to bring vague troubles upon the jurors from the socialist bloc.[85] At first, the conversation among jurors was unusually calm: there were no films worth fighting over. The bored jurors began to invent special citations and pass jokes.[86] But then they watched 8½. And now they had their Grand Prix film. Kramer was relieved and proud: "There was only one true work of art at our festival. This is the singular film that we have searched for, that we can show to the entire world, [saying] it received a prize, here, at the Moscow festival."[87] Jean Marais sensed in it "a new language." Bulgarian critic Emil Petrov could not shake off the "incredible power" of the film: "Watching it put me in an emotional state that continues still and that I cannot explain to myself. I cannot find logical categories with which to understand it." For Polish director Jan Rybkowski, Fellini's film was "exceptional."[88]

The prize was another matter. Chukhrai's deputy, film and literary critic Aleksandr Karaganov, who served as a member of the commission for the selection of films from capitalist countries in the early 1960s, disagreed—not about 8½, but about the prize. He may have even liked the film; years later he would write lovingly about his "encounters" with Fellini. But Karaganov also knew that awarding the Grand Prix to 8½ would scandalize state leaders across the socialist world. The film did not match the festival's motto of "peace, humanism, and friendship among peoples" as Soviet cultural bureaucrats understood it. And audience response to the film was "divided"; in other words, it put some people to sleep.[89] When discussing Fellini, socialist critics liked to focus on the final scenes of *The Nights of Cabiria*, in which Cabiria emerged from despair to find herself surrounded by merrymaking youths. They wore clownish hats, played musical instruments, and danced, and her inadvertent smile shone through tears. This was Cabiria's, and the film's, and the world's redemption.[90] 8½ ended with a carnival as well, but now it was monstrous (literally: fish!), not hopeful. The unresolved anguish set 8½ apart from *The Nights of Cabiria* in Chukhrai's opinion, too. He took a clear and strong position: while anybody could understand and empathize with Cabiria (hence, the film's humanism), 8½ was opaque for ordinary viewers. As Chukhrai put it: "Dozens of people, many, many people in the audience . . . are simple people. And we, the Soviet delegation, have to take that into account. Why do I say that? Because this festival takes place neither in France, nor in Italy, nor even in Czechoslovakia . . . From the perspective of the cinema that we represent, we would consider it inappropriate, incorrect, and incomprehensible if the prize for humanism, for peace and friendship among peoples were to go to a film, whose main problem is the honest and profound self-analysis of a bourgeois artist."[91]

Amidei and Kramer took these arguments seriously, moving the conversation to the definition of humanism and the accessibility of art. Brazilian director Nelson Pereira dos Santos did not take the arguments seriously: it was politics, he called out, and "I don't want to adapt [to political pressure]." Neither did Jean Marais, who refused to engage in debate, insisted on immediate voting for the Grand Prix, and threatened to leave the jury. Satyajit Ray appealed for 8½ in the name "of peace and humanism"; Czechoslovak screenwriter Jan Procházka cried out in the language of "our heart"; and Kramer felt humiliated when his own noncompetition film, *Judgment at Nuremberg*, was declared progressive and Fellini's was not.[92] Slowly, and after several breaks, during which a conversation with Soviet officials may have taken place, jurors from Eastern Europe silenced the voice of the heart and broke with the Kramer and Marais position. The ballots were cast against the Grand Prix. Kramer, Amidei, and Marais walked out.[93] When the doors slammed, Chukhrai agreed to give the Grand Prix to

Fellini, with a special formulation: "for remarkable art, in which he expressed the inner struggle of an artist in search of truth."[94] Everybody must have been relieved by the Solomonic decision: some salvaged their integrity (Fellini did get the Grand Prix), others salvaged their party cards (but not for peace and friendship), and all voted unanimously.[95]

The fallout remained, however. Rumors circulated. Members of the jury emerged disillusioned and emotionally drained. Their disappointment with Moscow was all the deeper, because they had arrived committed to a vision of cinematic humanism with Moscow in the lead. For Kramer, the dispute was enervating: "as an individual, I cannot remain here, it is impossible for me to remain here."[96] Fellini arrived in Moscow at the last moment and at the ceremony spoke of this prize as especially dear to his heart for being awarded in the Soviet Union.[97] To the embittered jurors, Fellini's cheerful speech only added insult to injury. *The Nights of Cabiria* had been purchased and screened in ordinary movie theaters in 1960, as *The Road* would be in 1967, but 8½ and the rest of Fellini's films remained unavailable to broad audiences.[98] The 1963 Grand Prix winner would be shown in Soviet theaters only in 1988. The silence of the Soviet press, the failure to celebrate Fellini's award or to purchase the film, made Soviet obscurantism appear that much worse—and undermined the festival's authority.[99]

The Moscow festival remained in the shadow of Cannes. By the mid-1960s, whatever excitement there was had subsided. In 1965, the KGB alarmed the Central Committee with a report on the festival's sliding prestige: in-competition films were weak, while influential filmmakers declined invitations to the jury.[100] Most of the jurors came from the socialist bloc and were unknown in the transnational cinema world, faring hardly better at home. There were celebrities in attendance, to be sure, but as guests of the festival or participating casts, without an official role. Sophia Loren graced the covers of Soviet popular magazines, and Franklin Schaffner and Joseph Strick made laudatory statements for the press. The festival's seriousness dissipated. The Americans, French, and Italians brought "entertaining pictures, meant for a popular audience and for raising profits." Meanwhile, the festival became a liability for Soviet security. Vladimir Semichastnyi, head of the KGB, saw the event as an invitation to foreign intelligence and to "propaganda for the Western way of life," suspecting State Department appointees in the American delegation and uncovering spies among the French and the Japanese. He even surmised that "weak and worthless films" were part of a comprehensive operation to subvert the festival.[101]

Every two years, the festival opened and closed according to a ritual that soon grew tired. But the films remained. In-competition pictures were screened broadly in Moscow, Leningrad, Kiev, and other republican capitals.[102] The Ministry of Culture made a commitment to purchase a careful selection of the winning films. On top of those, Sovexportfilm bought many films screened in and out of competition. Central Television disseminated out-of-competition movies as well. Their commercial release in the Soviet Union compensated, in part, for festival expenses.[103] Despite the anticommercial rhetoric, hefty business went on at the Moscow festival. In 1961, over thirty foreign distributors, selected by Sovexportfilm and embassy staff, were invited to send representatives. Yet more entrepreneurs came as unusual "tourists." Sovexportfilm officials and their guests spent many hours watching movies and "striking deals" worth hundreds of thousands of convertible rubles.[104] And that was how Vittorio De Sica's *Marriage Italian Style*, Luchino Visconti's *Rocco and His Brothers*, Pietro Germi's *Seduced and Abandoned*, *The Great Race* (dir. Blake Edwards), *The Magnificent Seven* (dir. John Sturges), *Campbell's Kingdom* (dir. Ralph Thomas), *Room at the Top* by Jack Clayton, *My Uncle* by Jacques Tati, *Babette Goes to War* (dir. Christian-Jaque), and many more cinematic attractions made it to the Soviet Union.

The Double

While cultural exchanges and the festival circuit determined what films would arrive in the Soviet Union, domestic translation practices defined how these movies would sound and feel. Dubbing and subtitling coexisted for much of the Soviet cinematic engagement with both sound and foreignness, but from the mid-1950s on, commercial release relied primarily on dubbing. Different politics and aesthetic principles animated these translation choices.[105]

During the global transition to sound in the late 1920s, when American and German companies had first dubbed films for export, the ventriloquism of the dub had disconcerted audiences across Europe. Dubbing erased original voices in an operation that felt eerie to spectators then and that some scholars have described as violent.[106] By preserving the actors' voices, subtitles acknowledged the uniqueness of languages and respected vocalization as part of the artistry. In turn, subtitles have been intended for audiences who can appreciate the sound of foreign speech.[107] Subtitles are not subtle: they do not pretend to convey nuances or dialogues in entirety. They presuppose an audience capable of imaginative readings—and, moreover, require such an audience: literate, tolerant of split attention, and willing to forgo mediation.

The Soviet project of unprecedented cultural accessibility militated against subtitles. The first audiences had been barely literate, so the politicized visual arts of the 1920s and 1930s had spoken in stark images that did not require reading fluency. Well into the 1960s, dubbing directors continued to bring up the challenges of speedy reading. It was no longer a matter of basic literacy, of course: now they were concerned with pleasure. The effort to read subtitles detracted from the enjoyment of camerawork and acting. "Those who manage to read do not grasp the image. The acting, that is, what people have come to watch, disappears entirely," complained dubbing director Aleksandr Andrievskii about his own experience of juggling subtitles and images, "and, most likely, in factories, on the periphery, on collective farms, there are people with weaker reading habits than mine, they have an even harder time, and see neither the image nor the subtitles."[108] Subtitles provoked a schizophrenic movement of the eyes from the center of the screen to the bottom and back. Diffusing attention, subtitles undermined the immediacy and emotional impact of the image. Moreover, the visibility of subtitles depended on the architecture of the theater. In the Soviet Union, raked seating, introduced during the Moscow Youth Festival, represented a major breakthrough in theater construction. But that was in the republican capitals and urban centers. In much of the country, movie theaters had flat floors, and subtitles were simply invisible.[109] Subtitles highlighted the exclusivity of privileged places (the capitals) and literate audiences.

In the mid-1950s, the dream of cultural accessibility took another, international turn. Exchanges "among the nations of the globe" were to reach people high and low, far from Moscow, "the broadest masses," in Andrievskii's words. In this vision of democratized cross-cultural interactions, film had a decisive role. Scholarly contacts were for a "relatively narrow circle of highly qualified intelligentsia." Foreign art exhibitions and theatrical performances were "the domain of inhabitants of large capital cities and of tourists who travel to other countries."[110] For millions of people, however, "especially for people on the periphery," movies offered one of the few contacts with foreign cultures. Andrievskii did not reference these millions metaphorically: in 1959, the projected data on viewers of 150 foreign films slated for release climbed to 1.33 billion people, or, on average, 30 million people per picture. As dubbers liked to emphasize, they "returned internationalism to the art of (sound) cinema."[111]

That said, dubbing often has implied dissimulation, whereas subtitles have been described in the vocabulary of honesty and authenticity. Dubbing hides its operation behind synchrony and so opens the door to trickery: different intonations, imperceptible shifts in connotation, or significant excisions.[112] And it is a small step from dissimulation to censorship. However, in the Soviet Union, the mode of censorship was neither scissors nor dubs. It was subtitles, which distribution officials used to "restrict" audiences "artificially." The general understanding among cinema bureaucrats was that few people would enjoy a subtitled film. This was precisely why the Administration for Cinefication and Distribution relied on subtitles when diplomatic protocol required Sovexportfilm to purchase and screen pictures that its own officials or those from the Ministry of Culture disliked. According to the Administration's deputy director, "we are not interested in having a large number of viewers for all films. Let us be frank—the release of some things will be a pure formality [to say] that we have fulfilled our obligation." In 1960, for example, Sovexportfilm committed to purchasing 160 foreign pictures. Fifty of them were slated, "alas, for subtitling," and the rest would be dubbed and "distributed for real."[113]

With few exceptions, pictures that needed significant and obvious modifications were not purchased. As with translated prose, Sovexportfilm and distribution authorities were circumspect when it came to cutting. Politically motivated excisions were rare. Depictions of violence would be condensed but preserved when they had political efficacy as a critique of bourgeois society. Hugo del Carril's *Dark River* (1952) performed this ideological work perfectly, portraying inhuman plantation labor and the dawn of class struggle. But during translation, the film lost scenes that a Ministry of Culture commission judged "naturalistic": a floating corpse, a graphic mud tussle and murder by choking and drowning.[114] Few films with graphic violence, however, were purchased in the first place.[115]

Sexual episodes were the main target of cuts, but what constituted a sexual episode evolved over decades. In the 1950s, imported films did not show much nudity, while bare shoulders and suggestive undressing remained unedited. Rock 'n' roll footage, which the Soviet press branded as erotic, was not excised. Scenes with prostitutes were kept intact. When the Ministry of Culture recommended films for acquisition, it reassured the Central Committee's Cultural Department that the appropriate excisions would be made.[116] But these promises could well go unfulfilled, perhaps for reasons of bureaucratic oversight and expectations of profitability. To give a scandalous example, in 1956, Yorgos Javellas's *The Counterfeit Coin* was released uncut—despite kissing scenes and a prostitute who rolled down her stockings while wearing nothing but a bodice; despite, as well, the Ministry's pledge to "remove erotic shots" and restrict distribution. Distribution authorities advertised the film extensively and printed more than a thousand copies for wide release, nearly 400 of them on 16mm film for rural projectors. The Central Committee's Cultural Department had directed the Ministry to withdraw uncut copies from Moscow's theaters, only to discover that several days later Muscovites were still watching the prostitute undress for a coin.[117] Ultimately, uncensored copies may have been removed from Moscow, but hundreds were dispersed across the Soviet Union, to provincial towns and collective farms. Here, for once, was a disadvantage of privileged places: Moscow and other capitals were too close to the ideological apparatus for uncensored copies to circulate freely or for long. Finally, most excisions grew out of showtime restrictions, rather than worries about undesirable information or imagery. Billy Wilder's *Some Like It Hot* was condensed by about twenty-five minutes over nearly thirty cuts. Only one expunged scene can be construed as "erotic": the prolonged kissing on a yacht. The rest were snippets of dialogues, technical edits, which reduced the two-hour film to fit the standard ninety-minute runtime.

It was not the censorial impulse, but the aesthetic concern for the integrity of the image that lay at the foundation of Soviet dubbing. From the avant-garde, Soviet cinematic translators inherited an enduring reverence for the wholeness of the frame, which subtitles threatened to disfigure. Whereas present-day theoreticians consider dubbing destructive of the original soundtrack, Soviet filmmakers called subtitles a monstrosity that "vandalized the visual texture of the picture." In the hierarchy of film elements, the image reigned supreme, and for its sake, Soviet filmmakers and distributors were willing to sacrifice speech.[118]

From experiments with sound in the late 1920s and early 1930s dubbing also inherited a set of concepts. In the Soviet Union, as elsewhere, the approach to sound had favored the eyes rather than the ears. The soundtrack's purpose was to confirm the reality of action on the screen. To do so, to retain "naturalness," sound would have to emanate from an identifiable source. If there was music, then there would have to be a piano, an orchestra, or a singer. If there was speech, then the speaker's face would have to be visible.[119] Making the source of speech visible required synchrony. At the beginning of the talkies era, avant-garde filmmakers feared synchronous speech as a return to traditional theater. They worried precisely about that illusion of naturalness and experimented with using sounds in juxtaposition to images. But another way of thinking about synchronicity was poetry or music.[120] In the late 1920s and early 1930s, music theoreticians viewed rhythm as the organizing connection between sound and image and drafted diagrams, similar to musical notations, of the rhythmic structure of speech.[121] Before words were units of meaning, they formed a pattern of breathing and lip movements. As speech arrived on the screen, voice trainers and actors turned to phonology in an intense study of the relationship among language, its visual articulation, and its affective power. It was not the words that helped to interpret faces but faces that set the interpretive frame for the words. Widely seen as responsible for the "emotional coloration" of language, lips ("ironic crooked smile, corners of the mouth mournfully lowered") preoccupied many experts involved in merging image and speech.[122] But to animate lips on the screen, sync actors watched a soundless track first. They taught the screen to speak by working from the postulates of silent cinema: by reading lips. Synchrony as an imperative was born with sound—and of the very discomfort with speech.

The principles and experiences—phonetic analysis, voice training, rhythmic notations—developed during the transition to sound in 1928–1935 defined the Soviet approach to dubbing. Professionals spoke about dubbing in the same vocabulary of musicality and rhythm. Russian scripts of foreign films bore notational marks for lip articulation: a coded, parallel language. Dubbers identified poetic translation and the constraints of the meter as the closest analog to their own work.[123] The point of dubbing, of course, was to render foreign speech accessible, but the image remained paramount and set dubbing parameters. Reading silent lips, without the soundtrack, was the dubbers' distress, joy, and obsession.[124] Dubbing admitted no secrets or silences: even when there was no sound, so long as lips on the screen moved, actors had to speak, or viewers would lose faith. As Sara Shaikevich, a prose translator who worked extensively in cinema, noted, dubbing made explicit what was only implied in the original. Where a child cried for her mother because she was hungry, Shaikevich had her actually say, "I am hungry." Her translations of film scripts revealed what she, having watched the original, understood "and viewers d[id] not," or, on the contrary, "eliminate[d] everything unintelligible" that could not be verbalized.[125]

Soviet dubbing culture insisted on all forms of synchrony, phonetic, kinetic, and temporal. Script translators faced a challenge that did not trouble prose translators: the text would have to be performable. Whereas literary translators worked with lexicons, dubbers worked with visible phonemes. The reel was cut into hundreds of tiny segments. Each was projected ("looped") repeatedly as the translator and sync assistant aligned dialogues with the articulation of labial consonants and rounded vowels on the screen, in perfect agreement with lip movements, phrase length, breathing, and pauses.[126] The text they created went to the dubbing director and actors, who had multiple takes recorded in loops, until they found "inimitable breathing, intonations."[127] Then, film editors matched the Russian soundtrack to the foreign visual track, and rerecorded everything, together with music and sound effects. Dubbers treated the soundtrack as a unity. When the original noise remained a backdrop to dubbed Russian speech, they heard something incongruous. Sound effects were restaged and recorded along with Russian dialogue, welding the disparate acoustic elements into an organic whole.[128] The process aimed to recreate the soundtrack completely.

Inimitable breathing and intonations were the actors' mission. They stood in a dark room before a microphone, eyes transfixed on the screen, to become the double. Dubbing directors sought out Soviet look-alikes: voice impersonators whose physical appearance recalled that of foreign actors. The assumption was that the physical constitution determined voice qualities, and similar physiques would result in matching voices.[129] Doubling was the moment when the actors' senses were most acute. The intensity of perception came from strenuous work with the screen; one dubber confessed that casting left "an actor all shaking."[130] Accomplished performers often found themselves unable to do it. The screen and cycling loop were so oppressive that some people instinctively turned away.[131]

The darkness in which dubbers toiled was not only literal (the recording rooms were "dark, stuffy"), but also metaphorical.[132] Dubbers trailed in the shadows of the directorial corps and remained peripheral as translators. Nobody doubted the importance of cinematic translation, which, as

a technological and performative experiment, attracted actors of great repute. Yet, dubbing occupied the lowest rung in the hierarchy of the arts. It
was an unspoken "thoroughfare" to "the so-called big cinema" or "fodder
[for actors] during downtime."[133] Even throughout the "golden age" of dubbing in the mid-to-late 1950s, Ministry of Culture officials thought of it as a
second-rate job. Behind the backs of dubbing directors, colleagues called
them "copyists."[134] Until the 1960s, dubbing directors and sync assistants
were excluded from the Union of Cinematographers.[135] The dubbers were
on the fringes even institutionally, as they had no premises of their own.
They operated in four established central studios, the Moscow and Leningrad Studios (Mosfil'm, Lenfil'm), the Gorky Studio, and the Animated
Film Studio (Soiuzmul'tfil'm). The Gorky Studio was the primary dubbing location in the country, both in the number of films it translated and
in the quality of translation—synchronization of the kind that the Soviet
dubbing community considered flawless.[136]

More mobile than directors, actors jump-started their screen careers in
dubbing or came briefly to the dark recording rooms from the limelight
and fame. Most dubbing actors had been trained in the best theater schools
and felt themselves destined for greatness. Then something happened:
war, arrest, personal tragedy, or temporary downtime. Dubbing seemed to
right the wrongs wrought by bad luck. For the young theater actor Zinovii
Gerdt, dubbing became the only path to the screen. Badly wounded
during the war, Gerdt spent two years in hospitals as doctors struggled to
save his leg; after multiple surgeries, he remained lame for life. His stage
career seemed over before it had even begun: "At first, it was a terrible tragedy.
I thought that an actor cannot limp, and I could not live without the theater."[137] While convalescing, Gerdt saw a show of Sergei Obraztsov's State
Puppet Theater. This apparition from his prewar life suggested a performance that could execute another kind of surgery, separating his voice
from his injuries. After the war, Gerdt arrived at the theater on crutches to
audition, recited poetry to Obraztsov for forty-five minutes, and found his
creative niche.[138]

The soundtrack in cinema is akin to a ventriloquist who moves his
dummy in sync with his speech and displaces onto his characters words
that he dare not speak in his own name.[139] In Gerdt's case, the ventriloquist metaphor is literally true: he spoke through puppets before speaking
for the screen. His first dubbing work was Christian-Jaque's *Fanfan the
Tulip*, starring Gérard Philipe and Gina Lollobrigida. Philipe's Fanfan, a

soldier of fortune, joined the army in pursuit of fame and marriage to Louis XV's daughter—and fell in love with the commoner Adeline (Lollobrigida), who predicted his glory. The enduring popularity of this film eclipsed much else. To this day, *Fanfan* stands among the emblems of the Thaw, its sequences incorporated into Soviet films as mnemonic references to the 1950s. For the Soviet image of *Fanfan*—casual irony and a fount of expressions that became idiomatic—the discreet "historian," a voice-over narrator offering tongue-in-cheek commentary, was just as important as Philipe himself. That historian was Gerdt. *Fanfan*'s dubbing director had one of Gerdt's puppet characters in mind when he invited the ventriloquist to the Gorky Studio. This character, Devil from the buffoonery "The Devil's Windmill," was sarcastic, refined, and unruffled. His gestures were elegant, his smile ironic, his attitude philosophical: evil was an art.[140] It was this irreverence and sangfroid that the dubbing director wanted to convey in *Fanfan*.[141] Gerdt liked to say that he not only read the text, but also "remade it, bringing it closer to the manner of my devil."[142] In the eyes (or ears) of filmmaker Petr Todorovskii, Gerdt's voice "infused the film with a typically French charm"—as if a French film was somehow not quite French until the Russian dub endowed it with charm.[143] In fact, however, Gerdt did not rewrite the text, and the translation was entirely faithful.

But he did give *sound* to endearing clichés about Gallic humor, lightheartedness, daredevil attitude, and gallantry. *Fanfan*'s swashbuckling romance lent itself to just such a project. Here were secret passages, vaulted castles, spectacular chases on horseback, mistaken identities, a dashing hero, a curvaceous heroine—and, of course, plenty of fencing, filmed in fast motion that exposed the unreality of the action. The film spoofed big ideas: the Seven Years' War was a droll affair; no authority was sacred and all authorities were despotic; history was moved neither by great men nor by class struggle, but by chance, mistake, and fortune telling; love was a game or a gamble; death was an occasion for chivalry and witticism. *Fanfan* was thoroughly silly, and its weightlessness has been disparaged by serious critics wherever they are found. But precisely its weightlessness and silliness were a revelation in the Soviet Union. The film laughed at itself at every turn and subverted historical fact and common sense. And the Soviet version owed much of its humor to Gerdt's historian. Gerdt's matter-of-fact narration flowed in one sweeping breath. Old-fashioned turns of phrase elevated his speech, but the mocking undertones sabotaged any pathos.

Gerdt made audible something one only read in books and heard in the mind's ear.

After *Fanfan*, invitations to dubbing sets overwhelmed Gerdt's phone line. For much of his dubbing (and acting) career, Gerdt would reenact the historian's indulgent, ironic, and worldly-wise intonation. He next played the informal and judicious narrator in Julio Saraceni's musical *The Age of Love*, another sensation of the mid-1950s. The film's melodramatic plot revolved around the love affairs of a father and son. As a young man, the father had fallen in love with an actress, only to have the affair quashed by his own father. Decades later, the story repeated, with a happier ending: the son fell in love with the daughter, herself an actress, of the very same woman his father had romanced so many years before. All ended in a musical performance and a kiss. Argentine actress Lolita Torres played both mother and daughter.

The Age of Love is a perfect example of how dubbing divulged assumptions, leaving nothing unsaid. Thoughts and memories only hinted at in the original were fully verbalized in the dub, and silences were expunged. Gerdt's narrator filled chronological gaps. He was entirely unconstrained, because there was no voice-over in the original: he was a new character, a Soviet invention, created to explicate the action. Gerdt told the father's love story as a recollection of the old man who had severed his son's affair. Alone with his thoughts, the old man looked at quivering leaves and rain in the window, and the past unfolded. In the original, this bridging shot between past and present was self-evident. In the Soviet version, Gerdt announced that link. The Russian voice-over also enunciated written texts—posters, letters, newspapers, business cards, banknotes. These were remade in translation: different paper, different handwriting and lettering, with, however, some visual marks of the original (stamp, state coat, portrait, Latin letters). There was more writing in the dubbed film than in the original: dubbers inserted billboards, posters, and signs in Russian to stall time when they needed to finish a dialogue or a poetic translation. Such inserts were flash cuts, taking only a moment, enough for the mind's eye to register Russian words, but not enough to contemplate the signs and realize their impossibility in Buenos Aires.[144] The subliminal effect was a subtle transposition, as if this were a Soviet film about foreign life. The combination of different languages and material realities created a sense of forgery.

Dubbers montaged these textual inserts so that translation of songs would not overlay the singing. To a great degree, the melodies were responsible for the film's tremendous success in the Soviet Union. The first Soviet incarnation of these songs fused with Gerdt's poetry reading. He did not declaim verse—he persuaded, paused as if searching for the right words, and, finding them, rushed forth.[145] Directly addressing the viewers, Gerdt positioned himself in their world: "Here is this little song," or "Let us listen to what she sings to her beloved." He was one of them, practically inciting viewers to sing. But his presence was also diegetic—so much so that when musical numbers interrupted the story, he too broke into song, seemingly unable to contain himself. The apparent spontaneity of the moment imparted the translation with ease and intimacy; at the end of the song, he playfully spoke the last word.

The lyrics told of jealousy, unification, and lives lived happily ever after. Combined with the props, the dancing, and Gerdt's translation, the songs also told of another world: a cardboard baroque—an old street, arched windows, flowers overgrowing from balconies, a tavern interior, or a fin-de-siècle square framed by streetlights. In Gerdt's reading, one of the most frequently reproduced pieces, "Coimbra Divina," was fanciful and nostalgic for an inaccessible, perhaps implausible, place of "towers, ancient stones," "our miraculous Portuguese sky," and the city of Coimbra, kept awake by "ringing guitars." In this "heavenly" place, girls danced to fado "under the moon" and boys looked at them "with loving eyes." Moonlight drowned the town in silver, as the verse swelled with images of paradise: "a brook, flowing down the mount / And the foliage of a nighttime garden." A lineup of guitarists and dancers wearing headscarves and wide-brimmed hats performed this idyll. The song left Soviet movie theaters at once. Enthusiasts who went to see the film multiple times transcribed the words. Military wives abiding by garrison regimen found comfort in the soundtrack, spinning the records all day on the Radiola. The music cut into the memories of their children, who still hate it for the mothers' obsession.[146] Hearing the first notes of "Coimbra Divina" on the radio compelled people to drop whatever they were doing, even studying for exams in the middle of the night.[147] Beyond the film, the song multiplied: new poets and performers added their own variations.

Dubbing directors often asserted that Soviet versions surpassed the originals.[148] They lionized the actors for discerning something essential, the very pith of screen characters, the task that, ostensibly, belonged to foreign actors.[149] Nuance, sensitivity, intonation: nobody could say precisely what that something was. But just as literary translators relinquished analytical categories before the power of love, when all was said and done—takes looped, projectors turned off, lights turned on—dubbers watched their own work and beheld a miracle. And perhaps this language of the marvelous was not too far-fetched, for they dealt in illusions: foreign actors spoke in a Russian voice.[150] Dubbing artists reveled in this effect. The response from viewers was endearing in its innocence. Dubbers laughed when the Gorky Studio received viewers' letters asking how they "recreated the same action with Russian performers." This was a laughter of satisfaction: they were able to induce "faith in a miracle" and thought of their powers as demiurgical.[151] Occasionally, even their colleagues were mystified and took a few minutes to "understand whether this is a Soviet picture or not."[152] During festival premieres of dubbed films, Soviet translators cast stolen glances at the creators of the originals to observe their astonishment. Watching the Soviet version of his *The Counterfeit Coin*, Yorgos Javellas became convinced that the studio had hired a Greek actor fluent in Russian. "The manner [of speech], the timbre [of voice] were indistinguishable" from the Greek, only the words were different.[153]

This was a fabrication of the image of speech. Unlike literary translation, dubbing did not aim to turn a foreign film into "a fact of Russian culture." The visual sequences—from faces and clothes to streets, landscapes, and interiors—resisted such transformations. Dubbers accepted foreignness. Their ambition was not to disguise foreign speech as Russian, but to convey in Russian "the structure" and pace of other languages, the equivalence of gestural and verbal expression.[154] Dubbed films retained foreign elements, while hiding the work of translators and actors who created Russian soundtracks. Much has been written about the invisibility of the literary translator and about domesticating translations that conceal their work.[155] But in Soviet culture, the most domesticated texts—"books about us"—were produced by highly vocal and visible translators who did little to suppress their presence in the texts. By contrast, dubbing, with its traces of another life, was the creation of truly invisible translators.

Neorealism as Deliverance and Loss

Dubbing was rooted in vernacular and visual speech that could be performed with ease. Script translators strove for "natural," colloquial language, the kind people use at home and in the streets. But just as dubbed pictures began to fill showtimes, in domestic cinema, filmmakers searched for mundane intonations as a refuge from sloganeering.[156] Dubbing modeled visually expressive speech and entangled Western films in the Thaw quest for veracity. Those Western films, as it happened, came from Italy.

Between mid-1953 and early 1954, half a dozen Italian films entered the Gorky Studio's dubbing plans. Some of them, like Eduardo De Filippo's *Side Street Story* and Giuseppe De Santis's *No Peace Under the Olive Trees*, appeared in theaters already in late 1953. They were joined by other pictures in an uninterrupted gush: De Santis's *Rome, 11 O'Clock*, Renato Castellani's *Two Cents Worth of Hope*, and Pietro Germi's *The Path of Hope* in 1954; De Santis's *A Husband for Anna*, Luciano Emmer's *Three Girls from Rome*, and Luigi Comencini's *Bread, Love and Dreams* in 1956 during the first Italian film festival; *Bellissima* by Visconti and *At the Edge of the City* by Carlo Lizzani in 1957; Lizzani's *Chronicle of Poor Lovers*, Germi's *The Railroad Man*, and De Sica's *The Roof* in 1958.[157] Neorealism was an international phenomenon, perhaps nowhere as consequential as in the Soviet Union.[158] Conversely, no other national cinema or stylistic movement resonated in Soviet culture as profoundly as neorealism. In 1956, Italian pictures formed the core of Western films in commercial release. The Soviet press was saturated with Italian names; periodicals published news from Italian filming sets and translations of Italian film scripts.[159] People who followed the cinematic press read about more films than they would ever see. Whereas in the mid-to-late 1950s neorealism was growing passé in Italy, in the Soviet Union it was emerging as the dominant aesthetic idiom.

This happened, in part, because there were political affinities between firebrand Italian directors and the Soviet establishment. Several neorealists—Giuseppe De Santis, Luchino Visconti, and Carlo Lizzani— were card-carrying communists; many had fought in the Resistance; and all were leftists who abhorred the commercialization of culture and took social issues to heart.[160] Italian filmmakers reinforced these political connections by claiming the Soviet cinematic avant-garde, Sergei Eisenstein and Vsevolod Pudovkin, as their teachers. *Battleship Potemkin* had been the first Soviet film that De Santis had seen: watching it had turned into an act of defiance when fascist police arrived to break up the screening.[161] Soviet directors cherished such stories and recognized themselves and their own 1920s at the Italian film festival in 1956.[162]

Soviet commentators saw a fundamental unity in filmmakers as different as Renato Castellani, Lizzani, Visconti, and Vittorio De Sica: neorealism was social(ist) politics arising from a moral condemnation of poverty. Unemployment, hunger, and homelessness were the classical themes of canonical films, De Sica's *Umberto D.* and *The Roof* or Visconti's *The Earth Trembles.* Drifting across neorealist pictures, from *Two Cents Worth of Hope* and *Rome, 11 O'Clock* to *Umberto D.* and *Bicycle Thieves,* the sad figures of the unemployed gave proof to accepted Soviet wisdom. Here was an exposé of capitalism's miserable reality—a cinema "of the underprivileged," as the Soviet filmmaker Abram Room called it—and an affirmation of human solidarity. Neorealist directors abandoned pavilions, broke the spell of the Hollywood-inspired studio system, and went into the streets to film on location. But the fact that it was not just any location made an immense difference for Soviet audiences. A sympathetic elaboration of upper-class life would not qualify as realism. The neorealist camera paused "in narrow side streets," scuttled before rundown buildings, wandered amid laundry hanging outside, rested in abandoned lots, and entered cramped quarters. These locations made for realism in Soviet critical eyes.[163]

Neorealism showed cruel suffering; "the truthful screen" was harsh and unsentimental. Theater critic Abram Gurvich wrote about the way ugly realism plunged audiences into dejection. Habituated to happy endings, he was "shaken" by such finales as the one in Giuseppe De Santis's *Rome, 11 O'Clock.* The film's action developed in the span of one day, during which hundreds of women came to interview for a single typist position. De Santis chose several of them to tell stories that emerged from scraps of conversations in a queue, facial play and gesture, clothes and accessories. Under the weight of the queue, the building's old staircase collapsed in an apocalyptic scene: din and dust, screams and prayers, a gaping hole filmed from above and below, beams protruding or hanging by a thread, and parts of women's bodies, as if severed. At night, the camera followed the girl who had been the first in line the morning before, accompanying her to the remnants of the building. The typist position had not been filled on account of the accident: again, she was the first in line. The film began and ended in the same way, at the same place, as if nothing had happened. Gurvich found this understatement heart-wrenching in its "dreariness and ordinariness." If not a happy end, then a fighting one, a spat, a scream, an explosion—these would have brought closure; but the "nothing happened" ending, motionless and voiceless, "freezes the soul, . . . terrifies more than all the nightmares of the day."[164]

Critiquing capitalism, however, was not the main impetus for the intensity of Soviet engagement with neorealism. The main reason was the moment of the mid-1950s itself. Italian pictures arrived in a rapidly changing film culture, from production, distribution, and projection technology, to genres, soundtrack, plot conventions, and editing.[165] The rush of Italian movies intersected with Soviet debates about the nature of cinema, its specificity, its relationship to literature and theater. These were not new concerns; the avant-garde had reflected on the same issues. The 1950s rewound the 1920s, but with the contrite experience of "film hunger" during Stalin's last years, when the industry had produced very few pictures. According to a 1948 resolution of the Council of Ministers, it was quality that mattered, not quantity—a demand for perfection intrinsic to Stalinist cinema more broadly.[166] The Ministry of Cinematography instructed studios to produce grand masterpieces, mainly historical epics and biopics. At its lowest point in 1951, the industry released only nine pictures.[167] This, then, was a dark age against which the cinematic discourse of the Thaw restaged a new renaissance.

Just as moviegoers were watching Italian films in the mid-1950s, something new was happening in neighborhood theaters. The Ministry of Culture abandoned the idea of grand masterpieces and mandated a swift expansion of the industry. This policy resulted in thirty-eight films in 1954 and sixty-five the next year, while 135 pictures were in production during 1956, of which seventy-five were to be released that year and the rest in 1957. No neighborhood with a movie theater remained unaffected.[168] The policy had several implications. Since it would be difficult to shoot, say, 100 historical epics in a year, the target numbers required diversification of genres and topics.[169] Soon, studios were making dozens of comedies, adventure and crime dramas, and movies for children and adolescents. Until then, Soviet cinema had been the preserve of filmmakers who had come of age in the 1920s and early 1930s.[170] While this generation was not eclipsed, the Thaw witnessed a significant expansion of the directorial corps. Largely because so many new faces and new films had entered the scene, the cinematic press of the mid-to-late 1950s was infused with a strong sense of rupture.[171] That sense was fundamental to both Italian and Soviet understandings of how to express political circumstances in cinema. Italian filmmakers argued that they had worked from scratch, rejecting fascist escapism and Hollywood commercialism. This argument perfectly corresponded with the perception of a break in the Soviet film industry after

1954. That celebrated neorealists had started their careers in Vittorio Mussolini's Cinecittà, that their documentary aesthetics owed much to the Light Institute of the fascist years, and that new social dramas bore striking similarities to the melodramas of the late 1930s went unmentioned in Soviet writings on Italian cinema.[172] Neorealism arose ex nihilo, on the ruins of fascism.[173]

As the renaissance paradigm would have it, Thaw cinema embraced the individual, the emotional, and the corporal. But these themes—attention to "ordinary people," the contention that passion made for emotional veracity and that details and objects conveyed authenticity—first had evolved in discussions of neorealism.

The idea of "the ordinary person" and the sense of new times in Soviet discourse converged from the beginning.[174] From the perspective of the mid-1950s, the protagonist of late Stalinist films was not quite right. Impeccable heroic figures had obstructed "the ordinary Soviet person." War films foregrounding generals were a point of intense, if somewhat duplicitous, indignation for "forgetting the Russian soldier."[175] Collective farm musical comedies became a symbol of all that was wrong with Stalinist cinema, in which ordinary people had experienced no hardships or tragedies, only "banquets, congratulatory speeches," "feasting, and merriment." The world of collective farm musicals had been entirely stylized. Now they were seen as the biggest "varnishing of reality"—that is, the biggest lie.[176] "The common man," "simple" and "everyday," became the mainstay of the mid-1950s cinema.

For veteran director Mikhail Romm, the problem with late Stalinist cinema was a certain emotional disposition, "cautiously cool, ornamental, [and] rational." In Thaw culture, rational and ornamental were coded negative, while impulsivity and simplicity were a virtue. Filmmakers looked back on the cinema of the late 1940s as indifferent.[177] The perfectly constituted frames were static; the heroes were static, too. These immobile films left viewers unmoved. Romm argued that Western films were so popular in the Soviet Union because they posed "questions of morality and everyday life."[178] Whether in the neorealist *A Husband for Anna* or the costume drama *The Red and the Black*, passions raged, eyes flared, lips interlocked, and the camera lingered on long kisses and unmade beds. Representations of romantic love became a testing ground of emotional veracity. By the mid-1950s, Soviet cinema had learned to be afraid of love. In the 1930s and 1940s, indeed, well into the 1950s, screen protagonists fell in love with politically conscious and socially useful counterparts. Love was sublimated into labor and subsumed in the collective. To speak of love, people sang, and, as a replacement of lovemaking, frolicked and ran after each other.[179] Romm and his colleagues—the generation that had come to cinema in the 1920s—wanted an emotional outburst.[180] One of the first impulses of Thaw culture was to reject stylized and ideologically correct love.[181]

In the ethical vocabulary of the Thaw, the emotional indifference of the late 1940s was closely related to falsity.[182] Of course, such interpretations were fallacies that took cinema for "reality" and judged stylization a lie. (This aesthetic operation can be compared to calling the Hollywood musicals of the 1930s "unreal.") In Thaw criticism, implausible plots, nonsensical situations, or unpersuasive acting were not merely a professional failure, but a moral one as well—an ill heritage, a bad habit. That ill heritage was theatricality; that bad habit was verbosity. Close-ups, superimpositions, and tracking shots had all but disappeared in the late 1940s, and the only way to make a statement was to speak it. Soviet films talked so excessively that the *Great Soviet Encyclopedia* defined "the art of cinema" as the art of the word.[183] Speech reached a beaming pitch of declamation, now seen as a travesty of realism.[184] This vision deliberately simplified Stalinist films as emotionless, static, declamatory, and deceitful. With an acute sense of the historical moment, Thaw critics and filmmakers ignored the many strands of Stalinist cinema, setting themselves against the aesthetics of the late 1940s and early 1950s.

These conversations about the verbosity and theatricality of late Stalinist cinema brought to the fore the great old problem of the avant-garde: cinema's specificity.[185] Was it theater by other technical means? Did film unfold a literary narrative? Yes, it did, the director Sergei Gerasimov insisted in a controversial opinion delivered to the Second Writers' Congress in 1954. In this antiauteur conception, a film was born from the screenplay's polished text, rather than in the seams between shots.[186] A contrary opinion defended the primacy of the image. The problem with late Stalinist film, in the director Aleksandr Dovzhenko's formulation, was that it had "lost the language of things" and did "not aspire toward spectacle."[187] Other commentators agreed: credibility would come from "the brand of cigarettes that the protagonist smokes, the page from a calendar, the style and condition of clothes"—in other words, from the precision of "detail."[188] However one defined cinema, be it as movement, image, or corporeal experience, autonomous speech was an alien substance.[189]

In neorealism, Soviet critics and filmmakers discovered exactly what they were trying to accomplish. Here was a documentary, that is, nontheatrical, aesthetic. Middle ground and long takes, in which "life itself" moved in and out of the frame, enmeshed the characters in the streets.[190] Snatched for a moment from "the flow of life," brought into focus, and released back, neorealist stories continued to evolve—only the viewers dispersed, and the theater locked its doors. The people on the screen thus existed apart from the validating eyes of the audience.[191] In *Rome, 11 O'Clock*, the finale gave viewers an opportunity to invent off-screen fates for the protagonists. The post- and off-screen lives of neorealist characters rendered their faces long familiar. In turn, the possibility of recognition accounted for their credibility.[192] Leaving the theaters, people carried away a faint picture of another life.

Italian films were celebrated for their unbridled expressivity of gesture and facial play. As the director Abram Room surmised, much of the drama in *Rome, 11 O'Clock* hinged on "manners, actions, gestures, movements," rather than dialogue.[193] Although Steno and Mario Monicelli's *Cops and Robbers*, so beloved in the Soviet Union, was garrulous, speech itself was different in Italian films. Here, exchanges between Aldo Fabrizi's cop and Totò's robber were earthy and temperamental. Commonplace speech in Italian pictures conveyed a sense of "life as it is," where "we do not speak in phrases conceived in advance, where words are always to some degree careless . . . [where] there are many omissions and interjections." The critic Anri Vartanov judged this torrential speech manifestly cinematographic.[194] Other neorealist films indulged in regional and social vernaculars— distinctive, dense with day-to-day realities, and convincing. Visconti's *The Earth Trembles*, filmed in Sicilian, and De Sica's *The Roof*, which reveled in the social accuracy of bricklayers' language, offered a solution to the generic idiom of Stalinist cinema that so embarrassed filmmakers in the late 1950s. Soviet commentators were fascinated with the authenticity effect of nonprofessional speech. During the shooting of *The Roof*, they followed intently De Sica's search for "a real type, who would speak and move as a man of the people."[195] Dubbing, which demanded effortlessly flowing speech, inadvertently participated in the Thaw quest for expressivity and naturalness. After all, dubbers sacrificed literal precision for the sake of articulation and gesture. Vartanov argued that in cinematic dialogues, as in dubbing, words were interchangeable. Rather than discrete words, gestures were the source of aesthetic power.[196]

Finally, here were films in which things spoke more clearly than words. The neorealist screen meticulously catalogued purses, shoes, cots, curtains and linen, worn-out suits, scraped building walls, porticos as witnesses to past elegance, and shutters flung open at morn. In *Bicycle Thieves*, symbolic repetition of bedsheets, bicycle rows, and bowls of soup amplified a leftist political message amid the prolonged silences of the main character. In *Side Street Story* and *A Husband for Anna*, uneven cobbled pavement was squeezed between rows of buildings. Ropes bedecked with washed linen stretched across the alleys, connecting windows on opposite sides of the street. Billboards and movie posters were an urban backdrop, anchoring viewers in a particular era. Warning about the ills of cinematic prolixity, the screenwriter Evgenii Gabrilovich cited as an example the dense material world of Italian films, "all these discolored oleographs of Madonna and advertisement boards hanging on chipped walls."[197] Topographic specificity prompted Soviet critics to think of recognizable vistas: "In *Rome, 11 O'Clock*, the geography of the city is shown so convincingly that, it seems, if you arrived in Rome, you would not be lost."[198]

Across Western Europe, critics and filmmakers wrote about on-location shooting, nonprofessional actors, leftist politics, and the erotic charge of neorealist pictures. But neorealist objects were rarely noticed.[199] For Soviet observers, however, things were a focal and liberating aspect of new Italian cinema. Soviet readings of neorealist materiality were thoroughly Aesopian, with a remarkable degree of identification between Soviet reality and Italian movies. Film and theater critic Inna Solov'eva, in *Italian Cinema*, a culmination of the 1950s interpretive efforts, spoke of fascist cinema as decorative and ornamental, in terms appropriated from the domestic context. Facade, duplicity, grandiosity, mendacity, and noisy slogans: Solov'eva's vocabulary was as much about the Soviet Union as about Italy.[200] It was also cut from the same cloth as interpretations of Remarque and Hemingway, and indeed, Hemingway was an occasional analogy in Soviet thinking on neorealism. "Poverty ruled [the neorealist] world," wrote essayist and theater critic Boris Zingerman, "but not counterfeit, sham values. Here, mended laundry hung on a rope stretched above the slums, but there were no requisite painted props."[201] In Solov'eva's words, these painted props (*raskrashennye dekoratsii, nakrashennost'*, with connotations of kitsch and theater) were a verbatim reproduction of lamentations about late Stalinist cinema. Against fascism's "falsity" and abstract "official values," neorealism counterposed a world of "tangible things."[202] Linking the concreteness of neorealism to that of the Renaissance, Zingerman wrote about the joys of materiality, of "reveling in the discovery of the world"—as if emerging from a long illness, when one's first encounter with the world is sensual, rather than cerebral. Things were so important because Soviet filmmakers read themselves into the Italian context.[203]

The most conspicuously neorealist of the Soviet 1950s films was Lev Kulidzhanov and Yakov Segel"s *The House I Live In* (1957), produced, like dubs from the Italian, at the Gorky Studio. The movie told intimate stories in distinctly private settings. As in *Rome, 11 O'Clock* or *Side Street Story*, the film's unifying center was a building. It was a safe harbor, where people returned for a short break from geological expeditions or from the war, crippled. The building was a dark solidity aglow with lit windows at night; at dawn, a silhouette dissolving in the fog; during the day, a white blot flooded by sunrays. It was a new construction on the outskirts of Moscow, located on a plateau beneath an empty hill. Beams and heaps of dirt were piled in the courtyard. They brought to mind De Sica's *The Roof*, a tale of homelessness, whose setting was an empty lot, a hilly piece of earth, with grass, bars, and sticks. In desperation, a newlywed couple with no place of their own resolved to build, illegally, a shack on the outskirts of Rome. They would have to do this in the course of a night and cover it with a roof before dawn, if they were to call it home; otherwise, the police would demolish it. De Sica's picture pivoted on suspense and the frantic action of class solidarity. In the darkness, figures laying bricks scurried back and forth, illuminated by a kerosene lamp that flickered nervously and cast deep shadows.

But in *The House I Live In*, there was no narrative suspense or temporal intensity. It was a slow film that performed "the flow of life" quite literally.[204] Here people were born, grew up, fell in love, aged, and everything began again. Despite the traumas of love and war, the ending was nearly the same as the beginning (recall, again, *Rome, 11 O'Clock*). None of the actors was prominent at the time. The choice of unfamiliar and "commonplace" faces was intentional: the equivalent of neorealist characters from the crowd.[205] To create a sense of veracity—"life as it is"—Kulidzhanov and Segel' montaged documentary sequences into this feature film, iconic ones of troops departing for the defense of Moscow in the winter of 1941–1942. The camera zoomed in on their faces: in one, viewers recognized the film's main protagonist, Serezha. Embedding Serezha in such familiar historical shots erased the line between a documentary and a feature film.[206]

Figure 4.2. *The House I Live In,* directed by Lev Kulidzhanov and Yakov Segel',
Gorky Film Studio, 1957.

Photo provided by Cinematheque of the Russian Federation (Gosfil'mofond).

Intimacy and documentary veracity came together in the directors' attention to material objects, openly referencing Italian cinema. White bedsheets drying in the sun were a refrain in *The House.* The film's opening
revealed a wall with flaking plaster and a wooden fence in the foreground.
Behind it, another wall fragment suggested architectural disorder, and, in
the center of the frame, drying laundry flailed in the air. The bicycle in
The House recalled De Sica's classic *Bicycle Thieves.* But whereas in De
Sica's picture the bicycle was vital for the plot, in *The House* it served atmospheric and expressive functions. Holding onto the bicycle, Serezha and
his love interest, Galia, wandered through nighttime Moscow. They walked
alongside the embankment, following the curves of the Moscow River; descended to the quivering water as it grew lighter with daybreak; and ran
up the stairs of a bridge, while the camera lingered on the bicycle, which
represented youth and escape.

Figure 4.3. *Rome, 11 O'Clock*, directed by Guiseppe De Santis, Titanus, 1952.
Photo provided by Cinematheque of the Russian Federation (Gosfil'mofond).

The precipitous photography from dramatically high and low angles in the penultimate sequence of *The House* echoed the penultimate sequence of *Rome, 11 O'Clock*. The arrangement of the frames was nearly identical in both films: small, smitten figures looked at each other from above and below on the staircase in perspectives alternating abruptly. In De Santis's picture, a man raised his head to see his panic-stricken wife leaning over the orifice left from the wreckage of the staircase. As he sprinted to the top floor to rescue her, the camera directed the viewer's gaze, via a sharp vertical line, to the remnants of the stair landing above. In the Soviet picture, Serezha ran down the staircase and halted to look up through the aperture at his brother, who told him that Galia had been killed during the war. From a perfectly vertical perspective, the camera fell on Serezha as he came to realize her death. Staircases at sharp angles, courtyards of continuous facades, and romantic walks through nighttime cities would become axiomatic in Thaw films. Atmospheric sequences of

Figure 4.4. *The House I Live In,* directed by Lev Kulidzhanov and Yakov Segel', Gorky Film Studio, 1957.
Photo provided by Cinematheque of the Russian Federation (Gosfil'mofond).

"life as it is" turned into a new convention, no less routinized than those of Stalinist cinema.

Almost as soon as material "details," "ordinary people," and the chaotic flow of urban life appeared in Soviet films, critics began to signal their alarm and to yearn for the heroic. Nighttime streets gleamed in the rain; sunrays cast bright patches on walls; the cobblestones of old Moscow appeared shaded in pencil. Boys in plaid shirts and girls in swing dresses wandered the streets unsure of their calling. Have we not, asked some critics, seen this somewhere already? "Why the director needed these nearly documentary shots is unclear, but where this came from is clear. It is well-known that Italian filmmakers shoot authentic city streets or neighborhoods and, instead of actors, widely use suitable types in the background."[207] Whereas in the mid-1950s, neorealism was a singular salvation from all that seemed wrong with Stalinist cinema, within a few years, those signature filming techniques had become annoying. The attempt to

Figure 4.5. *Rome, 11 O'Clock*, directed by Guiseppe De Santis, Titanus, 1952.
Photo provided by Cinematheque of the Russian Federation (Gosfil'mofond).

depict the lives of ordinary people transformed the grand Soviet collective into fragmented commonplaces.[208] In Italian films, life was public and communal. Intimacy required a crowd in *The Roof*, in which the couple relied on the collective in order to be alone. But in neorealism-inspired Soviet films, people on the screen were "busy with their private affairs and trivial passions, boring, gray, anonymous."[209] Recall the enthusiasm for the postscreen lives of neorealist characters, who could merge with the crowd and appear somewhere nearby—in our courtyard, in the building across the street, in that queue, or at this bus stop. That possibility now made them forgettable. "The day after watching the film, its images dissolve[d] in memory," director Aleksandr Zarkhi said of Soviet "imitators," who made movies "as Italians [*pod ital'iantsev*]."[210] The neorealist spirit had been defiant: De Santis, De Sica, and others had repudiated commercial cinema, bourgeois morality, and the social ills of capitalism. But if in Italian films, "location vividly illustrated" a critique of bourgeois society, in Soviet ones, on-location shooting was a conspicuous "device" in which critics could find no purpose.[211] Poeticizing the physical environment and everyday life erased the heroic.[212] A striking, audacious protagonist had vanished. What remained was laundry drying in a courtyard. When this quintessential symbol of Italian cinema appeared in domestic films, critics greeted it with mockery and called it "microrealism."[213]

This mockery accompanied a reevaluation of Italian films. In the mid-1950s, it was enough that people left theaters with a knot in their throats after watching *Cops and Robbers*. Nobody protested in this film; only a fat cop, panting and clasping his chest, chased a scrawny, limping thief through muddy outskirts. In this tender picture, both were comical, vulnerable, and wretched. But in the late 1950s, sad realism seemed to have turned into an all-forgiving sentimentalism. What was neorealism, and what remained of it? According to Inna Solov'eva's explanation, what killed neorealism were its imitators, including, presumably, the Soviet ones. Multiplied from film to film, the road and the child, penniless couples in love, endearing black marketeers, overpopulated neighborhoods, and overcrowded interiors had become commodities. Poverty proved "photogenic": "the peeling wall turned out to be an aesthetic phenomenon." "Drying linen" made for a "fashionable shooting backdrop."[214] This was an ironic end for an aesthetic that had emerged in rebellion against the commercialization of art.

In the late 1950s, important voices began to call for a cinema that offered a model of life, rather than life itself, for figures towering over the crowd, rather than faces snatched from its flow.[215] But this was a losing position: the neorealist aesthetic survived all critical campaigns.

In the process, neorealism was reinterpreted in an elitist key as plotless cinema. A Chekhovian mind-set became the defining lens for watching neorealist films in the mid-to-late 1960s. Neorealist classics were often built around an accident, with shots edited sequentially, rather than contrapuntually. Scriptwriter and neorealist theoretician Cesare Zavattini's statements about the possibilities of high drama in chance encounters sounded Chekhovian to Soviet critical ears. So did Zavattini's rejection of extraordinary characters.[216] Chekhov had dreamed of a drama in which people would dine, talk about the weather, and play billiards while their lives fell apart. In the late 1960s, Viktor Demin, a film critic and future editor of the popular illustrated monthly *Soviet Screen*, proclaimed the arrival of cinema "without intrigue," of film in which "nothing happens." In his ironic book for connoisseurs, Demin applied a "Chekhovian key" to unlock the cinema of "our days" in general and of Federico Fellini specifically. With Demin's book, the debate on literature and cinema came full circle. He demolished the argument for the primacy of dynamically moving images: the camera's specificity was not its ability to create an illusion of motion through editing, but its capacity for "description." If Demin wished to return narrative to the cinema, however, it was a new literature of subtext and a new theater of unmotivated actions and accidental encounters. In a Chekhovian work, time would flow slowly over two hours, a night, or nine days—an interminable prologue. Such a film would be "free": of subordinate episodes, because each would be equally important, of forced unity and teleological chronology. Demin found this freedom in Fellini, whose stories did not converge, as the fragments of our lives in real time fail to cohere. Of *La Dolce Vita*, Demin cited Fellini on the "chaotic" selection of episodes. In this film of "unconnected" "ordinary events" that the main protagonist Marcello experienced by happenstance, people dined and talked, while somewhere offstage and in the heart of hearts, life fell apart. Fellini subverted neorealism from within, exposing the limits of social action and of venerating the common man. But in the Soviet Union, Fellini and neorealism were related through the Chekhovian episodic and incoherent everyday. None of Fellini's characters was a King Lear, and all were Uncle Vanyas. Late socialism was Uncle Vanya's moment of "seeming inaction, seeming empty[ness]" that said so much to one's heart.[217]

Pornography at Harvest Time

Most of Fellini's films were exhibited in closed theaters for connoisseur audiences. The screenings—often of uncut copies with subtitles or simultaneous live translation, of films that would seldom, if ever, appear in commercial release—took place in "houses of cinema." In major cities, these clubs for professional filmmakers, with movie theaters, restaurants, and lounges, were patterned on Moscow's Central House of Cinema. As for the Moscow House of Cinema, in 1955, the district party committee found it dormant and unexciting, but within a year everything changed.[218] Nearly every month of 1956, the House was abuzz with lectures and screenings of foreign films: "the art of Italian director De Sica," "the art of Italian director Luciano Emmer," a presentation about traveling to "Mexico—New

York—Paris," evenings of Finnish, British, Greek, Argentine, and French cinemas. This kind of programming would become the House's major attraction.[219]

In principle, the Moscow House was closed to the broader public. In reality, during screenings of European and American pictures, the theater often descended into pandemonium. Viewers stood in the aisles, sat on the floor, and elbowed their way through the doors. A good number of people made it inside as friends, dates, and relations of club members. Passes to screenings served as bribes and gifts, a perfect way to thank a doctor or entice a woman. Several House members were caught obtaining extra passes, walking outside, and returning with people who had waited in the street.[220] Composer Nikita Bogoslovskii, who lived the life of the Moscow beau monde, spotted among the audience people he called "outsiders" and "unknowns," whom he happened to know by name: "the surgeon I. Knaper and wife, . . . the tailor Shnaider, ballerina Sharapova, models from the House of Fashion."[221] On the opening night of the first French festival in 1955, dozens of people entered the movie theater through the back door of the restaurant kitchen. Some tickets bore a forged inscription "for two," convincing enough to fool KGB agents assisting the House staff on this occasion.[222] Cultural events like the French film screenings belonged to the economy of shortages: the passes were prized commodities on the black market. People bought and sold "spare" or fake tickets in the streets, by the theater entrance and nearest subway station.[223] The rationale for the screenings was educational and aesthetic, but outsiders "seeping in from the street" were there for the forbidden fruit and threatened to undercut the respectability of Western film screenings.[224] Filmmakers on the House council spent years trying to figure out how to stem "the incursion" of "outsiders."[225] But no matter how vigilant the attendants or how harsh the identification policies the question was never solved. Restrictions merely invited ever more elaborate ways of cheating the system.

All the while, movies that Sovexportfilm purchased for commercial release circulated broadly and were an eye-catching presence in the expanding cityscapes of the 1950s and 1960s. Billboards and advertisements covered the facades of new theaters and nested in the niches between the columns of old ones.[226] Posters evoked foreign vistas. Etched in white, the buildings on each side of the Spanish Steps gave a dreamy depth to a placard for Luciano Emmer's *Three Girls from Rome*. A charcoal drawing of St. Paul's Cathedral, rooftops, and a bridge intimated a gray London in the background of a poster for Carol Reed's A *Kid for Two Farthings*. In a bill-board for René Clément's *The Walls of Malapaga*, dark blue rows of build-ings with yellow patches of windows and streetlights ran into the distance. Such displays became a visual refrain in Soviet cities, as if to suggest that infrastructural development—expansion of city boundaries, construction of new neighborhoods and new theaters—went hand-in-hand with the ex-pansion of geographical imagination. The posters used empty pictorial space to focus attention on central figures. Filling the entirety of a billboard, these head portraits, usually of women, communicated intense color and drama. Silvana Pampanini's face covered a poster for A *Husband for Anna*—her green eyes conveyed longing, soft brown curls enclosed apricot skin: Soviet posters had never been this openly inviting and sensual. In a placard for *Room at the Top*, Simone Signoret's portrait was rendered sug-gestively in charcoal, a pin-up to be found among a man's belongings. And indeed, the faces of Signoret, Pampanini, Gina Lollobrigida, Lolita Torres, Sophia Loren, Elizabeth Taylor, and Marina Vlady did adorn postcards, printed in runs of thousands by central agencies in Moscow and local ones in the republics. The ostensible purpose of such prints was didactic and informative. From a 1960 series of postcards, one could learn that Gina Lollobrigida "created portraits of simple girls from the people" in *Fanfan the Tulip* and *The Hunchback of Notre Dame* (dir. Jean Delannoy). But no matter: these were images of glamor—alluring smiles, sparkling eyes, long eyelashes, and bare shoulders. Billboards and postcards had eroti-cized Western films and created expectations even before viewers took their seats.[227]

That was in the big cities. But the story of film distribution is full of con-tradictions. The towns and settlements that appeared on the map in the mid-to-late 1950s were poorly connected to the rest of the country and had only a flimsy cultural infrastructure. Movies came to small towns and the countryside by mobile projection units, and they came infrequently, for lack of transportation, on account of great distances and inclement conditions. Projectionists had to travel by motorcycles, trucks, even by horse-drawn carriages or deer sleds along impassable roads in snow and mud.[228] As a result, new Soviet films, not to mention foreign ones, arrived in the Armenian countryside and remote settlements in Azerbaijan six to eight months after urban dwellers had seen them. In Russia, over the entire summer of 1955, collective farmers of the Vologda region watched just one movie.[229] According to the great Soviet dream of cultural accessibility,

Figure 4.6. Silvana Pampanini. Soviet film poster for *A Husband for Anna*.
Reproduced from KinoPoisk, https://www.kinopoisk.ru/picture/2372407/#. Artist unknown.

the countryside would have the same fare and viewing conditions as "the best" urban theaters.[230] Reality, however, offered worn-out projectors, poor sound, and unheated wooden structures with no seats. People brought chairs from home and waited many hours for the belated start of a screening, only to see the reel jam and tear.[231]

Yet films—Western ones among them—did come to small and remote places. The August 1956 schedule of screenings across the villages of Levkovka, Kozintsy, Savintsy, Demkovka, and Aleksandrovka in the Vinnitsa region, Ukraine, included Marc Allégret's *Julietta*, starring Jean Marais. Muscovites had seen it during the French film festival the year before.[232] A new state farm in western Kazakhstan, "Laborer" was established in 1955, at the start of Khrushchev's Virgin Lands program. The farm's workhands were young people who had volunteered in an outburst of idealism or had been drafted for a summer. They kept abreast of the news beyond the steppe and asked their equally young and strong-willed projectionist to bring Christian-Jaque's *The Charterhouse of Parma*. A barn served as a theater. It was here, on a makeshift screen, that Gerard Philipe's Fabrice del Dongo fenced with verve and pined after Clélia Conti.[233] In the main square of Chuvashia's capital Cheboksary, an enormous portrait of Fernandel announced the French comedy *Casimir* (dir. Richard Pottier).[234]

The billboards for *Fanfan the Tulip* or *A Husband for Anna* hung next to posters for Soviet movies, *The Height* (dir. Aleksandr Zarkhi) or *The House I Live In* (dir. Lev Kulidzhanov, Yakov Segel'). Programming that mixed domestic and foreign features alarmed officials. In early 1964, following the ideological panic of 1963, the Central Committee dispatched inspectors to the republics, where they examined theater offerings. They returned with identical reports: in venues big and small, central and peripheral, programming favored foreign movies. When Soviet reels were not gathering dust, or playing during the day to empty rooms, they were scheduled for the same showtimes as Western pictures, much to the Soviet disadvantage. Worse yet, Soviet productions sharing showtimes with lightweight Western fare were serious revolutionary dramas: in Daugavpils, Latvia, John Paddy Carstairs's *The Square Peg*, a farcical British war comedy, diverted viewers from *An Optimistic Tragedy* (dir. Samson Samsonov), and, a few years earlier, in the center of Moscow, Sergei Yutkevich's *Lenin in Poland* had competed for attention with *Some Like It Hot*.[235] Distributors and theater directors had a financial plan to fulfill yet were blamed for exhibiting films that brought revenues. To the ideological authorities, political negligence and commercial avarice explained the ubiquity of Western films. Otherwise, it was difficult to understand why the internationally recognized *Ballad of a Soldier, Fate of a Man*, or *Nine Days of One Year* (dir. Mikhail Romm) attracted just one-fifth of the viewership of Bernard Borderie's *Three Musketeers*. But such were the figures in Georgia: 53 percent of the population apparently saw *The Three Musketeers*, compared with 6.3 percent for *Ballad of a Soldier*, 8.3 percent for *Fate of a Man*, and 5.4 percent for *Nine Days of One Year*.[236] In Azerbaijan, *The Three Musketeers* enticed more than twice the number of people as the Soviet comedy *The Hussar Ballad* (dir. El'dar Riazanov). In Armenia, distributors tried to raise returns with the always-reliable *The Three Musketeers*, one of the great box office successes—inspectors called them "hits"—of the late Soviet decades.[237]

Dubbing reinforced the coexistence of Soviet and Western movies in the same theaters and brought them into the same interpretive space. Viewers compared, debated, and recalled them together. At first sight, little seems to connect sanitized love stories set at construction sites or tractor stations with *A Husband for Anna*. But for engaged viewers, who put their opinions on paper, there was more than meets the eye. Their letters to periodicals and institutions were forceful interventions—requests—meant to change film policy. These viewers took Soviet aesthetic populism seriously and saw themselves as cultural arbiters. Their crusading spirit revealed assumptions about cinema and audience expectations. Moviegoing was embedded in other urban experiences, sociabilities, and texts: what people read in the newspapers and saw in the streets influenced how they watched films. Western movies became entangled in a web of fleeting incidents and impressions, and of shifting norms of public behavior. These letters were mostly about Soviet films, but they mentioned Western ones, their frame of reference. No matter what film, one consistent theme ran through the viewers' letters spanning 1956–1962. Viewers called it pornography.

Beginning in 1956, it seemed to be everywhere, even in the Soviet production drama *The Height*, set at a new construction site, or the collective farm romance *It Began This Way* (dir. Lev Kulidzhanov, Yakov Segel'). Officials and censors from the Administration of Film Production were stunned. What pornography? Soviet pictures were puritanical to a fault; and "in foreign films, properly speaking, there are no pornographic episodes either, since they are excised before release." "It is difficult to understand what, precisely, you are protesting," the Administration's chief editor responded to a viewer's complaint in 1960, dismissing the cries against pornography.[238] Since what counts as pornography has been often contested and entirely contextual, a subjective and nonrational definition seems the only one possible. With that the case, viewers' visceral knowledge based on sight and physical sensations was as astute as anybody else's. "Pornography" was not a description of what they actually saw. It was a resentful language for what they found unnerving.

Moviegoing was a collective and public pastime, and its communalism defined the experience. There were few public places for people to spend time together; cafes were only beginning to appear, while the movies were very affordable. Theaters were often designed for socializing, with a snack bar, a dance band playing in the foyer, a smoking lounge, and reading rooms. Saturday evening, neighborhood theater: families, coworkers, friends, and dates had to share the darkness with people they knew.[239] Letters reflected sharp awareness of others—of their breathing, laughter, and silences. Watching close-ups of an on-screen kiss was deeply embarrassing. People sat dumbfounded, "ashamed."[240] Young men who took their girlfriends, or even wives, to the movies were baffled: the girl, the darkness, the intimacy on the screen, which itself went suggestively dark.[241] For women, the screen may have felt even more unsettling. As Lidiia Kalinchuk from Odessa supposed: "I am a middle-aged woman, I am forty-five years old, and it was simply unpleasant for me to watch scenes that have long been considered entirely intimate, so how does a young, modest woman, sitting next to a young man, feel?"[242] Laughter helped to conceal nervousness and awkwardness. But when people emerged into the foyer or the street, they felt awkward again and cursed, not only to decry the film but also to mask their unease.[243]

Viewers felt doubly discomfited in the presence of children and adolescents. Mothers complained about taking, in all innocence, their teenage sons to the movies and experiencing a sudden shock when "the secrets" never discussed at home appeared on the screen.[244] "I am an adult, a mother, but I could not watch this film," wrote M. N. Ur'evskaia from Mary, Turkmenistan, conveying her distress about a Finnish film, Toivo Särk-kä's *The Milkmaid,* one of the earliest in Europe to show nudity. On the screen, the milkmaid Hilja (Anneli Sauli) and her boyfriend romped in the fields, then dropped to the grass, kissing. The audience grew tense. Ur'evskaia struggled to describe how she had felt: "somehow awkward, ashamed of something." People sitting next to her dared not look at each other.[245] A viewer from Kiev wrote about the same tension permeating the darkness and fettering people to their seats, only he interpreted it differently, as a thrill: "The entire audience freezes in fascination when any hint, any intimation of nudity appears on the screen (foreign films . . .)."[246]

Mothers took their sons to see films like *The Milkmaid,* because, as Ol'ga Rubbo from Cheliabinsk wrote, Soviet cinema had no age restrictions, no warnings of sensitive content. This situation may have infantilized adults, but in Rubbo's opinion, the accessibility of all Soviet films to children was a cause for pride.[247] In fact, age restrictions first had emerged in the context of Western films captured in Germany and screened in Soviet theaters after the war. Still, in the 1950s, screening practices had not caught up with importation policies. Within a short time, distributors would learn to differentiate audiences by age and to classify as adult such films as André Hunebelle's *The Mysteries of Paris* and Pietro Germi's *Divorce Italian Style.*[248] But even when advertisement posters announced "Children under 16 not allowed," boys and girls found ways of getting inside a theater. In Põlva, Estonia, teachers raided movie theaters, hauling out adolescents who had traveled long distances to watch *The Mysteries of Paris*. In the Kafan district of southern Armenia, the Pioneer children's theater opened for evening screenings of films designated for adults, *That Hamilton Woman* (dir. Alexander Korda), *Thérèse Raquin* (dir. Marcel Carné), *The Blonde Witch* (dir. André Michel), and Emilio Fernández's *A Date of Love*. It is unclear if the theater admitted children to these after-hours screenings, but, it appears, the trademark of a children's theater masked romantic dramas.[249] And in the countryside, parents often took children to movies meant for adults.[250] Regardless of age, everybody watched the same films, Western or Soviet.

Many letter writers identified themselves as mothers or teachers, claiming moral authority and professional expertise. Most were middle-aged, pensioners, or of "an older formation, prewar youths," and found the films of the early 1960s "strange and painful to watch." They wrote as protectors of "our youth, our adolescents, school children."[251] Cinema could shape life in a bad way: "Ask doctors, how many girls have abortions. Even at thirteen," cautioned Francheska Sarksiva. She would not let her thirteen-year-old son watch a Soviet movie about first love.[252] Mothers worried, and warned about, imperiled health for life: images of "half-dressed women can trigger unhealthy longing in young men, longing that sometimes leads to sexual perversion."[253]

Half-dressed women on the Soviet screen? Viewers scrupulously trained their eyes on the slightest exposure, a bare female shoulder or leg. With particular annoyance, they studied the shots of women getting ready for bed: a wife removing her blouse to remain in an undershirt, her rotund shoulders uncovered, in *Alien Kin*; in *Kochubei*, a Cossack girl, appearing in the lodging of an officer and dropping her heavy coat to reveal a nightgown; or Aksin'ia, in *Quiet Flows the Don*, in undershirt, her arms exposed, resting her head on Grigorii's chest.[254] A self-described lover of cinema, P. S. Fomichev from Krasnodar watched *It Happened in Pen'kovo* (a countryside melodrama about the transformation of a dark village into a place of progress) in disbelief at the conspicuous display of flesh. "Soviet women with half-naked breasts, in undershirts—now they dress, now they undress," he noted about a tableau in which a young wife, wearing a shawl atop a plunging undershirt, served dinner to her husband.[255]

Although screen couples were paragons of physical attractiveness, viewers wrote of kissing scenes with revulsion. The camera magnified the kiss; the screen enlarged faces and figures beyond human proportions. As a film's only sexual experience, kissing carried an erotic charge—precisely because nothing else was shown and everything else was implied.[256] The fade-out after the kiss ignited imaginations, as viewers indignantly envisioned what happened in the ellipses beyond the kiss. Much of the resentment was a result of imaginary work invested in the fade-out. Viewers focused specifically on the proximity and enormity of enlarged heads: "Do not show close-ups of kissing."[257] In films of the 1930s through the early 1950s, love had been the domain of hints, portrayed "without even a single kiss," letter writers recalled approvingly.[258] Women's bodies had been concealed in shapeless suits or workers' overalls, approximating those worn by men.[259] Viewers understood pornography as divulging secrets.[260] Their letters spoke about "show" and "disclosure": moviegoers objected to being placed in a position of peeking and eavesdropping.[261] One letter revealed a telling slippage between voyeurism in a film and voyeurism imposed on viewers. Three friends, crane operators from Moscow, railed against the melodrama *Different Fates* (dir. Leonid Lukov). This unorthodox film, which foregrounded infidelity, scandal, and a relationship between a young woman and an older man, might have struck letter writers disagreeably.[262] But the crane operators did not remember the plot. They recalled "a scene of undressing." "The ailing hero sees a girl undressing to get ready for bed," noted their letter, rich in expletives. "Dammit, how [low] has cinema sunk! To show an undressing woman on a full-sized screen! In times past, it was a sign of good upbringing if a man turned away upon seeing something like that in life." Their memory played a trick, however. In the film, the ailing hero did look away. It was they, the viewers, who did not. And it was this viewing position—public voyeurism on an unsuspecting woman on the screen—that troubled the letter writers.[263]

The immediate analogy and the culprit were Western movies. People took cues from or found their anger reflected in the press. In 1960, the government newspaper *Izvestiia* initiated a discussion of indecorous comportment in the streets: young people conspicuously displayed affection in public, with men putting their arms around women's waists or shoulders. The newspaper tracked such "alien manners" to "foreign" and "the worst bourgeois films."[264] Viewers cited this discussion or sent clippings when crying "pornography."[265] They wrote of corrupting "foreignness [*inostran-shchina*]" that "seeped in" surreptitiously, "infiltrated" Soviet culture deviously.[266] Ol'ga Rubbo judged close-ups of kissing or bodily proximity ("stunning embraces") to be "'foreign' shots [*zagranichnye kadry*]." Her antimodel was Claude Autant-Lara's *The Red and the Black* with Gérard Philipe as Julien Sorel. She recalled how uncomfortable she had felt "seeing on the screen excessively explicit, intimate footage" in the French melodrama. Popular lore called such images "'Gérard-Philipe' shots [*filippzherarovskie*]."[267] Another viewer remarked on "conversations in bed" as a "script from Western European countries."[268] From France specifically, according to a group of elderly librarians living in provincial Nezhin in Ukraine; from France, where "nude women in bed, infinitely longing eyes, thirsting for carnal passion" brought box-office success. But Soviet cinema was about art and education, not profits. Why, then, "the unnecessary, alien" bed scenes? The librarians' letter opened with a French picture, Marcel Carné's *Thérèse Raquin*.[269]

Viewers' resentment and disorientation ran that much deeper, because they often mistook Western movies for Soviet ones about life in the West. They would have known they were watching a foreign production when they bought their tickets and the credits began, but at some point during the screening, the audience fell for the illusion of the Russian dub. G. S. Miroshnichenko from Izhevsk (Udmurt Autonomous Region) noticed "disgrace and debauchery" in five films. He assumed all five were made in the USSR. What two Soviet films, a Hungarian movie, a Czech one, and a French picture had in common were the Russian language, European atmosphere, and brief intimate scenes. The five films also shared Soviet screening and interpretive space. Five very different movies, and five examples of moral depravity "before the viewers' very eyes."[270] Viewers' letters were a remonstration about lost innocence, not only their children's, but also their own.

If in Soviet pictures on-screen kissing was shocking, in Western films it elicited no particular surprise. On the contrary, it was expected. People went to see Western movies anticipating something erotic. Only a handful of letter writers admitted this; certainly, it would not have been easy to request films with "pornographic content" and "various crimes."[271] These viewers spoke in the customary Soviet way, on behalf of "tens of thousands of moviegoers" and, moreover, of "many and many steadfast and morally upright" people. References to collectivities positioned the seekers of "pornography" among the mainstream. Their request, they suggested, was no less respectable than the requests of others. But they advanced a different notion of cinema—as entertainment, rather than moral instruction. They went to the movies to see something "beautiful and interesting."

And according to one such letter writer, A. Gaiduchenko from Kiev, there was nothing more beautiful (or interesting) than the naked body. With a good degree of intellectual hubris, Gaiduchenko justified his request using historical and aesthetic examples: since antiquity, people had admired the nude, and art offered for such admiration a dignified context. As an art, cinema was the right place for the nude body. Gaiduchenko stamped those who would disagree with him as reactionary and ignorant, "homebred Savonarolas and bigots, Pharisees persecuting the bathing Susanna." These dark forces expelled not only the body from the visual arts, but also art from the body—by imputing "pornography," "moral depravity," and "kowtowing before rotting, bourgeois culture" to the "delightful combination of girls' nude bodies, radiant blue sky, and blooming nature." Meanwhile, cinema without "the nude female body" had become "impoverished," "hopelessly boring," and "crammed with moralization." "Everybody is so sick" of watching upright stories, commented another, anonymous letter writer. In Western films, these viewers found salvation from the boredom of excessive moralizing: "show foreign movies, which do no such preaching, more frequently," for "people have grown to long for nudity in cinema."[272]

In turn, the passions on the screen, the actors renowned for their looks, the animated gestures in Italian films, and the hourglass dresses or sumptuous costumes in the French ignited emotions—impossible and senseless—that letter writers could not quite name. Twenty-eight-year-old Raisa Pesetskova from the town of Kropotkin in Kuban', found the words: "I very much want to have a long-distance affair with him." She saw Gérard Philipe in *The Charterhouse of Parma* and, smitten, returned to the theater three times. She could hardly wait for the next film to see "the hero of my soul." But most of all, she wished to correspond with him—that was the "long-distance affair" of her yearning, and she fancied Philipe "would not reject a letter from a Russian Soviet woman." Raisa knew that her letter may have sounded "strange or silly," but "that is how the heart can be," silly and strange, and she was "not embarrassed."[273] Others shied from such frank confessions, yet still admired Philipe's "talent and beauty," collected his photographs and biographical tidbits about him as "an actor and a person." They held their breath for *Fanfan the Tulip.*[274]

Ideological and educational worries revealed another expectation people brought to the movies. Viewers assumed that films were censored. Intimate scenes, however, suggested that censors were not doing their job. "But what are the censors doing?" demanded one letter writer in the language of party memoranda. He requested that his letter be forwarded to the Central Committee "for taking the necessary measures to purify pictures of vulgarity."[275] Maintaining the chastity of Soviet films required cutting merely a minute or two of "foreign shots," proposed a teacher from Vladimir.[276] And while at it, insisted another letter writer, "filthy things must be removed" from foreign pictures as well.[277] Cutting actual reels was one solution; the alternative was censorship during the selection process—censorship that would eliminate The Milkmaid, A Husband for Anna, the French comedy The Scandals of Clochemerle (dir. Pierre Chenal), and the Greek drama The Counterfeit Coin.[278] "Cut," "excise," "eliminate": when facing an incomprehensible life, viewers responded with an aggressive call for scissors.

One way to understand changes in notions of propriety and permissibility is to see "pornography" as a "frontier phenomenon," a step beyond the unspoken but widespread "moral sense of a community." Taboo topics, body parts, and language barriers, as well as the distinction between public and private, change along with this unstable frontier.[279] In the 1950s and early 1960s, Soviet screens were ahead of behavioral norms.[280] This is not to say that people did not kiss on park benches or walk with arms around each other's waists. They did, but Komsomol activists, middle-aged passersby, gossiping grannies, and caricaturists from satirical magazines saw promiscuity in such displays of affection. And of course, in films, intimate scenes *were* private, but the screen positioned viewers as intruders upon the intimacy of others. Critics back then and scholars ever since have celebrated Thaw cinema for innovative camerawork and for attention to everyday life. But nobody has appreciated just how novel and shocking the exposed bodies and unmade beds seemed to audiences at the time. A bare shoulder or leg flashed on the screen for seconds, but if viewers are to be believed, this revelation of flesh was a consequential Western import. In early Thaw films (1955–1957), the socialist realist plot and stock characterizations had not yet changed.[281] The camera shifted angles only modestly. The first innovation of Thaw cinema was none of the above: it was a repeal, however incremental, of certain bodily taboos.[282] "Pornography" as a shift in the frontiers of visibility may have been just the right word. What reads as obscurantism in viewers' letters actually registers with great sensitivity this initial, almost indiscernible, change.

Confronting the limits of physical display in mainstream cinema was common to the Soviet Union, Western Europe, and the United States.

European films were vital to the aesthetic and sexual revolutions on American screens as well. Between 1930 and 1968, with various degrees of stringency, the Production Code regulated morality in Hollywood movies. It homogenized production for adults and children; in the words of a censorship board director in Chicago, "If a picture is objectionable for a child, it is objectionable period." Only in 1968 would the rating system differentiate audiences.[283] In the United States of the 1950s and early 1960s, as in the Soviet Union, "foreign film" carried erotic connotations. American distributors screened Bergman and Fellini "as if they were shot in garages or in forest preserves," stressing sexual content in advertisements. In independent theaters, foreign pictures shared the screen with sexploitation movies. The 1950s represented an age of innocence nearing its twilight: "foreign films come from the outside to seduce or offend impressionable Americans who did not yet expect to see more than a kiss at the movies."[284] According to a historian of the American film industry, "the postwar high renaissance of foreign cinema" was instrumental in creating an audience who sought to escape the code and who helped to bring it down.[285]

Louis Malle's *The Lovers* did not make it to Soviet theaters, but it was cited by the press as an illustration of immoral capitalist filmmaking that thrived on "pornography." The film did, however, make it to the United States, only to occasion a police raid on a Cleveland Heights theater, whose manager, Nico Jacobellis, was arrested. The film portrayed a French woman's tiresome life on a splendid estate with a husband whom she hated and a lover who annoyed her. An accidental meeting with another man liberated her. Their lovemaking scene was so lengthy and integral to the film's theme of social and sexual freedom that cuts were difficult to make. In several states, censors (consisting of police and clergy) mandated excisions. But in Ohio, an uncut print earned Jacobellis a conviction for obscenity. It took five years, multiple trials, and a Supreme Court decision to overturn the conviction. Such cases as *Jacobellis v. Ohio* were argued on the grounds of the First Amendment.[286] Habituating sexual openness in mainstream American cinema took Supreme Court decisions and foundational publications by sexologists, as well as the medical breakthrough of the pill, the sexual revolution on college campuses, the development of a public discourse on sex, and market research into the profitability of adult content and audience differentiation.[287]

Soviet audiences experienced none of these. They had no pill and no First Amendment.[288] In the 1950s and 1960s, across Europe and the United

States, pushing visual boundaries in mainstream filmmaking was a shared and mutually constitutive process; the Soviet Union did not escape its reach. The result, however, was different. In its late decades, Soviet cinema was one long kiss in an adulterous affair. But when the kiss ended, there was no fade-out to guard the Soviets' innocence.

Dubbed Western films partook of two developments in Thaw cinema: the advance of a neorealist aesthetic and a subtle shift in the frontiers of visibility. Neorealism arrived in the Soviet Union amid far-reaching changes in the domestic industry and a concerted attack on the films of Stalin's last years. Obsession with the dangers of speech echoed the avant-garde writings of the 1920s. In bringing back these conversations, Thaw criticism shaped the image of Stalinist cinema as theatrical precisely in comparison with neorealism. For neorealism established a different model for watching cinema, reorienting audience expectations from dream factory to ethnographic accuracy. This was the initial context for seeing the theatricality, verbosity, coldness, and decorativeness of Stalinist films—a view that still dominates the critical vocabulary.

Dubbing created an uncommon setting for Russian at a time when filmmakers identified a crisis of language in the cinema. This setting was a palimpsest of realities, sounds, texts, objects, and faces, making Western films both accessible for understanding and foreign in everything else. Nobody called this Russian language revolutionary, but, dictated by behaviors and gestures on the screen, it was faster and more expressive than the celluloid speech people had heard until then. The truly revolutionary experience, however, came from raging passions, interlocking lips, and falling robes. Something licentious was expected of Western films: they evoked beautiful people and risqué scenes by definition. And so, even as Western films became ingrained on neighborhood billboards and postcard collections, they retained a patina of inaccessibility.

5

Barbarians in the Temple of Art

The Russian soundtrack made intelligible the images in dubbed films, but canvases were not supposed to require a soundtrack. They were supposed to speak more clearly than words. Transparency of content was pivotal to Soviet aesthetic theory and creative practice.[1] As in literary translation, professional and popular approaches to foreign paintings were based on the assumption that there were no inscrutable experiences or impenetrable cultures, no matter how distant in time and place. National cultures were unique, to be sure, but art was to present universal themes and convey universal values. During the Thaw, however, most Western art exhibitions included modernist paintings that frustrated expectations of narrative transparency. Defying the narrow confines of representational realism, modernist pictures resisted integration into Soviet urban life.

Just as in cinema, a fundamental conflict in the art world centered on the autonomy of visual language. Much of Thaw criticism crusaded for the specificity of painting, for expressivity of color and line. Increasingly, artists and even viewers also asserted that painting was irreducible to a storyline. This quarrel between the visual and the narrative dominated the conversation about realism's shifting borders.[2] Realist figuration was the main creed of Soviet visual culture. During the Thaw, longstanding definitional certainty—previously, how to understand realism had been undoubtable—gave way to ambiguity.[3] Reassessment of realism began with impressionism, which, during the late 1950s and 1960s, would be incorporated into the cultural canon. At the same time, American artist Rockwell Kent shone a different light on realism, a light that was vibrant, fantastic, and translucent. Throughout his career, Kent inveighed against cubism, expressionism, abstraction, and any kind of nonfigurative art. Perhaps only in the Soviet Union could his paintings have shared exhibition space with his philosophical and artistic opposite, Pablo Picasso. Kent's landscapes and Picasso's early portraits introduced into Soviet visual culture distorted perspective, exaggerated figures, and color laden with emotion. Picasso exposed the ultimate boundaries of realism.

Paintings often strike emotional, preverbal chords.[4] But words permeated the Soviet experience of Western modernism: catalogues, newspaper articles, radio programs, visitor books, and the fleeting remarks people exchanged in museum halls. These printed, handwritten, and spoken words were interpretations, often political, of Soviet culture and Stalin's legacy. As viewers faced hard-to-decipher expressionist or abstract canvases, lines and color blots elicited reactions whose central themes were revelation and barbarity. People who penned comments and letters about an epiphany in the museum asserted subjective perceptions and appealed for tolerance of the inexplicable. More prevalent, however, was a fear of new barbarians. Soviet viewers revered museums as temples of art. When modernist paintings escaped understanding, they seemed to desecrate the museum and to question viewers' cultural fluency. In anxiety and anger about a barbarian invasion, translation reached its limits.

In the Museum

Western art exhibitions arrived in the culture of socialist realism, the official aesthetic doctrine established in 1932–1934 and solidified by the end of that decade. Socialist realist artworks conveyed a vision of the future, of Soviet life as it should be: exultation, abundance, grandiosity, and revolutionary resolve. This utopian world was the socialism of the formula; realism meant accessibility, classical figuration, and narrativity. Literature served as the model for the visual arts. Critics evaluated paintings for plotline and psychological characterization, while viewers were encouraged to commit their impressions to museum comment books.[5] Soviet paintings were made for "the people" (workers and peasants) in an intellectual culture beholden to the Russian realism of the nineteenth century. Literariness was at the heart of that painterly tradition, which had evolved in dialogue with prose and which prized storytelling by visual means. Nineteenth-century artists and critics saw literature as a source of painting's legitimacy and of Russian cultural uniqueness. Between the 1840s and the 1880s, a new, socially conscious generation of painters took to the streets and villages to document the life of the insulted and the injured. But as artists immersed themselves in the world of their subjects, in an attempt to erase the difference between art and life, they came upon the impossibility of accessing and representing reality. Literary analogies spurred artists to reflect on the specificity of painterly representation. This tension between the visual and the verbal was fundamental to the realist tradition.[6] Socialist realism, in turn, pilfered from the nineteenth century and from artistic movements spanning the Renaissance to the avant-garde. It was all of these and none, as it set out to shape reality in its own likeness.[7] Life-creating as it was, socialist realism was also restrictive and repressive. Treating modernism as a nemesis, socialist realists purged themselves and their colleagues of deformation and dramatic expression, of experiments with form and color.[8] And they exorcised modernist artworks from Soviet museums.

The Soviet Union had inherited one of the earliest and richest collections of modern art, assembled primarily by two wealthy merchants, Sergei Shchukin and Ivan Morozov, who spent the years between the 1890s and 1914 acquiring a vast array of canvases. A visionary collector, Shchukin was among the first to realize the importance of Picasso and Matisse and to purchase their paintings for his sumptuous home, which doubled as a museum. Morozov, meanwhile, put together an impressive Cézanne collection and many fauvist paintings as well.[9] For his home exposition, Morozov commissioned sculptures from Aristide Maillol and paintings from Pierre Bonnard; Maurice Denis complemented existing murals with additional images. In early 1918, the Soviet government nationalized both collections, transforming them into the First and Second Museums of Contemporary Western Art. In 1921, the two museums were unified under the same directorship, and in 1928, they were moved under the same roof. The 1920s were years of development, when the museum received paintings from other nationalized collections, from artists themselves, and through painstaking acquisition despite very modest means. By the end of the decade, the museum's exceptional holdings included some 700 artworks: three rooms with Picasso, and yet other halls with Matisse, Monet, van Gogh, Cézanne, Gauguin, Denis, Renoir. The museum was staffed by young art historians, who traveled to Europe in the late 1920s to purchase prints, talk to artists, walk the Parisian streets depicted in the paintings, and research their dissertations. They would go on to hang paintings, create expositions, and guide visitors through Western art exhibitions during the Thaw.[10]

In the 1930s, the museum made two fundamental turnarounds. Early in the decade, administrative higher-ups compelled it to characterize paintings and its own work according to class categories. The staff had to rethink how to write art history and how to display paintings. The nascent aesthetic dogma portrayed the evolution of painterly styles as a (class) struggle, with notions of "decline" and "degradation" guiding interpretations of Western modernism. The second half of the 1930s brought another turnabout: instead of class struggle, the emphasis was now on realism. But much of the museum's original collection contradicted the new creed. In 1937, the All-Union Committee for the Arts, which oversaw all cultural institutions, ordered the museum to shift the focus of its permanent collection to realism and to acquire paintings from the late eighteenth and first half of the nineteenth centuries. Shortly, curators started taking down modernist pictures. Although the impressionists remained for the time being, Matisse, Léger, Picasso, and others began to disappear. By the late 1930s, modern art had come to occupy just one room.[11]

Finally, in 1948, the museum was disbanded. Upon returning from wartime evacuation, the staff had not even begun to unpack the paintings before the premises became prey to various institutional appetites. A commission led by Aleksandr Gerasimov, a prolific painter of Stalin's portraits, demanded the museum's building for the recently founded Academy of Arts. The next several days saw much scrambling behind closed doors, frantic pleas, and empty reassurances. Tensions boiled over when Kliment Voroshilov, accompanied by Gerasimov and an entourage of officials, descended upon the museum and ordered curators to present Matisse's *Music* and *Dance* for their inspection. They wanted to see firsthand the paintings' many objectionable characteristics—silhouetted red figures, flattened perspective, and simplified green-and-blue landscapes. One demoralized curator would remember the officials' derision for the rest of her life. The end came shortly thereafter when the Council of Ministers ordered the museum to close. The very curators who had assembled the museum's holdings now had to pack up and oversee the move. The paintings were divided between Moscow's Pushkin Museum of Fine Arts and Leningrad's Hermitage, where they were consigned to storage rooms for the next seven to eight years.[12] Only in 1954–1955 did some of these canvases emerge from hiding.

As they did, they shared space with an array of works from traveling exhibitions, staged mostly in Moscow, Leningrad, and occasionally in republican capitals: French Art, XV–XX centuries (1955), Mexican Graphic Art (1955), French 19th-century Painting (1956), Pablo Picasso (1956, 1966),

British Art (1956), "Looking at People": Eight Contemporary English Artists (1957), Contemporary Italian Graphics and Drawings (1957), International Exhibition of Fine and Applied Arts, VI International Festival of Youth and Students (1957), Rockwell Kent (1957–1958, 1960), Albert Marquet (1958), Contemporary Graphics from Argentina, Brazil, Mexico (1958), British Painting (1960), The Art of Mexico (1960), French Art (1961), Renato Guttuso (1961), Fernand Léger (1962–1963), French Art from the Hermitage (1964), to name the most prominent.

Viewers brought certain expectations to these exhibitions at the Pushkin Museum and elsewhere. The socialist realist aesthetic underscored reading as the reception model for the other arts. Museum visitors attempted to "read" artworks as illustrations of events, lives, and stories, explicitly comparing paintings to books. A painting's "content"—a word that dominated the vocabulary of both professionals and the lay public—had to be "accessible," easy to read for plot, characterization of protagonists, and ultimate lessons.[13] Viewers searched paintings for facts "about nature," about "everyday life," "external appearance, . . . character" of a people.[14] Sometimes they used comment books to elaborate their own "readings" of paintings and supplied their addresses so that artists, museum administrators, or some other authority would let them know whether their interpretations were correct.[15] Such expectations were grounded in the assumption that other cultures were readily accessible as long as the narrative devices allowed for intelligible reading. But modernist paintings—especially abstract expressionist works, which first arrived in 1957—offered no coherent stories. Viewers faced a distressing nothingness that defied description and a fragmentation of form that frightened them: "nothing for the heart, nothing for the mind."[16] Staring at shapes, colors, and broken lines, they found little that fostered the sense of human contact they expected from art.[17]

Much of what museum visitors knew about modern Western art came from the invective rhetoric of Soviet newspapers. Visitors' comments showed different ways of asserting judgment without relinquishing the customary framework of newspaper censure: "What we had only read about earlier, has now, after seeing the exhibition, become clear." Other comments highlighted the experience of seeing versus reading: "For us, it is a newly discovered world. Our eyes have been opened."[18] Indeed, references to recovering eyesight, to clarity, to the revealed and the hidden were widespread in responses that otherwise registered very divergent aesthetic preferences. Whether they expressed passionate admiration or adamant dislike of modernist paintings, comments both drew on the language of secrecy and disavowed its hiding devices—locks, walls, curtains, screens. In the words of a party member at a 1955 exhibition of French art, "for twenty years," since 1935, "[this] has been kept secret, but the radiance of true art will break through all obstacles, all screens, all walls, all curtains. And it becomes clear that it is *impossible to hide* such treasures . . . and once again to seal up in the darkness of the archives what belongs to the people. Thus taught the great Lenin."[19] Suspicion continued to grow: "The works of the cubists are kept hidden"; "We hide our treasures and keep them in storerooms"; "Why has the Museum of Contemporary Western Art (on Kropotkin Street) been hermetically shut since 1941? Strange!"[20]

Newspapers, though, were not the only sources of knowledge. Older museum visitors brought cultural memories of the 1920s, challenging the assumptions of professional critics and historians that Thaw-era viewers rejected modernism because they had never seen it.[21] Some not only remembered but also cited the 1920s avant-garde as further proof of realism's superiority and decisive triumph. These viewers called for publications about "the epoch of our 1920s—that is, the epoch of 'futurism,' 'cubism,' . . . and so on and so forth." Such publications would dispel the sense of novelty, showing that modernism "for us is already a thing of the past (and thank God!!!)." Contemporary European art thus appeared hostage to Russian modernism.[22]

Viewers also came with names, facts, and stories they had read in various books,[23] and with a Soviet aesthetic education that elevated the "Great Masterpieces." People took pride in knowing the names of old masters and the titles of old paintings. It was at once their personal accomplishment and a feat of the whole country, analogous to reciting Pushkin's poems by heart or boasting Zola's collected works in one's home library. Some names were Russian—Surikov, Repin, Shishkin, Serov; others—Leonardo da Vinci, Michelangelo, Titian, Rubens, and Rafael—became Russian as a result of Soviet custodianship over European classical patrimony.[24] Soviet faith in human invincibility embraced Renaissance anthropocentrism and its cult of Great Men, while rejecting its individualism. The Soviet Union laid claim to the Renaissance heritage, especially after World War II, when the Soviets presumed that they had saved Europe from barbarity. In the late 1940s and early 1950s, Soviet historians and art critics waged a holy war "in defense of the Renaissance"; it was not a "narrow academic" matter, but "of central importance for . . . our growing socialist culture."[25] The Renaissance was the highest stage of realism, and its masterpieces were the gold standard of human achievement. In viewers' observations throughout the 1950s, the Renaissance remained the aesthetic ideal. This was what they meant when writing about beauty and pleasure, about art that enraptures. Accessibility alone was not what museumgoers demanded; they shared a common—Romantic—understanding of aesthetic experience as elation, ennoblement of feelings, and harmony.[26]

If the Renaissance stood for the Golden Age, then the "Stone Age" in visitors' comments represented the idea of cultural decline in the West, culminating in twentieth-century capitalism. Art seemed to be dying out: the images created by present-day Western "cavemen" signified the extinction of culture, at least culture as it was understood in the Soviet Union.[27] The notion of Western "barbarity" had been readily available since the war, when it had gained wide currency. Some viewers sought the roots of modernist disembodiment in Hitler's Germany and meant their comparisons of Nazism and modernism literally.[28] Most museumgoers knew nothing about Nazi art or the comparable fates of the avant-garde in Germany and in their own country. Insistently and innocently, they spoke of modernism as "the art of degenerates," proposing to preserve some samples for "a museum of pathology," while burning the rest.[29] Disruption of the human form—of the classical body—was especially distressing. Enlarged hands or feet, elongated bodies, and distorted facial features scared viewers: why make people ugly, they protested. "Looking at People," a 1957 exhibition from England, included several portraits that one comment writer saw as "horrifying cretins," "disfigured . . ." or "robots without a face or a mind." At that same exhibition, the factory worker Ivanova thought the sculptor George Fullard had given his *Skipping Girl* an elongated, angular torso and arms because "he simply hated people, their feelings." Fernand Léger's workers "bore the marks of degeneracy," according to another viewer; their faces, all alike, disclosed no inner world.[30] Within the Renaissance paradigm, Italian artworks at the Moscow Youth Festival and the Italian Graphics exhibition (both in 1957) were especially shocking. It was, wrote a serviceman, "scary to think that Italian artists [were] capable of such splatter, which shows the degradation of art. How can this possibly be compared to the past? Italy, whose name is associated with magnificent and unsurpassed examples of visual art, has come to exhibiting such trash." In the collective mind's eye, that magnificent and unsurpassed vision was Rafael's *The Sistine Madonna*. "Dear Italy! The country of great masters! How have you come to this? Where is your true art?"[31]

In the comments, animals symbolized cultural regress. The popular magazine *Little Flame* and the satirical *Crocodile* periodically ran stories and caricatures about nonhuman paintings. Betsy the monkey and Jack the donkey dipped their tails into buckets of paint, then gleefully and indiscriminately splashed colors to the satisfaction of capitalist dealers. Fat capitalists wearing black tuxedos and top hats, zany bohemian artists in berets and narrow pants, conceited art critics, and ladies in sleeveless dresses pulled above their knees were all depicted feasting at a table tipped to one side, in an atmosphere of complete abandon, sexual license, and general chaos.[32] In these caricatures, humans looked a bit like animals, pointing to the fate awaiting culture: "the utmost crisis," "the twilight of European culture," concluded many viewers.[33] In the tradition of Jean de La Fontaine's and Ivan Krylov's fables, one visitor at the Youth Festival exhibition composed a dialogue between an artist and a monkey—or rather, the monkey's monologue, the artist being a docile disciple. In this fable about deception, the monkey took pity on the inept artist and taught him the skills of her trade:

> I do not labor painstakingly at night
> And my ideas are quite simple;
> First I throw some paint
> Upon both dirty and clean canvases.
>> Then, perfecting my method,
>> I draw a circle and a dot, again a patch of color,
>> And then the title of the painting, "Weather."
>> It all takes only one sitting.[34]

Viewers reminded each other about the famous monkey Betsy, donkeys and their painting tails, pigs and feeding-trays, a whole "zoo"—and, as befitting a zoo, dirt, dirt everywhere.[35] People incessantly pointed to animals and barbarians, to paints anybody can splatter across a canvas. After all, they believed that making art required craftsmanship, something scrupulous and special.[36] Even as they had been taught that painting ought to reflect life, they understood art as separate from the mundane and unremarkable.

For these viewers, looking at modernist paintings was not a detached, intellectual activity: people did not consult labels, shrug their shoulders,

Figure 5.1. Fedor Reshetnikov, central part of the triptych *The Mysteries of Abstraction*, 1961, Tretyakov Gallery.

Published by permission of Liubov' Fedorovna Reshetnikova.

and move on. They were violently shocked and experienced the disgust physically.[37] The canvases at the Youth Festival elicited (psycho)somatic responses: "It was vile," "nasty," "repugnant," so much so that one person felt nauseated, "as if [he] had drunk warm soap water."[38] Viewers complained of severe headaches, depression, and exhaustion, and rushed to leave these exhibitions.[39] The museum experience may well have included not only metaphoric but also real headaches and queasiness, since the crowds were huge, the space was stifling, the entrances and exits were jammed, and the debates were unrelenting. Sometimes people did not know exactly what was wrong with them. It escaped definition, this "grim, dejected feeling." The pictures were literally dangerous, giving no respite, not even after visitors had left them behind. The "vile impression[s]" were "indelible, ineradicable," and transformed into nightmares.[40] Viewers shifted the burden of their own malaise onto the artists. Time and again, artists were counseled to seek treatment for schizophrenia or were mocked as psychiatric patients, and doctors bore witness: "As the chief doctor of a mental ward, I must note with regret that the art of my patients is not inferior to the best 'masterpieces' of Western European artists. I would have been happy to admit them to my medical institution."[41]

This line of reasoning—or rather, abnegation of reason—overlapped with the analysis of capitalist degeneration to confirm the familiar dichotomy. The capitalist West was decrepit and decaying, practically on the verge of extinction; its art was decadence's last spasm and senility's last vision.[42] Its communist antipode was "youth"—an image that resonated strongly in Soviet culture. All the more reason to worry about young people becoming contaminated by capitalism's hallucinations. Unwavering pedagogues pushed medical metaphors the furthest: to the threat of contagion. They wrote about a "virus," an "infection" poisoning innocent students, and called attention to unidentified "young men" who propagandized abstract art.[43] Teacher Rudaeva from Moscow's school no. 72 described one such scene at the Youth Festival exhibition: "I was a witness to how a young, inexperienced man, with foam at his mouth, defended the novelty of 'cubism.' He played the hypocrite, calling on others to do the same, and, worst of all, he was convinced that understanding, studying, feeling realist art is not worth the trouble."[44]

One explanation for such responses can be found in Soviet viewers' prolonged exposure to socialist realism—an observation they themselves made at the time.[45] Abstractions seemed odd next to familiar realist paintings, and people had very little information to temper the rawness of their reactions. But the Soviet language of condemnation did not differ much from the usual tropes of antimodernism the world over. Since the mid-nineteenth century, daubs, donkeys, and the mentally deranged had been staples in critiques of modernism, whether in New York, London, or Paris. In 1863, critics and audiences at the Salon des Refusés had scorned Édouard Manet's *The Luncheon on the Grass* for lack of craftsmanship and composition. In the twentieth century, this judgment would be reflected in the commonplace refrain that "a child of six could do it." Impressionist brushstrokes had been ridiculed as daubs thrown onto canvases in jest or in ignorance, and critics had called the paintings dirty.[46] At the turn of the century, antimodernism fused with panic about degeneration to produce a medical interpretation of cultural crisis: expressively distorted faces and figures presented visible proof of the painters' mental illness. In the 1910s and 1920s, German museum visitors compared avant-gardists to children and barbarians and likened their displays to madhouses. The Nazis radicalized these ideas and viewers' resentment in their own exhibition of modern ("degenerate") art, whose catalogues and supporting texts on the walls spoke about garbage, decay, and madness.[47] Although during the Cold War, Western governments exploited abstract expressionism as an emblem of freedom, ordinary patrons continued to dismiss the brightly colored stripes of a Barnett Newman—anybody can do this. No matter what country, people feared, ridiculed, or rejected the transgression of aesthetic norms.[48]

But why should canvases painted in distant countries become such a personal affront for Soviet viewers? Why the spirited arguments and intense emotions?

The arguments in comment books were not so much about the paintings on display as about a collective identity defined by "being cultured."[49] Such expressions as "uncultured," "having little culture," "being truly cultured," "the growth of our culture," "narrow-mindedness," "crass ignorance," "in bad taste," and "philistinism" (*poshlost'*) conveyed the commenters' sense of moral superiority on the one hand and cultural insecurity on the other.[50] Poshlost', indeed, had assumed its pejorative meaning and its Russian specificity in nineteenth-century literature precisely in the context of the Russian encounter with Western fashions.[51] Pride and prejudice characterized a similar encounter in the mid-twentieth century.[52] A central claim of socialist realism was that the revolution had released culture—with a capital C—from class fetters and made it available to the people in schools, institutes, evening classes, lectures, and newspapers.

Modern art exhibitions from the West, however, cast doubt on Soviet viewers' cultural literacy. They knew well which objects were worthy of display at museums, described in the Romantic idiom as "shrines" of culture and "temples" of art.[53] These metaphors recalled the temples of antiquity; museums, for their part, enacted the metaphors in marble and stone. The first collections of French, Prussian, and British museums had consisted of classical statues or their plaster imitations. The famed museums built or redesigned during the nineteenth century, among them the Altes Museum in Berlin and the British Museum in London, had been cast in a neoclassical mold. The turn of the twentieth century had brought to museum architecture another wave of neoclassical friezes, porticos, columns, and grand stairways. In the United States, the period spanning the 1890s to 1930s had been a great era of museum building, much of it following classical models.[54] And in Moscow, the future Pushkin Museum of Fine Arts, built in 1898–1912 as a repository of classical works, presented an Ionic colonnade copied from the Temple of Apteros Nike on the Acropolis and a Parthenon frieze copied from the British Museum.[55] The silent halls of these museums encouraged reverence in the presence of art. As museumgoers walked up the grand stairways and passed through Palladian portals, they left the profane everyday to enter a sanctuary—experiencing art required separation from the world.[56] This understanding of art originated with the German Romantics, who had given currency to the temple metaphor. Exhibitions of Western modernism made Soviet audiences shudder at the "desecration of the museum." A viewer at the 1957 "Looking at People" exhibition from England thought the pictures "disgraced the walls of the Pushkin Museum." Several years later, another collection from England, which, according to the museum's documents, included "ten modernists," spurred one pensioner to protest the "defilement" of the museum, a place that should be respected as "a temple of art and a sanctuary." In his words, "abstract painting" was "an assault on civilization and people's tastes." Teacher G. E. Izotov, visiting Moscow from Kazan' in 1963, sounded the same refrain at a show of Fernand Léger's work, noting the profanity and desecration. Museumgoers wrote of the paintings as blasphemous and of the shame they felt at witnessing the violation of the temple.[57]

Because viewers could not anchor modern art in their definition of culture, they could not find a place for it in the museum either. Yet, exhibitions of modernist paintings were now sponsored by the Soviet government and displayed in art galleries as aesthetically valuable.[58] Visitors responded with surprise and incomprehension, but most surprising for them was their own incomprehension: "I look in astonishment: I am a Soviet viewer, and it seems to me that I am not so stupid, but I could not understand many paintings, despite my wish to do so."[59] The overwhelming majority of comment writers boasted higher education. Most were professionals. Many of those who left censuring and angry responses were doctors, researchers, professors, and Academy of Sciences affiliates.[60] When the meaning of paintings eluded them, people turned defensive about their acumen—and, by extension, about the Soviet project of cultural accessibility that had shaped them as an audience. They sought to expose modernism and its defenders for a lack of culture before anybody had a chance to strip them of their own claims to it.[61]

The collapse of customary boundaries between meaning and senselessness, culture and barbarity, health and illness was almost a natural—and certainly a national—disaster, depicted as a powerful torrent threatening to engulf the country. Comments repeatedly conveyed a sense of crumbling certainties: "I am scared, could this wave sweep over us?"; "I am scared to call this art"; "I am frightened"; "I am offended and scared."[62] Most powerfully, gaps in understanding were exposed not in abusive speech, which, after all, requires making sense—even if by negation—but in silence. Words ceased, language stopped: "I have no words," "no words, no words, no words," intoned the commenters.[63]

The boundary between the familiar and the foreign overlaid the cultural geography of Moscow. In viewers' comments, the Tretyakov Gallery functioned as an alternative center of culture and a symbolic counterpart to modernist exhibitions. As a shrine to realism, the Tretyakov Gallery was thought to inspire good aesthetic judgment.[64] But it did more than demonstrate the superiority of realism. From the beginning, the gallery's founder, Pavel Tretyakov, had intended it to affirm the Russian national genius.[65] The Tretyakov was a place where one could be both cultured and Russian; it was a shelter from the absurd, chaotic, and threatening world of Western modernism. The gallery's very name provided such comforting constancy and familiarity that one viewer turned it into a cozy adjective: "our very own, Tretyakovian." Or, as another visitor commented in 1957: "There was the epoch of the Renaissance in the West. Now Western art has entered an epoch of degeneration. The center of world art has clearly migrated to the East."[66] The path of this migration ran from the Pushkin Museum to the Tretyakov Gallery.

Reclaiming Impressionism, 1947–1967

Renaissance standards of beauty began to wane during the Thaw. In the new story of European art that emerged then, impressionism took center stage.

Impressionism owed its significance in Soviet visual culture of the mid-to-late 1950s to its notoriety during the preceding decade. Actually, impressionism had been a battleground for debates about foreign inflections in Russian culture and the nature of representation since the late nineteenth century, when impressionist canvases initially had appeared and made an impact in Russia. In Moscow, as in Paris, passions had raged at the first impressionist exhibitions. Famous painters stormed out, slamming doors in fury, while restless young artists were torn between their teachers and the exciting new world beyond realism. At stake in these clashes was the relationship among objective reality, subjective vision, and artistic representation. The Russian realist tradition obliged the artist to represent objective reality faithfully.[67] But impressionism denied the possibility of objective, dependable knowledge and faithful, fixed rendition. A subjective vision of an ever-shifting reality and the power of modulating light to alter perception were central to impressionism.

Like prerevolutionary commentators, their Soviet successors in the 1920s and early 1930s attacked the impressionists for individualism, which suggested a personal vision, ephemeral and socially irrelevant—whereas realist art elevated the collective, the objective, and the socially transformative. For others, impressionism, as a study of the effects of light, meant naked scientism devoid of feeling—whereas socialist art was supposed to inspire and mobilize. To be sure, there were critics who declared that impressionism was a novel aesthetic suitable for a revolutionary society. But from the mid-1930s on, and especially after *Pravda*'s concerted "antiformalist" campaign of 1936, impressionism was treated as an outpost of "formalism."[68] This aggressive campaign affected all creative fields and solidified socialist realism around key principles: realist form ensured accessibility; canvases were to offer behavioral models; and painting was to be "beautiful," conforming to classical norms, while "ugliness" suggested devious politics. The press equated realism with "simplicity." Appeals to "unambiguousness" and "clarity" indicated that formal experiments could not be understood by mass audiences and would not be tolerated by the party. Moreover, according to menacing *Pravda* articles, incomprehensible paintings could hide bourgeois ideological content.[69] When "simplicity" became the chief aesthetic criterion, the subjectivity and chance essential to impressionism signaled cultural decline.

Impressionism commanded such passions for another reason as well. The place of French culture in Russia and of Russian culture in Europe figured prominently in these debates. In the nineteenth century, anti-impressionism had been the ideology of Francophobes. To the enthusiasts of the French art scene, Russian patriots had argued back in the language of cultural uniqueness.[70] This argument unfurled with renewed bile during the anticosmopolitan campaign of the late 1940s and early 1950s. In 1949, impressionism became Soviet art's wicked alter ego, a metaphor for everything that was aesthetically unacceptable. But the anticosmopolitan critics did not reject plein air, luminous palette, or studies of light and its effects on color. They simply claimed Russian primacy, dating plein air to nineteenth-century painters Sil'vestr Shchedrin and Aleksandr Ivanov.[71] In the xenophobic vocabulary of the late 1940s, impressionism lost historicity and became an "ism"—a freestanding term denoting decadence and foreign threat.[72] The anticosmopolitan campaign in the visual arts was distinctly Francophobic.[73] No insult was too severe for the French and their Russian followers, and there was hardly a journal that did not publish such abuse in the late 1940s and early 1950s.

In 1974, twenty-five years after the anticosmopolitan campaign, the Pushkin Museum commemorated the centenary of the first impressionist exhibition on the Boulevard des Capucines in Paris as "the frontline where the history of contemporary Western European art begins."[74] The museum's 1970 catalogue rejoiced in the impressionists as "the pride" of its collection and announced the names of the painters as a shared European heritage. This was an art that "defined the aesthetic face of Europe in the last one hundred years."[75] It had taken the Soviet art world almost a century to arrive at this conclusion. Much of this process of acceptance and habituation happened during the Thaw.

Before critical reappraisal, impressionist paintings from the disbanded Museum of Contemporary Western Art reappeared on display at the Pushkin Museum and the Hermitage. In 1954, the Pushkin Museum reorganized

Figure 5.2. Exhibition of French art, Moscow, November 1955. Sovinformbiuro. Photographer: M. Ozerskii.

Photo provided by the Central State Archive of the City of Moscow, Archival negative no. 1-18180.

its regular exposition to include canvases by French impressionists, until then stacked in storage.[76] In 1955–1956, the museum opened two exhibitions of French art, the first from Soviet collections, the second on loan from France. The vast Soviet exhibition, ranging across six centuries, unfolded a story that culminated in "progressive art." In this history, impressionism was neither aberrant nor degenerate, but rather a transit point on the way to realism, ending with the communist artist André Fougeron. Yet, canvases from the mid-nineteenth to the early twentieth centuries were still separated from the rest of the exhibition, in a world of their own, a world of "cold contemplation" whose "nature, colors, forms" lacked certitude.[77] By contrast, for the organizers of the exhibition on loan from France, impressionism was the final destination.[78] For this event, Soviet curators wrote explications, markedly different from the descriptive accounts of Romanticism or neoclassicism, that presented facts, refrained from prescribing correct interpretations, and left viewers to decide what the paintings meant.[79]

The paintings from France returned home, but the explications that Soviet curators had written stayed on. The history they presented passed from one exhibition to the next. Earlier, the impressionists had been blamed for initiating the disintegration of form in cubism, surrealism, or tachisme. Soviet histories now presented them as legitimate precursors of "progressive art." By the mid-1960s, art critics had begun to link impressionism and socialist realism in a positive relationship. Evgenii Yakovlev, assistant professor of aesthetics at Moscow State University, argued that impressionism and socialist realism defied "naked rationalism" and created a vibrant, emotional world. He focused on the brightness of colors, the beauty of nature, and the centrality of man to both; in his analysis, socialist realism—like impressionism—was about "delight in the sensual beauty of the world, nature, and man." No longer "the art of bourgeois modernism," impressionism was now called "humanist."[80]

Expunged from art history for its Frenchness, impressionism returned as a specifically French phenomenon. In the mid-to-late 1950s, it was draped in the charm of a belated love affair with France. The impressionists' Paris was also Gérard Philipe's and Yves Montand's Paris, and it was the Paris of Ilya Ehrenburg, the Soviet Union's main Francophile. At the turn of the century, Ehrenburg had lived in Paris as a revolutionary exile, a poet, a frequent presence in Montparnasse cafés, and a member of a circle of young modernist artists. During the 1930s and 1940s, he returned to Paris as a journalist, novelist, and Stalin's informal cultural envoy. Ehrenburg's place in Thaw culture and his authority among Soviet readers of the 1950s and 1960s cannot be overstated. His memoirs, *People, Years, Life,* restored to Soviet cultural knowledge dozens of names, artistic movements, and foreign places that had been obliterated from the public domain. Ehrenburg's Paris had ash-gray buildings and green grass in December. It was inhabited by street singers, kissing couples, respectable old men passing time in cafés, women in huge feather-bedecked hats, mischievous students, and indigent artists. It was crowded and colorful; it was a theater. On his first day in Paris it had rained—as in Renoir's *The Umbrellas* or Caillebotte's *Paris Street; Rainy Day.* Ehrenburg poeticized France in his old age with a tenderness he reserved for few other subjects.[81] In his memoirs, he resorted to an impressionist technique to depict Paris, taking up different incidents, associations, or, indeed, impressions in every paragraph and sentence. There was a description of the Seine embankment with bookstalls; suddenly an old man, who happened to be Anatole France, appeared; then Notre Dame, Chinese students, and Polish newspapers; tiny quarters where everyone knew everyone else; a parade of nude artists; and simply a carnival. In one paragraph readers encountered the poet Charles Péguy, whom Ehrenburg had once met, and the fifteenth-century highway robber François Villon, whose verse Ehrenburg had translated.[82] For him, impressionism meant a rejection of literariness, of a storyline; the impressionists "tried to depict the world the way we see and feel it . . . to convey their feelings through form and color."[83] Ehrenburg did much the same in his descriptions of Paris. Brought up on impressionist paintings, he also brought the impressionists to a countrywide audience in the late 1950s and early 1960s.

Ehrenburg embraced impressionism romantically, breathlessly—and defensively. In 1958, he published a prominent article, "The impressionists," in a collection of his essays, *French Notebooks*. Opening on a combative note, the article struck at dogmas of faith and habits of viewing. Ehrenburg withdrew authority from the very genre of critical articles, announcing the primacy of personal experience and divorcing the storyline from the visual: "It is difficult to talk about painting, painting must be seen. Words sometimes hinder the ability to see art." His own essay was not about painting. It was about words: "Painting cannot be narrated, but words can be refuted with [other] words."[84] And he used "other words" to contest the main postulates of socialist realism. The reason a painting could not be narrated, Ehrenburg declared, was that plotline was not its most important aspect: "Painting's effects are different in nature from those of literature . . . Composition, drawing, colors, a sense of light—this is the complex and, at the same time, straightforward language with which an artist expresses his thoughts and feelings." Ehrenburg called for historicism: "We must consider the work of writers or artists not in comparison with the masters of the past or the future, but as an expression of their own time." This meant abandoning progress and decline as categories of aesthetic analysis.[85]

In Ehrenburg's article, the impressionists were not decadent formalists. "They were great artists" and "modest, hard-working people" with a "passionate love for art, a yearning to see nature anew, to paint it differently."[86] For Soviet audiences, this portrayal sounded unusual, but the argument was familiar. This was a tale of toil and poverty, not a bohemian kind of poverty, but very real, desperate poverty, which in Soviet stories equaled moral superiority and guaranteed moral triumph. Ehrenburg offered a socialist realist account that linked art with economic circumstances and personal morality; and he presented a Romantic vision of the artist, in which suffering and genius were mutually reinforcing.[87] Ehrenburg anticipated the ridicule of antimodernists. He combed the contemporary French press and plucked out such judgments as "pathetic daub," "mentally ill in a fit of

delirium," and "it is difficult to say whether the artists behind such paintings are mentally ill or they hope their insolence gains them glory."[88] Besides the French press, Ehrenburg had at his fingertips another source
that shaped his thinking: Soviet comment books from exhibitions of
Western art. In the Pushkin Museum of the 1950s, he heard derision that
no doubt seemed familiar to him, an echo of the laughter that had greeted
impressionist paintings at the Salon of the 1860s and 1870s. As the president
of the Soviet-French friendship society, Ehrenburg visited most exhibitions
of French art and was deeply offended by the public's scorn.[89] In stringing
together quotations from the French press, he had domestic audiences in
mind: "One does not argue with fools from a distant past, but reminding
[people] of former folly is useful so as to embarrass the next generation of
jeering dolts."[90] It was for the domestic audience that Ehrenburg described
impressionism as a conflict between "sincerity" and polished but "cold"
hearts. "Sincerity," of course, was a code word of the Thaw, and Ehrenburg did not let his readers miss the moral clue.[91]

Ehrenburg's article on impressionism had several lives. In 1958–1959, he
published it in two modest editions of *French Notebooks*, and in 1960, he
read it on the radio, reaching millions of people across the country.[92] His
text moved these audiences: "There is no hint of calm narration. On the
contrary—such unusual passion, grace, and overwhelming power of
conviction that to withstand it, not to catch your exuberance . . . is almost
impossible," reflected a letter writer.[93] In Ehrenburg's voice quivering with
drama, listeners discerned melancholy notes and wrote about his special
intonation.[94] An elderly woman from Kazan', by her own admission "barely
literate in art" and staunchly conservative in her tastes, "believed in the
validity of his words . . . his intonations forced me to believe."[95] Margarita
Sheffer, a math teacher and music fan from Rostov-on-Don, sensed "something authentic" and unusual about this radio program: the "intonations
[we]re his own, not something recited by an announcer." "Sincerity" was
in the voice: not only in what he said, but in how he spoke.[96]

By the time of the radio lectures in 1960, debates among art critics had
petered out, and impressionist paintings had joined the permanent displays at the Pushkin Museum and the Hermitage. But for broad audiences,
especially beyond the capitals, Ehrenburg's broadcasts were not old news.
Print runs for his *French Notebooks* were very small by Soviet standards
(10,000 in 1958, 30,000 in 1959). Most copies sold out in Moscow, never
reaching provincial centers; those that did were sold under the counter by

the distributor and never actually appeared in bookstores. The majority of people who wrote Ehrenburg after the radio lectures—to thank him, ask questions, or share their thoughts—lived in provincial cities and had not heard of his book nor read his article about impressionism. To them, the lectures were full of new information, and they requested the text's publication or a repeat performance on the radio.[97] Many people visited museums in the capitals infrequently, and many more had never seen impressionist paintings. The lectures inspired Leningraders to make a pilgrimage to the Hermitage and seek out the artists Ehrenburg had touted.[98] But most letter writers—from Khar'kov, Odessa, Riga, Kostroma, Astrakhan', Rostov-on-Don, Chita, Kemerevo, Kazan', Ufa, Syktyvkar, Chernigov, Dneprope-trovsk—did not have this luxury. An engineer from Chita, R. Dmitriev, resented the privilege of place: "How much I envy Muscovites . . . The Muscovites saw the American exhibition, French theater, British Shakespeare. They saw Pablo Picasso! . . . And the Tretyakov Gallery? And the rest of domestic and foreign art . . . But for me, Moscow is off limits. A vacation once a year, fourteen days. And how can one see everything, have the time to examine [it all]?"[99] Traveling exhibitions, let alone Western ones, were a rare happening, and throughout the 1960s, the drabness of cultural life in the provinces was a prominent issue in newspapers and letters of complaint. Instead of exhibitions, the provinces occasionally received stacks of posters and postcards.[100] No quantity of reports and resolutions could change the dismal quality of these offerings. Prints of impressionist paintings were black and white, which "completely destroy[ed] the whole charm of color, light, and air in their canvases," grumbled letter writers from the town of Orekhovo-Zuevo near Moscow.[101] Citing Ehrenburg on the impossibility of describing painting, a couple from Kostroma demanded "publication of a colorful album in mass print runs and separate prints from an exhibition of impressionist canvases in Moscow."[102]

Such requests were prompted by a thirst for cultural knowledge. In the 1950s and early 1960s, public lectures on art at local clubs, libraries, and institutes made for popular pastimes. Several social developments fueled this curiosity: the first postwar generation had grown up and graduated from institutions of higher learning; the ranks of technical intelligentsia, engineers and doctors, became not only more numerous but also better educated than at any point since the revolution;[103] and the urban population enjoyed more leisure time. Ehrenburg's correspondents were mainly engineers, doctors, and students. One engineer struggled to be as erudite as

Ehrenburg and resolved to devote himself "to studying the beautiful: literature, painting, music, and much, much more." He knew some German and was "assiduously" learning French with his wife, a language teacher, but he yearned for more: "How can I reach my goal to the fullest?"[104] Aspiring "to understand the historical development of art and aesthetic problems more generally," Viktor Brovkin, a craftsman, buried himself in books. He lived in Kotlas (a former Gulag site in the Arkhangel'sk region) and signed up for correspondence courses at the Moscow House of People's Art. Viktor was proud of how much he had learned, "considering that I've been studying painting for only three years."[105]

These people did not read or listen passively. An elderly party instructor from Leningrad "listened attentively and transcribed" Ehrenburg's radio program. A husband and wife from the Kokchetav region in Kazakhstan "took notes on everything we could." And the village history teacher N. G. Komarov used the radio lectures when leading an art history club in school.[106] The problem of impressionism spurred people to pursue comparative and cross-referential readings. They had several sources at their disposal: old books published before the war or the revolution, contemporary newspapers (especially *Pravda* and *Literary Gazette*), specialized art journals, and *The Great Soviet Encyclopedia*. Some old publications in foreign languages were of limited help. Unable to read them, people nonetheless kept such books as Julius Meier-Graefe's *Impressionisten* as family mementos or tokens of another world. Although he did not read French, Mikhail Dmitrievich Nirod, a persistent letter writer, treasured for "half of [his] life" Camille Mauclair's *L'impressionnisme, son histoire, son esthétique, ses maîtres.*[107] In the late 1950s, art criticism from the West, such as Lionello Venturi's *Impressionists and Symbolists* in Russian translation, began to reach a wider, nonprofessional audience.[108] Aleksandr Sergeevich Samokhin, a retired engineer with free time and a habit of systematizing information, checked Ehrenburg's arguments against those of Venturi. He did not take the radio lectures on faith, but followed art criticism in specialized publications, compared various texts, and methodically hunted through bibliographies for more titles. Reading Venturi and Ehrenburg prompted Samokhin to search for a Marxist-Leninist perspective, which he found in a collection of articles, *On Painting*, produced by the Academy of Arts in 1959. Seeking other professional publications, he perused the journal *Art* and scouted Venturi's bibliography. He took notes and jotted down quotations. His was a proactive reading that collated multiple perspectives.[109]

Figure 5.3. At the entrance to the Exhibition of West European art from the Louvre and other French museums, August 8, 1965. TASS. Photographer: V. Koshevoi.

Photo provided by the Central State Archive of the City of Moscow, Archival negative no. 0-20302.

Ehrenburg's article about impressionism and his memoirs sent readers to an authoritative text that promised all the answers, *The Great Soviet Encyclopedia*. But instead of answers, some discovered more questions and others only insults. After listening to Ehrenburg's lectures, M. Ditiakina, from Kazan', consulted the encyclopedia, which "has helped [her] so much in life," and which told her that impressionism was "a decadent movement of bourgeois art." Mixed feelings beset her. She was distressed, but not embarrassed, self-righteous, but with a hint of self-doubt. She admitted: "Listening to Ehrenburg's story about how people, the crowd, had mocked this art as clumsy daubs of paint, I thought that I would have probably sided with the opinion of this crowd. Such art is <u>incomprehensible</u> to me." Had her letter stopped here, the lectures would have made little difference. But Ditiakina continued: "I very much regretted that I didn't know at all the paintings he had spoken about; now, it is necessary to take an interest, that is, to get them and look at them . . . I will try to get impressionist paintings [i.e., prints] and then decide whether I am with them or against them." We do not know what she ultimately decided. But what had changed—and *this* is important—was the process of making decisions. Ditiakina thought it necessary *to see* the paintings, if only in reproduction, before evaluating them.[110] This was the end of encyclopedic certainties.

The impressionists elicited such tremendous interest and energetic readings, because at stake was information hierarchy, enforced ignorance, and cultural privilege. People wrote about Ehrenburg's "rehabilitation" of impressionism in the politically laden terminology of the Thaw. They talked about its "persecution" and underlined for emphasis: "in the 1940s, impressionism was <u>forbidden</u>."[111] They blamed the Soviet press, critics, educators—the authorities (recall the commanding encyclopedia entries)—thereby freeing themselves from the burden of incomprehension. And they voiced their assertions in a tone that was disconcerted, sarcastic, and downright hostile. When Ehrenburg suffered media attacks during the ideological campaign of 1962–1963, he found his mailbox flooded with letters tender and thankful, but also aggressive.[112] The rhetorical vehemence was aimed at the authoritative "them":

> They drum into our heads through newspapers and the radio
> that abstract and modernist art is terrible. [T]hey try to con-
> vince us that the impressionists were decadent and their art was
> degenerate. . . . What do we know about the art of the West

besides what we hear on the radio or read in the newspapers? One discovers the truth by comparison. We have nothing to use for comparison . . . It appears that they pull the wool over our eyes intentionally.[113]

Impressionism stimulated self-reflection in Soviet viewers and readers. As a model for seeing nature and painting, impressionism was grounded in a new autonomy of perception, in a vision independent both of critical interpretations and of stable, external conditions. Elusive and ambiguous, impressionism demanded active audience engagement in the creation of meaning. The pictures were open-ended.[114] Impressionists painted ephemeral experiences and transient states of nature; the world of their paintings was in flux, fragmented. Figures and objects melted away before the eyes of the beholder, requiring viewers to reassemble images. Vision became entirely subjective, and herein lay the political significance of the impressionist aesthetic for Soviet audiences. Faith in encyclopedic authorities, unambiguous answers, and correct interpretations was on the wane. In inviting viewers' participation, impressionism allowed for a multiplicity of meanings, admitted subjective interpretations, and invested trust in the eyes—ordinary human eyes.

Toward the Shores of Realism, 1957–1962

With the reappearance of impressionist canvases on museum walls, the sealed borders of socialist realism began to open. Viewers discovered a figurative art beyond verisimilitude, a realism that retained representational likeness but dispensed with detailed delineation, naturalistic color, and the illusion of objectivity. They discovered such realism in the American painter Rockwell Kent (1882–1971). Kent built his flattened landscapes on sharp and simplified geometrical planes and used decorative, vibrant color. As museum visitors came to recognize at his exhibitions, realism was in the eyes of the beholder—as well as in the beholder's experiences and physical sensations. The Soviet cultural establishment embraced Kent as a great realist. But for viewers, his realism was unusual and startling.

Kent belonged to a coterie of foreign intellectuals lavishly courted and smugly paraded by the Ministry of Culture as "friends of the Soviet people." His heyday in the United States had been in the 1930s, when he had illustrated books by Herman Melville, Walt Whitman, and others. Kent's *Moby Dick* illustrations had helped to propel the novel to the status of an American classic. On the eve of World War II, he joined the antifascist struggle, and the German invasion of the Soviet Union confirmed his leftist sympathies. Although he never became a card-carrying communist, he retained loyalty to the cause of peace and disarmament and, despite his intense American patriotism, to the Soviet Union as well. In fact, he first had appeared there for a Peace Congress in 1950. His artworks arrived in the Soviet Union seven years later in a one-man show of unprecedented publicity. A succession of bouquets and banquets followed in the next decade. Throughout his life in art and politics, Kent imagined "a land where . . . beauty was the common environment and people lived together in unending happiness." The Soviet Union seemed to have come close.[115] He never ceased to marvel at rose gardens and caviar breakfasts, at the enormous crowds queuing to see his art, and at the warmth and wit of his intelligentsia friends.[116] His paintings and prints entered museums across the Soviet Union to find a ready-made home.

Kent's politics and realism would seem to have made him a natural choice for Soviet cultural authorities. He was not their first choice, however. Kent's story is emblematic of transnational personal relationships between Soviet commissioners and Western leftists. But the story also belongs in the history of official cultural exchanges—even though, or precisely because, this relationship skirted diplomatic protocols and, instead, compensated for the failure of official Soviet-American negotiations. The Kent story illuminates an overlooked connection between Soviet formal diplomacy and informal dealings with Western fellow travelers. Kent's paintings appeared in the Soviet Union when attempts at official exchanges either collapsed or left Soviet cultural bureaucrats disappointed. The most prominent of such undertakings was the 1959 American National Exhibition in Moscow under the Lacy-Zarubin agreement. The origins of this exposition—and therefore those of Kent's Soviet life—lie in 1955–1956.

In the mid-1950s, quick to realize the advantages of Khrushchev's peaceful coexistence, American entrepreneurs barraged the Ministry of Culture with proposals for performances and exhibitions. Soviet cultural officials greeted these offers with open arms as opportunities to fulfill the new party course, as an excuse to expand their own travel engagements, and as evidence of the Soviet Union's growing prestige. American galleries also stood to gain from the exchange of art exhibitions. Under the pretext of cultural programs, museums across the United States and Europe would spend the next several decades trying to negotiate the loan of modernist paintings from the former Morozov and Shchukin collections. In 1955–1956, the most energetic initiative came from a most unlikely partner—New York's Museum of Modern Art (MoMA), representing, in Soviet eyes, the world of abstract blotches. In late spring of 1956, its delegation arrived in Moscow. It consisted of the museum's director, René d'Harnoncourt; its president, William Burden; and "the most powerful tastemaker" in the world of modern art, Alfred Barr Jr.[117]

Their first days in the Soviet Union and first talks at the Ministry of Culture left the Americans so "impressed" by the Soviet commitment to exchanges that they declared the negotiations a success. The Soviet Union would send two exhibitions—French impressionism and Russian nineteenth-century realism—in exchange for nineteenth-century American paintings. Before long, however, Soviet negotiators began to suspect that the Americans only cared about the impressionists and conceded Russian paintings as part of the bargain. The three modernists departed from the Mecca of realism with few achievements and invited Soviet colleagues to continue the talks in the United States.[118] That fall, 1956, the directors of the Tretyakov Gallery and the Pushkin Museum, Polikarp Lebedev and Aleksandr Zamoshkin, visited more than twenty museums across the United States.[119] Again, an exchange of exhibitions seemed a fait accompli: American paintings appeared in the Ministry of Culture's prospective plans for 1957.[120]

The Hungarian Revolution disrupted these plans. Negotiations in New York took place on November 3, 1956; fewer than twelve hours later, Soviet troops entered Budapest. Although the lists of paintings were still being drawn up in New York, spirits had already dampened, and not much came of this trip either. But even as the emerging outlines of cultural diplomacy were dissolving, Zamoshkin and Lebedev urged the Ministry of Culture "to press for an exchange of exhibitions."[121] They had reason to hope. After all, negotiations were "postpone[ed] for a decent interval," but not forever.[122] By mid-1957, everyone seemed invested in the endeavor again,[123] but months of bureaucratic delays, not to mention events in Hungary, had sapped the project's relevance. It quietly slipped from annual plans and passed into oblivion.

The project reemerged in 1958–1959, now as part of a far more ambitious initiative: bilateral cultural exchanges and the American National Exhibition in Moscow. But once art was written into bilateral agreements, Soviet authorities lost influence over the selection of paintings. In 1956, the MoMA representatives had sent preliminary lists of American paintings to Moscow and consulted Zamoshkin and Lebedev about their preferences. Soviet commissioners could, and did, request that some paintings be removed and others added—portraits, "good realist landscapes," and "scenes from the life of Indians."[124] They would not exercise this prerogative again. The overarching purpose of the American Exhibition, according to the US embassy in Moscow, was to "demonstrate . . . our superiority both technically and in living standards."[125] The main site of the exhibition, a 400-foot fan-shaped glass pavilion, was a consumer paradise that also housed artworks. Unlike the MoMA's unrealized project, here at the American Exhibition, the art display was an expressly propagandistic undertaking. During the 1956 negotiations in New York, decisions had been made according to aesthetic criteria.[126] But in 1959, a jury chose paintings for the political effect they were expected to have on Soviet audiences: Eugene Speicher's *Red Moore: The Blacksmith* for its realism, which "the Russians would readily understand and accept"; Andrew Wyeth's *The Children's Doctor*, for its "imagination, sensitivity and artistry . . . qualities with which Russian portraiture is not endowed"; Jack Levine's *Welcome Home*, a scandalous satire on the American military, to "show the artists' freedom to deal in this manner with a subject toward which the Russians must show only laudatory respect"; and Jackson Pollock's *Cathedral*, for its sheer strangeness. For the jury, this assortment embodied an idea so grand it could hardly be represented at all.[127] Since the early 1950s, art exhibitions had been a pillar of American cultural diplomacy in Western Europe, where the US Information Agency sought to complement images of consumer abundance and Hollywood gloss with avant-garde achievements.[128] During this decade, American art critics, artists, and the MoMA International Council developed a putative link between abstract expressionism and democracy.[129] The MoMA's René d'Harnoncourt spoke about the capacity of modern art to symbolize a society where individualism and pluralism flourished. He found "a good name for such a society" and called it democracy; its foil went by the bad name of totalitarianism.[130] The 1959 art exhibition in Moscow was an attempt to display democracy in a glass pavilion.

Among Soviet visitors and future memoirists, the glass pavilion was legendary for the miracle kitchen filled with domestic appliances, the auto show, and the bookstands with colorful magazines.[131] Following a policy adopted in Europe during the 1950s, the curators of the art show in Moscow's Sokol'niki Park wanted to counter the image of Americans as "cultural barbarians": to show that America had a soul to accompany the body.[132] But by surrounding paintings with cars, soft drinks, television sets, sewing machines, sports gear, and other motley things in a space "somewhat resembling a huge jungle-gym," American organizers achieved nearly the opposite effect.[133] For Soviet viewers, reducing artworks to one more consumer item could only reinforce that image of "cultural barbarians."[134] The context had a de-familiarizing effect, and, upon encountering abstract expressionism (Pollock's *Cathedral*), visitors complained about confusion and disorientation. Their comments drew explicit contrasts between art and appliances: "I liked the cars. The art is repulsive." "I liked the wonder-kitchen and apartment furniture very much. The picture gallery is absolutely no good." "Especially good are the machines and the typical home. The abstract paintings are rubbish." "I was quite impressed by: the kitchen, automotive vehicles, and television . . . No impression was created by the paintings."[135]

When the MoMA's 1956 project faltered, Rockwell Kent received an invitation to send his paintings to the Soviet Union. The invitation, offered in the spring of 1957, came from Tat'iana Mamedova, the cultural attaché involved in the MoMA negotiations.[136] As a replacement for the MoMA endeavor, Kent's exhibition held out hope, in Mamedova's words, "that this event will be followed by other projects of more extended mutual Soviet-American cultural exchanges."[137] The vision of an exhibition as the first step toward a broad cultural agreement underpinned the Soviet Embassy's and the Ministry of Culture's negotiations with both the MoMA and Rockwell Kent. He was invited neither as a "progressive artist" nor as a "fighter for peace"—appellations that would appear later—but as "a representative American artist" for the purposes "of cultural interchange."[138] Kent felt honored precisely on this count. It had been a long time since anyone had addressed him as a representative of America; more often, for his participation in leftist causes, he was judged un-American and subpoenaed by the House Un-American Activities Committee (HUAC).[139] This insult to his patriotism weighed heavily on him. Accepting the invitation to send his exhibition to the USSR, Kent wrote to the Soviet All-Union Society for Cultural Ties with Foreign Countries: "That an American should be so honored should be a cause of pride to all of us . . . Believe me, I will do my utmost to assemble a collection that will do honor to my country."[140]

Halfway through the exhibition's tour of the Soviet Union in 1957–1959, Kent wrote to a friend: "What has particularly pleased me in the reviews has been that the pictures and their painter have been received as typical and representative of America."[141]

His delight was short-lived. While his artworks were on their way home from the Soviet Union, the paintings for the 1959 National Exhibition—the ones meant to represent America in its quintessential diversity—were about to sail for Moscow. And the Exhibition's American organizers excluded Kent.[142] Perhaps this was the proverbial last straw in his protracted but unsuccessful efforts to reestablish a niche in the American artistic community. In the 1920s–1930s, Kent had enjoyed popularity as a master of book design.[143] But with the onset of the Cold War and abstract expressionism, which for Kent were one and the same ("Abstraction is the cultural counterpart of the atom bomb," he used to say), most doors in the art world closed for him. In his old age, he took stock of his paintings, which were either stored, sadly unwanted, in his wooden studio, where they could easily perish, or dispersed throughout the country, he knew not where. And so, Kent decided to present a gift of his unsold paintings, about eighty in all, plus books, manuscripts, and over 800 prints to the Soviet Union.

He defended his decision to the American public by relating how, seven years earlier, the Farnsworth Art Museum in his beloved Maine had accepted the paintings, only to rescind its offer after the artist's appearance before the HUAC.[144] However, Kent never explained why it had taken him seven years to act on his grudge. The timing of the gift points to the American National Exhibition as a motivating factor. Both in 1957–1958 and 1960–1961, the arrival of Kent's artworks in the Soviet Union followed frustration over official cultural exchange.

Kent sought a public for his art.[145] What impressed him deeply about his shows in the Soviet Union was the sheer number of people who came to see them. Kent's private letters written at the time of the exhibitions were full of numbers—1,500 to 2,000 people a day, altogether perhaps 500,000 in Moscow and Leningrad and close to a million around the country, "with such crowds . . . that people had to be turned away."[146] And then there were his books and illustrations of *Moby Dick*, all printed by the thousands in multiple press runs, bringing Kent unexpectedly large checks from Soviet publishers.[147] He reveled in laudatory reviews and invitations to people's homes, public discussions, and art congresses—so much attention and affection showered upon an artist sorely missing it.[148] Kent realized "the simple fact": "In the course of five or six exhibitions held in one short year in the Soviet Union, many times more people have seen and loved my work than in the whole course of my long life in America . . . My pictures are for them."[149] His public statements contrasted American and Soviet audiences. The Americans were either ignorant or so conceited and elitist that they wanted to suppress realism. The Soviets, however, were a cultured people capable of appreciating true art.[150] This was a familiar image in the Soviet press and one with which many viewers readily identified. They wrote to Kent to confirm this projection: "Your noble art will be cared for and loved by the Soviet people. Your creations have found their home"; "You can't find a more grateful admirer of your art than Soviet man"; "This gift was directed to the most proper place: we, the Soviet people, know how to appreciate beauty."[151]

In turn, Kent embodied the America of the Russian imagination—the America of the sun-kissed Southland and the arduous trails of the North; of pragmatic know-how, impenitent individualism, and reckless courage; of white fangs and last Mohicans. And this was precisely Kent's appeal. Although his exhibitions lacked the allure of forbidden fruit, Kent's persona and art resonated with another central narrative of the Thaw: the romanticism of remote places, the adventures of harsh terrains. In Thaw fiction, cities as seats of power were morally tarnished, so writers sent their young characters far from Moscow in search of purity and truth.[152] Young people followed suit, trading the capitals for bonfires, uncharted trails, and mountain peaks, where manhood and friendship could flourish. "The thicket of Northern forests will teach true friendship, faithfulness that needs no words," promised the poet and singer Yuri Vizbor, who transformed snow tourism into intimate verse.[153] Tourist clubs mushroomed in institutions of higher learning; geology became the most romantic college major; and young men dreamed of high seas.[154] Vizbor provided such dreamers with a poetic geography and supplied poetry with an array of objects: skis leaning against a stove, damp tents, ginger-colored tobacco—in short, the stuff that men are made of. Besides composing songs, traveling across the tundra, and broadcasting these experiences over the radio, Vizbor painted the same landscapes: blue and violet snow-covered mountain peaks, crimson sunsets, dark green firs. He liked to give his pictures to friends and to hang them on the walls of his room in a communal apartment. And he liked the paintings of Rockwell Kent.[155]

Kent himself was an enthusiastic traveler. He came of age in Theodore Roosevelt's America preoccupied with Strenuous Life and ready to answer *The Call of the Wild*.[156] Time and again, Kent would depart for the pristine and harsh wilderness of the North in search of self-discovery and self-fulfillment; but it was in Greenland, on the island of Igdlorssuit, that he found his place on earth. He arrived in Greenland as pirates and romantic heroes do—after a shipwreck. There, traveling by dog sleds with paints and canvases, camping alone for days on end, abiding by no man's law, he embodied a script written by one of his favorite authors, Jack London.[157] In turn, Kent's paintings can serve as companion pieces to London's stories.

Soviet museumgoers also had read and loved Jack London, and they understood Kent's paintings in terms of London's stories. They knew whence white expanses, dog sleds, and tough men had come. Bearing as titles little more than geographic and meteorological designations, the paintings made "white islands on the map" come alive for viewers.[158] As for maps, Kent drew them with embellishments: compasses in upper corners, arrows pointing in four directions, human figures representing the elements, and Neptune, the lord of high seas, overseeing it all. These maps resembled rugged scrolls that chart paths to hidden treasures or inform of shipwrecks. Kent illustrated his writings with such maps; most of his books were accounts of travels, exploits, and life in the wild among the natives. The Foreign Literature Publishing House or the State Publishing House usually printed Russian translations. Not so Kent's *Greenland Journal*, *N by E*, *Salamina*, *Voyaging*, and *Wilderness*, which were produced by publishing houses that specialized in geography and youth literature. His works belonged to the world of Soviet childhood—the world of Jules Verne, James Fenimore Cooper, Robert Louis Stevenson, and Jack London, of course.

From childhood books, viewers knew what Kent's paintings were about: "the rough, difficult, and heroic life of the brave and courageous people of the North," "the people, morose and manly, with their uneasy life and tenacious labor," "remarkable, courageous . . . in their struggle with rigorous nature."[159] These were comments from the exhibition of Kent's artworks that visited Sverdlovsk and Irkutsk in 1961–1962. One viewer was "involuntarily reminded of Jack London." Others read his remarks and agreed: "Rockwell Kent is Jack London in visual art." A student from the Leningrad Pharmaceutical Institute not only recalled London at Kent's exhibition, he also envisioned Kent's paintings when reading Jack London.[160] Viewers did not miss other literary analogies: "I think I won't be mistaken if I compare R. Kent to another great American, Ernest Hemingway."[161] Even when Hemingway was not named, the implicit comparison ran through the comment books. Students addressed Kent as "old man" at a time when this was a standard greeting and a compliment among young people. For them, Kent belonged to a brotherhood of "old men" and "good guys" by virtue of his "sincerity," of the understatement in his paintings: "There is no gold, no empty phrase, no gloss."[162] He wasted no words—"where the word ends, there Kent begins"; his landscapes were "laconic."[163] Such combinations of disparate adjectives—"tender and tough"—with which viewers described Kent and his paintings were also used to invoke Hemingway's characters, who shunned lofty words and hid tenderness behind affected roughness.[164]

Viewers often knew Kent's wild landscapes firsthand.[165] His paintings were habituated in Soviet visual culture thanks to recognition, rather than revelation. Among the people who left comments or wrote to Kent were explorers and geologists, geophysicists from Buriatiia, radio technicians from Angarsk, and hydraulic engineers from Sakhalin, sailors, captains, young men dreaming of adventures, and inhabitants of Murmansk and Arkhangel'sk in the Soviet North. Some of them had spent long stretches of time among sea storms and snowdrifts, and others aspired to do so. The paintings moved a pilot who often sailed in the North to feel anew "all the beauty, all the courage of the 'barbarian' and great North."[166] A student from Rostov who had been to the polar circle responded the same way. For two years, he had carried a memory, unable to articulate it until Kent did it for him: "What I saw here [at the exhibition] shook me up . . . This is a <u>real</u> bard of the North!"[167] To look at Kent's canvases was to experience the North vicariously: "you feel like taking a deep breath—to your very heart—and breathe in this strong cold air flowing from the canvas."[168] One visitor wanted "to walk into the paintings," while another "walked into every painting and [now] stood at that very place where Rockwell Kent had stood."[169]

Kent's radiant colors and forms, almost abstract in their simplicity, produced landscapes so stylized as to raise for exhibition visitors the question of realism.[170] The paintings may have inspired dichotomous viewing because they were built on contrasts: of black and white, background and foreground, intersecting horizontal and vertical planes (stripes of sea, snow, and skies pierced by trees, mountains, and icebergs), gigantic mountains and tiny human figures. Some people felt the paintings static and compared them to icons or advertisement posters.[171] But others were enchanted: "What colors! We see such [colors] for the first time"; "The brightness of colors is something unusually new. I am not used to it."[172] Although the Soviet press unequivocally placed Kent in the realist tradition, viewers wondered about the realism of an artist painting nature with fantastic turquoise and orange that looked more decorative than natural. Again, definitional certainties were unhinged: what was realism, and what was not? Some people at Kent's exhibitions even suspected that he was an abstractionist and drew on the antimodernist vocabulary of senility and charlatanry in their comments.[173]

Their answers to the question of realism depended on personal visions, rather than established criteria, on subjective interpretations of nature and man. Viewers maintained that Kent's realism was of a different kind, because reality itself was different in the North. "Purely classical art" could not accommodate the intensity of the landscape.[174] Some museumgoers thought that glowing colors and a degree of abstraction were justified in expressing "the stern, impregnable nature of North America."[175] Inclement elements appeared all the more omnipotent and arresting compared to the marginality and fragility of human figures in Kent's landscapes. As one viewer noted, "in the paintings' majestic kingdom of nature, the majority of people are irrelevant." When humans intruded into this kingdom, nature was the vanquisher.[176] Viewers who faulted the paintings for abstraction and lack of ideas "felt that the artist had painted the pictures in a state of total merging with nature. No conception, no design."[177] But those visitors who respected nature as indomitable also accepted Kent's fantastic realism.[178]

While Kent's pictures traveled across the country, young Soviet painters, along with poets, geologists, and radio operators, went to the tundra and the taiga in search of new heroes. In principle, the new heroes—builders of bridges and hydroelectric stations, raftspeople, fitters, and fishermen— were to be the same as the iconic representations of the first five-year plan (1928–1932). The artists came back, however, with different protagonists and different landscapes: mountainous terrain, barren and murky, divided into contrasting bands of foreground and background, rendered flatly, with crude, prominent brushstrokes. Nikolai Andronov's construction workers at the *Kuibyshev Hydroelectric Station* were clumsy, his monumental *Fitter* was schematic. Pavel Nikonov's *Fishermen* were flattened, somewhat distorted figures whose faces were barely visible to viewers, while the workers in his *Our Workdays* were coarsely painted, rough, and angular. In the late 1950s and early 1960s, these and similar conspicuously joyless paintings were examples of "severe style," as it was termed at the time. Generalization and monumentality, hyperbole or understatement, and, indeed, severity were its stylistic features.[179] If socialist realism demanded classical figuration and polished surfaces, then the exaggerated hands or feet, angular faces, and pronounced brushstrokes were indications of "truth," of unvarnished "life as it is," so prized during the Thaw.[180] Kent's paintings arrived just as "severe style" was born, defined, and consolidated. Losing the mystique of foreignness, his images became virtually indistinguishable from numerous landscapes painted not that far from Moscow.

As they crossed geopolitical and aesthetic borders, paintings moved from the margins of their original cultures to the center of the target culture. The very decision to import something elevated an object of translation from triviality.[181] Soviet critics and museum officials had no illusions about Rockwell Kent's place in the American art scene and did not keep it a secret from audiences. In fact, thanks to Kent's manifest marginality at home, translation repositioned him as a major realist painter and a true representative of American culture. Soviet hospitality rituals brought him to extraordinary, if brief, prominence. In presenting the gift of his collection to the Soviet Union, Kent turned out to be right, or simply lucky. He would never enter the artistic pantheon in Russia, but, long forgotten in the United States, he is still exhibited periodically and with a good deal of publicity at the Pushkin Museum.

Picasso in Thaw Culture, 1956–1966

While the impressionists had exonerated subjective vision, and Kent had broadened the definition of realism, it was Pablo Picasso who pushed audiences beyond realism. His 1956 exhibition in Moscow and Leningrad has acquired an epic significance in the memoirs of underground artists, political dissidents, and ordinary people who came of age during the Thaw. In memoirs, the exhibition functions as a biographical milestone and a shorthand notation for the Thaw itself: "suddenly, the Picasso exhibition was opened"; "and so, it was the year 1956."[182] Accounts of the exhibition describe clamor and commotion: large crowds break through museum gates; people speak loudly and agitatedly; outlandish young men defend modernism passionately, while equally earnest guardians of socialist realism try to shout them down. In the words of one such young man, "I would join the arguing crowd, reach its center, and there, losing my voice and gesticulating violently, try to convince."[183] When words failed to convince, museumgoers occasionally came to blows: "What an event that was, the artist's fans and his defamers scuffled at the entrance to the Hermitage." At the Pushkin Museum, it was "so loud that the police were called," but this could not prevent young people from expelling a particularly vociferous opponent of Picasso's work.[184] The dominant experience of the exhibition was revelation, "such as we hadn't seen": "For us everything was 'ah!'"[185]

In 1956, Picasso was not altogether fresh news in the Soviet Union. During the first postrevolutionary years, Soviet observers had written about him astutely and thoughtfully, if not always sympathetically. His drawings had been displayed in the 1920s, and throughout the first half of the 1930s, plans for a large exhibition of French art had consistently included Picasso.[186] Above all, Moscow's Museum of Contemporary Western Art had been home to one of the world's best collections of his early work. What made Picasso fresh news in the mid-1950s was his ambiguous place in the politics of the late 1940s. On the one hand, he was a prominent member of the French Communist Party, who generously devoted his time and money to communist causes; on the other hand, during the anticosmopolitan campaign, he was deemed an artistic persona non grata.[187] Anticosmopolitanism bequeathed these tensions to the 1956 exhibition planners.

The exhibition was the work of the All-Union Society for Cultural Ties with Foreign Countries (VOKS) and its "sector of the friends of French science and culture," under Ilya Ehrenburg's leadership. An avant-garde poet and expatriate in Paris at the turn of the century, Ehrenburg had frequented the same bohemian circles as Picasso, and the two maintained a warm relationship throughout the 1930s and 1940s. Ehrenburg associated Picasso with cultural cataclysms, abiding youthful idealism, and nostalgia for the Paris of his own youth.[188] The Picasso exhibition was a deeply personal matter for him. He appealed to the Central Committee, and his strategy worked: in September 1956, it approved the exhibition.[189] The timing, however, was hardly propitious. The idea of a Picasso exhibition had been initially broached in 1954, and perhaps that would have been a more congenial year, when even the president of the arch-conservative Academy of Arts, Aleksandr Gerasimov, was willing to greet Picasso in person.[190] But in the intervening two years, members of the artistic unions had begun talking about "creative freedom." In late 1953 and early 1954, several articles in professional art journals revealed that true socialist realism embraced different "forms, styles, and genres," not to mention "creative initiative."[191] Art regained a lofty purpose: at professional forums, artists spoke in ethical, even religious, terms about their erstwhile betrayal of a high calling for the sake of politics.[192] In early 1956, a closed party meeting of the Moscow branch of the Artists' Union (MOSKh) witnessed the most concerted effort yet to extend the parameters of socialist realism. There, one after another, artists stood up to challenge the concept of realism delimited by nineteenth-century Russian genre painting. MOSKh went so far as to propose reopening the Museum of Contemporary Western Art.[193] In fall and winter of 1956, on the eve of the First All-Union Congress of Soviet Artists, the discourse in the art press became especially divisive. Debates focused on how and who should define realism, and how much subjectivity, individuality, and stylistic diversity the concept allowed.[194] Picasso was rarely mentioned in these early meetings and debates, but they constituted the environment in which his exhibition took place. In the feverish atmosphere of calls for "creative freedom," the Picasso exhibition portended yet more discussions, more provocative statements, more unwelcome comparisons.

Therefore, the Central Committee's resolution mandated a "small" show, with drawings and prints from Soviet museums and private collections, and with little advance publicity. The exhibition was to be handled entirely by VOKS, so that Picasso would be celebrated not so much for his art as for his politics. The Academy of Arts would deliberately remain in the background. For VOKS officials, however, the academy's participation was crucial, as it would lend the exhibition cultural legitimacy.[195] At the Pushkin Museum and the Hermitage, curators were accustomed to following annual and quarterly plans, which included educating consultants and preparing catalogues, posters, and press announcements. But in this case, Pushkin Museum experts were not trained to explain the artworks correctly; no posters publicized the exhibition; no catalogues were printed; and Picasso did not become a topic of a learned conversation at the museum's "academic council."[196] Many museumgoers in Moscow and Leningrad were "indignant about the absence of a consultant at this exhibition, where he [was] especially necessary."[197] After the exhibition, in its annual report to the Ministry of Culture, the Pushkin Museum could do no better than offer excuses: "The Picasso exhibition was not planned."[198] The Central Committee's hush-hush strategy had important, if unanticipated, consequences for how viewers experienced this event—as confusion, loss of control, and unconstrained speech.

While VOKS did not quite get its wish for the academy's participation and for publicity, neither did the Central Committee get its wish for a small affair. As it happened, Picasso himself did not share the Central Committee's plans.[199] He insisted on a chronologically and stylistically broad retrospective—and he handpicked from his personal collection twenty-five paintings that conveyed the diversity of his approaches and interests. Each stylistic milestone was exemplified by an artwork, ranging from the realist portraits of Picasso's mother, his first wife Olga, and his son Paulo as Harlequin and Pierrot, to the early 1950s paintings and prints of his children, Claude and Paloma, with distorted bodies and overblown faces. The early 1920s were also represented by a massive, sculpturesque *Maternity. Seated Woman with a Book*, consisting of rectangular patches, and *Musical Instruments* complemented the cubist paintings in the Soviet museums. The 1930s were to begin with the merry *Still Life on a Pedestal Table* and to end with the ferocious *Cat and Bird*. Along the way, there were several multiview paintings with dislocated facial features, *Woman with a Book* and *Woman with Yellow Hair*. Picasso appears to have kept his audience in mind and did not forget the more palatable preparatory sketches for *Man with a Lamb* and two drawings of doves.[200]

To the chagrin of Soviet officials, Picasso had sent his paintings, drawings, and ceramics to the Soviet Embassy in Paris before they had a chance to object or dissuade him. There the artworks sat, waiting to be shipped to the Soviet Union. Returning them would have been an unthinkable affront to Western leftist intellectuals, and so the artworks were accepted.[201] Soviet curators supplemented the show with items from the Shchukin and Morozov collections.[202] To demonstrate "the early, realist phase," the exhibition at the Hermitage was augmented with the tragic, angular, and lonely figures of the Blue period: *Absinthe Drinker, The Two Sisters, Portrait of Soler,* and *Portrait of Jaime Sabartés*. The curators of the Western European art department, who had spent most of their lives in the museum and recalled the anticosmopolitan campaign with a collective shudder, also wished for a wide-ranging exhibition. They presented cubist guitars, violins, clarinets, and pears, as well as *Woman with a Fan, Dance of the Veils,* and *Three Women*. Many years later, one of the curators would recall, "You had to witness it, how there was nothing, and then [the paintings] returned" from their exile in the vaults.[203]

As the paintings returned, the two museums lost the atmosphere of restrained contemplation befitting "temples of culture." At the Pushkin Museum, visitors queued for five hours in the cold of late fall and early winter; exposition rooms were crammed; people elbowed each other and shouted.[204] These excited passions were not primarily about transparency of content; viewers conceded that much of Picasso was not easily accessible. What troubled them was whether Picasso spoke "the truth," even when they did not understand his means of doing so. Comment writers used the prevalent vocabulary of sincerity and truth seeking. For many, it was "not always intelligible, but, surely, . . . enormous and sincere art. For it is said, 'seek and thou shall find'"—Picasso's very quest assured his honesty. While for some people Picasso was a truth seeker, for others he was a truth teller; as several students affirmed in a comment, "Picasso would not lie to us."[205] Those viewers who detested the paintings spoke in similar terms: "No, true Soviet youth would not be deceived by Picasso. There is no secret and no mysticism in his 'works.'"[206] Their comments were filled with evocations of deception: "mockery," "distorted mirrors," "grimacing," "palming off," "mystery," "enigma," "devilry," "seduction." The show felt like a prank or a lie: Was Picasso serious? Or maybe it was a trick, and we are supposed to laugh with him, lest he laugh at us?[207] What today may sound like a regurgitation of newspaper speak was for them the expression of thoughtful, independent, "courageous, honest," "private opinion," in opposition to "the official opinion."[208] Was this not an officially sanctioned exhibition? Was it not held in the Soviet shrine of high culture?[209] And did not Ehrenburg, the Soviet Union's chief connoisseur of art, liken Picasso to the "Renaissance masters," to "his great predecessors Michelangelo, Rembrandt, Goya," to Leonardo da Vinci himself?[210]

Ehrenburg did even more to disarm potential critics. While professional art periodicals remained silent, the journal *Foreign Literature* featured his article "The Drawings of Pablo Picasso." The article made that issue of the journal a bibliographic rarity, perpetually missing from regional libraries.[211] Published on the eve of the exhibition, the article situated Picasso within the confrontation between revolution and reaction, good and evil that Ehrenburg's readers understood best. It began with Picasso's childhood and his introduction to the art world via drawings of doves; at the end of the article, as the aged artist sent his doves to all corners of the earth, the child in the artist returned. "Picasso's doves are astonishingly pure, moving, and also defenseless, like a child, and invincible, like the people's conscience." Picasso was an "artist-revolutionary," a "furious rebel," "the greatest inventor." So iconoclastic and groundbreaking was his art that it made him vulnerable to charges of "Bolshevism in painting"—charges whose validity he confirmed by becoming a communist in life.[212] Picasso's detractors were the paradigmatic forces of evil, Hitler and Truman, the former having banished his paintings from museums, the latter having labeled his art "depraved" and "corrupting." In Ehrenburg's quotations, the two used rhetoric similar to that of Soviet critics in the 1940s.[213]

People often had read this article before visiting the museum and responded to it, directly or indirectly, in their comments. The scant information then available about Picasso, including Ehrenburg's article, which allocated much space to the creation of *Guernica* from the debris of the destroyed city, focused on Picasso's membership in the Communist Party, his 1950 International Peace Prize, and his antiwar stance in painting and politics. But viewers had trouble reconciling communism with cubism. An elderly woman had seen a Picasso painting in the 1920s and now faced "three or four terrible women," "a revoltingly concocted picture . . . (where do you see naked women of brown color?)" She was astonished to learn from an encyclopedia that this same artist was "a communist and our contemporary, and that he had drawn the 'peace dove,' a symbol of peace."[214] Perhaps, suggested another viewer, E. I. Bliumina, writing to Ehrenburg from Viatka in Belorussia, the distorted pictures were accidental, while Picasso's dove, "which, without a doubt, has nothing to do with abstractionism, but, on the contrary, has great realist meaning," was the core of his work.[215]

Or perhaps what viewers encountered was not cubism, but an unfamiliar form of realism. According to one student, this "realism" "was the most correct and most truthful, most necessary" kind of realism, more so than replicas of the classics. It was a realism of the twentieth century, "in which everything is movement and swiftness of perception"; it was a realism for the young, who "feel our age in Picasso's paintings." Such comments registered keen awareness of generation and time: "our era," the distinctiveness of the twentieth century, and Picasso's unique capacity to respond to its terror and thrill. Identifying themselves with "the era" and its chronicler, viewers insisted that the paintings' realism came not from timelessness but from temporal immediacy.[216] Just as acutely, some people recognized that they were living in a special year and described 1956 as a watershed.

The opening of the exhibition was central to this recognition. One student thought it was "the greatest event in our cultural life, at least in the last ten years"—or even in several decades, as Ehrenburg, in a legendary statement, told the frenzied crowd anxious to get into the museum: "Comrades, you have waited for this exhibition for twenty-five years, now wait calmly for twenty-five minutes."[217] The exhibition was an invitation to rebel against the past—as Picasso had done.

For those who exalted in Picasso, "the past" was the Stalinist past, and it meant obscurantism, obsoleteness, and isolationism, or, in the words of Ehrenburg's readers, the "Great Wall of China" separating "us from Western culture."[218] After reading Ehrenburg's memoirs in 1963, twenty-six-year-old engineer M. Avaev extracted the phrase "iron curtain" from newspaper denunciations of capitalism and imperialism and projected it onto the domestic cultural context: "An iron curtain used to divide art into official art and art for the soul, for the people. The great artists who had belonged to movements other than socialist realism had been a proscribed subject . . . during the time of the cult of personality." Between the "time of the cult of personality" and 1963, Avaev and the generation for whom he claimed to speak had realized just "how uneducated we are, how 'gray' we are."[219]

Similarly, a twenty-four-year-old soldier blamed a "lack of education" for his inability to understand Picasso. A former mechanic trained at a factory technical school and now serving in the army, Aleksandr Liakhovitskii visited the Picasso exhibition at the Hermitage during a trip to Leningrad in 1956. To his "great regret, most of the paintings were not yet altogether clear for [him]," but he was convinced that diligent study would bring a better understanding. Aleksandr compared Picasso to the early Mayakovsky, whom he studied "line by line," "sometimes in the evenings, together" with his fellow servicemen. Wishing to master Picasso in the same way, he searched for information everywhere in Leningrad and Narva, where he had been stationed, but "there [was] nothing to read about [the paintings], and almost nobody to ask." And so, several years after the exhibition, in pursuit of the images (*Cat and Bird, The Two Saltimbanques*) that had seized his memory, Aleksandr wrote to Ehrenburg asking for photographs of Picasso's paintings. In response, Ehrenburg sent some reprints, and we can envision how young men from military unit 41035 scrutinized these pictures.[220]

Picasso's was not yet an intelligible art, but it was nonetheless breathtaking. And it was not yet too late, but it was already too little: "We want [to see] Matisse after Picasso. We want [a] fuller exhibition of Picasso's production. We want the freedom of the [*sic*] discussion."[221] At the Picasso exhibition, museumgoers got exactly what they wanted; the Pushkin Museum personnel, unprepared and overwhelmed, simply ceded the parquet battleground. "Viewers interpret[ed] on their own, argue[d]," and were delighted: "[There were] discussions at the exhibition, conversations," "heated arguments . . . debates right here, in the gallery, all highly portentous."[222]

It was all highly portentous because, in 1956–1957, heated arguments and debates broke out in student dormitories, Komsomol cells, editorial offices, artists' meetings, and city squares. Without official approval but with "artistic freedom" as their slogan, students gathered to talk about Picasso in several institutes and at Moscow State University.[223] In Leningrad, debate spilled beyond the Hermitage onto the streets when students decided to hold a discussion in Arts Square, for lack of a better place. They gathered, only to postpone the meeting until the following week—a plan that the local party authorities interpreted as malicious. According to the regional party secretary, the meeting's instigators were "a small group of students," perhaps the same ones who, at the Hermitage, "displayed an uncritical attitude toward formalist works of foreign art, considering Picasso's paintings the highest accomplishment." But according to the meeting's participants, "there was nothing illicit there"; they came to talk about art, not politics. On the evening of December 21, the students (300 to 500 people by various counts) gathered again, but some were promptly apprehended by the police before they had a chance to start their discussion.

Having been ordered to disperse, the students walked to the Leningrad branch of the Artists' Union (LOSKh).[224] Just then, a select group of viewers, many from the factory bench, assembled at LOSKh to evaluate an exhibition of Leningrad artists. Until the students arrived, the viewers' conference had proceeded according to the customary Soviet ritual of criticism and self-criticism, so that "the artists [could] better realize weaknesses and deficiencies in their creative activity." The student intruders, professing admiration for Picasso and comparing him to Beethoven, argued that "true" art was inaccessible to the masses. Appreciating "true" art was the prerogative of people with special acumen and aesthetic sensibilities. Local party officials had little doubt that the Leningrad University and Conservatory students positioned themselves among the elect. Nonetheless, the regional party committee concluded its report to Moscow on a reassuring note: it was "taking measures . . . to suppress the encroachments of hostile anti-Soviet elements," the Artists' Union "strengthened the propaganda of socialist realism in visual art," and, in any case, such hostile elements were few.[225]

The Central Committee, however, was not convinced, because the arguments were only tenuously about Picasso.[226] They were about Soviet art—indeed, politics—and Picasso's name was shorthand for everything that domestic culture was not. Words already had triumphed over images at the Hermitage, where, according to one curator, "the audience no longer looked at the paintings . . . [She] recall[s] how [she] wanted to say, for God's sake, just look at the paintings."[227] But many were too busy arguing, their aesthetic pronouncements easily mistaken for political attitudes or ethical comportment. Viewers who declared, "My grandson can draw this ten times better," risked hearing the retort, "But it is clear that you've been a police informer."[228] On December 21, the most rousing address, delivered by Conservatory student Yuliia Krasovskaia, became a city legend overnight, both for its content and for the arrest of its author. The speech was not about Picasso's art per se. Rather, his name connoted the very possibility of divergent opinions:

> About the Picasso exhibition. I am not a Picasso apologist . . .
> Maybe I am not mature enough, maybe this is not real art. One thing was exciting there—the atmosphere of lively debate, when people wanted to discover how art should develop.
>
> The problem is that the concept of socialist realism, which has been hammered into our heads since grade school, has completely discredited itself. /Applause/
>
> In my opinion, socialist realism as such does not exist. /Applause/ . . .
>
> They say that students reject socialist realism. That's nonsense! We do not reject it; we don't see it. Show us [socialist realism] and we will gladly stand by it. /Applause/

More than art was at stake for Krasovskaia and her audience: "Comrades, I want to say that even in my short life, I have noticed how we have a very stagnant atmosphere not only in painting, not only in music, . . . but generally in all public opinions." As Krasovskaia announced, "we came here to finally talk about something, but a police unit followed us." In her rendering, students were like prisoners or camp inmates, and innocence and youth were pitted against brutal force.[229] "Picasso," "students," and police squadrons were figurative terms as much as a reality of 1956.

The identification of the seventy-five-year-old Picasso with youthfulness was strong enough to make its way into participants' memoirs. Boris Vail', presenting the Picasso affair as a milestone on his way to political dissent, recalled the LOSKh auditorium, where spatial divisions corresponded to generational ones—the "decorous public" in the stalls, the students, some with long hair, in the gallery.[230] "The respectable public," established artists, party officials, university administrators, and other adults likewise depicted Picasso's admirers as bohemians: disheveled, unkempt youth wearing narrow trousers.[231] These associations lived on beyond the exhibition, beyond 1956, to resonate in literature. In his 1960 poem "The Nihilist," Evgenii Evtushenko paired Picasso with innocence and youth. This was how authorities in school and at home saw the poem's protagonist, a student who loved Picasso, rejected socialist realism, committed stock ideological offenses, and appeared a hopeless case. But in the end, "the nihilist" saved a friend's life, losing his own in the process, and thereby proved his moral superiority. His death redeemed all that he had embraced in life— Picasso, slim-legged trousers, passionate arguments.[232]

Report after report from all levels of the Komsomol and the party described the passionate arguments, unauthorized meetings, brazen captiousness, and "demagogic speeches" occurring in institutions of higher learning across the country. Labeled as "demagogues," "nihilists," "wavering intellectuals," or "accidental elements," students seized public spaces to deliver their "pessimistic pronouncements" and "unhealthy views." All this— especially the zeal, ostentation, and scale—looked so bizarre that municipal party authorities dispatched special inspectors to various universities; the inspectors, for their part, could do no better to explain the situation than to point fingers at fictitious "outsiders" of questionable morals.[233] "Style-chasers" and "vulgar women" "infiltrated" the Picasso discussion at the Architectural Institute. There, professors and party officials surrendered the podium to "students from other universities," who "underrated the achievements of Soviet art, . . . defamed our art and Soviet reality."[234] The discussion on "Poetry and Public Life" at the Gorky Literature Institute also went amiss; the atmosphere was "unhealthy," there were whistles and catcalling, and some speakers abandoned party guidance for alternative authorities—chief among them, Picasso.[235] Central to what had gone awry that year was the fact of the discussion itself: the idea of unhampered speech, the right of assembly, open criticism, uninhibited conversation, and creativity.[236] Particularly farsighted authorities, like the director of the Moscow Pedagogical Institute, moved swiftly to nip Picasso discussions in the bud. He was afraid, not of the unfamiliar art itself, but of the symbolic associations with debate and publicity that "Picasso" unleashed in the course of the exhibition. "The discussion," he cautioned, "could have become an anarchic rally on any issue."[237]

In 1956, many young people "sought a Teacher, with a capital T," and half a century later, they would recall this search and the "astound[ing]" Picasso exhibition in the same line of thought.[238] The Great Father was gone and the Great Family was in disarray. To paraphrase another poem by Evtushenko, nobody really wanted to be "Stalin's heir."[239] Progeny without patrimony, they became Picasso's heirs.

After the exhibition, Picasso remained a conspicuous presence in conversations and museum catalogues. In the late 1950s and early 1960s, firsthand accounts of "a visit to Picasso" proliferated in the Soviet press, reaching far more people than the thousands who came to the Pushkin Museum and the Hermitage in 1956. Before critics could generate a professional assessment of Picasso's art, the image of Picasso as "a compelling cultural hero" had emerged in biographical and anecdotal sketches.[240] His Soviet acquaintances singled out characteristics that reflected their own aesthetic and political world at least as much as that of their hero. Consider the prominent themes: the innocence of the artist-child; the spontaneity of the artist as *homo ludens*; modesty, austerity, and unpretentiousness; and an attachment to folklore and national traditions as proof of the artist's connection to "the people." Developed by the literati, these images became the building blocks in interpretive articles that multiplied in the 1960s.

Personal testimonies and the portrait they offered were key to the process whereby the Soviet cultural establishment admitted Picasso into its pantheon of classics. Through a series of encounters and conversations with Picasso, the avant-garde filmmaker turned propagandist Sergei Yutkevich presented the artist as an *ingénu*. A Francophile, Yutkevich traveled to France frequently as a member of Soviet delegations and a juror at the Cannes film festival; he did not pass up opportunities to visit Picasso. The artist of his descriptions was an unassuming man of the people: Picasso's villa "[wa]s furnished modestly," even "ascetically"; he invariably wore a black sweater, while his formal attire, buried deep in some closet, was wrinkled, faded, and outmoded.[241] A decade later, in a radio program about Picasso, Yutkevich would refer to him as a "hospitable French toiler," his black sweater now fashioned into the recognizable outfit of "dockers, metal workers, or freight drivers."[242] As for fame, "he does not think about his fame at all, and every time he receives yet another proof of it, he is surprised like a spontaneous child." "Child" was another of Yutkevich's recurrent characterizations: Picasso dressed up in costumes, assumed various gaits, or wore a clown's nose.[243]

Other writings of the 1960s echoed these stories of pranks and transformations and depicted Picasso as a teller of fairy tales or as a fairy-tale creature himself ("a legendary troll"). His art assumed magical qualities.[244] In one of the more insightful and sympathetic essays on Picasso's fantasy world, literary critic Dmitrii Moldavskii discussed cubism as "a striving for simplicity and clarity" akin to the "folk ornaments of the European peoples."[245] Moldavskii became a devotee of Picasso after seeing the artist's drawings on the walls of Yutkevich's apartment—a small gallery the film-maker used to assess the sensibilities of his visitors. Having passed this test, Moldavskii went on to investigate Picasso's impact on Yutkevich's cinematography and on the prose of writer Valentin Kataev.[246] For his part, Kataev took the artist's child-like simplicity a step further—to accessibility. "Picasso has a child's soul, pure, primeval, lucid," and that was why, according to Kataev, adults failed to understand him, but children "unravel in a split second the secret intention of the artist-genius."[247] These techniques of familiarization underpinned critical attempts to explain and popularize Picasso during the 1960s.

Knowing that most of their readers had not seen his art, critics recounted feelings and associations triggered by the paintings. They tried to exemplify the mental work that goes (or should go) into aesthetic reception.[248] Much of this work was associational, requiring viewers to "make inferences from images": "The objects are linked; they speak to each other . . . The contours of a woman's face take the oval shape of a dove. The brows wreathe into an olive branch. And what is this? Hair? Or the wings of a dove?"[249] Most authors agreed that Picasso's pictures reflected not reality but its refraction in the artist's mind, and they increasingly saw nothing wrong with this.[250] Picasso popularizers broke the pictures down into their constituent elements and explained the effects of deformation and use of color.[251]

The authors who most consistently engaged the reader-viewer in this way were Igor' Golomshtok, a specialist in contemporary Western art, and Andrei Siniavskii, a literary scholar. Their 1960 brochure *Picasso* was the first professional study of the artist published in Russian since 1933. Golomshtok and Siniavskii abandoned the obsession with narrative that characterized Soviet art criticism. Instead, true to their thesis that Picasso created "paintings as concepts, paintings as symbols," they interpreted hidden meanings in his work. Golomshtok had worked as a guide at the Picasso exhibition in 1956 and was experienced in answering viewers' questions. The two authors anticipated readers' reactions, wrote about an "unprepared gaze" and a "first encounter," and structured the brochure as an instructional manual, alternating illustrations and explanations.[252] A product of cross-disciplinary, literary and visual analyses, the brochure attested to the Soviet literati's infatuation with Picasso. Accompanied by Ehrenburg's personal account and a version of his 1956 article, the brochure also represented the symbiosis of scholarly and memoiristic writing that was central to Picasso's domestication in the Soviet Union.[253]

Just as the brochure was going to press, the journal *Novyi mir* began to serialize Ehrenburg's memoirs *People, Years, Life*. The first volume contained an entire chapter about Picasso. It was much the same text as Ehrenburg's 1956 article and the brochure's account, but printed in *Novyi mir*, it reached a wider audience than any previous publication. The chapter looked at Picasso through the prism of Ehrenburg's own life and the life of prewar and wartime Europe. Ehrenburg placed Picasso among other exiles in Paris, amid their pranks, prophesies, poverty, and scandals; he reappeared in the narrative when Ehrenburg wrote about personal crisis and confusion in times of general foreboding and apocalyptic expectations. Even the structure of the memoirs confirmed Picasso's place among momentous events—the chapter was set between a frenzied account of World War I and the news of the tsar's abdication.[254] By thus positioning Picasso, the memoirs legitimized him as a subject of scholarly inquiries and poetic musings.

Without Ehrenburg's memoirs, it is impossible to make sense of the outpouring of Picasso-related poetry in the 1960s. In Pavel Antokol'skii's poetic cycle "Picasso," the atmosphere was decidedly fin-de-siècle ("Merriment and ruin all around"). Like Ehrenburg's memoirs, the poem placed Picasso "on the brink of two worlds," on the "eve" of World War I, amid revolutionary "fireballs" that illuminated the "utter darkness" of "the night" enveloping Europe.[255] Antokol'skii's Picasso was a prophet, who confronted God about the principles of creation. Picasso occupied a special place in Antokol'skii's universe. He kept the artist's portrait on the wall across from his desk; he "liked the Kabbala of names: Pablo Picasso . . . Pablo Antokol'skii."[256]

Picasso was thus mediated for Soviet readers through the poetic Word. And one of the most powerful, as well as officially recognized, poetic words belonged to Vladimir Mayakovsky. He had visited Picasso's studio in 1922 and jotted down brief, complimentary impressions, which were endlessly reproduced in the 1960s.[257] In legitimizing Picasso's demolition of form, in discussing cubism more generally, critics relied on the poet's name and clout. They excerpted Mayakovsky's verses as explanations for Picasso's images and identified both as "rebels" against bourgeois society.[258] In the late 1950s and early 1960s, Mayakovsky's posthumous popularity was at its peak. The new monument to him in central Moscow became a symbolic hub of youthful creativity and protest. "Young poets" claimed his mentorship and mixed his rhymes with their own.[259] Many who wrote about Picasso originally had trained as Mayakovsky scholars or had been profoundly affected by his poetry.

The comparison was not merely an expedient justification. Mayakovsky provided the conceptual basis for understanding Picasso. In a study of interactions between painting and poetry, the literary scholar Vladimir Al'fonsov confirmed aesthetic affinities between Mayakovsky and Picasso. As Al'fonsov saw it, both communicated through complex associations. Both deformed images to achieve maximum expressiveness. And both abandoned "individualized narratives" for universalized statements, such as *Guernica*, which Al'fonsov and others considered a Mayakovskian painting.[260] Perhaps nowhere else, save for France, was Picasso such a recurrent poetic presence—as a common noun, a dedication, and a companion of gods. Ultimately, when critics had to identify Picasso in one precise word, they called him a poet.[261]

In 1966–1967, a version of Ehrenburg's memoirs appeared together with scholarly analyses in the first Picasso album. This volume explored Picasso's themes, colors, allegories, and "special aesthetic universe" in a way that left readers with no doubt: "It is unquestionable; Picasso is a veritable artistic genius." Opening with Picasso's signature rendered in Cyrillic, the album was an instructional guide for reading his artworks; every page contained four or five illustrations with explanations about the effects of lines, distortions, decorativeness, and symbolic and historical references.[262] The album summed up the decade's efforts at teaching audiences how to look at new art.

The occasion for the album was another Picasso exhibition in Moscow and Leningrad, held in 1966 to mark his eighty-fifth birthday. This time the focus was on graphics, with some familiar drawings, lithographs, and ceramics from Soviet collections, plus over a hundred prints from the Louise Leiris Gallery in Paris. The pride of the exhibition was a selection of engravings from the *Vollard Suite* with neoclassical figuration and mythological subjects (the series *The Sculptor's Studio*, *The Minotaur*, and *The Blind Minotaur*). On display, too, were *The Painter and His Model* of 1954 and 1963–1964—prints in which Picasso reassessed the problem of artistic creation. These, as well as *The Smoker* series, presented distorted figures and faces, but the retrospective also included the 1954 classicist explorations of masquerade and voyeurism, *Dance of the Banderillas* and *The Rehearsal*.[263] Unlike ten years earlier, this event received press coverage, a catalogue, and an album. Much of this output was a discourse on genius, with images developed in the preceding decade: Picasso as homo ludens, magician, child.[264] In homage, Soviet newspapers printed reportage from France, in which journalists told of the Picasso retrospective in Paris and popular festivities in Vallauris, where he had lived in the 1950s. These reports placed the Soviet Union in a worldwide community of Picasso admirers; "all of mankind" celebrated the artist, and *Pravda* wished to leave nobody behind, reprinting the news in its provincial edition.[265]

Accordingly, viewers came to the 1966 exhibition with certain expectations about Picasso. If a single common thread ran through the comment book, it was citations of his "great name" and "indisputable authority." And yet, almost 70 percent of comment writers did dispute his authority—and not only his, for they responded as much to what they had read about Picasso as to what they saw at the exhibition.[266] In structure, hostile comments followed the logic of a rebuff, restating the accepted position ("with all due respect to Picasso as a public figure"; "there is an illustrious signature"; "despite his universal recognition") and proceeding to its negation ("but none of this means that we should propagandize him here in Russia"). Many challenged the status of the name itself: "The name of the author and his deeds will be forgotten by posterity."[267] They had read about Picasso's politics, his fame, his genius, and much of their resentment came from frustrated expectations, from feelings of having been cheated. "Is this Picasso?!" viewers repeatedly asked.[268] "I came to the Picasso exhibition with great interest. And I am leaving with even greater disappointment. I don't know what the organizers of the exhibition wanted to show, but they clearly did not show us what we respected in the artist," wrote one official. A student found the exhibition "offensive" for its "mediocrity," for the lack of something "significant," something one would expect from "a world-famous artist, intelligent, subtle."[269] Viewers who left negative comments frequently spoke of disenchantment, of the long-awaited and longed-for "meeting" with Picasso, of the respect and love they had accorded the artist, a genius and a hero.[270]

When people professed their love for Picasso, they meant his *Young Acrobat on a Ball* and, more generally, his paintings of the Blue and Rose periods in Soviet museums.[271] *Young Acrobat on a Ball*, on display at the Pushkin Museum since the mid-1950s, was one of the most frequently reproduced foreign paintings in popular publications.[272] Viewers, thus, had in mind *their* Picasso. Konstantin Otpiakin, an elderly teacher who had reservations about the present exhibition, still admired Picasso's "large paintings in the Pushkin Museum." Although outraged by the drawings, another visitor, technician Tat'iana Vasilenko, modified her verdict: "Some pictures at this exhibition are not so bad, but the best ones are the acquisitions of our museum."[273] The Pushkin Museum thus helped viewers to acclaim—and to claim—the familiar Picasso: the one who *had become* familiar in the course of the decade.

As for those viewers who welcomed the exhibition, they too found the pictures "incomprehensible, . . . unusual, strange."[274] Yet, their self-referential vocabulary was (or became) different. By 1966, new words were appearing in the comments. In addition to "we," people now wrote of "the self" and "the soul," asserting its primacy over reason. They may not have understood the images, but "understanding everything was not necessary"; it was what happened to "the soul" that mattered.[275] They were willing to let Picasso into their world or to take a precarious journey into his. One visitor, who hoped to become an art critic some day, interpreted this journey as a merging of his own world with that of the artist: "Picasso [is] a philosopher who seeks (not in the sense of art but in the sense of life) and reflects his vision of reality in his own way . . . Picasso asserts himself and announces himself . . . and reverberates in my soul."[276] Reverberated almost literally, for viewers now described their visual experiences as audible: "everything is alive, it all rings," "the engravings are sonorous, ringing." In *The Rehearsal*, student L. Kraipova "could hear the rhythmic music of the man with the tambourine—tam-tam-tam."[277]

Music, but not noise. This is perhaps the most important difference between 1956 and 1966. During the opening ceremony at the 1956 exhibition, Ehrenburg had felt that Picasso was right there, standing behind a curtain, and it would take only a hand's motion to reveal his presence.[278] He was not the only one who felt this way. In 1956 Picasso was everywhere—as an enigma, a metaphor, and a cause. Picasso's presence was so palpable because it merged most immediately and memorably with student unrest and most organically with the nascent reevaluation of aesthetic values. Picasso's art was not the focus of student unrest and of grumbling in the creative unions, but he served as a convenient and prominent metaphor for expressing discontent and expectations. In 1966, the intense physical reactions of 1956, the scuffles and screaming, were no more. There were conversations, to be sure, and rather strong emotions were evident in the comments, but there was no scandal, commotion, or display of passions.[279] The projection of politics onto art had become less immediate, while political debate had shifted to other, covert places. Gone were the insistence on truth and the demand for open discussions and creative freedom. Viewers no longer thought of art exhibitions as revelatory experiences or opportunities to stage urgent debates. When the dissidents of the mid-1960s assembled in city squares, they had no plans to discuss art; they carried political slogans. Gone, too, was the confrontational stance with which a young generation had announced its presence in 1956. In 1966 the audience consisted mostly of middle-aged people, whose serious, concentrated faces were captured in photographs and documentary sequences filmed at the exhibition.[280] Few comments associated Picasso with youth, unhampered discussion, freedom, or revelation.[281] The 1966 exhibition never entered the lore of youth culture; nor did it become a memoiristic myth. By the late 1960s, museums once again had become places of detached contemplation.

Western art exhibitions stirred violent passions, because modernist paintings challenged deep-seated notions of culture and the prevalent narrative of Russian-Soviet cultural ascendancy. What created such a shocking and upending effect were not only stylistically unfamiliar artworks but the violation, time and again, of the sacred space of the museum. The thousands of angry, bitter, mocking, or abusive comments that viewers felt compelled to write were fundamentally about barbarity, the most basic notion of foreignness. This theme overlaid others: true art versus charlatanry, painterliness versus literariness, the Soviet Union versus the West. Viewers remarked on cultural regression in the West and attributed modernist paintings to primitive man, deranged minds, or destructive impulses. The Soviet Union, by contrast, was the preserve of culture in a world gone mad, animalistic, and brutal. Russian ascendancy was made possible by Soviet socialism: this was a point both of dogma and conceit. It was next to this exclamatory point that Western art exhibitions, and the Thaw more broadly, put a question mark. Arrogance upon encountering languages (including visual languages) that we do not understand is common to our post-Babelian provincialism.[282] Soviet specificity lay in the entrenched assumption of cultural transparency: foreign life was not opaque, and the key to understanding it was art, particularly painting. The universality of images had long been taken for granted, until modernist exhibitions from the West began arriving in the mid-1950s.

At these exhibitions people discovered alternative definitions of art and sometimes sadly confessed to the absence of culture in the Soviet Union. An emerging new sensibility was marked by greater tolerance, cultural relativism, and a more expansive understanding of painting beyond classical notions of beauty and harmony. This sensibility called for "modesty" about Russian-Soviet ascendancy and the cultural fluency of the Soviet people.[283] Perhaps Russian-Soviet culture was neither central to the rest of the world nor the quintessence of its best achievements—"we have fallen behind the West," "hopelessly, by a hundred years," and "our aesthetic taste is blatantly backward, illiterate," "how poorly, absurdly, . . . stupidly, and barbarously we understand art in all of its complexity and multiplicity."[284] Such comments overturned the discourse on the barbarity of others. Now, some Soviet viewers were calling themselves barbarian. The location of "true art," identified with great confidence as the Tretyakov Gallery in the historic center of Moscow, was gradually moving elsewhere: to the margins of Soviet culture and even beyond its geopolitical and ideological borders—to the West. Something was thus lost at these exhibitions: stable definitions, cultural confidence (or arrogance), a sense of transparency and coherence, as well as a certain innocence.

It is remarkable just how far from the Pushkin Museum in Moscow or Arts Square in Leningrad the aesthetic ideas, foreign names, and brash language circulated. Those who were unable to visit museums had access to these ideas through books and albums; and where the printed word did not reach, the radio did. Soviet visual culture was made in the virtual spaces of radio lectures, popularizing brochures, exquisite memoirs, encyclopedia invectives, and readers' letters. Thanks to the radio and print, the geography of curiosity, self-doubt, and polemical rage spanned the Russian-speaking population around the country, and everywhere these aesthetic experiences were politically and culturally divisive.[285]

From consulting and cross-referencing encyclopedia entries to writing comments at museum exits, reading and writing were fundamental to visual experiences. Indeed, verbal texts were at the heart of Soviet visual culture from the 1930s through the 1950s. This was why the central conflict in the visual arts during the Thaw was about the specificity of the medium, about liberating painting from literature and vision from speech. As Ehrenburg boldly declared, and as many viewers would come to learn to their frustration or delight, paintings could not always be retold. Yet, the arguments for the autonomy of painting relied on literary narrative— on characterization, dramatization, and the act of retelling. Painting was still mediated through the literary Word. The very idea of the visual as a distinct experience was controversial and difficult to impress upon audiences. Modernist paintings displayed at Western art shows proved the least "translatable" of artifacts and were never comfortably domesticated in Soviet culture.[286]

6

Books and Borders

Exhibitions, books, movies, postcards, and art prints offered ways of journeying abroad. They defined the emotional and intellectual experiences of travel writing and reading, perhaps even of travel itself. Those privileged travelers who did visit Europe felt a startling sense of recognition: they already had seen it all in their mind's eye, and the trip only confirmed their earlier knowledge. Upon return, they brought back neorealist mise-en-scènes, Renaissance landscapes, the Paris of the impressionists, and a growing recognition that human bonds are universal.

In the Soviet Union, travel abroad was a textual work of the imagination. Travelers "read" cities. Trips were framed as literary and artistic pilgrimages and enclosed between covers.[1] For the country's most prolific traveler, Ilya Ehrenburg, cities were akin to books: they were dusty like old tomes, and he found refuge from insomnia in walking the streets, as one does in reading.[2] The book remained a centerpiece of travel experience and a prominent metaphor for the world. Journeys were mnemonic occasions for recalling books, each excursion entangled in a web of textual associations and stimulating further commentary on texts. As poet and translator Yakov Khelemskii explained, "every journey happens three times. The first is when the imagination travels in the footsteps of books, of beloved paintings, films, and dreams . . . The second journey happens in reality. And the third [one] you undertake upon returning, when you recollect and interpret your impressions." The first journey is the longest—it can last a lifetime.[3] For the majority of Soviet citizens, it was the only one available, lasting, indeed, a lifetime.

In Thaw culture, travelogue and memoir were intricately bound. As literary genres, the childhood memoir and the travelogue share a common history, the quest as a central plot, and an emotional disposition open to fantasy, misunderstandings, and wonder.[4] To go to Europe in the late 1950s and early 1960s was to cross time, relive childhood, and return home to mother's books and grandmother's stories.[5] Travel writers spoke of journeys and childhood in one breath: it was as children that they had made the first journey, vicariously, by reading. Childhood readings had transformed foreign cities into intimate and familiar sites. To the surprise of the travelers, they felt their long-awaited European journeys to be a return or a fleeting memory: after all, they had been there once upon a time. To a significant extent, the pleasure of the trip came from such moments of recognition.[6] As the origin of knowledge and wanderlust, "since childhood" was also the temporal referent for the audiences steeped in classical literature.[7]

Soviet travelogues were written for people who would never go abroad. Amid the chaotic flight, demographic catastrophes, and cataclysmic population movements of 1914–1956, a fundamental and unquestionable immobility marked the lives of the majority of the Soviet population. Throughout the 1930s, people were increasingly tied to places, in reality and imagination. The stiffest of restrictions on mobility was the impassability of Soviet borders. By the mid-1950s, closed borders had become the natural order of things, and travel abroad had become unthinkable.[8] Only in the late 1950s would people openly begin to question the normalcy of closed borders. By then, immobility had transformed any text into a travelogue: art historical studies, popular biographies, fiction, guidebooks, exhibition pictures, films, lectures, radio concerts, and memoirs. Closed geopolitical borders opened the borders of the genre.

Travel accounts raised questions of credibility and trust, questions characteristic of translation more broadly.[9] In the absence of firsthand experiences, how was one to verify and on what basis was one to believe these accounts? Countless pages hammered home the opposition between life under socialism and capitalism. According to Soviet propagandistic clichés, the Western world was inhabited by "ordinary peace-loving people," "fascist thugs," "fat cat" millionaires, and an honest, "progressive" intelligentsia. And there was the proverbial phrase—"let us turn the corner"—suggesting that merely a few steps from affluent shops, shiny cars, and fashionable people were dumpsters, dirt, dearth, and death. The travel genre was highly conventional, with obligatory itineraries, predictable encounters, and a stable ideological vocabulary.[10] For readers, these conventions were both meaningful and maddening. Evaluating the reality of such depictions was a matter of faith; people could only believe or disbelieve them. And increasingly, they had misgivings about poverty and misery, seeking instead representations of prosperity, comfort, and beauty. For everything else they saw and read—especially films—convinced them that Western life was incomparably better than their own.

The Politics of Tourism

Although for most people in the Soviet Union going abroad remained impossible, the Thaw witnessed a sustained discourse on the new accessibility of travel for all.[11] The expansion of foreign tourism was a cornerstone of peaceful coexistence. At the United Nations Assembly in June 1955, Foreign Minister Viacheslav Molotov announced the "first goals to be achieved" toward lasting peace ahead of the Geneva Summit. Among those goals, on a par with disarmament, dismantling military bases, and withdrawing allied troops from Germany, Molotov highlighted tourism.[12] Linking tourism to the reduction of conventional and nuclear weapons signified its new functions and importance. Between early 1955 and mid-1956, the Soviet government passed no fewer than five resolutions on the development of international tourism. The very concept of travel for pleasure was so thoroughly a political matter that the government allocated target numbers of foreign tourists according to specific diplomatic aims.[13] Tourism offered proof of new openness, determination in peace efforts, and innovation in international policy. Soviet peace campaigns were nothing new, but earlier initiatives had not been linked to cultural exchange and crossing borders. On the contrary, the previous widely propagandized "peace offensive" had served as the backdrop to the anticosmopolitan campaign; to rampant xenophobia, both popular and official; to the near-total absence of foreign visitors (save for diplomats and journalists); to closed borders and rejected visa applications.[14] Tourism was meant to tell the world that, this time, Soviet peace efforts went beyond propaganda.

In the next few years, the Soviet travel agency Intourist (established in 1929) revived its activities after the postwar standstill. Signing agreements with sixty-eight foreign firms, Intourist began building a substantial infrastructure to support foreign tourism and to welcome ever more foreigners with each passing year.[15] So many more, indeed, that in 1956 Intourist was overwhelmed by 28,000 visitors, more than 10,000 of them from capitalist countries. The next year, there were over 40,000 tourists, and in excess of 500,000 foreigners altogether, including businessmen, athletes, and members of delegations and diplomatic corps, some 30 percent of them from the capitalist world.[16] In 1960, 130,000 tourists were expected to visit the country, 50,000 from capitalist countries and 80,000 from the socialist bloc.[17] There were not enough hotel rooms, cars and buses, translators or staff with basic conversational knowledge of foreign languages. As Intourist officials realized, the number of sites for showcasing "Soviet accomplishments" was disappointingly paltry. Soon, tourists began to notice and tell others that they were all being shown the same handful of hospitals and factories.[18] On occasions, there was not even enough food.[19] It came as something of a shock that tourism is a seasonal activity. While staff and space were allotted according to an annual logic, the vast majority of tourists arrived in summer and early fall. "Chaos reigned," as 15,000 foreigners overran the capital in July and August 1956.[20] In those early years, 1955–1957, Intourist meetings were heady affairs. Officials brought bad news from all directions and all industries, but there also was intense excitement and a sense of novelty. No wonder so many things went amiss—after all, they were pioneers, or felt themselves as such, marveling at the pace of change.[21] In their eyes, time trouble made other troubles "forgivable." But in the eyes of the government other troubles were not forgivable: in September 1956, the Council of Ministers reprimanded Intourist chairman Vladimir Ankudinov and a host of lesser officials for massive failures in servicing tourists uncovered by an investigative commission from the Ministry of State Control.[22]

There was so much alarm in those initial years, because service was high-stakes politics. In the age of Sputnik and mass housing construction, tourism, like the Youth Festival, would allow foreigners to see for themselves that the country was no longer "backward, located somewhere on the fringes of world civilization," but industrialized, democratic, and modern.[23] Translators prided themselves on dispelling stories about bears, Ivans, and labor camps as "bourgeois propaganda" that "has seeped deeply into people's consciousness."[24] "For forty-two years, American propaganda has painted us in the eyes of Americans as some sort of uncouth, stymied people, uncultured, illiterate, impoverished, in tatters, [people] who don't know how to talk, who are afraid of a breeze of Western culture."[25] Indeed, translators' reports on work with foreigners registered a stereotyped amazement at how "ignorant foreigners were about Soviet life."[26] Tourists would learn, from the convincing power of personal experiences, that socialism did work—that, thanks to welfare provisions and noncapitalist labor relations, socialism was a more humane path to modern technology, productivity, and consumer society.[27] This was the veiled propagandistic purpose of tourism.

Tourist itineraries became openly propagandistic in 1960, in the wake of the U-2 spy plane crisis, as Soviet-American relations deteriorated rapidly and the East-West summit in Paris collapsed.[28] The fear of trafficking with foreigners had been always close to the surface, but in the early 1960s, amid a new spy mania, it reappeared with a vengeance. For the ideological commissions of those years, every foreigner was a potential spy or provocateur, and cultural exchange threatened to turn into a channel for "infiltration and espionage."[29] Tourism itself became suspect, although never to the same extent as in the late 1940s. In 1960–1961, several arrests of American tourists for espionage disrupted the optimistic vision of international travel as exchange and proximity.[30] In 1962, foreign tourism in general shrank by 22 percent—a striking number considering that in 1959, the goal had been to receive between 200,000 and 300,000 travelers a year.[31] Now, no foreigner was entirely innocent.[32]

But even as the tone of discussions at Intourist's governing board changed dramatically in 1962 to focus on the threat of espionage, "personal contacts" remained foundational to propaganda and counterpropaganda. It would not be an Intourist "translator who tells [foreigners] that Soviet people live in such and such way," but ordinary people "at a family dinner [over] a cup of tea." Officials from the Union of Soviet Friendship Societies (SSOD) shared with Intourist this "cup of tea" vision (or "a jug of beer" or "dinner on the grass").[33]

Among the many questions that foreign tourists posed during such informal conversations one was as inevitable as it was frequent and incessant: Why were there so few Soviet tourists abroad? Can Soviet citizens actually travel?[34]

Throughout the late Soviet decades, the significance of international tourism would remain qualitative, not numerical, and traffic across Soviet borders asymmetrical until the end. The earliest Central Committee resolution drafts on tourism were primarily concerned with the presence of foreigners in the Soviet Union and restricted Soviet citizens' foreign travel to the socialist bloc, at least for 1955. There were no provisions for tourism to capitalist countries, but vague wording allowed for a possibility of such trips "in the years to come," and indeed, plans for 1956 already included forays into Western Europe.[35] On January 3, 1956, the Central Committee passed a resolution "On the organization of trips of Soviet tourists abroad," spelling out the general procedures and ideological foundation.[36] Even earlier, in the fall of 1955, Intourist, in preparation for the next year, had started to collaborate on organizing such trips with the Central Union of Trade Unions.[37] Foreign tourism became standardized in the summer of 1957, as Intourist and the trade unions began to sell travel vouchers.[38] But the Central Committee's initial indecision would prove prescient. Every year, tourism to Eastern Europe continued to expand (in 1957, for example, over 80 percent of Soviet tourists went to socialist Europe).[39] Meanwhile, travel to Western Europe remained largely the domain of the cultural elite and carefully selected delegations.

Travel vouchers were not for anybody who wanted or had the means to buy them. The constitution of a tourist group was the work of professional unions and local party committees. Following a biographical questionnaire, the main document in the selection process was a recommendation letter, attesting to the potential tourist's personal qualities ("character") and countersigned by the secretary of a local party committee, the employer, and the chairman of a local trade union. The unions compiled lists of tourists for vetting by the police. After the KGB's judgment, the decision rested with regional party committees. "Character" meant not only political reliability, but also private ethics and comportment—everything from sobriety to faithfulness in marriage. Travel to the West would test the tourists' political acumen, as they would have to interpret material comforts within the proper Marxist framework and understand the inequalities behind that glittering world.[40]

More than a concept of political economy, capitalism was a temptation, demanding ethical choices. Evaluations of tourists before and after trips spoke in a distinctly moral language "about disagreeable actions"— disagreeable not necessarily in a strictly political sense, but in aesthetic and ethical terms, "starting with the [tourists'] appearance."[41] The Moscow Art Theater actors giving guest performances across Eastern Europe in 1956 were not tourists, but what happened during their trip was the Intourist officials' worst nightmare come true. The theater's eminent actors— bestowed with the rank of People's Artist—drank heavily and unremittingly in the company of foreigners, "surrounding themselves with the local artistic boheme." One struck friendships with foreigners "indiscriminately"; another "befriended" a local girl and "importunately demonstrated his friendship"; a third tried to borrow money from foreign citizens with vague promises to pay it back in Moscow. All were insolent, defiant, and conceited, but "the worst offender against ethical norms" was a member of the theater's party organization, who was there to uphold ethical norms. Alcohol, women, money, and boheme lurked behind the veneer of Soviet cultural accomplishments.[42] Permission to cross borders was itself a moral judgement. Trade unions offered travel vouchers as a reward for political activism and record-breaking feats of labor.[43] But Intourist and SSOD officials often found people journeying abroad disappointingly ordinary—not at all the ideological activists they were meant to be. Rather, they "had no definite position on unmasking bourgeois ideology" and delighted in tourism for its own sake.[44] The Central Committee resolution on tourism was quite clear, however: the point of travel was to display Soviet values, not to indulge in pleasure.[45]

In practice, the vetting was not as rigorous as the chain of command suggests. In the early 1960s, the ideological commission at the Moscow party committee discovered egregious cases of tourist groups "that included practically everybody who wanted to go." Bureaucratic carelessness was at fault: groups were assembled at the last moment, in one case "a day before departure." Dozens of them passed across the border in spurts, overwhelming border patrols.[46] The standard procedure included a stopover in Moscow for a predeparture briefing by the staff of Intourist's Department of Soviet tourism, but sometimes the briefing was done en route, or by Soviet embassy personnel upon arrival. And sometimes it was not done at all.[47] "In regional professional unions, you hardly can find 5–10 percent of people who had been abroad themselves. How can we ask them to offer briefings?"[48] Predeparture preparations were so inadequate that tourists confided in one Intourist official just how "scared" they were to be venturing abroad.[49] They often departed without a word about the country they would visit—and without much besides their own experiences to rely on for stories about the Soviet Union.[50]

The groups were accompanied by a trip leader, whose job was to enforce implicit behavioral norms and to report on the journey upon return. But trip leaders had a difficult time enforcing those norms and were even less successful when tourist groups included famous cultural figures—"they consider us nonentities," complained one such custodian.[51] Travelogues and memoirs reveal that tourists disparaged trip leaders as petty, inane, and, on occasion, malicious. They often would meet the tourists nearly at the border, or en route, and have no chance to establish rapport.[52] No wonder that tourists saw them as outsiders, intruders, and KGB officers. Given that the reports they filed—our archival record of travel experiences—border on surveillance, their bad reputation with tourists and later historians is not surprising.[53] But Intourist officials worried about trip supervisors as much as they did about tourists. Intourist knew that, like the Youth Festival, like art exhibitions and other intense moments of encounter, a journey abroad was a time out of the ordinary flow of time, even for overseers in positions of authority. "Abroad," they "display characteristics that we cannot always ascertain here," and it was in the specific "conditions of the experience abroad that they failed in their tasks."[54] Trip leaders failed, because they, too, often saw themselves as tourists and cherished the pleasures of the adventure.[55]

Tourists journeyed as groups, not individuals, and this was, perhaps, the most frustrating part of going abroad. The publicity surrounding the revival of international tourism ignited hopes of traveling individually. Many people thought they could simply travel—alone or in groups, for reasons personal or professional, to study, to hear foreign speech, or to see the world. An English teacher from the Kaliningrad region "very much want[ed] to visit England, to hear live the spoken language that I teach to our children."[56] A thirty-two-year-old electrician from Ust'-Kamenogorsk in Kazakhstan was determined to spend his "vacation abroad this time": three days in Hungary, four in Austria, six in France and Germany.[57] A fitter at a L'vov factory imagined she could study "in India, Indonesia, or some other country"—an incredible vision, attesting to how deeply the new discourse on internationalism had been democratized.[58] Was the opportunity for a female factory worker to study or an electrician to vacation not the Soviet Union's fundamental raison d'être? The Thaw only infused this Soviet project with a different imaginary geography. People wrote countless letters to Intourist, SSOD, and the State Committee for Cultural Relations with Foreign Countries asking for logistical help in visiting relatives abroad and seeking ways to invite foreign friends, usually from socialist Europe. A family of career MVD officers and party members struck a friendship and began to correspond with a family in Bucharest. "We would like to go see them, and to invite them over here [to Gorky], on the Volga. . . . not on a tour voucher, but as guests, the way I would want to travel to any part of the Soviet Union."[59] The response was always a no.[60] Only relatives were permitted to visit Soviet citizens in their private capacity. For their part, Soviet citizens—as individuals—could not visit relatives abroad, even in

Eastern Europe; until the late 1960s, all travel was collective.[61] This was another manifestation of asymmetry, for the Soviet Union did admit foreigners traveling alone.

Individual tourism was possible for renowned writers and artists, whose plans had to be approved by the Central Committee's Department for Travel. A rare privilege, these trips were an absolute value, even for the elite, among whom a key division was between those permitted and those forbidden (*vyezdnye/nevyezdnye*) to travel. The preciousness of such trips and the emotional significance of their very possibility are difficult to understand in our own world.[62] Foreign journeys justified any number of sacrifices and moral compromises. On occasion, these trips determined fundamental and enduring life choices; they shaped people in intimate ways, mind and body. Ekaterina Sheveleva was a prominent author and one of the best-traveled people in the literary establishment. She was a committed member of the Communist Party. Her publications were ideologically correct to the bone. Much of Sheveleva's writing was about her foreign travels to Europe, Japan, India, the United States, Egypt, and Syria. These tours meant the world to her. Or half the world; the other half was occupied by her politically incorrect love for a man she called her husband for forty-some years. A Lithuanian, he had participated in anti-Soviet resistance, served a prison term for his activities, and detested the Soviet regime to the end. For him, Sheveleva jeopardized her publishing career and party membership. She chose to ignore his infidelities, fought staunchly for his life in and out of hospitals, and honored his memory obsessively. Still, Sheveleva would not register the marriage officially—that would cost her the privilege of travel abroad. Reflecting on their relationship after his death, she would torment herself: "As it turns out, I traded Zhenia for trips abroad!" From year to year, she also pleaded with various authorities to grant him permission to journey with her. Her ideological commitment notwithstanding, she felt that his nevyezdnoi status "branded" him "in slavery." Both saw the privilege to travel as fundamental to their very humanity.[63]

One would think that the cultural elite, with their long-standing access to privileged opportunities, would benefit from the new foreign tourism. At first, however, these people were at a disadvantage. Travel vouchers were allocated through trade unions. But creative unions were not institutionalized within a workplace and received whatever vouchers remained after general distribution. In 1958, for example, the Union of Trade Unions earmarked for writers, artists, musicians, and filmmakers a mere 150 vouchers to the socialist bloc and just twenty vouchers to capitalist countries. The Writers' Union took the initiative in calling attention to the "unfavorable conditions" of creative unions compared with professional ones. Yet, for writers, argued Writers' Union chairman Aleksei Surkov, a sojourn abroad was a professional necessity, a source of inspiration, "immediately connected to [their] creative plans, work on a book, play, or screenplay."[64] This was also how artists and writers argued for individual, unregulated travel. The painter Pavel Korin asked for a Grand Tour of his own to gain "a deeper understanding of the treasures of world art in Rome, Venice, Florence, Milan, and Naples." From the perspective of Intourist chairman Vladimir Ankudinov, such trips set "a precedent for requests from other cultural figures" and were simply too expensive. He did not like to make exceptions for creative work, instead offering Korin "general twelve-day group tours." In this case, the Central Committee's Cultural Department upheld Ankudinov's position.[65]

Surkov's and Korin's logic was groundbreaking and unimaginable earlier. According to socialist realist traditions, writers and artists derived their inspiration from the factory, the collective farm, and the natural sweep of the motherland. That a writer or artist would need to travel abroad to "expand his horizons and enrich his themes" was becoming a legitimate idea in the age of cultural exchange—so legitimate that the Cultural Department of the Central Committee took heed and passed a resolution mandating a more equitable distribution of travel vouchers.[66] And so the late 1950s and 1960s ushered in a new age, or, more precisely, a return to the imperial art world's practice of sending Russian artists abroad, usually to Italy, to study the classics in European museums and to paint iconic vistas.

Artists journeyed with albums, pencils, and paints and brought back sketches and watercolors. SSOD's House of Friendship staged exhibitions of their drawings and photographs "portraying life" in foreign countries—a collective visual travelogue.[67] In comment books, visitors often complained that there was no publicity for events at the House, yet people learned of exhibitions by word of mouth and rushed to see sketches made in Rome ("Around Italy"), Paris ("France in the works of Soviet artists"), or New York ("In America").[68] Radio programs and publications reached a broad audience, particularly in the provinces. Among listeners and readers, the thirst for travel accounts was insatiable: people sought out books, scrutinized journals for drawings, tuned into radio programs, and attended lectures at local houses of culture and dormitories. Documentaries about foreign countries drew full houses. Readers wrote to cultural mediators with requests to speak on the radio about their journeys and with pleas for postcards of Italian cities or paintings from the Louvre.[69] These images would let them walk the streets in their mind's eye and hold—literally, in their hands—a fragment of that unreachable world.

The Book of Paris

For Soviet artists, writers, and readers, no city was more familiar than Paris; no city was as instantly recognizable. Paris was a memory first, prior to experience.[70] Soviet travelers often compared Paris to a book.[71] The writer Viktor Nekrasov opened his account of a brief Paris visit with quotations from nineteenth-century classics. They bore no quotation marks, however. Removed from their literary sources, they were anonymous, at once common knowledge and Nekrasov's personal recollection. Book-inspired memories assured that Paris would not be "foreign" for Soviet visitors, or that, while remaining foreigners, they could reclaim in Paris something of their own biographies.[72] The aged Romantic writer Konstantin Paustovksy thought the memory of Paris was more formative than the actual trip. His three days in Paris in 1956 offered an experience at once momentary and enduring. Paris, in his reflections, took travelers by "sudden charm" and "open[ed] up immediately." But the experience of the moment was possible only because of the drawn-out chronology of a lifetime. For your entire life, the books you read and the paintings you saw, Paustovsky proposed, had prepared you for this "encounter with Paris." "The moment you set foot in Paris, its charm suddenly takes possession of you . . . But only if you have known and loved Paris long before this first encounter"—if, in a way, you had been there before. Indeed, Paustovsky, his readers, and "every enlightened person" had been there before, "in one's imagination or in one's dreams."[73]

The Paris of Soviet travelogues was almost entirely a literary creation, and the journeys were first and foremost literary pilgrimages. French cinema was not a source of interpretations and predictable knowledge, nor was twentieth-century prose. The literary routes were of nineteenth-century provenance. Reprinted during the late 1950s as multi-volume collected works, Zola, Maupassant, Balzac, Flaubert, Stendhal, Hugo, and Dumas were code words, recalling adolescent readings and iconic pictures of Paris.

The Soviets' itineraries followed in d'Artagnan's footsteps, in those of Georges Duroy and Eugène de Rastignac, Denise Baudu and Julien Sorel. The Opéra called to mind Maupassant and Flaubert, and the Hôtel Excelsior Opéra suggested Maupassant again.[74] "Is this not the garret where Balzac's Lucien de Rubempré lived?" (from *The Human Comedy*). "Was this not the place of the barricades where Gavroche [from Victor Hugo's *Les Misérables*] fought so heroically? And there, towering over the roofs, is the stony mass of the Notre-Dame de Paris, whose ledges the hunchback Quasimodo scaled with monkey-like dexterity."[75] To natural scientist, consummate traveler, and writer Viktor Sytin, the "somber, endless side wall of the Louvre" was exactly as Alexandre Dumas had described it in *The Three Musketeers*.[76] Travelers expected to see the musketeers somehow, somewhere, the mid-twentieth century notwithstanding. Irina Freidlin, a young biologist who went to Paris as part of a scientific exchange program in the late 1960s, imagined musketeer history at a flea market. There, she found candlesticks, "some sort of fantastic vases," snuffboxes, rusty swords, and pistols, and thought somebody might one day "revive the noble knightly ritual of the duel."[77] Objects and buildings, as well as place-names like Poitou or Angoulême, belonged to Romantic history. The travelers and their readers knew of Poitou and Angoulême from Dumas's *Queen Margot* and other volumes in the trilogy. They called hotels and restaurants "coaching inns" and "eating-houses," as in nineteenth-century novels about seventeenth-century adventures.[78]

Zola's focal sites were signposts for Soviet travelers. There was not a travelogue that failed to describe Les Halles, the Parisian wholesale food market where produce, delivered at night, was sold to groceries and restaurants every morning. Soviet visitors went there to confirm what they had read in Zola's *The Belly of Paris* and brought back descriptions of gargantuan abundance, à la Zola indeed, citing his book for authority.[79] Like Zola's, their Les Halles was not only a site of plenty, but also of poverty and degradation, the rough manners of truck drivers, the crassness of prostitutes, and clochards sitting among empty cases.[80] Les Halles would be demolished in 1971, but throughout the 1960s, Parisian newspapers debated whether the marketplace should be destroyed and what should be built in its stead. Soviet travel writers summarized these debates and had strong opinions on the subject.[81] The marketplace was important to them as a literary landmark. The contrast between the silent, sleeping city and the crowded, busy activity of the market positioned Les Halles among the mythological scenarios that come alive at night. To reach this world apart, the Soviets had to traverse an empty Paris.[82]

Pacing the empty city on the way to Les Halles figured into a larger narrative focus on the streets. Travelers declared their indifference to museums in defiance of touristic practices. Instead, they relished the streets. En route to Paris, Nekrasov wrote out a detailed schedule according to a guidebook distributed on the plane. He planned to visit museums from 10 am to 6 pm; after the museums, he would go to the theater and spend the evenings at the Moulin Rouge or Folies Bergère. Upon arriving in Paris, however, he jettisoned his schedule and skipped even the Louvre. "It is a crime, I know. To be in Paris and not to see the Venus of Milo and the Mona Lisa . . . [But I] exchanged the treasures of the Louvre for the Parisian streets." Bypassing traditional museum destinations, tourists used the few precious days in Paris to observe life from a sidewalk café, converse with strangers in a park, take the subway without purpose or destination in mind, and meander "where your feet take you, if they can still hold you, that is."[83]

The café allowed them, foreigners, to participate in a native pastime as they tried to blend in with the French.[84] Travelers lovingly described tables, chairs, and saucers, everything miniature and delightful. In an effortless scene from a generic European novel, Soviet tourists would order a diminutively elegant "small cup of coffee" and water with "two ice cubes," which sounded classy. They itemized what they ordered: toast, brioche, roast beef, croque monsieur, cheese, oysters, baguette, and, "it goes without saying," red and white wine—there was an extra-culinary pleasure in such enumeration of food.[85] Everything was served by a garçon, and travel writers insisted on using the Russified French, as in translations of French classics or in nineteenth-century Russian literature.[86] Installing themselves (along with everybody else in the multinational touristic crowd) at tiny tables on the sidewalks, they watched other people, all watching one another, and created for Soviet readers pictures from an exhibit of French social types.[87]

One of the most curious sights Soviet travelers noticed was couples kissing in public and in oblivion. In Soviet accounts, they became an obligatory attribute of Parisian life. Kissing couples represented the French lightheartedness of Soviet clichés; they were an endearing symbol of the none-too-discreet charm of Western life. From his café observatory, the biologist Andrei Kursanov first noticed "a couple in love": "Their coffee had long gotten cold, but they were immersed in a sweet conversation and from time to time kissed tenderly." With a nod of acceptance, Kursanov explained this unusual situation to his readers: it is quite normal in Paris for couples to "kiss everywhere, in the streets, in the restaurants, at the movies and in the subway," and nobody notices or cares.[88] At times, Soviet travelers became silent participants in an exchange of stolen glances. The artist Aleksandr Zhitomirskii fixated on two youths and caught the eyes of the girl. Surreptitiously, she returned his gaze from behind the shoulder of her boyfriend, aware of the situation's exhibitionism and involving Zhitomirskii as a voyeur in their kiss. Among his sketches from that trip is a drawing of the girl's face, almost hidden behind the wide back of a man; she looks out from the corner of one eye.[89]

The counterpoint to the charming prospect of café rituals and kissing couples' youthful insouciance was nighttime Paris. Soviet tourists arrived with Parisian nightlife on their minds: "Everyone knows that Paris is the city of sleepless nights. Show us this Paris, please, do show it to us."[90] They sought out this Paris; and walking the streets, they marveled at the quiet sleepiness of the night. The dawning realization that "Paris goes to bed early" served to break the stereotype and, in the process, became a new stereotype, to be endlessly repeated in Soviet travelogues.[91] But travelers knew where they wanted cabs to take them, asking passersby for directions and eliciting winking smiles.[92] And what they found there was every bit as bad as they had imagined. Written with zealous opprobrium, the pages devoted to the Place Pigalle were among the most vivid and fast-paced in Soviet travelogues. In the first moment, the visitors were overpowered by neon lights. Viktor Sytin heaped iridescent impressions, fragments of images and foreign words, "coca-cola," "vedette," as they flashed on cornices. He felt the lights as aggressive, "furious," "attacking you from all directions."[93] The writer Semen Shurtakov *heard* the visual attack. "Deafening" lights merged with the music emanating from bars and restaurants, "slow, mournful, viscid, or rabid rhythmic twitches." The analogy between pulsating music and lights created a feeling of mad movement and testifies to how overcome the travelers felt—to the point where their senses were confounded.[94]

In the second moment, they were beleaguered by sexual propositions. In Sytin's writings, the din of crowds, music, and cars collided with the suggestive whisper of pimps ("insolent fellows, ironed and decked out fashionably").[95] The whisper—the chill and sweetness of the forbidden—made Soviet travelers shiver. They tried to rush past, but strangers besieged them. Travelogues presented these encounters in the Place Pigalle as intrusive, corporeal, and almost violent: hands grabbed them, yanked at their sleeves, trying to pull them into strip clubs and peep shows, old, vulgar, and masculine prostitutes blocked their way, calling out in hoarse voices, "hello, boys."[96] The prostitutes mistook the Soviets, as they did all foreigners, for universalized Americans. The Place Pigalle was part of despised cosmopolitan pastimes, complete with "noisy Americans, smug Germans, animated Africans, restrained and surprised white-haired Scandinavians and Britons, black-eyed, dark-skinned sons of Oceania, Indians, [and] Japanese." Many signs were in English, and those "insolent fellows" addressed Soviet tourists in English, too.[97] Travelogues depicted the Place Pigalle as an environment wholly alien to "real Frenchmen." The "real" Paris was the Paris that went to bed early.[98] Soviet travelers thus found themselves in a doubly alien space and retreated in fright. In fact, however, love for hire was what they came to see at the Place Pigalle.[99]

But there was something redeeming about this location: it had been a battleground of the Paris Commune. Looking for the Commune's traces was a unique feature of Soviet itineraries. Revolutionary landmarks were not included in standard tour circuits, so Soviet visitors had to chart the routes through Parisian streets on their own. Traveling to Commune-related sites became something of a scavenger hunt.[100] Soviet writers used the obligatory quest for the Commune—and for leftist landmarks generally, such as the street where Lenin had lived in exile—for other purposes: to fill their pages with exotic toponyms and detailed directions. For readers who would never go there themselves, the travelogue became a neighborhood guide of great precision:

> now onto Place de l'Hôtel-de-Ville, where the Paris Commune had been proclaimed. . . . I turn from rue de Castiglione onto noisy rue Saint-Honoré, which stretches several kilometers parallel to the Seine. Saint-Honoré is a narrow and rather winding old street. At the center, it is a street of expensive stores . . . a street of luxury, like the Rivoli, which runs parallel to it but closer to the Seine. Along rue de Rivoli, from Place de la Concorde until the small square before La Comédie-Française, one can walk under the arcades freely. . . . The square before La Comédie-Française is inviting and beautiful. Before the columns of the theater's facade, amid the trees, two fountains adorn [the square]. From here, it takes but a few steps to the beginning of

narrow rue de Richelieu. It originates right behind the theater. The side of the royal palace, Palais-Royal, and the gray, uncomely facade of the National Library's elongated building look onto it . . . Saint-Honoré continues beyond the Palais-Royal square. To reach Hotel de Ville, it is better to take rue de Rivoli, past Place du Châtelet and the Tour Saint-Jacques.[101]

While this pilgrimage positioned Soviet travelers as heirs to the Commune's legacy, the cultural effect of such inventories was a narrative map of Paris.[102] Soviet descriptions colored this map in a modulating green and gray-violet and enveloped it in a haze. Sometimes the fog was transparent, at other times thick, but always draped over buildings, distorting their size and shape.[103] Sytin saw the city's panorama from Montmartre in a "blue-gray mist." The Seine "gleamed of bluish steel." Evenings were violet.[104] Aleksandr Zhitomirskii loved this sad palette: "leaden Paris, with black damp patches and columns bathed to whiteness in the rain, [Paris] in a light violet haze."[105] It always rained. A sound, a feeling, a smell, a prism for seeing Paris, rain was a refrain in Soviet travelogues.[106] Rain covered the city in gloss. As Soviet artists painted the landscape, it glistened. This was the impressionists' Paris, part painting, part mirage, as travelers realized and granted canvases a reality beyond art.[107] Zhitomirskii relished Parisian "purity [and] transparency" and tried to transfer it onto paper. Rain was his helper: "Under a shroud of rain, drizzle first, then downpour, I sat drawing the Seine, the old bridge, and behind it, in the distance, gray buildings. . . . Water streamed down the paper," washing away the contours of buildings and creating precisely the ash haze that dominated Soviet travelogues.[108] The artist Yuri Neprintsev "felt something close to perplexity" when he tried to paint his first study in Paris. The buildings would vanish, as if "melting," and reappear in front of his eyes, all "draped in a light, vacillating, and shimmering fog." And thus he began to see the impressionists as a distinctly French phenomenon.[109] The written and visual travelogues of the late 1960s were prompted by—and belonged to—a culture that reevaluated impressionism; in turn, accounts of Paris validated impressionism as a version of realism.

Perhaps the main Soviet literary source for the gray and violet palette were Ilya Ehrenburg's chronicles of Paris, especially his memoir *People, Years, Life* and his postwar novel *The Storm*. Serialized in the early 1960s, *People, Years, Life* set an authoritative narrative and pace for writing

Paris: a memoir, it was also the most important Parisian travelogue of the Thaw years. The book depicted Paris in fragmented scenes hurriedly supplanting one another, each a quick contour without time or context. Ehrenburg's impressionistic tableaux were multiplied in subsequent travel accounts, which similarly outlined scenes and persons in just a few strokes or snapshots arranged in no particular order.[110] Travel itself was not Ehrenburg's focus, but in the memoir, people constantly crossed borders, sometimes moving effortlessly and creating the cosmopolitan environments of Paris in the 1910s, and at other times encountering difficulties. Then, Ehrenburg discussed visas, permission or inability to travel, and the feeling of being trapped. Much of the memoir took place in Paris; and chiming in to defend Ehrenburg from the press attack during the ideological panic of 1962–1963, readers filled letters with words of gratitude and sympathy, as well as with their own imaginings of Paris. In these letters, they recalled his postwar novel *The Storm* (1947).[111]

Like Ehrenburg's other novels, *The Storm* has passed into oblivion, but in the late 1940s and throughout the 1950s, readers celebrated it for its descriptions of Paris and for its foreign love plot between a French woman and a Russian man. The novel created a strong presence effect, transporting readers, young women especially (judging by Ehrenburg's mail), to Paris. *The Storm* contained these lines, which readers remembered and quoted in their letters well into the 1960s: "He fell in love with the lusterless enigmatic Seine, with the pavements—now a grayish blue and now violet, washed by the frequent rains and reflecting a swarm of restless lights—with the cool narrow streets, the raw air that smacked of the sea, and the profusion of flowers, beads, tears, the lugubrious gaiety of the crowds, which jested even on the brink of death. He fell in love with the gray, everyday, ordinary, and yet extraordinary Paris."[112] The lines struck in readers so familiar and sentimental a chord that some even borrowed Ehrenburg's palette and vision in speaking of impossible journeys. With no words of her own to convey her wistful affection for Paris, twenty-six-year-old Inna, a geologist and a graduate of Leningrad University, excerpted his sentences: "I so much love," she began, continuing with a quotation from the novel, "'the lusterless enigmatic Seine, with the pavements—now a grayish blue and now violet, washed by the frequent rains and reflecting a swarm of restless lights—with the cool narrow streets.'" The damp streets and dim lampposts reminded her of Claude Monet or Albert Marquet. To assure herself that Paris was not a painterly mirage, she again quoted from

Ehrenburg's novel: "I know there was Paris. Roses turned bright red under the lights of befogged windows."[113] Seventeen-year-old Natal'ia Filimonova recalled *The Storm* for a mauve atmosphere that she believed was Parisian: "pavement tinted lilac from the rain," chestnut trees, a park bench. Natal'ia participated in the novel, strongly identified with its heroine Mado, or felt herself to be the heroine: "It was I," she insisted, "who put dahlias where Léontine had died" and "[who] sat on Mado's bench." Gray and lilac Paris was not only melancholy, but also romantic; and Natal'ia wrote herself into the novel's emotional disposition. Love was a recurrent declaration in her letter: "I now know love. It is Mado . . . I love Mado very much."[114] Formal genre notwithstanding, people read *The Storm* and Ehrenburg's other books as travelogues. For travelogues were not only accounts of trips, but anything—colors, objects, details—that gave readers the means to journey vicariously.

Letter writers claimed to know Paris with a special knowledge "of the heart," and credited Ehrenburg as well as French nineteenth-century classics with an intimacy beyond factual information. Concerning "the elusive, ineffable spirit of Paris, of France," Leningrader Mila Orlova's knowledge was intuitive and atmospheric. "Although I have never been there, and although I might not have sufficient factual knowledge about France, I know this country, I know its people, its spirit, its mood," Mila wrote with certainty. This non sequitur was not a contradiction in terms, for "spirit" and "mood" cannot be appraised on the basis of verifiable data. They can only be sensed "subconsciously," as Mila put it; the inner vision revealed to her "much more" than newspapers and facts, "or maybe less, but something much more essential, inherent to true France." The country in her mind's eye was closer and truer still for having been invented by Mila herself.[115]

This knowledge of the heart was confirmed by a photography exhibit, "The Living Paris," sent from France in fulfillment of the cultural exchange agreement and displayed at the House of Friendship in January 1960. Among the sixty-five black-and-white photographs, which viewers consistently found too few, many were panoramic and multiplane. They foregrounded the Seine, for instance, with Île de la Cité and the Notre Dame in the background, or the Seine again, the camera spotlighting a fisherman, with the Pont Royal in the middle ground and the south facade of the Louvre in the distance. The exhibit celebrated the streets, training the lens on a railing or a building facade, yet never losing sight of the long shots.[116]

These photographs were akin to tourist postcards. And indeed, visitors, eager for a token of their trip, asked for copies of the photographs to be published as postcards, or for pictures "with Parisian views" to be sold at the exhibit.[117]

They regarded the exhibit as a chance to travel. "I have been to Paris! I have walked through its squares, palaces, and parks, and learned a bit about the life of Parisians," one excited visitor gushed in his comment; and the next viewer convinced himself that he, too, had made the trip.[118] People knew that such declarations were trite. Still, they indulged in linguistic conventions, because "you really do feel as if you took a little walk around Paris."[119] The photographs gave physical form to disembodied dreams and imaginings; thanks to the panoramic shots of buildings and avenues, "you begin to envision Paris so familiar from literature—the city of your heroes."[120] To convey the bookish knowledge they had brought with them, comment writers compiled lists of architectural landmarks.[121] Other fragments for assembling Paris were songs and, rarely, films. "I would have liked to see more pictures of life, scenes from real life under the sky and the roofs of Paris," explained a visitor, using the song "Under the Paris Sky," which the Soviets knew in Yves Montand's version, and René Clair's film *Under the Roofs of Paris*.[122]

The comments are striking for the numerous remarks written in French or, to be precise, in struggling French. Some statements were rendered in a single sentence, offering thanks to the photographers or a salutation at the conclusion of a comment in Russian. Others were slogans about friendship ("Long live . . .") and affirmations of amity, addressing the photographers as "dear friends." Often, the French was but a few misspelled and arbitrarily arranged words, which later visitors would correct in a display of their own sophistication.[123] Most remarks were not informative, and sharing an opinion was not their purpose. Visitors wrote in exclamation points: "Wondrous!" "Marvelous!" "Thank you, thank you thrice!" "Wonderful!" "Long live Paris!"[124] These comments were meant to demonstrate worldly conversance, so much so that when viewers did not have French, they wrote in broken English to say "It is all rait. Very good!!!" or "Just well exibition. Long live Paris!"[125] What mattered was the very use of foreign words. Whether in Russian, French, or nonsensical, the comments were written in the language of love. "Enchanted," visitors could not tear themselves away from the photographs and recited the affective verbs as an incantation: "I love France, I love Paris, I love the French."[126] They wrote their love into the history of the Russo-French cultural affair.[127] In Maya-kovsky's famous line—"I would want to live and die in Paris if there were not such a place as Moscow"—viewers found a ready-made idiom to express the proper configuration between home and abroad, compromising neither love of France nor patriotism.[128]

But amid the effusive comments and letters, a different reaction, resentful and hostile, occasionally surfaced. Visitors knew what the refrain about having been there, in the virtual reality of the photographs, meant: "the living Paris" was unreachable. The sentimental relish of place-names, foreign words, and minute detail was a function of this impossibility. Some in the audience grew downhearted at the imperative "cannot [*nel'zia*]" and the unrealizable desire "to travel to France, to see everything with our own eyes."[129] There was a trace of hope in such wishes. A. Alekseev believed that one day "in the near future, mutual understanding and trust will allow [us] to stroll in Paris."[130] There was anger in such wishes, too. Hiding none of his (or her?) impatience, another visitor emphasized "freedom": "to freely travel to Paris and to see the living Paris with living eyes. When will it finally come to pass: free travel for all!"[131]

With the new development of foreign tourism—and the publicity accompanying it—travel opportunities were seemingly within reach. Continued immobility was therefore all the more frustrating. Anna Vladimirovna Vasil'eva, a lecturer who taught French literature, took the apparent travel opportunities so seriously that she tried to join a tourist group going to France in the summer of 1957. She had spent much of her life dreaming of this trip: she "loved France" for the politically correct reason of "revolutionary storms," but also for a mood at once melancholy and "pungently sarcastic."[132] However, at the first step in the process—her place of employment, the Groznyi Pedagogical Institute—her prospects were rudely quashed: "You have no business [going] there," she was told. "Pardon me," she began her story, writing to Ehrenburg in bitterness: she esteemed the writer, yet envied him in a quiet, hopeless way.[133]

Anna Vladimirovna was emblematic of the manner in which people organized their hobbies and careers as surrogates for travel. Majoring in foreign languages and literatures was a prevalent choice for those who wished to inhabit childhood books.[134] But even imaginary journeys and academic attempts to dwell in the world of nineteenth-century classics sometimes proved as elusive as the actual trip. Twenty-four-year-old Natal'ia Teleteva majored in literature and French at the Ural State University in Sverdlovsk for bookish reasons, having "long grown to identify with the world of [Romain Rolland's] Jean-Christophe, with . . . a literary Paris, which I will probably never see, with its streets, familiar from Balzac, Maupassant, Zola." Natal'ia desperately wanted to continue living in this world—by going to graduate school and by teaching foreign literature and battling xenophobia. But her higher calling encountered bureaucratic obstacles: Khrushchev's 1958 education reforms required three years of work as a prerequisite for graduate admission. That is, "three years of life," she wrote in anguish, three years of "doing unclear what and for what purpose" in a hated, "mind-numbing" job as a librarian at the Ural State Forestry Engineering Institute. This prospect was especially depressing when her heart was filled with Parisian characters and scenery: "I clearly see the sweet Seine, where, at the bookstalls on the embankment, A. France would find his favorite antique in folio publications. And then Yves Montand sang about Paris, and [Louis] Aragon" wrote about it. Beyond her invented Paris were "quagmire, dirt, [and] stupidity of my coworkers (without exaggeration)"—in other words, the "quagmire, dirt, [and] stupidity" of Soviet institutions and of life in a provincial city. Her thesis on Zola was an escape from the job and the people she loathed, from the daily grind of Soviet reality.[135] Natal'ia's lament reveals the fragments that constituted the Parisian fantasy: literary works sanctioned and promoted by the ideological establishment, new cultic figures like Montand, and Soviet visionaries of internationalism like Ehrenburg. The letter conveyed a common melancholic disposition. "I love France, which I have never seen and probably will never see"—this line recurred in readers' mail and in comment books from exhibitions.[136]

The same hopeless immobility inspired various academic and popular texts that were actually hidden travelogues. In the 1960s, the young art historian Mikhail German wrote a biography of the artist Honoré Daumier as a virtual journey to France. Tellingly, the book began with the boy Honoré traveling from Marseille to Paris by yellow postal coach. The opening pages encompassed so much: the traditional script of a provincial arriving in Paris, à la d'Artagnan, Rastignac, Sorel, and any number of other literary young men determined to conquer the capital; German's own impossible journey, originating in and sublimated into texts; and the perception of France through the eyes of a child—a romantic lens particularly meaningful for German.[137] There had been a trip in German's childhood, too, but it was nothing like Honoré's journey. At the start of World War II, German had been evacuated aboard a crowded train from the intellectually resplendent

Leningrad to a dirty village.[138] It was in evacuation, "in half-darkness," "behind a huge Russian stove," that Mikhail first read Dumas, Hugo, and Jules Verne. *The Three Musketeers* was the strongest "childhood shock": he read the book with uncommon intensity. Although the illustrations were "magical" and the swashbuckling action was fantastic, the book had a greater reality than the evacuee's day-to-day existence. Mikhail retold this "best book in the world" to his friends; and together they turned the pitiful objects of their lives—an old straw hat, a rare biscuit, mother's festive cape, sticks and coins—into swords, pistols, Louis d'ors, and ruffled collars. German wore an old straw hat with a paper plume, his mother's lilac cape and lace collar; in their games he played Athos. With glue, paper, and scissors, he created what he would later call "stage props" for Hugo's *Ruy Blas*. For other props, he used empty cans cut out as swords and shields.[139] As an adult, he would aspire to write a historical novel of the kind he had read as a child, "like Dumas, of course (and this was the main thing!)."[140] His biography of Daumier recalled the theatrical props of his childhood games: "the dazzling houses of Saint-Germain . . . perfumed rooms . . . servants wearing silk stockings."[141]

With *Daumier*, German created not only a book or a character, but also Paris itself—"the creation of Paris [*sotvorenie Parizha*]" is what he would later call the process of writing, in a vocabulary echoing the story of Creation. This Paris was uniquely and solely his own: "I did not have to share it with anybody, its practically invented buildings, colors, and smells belonged to me alone, to my early childhood, [and] to Dumas."[142] *Daumier* was rich in descriptions inspired by childhood readings and historical research, and also, one senses, by the growing corpus of travel writings.[143] Honoré's encounter with Paris, as German imagined it, originated at the "leaden Seine," which colored everything in that proverbial gray. The sky was "faded," the buildings were "sad and ashen," the streets were dirty, and the boy felt melancholy. Slowly, however, as German sent him on long walks around the city, Honoré began to discover Paris.[144] There were streets whose twists, turns, and intersections German could visualize and whose names he savored: rue du Puits-de-l'Ermite, rue Saint-Denis, Quai d'Anjou, Galerie Véro-Dodat in "the labyrinth of narrow streets behind the Louvre."[145] German came to know Paris so intimately that his acquaintances, lucky to be going to France, sought his advice, "recognizing very well that I had never been there." When he failed in his first attempt to join an SSOD-sponsored tourist group to France, a colleague consoled him: "Mikhail Yur'evich, what do you need [this trip] for, you see and know it all already."[146] "It all" was Paris, the true hero of German's books.

German would see Paris many times, however, both in the Soviet and post-Soviet eras. He first went there in 1965 as part of a tourist group. A lifetime of imaginary work turning into reality; a recovery of childhood secrets apart from fellow Soviet tourists; a feeling of unique and uniquely deserved fortune—all combined to impart a sense of the miraculous to his initial experience of Paris.[147] German found his way around the city thanks, again, to Maupassant, Zola, and Dumas. Every street or building seemed to hold literary associations: "From the Pont des Arts, I looked onto the Cité, onto the towers of the Notre Dame, onto the buildings that receded back to the quai Malaquais, where Anatole France and his Pierre Nozière and his Sylvestre Bonnard had strolled." The beloved Dumas was a haunting presence.[148] On his second trip, German sought out rue du Pot-de-Fer, which held a special significance as the site where Athos, his childhood alter ego, had lived.[149] In the Marais, at the Place Royale (Place des Vosges today), he heard the din of swords "under the vaults" of the arcades and, as a souvenir, brought back a toy sword with the Paris coat of arms. Kitschy as it was, he loved it all the same and kept it on his desk for thirty years.[150] In cafés, he tried to do what characters "in books about France" do. He tried to write a letter—with a look of "Parisian pensiveness"—over "a small, heavy, porcelain cup" of "unwontedly thick coffee." But his excitement and relish for such details as sugar wrappings, long-handled spoons, and small, cast-iron tables betrayed a tourist.[151]

Despite it all, though, German was sad rather than joyous: that first trip was already shot through with a sense of loss. German's walks around the canonical tourist sites left him as bitter as he was elated. He was "tormented by the thought: my own, invented Paris will never exist again."[152] With each day, "the bookish Paris was dying." Dying was the city of German's sole proprietorship; the real Paris belonged to everybody. The very ability to create and recreate Paris with each book, painting, film, or song was dying as well. The real Paris had a finality of fact and stone, which left little room for creativity and for German as its creator.[153] On this first trip German experienced a moment of loneliness—when it rained, of course—that would beset his future trips to Paris.[154]

In 1972, German traveled to Paris in a private capacity, at the invitation of a distant uncle who had emigrated long ago. The permission to journey alone and stay in France for a month was an exception to the usual travel and surveillance practices. No longer an impossibility, Paris came to German at the price of humiliation: he had to complete dozens of forms, place his biography under a KGB microscope, and then rely on his wealthy uncle's wallet and goodwill. During this trip, Paris did not lose the enchantment of childhood, but German's feelings became darker and more complex. With despair and affectation in equal measure, he wanted to be a Parisian and "to entertain the thought that [Parisians] take you for one of their own."[155] The truth weighed on him in the evenings, when he felt lonely in his longing for Paris. But was he not there already? Was this trip not the ultimate fulfillment of adolescent dreams? He was in Paris. Moreover, he was in Paris alone, without oversight. And he had linguistic fluency and impeccable knowledge of the city's topography. But for the entire month, German lived in anticipation of departure; a week into his trip, he wrote in his diary "how little of France remains!" Hence the "eternal and hopeless, insatiable nostalgia" for Paris. The city "evaded me," he lamented, "even while I was there."[156] Having lost his "bookish" Paris, he could not find himself in the real one. Worse, upon returning to the Soviet Union, German felt himself a stranger at home. He became restless, yearning to travel to Paris again, unable to find a place in Leningrad, and feeling "superfluous there and here." With time and subsequent trips, he would realize that his Paris existed only at home, in Russia.[157]

The Passions of the Renaissance

While the Paris of Soviet cultural invocations was made from the fragments of nineteenth-century literature and painting, the experiences of Soviet travelers in Italy were structured by two visual traditions: the Renaissance as the painterly ideal and a source of emotional vocabulary, and cinematic neorealism as a prism for interpreting urban mise-en-scènes.

Soviet trips to Italy were scripted—experienced and written about—in the rich literary tradition of Russian (and other) fantasies of the peninsula.[158] The cultural elite was acutely self-conscious of their predecessors who had written about the Italy of universal beauty. What novelty could they bring to narratives that, over centuries, had been created about the Coliseum and Pompeii, St. Paul's and St. Mark's, Ponte dei Sospiri and Ponte Vecchio, The Last Supper and the Sistine Chapel? What images could they convey besides those that had been infinitely reproduced? How, Soviet authors

often asked, should they write Italy? These very misgivings were unorig-
inal, as they had plagued travel writing since the Romantics' search for
unique experiences and heightened emotions. From the Romantics, the
Soviet literary world inherited enduring ideas: a trip as a love affair; the
feminization of the "passionate" South; the validity of sensual, even irra-
tional knowledge; and the legitimacy of idiosyncratic visions.[159] The pen
of writer Sergei Smirnov failed at "description," for it had all been said
before; he could only offer his own "perceptions" and "impressions."[160]
Theater historian and critic Grigorii Boiadzhiev insisted on the right to
his personal vision, fallible though it might be, and hence to subjective
writing: "I want to defend," he submitted to his readers, "this freedom and
sincerity of my perception." He initially endeavored to compose a diaristic
travelogue, conveying the immediacy of impressions without consulting
other books and without editing. He wanted to transform "great artistic
monuments" into moments of empathy particular to the theatrical act, to
take paintings out of art history books and experience them firsthand as
drama.[161] Smirnov and Boiadzhiev asserted the interpretive legitimacy of
their "perceptions"; their feelings and fantasy mattered.

The Italy of their fantasies originated in childhood, and Soviet travelogues were filled with allusions to a tender age. The painter Sergei Gerasimov knew Renaissance artists "from childhood."[162] "With all the might
of youthful imagination, we fancied how 'one day' (when we grow up!) we
will wander the streets of Rome and Florence and glide along Venetian
canals," recalled art critic Genrikh Nedoshivin, "we were held captive by
the dream of a trip to Italy."[163] For Boiadzhiev, Venice felt like a "children's
joyful kingdom," overflowing with toys: "bugles, golden china, glass balls,
blinding illumination of the sun frolicking upon all this," and dolls,
"beauties with golden hair in nylon dresses, each the size of a five-year-old
girl, in her own box resembling a castle, and these stacked castles creating an entire kingdom populated by princesses."[164] The names of Italian
cities were a meaningful vocabulary of adolescent pastimes; in adulthood,
they joined other code words for childhood itself. Sergei Smirnov compared the romantic cachet of Naples to that of the Amazon and Orinoco, to
the Zambezi, Ganges, and Mount Kilimanjaro—a real but nonetheless
mythical geography of adolescent adventures in "cherished faraway lands."
According to Smirnov, every child has such an imaginary faraway land, "a
wondrous city," in which he lives out heroic stories from books and movies.
Adults retain a special fondness for the imaginary lands of their childhood:

even in old age, these place-names "hold miraculous meaning" and "force the heart to skip a beat." Smirnov's cherished and wondrous place of childhood escape was Naples, the very word "touching the most secret of heartstrings." There was music in the word and "a stirring call of the south and the sea." When, as an adult, Smirnov finally arrived in Naples, he dropped his things off and ran onto the street "in feverish impatience."[165]

Foreign toponyms were a magical language. In his travelogue *Around Italian Cities*, translator Georgii Bogemskii named fountains, squares, palaces, fortresses, churches, roads, streets, cafés, buildings, monuments, heroes past and present—everything received an annunciation. Any randomly chosen sentence read like this: "Near the Castello Sforzesco, between Via Boccaccio and the long avenue Corso Magenta, towers the Church of Santa Maria delle Grazie."[166] The church is the location of Leonardo's *The Last Supper*, to which Bogemskii devoted less space than to listing streets in Milan and elsewhere. The narrative pleasure of this very political book was in the naming, which Bogemskii did with cartographic precision and relish.[167] This was the book's significance for the mid-1950s. Place-names were more than geographic designations. Incomprehensible of yet as locations on the map, they were aesthetically meaningful: incantations, recitatives, prayers, verses. Literal meaning would have threatened their aesthetic value.

Travelers knew exactly what they would see and what colors their visions would be. They entered painted landscapes, where everything seemed instantly recognizable.[168] The distinction between immediate landscapes and the enigmatic backgrounds of Renaissance paintings was entirely erased. Traveling by train, the art historian Yuri Kolpinskii relived his museum experiences, for beyond the windows were Renaissance pastorals: "the gray crests of the Alps, shrouded in clouds, somewhere in the background, and here, among soft hills, under the sun sparkles a rivulet, which has preserved the swiftness of the running start it took from the mountains." This panorama echoed the background in Titian's *The Presentation of the Virgin Mary at the Temple*, a fragment of which Kolpinskii included in his book.[169] Nedoshivin could swear that an old woman he saw selling fish at a market on via Garibaldi in Venice "was a twin look-alike of an old woman sitting by the staircase" in Titian's *Presentation*, and that "the flask of wine" he saw in a Giudecca trattoria was "exactly" like the ones Paolo Veronese had painted.[170] Fruit and vegetable markets and carts with herbal produce were inevitably called "still lives."[171] The artist Semen Chuikov was surprised by this feeling of recognition (*uznavanie*), experiencing the moment of arrival in Rome as a return—a return because his knowledge of Roman topography was primordial, preexperiential.[172] Even the smell and the air were captured in a memory: in Milan, Konstantin Paustovsky was haunted by a strange sensation, against all reason and fact, that "in distant youth, I had lived in this city once upon a time and had felt its unmovable, yellowish heat."[173] Soviet tales of Italy were permeated with a nostalgic and elated sense of a return to a place where the travelers had never been.

Accounts of Italian tours were often written by art historians or artists, as a textual equivalent of their sketches. Words took the place of paints, and the written page turned into a palette. Artists strove to capture in writing the modulation of color. In turn, professional authors embraced a painterly technique; color was at the heart of their texts. Halftones and mixed pigments were Yuri Kolpinskii's credo: for him, turning the foreign into the familiar required an eye that could see the hues in-between.[174] The photographs with which Kolpinskii illustrated his book were black and white, but his prose colored them: Venetian canals in "trembling ripples" of green and blue, "the walls of old houses and palaces" in "gray, marble-white pink, and brown," and the spread of pigeon wings in "pink, warm-gray, and white." For morning impressions of Venice, Kolpinskii blended a tender and transparent palette, creating weightlessness.[175] For other moods and vistas, he delineated chiaroscuro. As in Caravaggio or Bellini, where shadows were pierced by gold and red, in Kolpinskii's exalting depiction, the "sky above Venice . . . was enveloped in the solemn shine of a golden sunset," while "the stripes of clouds were afire with royal purple" and "dusky crimson." Kolpinskii painted the Tuscan countryside with: "dark-green crowns of gardens and groves . . . rusty brown patches of vineyard land far in the distance . . . iridescent silveriness of olive groves, and remote hills in foggy-gray lilac." Distant silver and lilac created a mythical landscape, at once lush and ethereal, a scriptural land of milk and honey.[176]

For readers who would never travel there, the land of milk and honey had a precise topography. These travelogues were guidebooks, retelling city maps, and art historical treatises, leading readers through museums. Such was art historian Valerii Prokof'ev's *Around Italy*, which included foldout grid maps. Prokof'ev gave exact directions to monuments and museums. Readers could make right and left turns with him and pursue his itineraries as the maps unfolded: "walk to the middle of the street and turn to look back," "crossing the bridge and turning right along the Arno, in just several steps we see the Uffizi."[177] The book's illustrations positioned the reader as participant and spectator. Arches or windows, shown at close range to amplify details, framed views onto broader terrains. In one instance, the laced pinnacles and spires of the Milan Cathedral were pictured through an opening of a semicircular flying buttress.[178] In another, a rectangular arch—an ancient portal or part of a colonnade—revealed a modern high-rise. Looking through portals, the reader became an insider.[179] Attentive to touch, smell, and the physical environment, Prokof'ev recreated the sensory experience of buildings.[180] He situated his readers in the Basilica of St. Paul Outside the Walls by conveying the emotional effect not of architectural materiality but of immaterial light, dusk, and color. "You"—the armchair traveler—"you sense physically how you walk from darkness to light." Oddly, for a book about paintings and vistas, Prokof'ev imagined his traveler as someone nearly blind, or "blinded" by the mysterious radiance of St. Paul Outside the Walls, powerless to resist its sensual allure, sleepwalking through interlacing streaks of light. This was a scene of surrender, a scene of "enticement" and "desire."[181]

For Soviets, Italy was a story of passion. The world Soviet travel writers envisioned through the prism of romanticized history and poetry was terrible and beautiful: love, lust, power, murder, money, betrayal. It was the world of the Medicis and the Borgias, Orsinis and Colonnas, Montagues and Capulets, Othellos and Iagos. In Venice, tourists always sought out the Statue of Colleoni, a regular stop on Soviet itineraries, while the artists among them sketched it compulsively and included its likeness in the travelogues. Some recalled the copy in the Pushkin Museum, which had been their earliest introduction to, or memory of, the Renaissance and Italy.[182] The *condottiero*'s ferocious face signified "worldly passions" that Soviet travel accounts expected of the Renaissance.[183] In the Doge's Palace, in the Colleoni, indeed, in all of Renaissance art, Soviet authors extolled masculine power. The virility and intensity of the Renaissance was a common refrain in the travelogues.[184] Tintoretto and Michelangelo were heroes for Soviet travelers, who viewed paintings through the secular lens of Man Ascendant. They marveled at Tintoretto's "furious" pace and productivity and could not believe that one man had created the paintings in La Scuola Grande di San Rocco. His canvases were "immense" without measure; the drama of his battle scenes was "impetuous"; and his colors gave the canvases "a cold passion (*strastnost'*) [and] almost explosive power."[185]

In the streets of the 1950s and 1960s, Soviet visitors found the same raw emotions and unique expressivity that they saw in old paintings—only now it was cinema that defined modern Italy. Acquaintances and passersby appeared to these travelers "as characters from a neorealist film, who had come off the screen." Sergei Smirnov's new friend, Francesco Capurro, had "an unusually expressive face, lively, fiery eyes . . . eloquent features, and typically Italian gestures," exactly like cinema characters; and, Smirnov joked, he "avoided an acting career only because the famous Italian directors De Santis or De Sica hadn't met him."[186] In an itinerant trader advertising his wares with humor and verve, the painter Semen Chuikov saw Totò, a comedian beloved in the Soviet Union after the screenings of *Side Street Story, Cops and Robbers, The Gold of Naples,* and *The Law is the Law.* "Who imitates whom?" The trader, pulling up his slipping trousers, "copies Totò," or the actor "caricatures little people like" this trader? Either way, on a train, Chuikov encountered a manifest "character from an Italian neorealist film. And exactly as in those films, the passengers chaffed him in a somewhat coarse and unceremonious manner, as if he were a close buddy of theirs."[187] In the street, the artist Yuri Pimenov spotted an anonymous film star: "a long-legged, tall beauty from the movies." Rather than a fashionable boutique, an affluent hotel, or a sleek car, however, she entered "some little shop and several minutes later, started sweeping and washing the floor. Her light body, her exquisite head with dark hair moved in the dimness of the small room."[188] Maybe she was an ordinary girl with a star's beauty, or maybe cinema was the interpretive lens for seeing beauty; whatever the case, in Italy, street and cinema fused. Even such marks of ordinary life as time were cinematic reminders. A walk through Roman streets at eleven o'clock in the morning was recorded as *Rome, 11 O'Clock:* "the same eleven o'clock when unmovable hands [of the clock] froze in an old picture. Remember?"[189] As in films, "dark street corners" were inhabited by "made-up, pathetic Cabirias."[190] Chuikov recognized Cabiria's "voice and manner" in a street brawl. A young woman, who reminded him of Cabiria, advanced toward her opponent, and the small square filled with an audience watching "the unfolding action" from the windows and balconies—a situation evocative of Fellini's classic.[191]

Soviet travelers gauged what was "real" Italy and what was not according to preconceived notions shaped by cinema. For Bogemskii, the "real Naples" was such as depicted in *Side Street Story,* Eduardo De Filippo's half-bitter,

Figure 6.1. Yuri Pimenov, *A Venetian Girl*, 1958.

half-comedic play. In addition to translating De Filippo's script, Bogemskii devoted much of his professional life to Italian cinema. He collected
clippings from the Italian press and published them in Russian translation, compiled film scripts, and wrote a biography of Vittorio De Sica. In
his travelogue, Bogemskii created an implicit community of "Soviet
viewers" united by a shared source of knowledge: *Rome, Open City, Bicycle Thieves, Rome, 11 O'Clock*.[192] Viktor Nekrasov wished he had more
time in Naples, so he could "stroll [the streets], loaf about the markets,
[and] meet the characters from Eduardo De Filippo's pictures." That he
would meet them in the streets he had no doubt: Soviet visitors assumed,
even before traveling, that Italian films were true to life. They met De
Filippo's and De Santis's protagonists because they had prepared themselves for such a meeting. As Nekrasov put it, "we encountered a real
Neapolitan, exactly as we imagined Neapolitans." He was named the part,
Dante-Buonarotto.[193]

In depicting Naples or Trastevere in Rome, travel writers created
their own neorealist film. Travelogues described buxom and disheveled
women, sitting by doorsteps or looking out of windows, cleaning beans,
flinging soapy water or slops, bargaining with itinerant traders, and yelling
at each other; their slender, beautiful daughters rushing to a date; their husbands working, complaining about unemployment, and debating politics
in the street; and their children, unwashed, poorly dressed, but spirited and
cheerful. The narrow passageways were noisy and crowded. Junkmen,
traders in fried fish, currency dealers, paupers—everybody was here.[194]

In these neorealist mise-en-scènes, drying laundry, stretched across the
street from building to building, was a principal attribute. By the late 1950s,
laundry fluttering in mid-air had become an Italianesque visual cliché: a
staple of Soviet travelogues and sketches, conveying a life at once tragic and
"charming." Soviet artists pursued narrow side streets for what appeared to
be quintessential Italianness: "frayed, multicolored buildings, . . . covered
with laundry."[195] The white patches of laundry brightened the browns and
dirty yellows of the buildings in Semen Chuikov's oil studies. The sheets
and nightgowns cast deep shadows and enclosed the viewer within the
intimate world of someone else's life.[196] Chuikov rendered these alleys,
apartment buildings with peeling paint, these architectural heaps of balconies, window shutters, and staircases, these claustrophobic, vertical
cityscapes in a patchwork of large strokes of scorched yellows, oranges,
and browns, muddy violets and grays. For instance, in his series "Rome.

Figure 6.2. Semen Chuikov, *Rome, Piazza de'Renzi*, 1963.
Published by permission of Ivan Semenovich Chuikov.

Trastevere," the cityscapes were monotonous and often devoid of people. Drying laundry—colorful scraps of textile that Chuikov called garlands—added a touch of playfulness, an ornament, to the back alley. The artist Anatolii Kokorin felt keenly the constricted space of side streets, as if the walls tightly enfolded the space between buildings, with but "a scrap of blue sky" visible "high above." He sketched "poor Venetian neighborhoods" from a frontal lower viewpoint, capturing the narrowing alley in a series of acute angles.[197] By contrast, his drawings of central avenues and squares presented panoramic sights from a side glance revealing a busy crowd in motion or from a bird's-eye view, with ink blots for human figures, with the roofs of cars and buses, and with a sense of wide space.

Not everyone delighted in narrow alleys, flapping laundry, and slops. Smirnov "turned the corner" from wide avenues filled with festive crowds, glimmering shop windows, and posh autos. Beyond the corner was a dark, narrow street, but he did not find the colorful scenes from Italian films. What he found was a pervasive and uncinematic stench. As he crossed the alley, Smirnov grew sick from "stale, washed off laundry, kitchen stink, the reek of some rotting refuse," and "thick, unmoving" air.[198] His visceral reaction notwithstanding, Smirnov's experience sounds all too ideologically correct, and indeed, these rancid streets were not only places of disease; they were also spaces of politics. It was here, on these "darkened walls," that travelers discovered, to their satisfaction, political scribbles: "Peace!"; "Long live the Soviet Union!"; and "Yankee, go home!"[199] Soviet travelogues took readers to leftist enclaves, the streets and buildings associated with communist offices and actions.[200] The topography of radicalism continued with the sites of the antifascist underground. This was the source of ideological affinity that Soviet visitors felt for their hosts. In the stories of the Resistance, Italians were no longer comically impulsive. The passion was reticent and courageous, the language economical.[201]

Fueling artistic and political passions was an insane, improbable love. In the Soviet iteration of the European Romantic tradition, Italy was a woman; in turn, the woman was a central figure in these literary works.[202] The writer Boris Evgen'ev, in a book of essays documenting the Italian traces in his life, drew on a sensual vocabulary. For this travelogue was one man's, but also a collective confession of love: Evgen'ev's impossible first love for a girl named Francesca and the loves of great Russian expatriates. His account was haunted by apparitions of women. Repeatedly, the voyage turned into voyeurism. Evgen'ev wished to "spy on [a foreign life] furtively, as if through a chink, to see it untidy, domestic."[203] Already in the opening pages, as his tour bus passed by small towns en route from Rome to Naples, Evgen'ev spotted "a beauty with luxuriant hair" in the street and wished he could stop and trade smiles with her.[204] In a roadside trattoria, he encountered Mariella, "very young, very pretty, swarthy, thin, her pink sweater fitting snuggly over her small, high chest." "A devilish girl," she walked, "wiggling her round behind draped in a little skirt," gave men "an alluring, mysterious smile," and Evgen'ev at once invented a "neorealist" drama. According to his imaginary screenplay, the owner of the trattoria was "pathetically, timidly in love" with the girl, while his "fat, ample-bosomed, shaggy wife" silently hated and feared her, and the girl, in turn, waited for her prince in "an extravagant, low, square-shaped Cadillac" who would "take her away."[205] In Venice, as he glided past Palazzo Corner, Ca' Pesaro and Ca' Foscari, he imagined "a lovely female face in one of the windows appearing but for a moment," and "the figure of a man, wrapped in a black cloak, with white, long-nosed bauta mask under his cocked hat, who rushes across these green, molding stairs." Upon arriving in Naples late in the evening, Evgen'ev saw in an open window across the street a lonely, "aging, large woman, in a robe with bright flower pattern"; she paced up and down, smoking, as if waiting for somebody.[206]

Woman was Evgen'ev's symbolic juxtaposition of home and abroad, Russia and Italy. An excursion into the obscure seventeenth-century biography of Ivan Chemodanov, Muscovy's ambassador to Venice, inspired Evgen'ev to reflect on dislocation and nostalgia. Evgen'ev wrote an emotional drama into Chemodanov's biography—the drama of seeing another world and losing peace of mind. He imagined Chemodanov's life in Italy as burdensome service. Visibly out of place at the Venetian court, the Muscovite had longed to return home. But a longing worse than homesickness awaited him upon return. As he once dreamt of Muscovy in Venice, he now dreamt of Venice in Muscovy. In the snowy night, in a stuffy room, the Chemodanov of Evgen'ev's poetic musings could not sleep: "Time and again during sleepless nights, a moist, salty wind from the Venetian Lagoon blew into [his] hot, sweaty face. In the dusk of the room, warmed by the flickering lights of icon-lamps, [he] could hear water purling, foaming under a mighty stroke of an oar. And the floor rocked, as if [he] sat in a gondola, gliding along a canal . . . Or, suddenly, [he] would sense the smell of cypresses, heated by the sun. . . . Anguish, sick at heart!" Chemodanov's Venetian apparition in the midst of a Moscow snowstorm included a woman—"a cursed Venetian red-haired girl, jolly and capricious," very different from his lethargic Russian wife, "imbecilic," "fluffy, white-skinned" "broody hen," sleeping while he dreamt of Venice.[207]

Like Evgen'ev, most Soviet travel writers associated Italy with carnal pleasures. They spoke of arrival as drunken revelry. Walking in Florence, riding along via Appia, or gazing at seaside panoramas were sensual experiences—enveloping their bodies in "sweetness." Sensual as well was art itself. Prokof'ev described the gold mosaic in Ravenna's Mausoleum of Galla Placidia as "intoxicating, sensuous," and "mysteriously tender."[208] For Chuikov, classical sculptures were alive. He saw the folds of their tunics "stirring, fluttering," took pleasure in drawing them, and chose a quick sketch, rather than detailed shading, to convey their dynamism. With the sculptures, as with a real woman, he "experienced wondrous hours," "ineffable bliss."[209]

But for all the corporeality of these experiences, the Italian trip appeared illusory. Even while in Venice, Prokof'ev kept thinking: "Does it exist, this city?" He devoted several hundred pages to Renaissance architecture; his book was about stone, brick, marble, and bronze, as tangible as matter gets. Yet, his memory preserved Venice as "something fantastic, almost unreal," arising from the waters like a miraculous vision. It glides, it moves, it "loses all connection with the ground."[210] Bogemskii warned that something like that would happen if travelers did not arm themselves with the knowledge of local politics and glided in a gondola along the Grand Canal, rather than "turning the corner" onto those dark and dismal alleys. He did turn the corner, but still spoke about Venice as "suspended in the air between earth and heaven."[211] Even for Chuikov, who had reflected on the tangibility of claustrophobic side streets and on the vivacity of antique sculptures, Italy began to lose its reality shortly after departure. He had not yet arrived home when he thought of Italy as an apparition. A ticket from Florence to Rome—an ephemeral piece—remained as proof of something that happened "long ago and was not very real" anyway.[212]

The Failure of Recognition

In France and Italy, Soviet travelers were unpleasantly struck by a pervasive American presence. Hollywood cinema—Westerns and horror films—occupied the best and biggest movie theaters, while garish posters festooned building facades in old city centers: cowboys, blondes baring their shoulders, vampires, monsters, King Kongs, and gangsters. Nighttime Paris was infused with jazz and rock 'n' roll. American soldiers and tourists were loud, ignorant, smug, and mercantile. In Soviet accounts of Italy, a frequent scenario, set in a museum, had a guide's learned monologue abruptly interrupted by an American asking about the price of a priceless masterpiece. Americans purchased mass-produced souvenirs, fell for ersatz culture, and splurged big money in the conviction that everything can be bought. Their tastelessly bright clothing and crude manners conspicuously set them apart.[213]

That was the Soviet portrayal of Americans in Europe. Americans appeared quite different at home, where Soviet journalists and writers began to visit them in 1955. Travelers had read American nineteenth- and twentieth-century fiction, and now searched their literary memories for referents. They "knew" the names and places: James Fenimore Cooper, Mayne Reid, Mark Twain, Jack London, and Theodore Dreiser. For Soviet visitors, the journey from Salt Lake City to California could follow "the romantic roads of Mark Twain, Jack London, [and] O. Henry, through the cities and towns that in the middle of the past century had acquired a noisy reputation as the centers of fabled profits, as the hotbed of 'the Gold Rush.'"[214] At the New York Stock Exchange, Soviet journalists relied on Theodore Dreiser for the context in which to make sense of stock trading. They did not have "the nerve" to reveal their novelistic source of information to their American guides.[215] Hemingway's *The Old Man and the Sea*, published in *Foreign Literature* in 1955, was a stylistically modernized variation on Cooper's and London's heroes. The Soviets, who traveled to a Utah mining town (perhaps Bingham Canyon) that same year, spotted in a tiny tourist shop an old man "with the face of a Hemingway character or even Hemingway himself." Hemingway's portrait also hung in the shop.[216] In San Francisco, walking by the ocean one morning, they encountered another Hemingway: an old fisherman, his face "weather-beaten," as the cliché went, "with a hawk's nose," wearing high boots, a tarpaulin jacket, and faded hat. He was parsimonious with words. The analogy was complete: "How wonderful was this old fisherman by the stormy ocean—the old man and the sea. Hemingway!"[217]

However delightful they were, Hemingway look-alikes were all that struck a familiar chord for Soviet travelers. For, unlike in Europe, in the United States, literature, cinema, and painting largely failed to effect recognition. In a much-publicized 1955 trip, seven prominent journalists (editors-in-chief of the most influential Soviet periodicals, who were also translators, poets, and prose writers) traveled to the United States for a cross-country journey.[218] Arriving at various destinations with novelistic reminiscences in mind, they discovered a reality that did not conform to their literary expectations. "Discovery" beyond books—a ready-made metaphor for landing in America—was a central theme in their travelogues. This was the first trip explicitly under the sign of "peaceful coexistence." In 1955, the Soviet and American governments began a conversation on some form of cultural exchange, a conversation that, three years later, would become the famous Lacy-Zarubin agreement. As a gesture of goodwill and an exercise in public diplomacy, the two governments sponsored delegations of agriculturalists and journalists. The reciprocal trips of the journalists spurred a long paper trail on both sides: newspaper reports, travelogues, and secret documents.[219]

Among Soviet accounts of that trip, Boris Polevoi's *American Diaries* (1956) was the most notable and representative of the "peaceful coexistence" mantra. A journalist for the Communist Party newspaper *Pravda*, Polevoi was a prominent figure in the writers' guild and an astute politician. In addition to the printed travelogue, he also wrote a different kind of narrative: an unpublished piece of cultural reconnaissance for the Central Committee. The two texts, the travelogue and the policy memo, have more in common than meets the eye. In his policy recommendations, Polevoi argued for rethinking Soviet propaganda, information gathering, and views of the United States.[220] This was a pragmatic document, but its subtext was the failure of literary recognition: the epistemological basis of Soviet perceptions—nineteenth- and early twentieth-century prose— seemed thoroughly outdated. Although *American Diaries* was about "open doors," tolerance of different peoples and points of view, and conversations in gestures that needed no translation, at the end of the travelogue, Polevoi confessed failure.[221] For all the talk of mutual understanding, America "remain[ed] as faraway, alien [*chuzhaia*], interesting, and somewhat incomprehensible" as it had been at the start of the journey: "another planet."[222]

Rather than American fiction, the journalists found Soviet travelogues from the 1920s and 1930s to provide a more helpful lens. Polevoi styled *American Diaries* as an updated version of Ilya Il'f and Evgenii Petrov's *American Road Trip* (1936), in which the popular satirists created a situational memory for future Soviet travelers.[223] Polevoi and his colleagues journeyed practically in Il'f and Petrov's footsteps and, throughout the trip, checked the United States of the 1950s against the earlier portrayal. Beyond the big cities, the scenery turned "one-storied," an image and expression coined by Il'f and Petrov to describe small-town life, slow-paced, provincial, and personal, in contrast to the anonymous skyscrapers of the metropoles.[224] Polevoi confirmed the depiction: "Yes, Il'f and Petrov were right . . . we drove into one-storied America, the country of small estates, good roads, gas stations, stores where one could buy everything, from a toothbrush to an automobile."[225] This America was a welcoming and convenient place, and Polevoi did not hide his admiration for its comforts and regularity. He and other Soviet travelers fixated on cars, whose significance struck them as odd. The car was everywhere: a necessity, a source of prestige, an article of devotion, a place of amorous rendezvous, and an object of dreams. Polevoi was astonished by car production, seasonal displays at dealerships, and drive-in movie theaters. The word itself, which he transliterated in Russian (*kar*), as Il'f and Petrov had done, invaded his travelogue, hiding in direct speech, translated signs, and authorial text.[226] With such repetition, Polevoi and his fellow journalists rewrote, and perhaps relived, Il'f and Petrov's iconic trip for a new age. They even looked up a key protagonist from *American Road Trip*, Dr. Reynolds—"yes, yes, the same Reynolds who had . . . taken Ilya Il'f and Evgenii Petrov to see the construction of the now famous Oakland [Bay] Bridge." Polevoi did meet Dr. Reynolds and his wife, and although he spoke no English, he understood them anyway, as had Il'f and Petrov.[227] One would be tempted to read Polevoi's gentle humor, quiet respect, and feigned sadness for the imperfections of capitalist life as an expression of the "spirit of Geneva." But, in fact, it was conditioned by Il'f and Petrov's narrative style of the 1930s.[228]

Il'f and Petrov had pioneered the Soviet notion of "ordinary Americans," telling their stories and printing their photographs. "The ordinary American" became the dominant figure and interpretive lens in Thaw travelogues.[229] The main protagonists of *American Diaries* were common people, not the philistine snobs in gaudy outfits whom the Soviets encountered in Europe. Thus, for example, a car mechanic, on whose door the journalists knocked late one evening and whose family greeted them affably. His house embodied the American dream, of which Polevoi wrote with approving indulgence and benevolent condescension. Polevoi spelled all creature comforts in the diminutive, to indicate the smallness of spirit. The mechanic's "little house" boasted a refrigerator, a television set, "a tiny kitchenette" with "sparkling little pots"; the mechanic's wife wore "a little robe." The family had three children and feared war. War and peace were the main subjects of that evening's conversations—as well as of all other conversations.[230] The ordinary Americans whom Polevoi encountered spoke, unaware, in a perfectly Soviet idiom of "peaceful coexistence."[231]

In Polevoi's travelogue just about everybody, including millionaires, newspaper moguls, and movie stars, was an "ordinary American." In Cleveland, Soviet journalists visited the great financier Cyrus S. Eaton, a devotee and funder of the peace cause. Polevoi described the man and his home as humble: his manners and dress were simple, his "baggy jacket" was not particularly fashionable, the furniture was old and worn out, the living room was graced with a "modest fireplace" and "antique candlesticks." They felt comfortable around him and in his home—there were no "aristocratic ceremonies."[232] Grace Kelly was likewise modest, even self-effacing. Dressed "artlessly, in a white cotton blouse and a similar dark skirt, with no jewelry," she looked like "thousands of working girls, who so skillfully and confidently, with knowledge and great conscientiousness, work in endless American offices." Her image "destroyed the standard perceptions of Hollywood prima donnas."[233]

In Soviet travelogues, the America of "ordinary people" was naive, unpretentious, and easygoing; it was a country of commoners with a common-sense morality.[234] Their tastes were unrefined—try the "bland," "standardized" food.[235] Their speech was unaffected: they spoke their minds straightforwardly, to the point of "rudeness," and did not pass an opportunity for a "salty joke." Energetic and sociable, they approached Soviet travelers in public places to ask questions and shake hands.[236] And yet, there was something dissimulating about ordinary Americans: their smiles. Polevoi did not attempt to reconcile dissimulation and frankness. He only registered a gap in comprehension when it came to that wide smile, which hid more than it revealed. "An American must always look content and successful, he must always smile, no matter how he feels inside." "Keep smiling!" Polevoi, refusing to understand this disguise, spelled in Cyrillic a favorite American dictum to capture its sound and strangeness.[237]

In 1960, Viktor Nekrasov went to the United States with a tour group and wrote a controversial and, at the time, famous travelogue.[238] Nekrasov had penned several books, but until this account brought him *succès de scandale,* he was known to readers for the most Remarquean novel in Soviet literature, *Front-line Stalingrad* (1946), about male friendships, understated emotions, the chaos of war, and the impossibility of reentering peacetime. Himself a combat engineer at Stalingrad, Nekrasov had joined the Communist Party during the war. Yet, his travelogue was animated by a contrarian spirit as he rejected the conventions of Soviet travel writing, specifically, "turning the corner" in pursuit of slums.[239] He asserted the author's right to a subjective vision and used the trip as an opportunity to comment on domestic culture. He found Mayne Reid and James Fenimore Cooper irrelevant and dispensed with prior knowledge, including Il'f and Petrov.[240] But the one conventional plotline Nekrasov did not eschew was the depiction of "ordinary Americans" as "trusting," "affable," and "easygoing." "Simple" people, they hated formalities, liked to have fun, and loved a strong drink and a good joke. Their naïveté and sociability bordered on the childlike; Nekrasov characterized them as "infantile" for avoiding serious philosophical and political conversations.[241] However, just as Polevoi thought their smiles were a mask, Nekrasov found something that set the limits to the naïveté and cheerfulness of "the ordinary American." That something was money. Nekrasov created a portrait of the American as calculating, pragmatic, and egotistical, occupied by a singular pursuit of "business" to the exclusion of the common good. Indeed, collective responsibility seemed inimical to the average citizen, nor was this his individual fault. After all, business and self-interest were societal norms.[242] These were the first inklings about American frankness, simplicity, and good nature; but the stereotype persisted through travel accounts—until émigré literature and experience destroyed it.

The ordinary American was the Soviet authors' invention and interlocutor. Polevoi took an ordinary American ("a small house . . . a good car," two kids) by the name of John Smith for an imaginary travel companion. Polevoi had met "Smith" at the Elbe in April 1945, during an encounter between Soviet and American troops. In the discourse on "peaceful coexistence," this encounter was a propagandistic highlight; and Polevoi dedicated the travelogue to the memory of the Elbe.[243] In *American Diaries*, Polevoi portrayed the fraternizing of Allied combatants as intimate and "lyrical." Soviet and American soldiers exchanged objects (lighters, buttons), food, drink, song, dance, and flowers. John Smith and Boris Polevoi traded the most precious things they had. Polevoi took the red star off his cap; in return, the American gave a picture of his wife and children, his own inscription "To the Russian ally in eternal friendship. John Smith. 1945, Elbe" doubling his wife's "We are waiting for you."[244]

Polevoi organized his travelogue around a quest to find John Smith. He did not find that particular John Smith. But he did find an archetypical Smith, a figure Polevoi used to stage situations of ideological significance as dialogues with "the ordinary American." A visit to the Stock Exchange, where Soviet journalists learned that citizens of average means were shareholders, concluded with one such conversation: Polevoi envisioned Smith as a small shareholder. The invented Smith defended his proud co-ownership with an argument for a new capitalism that spread wealth more broadly. Polevoi exposed the argument as a lie to co-opt ordinary people, credulous like John Smith, into the workings of capitalism.[245] But even as he revealed Smith's gullibility, Polevoi consistently appealed to that common humanity of the Elbe, calling Smith "my old wartime comrade." The very last words of the travelogue were meant for him: "Give me your hand, my American buddy, let us embrace like we did back then, in a faraway German land."[246]

Viktor Nekrasov had his own John Smith, named Patrick Stanley, whom he met on the last night of the Soviets' sojourn in New York. The friendship they struck belonged to the same wartime brotherhood. Stanley was a "lieutenant," "a gunner and radio operator," who had fought in Ukraine, practically Nekrasov's comrade-in-arms. Middle-aged, with graying temples, Stanley was still tough; he spoke matter-of-factly, his statements were terse and his feelings hidden in the subtext. Their conversation was styled after Hemingway. They chanced upon each other at a bar, drank beer, but talked about stronger things.[247] Nekrasov did not record the conversation as a dialogue. Rather, he spoke both for himself and for his interlocutor, merging the two lines and perspectives into a monologue. That was because Nekrasov indeed talked to himself: there was no Patrick Stanley. Nekrasov invented him, along "with this whole story of a nighttime trip." He invented it all because he so intensely wanted for Patrick Stanley, the ordinary American, to cross his path and to speak in a universal language of wartime brotherhood and strong drink.[248] On the plane home, Nekrasov fancied "flying over America, over France, over the whole earth." This was a quintessentially Thaw fantasy.[249]

While Il'f and Petrov scripted the small town and the ordinary American, the revolutionary writer and founder of Soviet literature Maxim Gorky supplied the images of the big city. In his apocalyptic vision of New York in 1906, the soiled and stocky metropolis was an iron beast that had swallowed millions of people, who now inhabited the dark intestines of its avenues and streets. The shadows of silent skyscrapers and "the terrifying abundance" of "insolent" "yellow lights" (which Gorky called "molten Gold") recurred in later Soviet descriptions and drawings.[250] In Polevoi's account, the skyscrapers appeared dark and heavy, their weight pressing upon readers in such metaphors as "electric iron" for the New York Times building.[251] New York felt narrow. Its streets at the feet of skyscrapers reminded Polevoi of constricted ravines: "When the lights went out at night and only two-three illuminated windows loomed up high, it was as if you were walking on the bottom of a deep gorge, while there, at the top, glowed the bonfires of hunters or shepherds." The city was a sediment formed by a natural cataclysm of enormous proportions, "squeezed out of the earth by some titanic forces." The noise of the subway resonated with this picture: the bowels of the earth from whence the city had emerged continued to roar, tremble, exhale heat, and exude foul breath.[252] Polevoi's geological metaphors recalled Gorky's images from the (super)natural repertory of the city-monster breathing fire. Nekrasov, too, resorted to geological and natural analogies for describing New York. The "city-octopus," resembling Gorky's monster, lay "in the ravines" between skyscrapers. From the top of the Empire State Building, he observed that "dozens of skyscrapers crowd upon a vast space, and among them, like in gorges, crawl some kind of ants and race tiny cars." As he stood, the wind "fanning," he likened the feeling of elevation (in the sense of both the building's height and human conquest of the elements) to rising atop Mount Elbrus.[253]

In the graphic artist Orest Vereiskii's sketches of New York and Chicago, the low vantage point created a sense of American streets as ravines and gorges indeed. A member of the governing board of the Institute of Soviet-American Relations, Vereiskii was an authority on the United States among visual artists. In the 1960s, he traveled there twice for reciprocal exchanges of artists and graphic arts exhibits. While on official missions, Vereiskii filled his albums with drawings and watercolors, which he displayed at the House of Friendship. His skyscrapers rose as harsh massifs. In a sketch of Park Avenue, the angular edges of the dark silhouette in the foreground cut the sharp lines of the contrasting white skyscraper behind it. These monochrome colossi competed with the checkered background of windows from yet other buildings. And a small human figure was lost in the lower corner. In a Chicago drawing, the viewer, positioned on the ground, was jammed between two rows of protruding metal constructions—building staircases. In another picture from Chicago, low, dark railroad tracks, observed from below, functioned as the sky and the ceiling. Dominating the work, their mass pushed the source of light to the very edge of the paper and beyond.[254]

The aesthetics of unadorned geometry was "strange" for Soviet visitors.[255] They saw the proliferation of vertical lines as evidence of technical genius but not of cultural refinement. Yet they admired the architectural virtuosity and called it beautiful.[256] Nekrasov sang the skyscrapers' uniqueness and allure. "I saw many faceless cities in America, each like the next so you cannot tell [them] apart: Buffalo, Detroit, something else, all have merged, but not New York or Chicago. They have their own face, their own charm, their own soul," breathtaking even if "foreign to me."[257] Nekrasov had trained in architecture in the early 1930s, at a time when constructivism was the byword of new socialist housing. In the travelogue, he spoke as a layman whose professional knowledge lent him credence. Whereas other Soviet authors disparaged the skyscrapers as bulky and overpowering,

Figure 6.3. Orest Vereiskii, *Chicago Subway,* 1964.
Published by permission of Anna Orestovna Khmeleva née Vereiskaia.

Nekrasov experienced them as "airy [and] translucent." He adored "the accentuated urbanism" of glass and steel. There was even something playful in those titanic buildings—the way they looked into and reflected in each other's windows.[258] Nekrasov poeticized the skyscrapers at dawn; illuminated by the rising sun, they were not the nighttime monsters of Polevoi's description. Chicago's Prudential Building (today's One Prudential Plaza) "burn[ed]" as its windows reflected "the low November sun."[259] The Empire State Building emerged from "the morning fog" suddenly, its pinnacle "pink from the sun [and] the shine of windows." Walking around Manhattan, Nekrasov "understood the beauty of this enormous, contradictory city."[260] He also understood, he assured his readers, the problems of living— or not living—amid skyscrapers. But his appreciation was not for skyscrapers as a solution to housing needs. It was, rather, for "the image": the image of the city and its picture-perfect skyline that "looks good only on postcards and is liked only by tourists."[261] Nekrasov, however, was not embarrassed by being a tourist. In his account, the Soviet group behaved like

other visitors: they posed for pictures in Times Square, gaped at the huge
Camel billboard, and went to the movies to see Elvis, "the idol of American
girls."[262]

Nekrasov's unapologetic espousal of postcard vistas and tourist perspectives entangled him in the ideological campaign of 1962–1963. The
campaign was directed against modernist and Western inflections in literature, sculpture, and painting; but Nekrasov's failure "to turn the corner"
from gleaming avenues to alleys where the hungry rummaged through
trash cans was a sure sign of the old kowtowing to the West. According to
an anonymous editorial in the government newspaper *Izvestiia*, Nekrasov's
travelogue was factually mistaken and ideologically misguided in admiring
American goods, skyscrapers, and services, while overlooking destitution,
crime, racism, and cultural degradation. Hence, the editorial's doubly sarcastic title "A Tourist with a Walking Stick," implying that the travelogue
was superficial and frivolous. The antitourist discourse suggested that
Nekrasov had been fooled by the capitalist facade, and the walking stick
added a touch of social snobbery to the writer's image. His critical comparisons between the United States and the Soviet Union, to the latter's
disadvantage, indicated that he may have been malevolently unpatriotic
rather than innocently gullible; the editorial judged the travelogue offensive to "the sacred feelings of Soviet man."[263] Even before the editorial,
Nekrasov's conduct raised a few indignant eyebrows: the trip leader reported
that he had meandered alone in New York, consorted with unknown Americans late into the night in Washington, visited Russian émigrés, and, according to the KGB, enjoyed the company of "women of ill repute."[264] In
quick succession, the republican newspaper *Literary Ukraine* followed with
its own damning publication, and the Communist Party committee at the
Ukrainian Writers' Union censured the travelogue. Against all reproofs,
Nekrasov defended his portrayal of the trip.[265] In Soviet rituals of criticism
and self-criticism, such defiance meant political rottenness. At the June 1963
Central Committee plenum on ideology, Khrushchev berated Nekrasov
for losing "the precious qualities of a communist, the sense of party-
mindedness" and "degenerating" so low as to uphold "a mistaken personal opinion" against higher-order party criticism.[266] Four months later,
the Kiev regional party committee gave Nekrasov a severe reprimand and
a warning. By then, journals and publishing houses had stopped printing
his works, while rumors in Kiev claimed that libraries withdrew his
novels from circulation.[267]

In the days following the *Izvestiia* attack, the phone in Nekrasov's apartment rang continuously. Friends and strangers were calling to express "naive indignation," as Nekrasov's aunt described it.[268] Readers' letters conveyed a mix of trusting support and irate rejection of the propagandistic conventions in writing about Western countries. They knew the scenarios and truisms by heart: "hunger, unemployment, and poverty."[269] Fabricating an endless array of interchangeable, derogatory formulas did not require going anywhere, suggested one letter writer, putting "travelers" in quotation marks.[270] So pervasive and unvarying were these clichés that the socioeconomic vocabulary had lost all credibility with readers. For Efrosiniia Pokryshkina, a homemaker from a settlement in the Krasnodarskii region, such texts merged into the all-encompassing darkness of capitalism. She listed common descriptions of capitalist cities: "sullen, colossal [buildings] or hovels, dirty side streets or central avenues, . . . where intrusive lights roar and glitter, and where gasoline saturates [the air]." Not only this manmade world, but nature, too, was somehow wrong. "It turns out," she wrote in disbelief, "that even the sun shines in another country differently than here." Soviet travelers seemed to be perpetually caught in bad weather, either "overcast, foggy" or "impossibly hot." Much as she tried, Pokryshkina could not find likeable foreigners. The extremes of poverty and prosperity disfigured their features—the workers' faces were "emaciated [and] pale, [their] cheeks hollow," and the wealthy had "dim-witted expressions, angry, [and] crude." Such uniform images may have been dubious, but they nonetheless had insidious power. Pokryshkina noticed that her children were especially receptive to "dark" portrayals. "My oldest daughter is already in sixth grade, but in her imagination, people living abroad are as scary as depicted in newspaper caricatures and as nasty as fascists, and try convincing her that they are people just like us, that they are not nasty, and that not everybody there wants war." Pokryshkina knew better. Although she did not claim cultural sophistication (her writing was colloquial, and she called herself "an ordinary woman"), she loved "geography," pursued "books [and] brochures that describe the countries of our planet," and was keenly interested in "the life [and] customs" of other peoples. Yet she, too, could not escape what she called "a shroud" of negative stereotypes "over my eyes."[271]

Amid this publishing output, Nekrasov's travelogue stood apart for its originality, which readers received as "the truth." Most letters applauded Nekrasov for "sincerity," for "an unprejudiced," "objective," and "honest" portrayal of American life.[272] What was Nekrasov's "truth," and how could people who had never been to the United States evaluate it?

What made his prose "sincere," in the terminology of the Thaw, was Nekrasov's informal and subjective tone, which invited dialogue. The account was conspicuously autobiographical, his foreign impressions fusing with intimate memories of home. His "I," rather than the collective "we" of Soviet travelers, admitted the subjectivities of his readers. They felt that he neither preached nor imposed himself but allowed for their comparisons and judgments—a reading experience they found "unusual."[273] For letter writer V. Karpov, from the working-class town Severnyi near Moscow, Nekrasov's truth was not solely in what he wrote but also in how: in the textual space for "a conversation of equals."[274] Perhaps it was this space for dialogue that urged people to read together. "It is impossible to read your things alone," explained a young woman from Rostov-on-Don; these texts were for sharing, and she read the American account with her husband. Her friends, too, read the travelogue in the company of others.[275] Nekrasov broke through the enduring narrative conventions of Soviet travel writing. Not only did his intonation differ, not only did he commend the sights that were usually condemned, but he also ridiculed the familiar travel routes and writing tropes. Hence, readers described the travelogue's effect as a "fresh wind" and "clean breeze": "a conscientious search for truth . . . where it has not existed for a long time, in surveys of the life and mores of the capitalist world."[276] For the young woman from Rostov-on-Don and for her roommates, Nekrasov's "truth" was a "departure from the predictable plan," a "lively and witty story" instead of deadpan politics—and they believed him.[277] Another letter writer, a Muscovite, equated "unorthodox thoughts" with "truthful information" and traced both to Nekrasov's disdain for "the paucity of tourist itineraries with their obligatory schedules and the tour guide's constant fear of losing the travelers entrusted to him (like in daycare)."[278] Readers suspected that Nekrasov was "hit over the head with a walking stick" precisely for the unusual portrayal of something that had been formalized, inflexible, and taken for granted. They readily accepted unconventionality as truth.

In this reading culture, Nekrasov's text assumed an ethical charge beyond its purpose or subject, for it joined the 1962–1963 reevaluation of political violence under Stalin. This breezy travelogue with a humorous touch had nothing to do with the Stalinist past. But it was published in the same volume of the journal *Novyi mir* as Aleksandr Solzhenitsyn's *One Day in the Life of Ivan Denisovich*, which gave Soviet readers their first look at the Gulag's barracks, guard towers, and eternal camp sentences. Nekrasov's travelogue also overlapped with the serialization of Ilya Ehrenburg's *People, Years, Life*, where the aged writer contemplated the Stalin phenomenon, described arrests among the cultural elite, and put forth the question of personal and collective responsibility for the Terror.[279] Responding to Solzhenitsyn's novella and Ehrenburg's memoirs, readers reflected on the media vilification campaigns of the 1930s as enabling mass violence.[280] In this unhinged moral environment, with the Soviet press implicated in the repressive apparatus, came the assault on Nekrasov's travelogue. I. Efimov had not read Nekrasov's book. He responded not to the travelogue, but to a censuring article in whose "tone" he heard "a police shout" from "the cruelest of times, . . . a complete suppression of freedom of the press."[281] Almost all letter writers linked the attack on Nekrasov to "the recent, [and] not particularly happy, past." The unsupported political accusations were chilling.[282] An anonymous "well-wisher," who was afraid to sign his name and embarrassed by his fear, thought there was nothing "new or unpredictable" to the campaign against Nekrasov. "For many decades, such has been the fate," he remarked gloomily, "of all honest people who try to say or write what they think."[283] Readers pictured Nekrasov as an exemplar of moral probity who would not trade "the truth" for material comforts.[284] For them, "the truth" of Nekrasov's travelogue about a country they had never visited was a moral ethos and an emotional disposition. Truth was not intrinsic to the text; rather, it accrued from political context. Nekrasov's truth was the opposite of the newspaper lie. Readers admitted no possibility of multiple truths—it was unfathomable that there might have been any substance to the loathed Soviet stereotypes of life in the West. And thus, Western imaginings became an ethical territory of courage.

The author of that anonymous *Izvestiia* editorial against Nekrasov was the journalist Melor Sturua. An *Izvestiia* reporter first stationed in New York in 1968, then in Washington, DC, in the late 1970s, Sturua was a prolific and notorious commentator on the United States in Soviet popular media. His first American texts, from the late 1960s, were aggressively anti-American. An attentive and clever stylist, he wrote with rhetorical flair and bile. Sturua's America was an ideological entity, often lacking physical specificity. Unlike other accounts of foreign countries, whatever the genre, Sturua's writings did not convey a sense of place: readers could not claim to have traveled to the United States, walked along this street or stood next to that monument. The American cities of his stories did not feel like anything—smell, color, and texture were absent from Sturua's prose. So were "ordinary Americans." Sturua's protagonists were leading politicians, film stars, entertainment moguls, and criminals.[285] He used some of the biggest names in American politics and culture to craft detective stories. In these morality tales, the police were often present, and there were many machinations with Lady Justice.

Sturua shone a sinister light on America. Nothing was innocent, not even pastoral landscapes. Sturua's descriptions served as a backdrop to political drama. Thus, a depiction of the wooden, decrepit Dike Bridge opened a story about Senator Ted Kennedy and the drowning of Mary Jo Kopechne.[286] Sturua's picture of the Cape Cod landscape and cottages was a stage piece for scandal. Indeed, scandal—commotion, publicity, and manipulation of information—was at the heart of his stories. Sturua exposed the legal and media stratagems to salvage the senator's reputation and condemned American society for the cynicism with which personal tragedies were used in big-power politics.[287] Journalism was a farce, motivated by "thirst" for entertainment, power, and smut.[288] Especially for smut: the press reflected, savored, and publicized "the vile passions of high society." Sturua wrote several essays about the porn industry, beauty contests, and other forms of infatuation with the female body, arguing for the centrality of sex to the moral fabric of American society. He saw Americans as both promiscuous and puritanical: "a gigantic petty soul, sanctimonious, sentimental, and conceited," proclaiming Victorian morality, on the one hand, and seeking lascivious experiences clandestinely, on the other.[289]

Money and commerce were the leitmotif in Sturua's American writings. Everybody was a sellout, and everything was for sale. Indeed, several stories were about people for hire, or that is how Sturua presented the lives of Judy Garland, Louis Armstrong, Muhammad Ali, and Rocky Marciano.[290] An astute observer of American popular culture and media, Sturua discerned the construction of events and personalities for mass consumption. In his sweeping denunciation of consumer society, Sturua used "engineering"—the making of synthetic things—as a metaphor for counterfeit lives and feelings.[291] Lest his readers recall a different American code of honor—grace under pressure—from the beloved books by Jack London and Ernest Hemingway, Sturua reminded them: "Life is at once more and less complicated than the long novels of Jack London and the short stories of Ernest Hemingway."[292]

Their America was a literary invention beyond recognition.

The Thaw witnessed a tremendous explosion of travel writing. Resolutions on the expansion of foreign tourism were passed, old travel agencies were resuscitated, and new procedures and service standards were established. Foreigners began to visit the Soviet Union by the thousands. However, the reverse traffic—Soviet citizens traveling abroad, especially to capitalist countries—was highly asymmetrical. Discourse on travel compensated for restrictions and promised opportunities in the future. All sorts of texts— memoirs and novels, art history books and architectural guides, photography exhibits and postcards—functioned as travel writing. That was because travelogues not only reflected trips, but, more important, allowed readers and viewers who could not go abroad to travel vicariously.

Recognition haunted Soviet writers and artists in France and Italy. To their astonishment, they stepped into familiar reality, and they invoked childhood readings and dreams to make sense of this feeling of having been there. The travel writings of the 1950s and 1960s brought back the France and Italy of Soviet translations. Travelers also drew on new imports and visual experiences: impressionist paintings, which appeared in central museums and popular magazines in 1955, and neorealist films, which appeared in local movie theaters that same year. By contrast, the United States was an unfamiliar place, where literary sources failed to effect recognition. Created for people who could not ascertain the reality of foreign places, travel accounts raised the question of knowledge and veracity: how was anything to be believed? Readers and viewers had their own strategies. They searched for the first-person singular "I" as an attestation to the truth. The collective authorship of a "we" was dubious. They accepted unconventional or contrarian portrayals for accurate ones and turned a suspicious eye to Soviet set expressions. They took cues from political debates. And they aligned travelogues with what they knew from literary classics, new art, and cinema. The audiences' evaluations of veracity were moral judgments. It was thus that travel accounts, and Western imports in general, introduced the problem of credibility into a culture of information shortages.

The fundamental reality of that society was immobility in the context of ever-expanding print and visual space: ever more films, books, exhibitions, images, and words, without a possibility of firsthand experiences.

There was a tragic disconnect between the world people constructed out of travelogues and Western cultural imports and the monotony of their daily lives. They blamed the impossibility of travel for ennui, dissatisfaction with work, the drabness of location, and the triteness of aspirations. They ached for something they called "the fullness of life," and it included travel abroad. Immobility gave rise to wanderlust. "Meager, lacking richness, does not captivate me wholly," R. Dmitriev, an engineer from provincial Chita, lamented his life. "I want to live a life that would sprint like a fountain." At work, he fulfilled his duties, but found no outlet for creativity. He spent his free time reading nineteenth-century French classics, watching neorealist films, and seeking out the impressionists: "I love art. I especially enjoy Monet, Manet, Cézanne. On a business trip in Leningrad, I very often marveled at their paintings. And I felt something grand, something proud arising within me." Dmitriev's preoccupation with European stories and images moved him to dream of travel: "I want to see the world, the entire planet, and France first and foremost."[293]

The poignancy of such confessions emerged from a combination of resignation and protest. Against the odds of immobility, people loved the places that they had "never seen and probably will never see." Dmitriev's forbearance would have been understood by another provincial, a teacher with thwarted ambitions "to do something grand and real." R. A. Mesteliainen graduated from an institute and was sent to work in "a regional 'town,'" where he found ignorance and parochialism. "God forbid," he wrote, bemoaning the narrow-mindedness of local schools, "to recommend Stefan Zweig and *Colas Breugnon* to ninth-graders." His life turned dreary. But in defiant moments, Mesteliainen fancied "an opportunity to cross borders freely." He hinted at emigration as a hypothetical solution to the quest for travel. His intimation carried moral (self-)censure. There was something sinister, perhaps treasonous, about the idea: "I love my Motherland. Very much. . . . But sometimes it seems to me that I would be ready, that I would agree to go anywhere, to any country, if given a chance to do something truly novel. Is this dishonorable? I don't know."

What, in conditions of closed borders, could the future hold for people like this provincial teacher? He knew the answer: "Slippers, an old robe, a pipe, ailing eyes, Paris that remained unseen, *The Ring of the Nibelung* that remained unheard, books that remained unwritten . . . My God!"[294]

Epilogue
Exit: How Soviets Became Westerners

During détente, and again, perestroika, emigration became a possibility for hundreds of thousands of people who, over the decades, had fashioned their own West from the fragments available to them. Some were stripped of Soviet citizenship while traveling abroad. Others defected during tours or professional assignments. The majority, more than 350,000 people between 1971 and 1990, relinquished their Soviet citizenship and opted for provisional statelessness, promising, via signatures on a form issued by the Soviet Department of Visas and Registration, that they would not attempt to return.[1]

They made this promise because they were certain that beyond Soviet borders they would find the "good life" of abundance, mobility, excitement, and beauty, be it old winding streets or neon lights. The writer Sergei Dovlatov, a seismographer of late Soviet emigration, ascribed his own decision to emigrate to the "idea of Eden." Eden was America, the country of "cowboys, jeans, music records, and cocktails," inhabited by people whose elegance came from within, who were contemptuous of conventions and spoke in understatements.[2] This image originated in Hemingway's prose, translated and read as an ethical imperative under specific political circumstances. Indeed, the Russian émigré press returned several times to the decisive importance of "splendid" translations. The essayists Petr Vail' and Aleksandr Genis, who made their name with witty and perceptive comments about immigrants, credited "the Soviet school of translation" with creating both a great literature and an image of paradise.[3]

Unlike Dovlatov, most emigrants neither pondered nor articulated the sources of their Eden, but nevertheless were influenced by vague and generalized images when making life decisions. It was the emotional power of Edenic fantasy, rather than ethnic, religious, or political persecution, that the émigré press—whatever its political and aesthetic stripes—held responsible for emigration. Thus, the Munich-based *Veche*, an ultra-nationalist religious almanac, traced a direct line from infatuation with Western objects to emigration.[4] Meanwhile, the playful illustrated Russian weekly *Seven Days* from New York printed articles about Federico Fellini, with everything readers had long wanted to know but could not find in the Soviet press.[5]

Literary, painterly, and cinematic fantasies were also the main references for making sense of a new life. The layover in Italy, where anxious émigrés prepared for an interview at an American consulate, was a tongue-in-cheek "Roman holiday," after William Wyler's comedy, released in the Soviet Union in 1960.[6] In the United States, immigrants searched for "Salinger's characters, as if they were old friends who would not betray and who brought comfort in a strange land."[7] In Paris, the exiled artist Mikhail Shemiakin learned that Les Halles would be destroyed and, like his travelogue-writing compatriots, for whom "the Belly of Paris" represented a meaningful literary landmark, made sure to go there. He took more than 5,000 photographs—the foundation for a series of lithographs, "the Belly of Paris," in which humans and carcasses merged into grotesque new creatures.[8] Immigrant publications used Hemingway's titles as set expressions. Insider knowledge of an idiom's origins (without quotation marks) established a virtual community of authors and readers. As tourists in Paris, Russian-Americans still "summoned Hemingway's *A Moveable Feast* and traveled along roads inspired by reading Russian translations."[9]

On their first trips to France, émigrés were haunted by a "very strange feeling—something like a memory of the future." That feeling was recognition, the kind that Soviet travelers had experienced in the 1950s and 1960s. "It is delightful to recognize Europe the way [our] imagination had created it once upon a time," commented a new Russian-American in a perfectly Soviet sequential turn: reality complied with texts.[10] Vail' and Genis "knew everything about France, without ever having been there," and conveyed their knowledge in the language of possession: France was "our own."[11] When they did finally go there, their Parisian journey began at the Porte St. Antoine with a quotation common in Soviet travel writing: d'Artagnan (from *The Three Musketeers*) "remounted his yellow horse, which bore him without any further accident to the gate of St. Antoine at Paris." (Two decades earlier, Viktor Nekrasov had opened his French travelogue with this line as well.) On their last evening in Paris, Vail' and Genis "took a walk through the Tuileries Garden and turned by the Arc du Carrousel toward the Seine. The Pont Royal led us across the Voltaire Embankment to rue du Bac. A memorial plaque on building no. 1 read: 'Here lived a lieutenant of the King's musketeers Charles d'Artagnan.'"[12]

In those large suitcases that Soviet émigrés lugged across the world, among floral bedsheets and children's clothes, were books—collected works, printed in the late 1950s and early 1960s, of Honoré de Balzac, Émile Zola, Stefan Zweig, Guy de Maupassant, Sir Walter Scott, and John Galsworthy. Those suitcases also contained the beloved books of the Thaw: Hemingway in two volumes, bound in black with silver trim, Salinger's *The Catcher in the Rye* in Rait-Kovaleva's translation, and the "fat, green book," the 1959 edition of Remarque's *Three Comrades*. Some of the most durable and meaningful possessions that Soviet émigrés packed as tokens of the world they were about to leave were translations from the world they were about to enter. Late Soviet emigration was overdetermined by the "memory of the future."

Émigrés had imagined that all it took to live "the good life" was escaping the Soviet regime. In the Soviet Union, they had been teachers, engineers in design bureaus and railcar plants, dentists and pediatricians in district clinics, educated professionals, many of whom eventually would succeed in joining the European or American middle class. But cinematic and literary visions were slow to materialize. Émigré writings were consistent in the language of Paradise Lost.[13] Time and again, former Soviets assured the readers of their newspaper articles or interlocutors in grocery stores that the West or America was "not paradise, nor a branch of heaven on earth."[14] A deep sense of having been cheated permeated the fiction and press of late Soviet emigration. Decades later, with the advantage of hindsight, this disappointment does not seem surprising, given the quixotic hopes invested in the Western utopia.[15] Nor were Soviet émigrés unique in their disappointment: in the nineteenth century, "Russian Europeans" had arrived in Europe to find themselves strangers and their promised land a bourgeois quagmire—their tragedy became a cultural script.[16] But what Soviet émigrés experienced was not merely disappointment. It was dispossession.

The stories émigrés told, even those that end well, were about humiliation and loss. Dispossession began at home. Prose and poetry represented departure as destruction: émigrés squeezed their entire lives into several suitcases, having to decide what was worth taking and which relationships and mementos were to be excised forever. They stood helpless as their possessions flew across the counter when Soviet border guards searched their luggage. In the clumsy words of an amateur poet, who was grateful to have left anyway:

> Let us remember together,
> Let us remember together,
> And then forget forever.
>
> . . .
>
> Let us remember how we came here.
> Shirts, soap, shaver
> Tossed out of suitcases
> Onto the table, onto the floor
> A major is checking your luggage
> At customs in Chop.[17]

But this experience was not easy to forget, and the suitcases plagued émigré recollections.[18] Immigrants were pitiful for having hauled from the Soviet Union things that had been so difficult to procure and that turned out to be so unnecessary in their Western lives. Their new belongings were just as contemptible. Valerii Skorov, a hydrochemist and geography teacher from Leningrad, described the arrivals' source of furniture—and shame—in a song for guitar called "Garbage." The song conveyed both ridicule and empathy for immigrants who created their new life from trash cast off by natives. Discarded in Chicago's back alleys, "Color television sets/Mattresses still in packaging/Dishes, stylish furniture/Clean undergarments" were the ex-Soviets' "plunder." "Crouching" under the weight of these things, they imagined having outwitted "the bourgeois." Skorov's mockery masked hurt and commiseration: "When I remember emigration, I blush, I tremble" for "the most cultured people" now reduced to "rummaging through rubbish." Occasional English words in Russian transcription, especially the title "Garbich," highlighted the foreignness of the situation—or how degrading foreignness can be.[19]

Dumpsters as the ultimate periphery were a frequent setting of émigré prose. The most scandalous novel of third-wave emigration, Eduard Limonov's *It's Me, Eddie*, was about a Soviet immigrant as an outcast, a regular among the dumpsters and a fellow of the vagrants. A nonconformist poet in his former life, in America, Eddie lost his fame and his love. In anguish and sickness, "out of my fucking mind," "wrapped in a filthy overcoat I had found in the trash, my arm oozing pus, I was roaming through the New York February, picking scraps out of garbage cans and drinking the last drops from wine and liquor bottles."[20] His permanent home was the Winslow, an old and malodorous Madison Avenue hotel, its tiny rooms populated by Soviet immigrants who had not made it. This place, its dust and darkness, embarrassed them, sapping their motivation to do anything except wallow in misery.[21] Even with a room of his own, Eddie occasionally rummaged through the dumpster and wandered aimlessly, a habitué of the streets, who knew all the joints and was known to all the prostitutes. This endless meandering bespoke a fundamental homelessness. Limonov was unique among émigré artists, let alone average immigrants. His life and prose were épatage—his vulnerability and blunt anger on display, his offhandedly obscene language and graphic sex designed to shock readers. The novel was difficult to publish, and it did shock readers when it finally appeared in print. But one of the reasons it was outrageous was that it gave voice—screaming, wailing, offensive, explosive voice—to the mute despair of the average immigrant.

In Dmitrii Savitskii's novel *From Nowhere with Love*, the narrator is a Soviet émigré and vagrant in Paris.[22] Back at home, in the Soviet bohemian crowd, he had met a French woman of Russian origin, a translator who rendered translation unnecessary, a Russian soul in a French body. He followed her to Paris as a tourist intending to defect. There, abandoned by the woman of his fancy, he roamed the streets drunk and slept in a library during the day and under bridges at night. Other places of shelter were "a tiny, warm café in one of the alleys of Les Halles" and an "underground supermarket," housing "all the clochards, all the crazies of the city, marginals and hungry fags."[23] He bathed in the fountain in Place de la Concorde, freshened up at La Samaritaine with trial eau de cologne, and ate soup cooked for advertisement purposes at the Bazar de l'Hôtel de Ville.[24] Images of decay pervaded the Parisian pages: the smell of urine, the "foul" rain, the "smoldering" day, the "grimy copper" Seine, "muddy [and] sullied" mornings, "the thick, dirty air of the subway's endless tunnels," and the accentuated physicality of homelessness—unkempt beards, messy eating, prostrate bodies, on one of which he almost stepped.[25] This was the world of the proverbial Soviet "turn the corner" come true. Although Soviet émigrés rarely lived in and off Dumpsters, the pervasiveness of such settings in third-wave prose spoke to the depth of emotional and cultural marginalization.

The immigrants' new environment gave physical form to the insecurity and isolation of their lives. Their first settlements were anonymous, squalid, at once crowded and lonely. The buildings in New York's Brighton Beach evoked Maxim Gorky's description in *The City of the Yellow Devil* from the turn of the century. The subway stations in Paris were filthy, and immigrants sentimentally recalled the palatial Moscow metro.[26] The weather conspired against the new arrivals. The New York of émigré literature was always hot.[27] In Savitskii's novel, rain was the unceasing Parisian backdrop, a favorite Soviet scenario turned on its head. "Tedious like tooth ache," rain hurt in a dull kind of way. Rain "smelled of mold." It washed away the pleasures of walking, writing, or making love. Soaking clothes stuck to bodies, which clumsily tried to be rid of it—love had no chance.[28]

Families fell apart. The first years were exhausting, remembered in a vocabulary of warfare: immigrants "bravely battled with . . . English, with a new profession, with foreign customs," struggling to keep up with "the remarkable intensity of Western life."[29] But the collapse of "marriages that [in the Soviet Union] had withstood the test of decades" was irreducible to the stress of poverty or the time constraints of multiple jobs. The situation was so common as to become a topic of repeated analyses in the émigré press and so tragic as to become a prominent theme in émigré literature. According to the press, one of the strains was the reversal of traditional gender norms, as women became the primary breadwinners, while husbands looked for jobs, or, as often happened, gave up looking.[30] "We came to the United States three years ago. My wife enrolled in medical courses right away, getting a job half a year later. For me, all these years were a constant run of bad luck. All attempts to find a job failed. My English is atrocious. That is why the head of our family is my wife. She is the wage earner. I handle housework, cook, and pick up the children from school." Such was the tale of one I. A., who wrote to an émigré periodical, identifying himself as "chronically unemployed." The reversal of gender roles compounded the social humiliation of unemployment or employment below abilities and Soviet education: scientists drove taxis.[31]

The disintegration of self-esteem, men's more so than women's, permeated émigré prose. Their uneasy accent, social gaffes, odd jobs, and Soviet clothes made immigrants look ridiculous even in the eyes of their spouses. In literary representations, immigrants were physically repulsive, often unshaven and unkempt, too skinny or too fat. They slouched, shyly hiding their poverty.[32] Limonov's Eddie despised immigrants for "their main trait—depression." He loathed a neighbor, "the disheveled, stupid" "Uncle Sasha," who whimpered about how much he wanted to go back. But even as Eddie scorned them, he, too, wallowed in self-pity, mourning his former Soviet self: "Well, I was a poet, if you must know, a poet was I, an unofficial, underground poet. That's over forever, and now I am one of yours, I am scum."[33] Although nearly every page of Limonov's novel breathed hatred, *It's Me, Eddie* was also one of the most moving stories of love lost in twentieth-century Russian literature. He called his wife's departure "my tragedy," but it became an antiemigration manifesto when he implicated social inequality and marginalization as causes for the breakup.[34] For before losing her, he lost status (the high status of an unofficial poet) and linguistic mastery (the novel was filled with misspoken English, verbatim translations that render meaning absurd, and conspicuous self-awareness of poor English skills).[35] Limonov was one of the first to suggest, provocatively, that American society was as duplicitous as its Soviet counterpart, that Soviet immigrants had been seduced by visions of a beautiful life and then abandoned to their own devices in the face of chaos.[36] The loss of family should be counted among the losses of emigration.

The popular émigré press sought to ease family troubles with advice about intimate life. The illustrated weekly *Seven Days* took upon itself sex education with articles on prostitution, pornography, and the burlesque, as well as recommendations on personal hygiene and fashion, the art of seduction and ways to rekindle romance.[37] Printed in nearly every issue, such articles were an ideological statement. They endeavored to compensate for a lifetime of Soviet puritanism and to teach readers how to be Western men and women—comfortable with their sexuality, flirtatious but not vulgar, easygoing but not debauched, elegant and casual at once, like those beautiful people from films. "An erotic atmosphere is not at all a cinematic invention," *Seven Days* assured its readership in an article titled, after Hemingway, "A Moveable Feast."[38] "So long as we live in the West," admonished the newspaper, "where (for better or for worse, depending on how you look at it), they speak and write about everything candidly, we ought to master even this, previously taboo, sphere of life."[39] Sexuality was part of "freedom" as émigrés understood it.

Sex advice was an ideological statement in yet another way—as a language. Émigré literature decisively legitimized nonnormative speech for the printed page, a process that had begun back in the late 1950s and early 1960s, with the translation of Salinger and the search for words that were true to life. Initially, little of such nonnormative prose could be published in émigré periodicals, which preferred narrative realism and linguistic propriety. New journals, avant-garde, bohemian, and make-shift, working out of kitchens, sprang up under a slogan of stylistic plu-ralism to give space to obscene language, graphic sex, and violence.[40] Soon enough, physiological depictions emerged as the new norm in Russian émigré literature. As one reviewer complained, "Without obscenities and sex, writing seems to have become inappropriate."[41] Remaking Soviet people into Europeans and Americans would begin with language and the intimate world.

As they tried to reinvent themselves, many people grew convinced that their Western dreams were fulfilled at long last—or, rather, that their recently acquired middle-class life had been their Western dream all along. Immigrants tended to scorn any hint of discontent as evidence of failing (only "losers" grumble) and relished inventories of goods ("the villas of our immigration") as evidence of accomplishments. Next to discontent, immi-grants disparaged the conflation of life and literature for its impracticality and reliance on translations, "which, whether better or worse, always differ from originals."[42]

But even success stories were tinged with moral disapprobation. Es-pousing the morality of profit making proved no easier than other aspects of life in the West.[43] Émigré periodicals printed tales of morally dubious financial success, and one was never quite sure whether in celebration of Soviet tricksters or in travesty. Such, for example, was an interview with a newly minted insurance agent, who commenced his American life as a tailor, a skill he had mastered when preparing to leave Leningrad, tried his hand at his own business, drove a cab, and finally landed a job with an insurance company. Disdaining his American clients for naiveté and pro-vincialism, he made money off them and, as he joked, did so using his Russian exoticism shamelessly.[44] For readers, the moral lesson was not transparent: the result of such "initiative," they were told, was "today's America, with her cult of power, contempt for the law, [and] veneration of individualism," "greed, [and] desire to rule over others."[45] These lines could have been written by Melor Sturua for *Izvestiia*. They were com-posed, however, by an immigrant and published in a resolutely anti-Soviet journal. What if there had been some truth to Soviet propaganda?

Success was not only amoral; it was provincial and banal. So, too, was the West, according to astonished immigrants in the United States. The country of understated emotions and courageous adventurers, glamorous women and elegiac jazz turned out to be philistine, parochial, and calculating, as Soviet travelogues had warned all along.[46] Americans spent their weekends mowing the lawn, excelled at small talk, and knew their beneficiaries in case of death. This lifestyle was antithetical to many immigrants, whose reactions to their neighbors and colleagues oscillated between feelings of inferiority and disdain.[47] Immigrants had to reconsider the entire system of social worth, to learn financial planning, and to think of beneficiaries in case of death; but even as they did so, they held the new knowledge in moral contempt.[48] The sense of superiority with which Soviet immigrants spoke about their neighbors masked a desperate need to feel at home. Having moved from those squalid apartment buildings to middle-class neighborhoods, immigrants continued to feel at sea. Or, in the words of Savitskii's protagonist in Paris, "having left, the majority [of Soviet émigrés] did not arrive anywhere."[49]

But if anybody else doubted their belonging, immigrants protested vigorously. This is what filmmaker and journalist Ofra Bikel did in her documentary *The Russians Are Here*, aired in 1983 on PBS.[50] Perhaps no other representation of Soviet immigration in a host culture produced so vehement a reaction, with letters of protest, polemics in the press, threats of legal action by the Anti-Defamation League against PBS, and a street rally in Boston.[51] Bikel was interested "in the problem of freedom" and used interviews with Soviet immigrants to question the truths that Americans, purportedly, held self-evident: individualism, consumerism, competition. For immigrants, these turned into egoism, profit seeking, loneliness, and free rein for all. Many felt unappreciated; many felt out of place. The film showed success, too—people who had learned to play by the rules of the game, but remained equally unhappy. Bikel's subjects criticized the ethical foundations of the United States from a perspective that echoed Soviet writings on the West.

Although she did not disagree with them, she judged the interviewees harshly as homo sovieticus, who brought their unfreedom with them.[52] The film presented Soviet immigrants as a different breed of people. They were pitiful and socially awkward. They congregated in noisy crowds on Brighton Beach littered with trash.[53] Immigrants complained, as if anybody owed them anything, or cared. They were overemotional. Footage from a citizenship class showed them thanking the lecturer in unison, as children in kindergarten do.[54] In the film, they spoke with a thick accent. Muteness would have been less discomfiting. A circus, a moving exhibition, and a lesson in primitiveness, they must have watched themselves with embarrassment. Immigrants felt the film's offense viscerally. They would have liked to say—and to hear themselves say—that life turned out as they had imagined it in their book-inspired and cinematic dreams.

In the 1990s, the rest of the country essentially emigrated to the West. Emigration is an apt analogy for the disappearance of the Soviet Union, whose citizens found themselves foreigners at home. There was the same loss of statehood. The loss of social status and security. The loss of language. The loss of meaningful symbols and rituals. The loss of home and family.

By 1991, the Soviets had fashioned the West as the ultimate utopia. It seemed that a Western life of beauty and freedom was imminent, and all it took was doing away with the Soviet regime. In Svetlana Alexievich's oral history of the 1990s, participants defined freedom in much the same way as émigrés did: as abundance, choice, mobility, and forthright sexuality. One interviewee recalled with lingering relish the European places she had never been meant to see, only read about. She associated the end of the Soviet Union with open borders and opportunities "to see Paris . . . Or Spain . . . the Fiesta . . . the corrida"—in Hemingway's footsteps, of course.[55] But when the Soviet regime fell, freedom turned out differently, while beauty materialized for only the very few. The process of Soviet disintegration has left many citizens with a profound sense of having been wronged—a sense that surfaces in the press, in prose, and in political discourse. To be sure, a number of influential writers, journalists, bloggers, and academics evoke the 1990s as a time of newfound openness and uncontrolled information, indeed of freedom and democracy. They look back on those years as a counterpoint to present-day authoritarianism (tyranny, in their language). But the dominant depictions of the 1990s present a "time of troubles" and "mayhem," which people recall as wilderness and madness.[56] Opening to another world now has apocalyptic overtones: the implosion of the familiar one. The sentiment is not merely disappointment—this would be unsurprising and too forgiving. The sentiment is an acute sense of dispossession.

Soviet things so painstakingly accumulated turned out to be pitifully useless.[57] Ex-Soviets had to master an entire universe of mundane objects:

carton juice boxes, yogurt, hair conditioner, CD players, sneakers. Along the way, an entire universe of Soviet things was obliterated. Economic deprivation struck in 1992–1993, when prices were liberalized, industries privatized, and state subsidies disappeared. This "shock therapy" seemingly paved the fastest route to the West. Rapidly, indeed, people saw their jobs and life savings wiped out.[58] Disproportionately affected, engineers, teachers, doctors, and retirees survived by selling anything they could, from cucumbers grown on balconies to Soviet belongings: oversized undergarments, World War II medals, books. Their pathetic wares laid out on crates, they stood in rows along roads or under tents in open-air markets. They lugged to used bookstores Balzac's *Collected Works*, tomes by Zola, Maupassant, Walter Scott, and John Galsworthy, and the treasured books of the Thaw, Hemingway in two volumes, Salinger in Rait-Kovaleva's translation.[59] These were, perhaps, the most unwanted of things. Western tourists bought World War II medals as souvenirs, but who needed a Soviet translation of Hemingway? Cultural dispossession was an intimate tragedy as people traded their youthful infatuations.

Many also forfeited their homes. Some were expelled by relatives in rough and anxious times. Others were defrauded in the course of privatization, when the government allowed citizens to become the owners of their apartments. Communal apartments were consolidated and remodeled into sumptuous flats with the latest Western conveniences, while former inhabitants were evicted or resettled. Countless people found themselves in the streets.[60] In big Russian cities of the 1990s, the homeless were ubiquitous. During the day, they scavenged; worked menial jobs, sweeping streets and selling odds and ends in kiosks; or collected objects that others left behind. At night, they found warmth in subway stations and foul-smelling attics or staircase landings, where they slept on heaps of newspapers. They were "Soviet leftovers," in the words of an anthropologist of homelessness in Russia.[61] Or, perhaps, the residues of Westernization.

The émigré nightmare turned into a Russian reality. So common and wretched were the homeless that they became a dominant symbol of the human catastrophe that was Russia's new capitalism. Writers gave philosophical underpinnings to this experience of dislocation. In *Matisse*, Aleksandr Ilichevskii's Russian Booker Prize winner about the 1990s and homelessness, Western imports of the late Soviet decades served as a faint memory of elegance and beauty that did not materialize. As the Soviet Union disintegrated, the book's central character, Korolev, lost his scholarly calling, the scientific institute where he had worked, the woman he loved, and friends, who had emigrated or died. But he gained something as well: a car and an apartment—only to abandon these trappings of stability, willingly, willfully, for a life in attics and subway stations. Korolev abandoned it all from despair over servility before uncouth bosses, from hatred of a new unfreedom ("slavery," in the novel's language, "slavery reigning all around"). Amid degradation, loneliness, stench, lice, and "eschatological" ruin, Soviet-made Westernisms hovered as biographical facts, dreams, and apparitions. There had been Italy, Spain, and Brazil in Korolev's childhood, when he had believed these were "different names of the same country." There had been an erotic experience of jazz as an adolescent. There had been the act of reading Salinger as a student at a physics-mathematics institute. In Korolev's building lived a quintessential figure of Thaw-era cinematic imports. A prostitute, she "resemble[d] an actress from a 1950s Italian film about the life of a fishing village." There was, finally, Matisse, his beloved artist. Korolev dreamed of Matisse in the guise of a prophet, with an unkempt beard and broken pince-nez. Matisse's bird cages were empty, and Korolev took to the streets. Beaten to a pulp, the vagrant Korolev hallucinated about "a wild red dance. The dancers, red like the flames, whirled around his eyeballs in a mad twirl across a blue plane." He finally saw Matisse for real—the artist and his model—through a restaurant window, as they selected lobsters on a silver platter. The model's back was bare, her beauty was stunning, and she coolly stared back at the tramp with shaggy hair and bruised face.[62]

The loss of social status afflicted most Soviets, but men more so than women. As industry crumbled, the market reduced many men to a shadow of their former breadwinning selves. Unable to provide for their families, they worked odd jobs, failed to make ends meet, felt inadequate, took to alcohol. According to anthropologists and demographers, this sense of irrelevance was at the root of the 1992–1994 mortality crisis. Death took a heavier toll on men: they died in greater numbers and at an earlier age than women. Although the reversal of gender norms that emigrants experienced did not happen to the same degree, the uncertainty and misery of the 1990s stressed marriages to an extreme. That stress on the family should be counted among the fallouts of Westernization. Flagging self-respect was emblematic of the larger irrelevance of Soviet labors, skills, and lives.[63] Traditional Soviet occupations fell by the wayside as bankers, entrepreneurs, security guards, and hitmen appeared on the scene.

The despoliation of the 1990s coexisted with, indeed produced, new and ostentatious wealth. Success was glamorous and immoral. Popular lore derided the entrepreneurs of the 1990s. Journalistic and cinematic clichés represented them as greedy, vulgar, and thuggish, Mafiosi without the Corleones' elegance, Sicilian landscapes, or the charm of Nino Rota's score. Sudden wealth had always been suspect as criminal, but never more so than in the 1990s, when much of it was, indeed, criminal, when racketeering thrived, violence was wanton, film and fiction profiled villains, and entrepreneurship became legitimate after seventy years of interdiction.[64] All this was bound up with the Western utopia, which did materialize for some people. Western were the clothes, cars, and appliances of the nouveaux riches. Western was their wheeling and dealing. They journeyed to Nice and New York with an ease previously unimaginable, except in romanticized Soviet travel accounts that had given little place to documents, permissions, or checkpoints. Abroad, they enjoyed beaches and bars and picture-perfect luxury from glossy magazines. They were called the new Russians, and they inhabited foreign spaces, opulent apartments and cottages.[65]

Reconstruction of buildings and interiors, which looked markedly un-Soviet, was billed as Euro-renovation. "Euro" meant wholesale obliteration of the Soviet material world, of familiar sights, colors, and textures, from wallpaper and window frames to ceilings and floors. Ceilings were now layered with drywall; vinyl wallcoverings replaced wallpaper with fading flowers. Tile mosaics, sparkling vanities, and roomy leather sofas in soft orange created a non-Soviet domesticity, slick and sexy. The new interiors looked like something out of a 1970s-era French or American film about the jaded life of the bourgeoisie. At the turn of the century, public "Euro" enclaves, glass structures gleaming outside under sunrays and flooded by electric lights inside, dotted the big cities. These futuristic spaces (many were actually called "city" and "metropolis") housed Western boutiques, technology, perfumeries, and patisseries. Urban renovation was not merely about repairs. It was about transforming Soviet streets and homes into (a semblance of) Western ones.[66]

This transformation was broadcast across urban landscapes. In big cities, one could hardly turn the proverbial corner without encountering foreign words. Homey Pepsi and Marlboro kiosks were scattered inconspicuously in the streets of the early 1990s, with only the Latin letters painted on the canopy to mark their difference. Soon, the letters grew bigger and the signs more colorful. Bus stop booths showcased advertisements for Opel Astra. People queued at the Rifle jeans store on Kuznetskii Bridge in Moscow— "Rifle" leaped from the store's every window, in red, in all caps. Trollies spelled Kaiser on the side and clarified in Russian "German household technology." If the Youth Festival had once brought cardboard cities and literary characters to Moscow's Tverskaia and Pushkin streets, the 1990s brought a different three-dimensional décor: an oversized Coca-Cola can and a West cigarette box. High on the rooftops, in place of red banners with party slogans, Latin letters spelled out Gillette and Sanyo. By the turn of the century, rows of boutiques graced city centers and glimmering shopping malls: Gucci, Motivi, Ecco, Camelot "super-fashionable shoes," and Carlo Pazolini footwear from Italy. The display windows of subway kiosks showcased multihued perfume boxes, stacks of Boss, Calvin Klein, Bulgari, Opium, Lacoste, Amor. On television, sensual lips blew frost across the screen, promoting Orbit "snow-white." Beautiful women turned their heads and let luxurious hair swirl, promising that with Garnier Fructis anybody could have a mane like that. Gallina Blanca soups from Spain filled kitchen cabinets.

Latin letters and foreign words in Russian transcription invaded homes, streets, and conversations. New consumer goods, food, technology, political concepts, financial dealings, bodily practices, and occupations required a new vocabulary.[67] Much of it drew on English and relied on loanwords with Russified prefixes and endings. Russian transcriptions of Western companies, products, and terms read like a page from émigré prose: this was how immigrants proclaimed the strangeness of their new life as well as their linguistic embarrassment. By the end of the 1990s, Russian linguists were busy compiling dictionaries of the latest terms. But before taking on concrete social meaning, foreign words were a pervasive visual presence and a sound medley. They were also a symbol of Russia's misfortune printed on signs of various kinds. They provoked anger among people who could not afford the lifestyle that the words signified.[68] The relentless advertising was an aggression upon the eyes, much the same way that Soviet travelogues about the West had described it. Hence, by the late 1990s, linguists were not only compiling dictionaries; some were also leading a campaign for the protection of the Russian language. Radio and television programs advised audiences on questions of grammar and proper usage. Behind genteel linguistic exchanges was a moral panic about a foreign invasion.[69]

But the revolution in the Russian language was deeper than the signs on storefronts and words designating new practices. At long last, prohibitions of propriety fell. A mainstay of print for some two centuries, the linguistic norm suddenly disintegrated. Substandard speech of various kinds—youth, urban, criminal, and most shockingly, obscene—overran Russian prose and journalism. What is more, the 1990s idealized crudeness as a new authenticity for rugged, new times. Expletives were the language of the people and thus democratic. They were also fascinating, like everything else that had been taboo earlier, so the mid-1990s witnessed a boom in dictionaries of Russian cusswords.[70] As in the early 1960s, vernacular speech was a battle cry against the stale truisms of the old Soviet language. It was no accident that perestroika had emphasized oral genres and public debates. The Soviet foe was immobile and sacred—against it rushed profane words from the street. One can look at the collapse of verbal taboos as social liberation or as social downfall, and both interpretations were in play in the 1990s. Either way, Soviet speak was profoundly discredited, and the victory of the street was final. What had begun in the late 1950s and early 1960s came to fruition in the 1990s, when sex and violence found a graphic language.[71] And it was a ubiquitous language. In the streets, girls wearing denim or leather miniskirts promised flirtation, and more. Advertisements promised seduction. Books promised intimate advice. Magazines promised arousal. After 1 am, Russian television turned to pornography. The original was in English or French, voiced over as an emotionless echo by a narrator. Love had every chance, no matter the weather.

In the early 1990s, Western observers hailed the Westernization of Russian streets, homes, and speech as the coming of freedom: as the coming, in other words, of choice. The choice to read what you wish, to watch what intrigues you, to go where you please. But in the course of the 1990s, Westernization, as well as freedom and choice, became associated with the dissolution of social bonds and behavioral norms, with the marginalization of much of the population and entire fields of knowledge—a new unfreedom, as in Ilichevskii's *Matisse*. Soviet obsoleteness meant the ultimate marginalization of Russia itself, which, in the 1990s, was entirely irrelevant to the West and the world. Irrelevant was the country whose identity throughout the twentieth century had been grounded in its worldwide centrality as the first socialist society, the vanquisher of fascism, the torchbearer of progress, the exemplar of internationalism, and the realm of great culture. By the end of the century, Russia, particularist and peripheral, had little to offer to the world and no promising narrative to share. Or, in Ilichevskii's words, "Nobody, save for God, needs this country."[72]

The Soviet Union and the West are usually treated as antitheses. However, in conditions characterized by information shortages, Soviet and Western utopias had become entwined. To an extraordinary degree, late Soviet life was suffused with non-Soviet things, films, sounds, and stories. Some of these were unofficial, but most were perfectly legitimate, albeit in drastically short supply; some of these were eye-catching, but most were invisible, an ordinary part of ordinary lives. All were to die for. Their presence created a hybrid culture that defied neat classifications. The Soviet Union has been deemed a closed society. It was governed by censorship; information scarcity was a basic fact of everyday life; and social hierarchy was closely related to information access. But in the late Soviet decades, an abundance of cultural material was imported, displayed in museums, translated, and dubbed. By contrast, a modest share of the world's literary traffic consisted of translations into English, and the ostensibly open American society was notoriously inaccessible to foreign films.[73] To be sure, the Soviet field of cultural imports was skewed and asymmetrical. But it was also increasingly capacious.

Soviet translations were possessive, transforming Western imports into intimate belongings. Translated books claimed to be originals in their own right. Dubbed films claimed to be better than originals. Although modernist paintings were often rejected, Soviet museums and their visitors claimed the European classical heritage. Soviet travelogues were retranslations of these earlier texts. Translations across the arts built on each other to constitute a distinct intertextual space that was intricately linked to the larger Soviet world. In turn, the larger Soviet world provided the language, meanings, and uses for Western imports. The end of that world overturned this situation of intimate ownership.

Soviet and Western utopias disintegrated together. When the borders were flung open, when the market came to regulate availability, and when foreign languages became common currency, while hard currency became a common language, translation lost its social weight. In the 1990s, translators found themselves in the uncharted territory of the market. To survive (translators speak of bread and hunger when they recall the early 1990s), they worked for a pittance, preferring short pieces, because "while you translate, the publisher may disappear, or you simply starve to death." They despised the texts they translated for the mass market. Unprofessionalism flourished. Even with the hindsight of the new millennium, some eminent translators look back on the late Soviet decades as a time of cultural refinement. Back then, they had translated the authors they loved and the books that held them captive. Yes, there had been censorship, but no hackwork; the market merely replaced "ideology" with "a publisher's fat wallet." And they had enjoyed distinguished status as people of the word and bearers of exclusive knowledge. Dubbing actors and directors grumble about post-Soviet times, too, when numerous studios threw together quick and cheap voice-overs with no care for artistry. Of course, the complaints represented only one side; the other side was comprised of translators and dubbers who preferred the market, if for no other reason than the absence of censorship and the prospect of profits and greater choice. All agreed, however, that with the end of the Soviet Union, the monopoly on information that translators and mediators had once enjoyed vanished.[74]

The grand translation project expired in dispossession. Western friends of the Soviet Union turned out to be marginal in their own cultures. There were other names, books, films, and paintings of which the Soviets knew nothing. The books and journal volumes that people cherished, passing from generation to generation, and the films that brought sweet memories belonged to somebody else or were greeted with indifference, sometimes even contempt, in their home countries. Dispossession is wasteful. In fact, to waste (*perevesti*) is one of the meanings of the Russian word for translation.[75] Post-Soviet cultural dispossession converted precious belongings into old junk not too different from other Soviet things of poor quality. Soviet audiences had been taught for decades to think of themselves as the most invested readers, as the most discerning viewers. Dispossession disrupted these norms. Scholars and journalists describe post-Soviet industrial decay, but the epistemological ruin was equally immense. People learned that their cultural predilections were outmoded, their ways of living books were juvenile, their expectations of paintings were unsophisticated and of cinema melodramatic or plainly crude. They had cultivated cultural capital devotedly but found themselves empty-handed. Mastery of Western imports had been pivotal for the Soviets' sense of accomplishment and personhood. Dispossession ripped apart this cultural core. In conventional understanding, dispossession refers to a loss of land, often through violent expulsion or cynical manipulation. But dispossession is not only an external economic condition. It concerns subjectivities and sentiments as much as acres or objects. It begets melancholy.[76]

The melancholy of dispossession stirs loving memories of a lost home. Western imports have joined other cultural moments and artifacts as subjects of nostalgic memorialization—for, indeed, Western imports, no less than other cultural moments and artifacts, represent the Soviet past. Communities of fans reminisce on the Internet, the most accessible archive of Sovietness, about the first time they saw Lolita Torres in *The Age of Love*: that movie theater, that evening, that Radiola spinning "Coimbra Divina." Others recall the heart-stopping moment of encountering Gérard Philipe or Yves Montand on the screen or the radio. And yet others ascribe the charm of Western films to the magical, sensual voices of the dubbers. Postcards, stamps, lighters, notebooks, and shawls with the Youth Festival daisy appear among online attempts to preserve Soviet material traces, along with images of old radios, World War II medals, teacup holders, and record labels. Despite a profound transformation of literary language, Vera Toper's translation of Hemingway's *The Sun Also Rises* and Evgeniia Kalashnikova's rendition of *A Farewell to Arms* continue to find readers. Challenges to canonical Soviet translations are seen as attacks on literary classics and on first, youthful love. And perhaps only in Russia does Remarque's *Three Comrades*, republished fifty-five times between 1991 and 2005, still bring bittersweet recognition. In 1999, Remarque again was at the center of controversy when Moscow's Contemporary Theater staged *Three Comrades*, with a script based on the 1958 translation. Like *Foreign Literature* editors and Cultural Department instructors forty years earlier, critics judged the play cheaply sentimental and found its success perplexing. But time and again, audiences gave it standing ovations. And people cried, convinced, once more, that "this is about our life, about our warped, cheated life." Was it "about our life," because the stage set evoked comparisons between Berlin in 1928 and Russian streets in the 1990s? Was it "about our life," because the actors prepared for their roles by watching film reels from the First Chechen War? Was it "about our life," because, as one critic put it sarcastically, the play was "a monument to the sixties"? Whatever the explanation, "there [were] moments when the audience [froze] in recognition."[77] *Three Comrades* was still about the three comrades from Nevsky.

As the Soviet Union disintegrated, its Western fragments served to inform thinking about the Soviet past and the Russian future. Perhaps nowhere is this better demonstrated than in Yuri Mamin's eccentric comedy *Window to Paris* (1993), which makes literal use of Russia's most famous metaphor—the window onto Europe hacked by Peter the Great (again in Pushkin's rendition). In the Leningrad of the Soviet twilight, a window of a rundown, cluttered communal apartment suddenly opens onto a Parisian roof. Accompanied by a group of incidental drinking companions, Nikolai, a zany musician, scatterbrained teacher, and intellectual down on his luck, sobers up to the sight of the Eiffel Tower. Thus the merrymakers begin their adventures. The film satirizes Soviet dreams and nightmares, rituals and idioms. There are the iconic postcard vistas, the neon lights of the capitalist city, the street cafés, and that resentful, plaintive saying "where you have never been and most likely will never go." There are conversations in gestures and Yves Montand's "Les Grands Boulevards," which Nikolai hums without understanding a word and which provides him the vocabulary for his fake, improvised French. There is the madness around Western goods, which the vulgar group plunders shamelessly, all the while arguing that the display of plenty is nothing more than garbage discarded by natives. There are the leftist itineraries that Soviet tourists endured so patiently and the alluring places where, they imagined, the wealthy live fast. Stranded in Paris, the film's last Russian communist appears before French comrades and appeals to socialist friendship. The French know what to do with Soviet guests: take them to the Communards' Wall at the Père Lachaise, which the Russians mistake for a restaurant styled after Maxim's.

And there is the question of emigration: fear, attraction, reproach, regret, determination. On his first night as an immigrant, Nikolai has a nightmare about the homeless life of a Soviet immigrant dressed in rags, stumbling through the rain and sleeping in piles of newspapers. The émigré promise—never to return—comes to haunt Nikolai when the window closes, and he finds himself trapped in paradise. He does manage to return to Petersburg, only to play Edith Piaf's "Padam, padam" in the street for some cash, to feel trapped again, and to look for a window that would take him back to Paris. The film is about post-Soviet opportunities, but the options are not so cut and dried. After all, Nikolai and his friends want to have it both ways, to live in the West of their imagination and in the Russia of their affection—to live, in other words, in Paris without leaving Saint Petersburg.

Abbreviations and Archives

Periodicals

AiSM	Arkhitektura i stroitel'stvo Moskvy
DN	Druzhba narodov
EK	Ezhegodnik kino
IK	Iskusstvo kino
IL	Inostrannaia literatura
KP	Komsomol'skaia pravda
LG	Literaturnaia gazeta
LiZh	Literatura i zhizn'
MG	Molodaia gvardiia
MZh	Mezhdunarodnaia zhizn'
NM	Novyi mir
SD	Sem' dnei
SE	Sovetskii ekran
SEMP	Sovetskii ezhegodnik mezhdunarodnogo prava
SR	Sovetskaia Rossiia
VF	Voprosy filosofii
VIMK	Vestnik istorii mirovoi kul'tury
VL	Voprosy literatury

Archives

d. (delo; plural dd.) = file
dok. (dokument) = document
ed. khr. (edinitsa khraneniia) = unit of preservation
f. (fond) = collection
l. (list; plural ll.) = page
ob. (oborot) = over
op. (opis') = inventory
per. (perechen') = inventory
sv. (sviazka) = bundle
t. (tom) = volume

RUSSIAN FEDERATION

AGE State Hermitage Archive
    f. 1   State Hermitage
AGMII Archive of the Pushkin State Museum of Fine Arts
    f. 5   Museum exhibitions
    f. 41   Personal collection: Ilya Ehrenburg
AKG Archive of the Gorky Film Studio
GARF State Archive of the Russian Federation
    f. A-501   The Ministry of Culture of the RSFSR
    f. 6903   The State Committee for Television and Radio
    f. 8131   The General Procuracy of the USSR
    f. 9401   The Ministry of Internal Affairs of the USSR (MVD)
    f. 9415   The Main Administration of the Militia of the Ministry
             of Internal Affairs
    f. 9425   The Main Directorate for the Protection of State
             Secrets in the Press (Glavlit)
    f. 9518   The Committee for Cultural Relations with Foreign
             Countries (GKKS)
    f. 9576   The Union of Soviet Friendship Societies (SSOD)
    f. 9612   Institutions for Administering Foreign Tourism in the
             USSR (Intourist)
Gosteleradio State Collection of Television and Radio
RGAKFD Russian State Archive of Film and Photo Documents
RGALI Russian State Archive for Literature and the Arts
    f. 613   The State Publishing House
    f. 631   The Union of Writers
    f. 634   Editorial board of the newspaper *Literaturnaia gazeta*
             (*Literary Gazette*)
    f. 1204   Personal collection: Ilya Ehrenburg
    f. 1573   Editorial board of the journal *Inostrannaia literatura*
             (*Foreign Literature*)
    f. 1702   Editorial board of the journal *Novyi mir* (*New World*)
    f. 2329   The Ministry of Culture, USSR
    f. 2453   Moscow Film Studio (Mosfil'm)
    f. 2458   The Directorship of Art Exhibitions and Panoramas,
             Ministry of Culture
    f. 2487   Central Studio of Documentary Films
    f. 2494   Association of Workers of Revolutionary
             Cinematography

	f. 2732	Personal collection: Sergei Obraztsov
	f. 2854	Personal collection: Ivan Kashkin
	f. 2900	The All-Union State Institute of Cinematography (VGIK)
	f. 2912	Editorial board of the journal *Iskusstvo kino* (*Art of Cinema*)
	f. 2918	The All-Union Association for the Export and Import of Films (Soveksportfil'm)
	f. 2923	Central House of Cinema
	f. 2924	Editorial board of the journal *Iunost'* (*Youth*)
	f. 2926	The Directorship of Exhibitions of the Artists' Union
	f. 2930	Central House of Actor(s) (TsDA)
	f. 2932	Central House of the Arts of the USSR (TsDRI)
	f. 2936	The Union of Filmmakers
	f. 2943	The Moscow organization of the Artists' Union
	f. 2944	The Council of Ministers' Cinematography Committee (Goskino)
RGANI	Russian State Archive of Contemporary History	
	f. 5	Apparat of the Central Committee of the CPSU
	f. 11	Commission on the Questions of Ideology and Culture
	f. 72	Ideological Commission
	f. 89	Collection of declassified documents
RGASPI	Russian State Archive of Socio-Political History	
	f. 17	Central Committee of the CPSU
	f. 606	Academy of Social Sciences, Central Committee of the Communist Party (AON)
RGASPI-M	Russian State Archive of Socio-Political History (formerly Center for the Preservation of Documents of Youth Organizations)	
	f. M-1	Central Committee of the Komsomol
	f. M-3	Committee for Youth Organizations
TsALIM	Moscow Municipal Archive for Literature and the Arts	
	f. 21	Central Exhibition Hall
	f. 138	Cinefication Department of the Moscow Municipal Administration of Culture
	f. 147	The Main Administration of Culture, Moscow
TsAOPIM	Moscow Municipal Central Archive of Socio-Political History	
	f. P-4	Moscow city committee of the Communist Party
	f. P-534	Party organization of the administration of the Writers' Union
	f. P-3991	Party organization of the Surikov Art Institute

f. P-1007   Party organization of the Moscow Municipal Artists'
             Union (MOSKh)
f. K-635   Moscow municipal Komsomol committee
f. K-4091   Sokol'niki district Komsomol committee
f. K-6083   Moscow State University Komsomol committee

TsMADSN   Moscow Municipal Archive of Audio-Visual Documents
TsMaM   Moscow Municipal Archive

f. 1609   Moscow State University

UNITED STATES

Archives of American Art, Smithsonian Institution
    Rockwell Kent papers (RKP)
    Richard McLanathan papers
Fales Library and Special Collections, New York University
    Remarque Papers: Erich Maria Remarque and Paulette Goddard Papers,
    Series 3, Box B, Folder 28
NARA   National Archives and Record Administration II
    RG Record Group 59 General Records of the Department of State
                        Central decimal files, 1955–1959
                        Central decimal files, 1960–1963
                        Subject files of the East-West contract staff
                            lot file 59D127
                        Subject files of the policy and guidance staff, 1946–1962
                            lot file 61D134
                        Bureau of cultural affairs: Country files of the
                        planning and development staff, 1955–1964
                            lot file 66D499
                        Bureau of European affairs: Records relating to
                        Soviet-US Relations, 1945–1966   lot file 69D162
                        Miscellaneous records of the bureau of public affairs
                            lot file 59D127
                        Records relating to the evaluation of cultural
                        programs and to staff visits overseas, 1952–1960
                            lot file 67D43
                        Records relating to fairs and expositions, 1959–1965
                            lot file 66D424
                        Office of the Assistant Secretary for Public Affairs:
                        Public Affairs   Subject Files, 1957–1961
                            lot file 62D92

Bureau of Cultural Affairs: Office of the Policy
and Coordination Staff: Subject files, 1961
    lot file 63D135
Bureau of Cultural Affairs: US Advisory Commission
on International Education and Cultural Affairs,
    Subject Files, 1948–1965   lot file 65D545
    lot file 66D221
RG Record Group 306 Records of the United States Information Agency
    Records relating to trade fairs, 1958–1966
    Records relating to the American National Exhibition
    in Moscow, 1957–1959
    Exhibition Division: Records concerning exhibits in
    foreign countries, 1955–1963
    Office of Research: "R" Reports, 1960–1963
    Office of Research: Special "S" Reports, 1953–1963
    Office of Exhibits: Comment books and lists of visitors
    related to US exhibits in the USSR, Rumania and
    Bulgaria
National Museum of American Art: General records
SIA   Smithsonian Institution Archive
Tamiment   Tamiment Institute Library, New York University
    Sally Belfrage Papers (SPB)

Appendix:
Assessing Responses to Cultural Imports

In examining the reception of Western imports in the Soviet Union, I have drawn on a vast array of commentary from citizens, including 1,100 letters from viewers and readers to central institutions and cultural figures and more than 6,000 entries in comment books from art exhibitions.

The letters include responses to the new cultural exchange policies, translated prose, radio programs, travelogues, and Western films in the context of Soviet ones and vice versa. The authors of these letters were teachers, librarians, doctors, engineers, and students. Students comprised nearly 30 percent of respondents to radio concerts of the French singer and actor Yves Montand in 1954–1956. Most of them were studying pedagogy and engineering. Secondary school teachers and engineers made up another 18 percent of letter writers. Among Ilya Ehrenburg's 206 correspondents about modern art, one hundred listed their professions. The majority (41 percent) were engineers and teachers (24 and 17 percent, respectively). Others were doctors, bookkeepers, and agronomists. They graduated from five-year colleges and specialized institutes of, for instance, forest management in Briansk, metallurgy in Magnitogorsk, water transport engineering in Leningrad, and construction in Odessa. Overall, of 550 letter writers who specified their jobs, the intellectual elite—writers, artists, filmmakers, translators, professors, doctoral students, researchers, and foreign affairs specialists—comprised a minority of just 12 percent. By contrast, teachers and engineers made up 23 percent, or twice as many. Only 9 percent of 550 letter writers with known occupations were workers. Letter writers were primarily urbanites; among the letters I examined, those from the countryside typically were penned by village teachers, librarians, bookkeepers, and agronomists.

The letters in my sample came from across the Soviet Union. Out of 808 letter writers who supplied their addresses, Muscovites and Leningraders accounted for 40 percent. Their share was lower among respondents writing about cinema (27 percent), translated literature (29 percent), and international affairs (27 percent). Moscow and Leningrad were home to the country's most prominent theaters, film studios, museums, libraries, and universities. Not surprisingly, these population-dense cultural capitals also hosted the most significant art exhibitions. Western entertainers performed primarily in the two cities and occasionally in Kiev, the USSR's third most important metropolis. Moscow was the site of mega-events, while Leningrad and republican capitals hosted smaller thematic festivals. It is, therefore, predictable that the residents of Moscow and Leningrad had better access to Western imports and thus figured prominently among the letter writers.

But Moscow and Leningrad did not dominate the corpus of letters. From 30 percent to 37 percent of letters came from the Soviet republics; most frequently from republican capitals (Kiev, Riga, Minsk, Baku, Tashkent, Ashkhabad, Tallinn, Frunze, Alma-Ata, Kishinev), industrial conglomerates (Stalino, Dnepropetrovsk, Khar'kov, Rustavi), urban centers (Odessa, L'vov, Gomel', Kaunas), and historic cities (Dzhambul). Ukraine stands out for the biggest share of letters, accounting for over 60 percent of all respondents from the republics. Roughly 30 percent to 40 percent of letter writers lived in the Russian provinces: in the major cities of Kazan', Gor'kii, Stavropol', Groznyi, Magnitogorsk, Barnaul, Kaluga, Saratov, Kaliningrad, Novosibirsk; in the central and southern hinterland, where outlaying districts were poorly provisioned; and in the far north and far east, where climate and distances were especially prohibitive. These letter writers' quest for culture, their searching engagement with Western imports, was a significant facet of the Thaw.

I have not treated these letters as statistically representative of a broader public opinion. The source base is eclectic and uneven. Letters were crafted in response to different genres, and their content varied widely in spirit, displaying everything from resentment to exultation. The recipients of these letters—both individuals and varying cultural institutions—adopted different archiving practices, with some saving massive quantities of correspondence and others winnowing the collection down to a few viewpoints. We will never know whether the letters that have been preserved are similar to the ones that were discarded. And despite letter writers' frequent insistence that they spoke for thousands of readers, for millions of viewers, it is a moot point as to whether they exemplified anyone's experiences other than their own. They were a self-selected group, more active than most, or more sentimental, wishing to share their emotional excess with the addressees. What these letters do well is speak for their authors. That is why I consider reception within the social environment and pay attention, insofar as the sources allow, to the place of Western imports in the biographies of individual letter writers. In reconstructing how people read books, how they looked at paintings and watched movies, I am interested not so much in representativeness as in the range of possible meanings.

Alongside the letters, I read comment books from exhibitions of modern Western art, photography, and Soviet travel drawings. The comments are a very different source in their physical and temporal aspects. In their letters, people could be as spontaneous or deliberate, curt or detailed as they wished. They had hours and weeks to work on their letters. They penned these in silence or with friends and "on behalf of collectives." When writing to cultural figures in whom they saw a confidant, people often assumed a confessional tone: these were intimate documents, meant for the eyes of a special person. Letter writers often received a response, even from institutions. Letters could evolve into a relationship, however unequal, sustained by protracted correspondence. By contrast, comments were always written in public, scribbled in a matter of minutes, and they retain the immediacy of anger or repartee. Momentary impressions, comments contained little biographical information. The comment book was an interactive, self-generating text that invited participation. People approached the comment book not only to write, but also to read the thoughts of others. Reading previous remarks prompted museumgoers to compose their own. The openness of the comment book, the possibility of surveillance, and the repetitiveness of the entries all justly raise doubts about the integrity of this source. However, under different conditions of writing—when, for example, in the early 1960s, museums replaced the bound comment book with loose sheets and closed collection boxes—viewers produced similar comments. Rather than seeing the comments as compromised or comment writing as performative (qualitatively different from any other public behavior), I searched for patterns. I found these patterns to be especially informative: repetitions and linguistic conventions revealed the frameworks, prior knowledge, expectations, and rituals surrounding Western imports.

Notes

Introduction

1. Metaphors and translation: *Thinking through Translation with Metaphors*, ed. James St. André (Manchester: St. Jerome Publishing, 2010).
2. Yuri Lotman and Boris Uspenskii, "'Pis'ma russkogo puteshestvennika' Karamzina i ikh mesto v razvitii russkoi kul'tury," in Yuri Lotman, *Karamzin* (Saint-Petersburg: Iskusstvo-SPb, 1997), 531.
3. Vladimir Kantor, *Russkii evropeets kak iavlenie kul'tury* (Moscow: ROSSPEN, 2001), 4–5, 104; idem, "Zapadnichestvo kak problema 'russkogo puti,'" in *Rossiia i Zapad: Dialog ili stolknovenie kul'tur. Sbornik statei* (Moscow: Rossiiskii institut kul'turologii, 2000), 6–7, 26; E. V. Alekseeva, *Diffuziia evropeiskikh innovatsii v Rossii (XVIII–nachalo XX vv.)* (Moscow: ROSSPEN, 2007), 91.
4. Kantor, *Russkii evropeets*, 61, 158, 336–337; Liudmila Chernaia, "Obraz 'Zapada' v russkoi kul'ture XI–XVII vv.," in *Rossiia i Zapad*, 32–35.
5. Modernization and its relationship to Westernization are important topics, but are not a subject of this book.
6. Alekseeva, *Diffuziia evropeiskikh innovatsii*, 104–119, 133–135; James Cracraft, *The Petrine Revolution in Russian Culture* (Cambridge, MA: Harvard University Press 2004).
7. Michael David-Fox, *Showcasing the Great Experiment: Cultural Diplomacy and Western Visitors to the Soviet Union, 1921–1941* (Oxford: Oxford University Press, 2012), 11.
8. Alekseeva, *Diffuziia evropeiskikh innovatsii*, 104, 133; *Rossiia i Zapad*, 26–27.
9. Alekseeva, *Diffuziia evropeiskikh innovatsii*, 133; James Cracraft, "Opposition to Peter the Great," in *Imperial Russia, 1700–1917: State, Society, Opposition*, ed. Ezra Mendelsohn and Marshall Shatz (DeKalb: Northern Illinois University Press, 1988), 22–36.
10. *Rossiia i Zapad*, 29, 33–34; Alekseeva, *Diffuziia evropeiskikh innovatsii*, 47.
11. Original formulation: Mikhail Shcherbatov, "O povrezhdenii nravov v Rossii" (1787).
12. Aleksandr Pushkin, Nikolai Gogol', Mikhail Saltykov-Shchedrin.

13. Kantor, *Russkii evropeets*; David-Fox, *Showcasing the Great Experiment*, 9–10.

14. Kantor, *Russkii evropeets*, 6–7, 581.

15. Marc Raeff, *Origins of the Russian Intelligentsia: the Eighteenth-Century Nobility* (New York: Harcourt, Brace & World, 1966).

16. Nicholas Riasanovsky, *Russia and the West in the Teaching of the Slavophiles: A Study of Romantic Ideology* (Gloucester, MA: P. Smith, 1965), 24, 60–114, 117–124, 157–719; Laura Engelstein, *Slavophile Empire: Imperial Russia's Illiberal Path* (Ithaca, NY: Cornell University Press, 2009), 99–124, esp. 111.

17. David-Fox, *Showcasing the Great Experiment*, 40–57; Liudmila Stern, *Western Intellectuals and the Soviet Union, 1920–40: From Red Square to the Left Bank* (London: Routledge, 2007).

18. David Brandenberger, *National Bolshevism: Stalinist Mass Culture and the Formation of Modern Russian National Identity, 1931–1956* (Cambridge, MA: Harvard University Press, 2002), 43–94. Isolationism grounded in "Sovietness," rather than Russian nationalism: Malte Rolf, "A Hall of Mirrors: Sovietizing Culture under Stalinism," *Slavic Review* 68:3 (Fall 2009): 601–630.

19. David-Fox, *Showcasing the Great Experiment*, 7–12; Stephen Kotkin, *Magnetic Mountain: Stalinism as Civilization* (Berkeley: University of California Press, 1995), 2, 30, 150–153, 184–187, 227–228, 236–237.

20. Katerina Clark, *Moscow, the Fourth Rome: Stalinism, Cosmopolitanism, and the Evolution of Soviet Culture, 1931–1941* (Cambridge, MA: Harvard University Press, 2011); David-Fox, *Showcasing the Great Experiment*; Lisa Kirschenbaum, *International Communism and the Spanish Civil War: Solidarity and Suspicion* (New York: Cambridge University Press, 2015), 15–66.

21. Clark, *Moscow, the Fourth Rome*, 95–100, 119–124, 137–145, 160–163, 312–329; Pauline Fairclough, *Classics for the Masses: Shaping Soviet Musical Identity under Lenin and Stalin* (New Haven, CT: Yale University Press, 2016), 6–8, 26–41, 101–133; Ekaterina Sal'nikova, *Sovetskaia kul'tura v dvizhenii: ot serediny 1930-kh k seredine 1980-kh. Vizual'nye obrazy, geroi, siuzhety. Otechestvennaia kul'tura za predelami "sovetskosti"* (Moscow: Izdatel'stvo LKI, 2008), 10–55.

22. Thomas Lahusen, "From Laughter 'Out of Sync' to Post-Synchronized Comedy: How the Stalinist Film Musical Caught Up with Hollywood and Overtook It," in *Socialist Cultures East and West: A Post-Cold War Reassessment*, ed. Dubravka Juraga and M. Keith Booker (Westport, CT: Praeger, 2002), 31–42; Rimgaila Salys, *The Musical Comedy Films of Grigorii Aleksandrov: Laughing Matters* (Chicago: University of Chicago Press, 2009); Clark, *Moscow, the Fourth Rome*, 186–192.

23. Clark, *Moscow, the Fourth Rome*, 151–157, 169–179, 271; Fairclough, *Classics for the Masses*, 9, 123–127; Benjamin Martin, *The Nazi-Fascist New Order for European Culture* (Cambridge, MA: Harvard University Press, 2016).

24. Clark, *Moscow, the Fourth Rome*, 169–179.

25. Ibid., 242–255; Kirschenbaum, *International Communism*, 73–79, 117–125, 131–137.

26. Vladimir Paperny, *Kul'tura "dva"* (Ann Arbor, MI: Ardis, 1985), 64–65; Iu. I. Igritskii, "Vospriiatie SSSR kak factor global'noi politicheskoi konfrontatsii," in *Rossiia i mir glazami drug druga: iz istorii vzaimovospriiatiia*, issue 2 (Moscow: Institut rossiiskoi istorii RAN, 2002), 198–217; A. V. Golubev, "'Mirovaia respublika' ili 'zakrytoe obshchestvo': SSSR v 1920–30-e gody," ibid., 277–306; idem, "'Tsar' Kitaiu ne verit . . .'. Soiuzniki v predstavlenii rossiiskogo ob-shchestva 1914–1945 gg.," in *Rossiia i mir glazami drug druga: iz istorii vzaimovospriiatiia*, issue 1 (Moscow: Institut rossiiskoi istorii RAN, 2000), 317–355; Violetta Gudkova, "Neputeshestvie kak literaturnyi fakt: obrazy Frantsii v proizvedeniiakh rossiiskikh pisatelei 1920–1930-kh godov," in *Rossiia i Frantsiia: XVIII–XX vv. Lotmanovskie chteniia* (Moscow: RGGU, 2013), 310–334, here 319–321; David-Fox, *Showcasing the Great Experiment*, 102; Emma Widdis, *Visions of a New Land: Soviet Film from the Revolution to the Second World War* (New Haven, CT: Yale University Press, 2003), 143–144, 153–154.

27. David-Fox, *Showcasing the Great Experiment*, 295–305; Kirschenbaum, *International Communism*, 29–30, 45–48; James Harris, *The Great Fear: Stalin's Terror of the 1930s* (Oxford: Oxford University Press, 2016), 32–34, 43–50, 105–110, 127–130, 141–160; Sergei Zhuravlev, *"Malen'kie liudi" i "bol'shaia istoriia." Inostrantsy moskovskogo Elektrozavoda v sovetskom obshchestve 1920kh–1930kh gg.* (Moscow: ROSSPEN, 2000), 294–333; Shawn Salmon, "To the Land of the Future: A History of Intourist and Travel to the Soviet Union, 1929–1991" (PhD diss., University of California, Berkeley, 2008), 98–104, 108–112.

28. David-Fox, *Showcasing the Great Experiment*, 299–300; Robert English, *Russia and the Idea of the West: Gorbachev, Intellectuals & and the End of the Cold War* (New York: Columbia University Press, 2000), 37–42.

29. David-Fox, *Showcasing the Great Experiment*, passim; Clark, *Moscow, the Fourth Rome*, passim.

30. Further discussion: Katerina Clark, "'Wait for Me and I Shall Return': The Early Thaw as a Reprise of Late Thirties Culture?" in *The Thaw: Soviet Society and Culture during the 1950s and 1960s*, ed. Denis Kozlov and Eleonory Gilburd (Toronto: University of Toronto Press, 2013), 85–108.

31. *Doklad N. S. Khrushcheva o kul'te lichnosti Stalina na XX s"ezde KPSS: Dokumenty* (Moscow: ROSSPEN, 2002); Polly Jones, *Myth, Memory, Trauma: Rethinking the Stalinist Past in the Soviet Union, 1953–70* (New Haven, CT: Yale University Press, 2013), 34–35.

32. Denis Kozlov, *The Readers of* Novyi mir: *Coming to Terms with the Stalinist Past* (Cambridge, MA: Harvard University Press, 2013); Jones, *Myth, Memory,*

Trauma, 19–21; Vladislav Zubok, *Zhivago's Children: The Last Russian Intelligentsia* (Cambridge, MA: Harvard University Press, 2011), 61–66.

33. Kozlov, *The Readers of Novyi mir*; Jones, *Myth, Memory, Trauma*, 21–28, 36.

34. D. M. Feldman, *Terminologiia vlasti: Sovetskie politicheskie terminy v istoriko-kul'turnom kontekste* (Moscow: Rossiiskii gosudarstvennyi gumanitarnyi universitet, 2006), 65–117.

35. A. V. Fateev, *Obraz vraga v sovetskoi propagande, 1945–1954 gg.* (Moscow: Institut rossiiskoi istorii RAN, 1999); Konstantin Azadovskii and Boris Egorov, "From Anti-Westernism to Anti-Semitism," *Journal of Cold War Studies* 4:1 (Winter 2002): 66–80. The connection between the opening to the West and the Terror theme: English, *Russia and the Idea of the West*, 63–64.

36. Henri Chambre, "Exit Joseph Stalin," *America*, June 30, 1956, 320–322; Philip Mosely, "Soviet Foreign Policy: New Goals or New Manners?" *Foreign Affairs* 34:4 (July 1957): 541–553; idem, "Russia Revisited: Moscow Dialogues, 1956," *Foreign Affairs* 39:1 (October 1956): 72–84; M. Searle Bates, "Is There a New Russia since Stalin?" *Christianity and Crisis*, November 11, 1957; Frederick C. Barghoorn, "De-Stalinization: Temporary Tactic or Long Term Trend?" *International Journal* 12:1 (Winter 1956–57): 24–33.

37. Further discussion: Kozlov and Gilburd, "The Thaw as an Event in Russian History," in *The Thaw*, 29–30.

38. The importance of physicality for the understanding and use of metaphors: George Lakoff and Mark Johnson, *Metaphors We Live By* (Chicago: University of Chicago Press, 1980), 56–60, 112, 117–121, 146, 175–182.

39. In the most common challenges to the metaphor, scholars argue that it 1) universalizes the aspirations of one group of intellectuals (those who invented it), but excludes conservatives who rejected reforms; 2) represents only the intelligentsia, whether in its elite or populist meanings, but not those who remained oblivious to change; 3) projects a rosy picture of the period that emerged only in retrospect, as a nostalgic memory. My reading of the metaphor differs in stressing its physical, atmospheric, expansive, and contingent connotations. The metaphor's life: Kozlov and Gilburd, "The Thaw," 18–23. Other perspectives: Nancy Condee, "Cultural Codes of the Thaw," in *Nikita Khrushchev*, ed. William Taubman, Sergei Khrushchev, and Abbott Gleason (New Haven, CT: Yale University Press, 2000), 160–176, esp. 169–175; Stephen Bittner, *The Many Lives of Khrushchev's Thaw: Experience and Memory in Moscow's Arbat* (Ithaca, NY: Cornell University Press, 2008), 2–13; Benjamin Tromly, *Making the Soviet Intelligentsia: Universities and Intellectual Life under Stalin and Khrushchev* (Cambridge: Cambridge University Press, 2014), 19–21.

40. For a similar approach: Bittner, *The Many Lives*, 10–11; Aleksandr Prokhorov, *Unasledovannyi diskurs: paradigma stalinskoi kul'tury v literature i kinematografe "ottepeli"* (Saint Petersburg: Akademicheskii proekt, 2007), 83–89; Erik

Scott, *Familiar Strangers: The Georgian Diaspora and the Evolution of Soviet Empire* (Oxford: Oxford University Press, 2016), 127, 141–154; Christine Evans, *Between Truth and Time: A History of Soviet Central Television* (New Haven, CT: Yale University Press, 2016), 3–5, 16–17, 96–97, 183–190; Alexei Yurchak, *Everything Was Forever, Until It Was No More: The Last Soviet Generation* (Princeton, NJ: Princeton University Press, 2006); Peter Schmelz, *Such Freedom, If Only Musical: Unofficial Soviet Music during the Thaw* (Oxford: Oxford University Press, 2009); Kristin Roth-Ey, *Moscow Prime Time: How the Soviet Union Built the Media Empire That Lost the Cultural Cold War* (Ithaca, NY: Cornell University Press, 2011), 5–6; Zubok, *Zhivago's Children*, 124–126.

41. Rossen Djagalov and Masha Salazkina, "Tashkent '68: A Cinematic Contact Zone," *Slavic Review* 75:2 (Summer 2016): 279–298; James Pickett, "Soviet Civilization through a Persian Lens: Iranian Intellectuals, Cultural Diplomacy, and Socialist Modernity, 1941–55," *Iranian Studies* 48:5 (2015): 805–826; Masha Kirasirova, "'Sons of Muslims' in Moscow: Soviet Central Asian Mediators to the Foreign East, 1955–1962," *Ab Imperio* 4 (2011): 106–132; Tobias Rupprecht, *Soviet Internationalism after Stalin: Interaction and Exchange between the USSR and Latin America during the Cold War* (Cambridge: Cambridge University Press, 2015); Anne Gorsuch, "'Cuba, My Love': The Romance of Revolutionary Cuba in the Soviet Sixties," *American Historical Review* 2 (2015): 497–526; Sudha Rajagopalan, *Indian Films in Soviet Cinemas: The Culture of Movie-going after Stalin* (Bloomington: Indiana University Press, 2008); Konstantin Bogdanov, "Negry v SSSR: Etnografiia mnimoi diaspory," *Antropologicheskii forum* 22 (2014): 103–142; Maxim Matusevich, "Expanding the Boundaries of the Black Atlantic beyond the Iron Curtain: African Students Encounter the Soviet Union," *Afroeurope@n Configurations: Readings and Projects*, ed. Sabrina Brancato (Newcastle upon Tyne: Cambridge Scholars Publishing, 2011), 58–80; idem, "Journeys of Hope: African Diaspora and the Soviet Society," *African Diaspora* 1:1 (2008): 53–85; Julie Hessler, "Death of an African Student in Moscow: Race, Politics, and the Cold War," *Cahiers du monde russe* 47:1 (2006): 33–63. More broadly: David Engerman, "The Second World's Third World," *Kritika: Explorations in Russian and Eurasian History* 12:1 (Winter 2011): 183–211.

42. Fundamental continuity: Michael David-Fox, *Crossing Borders: Modernity, Ideology, and Culture in Russia and the Soviet Union* (Pittsburgh: University of Pittsburgh Press, 2015), 48–71.

43. English, *Russia and the Idea of the West*, passim, esp. 194, 207–215, 220–225; "'Europe as a Common European Home': Address Given by Mikhail Gorbachev to the Council of Europe (Strasbourg, 6 July 1989)," http://chnm.gmu.edu/1989/archive/files/gorbachev-speech-7-6-89_e3ccb87237.pdf.

44. Alexei Kozlov, *"Kozel na sakse"—i tak vsiu zhizn'* (Moscow: Vagrius, 1998); Vasilii Aksenov, *V poiskakh grustnogo bebi: Kniga ob Amerike* (Moscow: Izdatel'stvo MAI, 1991); S. Frederick Starr, *Red and Hot: the Fate of Jazz in the Soviet Union, 1917–1980* (New York: Oxford University Press, 1983); Yurchak, *Everything Was Forever*, 181–190; Sergei Zhuk, *Rock and Roll in the Rocket City: The West, Identity, and Ideology in Soviet Dniepropetrovsk, 1960–1985* (Baltimore: Johns Hopkins University Press, 2010), 65–77, 81–89, 97–101. The nylon and neon America of European fantasies: Reinhold Wagnleitner, "The Empire of the Fun, or Talkin' Soviet Union Blues: The Sound of Freedom and U.S. Cultural Hegemony in Europe," *Diplomatic History* 23:3 (Summer 1999): 499–524.

45. Arthur Marwick, *The Sixties: Cultural Revolution in Britain, France, Italy, and the United States, c. 1958–c. 1974* (Oxford: Oxford University Press, 1998), 18, 36, 319, 329, 406, passim.

46. Victoria de Grazia, *Irresistible Empire: America's Advance through Twentieth-Century Europe* (Cambridge, MA: Harvard University Press, 2005).

47. *Decentering America*, ed. Jessica C. E. Gienow-Hecht (New York: Berghahn, 2007).

48. Emily Apter, *Against World Literature: On the Politics of Untranslatability* (London: Verso, 2013), 1–44, esp. 3–4, 9–10, 34–35; untranslatable remainders in all texts: Walter Benjamin, "The Translator's Task," in *The Translation Studies Reader*, 3rd ed., ed. Lawrence Venuti (New York: Routledge, 2012), 75–83, here 79, 81; the untranslatable in Romanticism: Antoine Berman, *The Experience of the Foreign: Culture and Translation in Romantic Germany* (Albany: State University of New York Press, 1992), 16, 118–120.

49. Reception as integral to translation: Gideon Toury, "The Nature and Role of Norms in Translation," in *The Translation Studies Reader*, 168–181.

50. Soviet claims to classical culture: Paperny, *Kul'tura "dva,"* 40; culture of the 1930s as "Great Appropriation": Clark, *Moscow, the Fourth Rome*, 27, 95–100, 307–328; appropriation as "ethnocentric translation" found in any culture: Berman, *The Experience of the Foreign*, 4; translation as accommodation and "arrival": Leon Burnett and Emily Lygo, "The Art of Accommodation: Introduction," in *The Art of Accommodation: Literary Translation in Russia*, ed. Burnett and Lygo (Bern: Peter Lang, 2013), 1–29.

51. Konstantin Bogdanov, *O krokodilakh v Rossii: Ocherki iz istorii zaimstvovanii i ekzotizmov* (Moscow: Novoe literaturnoe obozrenie, 2006).

52. Vladimir Dal', *Tolkovyi slovar' zhivogo velikorusskago iazyka* (St. Petersburg: M. O. Vol'f, 1912–1914), 4: 72–73. Other meanings: Yuri Lotman, "'Izgoi' i 'izgoinichestvo' kak sotsial'no-psikhologicheskaia pozitsiia v russkoi kul'ture preimushchestvenno dopetrovskogo perioda ('Svoe' i 'chuzhoe' v istorii russkoi kul'tury)," in *Istoriia i tipologiia russkoi kul'tury* (St. Petersburg: Iskusstvo-SPb,

2002), 222–232; Viacheslav Morozov, *Rossiia i drugie: Identichnost' i granitsy politicheskogo soobshchestva* (Moscow: Novoe literaturnoe obozrenie, 2009), 237–249; György Péteri, "The Occident Within—or the Drive for Exceptionalism and Modernity," *Kritika: Explorations in Russian and Eurasian History* 9:4 (Fall 2008): 929–937.

53. Further discussion: Brian James Baer, *Translation and the Making of Modern Russian Literature* (New York: Bloomsbury, 2016); Burnett and Lygo, "The Art of Accommodation," 9–20.

54. Yu. Levin, *Russkie perevodchiki XIX veka i razvitie khudozhestvennogo perevoda* (Leningrad: Nauka, 1985), 9; Maurice Friedberg, *Literary Translation in Russia: A Cultural History* (University Park: Pennsylvania State University Press, 1997), 28–32; Lawrence Venuti, *The Translator's Invisibility: A History of Translation*, 2nd ed. (New York: Routledge, 2008), 1–34.

55. Levin, *Russkie perevodchiki*, 23–24; Friedberg, *Literary Translation*, 43–45, 48–59, 63.

56. V. E. Bagno and T. A. Novichkova, "Imia: Svoe i chuzhoe," in *Chuzhoe imia* (St. Petersburg: Kanun, 2001), 5–14.

57. Susanna Witt, "The Shorthand of Empire: *Podstrochnik* Practices and the Making of Soviet Literature," *Ab Imperio* 3 (2013): 155–190.

58. Maria Khotimsky, "World Literature, Soviet Style: A Forgotten Episode in the History of the Idea," *Ab Imperio* 3 (2013): 119–154; Baer, *Translation and the Making*, 118; Burnett and Lygo, "The Art of Accommodation," 21–24; Friedberg, *Literary Translation*, 4–5.

59. V. Bagno and N. Kazanskii, "Perevodcheskaia 'nisha' v sovetskuiu epokhu i fenomen stikhotvornogo perevoda v XX veke," in *RES TRADUCTORICA: Perevod i sravnitel'noe izuchenie literatury: k vos'midesiatiletiiu Iu. D. Levina*, ed. Bagno (Saint Petersburg: Nauka, 2000), 50–65; Brian Baer, "Literary Translation and the Construction of a Soviet Intelligentsia," in *Translation, Resistance, Activism*, ed. Maria Tymoczko (Amherst: University of Massachusetts Press, 2010), 149–167.

60. See also: Baer, *Translation and the Making*, 11–12, 53.

61. Itamar Even-Zohar, "The Position of Translated Literature within the Literary Polysystem," in *The Translation Studies Reader*, 162–167, here 163–164. The significance of the moment and the importing culture's need: André Lefevere, "Mother Courage's Cucumbers: Text, System and Refraction in a Theory of Literature," in *The Translation Studies Reader*, 203–219, here 207; Burnett and Lygo, "The Art of Accommodation," 7–9.

62. Canon and translation: Mihály Szegedy-Maszák, *Literary Canons: National and International* (Budapest: Akadémiai Kiadó, 2001), 59–64.

63. Pascale Casanova, *The World Republic of Letters* (Cambridge, MA: Harvard University Press, 2004), 22–23.

64. Roth-Ey, *Moscow Prime Time*, 151, 168; William Jay Risch, *The Ukrainian West: Culture and the Fate of Empire in Soviet Lviv* (Cambridge, MA: Harvard University Press, 2011), 8, 11, 44–45, 82–97, 112–115, 211–215; idem, "A Soviet West: Nationhood, Regionalism, and Empire in the Annexed Western Borderlands," *Nationalities Papers* 43:1 (2015): 63–81, esp. 72–76; Zbigniew Wojnowski, "An Unlikely Bulwark of Sovietness: Cross-Border Travel and Soviet Patriotism in Western Ukraine, 1956–1985," in ibid., 82–101; Zhuk, *Rock and Roll*, 67–68, 83; Zubok, *Zhivago's Children*, 90; Anne Gorsuch, *All This Is Your World: Soviet Tourism at Home and Abroad after Stalin* (Oxford: Oxford University Press, 2011), 92; Maurice Friedberg, *A Decade of Euphoria: Western Literature in Post-Stalin Russia, 1954–64* (Bloomington: Indiana University Press, 1977), 59–60.

65. Correspondingly, films in the languages of Soviet republics were dubbed into Russian for all-Union and international festivals. G. Zargar'ian, "Iskusstvo perevoda fil'ma," in *Masterstvo perevoda: Sbornik dvenadtsatyi* (Moscow: Sovetskii pisatel', 1981), 109–153, here 112.

66. Perry Sherouse, "Quality, Comfort, and Ease: Remapping the Affordances of Russian Language in Tbilisi, Georgia" (PhD diss., University of Michigan, 2014), 124–151. Western mass culture as a channel of Russification: Zhuk, *Rock and Roll*, 121, 124, 167, 262–264, 314.

67. The significance of indirect translation and intermediary languages/texts: Witt, "The Shorthand"; Oleksandr Kal'nychenko, "A Sketch of the Ukrainian History of Translation of the 1920s," in *Between Cultures and Texts: Itineraries in Translation History*, ed. Antoine Chalvin, Anne Lange, and Daniele Monticelli (Frankfurt am Main: Peter Lang, 2011), 240–242.

68. Daniele Monticelli, "'Totalitarian Translation' as a Means of Forced Cultural Change: The Case of Postwar Soviet Estonia," in *Between Cultures and Texts*, 167–180; Daniele Monticelli and Anne Lange, "Translation and Totalitarianism: the Case of Soviet Estonia," *Translator* 20:1 (2014): 95–111.

69. Monticelli and Lange, "Translation."

70. RGALI f. 1573, op. 1, d. 106, ll. 103–104.

71. Scott, *Familiar Strangers*, 212–214, 231–233; Roth-Ey, *Moscow Prime Time*, 86–87; Friedberg, *A Decade of Euphoria*, 60; Baer, *Translation and the Making*, 62.

72. The people at the top of the Soviet cultural apparatus were mostly men. Rank-and-file translators were overwhelmingly women, and there were many women among rank-and-file literary and film critics. "Stalinist Westernizers": David-Fox, *Showcasing the Great Experiment*, 6–7, 219–227.

73. Clark, *Moscow, the Fourth Rome*, 32–39. In this book, cultural mediators act in a different capacity than they do in Clark's, even when we write about the same people. In Clark's study, their mediating activities bring them into dialogue with Western intellectuals, as the proselytizers for the Soviet cause and as the makers of a cosmopolitan Stalinist culture. Their circle of ad-

dressees and interlocutors are people like themselves. In my account, their efforts are directed at domestic audiences. Their work with readers' and viewers' letters—preservation, categorization, marginal notations, correspondence—allows us a view into their aspirations and conveys the importance of popular enlightenment for their sense of themselves.

74. Kendall Bailes, *Technology and Society under Lenin and Stalin* (Princeton, NJ: Princeton University Press, repr. 2015); Sheila Fitzpatrick, "Stalin and the Making of a New Elite," in *The Cultural Front: Power and Culture in Revolutionary Russia* (Ithaca, NY: Cornell University Press, 1992), 149–182; Tromly, *Making the Soviet Intelligentsia*, 3–9, 53–61; Zubok, *Zhivago's Children*, 21, 23–24, 34–35, 124. Like Zubok's protagonists, my subjects benefited from postwar Soviet education, but, unlike Zubok's intelligentsia, they did not become leading scientists, dissidents, diplomats, or architects of perestroika. They remained provincial teachers and factory engineers.

75. Kozlov, *The Readers of* Novyi mir, 402n61.

76. Fairclough, *Classics for the Masses*, 39–56; David-Fox, *Crossing Borders*, 64–66; Adele Barker, "The Culture Factory: Theorizing the Popular in the Old and New Russia," in *Consuming Russia: Popular Culture, Sex, and Society since Gorbachev* (Durham, NC: Duke University Press, 1999), 12–45; Vadim Volkov, "The Concept of *Kul'turnost*': Notes on the Stalinist Civilizing Process," in *Stalinism: New Directions*, ed. Sheila Fitzpatrick (New York: Routledge, 2000), 210–230.

77. B. A. Grushin, *Chetyre zhizni Rossii v zerkale oprosov obshchestvennogo mneniia. Epokha Khrushcheva* (Moscow: Progress-Traditsiia, 2001), 494; RGALI f. 1204, op. 2, d. 2616, l. 890b.

78. Roth-Ey, *Moscow Prime Time*, 3–5, 13–15, 98–106; Evans, *Between Truth and Time*, 49–81, 98–113; Stephen Lovell, *Russia in the Microphone Age: A History of Soviet Radio, 1919–1970* (Oxford: Oxford University Press, 2015), 182, 207–208; Joshua First, "From Spectator to 'Differentiated' Consumer: Film Audience Research in the Era of Developed Socialism (1965–1980)," *Kritika: Explorations in Russian and Eurasian History* 9:2 (2008): 317–344; idem, *Ukrainian Cinema: Belonging and Identity during the Soviet Thaw* (London: I. B. Tauris, 2015), 11, 183–192; David-Fox, *Crossing Borders*, 68–69.

79. Evgenii Dobrenko, *Formovka sovetskogo chitatelia: Sotsial'nye i esteticheskie predposylki retseptsii sovetskoi literatury* (Saint Petersburg: Akademicheskii proekt, 1997); Stephen Lovell, *The Russian Reading Revolution: Print Culture in the Soviet and Post-Soviet Eras* (New York: St. Martin's Press, 2000).

80. "K chitateliu," *Zhizn' muzeia. Biulleten' Gosudarstvennogo muzeia iziashchnykh iskusstv* 1 (May 1925): 1–2; A. A. Vol'ter, "K voprosu ob ekspozitsii v khudozhestvennykh muzeiakh," *Sovetskii muzei* 3 (May–June 1933): 54–62; N. I. Ruban, *Sovetskaia vlast' i muzeinoe stroitel'stvo na Dal'nem Vostoke Rossii*

(1920–1930-e gg.) (Khabarovsk: Khabarovskii kraevoi kraevedcheskii muzei im. N. I. Grodekova, 2002), 23, 34.

81. Roth-Ey, *Moscow Prime Time*, 3–5; Lovell, *Russia in the Microphone Age*, 8–11, 23–41, 51–67.

82. Kozlov, *The Readers of* Novyi mir, 24–43. Earlier example: Jochen Hellbeck, *Revolution on My Mind: Writing a Diary under Stalin* (Cambridge, MA: Harvard University Press, 2006); Zubok, *Zhivago's Children*, 21.

83. Sheila Fitzpatrick, *Everyday Stalinism: Ordinary Life in Extraordinary Times: Soviet Russia in the 1930s* (Oxford: Oxford University Press, 1999); Alena Ledeneva, *Russia's Economy of Favours: Blat, Networking and Informal Exchange* (Cambridge: Cambridge University Press, 1998).

84. Statement supported by regional studies: Tromly, *Making the Soviet Intelligentsia*, 219–230; Gleb Tsipursky, *Socialist Fun: Youth, Consumption & State-Sponsored Popular Culture in the Soviet Union, 1945–1970* (Pittsburgh: University of Pittsburgh Press, 2016); Risch, *The Ukrainian West*; Michaela Pohl, "From White Grave to Tselinograd to Astana: The Virgin Lands Opening, Khrushchev's Forgotten First Reform," in *The Thaw*, ed. Kozlov and Gilburd, 269–307; Donald Raleigh, *Soviet Baby Boomers: An Oral History of Russia's Cold War Generation* (Oxford: Oxford University Press, 2012); Oleg Leibovich, *V gorode M: Ocherki politicheskoi povsednevnosti sovetskoi provintsii v 40–50-kh godakh XX veka* (Perm': Permskii gosudarstvennyi tekhnicheskii universitet, 2005); idem, *Reforma i modernizatsiia v 1953–1964 gg.* (Perm': Izdatel'stvo Permskogo universiteta, 1993); English, *Russia and the Idea of the West*, 62–63.

85. Roth-Ey, *Moscow Prime Time*, passim; Kozlov, *The Readers of* Novyi mir, 28–29; Lovell, *Russia in the Microphone Age*, 142, 148–153, 157–158, 162.

86. The system of occupational distribution, the various schemes to evade it, and the shock of going from urban centers to a Central Asian village: Tromly, *Making the Soviet Intelligentsia*, 67–75; periphery-bound young people: Kelly Smith, *Moscow 1956: The Silenced Spring* (Cambridge, MA: Harvard University Press, 2017), 200–225.

87. See Appendix.

1. Soviet Internationalism

1. The shell is the emblem of the Santiago Order; the palace was built by Rodrigo Arias Maldonado, a knight of the Order.

2. GARF f. 9576, op. 1, d. 8, ll. 204–234.

3. Based on Anthony Colantuono, "The Mute Diplomat: Theorizing the Role of Images in Seventeenth-Century Political Negotiations," in *The Diplomacy of Art: Artistic Creation and Politics in Seicento Italy*, ed. Elizabeth Cropper (Milan: Nuova Alfa Editoriale, 2000), 51–76; Richard Arndt, *The First Resort*

of Kings: American Cultural Diplomacy in the Twentieth Century (Washington, DC: Potomac Books, 2005), 7–10; Mark Lamster, *Master of Shadows: the Secret Diplomatic Career of Painter Peter Paul Rubens* (New York: Nan A. Talese, 2009).

4. Akira Iriye, *Cultural Internationalism and World Order* (Baltimore: Johns Hopkins University Press, 1997).

5. Katerina Clark, *Moscow, the Fourth Rome: Stalinism, Cosmopolitanism, and the Evolution of Soviet Culture, 1931–1941* (Cambridge, MA: Harvard University Press, 2011), 155, passim; Kiril Tomoff, *Virtuosi Abroad: Soviet Music and Imperial Competition during the Early Cold War, 1945–1958* (Ithaca, NY: Cornell University Press, 2015), 10–12; Benjamin Martin, *The Nazi-Fascist New Order for European Culture* (Cambridge, MA: Harvard University Press, 2016), 3, 121; Michael David-Fox, *Showcasing the Great Experiment: Cultural Diplomacy and Western Visitors to the Soviet Union, 1921–1941* (Oxford: Oxford University Press, 2012), passim; Liudmila Stern, *Western Intellectuals and the Soviet Union, 1920–1940: From Red Square to the Left Bank* (London: Routledge, 2007).

6. Iriye, *Cultural Internationalism*, 20–33, 54–58, 60–67, 70–74, 76–79 (Trotsky quotation: 15); Mark Mazower, *Governing the World: the History of an Idea* (New York: Penguin Press, 2012), 38–47, 66–153; Zoë Druick, "The International Educational Cinematography Institute, Reactionary Modernism, and the Formation of Film Studies," *Canadian Journal of Film Studies* 16:1 (Spring 2007): 80–97; idem, "'Reaching the Multimillions': Liberal Internationalism and the Establishment of Documentary Film," in *Inventing Film Studies*, ed. Lee Grieveson and Haidee Wasson (Durham, NC: Duke University Press, 2008), 66–92.

7. David-Fox, *Showcasing the Great Experiment*, 40, 61–89; Liudmila Stern, "The Background History of Creation of the French Rapprochement Society *The New Russia* (Based on Unpublished VOKS Documents)," *Australian Slavonic and East European Studies* 11:1–2 (1997): 143–160; Jean-François Fayet, *VOKS: Le laboratoire helvétique. Histoire de la diplomatie culturelle soviétique durant l'entre-deux-guerres* (Chêne-Bourg: Georg, 2014), 257–279, 281–292.

8. Arndt, *The First Resort of Kings*, 26, 37–38; Gregory Paschalidis, "Exporting National Culture: Histories of Cultural Institutes Abroad," *International Journal of Cultural Policy* 15:3 (2009): 275–289.

9. David-Fox, *Showcasing the Great Experiment*, 29–35, 40–46, 58–60, 192–193; Stern, *Western Intellectuals*, 120–128, 155–158.

10. David-Fox, *Showcasing the Great Experiment*, 98–127.

11. Ibid., 26, 46–54, 122, 227–246, 315.

12. Ibid., 193, 295–296, 312–323.

13. Martin, *The Nazi-Fascist New Order*, 6–7, 15, 20–21.

14. Ibid., 4–5, 13–14 , 34–40, 65–70.

15. Ibid., 16–17, 32–33, 52–59.

16. Ibid., 9, 27–29.

17. Ibid., 60–62, 76–79, 102–104.

18. Ibid., 74–76, 96–97, 109–122.

19. Ibid., 21, 84–90.

20. Arndt, *The First Resort of Kings*, 31–32, 38–39; Nicholas Cull, *The Cold War and the United States Information Agency: American Propaganda and Public Diplomacy, 1945–1989* (Cambridge: Cambridge University Press, 2008), 11.

21. Cull, *The Cold War and the United States*, 5, 10.

22. Frank Ninkovich, *The Diplomacy of Ideas: U.S. Foreign Policy and Cultural Relations, 1928–1950* (Cambridge: Cambridge University Press, 1981), 8–34.

23. Ibid., 24–31; Justin Hart, *Empire of Ideas: The Origins of Public Diplomacy and the Transformation of U.S. Foreign Policy* (Oxford: Oxford University Press, 2013), 3–4, 15–39.

24. Hart, *Empire of Ideas*, 20, 41–43, 46–52, 59–68, 71–86, 95–106; Ninkovich, *The Diplomacy of Ideas*, 36–39; Cull, *The Cold War and the United States*, 11–20; Darlene Sadlier, *Americans All: Good Neighbor Cultural Diplomacy in World War II* (Austin: University of Texas Press, 2012), 10–33, 84–157.

25. Cull, *The Cold War and the United States*, 13–15.

26. Ibid., 22–23, 27–37, 39–41, 52–53, 63–66, 100–114; Hart, *Empire of Ideas*, 111–118, 128–133.

27. Alessandro Brogi, *Confronting America: The Cold War between the United States and the Communists in France and Italy* (Chapel Hill: University of North Carolina Press, 2011), 13–19, 24–33, 53–60, 72–74, 82–86.

28. The Soviets' inept and inert cultural outreach to the socialist bloc: Patryk Babiracki, *Soviet Soft Power in Poland: Culture and the Making of Stalin's New Empire, 1943–1957* (Chapel Hill: University of North Carolina Press, 2015), 63–67, 72–74, esp. 79–89.

29. Zhorzh [Georges] Marten and Vol'f Sedykh, *Moskva-Parizh: Velenie serdtsa i razuma* (Moscow: Mezhdunarodnye otnosheniia, 1998), 29–49; Thomas Gomart, *Double détente: les relations franco-soviétiques de 1958 à 1964* (Paris: Publications de la Sorbonne, 2003), 102–103, 109, 115–116. On France-USSR's political composition, dominated by communists: ibid., 107–109.

30. RGANI f. 5, op. 36, d. 11, ll. 93–94; GARF f. 9576, op. 2, d. 129, l. 238; ibid., d. 90, l. 184.

31. RGANI f. 5, op. 36, d. 11, ll. 91–92.

32. Cull, *The Cold War and the United States*, 45–46 (quotation: 45).

33. Sadlier, *Americans All*, 171–173; Ninkovich, *The Diplomacy of Ideas*, 18, 45, 92, 114, 117; Cull, *The Cold War and the United States*, 56–57; Hart, *Empire of Ideas*, 87.

34. Cull, *The Cold War and the United States*, 114–115; Helen Franc, "The Early Years of the International Program and Council," in *The Museum of Modern Art at Mid-Century, At Home and Abroad* (New York: The Museum of Modern Art, 1994), 109–149, here 118–119, 124–128; Robert Elder, *The Information Machine: The United States Information Agency and American Foreign Policy* (Syracuse, NY: Syracuse University Press, 1968), 36–39; David Monod, "Disguise, Containment and the *Porgy and Bess* Revival of 1952–1956," *Journal of American Studies* 35: 2 (2001): 275–312.

35. Saki Dockrill and Günter Bischof, "Geneva: The Fleeting Opportunity for Détente," in *Cold War Respite: The Geneva Summit of 1955*, ed. Dockrill and Bischoff (Baton Rouge: Louisiana State University Press, 2000), 1–20; William Taubman, *Khrushchev: The Man and His Era* (New York: W. W. Norton, 2003), 349–353.

36. See David Caute, *The Dancer Defects: The Struggle for Cultural Supremacy during the Cold War* (Oxford: Oxford University Press, 2003); Greg Castillo, *Cold War on the Home Front: The Soft Power of Midcentury Design* (Minneapolis: University of Minnesota Press, 2010); Greg Barnhisel, *Cold War Modernists: Art, Literature, and American Cultural Diplomacy* (New York: Columbia University Press, 2015).

37. N. S. Khrushchev, *The Report of the Central Committee of the Communist Party of the Soviet Union to the 20th Party Congress* (Ottawa: The Press Office of the USSR Embassy in Canada, 1956), 19–23, 29–46; "Programma Kommunisticheskoi partii Sovetskogo Soiuza," in *Materialy XXII s'ezda KPSS* (Moscow: Gosudarstvennoe izdatel'stvo politicheskoi literatury, 1962), 361–365; G. I. Tunkin, "XXII s"ezd KPSS i mezhdunarodnoe pravo," *SEMP-1961* (1962): 15–28.

38. "Otvet tovarishcha Stalina na voprosy gruppy redaktorov amerikanskikh gazet" and "Pribytie v Moskvu uchastnikov Mezhdunarodnogo soveshchaniia," *Pravda*, April 2, 1952; Margot Light, *The Soviet Theory of International Relations* (New York: St. Martin's Press, 1988), 37–41; A. A. Danilov and A. V. Pyzhikov, *Rozhdenie sverkhderzhavy: SSSR v pervye poslevoennye gody* (Moscow: ROSSPEN, 2001), 80–86.

39. G. M. Malenkov, "Rech' na piatoi sessii Verkhovnogo Soveta SSSR," *Kommunist* 12 (1953): 12–34, here 26–31; E. Voznesenskii, "Vzaimnoe doverie i druzhba—osnova dobrososedskikh otnoshenii mezhdu SSSR i Finliandiei," *Kommunist* 17 (1954): 85–97; "Za mirnoe uregulirovanie mezhdunarodnykh voprosov," *Kommunist* 13 (1953): 36–48; A. Leont'ev, "O mirnom sosushchestvovanii dvukh sistem," *Kommunist* 13 (1954): 43–58; A. Solodovnikov, "Mezhdunarodnye kul'turnye sviazi," *MZh* 2 (December 1954): 100–110. This change was reflected in diplomatic dictionaries: Vyshinskii's 1950 dictionary contained no entry on cultural cooperation, but a well-elaborated entry on "trade

agreements," while Gromyko's 1960 dictionary contained entries on "cultural cooperation" and "scientific and technological cooperation." *Diplomaticheskii slovar'*, ed. A. Ia. Vyshinskii (Moscow: Gosudarstvennoe izdatel'stvo politicheskoi literatury, 1948, 1950), 1:846, 2:818–819; *Diplomaticheskii slovar'*, ed. A. A. Gromyko (Moscow: Gosudarstvennoe izdatel'stvo politicheskoi literatury, 1960, 1961, 1964), 2:154–156, 378–380.

40. G. A. Mozhaev, "Kul'turnye sviazi sluzhat ukrepleniiu mira i druzhby mezhdu narodami," *VIMK* 5 (1961): 74–91, here 78.

41. Idem., *Mezhdunarodnye kul'turnye sviazi SSSR* (Moscow: Znanie, 1959), 3, 8, 20.

42. V. I. Lenin, *Sobranie sochinenii* (Moscow: Gosudarstvennoe izdatel'stvo politicheskoi literatury, 1948), 20:8, 16; 27:278, 376; 29:54–55; 31:259–265, 343.

43. Mozhaev, "Kul'turnye sviazi," 78; a similar formulation by Mozhaev's superior in the diplomatic corps: S. K. Romanovskii, *Sredstvo sblizheniia narodov: O zarubezhnykh kul'turnykh i nauchnykh sviaziakh Sovetskogo Soiuza* (Moscow: Znanie, 1965), 29.

44. Solodovnikov, "Mezhdunarodnye kul'turnye sviazi," 104; GARF f. 9576, op. 2, d. 4, ll. 105–106; E. A. Baller, "Problema preemstvennosti v razvitii kul'tury," *VIMK* 5 (1961): 14–29.

45. Solodovnikov, "Mezhdunarodnye kul'turnye sviazi," 101.

46. GARF f. 9576, op. 2, d. 4, l. 99; Mozhaev, "Kul'turnye sviazi," 78–79, 82–83. Cosmopolitanism, universalism, and related notions of common humanity: Catherine Lu, "The One and Many Faces of Cosmopolitanism," *Journal of Political Philosophy* 8:2 (2000): 244–267.

47. "Materialy k planu 5-go toma 'Istorii nauchnogo i kul'turnogo razvitiia chelovechestva,'" *VIMK* 4 (1957):146–178.

48. "Prospekt istorii mirovoi kul'tury," *VIMK* 25:1 (1961): 98–111, here 99.

49. The journal reviewed international scholarship. Its own articles came with summaries in English. It was emblematic of other scholarly periodicals, which now added rubrics on foreign developments: critical bibliographies, calendar chronicles, and summaries in English or French.

50. Robert English, *Russia and the Idea of the West: Gorbachev, Intellectuals & the End of the Cold War* (New York: Columbia University Press, 2000), 70–80, 87–113, 125–155; quotations: 89, 140, 144; Ted Hopf, *Reconstructing the Cold War: The Early Years, 1945–1958* (New York: Oxford University Press, 2012), 251.

51. In Vladimir Dal''s dictionary, tsivilizatsiia did not have associations with culture and carried solely political meaning (civic consciousness): *Tolkovyi slovar' zhivogo velikorusskago iazyka* (St. Petersburg: M. O. Vol'f, 1909), 4:1259. Soviet dictionaries included material and artistic culture as one of the definitions of tsivilizatsiia. In the authoritative dictionary of the 1930s, the entry included barbarity as a stage preceding civilization: *Tolkovyi slovar' russkogo iazyka*, ed. B. M. Volin and D. N. Ushakov (Moscow: Gosudarst-

vennoe izd-vo inostrannykh i natsional'nykh slovarei, 1940), 1222. Dictionaries from the late 1950s–1960s listed stages of development from barbarity to civilization as "outdated": *Slovar' russkogo iazyka*, ed. S. I. Ozhegov (Moscow: Gosudarstvennoe izdatel'stvo inostrannykh i natsional'nykh slovarei, 1961), 882; *Slovar' russkogo iazyka*, ed. S. I. Ozhegov (Moscow: Izdatel'stvo sovetskaia entsiklopediia, 1968), 860.

52. Norbert Elias, *The Civilizing Process: Sociogenetic and Psychogenetic Investigations* (Oxford: Blackwell Publishers, 2000), 32–35, 365–447; Lucien Febvre, *"Civilisation:* Evolution of a Word and a Group of Ideas," in *A New Kind of History: From the Writings of Febvre*, ed. Peter Burke (New York: Harper & Row, 1973), 219–257; the Soviet case: Sheila Fitzpatrick, "Becoming Cultured: Socialist Realism and the Representation of Privilege and Taste," in *The Cultural Front: Power and Culture in Revolutionary Russia* (Ithaca, NY: Cornell University Press, 1992), 218–219; *Constructing Russian Culture in the Age of Revolution: 1881–1940*, ed. Catriona Kelly and David Shepherd (Oxford: Oxford University Press, 1998), 295–297.

53. Fevre, *"Civilisation,"* 234–238; Prasenjit Duara, "The Discourse of Civilization and Decolonization," *Journal of World History* 15:1 (March 2004): 1–5.

54. Dina Khapaeva, *Vremia kosmopolitizma: Ocherki intellektual'noi istorii* (Saint Petersburg: Izdatel'stvo zhurnala "Zvezda," 2002), 86–87; *Filosofskii entsiklopedicheskii slovar'* (Moscow: INFRA-M, 1997), 507–508.

55. Ts. G. Arzakan'ian, "Kul'tura i tsivilizatsiia: Problemy teorii i istorii," *VIMK* 3 (1961): 52–73, here 68–69; Baller, "Problema preemstvennosti," passim.

56. Clark, *Moscow, the Fourth Rome*, 169–192; "Internatsional'naia literatura," in *Ocherki istorii russkoi sovetskoi zhurnalistiki, 1933–1945* (Moscow: Nauka, 1968), 403–443, here 423, 427–433.

57. V. P. Tugarinov, *O tsennostiakh zhizni i kul'tury* (Leningrad: Izdatel'stvo Leningradskogo universiteta, 1960); RGASPI f. 606, op. 1, d. 486, ll. 3, 15–20, 60–62, 67–72, 77–79.

58. "Rech' tovarishcha G. M. Malenkova," *Pravda*, March 13, 1954; David Holloway, *Stalin and the Bomb: The Soviet Union and Atomic Energy, 1939–1956* (New Haven, CT: Yale University Press, 1994), 336–340; Vladislav Zubok and Constantine Pleshakov, *Inside the Kremlin's Cold War: From Stalin to Khrushchev* (Cambridge, MA: Harvard University Press, 1996), 166–169.

59. Hopf, *Reconstructing the Cold War*, 244–245; Zubok and Pleshakov, *Inside the Kremlin's Cold War*, 164–166; Vladislav Zubok, *A Failed Empire: The Soviet Union in the Cold War from Stalin to Gorbachev* (Chapel Hill: University of North Carolina Press, 2007), 124.

60. Light, *The Soviet Theory of International Relations*, 221–228; English, *Russia and the Idea of the West*, 50–51, 54; Zubok and Pleshakov, *Inside the Kremlin's Cold War*, 29–33, 184.

61. "Rech' predsedatelia Soveta Ministrov SSSR, deputata G. M. Malenkova," *Izvestiia*, April 27, 1954; "Sud'by mira i tsivilizatsii reshaiut narody," *Kommunist* 4 (March 1955): 12–22.

62. Holloway, *Stalin and the Bomb*, 340.

63. Tunkin, "XXII s"ezd," 18–19; G. I. Tunkin, *Zapisnye knizhki iurista-mezhdunarodnika* (Moscow: Kolo, 2014), 13.

64. Zubok, *A Failed Empire*, 129.

65. Ibid., 104–105; Zubok and Pleshakov, *Inside the Kremlin's Cold War*, 172.

66. English, *Russia and the Idea of the West*, 50–51, 55–56, 58, 61–62.

67. A. Nikonov, "V sovremennuiu epokhu voiny mogut byt' predotvrashcheny," *Kommunist* 6 (1956): 31–45; "Leninskii kurs na mirnoe sosushchestvovanie— general'naia liniia vneshnei politiki Sovetskogo Soiuza," *Kommunist* 11 (1957): 3–11; English, *Russia and the Idea of the West*, 55.

68. G. I. Tunkin, "Mirnoe sosushchestvovanie i mezhdunarodnoe pravo," *Sovetskoe gosudarstvo i pravo* 7 (1956): 3–13; idem, "Sorok let sosushchestvovaniia i mezhdunarodnoe pravo," *SEMP*-1958 (1959): 15–49; E. G. Panfilov, "Marksizm-Leninizm o demokraticheskom i spravedlivom mire," *VF* 4 (1958): 15–27.

69. *Traktaty o vechom mire* (Moscow: Izdatel'stvo sotsial'no-ekonomicheskoi literatury, 1963); I. S. Andreeva, "Vekovaia mechta chelovechestva," in ibid., 13–38.

70. Immanuel Kant, *Perpetual Peace: A Philosophical Essay* (London: Swan Sonnenschein & Co, [1795] 1903), 108–109, 113, 117–119, 128–136, 155; Allen W. Wood, "Kant's Project for Perpetual Peace," in *Cosmopolitics: Thinking and Feeling Beyond the Nation*, ed. Pheng Cheah and Bruce Robbins (Minneapolis: University of Minnesota Press, 1998), 59–76; Soviet reception: A. V. Glebov, "Vokrug traktata Kanta 'O vechnom mire,'" *VF* 2 (1958): 173–175.

71. Kant, *Perpetual Peace*, 156–157; Glebov, "Vokrug traktata," 173–175; B. T. Grigorian, "Filosofiia kul'tury Kanta," *VIMK* 3 (1959): 24–38.

72. Iu. Ia. Baskin, "Ideia 'vechnogo' mira v filosofskoi i politicheskoi literature novogo vremeni," *SEMP*-1964/1965 (1966): 190–201; ibid, *SEMP*-1966/1967 (1968): 166–178.

73. Soviet publications on various projects for "perpetual peace" explicitly referred to the Third Party Program: F. V. Konstantinov, "Predislovie," in *Traktaty o vechnom mire*, 3–12, here 10.

74. "Programma Kommunisticheskoi partii," 362–364, 419.

75. RGASPI f. 606, op. 1, d. 486, ll. 15–19, 43, 60.

76. RGANI f. 5, op. 36, d. 11, l. 98; GARF f. 9576, op. 1, d. 7, l. 46; ibid., op. 2, d. 9, l. 256; Zubok, *A Failed Empire*, 104.

77. David-Fox, *Showcasing the Great Experiment*, 207–283.

78. Aleksandr Pyzhikov, *Khrushchevskaia "ottepel'," 1953–1964* (Moscow: Olma-Press, 2002), 33, 90.

79. Ibid., 35, 136–137; George W. Breslauer, "Khrushchev Reconsidered," *Problems of Communism* (September–October 1976): 18–33, esp. 23–25.

80. Michael David-Fox, "From Illusory 'Society' to Intellectual 'Public': VOKS, International Travel, and Party-Intelligentsia Relations in the Interwar Period," *Contemporary European History* 11 (2002): 7–32, here 25.

81. Raisa Orlova, *Vospominaniia o neproshedshem vremeni. Moskva, 1961–1981 gg.* (Ann Arbor: Ardis, 1983), 103–118; V. N. Kuteishchikova, *Moskva—Mekhiko— Moskva: Doroga dlinoiu v zhizn'* (Moscow: Akademicheskii proekt, 2000), 8–12.

82. Johanna C. Granville, *The First Domino: International Decision Making during the Hungarian Crisis of 1956* (College Station: Texas A&M University Press, 2004), 88.

83. GARF f. 9576, op. 2, d. 75, ll. 2–3, 208.

84. RGANI f. 89, per. 46, dok. 28, ll. 5–6.

85. GARF f. 9576, op. 2, d. 75, ll. 15, 440; Solodovnikov, "Mezhdunarodnye kul'turnye sviazi," 101.

86. GARF f. 9576, op. 2, d. 75, ll. 9–11; ibid., d. 86, ll. 30, 121; ibid., d. 7, ll. 80, 114–115; ibid., d. 9, ll. 20–21.

87. A discussion of this phenomenon: Pyzhikov, *Khrushchevskaia "ottepel'*," 136–137.

88. GARF f. 9576, op. 2, d. 120, ll. 35, 37.

89. Ibid., op. 6, d. 33, l. 4.

90. Ibid., ll. 47–47a.

91. Ibid., l. 12.

92. Ibid., op. 2, d. 7, l. 57; ibid., d. 9, ll. 170–171 [new pagination]; ibid., dd. 36–37, passim; ibid., d. 67, l. 6. Membership in sections by interests was individual, but limited to important figures in various fields: ibid., d. 7, ll. 10–15.

93. Ibid., d. 82, l. 186.

94. Ibid., l. 129; ibid., d. 9, l. 25.

95. RGALI f. 1204, op. 2, d. 2601, ll. 94–940b.

96. GARF f. 9576, op. 1, d. 387, l. 115.

97. Solodovnikov, "Mezhdunarodnye kul'turnye sviazi," 100–101.

98. GARF f. 9576, op. 2, d. 4, passim.

99. Ibid., op. 1, d. 386, l. 66.

100. Kenneth Osgood, *Total Cold War: Eisenhower's Secret Propaganda Battle at Home and Abroad* (Lawrence: University Press of Kansas, 2006), 229–244.

101. GARF f. 9576, op. 1, d. 388, ll. 83, 141–143.

102. GARF f. 9518, op. 1, d. 50, ll. 31, 36, 37; ibid., d. 11, l. 146.

103. Ibid., d. 20, l. 84.

104. See Chapter 6; Anne Gorsuch, *All This Is Your World: Soviet Tourism at Home and Abroad after Stalin* (Oxford: Oxford University Press, 2011), 1–25.

105. GARF f. 9612, op. 1, d. 373, l. 5.

106. See Chapter 2.

107. GARF f. 9576, op. 1, d. 388, ll. 157–159; ibid., d. 90, l. 172.

108. Ibid., d. 388, ll. 34, 208–209.

109. Ibid., op. 2, d. 9, ll. 62–63 [new pagination].

110. Ibid., op. 1, d. 388, ll. 34, 158–159.

111. Nigel Gould-Davies, "The Logic of Soviet Cultural Diplomacy," *Diplomatic History* 27:2 (April 2003): 193–214.

112. RGANI f. 5, op. 36, d. 4, ll. 40–78.

113. Marten and Sedykh, *Moskva-Parizh*, 80–82; *"Ot Atlantiki do Urala": Sovetsko-frantsuzskie otnosheniia, 1956–1973: Dokumenty* (Moscow: Mezhdunarodnyi fond "Demokratiia," 2015), 31.

114. Colette Barbier, "French Policy Aims at Geneva," in *Cold War Respite*, 113–115.

115. M. Narinskii, "Vizit frantsuzskoi pravitel'stvennoi delegatsii v SSSR v 1956 godu," in *SSSR, Frantsiia i ob"edinenie Evropy (1945–1957)*, ed. Narinskii (Moscow: MGIMO-Universitet, 2008), 198–216, here 198, 204.

116. *"Ot Atlantiki do Urala,"* 18–22.

117. RGANI f. 5, op. 28, d. 367, l. 82; *Vystavka frantsuzskogo iskusstva, XV–XX vv. Katalog* (Moscow: Iskusstvo, 1955).

118. K. Sitnik, "Vysokie traditsii (Zametki o vystavke frantsuzskogo iskusstva)," *Iskusstvo* 3 (1956): 39–54.

119. RGANI f. 5, op. 36, d. 7, ll. 120–123; RGALI f. 2329, op. 8, d. 364, ll. 127, 143–146.

120. RGALI f. 2329, op. 8, d. 365, l. 128.

121. *"Ot Atlantiki do Urala,"* 32; *Deklaratsii, zaiavleniia i kommiunike Sovetskogo pravitel'stva s pravitel'stvami inostrannykh gosudarstv, 1954–1957 gg.* (Moscow: Gosudarstvennoe izdatel'stvo politicheskoi literatury, 1957), 262–270; Gomart, *Double détente*, 199–201.

122. RGANI, f. 5, op. 36, d. 11, l. 17.

123. Ibid., ll. 17–21, 86–87; RGALI f. 2329, op. 8, d. 239, ll. 130–132; Marietta Shaginian, "Na vystavke angliiskoi knigi," *Pravda*, March 24, 1956; idem, "Na vystavke angliiskogo iskusstva," *Pravda*, March 25, 1956; Samuil Marshak, "Dorogi druzhby," *Pravda*, April 1, 1956; David Oistrakh, "Desiat' dnei v Anglii," *LG*, April 12, 1956; "Kul'turnyi obmen mezhdu SSSR i Angliei," *LG*, March 29, 1956.

124. GARF f. 9518, op. 1, d. 168, l. 46; RGALI f. 2329, op. 8, d. 235, ll. 123–126; ibid., d. 239, ll. 39–47, 134–135; RGANI f. 5, op. 30, d. 161, ll. 113–116.

125. Simon Miles, "Carving a Diplomatic Niche?: The April 1956 Soviet Visit to Britain," *Diplomacy & Statecraft* 24 (2013): 579–596; Mark Smith, "Peaceful Coexistence at All Costs: Cold War Exchanges between Britain and the Soviet Union in 1956," *Cold War History* 12:3 (2012): 537–558; Kathleen Smith,

Moscow 1956: The Silenced Spring (Cambridge, MA: Harvard University Press, 2017), 231–238; Taubman, *Khrushchev: The Man and His Era*, 355–358.

126. The entanglement of the Hungarian Revolution and the Suez crisis: Sabine Jansen, "La crise de Budapest dans les relations franco-soviétiques," in *Les crises dans les relations franco–soviétiques (1954–1991)*, ed. Mikhaïl Narinskiy and Maurice Vaïsse (Paris: Editions A. Pedone, 2009), 55–71.

127. Classical music and ballet: Tomoff, *Virtuosi Abroad*, 3, 13–14, 72–80, 115–131; Christina Ezrahi, *Swans of the Kremlin: Ballet and Power in Soviet Russia* (Pittsburgh: University of Pittsburgh Press, 2012), 137–168.

128. GARF f. 9518, op. 1, d. 276, ll. 23, 44, 50–51, 58–60; RGANI f. 5, op. 36, d. 43, ll. 116–118; ibid., d. 304, ll. 2, 10.

129. Victor Rosenberg, *Soviet-American Relations, 1953–1960: Diplomacy and Cultural Exchange during the Eisenhower Presidency* (Jefferson, NC: Mc-Farland & Co, 2005), 126–127.

130. RGANI f. 5, op. 36, d. 43, ll. 116–118; ibid., op. 30, d. 235, ll. 103, 128–129; ibid., d. 370, l. 76; GARF f. 9518, op. 1, d. 276, ll. 21–24, 76–77; ibid., d. 166, ll. 124–126.

131. GARF f. 9518, op. 1, d. 276, ll. 46–55.

132. Ibid., d. 346, l. 83.

133. Paraphrase of: Truman Capote, *The Muses Are Heard: An Account* (New York: Random House, 1956), 60.

134. RGANI f. 5, op. 55, d. 22, ll. 107–113; Rosenberg, *Soviet-American Relations*, 129.

135. GARF f. 9518, op. 1, d. 346, ll. 54–59, 66, 68.

136. Ibid., ll. 64, 81; Rosenberg, *Soviet-American Relations*, 129–132.

137. RGANI f. 5, op. 30, d. 274, l. 21; GARF f. 9518, op. 1, d. 166, ll. 1, 19, 230.

138. GARF f. 9518, op. 1, d. 166, ll. 5–6, 10–11, 26, 96, 112–113, 230–231, 238.

139. Ibid., d. 168, ll. 29–36.

140. G. E. Gigolaev, "Luka P'etromarki—ital'ianskii posol v Moskve (1958–1961 gg.)," in *Rossiia i Italiia: Ital'iantsy v Rossii ot Drevnei Rusi do nashkh dnei* issue 6 (Moscow: URSS, 2015), 353–360, here 354, 357–358.

141. RGANI f. 5, op. 30, d. 338, ll. 15, 23–31; Gronchi's visit: Gigolaev, "Luka P'etromarki," 356–357; Dzh. [Giulio] Andreotti, "O vstrechakh s Khrush-chevym," *Kentavr* (July–August 1992): 75–86; "In Dispraise of Macaroni," *Time*, February 22, 1960.

142. See Chapters 4 and 5; Rosenberg, *Soviet-American Relations*, 102–103. Impact on friendship societies: Gomart, *Double détente*, 108.

143. See Chapters 4 and 5.

144. RGANI f. 5, op. 36, d. 43, l. 118 (quotation); ibid., op. 30, d. 235, l. 103; GARF f. 9518, op. 1, d. 276, ll. 33–35; Jansen, "La crise de Budapest," 64.

145. Rosenberg, *Soviet-American Relations*, 109, 113; Psychological war: Walter L. Hixson, *Parting the Curtain: Propaganda, Culture, and the Cold War, 1945–1961* (New York: St. Martin's Press, 1997).

146. N. A. Erofeev, *Tumannyi Al'bion: Angliia i anglichane glazami russkikh, 1825–1853 gg.* (Moscow: Nauka, 1982).

147. Also: Smith, "Peaceful Coexistence"; Rosenberg, *Soviet-American Relations,* 133; Norman Saul, "The Program that Shattered the Iron Curtain: The Lacy-Zarubin (Eisenhower-Khrushchev) Agreement of January 1958," in *New Perspectives on Russian-American Relations,* ed. William Benton Whisenhunt and Norman E. Saul (New York: Routledge, 2016), 234.

148. See Chapter 5; Smith, *Moscow 1956,* 73, 161–165, 299–305; Vladislav Zubok, *Zhivago's Children: The Last Russian Intelligentsia* (Cambridge, MA: Harvard University Press, 2011), 67–69, 80–81.

149. Smith, *Moscow 1956,* 308–309.

150. TsAOPIM f. 4, op. 139, dd. 32, 53, 67, 69; *Ideologicheskie komissii TsK KPSS, 1958–1964: Dokumenty* (Moscow: ROSSPEN, 2000).

151. On the exhibition: Nina Moleva, *Manezh. God 1962: Khronika-razmyshlenie* (Moscow: Sovetskii pisatel', 1989); Susan E. Reid, "In the Name of the People: The Manège Affair Revisited," *Kritika: Explorations in Russian and Eurasian History* 6:4 (2005): 673–716.

152. *Ideologicheskie komissii,* 293–378; Ernst Neizvestnyi, *Govorit Neizvestnyi* (Frankfurt am Main: Possev-Verlag, 1984), 5–21; Mikhail Romm, *Kak v kino: Ustnye rasskazy* (Nizhnii Novgorod: Dekom, 2003), 179–226 (quotation: 187); Zubok, *Zhivago's Children,* 210–219.

153. Denis Kozlov, *The Readers of Novyi mir: Coming to Terms with the Stalinist Past* (Cambridge, MA: Harvard University Press, 2013), 187–189.

154. RGANI f. 5, op. 30, d. 304, ll. 78–84; Gould-Davies, "The Logic of Soviet," 206.

155. RGANI f. 5, op. 30, d. 235, ll. 62–64.

156. Mozhaev, "Kul'turnye sviazi," 86–90.

157. David-Fox, *Showcasing the Great Experiment,* 323.

158. David Brandenberger, *National Bolshevism: Stalinist Mass Culture and the Formation of Modern Russian National Identity, 1931–1956* (Cambridge, MA: Harvard University Press, 2002), 28, 58–59, 109, 123–129, 132, 141–143, 186–196.

159. Rachel Applebaum, "Friendship of the Peoples: Soviet-Czechoslovak Cultural and Social Contacts from the Battle for Prague to the Prague Spring, 1945–1969" (PhD diss., University of Chicago, 2012).

160. Madeleine Herren, "Governmental Internationalism and the Beginning of a New World Order in the Late Nineteenth Century," in *The Mechanics of Internationalism: Culture, Society, and Politics from the 1840s to the First World War,* ed. Martin Geyer and Johannes Paulmann (Oxford: Oxford University Press, 2001), 121–144.

161. "Programma Kommunisticheskoi partii," 363.

2. The Tower of Babel

1. Arika Okrent, *In the Land of Invented Languages* (New York: Spiegel and Grau, 2009), 284; Marina Yaguello, *Lunatic Lovers of Language: Imaginary Languages and Their Inventors* (London: Athlone, 1991), xiv; Sarah L. Higley, *Hildegard of Bingen's Unknown Language* (New York: Palgrave Macmillan, 2007), 63–64. A different interpretation of the festival as a propagandistic enterprise: Kristin Roth-Ey, "'Loose Girls' on the Loose?: Sex, Propaganda and the 1957 Youth Festival," in *Women in the Khrushchev Era*, ed. Melanie Ilič, Susan E. Reid, and Lynne Attwood (New York: Palgrave Macmillan, 2004), 75–95; Pia Koivunen, "The Moscow 1957 Youth Festival: Propagating a New Peaceful Image of the Soviet Union," in *Soviet State and Society under Nikita Khrushchev*, ed. Melanie Ilič and Jeremy Smith (New York: Routledge, 2009), 46–65.

2. Marina Khachaturova, "Na zare tumannoi iunosti," in *Polveka na Mokhovoi (1947–1997)* (Moscow: Izdatel'stvo Moskovskogo universiteta, 1997), 168.

3. Viacheslav Kabanov, *Odnazhdy prisnilos'. Zapiski diletanta* (Moscow: Materik, 2000), 150.

4. A. M. Biriukov, "Sovsem nedavno, letom 57-go," in *Proshchanie so Zmeem: Rasskazy i povesti* (Magadan: Kordis, 2003), 148, 159.

5. Alexei Kozlov, "*Kozel na sakse"—i tak vsiu zhizn'* (Moscow: Vagrius, 1998), 100.

6. RGASPI f. M-3, op. 15, d. 83, l. 95; ibid., d. 19, l. 4; *Vsemirnaia federatsiia demokraticheskoi molodezhi. Daty i sobytiia (1945–75)* (Moscow: Vysshaia komsomol'skaia shkola pri TsK VLKSM, 1975); A. Kurantov, *Prazdnik molodosti: Vsesoiuznyi i VI Vsemirnyi festivali molodezhi (v pomoshch' lektoru)* (Moscow: Gosudarstvennoe izdatel'stvo kul'turno-prosvetitel'noi literatury, 1957), 5–12; Jöel Kotek, *Students and the Cold War* (New York: St. Martin's Press, 1996), 107–124, 189–199; Nils Apeland, *Communist Front Youth Organizations* (Bombay: Popular Book Deposit, 1959), 35–47.

7. Kotek, *Students and the Cold War*, 63–106.

8. RGANI f. 5, op. 28, d. 454, ll. 5–6, 49–53, 95–105; ibid., op. 30, d. 233, ll. 37–38.

9. RGASPI f. M-3, op. 15, d. 1, l. 35.

10. Ibid., d. 83, ll. 1, 102–103; ibid., d. 40, ll. 6–7; TsAOPIM f. 4, op. 113, d. 23, ll. 30–32; RGANI f. 5, op. 28, d. 454, l. 7; Margaret Peacock, "The Perils of Building Cold War Consensus at the 1957 Moscow World Festival of Youth and Students," *Cold War History* 12:3 (2012): 515–535, here 528–529; Gleb Tsipursky, *Socialist Fun: Youth, Consumption, and State-Sponsored Popular Culture in the Cold War Soviet Union, 1945–1970* (Pittsburgh: University of Pittsburgh Press, 2016), 139–140; *Prazdnik mira i druzhby* (Moscow: Molodaia gvardiia, 1958), 39.

11. RGASPI f. M-3, op. 15, d. 197, ll. 130–131; ibid., d. 19, l. 22; ibid., d. 199, l. 186; RGANI f. 5, op. 33, d. 31, l. 18; Malcolm Nixon, "Doreen Casey and the Impact of Ballroom Dancing on Nikita Khrushchev," *Dance Today* 47:14 (November 2002).

12. RGASPI f. M-3, op. 15, d. 2, l. 34.

13. Ibid., d. 22, ll. 5, 9, 35–36; ibid., d. 83, l. 97; ibid., d. 204, l. 52; ibid., d. 197, ll. 63–64; RGANI f. 5, op. 30, d. 233, l. 157; Nixon, "Doreen Casey."

14. RGASPI f. M-3, op. 15, d. 22, l. 46; ibid., d. 35, l. 22.

15. For example: Vas. Zakharchenko, *Festival'* (Moscow: Molodaia gvardiia, 1953), 28–35.

16. RGASPI f. M-3, op. 15, d. 2, ll. 17, 22–25; ibid., d. 84, l. 12; TsALIM f. 147, op. 1, d. 539, l. 18; A. P. Shemarulina, *Vsemirnye festivali molodezhi i studentov za mir i druzhbu* (Moscow: Znanie, 1957), 21.

17. The International Preparatory Committee included dozens of famous people from youth organizations, the academy, and the arts; most were figureheads. The inner circle was limited to the WFDY leaders, heads of the IUS, and Soviet Komsomol leaders. *VI Vsemirnyi festival' molodezhi i studentov: sbornik materialov* (Moscow: Molodaia gvardiia, 1958), 12–16; RGASPI f. M-3, op. 15, d. 21.

18. RGASPI f. M-3, op. 15, d. 21, ll. 9, 11; ibid., d. 22, l. 18.

19. Ibid., d. 8, l. 76; ibid., d. 197, l. 76; Alex Jupp, *A Canadian Looks at the USSR: A Firsthand View of Russian Life during the World Youth Festival* (New York: Exposition Press, 1958), 15; Sally Belfrage, *A Room in Moscow* (New York: A. Deutsch, 1959), 7.

20. RGASPI f. M-3, op. 15, d. 83, ll. 45, 104; ibid., d. 198, ll. 29, 34; ibid., d. 199, ll. 3, 30.

21. Ibid., d. 43, l. 37.

22. Ibid. d. 43, l. 37; ibid., d. 13, l. 101; Belfrage, *A Room,* 5.

23. TsALIM f. 147, op. 1, d. 517, l. 10; RGASPI f. M-3, op. 15, d. 13, l. 53; RGANI f. 5, op. 28, d. 454, l. 86.

24. RGASPI f. M-3, op. 15, d. 204, ll. 91–92.

25. Ibid., d. 193, l. 40.

26. Ibid., d. 83, ll. 6–7; ibid., d. 197, ll. 59–60, 100, 125–127; ibid., d. 199, ll. 1, 8–9, 24, 73; ibid., d. 200, l. 59; Pia Koivunen, "Friends, 'Potential Friends,' and Enemies: Reimagining Soviet Relations to the First, Second, and Third Worlds at the Moscow 1957 Youth Festival," in *Socialist Internationalism in the Cold War: Exploring the Second World,* ed. Patryk Babiracki and Austin Jersild (Basingstoke: Palgrave Macmillan, 2016), 219–247, here 224.

27. James von Geldern, *Bolshevik Festivals, 1917–1920* (Berkeley: University of California Press, 1993); Richard Stites, *Revolutionary Dreams: Utopian Vision and Experimental Life in the Russian Revolution* (Oxford: Oxford University Press, 1989), 97–100.

28. Rosalinde Sartorti, "Stalinism and Carnival: Organisation and Aesthetics of Political Holidays," in *The Culture of the Stalin Period*, ed. Hans Günther (New York: St. Martin's Press, 1990), 41–77; Sheila Fitzpatrick, *Everyday Stalinism. Ordinary Life in Extraordinary Times: Soviet Russia in the 1930s* (Oxford: Oxford University Press, 1999), 93–95: Karl Schlögel, *Moscow 1937* (Cambridge: Polity Press, 2012), 248–254, 404–410.

29. Betti Glan, *Prazdnik vsegda s nami* (Moscow: Soiuz teatral'nykh deiatelei, 1988), 15–41, 46–85, 126–131; *Massovye prazdniki i zrelishcha* (Moscow: Iskusstvo, 1961), 19–21, 72–85, 102.

30. Glan designed her festivals during the peak of Stalinist repressions; her park was the public face and the alternative reality of the terror. Katharina Kucher, *Park Gor'kogo: kul'tura dosuga v stalinskuiu epokhu, 1928–1941* (Moscow: ROSSPEN, 2012), 130–148, 157–178; Schlögel, *Moscow 1937*, 404–410.

31. Mikhail Ladur, *Iskusstvo dlia millionov. Zametki khudozhnika* (Moscow: Sovetskii khudozhnik, 1983), 6, 16, 19–20, 100–104; Glan, *Prazdnik vsegda*, 86–90. Physical culture parades and their aesthetics: Mike O'Mahony, *Sport in the USSR: Physical Culture—Visual Culture* (London: Reaktion, 2006), 21–96; Petr Roubal, "Politics of Gymnastics: Mass Gymnastic Displays under Communism in Central and Eastern Europe," *Body & Society* 9: 2 (2003): 1–25; *Massovye prazdniki*, 90–99.

32. *Massovye prazdniki*, 160; see also Stephen V. Bittner, "Green Cities and Orderly Streets: Space and Culture in Moscow, 1928–1933," *Journal of Urban History* 25:1 (November 1998): 22–56, here 36–40.

33. Glan, *Prazdnik vsegda*, 132–140; Boris Knoblok, *Grani prizvaniia* (Moscow: Vserossiiskoe teatral'noe obshchestvo, 1986), 371–402.

34. RGASPI f. M-3, op. 15, d. 19, ll. 9, 15, 21; ibid., d. 10, l. 117.

35. Ibid., d. 10, l. 62.

36. Ibid., ll. 60, 117–118; ibid., d. 19, l. 16; TsALIM f. 147, op. 1, d. 524, l. 15.

37. Knoblok, *Grani prizvaniia*, 383; N. Balabanova, "Ukrasim doma k festivaliu," *Bloknot agitatora* 17 (944) (June 1957): 15–23; RGASPI f. M-3, op. 15, d. 10, ll. 58–59; ibid., d. 7, l. 66; TsALIM f. 147, op. 1, d. 542, l. 167; TsAADM nos. 0–26923, 0–6487.

38. RGASPI f. M-3, op. 15, d. 10, ll. 62, 148–149, 153; *Prazdnik mira i druzhby*, 59–60.

39. G. Senchakova, "Emblema Vsemirnogo," *Vecherniaia Moskva*, July 6, 1957; Peacock, "The Perils of Building," 520. Earlier festivals were symbolized by the globe and young people's silhouettes. Future youth festivals would adopt some version of the daisy. The Olympic emblem had been adopted as the symbol of the Games in 1920 and gained wide recognition during the 1936 Berlin Games. The Berlin Games were probably the most (in)famous attempt to hijack an international event for a national ceremonial order. In thinking through the relationship between the festival and Soviet holidays, I have kept in mind the

Nazi claims to international legitimacy through hosting the Games and the imposition of Nazi rituals on the Olympic ceremonies. (Guy Walters, *Berlin Games: How the Nazis Stole the Olympic Dream* [New York: Perennial, 2006]; Anton Rippon, *Hitler's Olympics: The Story of the 1936 Nazi Games* [Barnsley: Pen and Sword, 2006]). Despite some similarities between the festival and Soviet holidays, and between the festival and the Berlin Games, I see the festival as substantially different.

40. Glan, *Prazdnik vsegda*, 165–170.

41. RGASPI f. M-3, op. 15, d. 13, l. 96; ibid., d. 84, l. 19; ibid., d. 10, l. 60.

42. RGASPI f. M-3, op. 15, d. 13, ll. 95–96; A. A. Konovich, *Teatralizovannye prazdniki i obriady v SSSR* (Moscow: Vysshaia shkola, 1990), 44–45; *Massovye prazdniki*, 120.

43. TsALIM f. 147, op. 1, d. 524, ll. 28–30; ibid., d. 546, l. 18; Knoblok, *Grani prizvaniia*, 392–393; Vasilii Ardamatskii, *Piat' lepestkov. Reportazh o VI Vsemirnom festivale molodezhi i studentov v Moskve* (Moscow: Gosudarstvennoe izdatel'stvo detskoi literatury, 1958), 85–86.

44. Knoblok, *Grani prizvaniia*, 393.

45. Maksimilian Nemchinskii, *Tsirk Rossii naperegonki so vremenem: Modeli tsirkovykh spektaklei 1920–1990 godov* (Moscow: GITIS, 2004), 260.

46. TsALIM f. 147, op. 1, d. 533, ll. 39–40; *Massovye prazdniki*, 164.

47. RGASPI f. M-3, op. 15, d. 12, l. 132. Note, however, the huge success of the bear mascot at the 1980 Olympic Games in Moscow.

48. Ibid., d. 10, l. 59.

49. Ibid., ll. 120, 154; ibid., d. 12, l. 132.

50. Knoblok, *Grani prizvaniia*, 382–383 (quotation); *Sovetskoe dekorativnoe iskusstvo, 1945–1975. Ocherki* (Moscow: Iskusstvo, 1989), 191; Liliana Rozanova, "My vdvatsaterom shagaem po Moskve," in *Tri dnia otpuska* (Moscow: Molodaia gvardiia, 1973), 394; RGASPI f. M-3, op. 15, d. 10, l. 118; RGAKFD no. 1-19325.

51. Armen Medvedev, *Territoriia kino* (Moscow: Vagrius, 2001), 91.

52. *Sovetskoe dekorativnoe*, 190; Gulliver atop a car: *Massovye prazdniki*, 161.

53. *Sovetskoe dekorativnoe*, 191; *Massovye prazdniki*, 164–165; TsALIM f. 147, op. 1, d. 524, l. 11.

54. TsALIM f. 147, op. 1, d. 524, ll. 44–53; Glan, *Prazdnik vsegda*, 132–141; *Massovye prazdniki*, 142–158, 312–317; RGASPI f. M-3, op. 15, d. 19, l. 19.

55. Glan, *Prazdnik vsegda*, 136.

56. TsALIM f. 147, op. 1, d. 524, l. 44.

57. Konovich, *Teatralizovannye prazdniki*, 44; V. I. Berezkin, *Sovetskaia stsenografiia, 1917–1941* (Moscow: Nauka, 1990), 21–24.

58. Konovich, *Teatralizovannye prazdniki*, 44–45; RGASPI f. M-3, op. 15, d. 13, ll. 95–96; *Massovye prazdniki*, 120–121; RGAKFD no. 1-20123.

59. RGASPI f. M-3, op. 15, d. 40, l. 14.

60. Knoblok, *Grani prizvaniia*, 392–393.

61. *Sovetskoe dekorativnoe*, 189; Konovich, *Teatralizovannye prazdniki*, 44.

62. Most buildings along this road were built in 1937–1940 and 1949–1953; both waves of construction were spurred by the 1935 Plan for the Reconstruction of Moscow; "Za gody rekonstruktsii," *AiSM* 10 (October 1957): 17–24.

63. TsALIM f. 147, op. 1, d. 470, l. 7.

64. Ibid., d. 539, l. 34; ibid., d. 538, ll. 183–186; *Moskva: Arkhitekturnye pamiatniki* (Moscow: Izogiz, 1957); *Moskva. Moscow. Moscou. Moskau* (Moscow: Gosudarstvennoe izdatel'stvo izobrazitel'nogo iskusstva, 1956); *Moskva: fotoetiudy* (Moscow: Moskovskii rabochii, 1957). Representations of Moscow: "Glazami shofera taksi. Rasskaz Dmitriia Beliaeva," *Festival'* 1 (September–October 1956): 7; "Moskva—gorod festivalia. Shofer Dmitrii Beliaev prodolzhaet rasskaz," *Festival'* 2 (November 1956): n.p; "Moskva—gorod festivalia. Tretii rasskaz shofera taksi Dmitriia Beliaeva," *Festival'* 3 (December 1956): n.p.

65. Belfrage, *A Room*, 5–6.

66. RGALI f. 2487, op. 1, d. 196, l. 10.

67. Ibid., l. 22.

68. Ibid., ll. 17, 55.

69. *Moskva: Sputnik turista* (Moscow: Moskovskii rabochii, 1957), 242–243; A. V. Ikonnikov, *Arkhitektura XX veka: Utopii i real'nost'* (Moscow: Progress-Traditsiia, 2001), 1: 429–431; Vladimir Paperny, *Kul'tura "dva"* (Ann Arbor, MI: Ardis, 1985), 143–145.

70. RGASPI f. M-3, op. 15, d. 35, ll. 17–18.

71. TsMAM f. 346, op. 1, d. 1132, ll. 4–11, 30–32; ibid., d. 1131, l. 11.

72. Ibid., d. 1132, ll. 30–31.

73. RGASPI f. M-3, op. 15, d. 10, l. 57.

74. Ibid., d. 13, l. 115; ibid., d. 6, ll. 15–16, 27–30.

75. Ibid., d. 48, ll. 47–58; ibid., d. 35, l. 17; TsMAM f. 346, op. 1, d. 1128, l. 61.

76. RGASPI f. M-3, op. 15, d. 48, ll. 42, 51, 58.

77. Ibid., d. 4, ll. 2–10; TsMAM f. 346, op. 1, d. 1129, ll. 20–21; ibid., d. 1128, l. 60. Soviet participants from across the USSR were housed in dormitories, military barracks, and schools: ibid., l. 61; RGANI f. 5, op. 28, d. 454, ll. 87–88.

78. TsMAM f. 346, op. 1, d. 1128, ll. 12–13, 20–21; RGASPI f. M-3, op. 15, d. 6, l. 41; ibid., d. 7, ll. 85–87.

79. RGASPI f. M-3, op. 15, d. 10, ll. 92–94; ibid., d. 13, ll. 71–72; TsALIM f. 147, op. 1, d. 542, l. 181.

80. Belfrage, *A Room*, 8 (quotation); RGASPI f. M-3, op. 15, d. 83, l. 26; ibid., d. 7, ll. 56–57; TsALIM f. 147, op. 1, d. 542, ll. 183–184.

81. RGASPI f. M-3, op. 15, d. 1, ll. 1–13; RGANI f. 5, op. 28, d. 454, ll. 83, 85; "Otkrytyi plavatel'nyi bassein 'Moskva,'" *AiSM* 8 (August 1957): 9–10; N. Gaigarov, "Plavatel'nyi bassein 'Dinamo,'" *AiSM* 9 (September 1957): 30–32.

82. RGASPI f. M-3, op. 15, d. 2, ll. 20–21.

83. V. M. Chekmarev, *Stalinskaia Moskva: Stanovlenie gradostroitel'noi temy "mirovoi kommunisticheskoi stolitsy"* (Moscow: Sputnik+, 2010), 10–11, 37, 53.

84. M. Bass, "Stroitel'stvo kompleksa sportivnykh sooruzhenii v Luzhnikakh," *AiSM* 1 (January 1956): 19–26; "Tsentral'nyi stadion postroen!" *AiSM* 8 (August 1956): 15–18; S. Elizarov, "Ozelenenie territorii Luzhnikov," *AiSM* 5 (May 1956): n.p. insert between 16 and 17; A. Kashirskii, "Chto pokazala priemka otkrytogo plavatel'nogo basseina i maloi sportivnoi areny," *AiSM* 9 (September 1956): 10–14; "Novaia Luzhnetskaia naberezhnaia. Tsentral'nyi skhod k Moskve-reke," *AiSM* 2 (February 1956): 13–14.

85. RGASPI f. M-3, op. 15, d. 6, ll. 17, 31–38; ibid., d. 7, ll. 3–14; TsALIM f. 147, op. 1, d. 520, ll. 23–24.

86. "Moskva gotovitsia k festivaliu," *AiSM* 9 (September 1956): inside cover; TsALIM f. 147, op. 1, d. 546, ll. 18–19; ibid., d. 538, l. 141; ibid., d. 528, ll. 5–9; RGASPI f. M-3, op. 15, d. 6, ll. 86, 90–91. On the green city movement in the 1920s and 1930s: Bittner, "Green Cities and Orderly Streets."

87. A. Ivanov, "Dlia tekushchego stroitel'stva. Proekty novykh kinoteatrov," *AiSM* 6 (June 1956): 21–24; Iu. Sheverdiaev, "Shirokoekrannyi kinoteatr na Pushkinskoi ploshchadi," *AiSM* 2 (February 1958): 14–16; "Panoramnyi kinoteatr 'Mir,'" *AiSM* 3 (1958): 23–26; V. Shul'gin, "Pervaia krugovaia kinopanorama," *AiSM* 7 (July 1959): 28–29.

88. TsALIM f. 147, op. 1, d. 541, ll. 5–6; ibid., d. 546, ll. 13–16; ibid., d. 538, ll. 68, 89–90; TsALIM f. 138, op. 1, d. 43, ll. 10–12.

89. Iu. Gnedovskii, "Voprosy proektirovaniia krupnykh kinozalov," *AiSM* 5 (May 1956): 27–32.

90. RGANI f. 5, op. 30, d. 233, ll. 87–88.

91. RGASPI f. 3, op. 15, d. 10, l. 15; Vladislav Zubok, *Zhivago's Children: The Last Russian Intelligentsia* (Cambridge, MA: Harvard University Press, 2011), 103. On policy toward such people in general: Sheila Fitzpatrick, "Social Parasites: How Tramps, Idle Youth, and Busy Entrepreneurs Impeded the Soviet March to Communism," *Cahiers du monde russe* 47:1–2 (2006): 377–408.

92. GARF f. 9401, op. 2, d. 491, ll. 150–151.

93. Ibid.; RGASPI f. M-3, op. 15, d. 43, ll. 5, 7, 10. Investigations and arrests continued during the festival: GARF f. 9415, op. 3, d. 315, ll. 7, 19, 44.

94. RGANI f. 5, op. 30, d. 245, ll. 264–265; 58–10: *Nadzornye proizvodstva Prokuratury SSSR po delam ob antisovetskoi agitatsii i propagande. Mart 1953–1991* (Moscow: Mezhdunarodnyi fond Demokratiia, 1999), 280, 285, 318.

95. GARF f. 9415, op. 3, d. 315, l. 18.

96. V. G. Shevchenko, *Materialy k lektsii na temu "Moskovskii festival' za mir i druzhbu"* (Moscow: n.p., 1957), 43–45; RGASPI f. M-3, op. 15, d. 83, l. 107; ibid., d. 265, l. 86.

97. Ibid., d. 3, ll. 207–214; ibid., d. 4, l. 18; ibid., d. 194, entire.

98. Ibid., d. 13, ll. 92–93, 105; ibid., d. 6, l. 40; TsALIM f. 147, op. 1, d. 523, ll. 32–33; ibid., d. 539, l. 57; TsMAM f. 346, op. 1, d. 1137, l. 65.

99. N. Lesovoi, "Rabotniki predpriiatii bytovogo obsluzhivaniia, gotov'tes' k festivaliu!" *Bloknot agitatora* 16 (943) (June 1957): 13–19, here 17–18.

100. TsMAM f. 346, op. 1, d. 1128, ll. 70–71; TsALIM f. 147, op. 1, d. 523, ll. 34–35; M. Davydov, "Molodye moskvichi, gotov'tes' k festivaliu!" in *Bloknot agitatora k festivaliu (otdely propagandy i agitatsii MK i MGK SSSR)* (Moscow: Moskovskaia pravda, 1957), 32.

101. RGASPI f. M-3, op. 15, d. 221, ll. 104–105; ibid., d. 149, ll. 126–127; ibid., d. 12, ll. 160–162; ibid., d. 3, ll. 203–214; RGASPI f. M-1, op. 4, d. 2369, l. 35; Peacock, "The Perils of Building," 520; Koivunen, "Friends," 225–226.

102. RGASPI f. M-3, op. 15, d. 170, ll. 169–170.

103. Ibid., d. 265, l. 84; TsALIM f. 147, op. 1, d. 538, l. 15; I. Buianov, "Radushno vstretim dorogikh gostei," in *Bloknot agitatora k festivaliu*, 104.

104. Buianov, "Radushno vstretim," 104; rubric "Poleznye frazy," *Festival'* 2 (November 1956); *Festival'* 3 (December 1956); *Festival'* 4 (January 1957).

105. TsALIM f. 147, op. 1, d. 546, l. 27.

106. Ibid., d. 528, l. 21; Buianov, "Radushno vstretim," 104.

107. RGASPI f. M-3, op. 15, d. 83, ll. 141–143.

108. *K VI Vsemirnomu festivaliu molodezhi i studentov (Rekomendatel'nye spiski khudozhestvennoi literatury i literatury ob iskusstve zarubezhnykh stran)* (Moscow: Gosudarstvennaia ordena Lenina biblioteka SSSR im. V. I. Lenina, 1957), 4–7.

109. TsALIM f. 147, op. 1, d. 546, l. 11; ibid., d. 538, l. 59.

110. TsAOPIM f. 4, op. 113, d. 23, l. 126; V. Panchenko, "Avtozavodtsy—k prazdniku iunosti," in *Bloknot agitatora k festivaliu*, 101; for more on the "Torch" club: Kurantov, *Prazdnik molodosti*, 35.

111. TsALIM f. 147, op. 1, d. 528, l. 3; ibid., d. 538, ll. 42–44.

112. *Festival'nyi sbornik no. 1. Sbornik sostavlen Orgkomitetom Stalinskogo raiona po podgotovke i provedeniiu festivalia* (Moscow: n. p., January–February, 1957), 5, 50.

113. Ibid., 50; GARF A-501, op. 1, d. 1636, l. 197. Demand for lectors who had written about foreign countries or had traveled abroad: TsALIM f. 147, op. 1, d. 546, l. 21; RGASPI f. M-3, op. 15, d. 19, l. 36.

114. TsALIM f. 147, op. 1, d. 528, l. 22.

115. Kozlov, *"Kozel na sakse,"* 70–71, 97.

116. TsALIM f. 147, op. 1, d. 528, l. 3.

117. Ibid., d. 518, ll. 2–3; TsAOPIM f. 4, op. 113, d. 23, ll. 5–6, 136.

118. TsAOPIM, f. 4, op. 13, d. 42, ll. 134, 147.

119. Anisim Gimmervert, *Maiia Kristalinskaia: Pesni, druz'ia i nedrugi* (Nizhnii Novgorod: Dekom, 2013), 51–56; "Pesni Maii Kristalinskoi peli vsei stranoi,"

http://ckop6b.narod.ru/kristallinskaya.htm#2; "'Opustela bez tebia Zemlia . . .':
Maiia Kristalinskaia—muzykal'nyi simvol pokoleniia," http://www.vilavi.ru/sud
/o81106/o81106.shtml.

120. RGALI f. 2732, op. 1, d. 1125, ll. 113–114.

121. Ibid., ll. 5, 15, 36–38, 86–88, 94–94ob.

122. *Festival'nyi sbornik*, 15–16.

123. TsAOPIM f. 4, op. 113, d. 23, l. 155.

124. Edita P'ekha, *Ot chistogo serdtsa* (Moscow: Izdatel'stvo "E," 2017); G.
Skorokhodov, *Zvezdy sovetskoi estrady* (Moscow: Sovetskii kompozitor, 1982),
84–87; *Russkaia sovetskaia estrada, 1956–1977. Ocherki istorii* (Moscow:
Iskusstvo, 1981), 270–272, 368–370; interview with Nikolai Vladimirovich
Eremchenko, March 13, 2003, unnumbered recording, TsMADSN.

125. Skorokhodov, *Zvezdy sovetskoi*, 84.

126. Gimmervert, *Maiia Kristalinskaia*, 81–86.

127. RGALI f. 2329, op. 3, d. 575, l. 3.

128. Ibid., ll. 3–4, 7–8 (quotation: l. 3).

129. RGANI f. 5, op. 36, d. 46, ll. 54–56; Ardamatskii, *Piat' lepestkov*, 8–9; Tsipursky,
Socialist Fun, 141. The TsDRI went on to represent the Soviet Union at the
festival upon Leonid Utesov's insistence and to receive a silver medal. (RGALI
f. 2329, op. 3, d. 575.)

130. RGASPI f. M-3, op. 15, d. 19, l. 25; TsAOPIM f. 4, op. 113, d. 23, l. 151; RGANI f.
5, op. 36, d. 46, l. 55.

131. RGASPI f. M-3, op. 15, d. 35, l. 23 (quotation); ibid., d. 265, l. 85.

132. TsALIM f. 147, op. 1, d. 548, ll. 101–102.

133. Ibid., ll. 130–132, 141–142.

134. RGASPI f. M-3, op. 15, d. 10, ll. 14, 32. Some soldiers changed into militia
uniforms; policemen, in turn, wore plainclothes. There are different numbers
for how many Komsomols patrolled the streets: by some counts 16,000, by
others 32,000. The numbers of militiamen and Komsomols were inversely
proportional; ultimately, festival planners settled on 30,000+ Komsomols and
11,000+ militiamen. Altogether there were 61,755 people policing the streets—
twice as many as there were foreigners. This number also included the
Ministry of Internal Affairs troops and students from military academies (8,500
and 4,000, respectively), and 6,000 janitors. Nonetheless, the police were
swamped, because, besides foreigners, there were also Muscovites, Soviet
delegates from across the country, and people who streamed into the capital.
GARF f. 9401, op. 2, d. 491, ll. 424, 428–429; RGASPI f. M-3, op. 15, d. 43, ll. 4,
17; ibid., d. 13, ll. 103, 151–152.

135. Biriukov, "Sovsem nedavno," 145–146.

136. Eremchenko interview; GARF f. 9415, op. 3, d. 315, l. 27; Ardamatskii, *Piat'
lepestkov*, 26.

137. Theater metaphors: Knoblok, *Grani prizvaniia*, 387; Rozanova, "My vdvat-saterom," 393.
138. *Prazdnik mira i druzhby*, 60–61; *Massovye prazdniki*, 117.
139. Knoblok, *Grani prizvaniia*, 389.
140. Biriukov, "Sovsem nedavno," 149; Ardamatskii, *Piat' lepestkov*, 35–36. Importance of touching foreigners: Roth-Ey, "'Loose,'" 79.
141. Ardamatskii, *Piat' lepestkov*, 36 (opening procession), 116–117, 124–125 (precious gifts: rings, pearl earrings).
142. RGASPI f. M-3, op. 15, d. 198, l. 38; GARF f. 9415, op. 3, d. 315, l. 26; Zubok, *Zhivago's Children*, 103–104.
143. Knoblok, *Grani prizvaniia*, 387.
144. Vasilii Katanian, *Loskutnoe odeialo* (Moscow: Vagrius, 2001), 143–144.
145. Biriukov, "Sovsem nedavno," 149.
146. RGALI f. 2487, op. 1, d. 446, ll. 237–238.
147. RGASPI f. M-3, op. 15, d. 134, ll. 4, 15; Aleksandr Khar'kovskii, "Opasnyi iazyk (zametki uchastnika)," http://miresperanto.com/historio/opasnyj_jazyk.htm.
148. GARF f. 9415, op. 3, d. 315, ll. 99, 110; RGASPI f. M-3, op. 15, d. 189, ll. 71, 96; ibid., d. 198, l. 62; ibid., d. 200, l. 223.
149. Rozanova, "My vdvatsaterom," 396, 401; *Prazdnik mira*, 204.
150. Nemchinskii, *Tsirk Rossii*, 260–261.
151. RGASPI f. M-3, op. 15, d. 124, l. 28; RGALI f. 2487, op. 1, d. 446, l. 13; RGAKFD no. 1-10702.
152. Dance and abandon: Barbara Ehrenreich, *Dancing in the Streets: A History of Collective Joy* (New York: Metropolitan Books / Henry Holt and Company, 2007).
153. RGAKFD no. 1-10633.
154. Rozanova, "My vdvatsaterom," 394–395; a different interpretation of such encounters: Roth-Ey, "'Loose,'" 85.
155. Ehrenreich, *Dancing in the Streets*, 23–27, passim.
156. RGAKFD no. 1-10702; RGALI f. 2487, op. 1, d. 446, l. 16.
157. RGAKFD no. 1-10633; RGALI f. 2487, op. 1, d. 341, ll. 13–14.
158. TsMAM f. 346, op. 1, d. 1129, ll. 27, 42–43; ibid., d. 1091, l. 126.
159. Rozanova, "My vdvatsaterom," 396; *Prazdnik mira*, 54.
160. "Mike Wallace Interviews," April 9, 1959, Tamiment, SBP 189, box 37, folder 3, 3–4.
161. "Notebooks. Moscow and China," Tamiment, SBP 189, box 4, folder 3.
162. "Office Memorandum 67c. Sally Belfrage on NBC 'Today' Show," March 20, 1959, Tamiment, SBP 189, box 37, folder 3 (quotation); "Letter of reader to J. Edgar Hoover, FBI," May 18, 1961, Ibid., box 37, folder 2; "Letter from Foreign Literature Publishing House," December 12, 1958, Ibid., box 25, folder 2 (quotation); RGANI f. 5, op. 33, d. 121, ll. 2–18.
163. "Notebooks. Moscow and China," Tamiment, SBP 189, box 4, folder 3.

164. Belfrage, *A Room*, 87.

165. "Notebooks. Moscow and China," Tamiment, SBP 189, box 4, folder 3.

166. Ibid.; Belfrage, *A Room*, 126–128.

167. Original grammar has been preserved. Andrei to Sally, September 29, 1960, Tamiment, SBP 189, box 24, folder 24.

168. RGASPI f. M-3, op. 15, d. 204, l. 38; GARF f. 9415, op. 3, d. 315, ll. 68–69.

169. Roth-Ey, "'Loose,'" 79–80, 87, 89–91.

170. Interview with Irina Iakovlevna [last name withheld], Moscow, May 25, 2003.

171. RGASPI f. M-3, op. 15, d. 200, l. 153.

172. Ibid., d. 193, ll. 2 (quotation), 5.

173. GARF f. 9415, op. 3, d. 315, ll. 112–113; GARF f. 9401, op. 2, d. 491, l. 433; Kozlov, "*Kozel na sakse*," 106–108; Zubok, *Zhivago's Children*, 109; Roth-Ey, "'Loose,'" 83–84.

174. RGASPI f. M-3, op. 15, d. 197, l. 94.

175. Eremchenko interview.

176. RGASPI f. M-3, op. 15, d. 197, ll. 65, 104; ibid., d. 221, ll. 45, 54; ibid., d. 200, l. 123; Zubok, *Zhivago's Children*, 105.

177. RGALI f. 2329, op. 3, d. 601, l. 22.

178. RGALI f. 2487, op. 1, d. 341, l. 14; ibid., d. 446, ll. 14–15; *Prazdnik mira*, 208.

179. RGALI f. 2329, op. 3, d. 591, ll. 50–51; ibid., d. 586, ll. 14–15, 20.

180. Ibid., d. 586, ll. 15–16, 23.

181. Ibid., ll. 19–20, 25.

182. RGASPI f. M-3, op. 15, d. 221, l. 83. The Soviets performed well in ballet contests, piano and violin, in all classical cultural forms, as well as folklore dancing and singing.

183. RGALI f. 2329, op. 3, d. 591, ll. 5, 24.

184. Ibid., d. 590, ll. 30–31.

185. N. Sheremet'evskaia, *Tanets na estrade* (Moscow: Iskusstvo, 1985), 287–302.

186. Eremchenko interview.

187. RGASPI f. M-3, op. 15, d. 192, ll. 26–29; ibid., d. 197, ll. 64–65; Tsipursky, *Socialist Fun*, 142.

188. RGASPI f. M-3, op. 15, d. 192, ll. 7–9, 13–14, 19, 33–34, 46, 48; ibid., d. 200, l. 216.

189. Eremchenko interview. At the time of the festival, Michel Legrand was twenty-five years old.

190. RGALI f. 2329, op. 3, d. 601, ll. 43 (quotation), 49–50 (quotation), 67.

191. Ibid., d. 590, l. 44.

192. Ibid., d. 591, ll. 21 (quotation), 35–36, 52.

193. Ibid., l. 52 (quotation); ibid., d. 601, ll. 43, 67, 74.

194. Festival moral panics and sexuality: Roth-Ey, "'Loose,'" 87, passim.

195. RGALI f. 2329, op. 3, d. 590, ll. 50–57.

196. Ibid., d. 591, ll. 23, 35.

197. RGASPI f. M-3, op. 15, d. 83, l. 38; RGANI f. 5, op. 30, d. 233, l. 190.

198. *Russkaia sovetskaia*, 345–349, 354–356; Kozlov, *"Kozel na sakse,"* 112–113; Zubok, *Zhivago's Children*, 112. Different interpretation: Tsipursky, *Socialist Fun*, 145–147, but also 167, 170–171.

199. GARF f. 8131, op. 36, d. 6174, ll. 34–36.

200. Ibid., l. 31.

201. Ibid., ll. 34–35; Il'ia Shatunovskii, "Prodavshie dushu," *KP*, August 30, 1960 (quotations).

202. Sally Belfrage to Dick, September 16, 1960, Tamiment, SBP 189, box 24, folder 24; Dick to Sally, February 11, 1961, ibid; Andrei to Sally, September 29, 1960, ibid.

203. Shatunovskii, "Prodavshie."

204. Mega-events and city infrastructure: Maurice Roche, *Mega-Events and Modernity: Olympics, Expos, and the Growth of Global Culture* (London: Routledge, 2000), 10, 25–26.

205. Interview with A. D. Shereshevskaia, St. Petersburg, July 24, 2004.

206. Interview with Marina Nikolaevna [last name withheld], Moscow, June 15, 2003.

207. Kozlov, *"Kozel na sakse,"* 354–355. There are structural parallels between the two events, including the international context, Hungary and Afghanistan.

208. Shereshevskaia interview.

209. RGASPI f. M-3, op. 15, d. 162, ll. 27–33.

210. Ibid., l. 18.

211. Ibid., d. 10, ll. 17–19, 35–39; RGALI f. 2329, op. 3, d. 592, ll. 100–101.

212. RGASPI f. M-3, op. 15, d. 146, ll. 6, 16–18, 31; ibid., d. 171, l. 14; ibid., d. 13, l. 19.

213. Ibid., d. 146, ll. 3, 26–27; V. Popov, "Vstrecha molodykh kinematografistov mira," *IK* 3 (March 1957): 119.

214. RGANI f. 5, op. 30, d. 233, l. 149; R. Iurenev, "Mezhdunarodnye kinofestivali," *SE* 15 (August 1959): 1, 4.

215. RGASPI f. M-3, op. 15, d. 147, l. 33.

216. GARF f. 6903, op. 15, d. 267, ll. 2–12; Zubok, *Zhivago's Children*, 105–106; Susan Reid, "Toward a New (Socialist) Realism: The Re-engagement with Western Modernism in the Khrushchev Thaw," in *Russian Art and the West: A Century of Dialogue in Painting, Architecture, and the Decorative Arts*, ed. Rosalind Blakesley and Susan E. Reid (DeKalb: Northern Illinois University Press, 2007), 227.

3. Books about Us

1. On aesthetic contemporaneity and compression: Emily Apter, *Against World Literature: On the Politics of Untranslatability* (London: Verso, 2013), 68.

2. The press involved included *Neva*, *NM*, *Zvezda*, *KP*, *LG*, *LiZh*, and *Izvestiia*.

3. Leontii Rakovskii, "Chuvstvo iazyka," *Zvezda* 2 (1962): 162–167, here 162–163; T. G. Vinokur, "Kogda 'kantseliarizmy' i 'shtampy' stanoviatsia opasnoi bolezn'iu?" in *Nasha rech': Kak my govorim i pishem*, ed. S. I. Ozhegov and V. P. Grigor'ev (Moscow: Znanie, 1965), 52–66; Kornei Chukovskii, *Za zhivoe, obraznoe slovo* (Moscow: Znanie, 1967), 31.

4. Alexei Yurchak, *Everything Was Forever, Until It Was No More: The Last Soviet Generation* (Princeton, NJ: Princeton University Press, 2006), 13–26.

5. Michael S. Gorham, *Speaking in Soviet Tongues: Language Culture and the Politics of Voice in Revolutionary Russia* (DeKalb: Northern Illinois University Press, 2003), 7–15, 39–42, 59–70.

6. Katerina Clark, *Petersburg: Crucible of Cultural Revolution* (Cambridge, MA: Harvard University Press, 1995), 224–241.

7. Also: Thomas Wolfe, *Governing Soviet Journalism: The Press and the Socialist Person after Stalin* (Bloomington: Indiana University Press, 2005), 38–70; Vladislav Zubok, *Zhivago's Children: The Last Russian Intelligentsia* (Cambridge, MA: Harvard University Press, 2011), 141–152.

8. 1920s: Clark, *Petersburg*, 105–106.

9. Kornei Chukovskii, *Zhivoi kak zhizn': razgovor o russkom iazyke* (Moscow: Molodaia gvardiia, 1962), 123; idem, *Dnevnik, 1901–1969* (Moscow: OLMA-Press, 2003), 2: 354, 358–360.

10. Chukovskii, *Za zhivoe, obraznoe*, 29, 36, 39.

11. Vit. Bianki, "Mysli vslukh," *Zvezda* 7 (July 1955): 136–138; Pavel Nilin, "Opasnost' ne tam . . . ," *NM* 4 (1958): 276–277; S. Radin, "Iazyk i slovar'. Pis'mo v redaktsiiu," *Zvezda* 1 (January 1959): 217–219.

12. Bianki, "Mysli vslukh," 138; Nilin, "Opasnost' ne tam," 277; Radin, "Iazyk i slovar'," 218; Igor' Kobzev, "Protiv oskuchneniia literaturnogo iazyka," *Neva* 3 (1959): 221–259; Lev Uspenskii, "Grazhdane, uchaite . . . ," *LG*, October 31, 1959; "Slovo chitatelei," *Izvestiia*, January 11, 1961.

13. Rakovskii, "Chuvstvo iazyka," 164; Leonid Borisov, "Vot tak govoriat i pishut," *Zvezda* 2 (1962): 169–170; S. Furtichev, "S russkogo na kazennyi," *Izvestiia*, January 11, 1961.

14. Denis Kozlov, *The Readers of Novyi mir: Coming to Terms with the Stalinist Past* (Cambridge, MA: Harvard University Press, 2013), 46–47. Insincerity and distrust as key aspects of sincerity: Kerry Sinanan and Tim Milnes, "Introduction," in *Romanticism, Sincerity and Authenticity*, ed. Tim Milnes and Kerry Sinanan (Basingstoke: Palgrave MacMillan, 2010), 1–28, here 12; Angela Esterhammer, "The Scandal of Sincerity: Wordsworth, Byron, Landon," in ibid., 101–119, here 113; Jane Wright, "Sincerity's Repetition: Carlyle, Tennyson and Other Repetitive Victorians," in ibid., 162–181, here 169; Ellen Rutten, *Sincerity After Communism: A Cultural History* (New Haven, CT: Yale University Press, 2017), 36–37.

15. Kozlov, *The Readers of* Novyi mir, 46–49 (quotation: 47), 60–65; Rutten, *Sincerity After Communism*, 41–42, 75–77 (for a different understanding of Pomerantsev's impact).

16. Rachel Platonov, *Singing the Self: Guitar Poetry, Community, and Identity in the Post-Stalin Period* (Evanston: Northwestern University Press, 2012), 20, 26–28, 52–53, 61–89; Oksana Bulgakowa, "Vocal Changes: Marlon Brando, Innokenty Smoktunovsky, and the Sound of the 1950s," in *Sound, Speech, Music in Soviet and Post-Soviet Cinema*, ed. Lilya Kaganovsky and Masha Salazkina (Bloomington: Indiana University Press, 2014), 145–161; Stephen Lovell, *Russia in the Microphone Age: A History of Soviet Radio, 1919–1970* (Oxford: Oxford University Press, 2015), 193–197; Simon Huxtable, "The Problem of Personality on Soviet Television, 1950s–1960s," *VIEW: Journal of European Television History & Culture* 3:5 (2012): 119–130. Imperfections and sincerity: Rutten, *Sincerity After Communism*, 60–62, 70.

17. Milnes and Sinanan, "Introduction," 24; Esterhammer, "The Scandal of Sincerity," 102–105, 113; Tim Milnes, "Making Sense of Sincerity in *The Prelude*," in *Romanticism, Sincerity and Authenticity*, 120–136, here 130; Jane Taylor, "'Why do you tear me from Myself?': Torture, Truth, and the Arts of the Counter-Reformation," in *The Rhetoric of Sincerity*, ed. Ernst van Alphen, Mieke Bal, and Carel Smith (Stanford, CA: Stanford University Press, 2009), 19–43, here 27.

18. Sincerity as a Romantic concept: Milnes and Sinanan, "Introduction," 1–6; Rutten, *Sincerity After Communism*, 48–49.

19. Herbert Read, *The Cult of Sincerity* (London: Faber and Faber, 1968), 15; Milnes and Sinanan, "Introduction," 11; Taylor, "'Why do you tear me from Myself?'" 19.

20. New languages and concepts in translation: Itamar Even-Zohar, "The Position of Translated Literature Within the Literary Polysystem," in *The Translation Studies Reader*, 3rd ed., ed. Lawrence Venuti (New York: Routledge, 2012), 162–167.

21. "Ob izdanii sovremennoi zarubezhnoi literatury," *LG*, March 18, 1954.

22. RGANI f. 5, op. 17, d. 490, ll. 254–259.

23. RGALI f. 1204, op. 2, d. 2606, ll. 29–290b.

24. RGALI f. 613, op. 8, d. 1512, ll. 7, 9; ibid., d. 1523, l. 6; ibid., d. 73, ll. 43–440b; RGALI f. 1573, op. 1, d. 63, l. 16.

25. RGALI f. 613, op. 8, d. 73, ll. 39, 50; RGALI f. 2646, op. 1, d. 702, ll. 10–11.

26. RGALI f. 1573, op. 1, d. 143, ll. 750b–75 [*sic*].

27. RGALI f. 2464, op. 1, d. 702, ll. 12–14.

28. Although translated prose appeared in various periodicals, only one other journal shared the same mandate, the Ukrainian *Universe* (*Vsesvit*), with a somewhat limited readership.

29. Kozlov, *The Readers of* Novyi mir, 29–36.

30. RGALI f. 1573, op. 1, d. 65, l. 96.

31. Ibid., d. 63, ll. 96–960b.

32. Ibid., l. 53.

33. Katerina Clark, *Moscow, the Fourth Rome: Stalinism, Cosmopolitanism, and the Evolution of Soviet Culture, 1931–1941* (Cambridge, MA: Harvard University Press, 2011), 160–162; "Internatsional'naia literatura," in *Ocherki istorii russkoi sovetskoi zhurnalistiki, 1933–1945* (Moscow: Nauka, 1968), 403–443, here 423, 427–433; Nailya Safiullina and Rachel Platonov, "Literary Translation and Soviet Cultural Politics in the 1930s: The Role of the Journal *Internacional'naja literatura*," *Russian Literature* 72: 2 (2012): 239–269, here 250–251. For an interpretation of the journal's domestic functions within the expanding reading culture of the 1930s, see: Nailya Safiullina, "Window to the West: From the Collection of Readers' Letters to the Journal *Internatsional'naia literatura*," *Slavonica* 15: 2 (November 2009): 128–161.

34. RGALI f. 1573, op. 5, d. 304, l. 10.

35. Ibid., op. 1, d. 3, l. 25.

36. Ibid., op. 5, d. 184, l. 37; ibid., d. 238, l. 42; ibid., op. 1, d. 113, l. 44.

37. Ibid., op. 1, d. 26, l. 57.

38. Ibid., d. 116, ll. 35, 40, 44–45; R. Orlova, "Chto znachit zhit' v shestidesiatye gody?" *NM* 5 (May 1963): 230–234; idem., "Korenitsia v samoi chelovechnosti . . . (o putiakh razvitiia amerikanskogo romana)," *VL* 8 (August 1961): 97–114; A. Elistratova, "'Tragicheskoe zhivotnoe—chelovek'. O dvukh romanakh Dzhona Apdaika," *IL* 12 (December 1963): 220–226; "Obsuzhdenie romana Grekhema Grina *Tikhii amerikanets*," *IL* 7 (July 1956): 198–206; M. Tugusheva, "Amerikanskaia tragediia 1960 goda," *VL* 6 (June 1960): 195–200; Samantha Sherry, *Discourses of Regulation and Resistance: Censoring Translation in the Stalin and Khrushchev Era Soviet Union* (Edinburgh: Edinburgh University Press, 2015), 108–109; Maurice Friedberg, *A Decade of Euphoria: Western Literature in Post-Stalin Russia, 1954–64* (Bloomington: Indiana University Press, 1977), 155–201.

39. RGALI f. 2854, op. 1, d. 359, ll. 58–68.

40. A similar argument for the 1930s: Safiullina and Platonov, "Literary Translation and Soviet Cultural Politics," 245–246, 254–255.

41. RGALI f. 613, op. 8, d. 1629, ll. 1–2, 4, 7.

42. *Ideologicheskie komissii TsK KPSS, 1958–1964. Dokumenty* (Moscow: ROSSPEN, 2000), 33–41, here 36.

43. Alberto Moravia, "Eroticism in Literature," in *Man as an End: A Defense of Humanism. Literary, Social, and Political Essays* (London: Secker & Warburg, 1965), 228–230.

44. Sexophobia in Soviet culture: I. S. Kon, *Seksual'naia kul'tura v Rossii: Klubnichka na berezke* (Moscow: OGI, 1997), 139–165; Herman Ermolaev,

Censorship in Soviet Literature, 1917–1991 (Lanham, MD: Rowman & Little-field Publishers, 1997), 42–46, 89–93, 131–134, 173–175; Sherry, *Discourses of Regulation and Resistance*, 124–131.

45. RGALI f. 1573, op. 5, d. 304, ll. 17–22; ibid., d. 307, ll. 6, 9, 12, 17–18. Also: Sherry, *Discourses of Regulation and Resistance*, 93–94, 106–107, 124–131, esp. 128; Brian Baer, "Translating Queer Texts in Soviet Russia: A Case Study in Productive Censorship," *Translation Studies* 4:1 (2011): 21–40.

46. Also: Ermolaev, *Censorship in Soviet Literature*, 46–47, 93–94, 175–176.

47. N. Balashov, "Na novom puti," *IL* 9 (September 1956): 198–201, here 199.

48. RGALI f. 1573, op. 1, d. 26, l. 68.

49. RGALI f. 1573, op. 1, d. 27, l. 34; ibid., d. 116, l. 33.

50. Henry Glade and Konstantin Bogatyrev, "The Soviet Version of Heinrich Böll's 'Gruppenbild mit Dame': The Translator as Censor," *University of Dayton Review* 12: 2 (Spring 1976): 51–56; Sherry, *Discourses of Regulation and Resistance*, 117–123.

51. RGALI f. 1573, op. 1, d. 158, ll. 3–8; Sherry, *Discourses of Regulation and Resistance*, 107–109, 111, 115.

52. RGALI f. 1573, op. 1, d. 5, l. 124; ibid., d. 15, ll. 10, 12, 24, 27, 31, 33, 47; ibid., d. 35, l. 32; ibid., d. 45, ll. 12, 44; ibid., d. 91, l. 118; ibid., d. 116, ll. 3–7, 46, 50; ibid., op. 3, d. 35, ll. 71–72, 81; ibid., d. 74, l. 107; ibid., op. 5, d. 242, l. 66; ibid., d. 304, ll. 11–12, 14, 15, 17–22; ibid., d. 308, l. 4; Sherry, *Discourses of Regulation and Resistance*, 113–114.

53. RGALI f. 1573, op. 5, d. 308, l. 4; Friedberg, *A Decade of Euphoria*, 23n15.

54. RGALI f. 1573, op. 1, d. 15, l. 10; ibid., op. 3, d. 63, l. 30; ibid., d. 88, ll. 8–80b, 20.

55. Ibid., op. 3, d. 160, ll. 14, 33–34, 63; Friedberg, *A Decade of Euphoria*, 21–22n10 (a different version of events), 46.

56. RGALI f. 1573, op. 1, d. 91, l. 118; ibid., op. 5, d. 304, l. 22.

57. Ibid., op. 3, d. 35, ll. 71–72, 81, 94; ibid., op. 1, d. 116, l. 50.

58. *Tsenzura v tsarskoi Rossii i Sovetskom Soiuze. Materialy konferentsii 24–27 maia 1993 g.* (Moscow: "Rudomino," 1995), 16, 30, 35–38; Sherry, *Discourses of Regulation and Resistance*, 124, passim.

59. Friedberg, *A Decade of Euphoria*, 16–57.

60. O. S. Ioffe and Iu. K. Tolstoi, *Osnovy sovetskogo grazhdanskogo zakonodatel'stva* (Leningrad: Izdatel'stvo Leningradskogo universiteta, 1962), 173–189.

61. RGALI f. 1573, op. 1, d. 35, l. 85; ibid., d. 49, ll. 56–57; ibid., d. 77, ll. 26–27, 34; ibid., d. 173, l. 87; ibid., op. 3, d. 90, ll. 67–68, 70; ibid., d. 91, ll. 8–9; RGALI f. 631, op. 26, d. 74, ll. 21–22; ibid., d. 87, ll. 10–17; RGANI f. 5, op. 36, d. 18, ll. 47–53, 96–99; ibid., d. 92, ll. 19–22; ibid., d. 134, ll. 170–172.

62. RGANI f. 5, op. 36, d. 18, ll. 97–98; ibid., op. 58, d. 27, ll. 81–98, 107. Honoring intellectual property rights did not necessarily require upholding worldwide

regulations; there was a less rigid alternative—the Soviet Union could have entered into bilateral copyright agreements and paid royalties in rubles. But the Central Committee would not sanction even such limited contracts.

63. RGANI f. 5, op. 58, d. 27, ll. 96–97.

64. On patronage: Sheila Fitzpatrick, "Patrons and Clients," in *Tear Off the Masks! Identity and Imposture in Twentieth-Century Russia* (Princeton, NJ: Princeton University Press, 2005), 182–202; Michael David-Fox, *Showcasing the Great Experiment: Cultural Diplomacy and Western Visitors to the Soviet Union, 1921–1941* (Oxford: Oxford University Press, 2012), 2–3, 90–97.

65. RGALI f. 1573, op. 1, d. 48, ll. 17–18; RGANI f. 5, op. 36, d. 2, ll. 15, 20.

66. RGANI f. 5, op. 17, d. 490, ll. 262–263.

67. Foreign writers knew they could ask for these benefits: RGANI f. 5, op. 17, d. 486, l. 231.

68. RGALI f. 1573, op. 5, d. 238, l. 23 (quotation); ibid., op. 1, d. 11, ll. 90–92, 96; ibid., d. 161, ll. 6, 118; ibid., d. 165, l. 64; ibid., op. 3, d. 58, l. 17; RGANI f. 5, op. 17, d. 490, l. 261; ibid., op. 36, d. 142, l. 7.

69. Traumatized by the Secret Speech, communist writer Roger Vailland experienced a professional and personal crisis. The Central Committee earmarked for him considerable sums in rubles and, unusually, in francs. *Dialog pisatelei: Iz istorii russko-frantsuzskikh kul'turnykh sviazei XX veka, 1920–1970* (Moscow: IMLI RAN, 2002), 413, 423, 671; Roger Vailland, *Écrits intimes* (Paris: Gallimard, 1968), 484–509; RGANI f. 5, op. 36, d. 18, ll. 43–44.

70. V. Stanevich, "Nekotorye voprosy perevoda prozy," *Masterstvo perevoda: Sbornik statei* (hereafter *Masterstvo-59*) (Moscow: Sovetskii pisatel', 1959), 46–70, here 49; M. Lorie, "O redakture khudozhestvennogo proizvedeniia," *Masterstvo-59*, 87–105, here 99.

71. Also: Andrei Azov, *Poverzhennye bukvalisty: Iz istorii khudozhestvennogo perevoda v SSSR v 1920–1960-e gody* (Moscow: Vysshaia shkola ekonomiki, 2013), 40–52, 94–106, 117–134; Sherry, *Discourses of Regulation and Resistance*, 27–30.

72. J. V. Stalin, "Marxism and the Problem of Linguistics," https://www.marxists.org/reference/archive/stalin/works/1950/jun/20.htm.

73. Stanevich, "Nekotorye voprosy," 49; N. Liubimov, "Perevod—iskusstvo," *Masterstvo perevoda. Sbornik, 1963* (hereafter *Masterstvo-63*) (Moscow: Sovetskii pisatel', 1964), 233–256, here 233, 249; Vl. Rossel's, "Radi shumiashchikh zelenykh vetvei," *Masterstvo perevoda. Sbornik, 1964* (hereafter *Masterstvo-64*) (Moscow: Sovetskii pisatel', 1965), 12–33, here 31; Iaan Kross, "Bez liubvi khoroshii perevod nemyslim," *Masterstvo perevoda, 1969* (hereafter *Masterstvo-69*) (Moscow: Sovetskii pisatel', 1970), 89–96.

74. RGALI f. 2854, op. 1, d. 130, ll. 10–11; P. Antokol'skii, "Chernyi khleb masterstva," *Masterstvo-63*, 5–12, here 7–8; R. Rait-Kovaleva, "Nit' Ariadny," in

Redaktor i perevod: Sbornik statei (Moscow: Izdatel'stvo "Kniga," 1965), 5–22, here 9; V. Levik, "O tochnosti i vernosti (Popytka perevodchika podelit'sia lichnym opytom)," *IL* 1 (January 1959): 186–192, here 187; the idea itself belongs to V. A. Zhukovskii, cited in Yu. Levin, "Ob istorizme v podkhode k istorii perevoda," *Masterstvo perevoda. Sbornik*, 1962 (hereafter *Masterstvo-62*) (Moscow: Sovetskii pisatel', 1963), 373–392, here 375.

75. RGALI f. 2854, op. 1, d. 125, l. 37; Antokol'skii, "Chernyi khleb," 6–7; "Tri napravleniia russkogo poeticheskogo perevoda," *Masterstvo-63*, 353–358, here 357; R. Mustafin, "Poeticheskaia intonatsiia perevodchika," *Masterstvo-64*, 34–50, here 35; S. Marshak, "Poeziia perevoda," *LG*, May 31, 1962; E. Etkind, "Iskusstvo perevodchika," *IL* 3 (March 1956): 199–205, here 200; Levik, "O tochnosti," 187, 190; idem, "Perevod kak iskusstvo," http://vvloo.narod.ru/vl-002 .htm.

76. Rait-Kovaleva, "Nit' Ariadny," 8.

77. RGALI f. 2854, op. 1, d. 130, ll. 1, 4, 6, 9.

78. "Na novom etape," *Masterstvo-62*, 507–511, here 507; Levik, "O tochnosti," 190.

79. P. Toper, "Predislovie," in Ivan Kashkin, *Dlia chitatelia-sovremennika: Stat'i i issledovaniia* (Moscow: Sovetskii pisatel', 1968), 5–14, here 8; Oleksii Kundzich, "Perevod i literaturnyi iazyk," *Masterstvo-59*, 7–45, here 7.

80. Rait-Kovaleva, "Nit' Ariadny," 5; S. Petrov, "O pol'ze prostorechiia," *Masterstvo-62*, 71–96, here 96; P. Toper, "Traditsii realizma (Russkie pisateli o khudozhestvennom perevode)," *DN* 5 (1953): 225–249, here 234.

81. A. Leites, "Vvedenie v obshchuiu teoriiu khudozhestvennogo perevoda. Programma kursa," *Masterstvo-64*, 252–270, here 260.

82. "Perevod—original—deistvitel'nost'," *Masterstvo-62*, 497–503, here 498; Vera Toper's translation of Dickens's *Hard Times* as "a work of Russian literature": M. Lorie, "Ob odnom khoroshem perevode ('Tiazhelye vremena' Dikkensa v perevode V. M. Toper)," *Masterstvo-64*, 98–117, here 100–107; RGALI f. 2854, op. 1, d. 130, l. 16.

83. Samuil Marshak, "Iskusstvo poeticheskogo portreta," *Masterstvo-59*, 245–250, here 249.

84. Kornei Chukovskii, "Marshak," *NM* 11 (1962): 224–228, here 227.

85. Aleksandr Tvardovskii, "Robert Berns v perevodakh S. Marshaka," in *Stat'i i zametki o literature* (Moscow: Sovetskii pisatel', 1961), 68–82, here 78–79; P. Karp and B. Tomashevskii, "Vysokoe masterstvo," *NM* 9 (1954): 233–244, here 234.

86. Marshak, "Poeziia"; Tvardovskii, "Robert Berns," 79; Chukovskii, "Marshak," 224–225; Lev Ozerov, "Vtoroe rozhdenie," *Masterstvo-59*, 276–286, here 276; Kross, "Bez liubvi," 89–96.

87. Ag. Gatov, "Spory po sushchestvu (K itogam mezhrespublikanskikh konferentsii)," *Masterstvo-63*, 331–348, here 339.

88. S. Markish, "Intonatsii russkogo Rable," *Masterstvo-63*, 134–156, here 135.

89. RGALI f. 2854, op. 1, d. 130, l. 4.

90. Linguistic argument: A. V. Fedorov, *Vvedenie v teoriiu perevoda* (Moscow: Izdatel'stvo literatury na inostrannykh iazykakh, 1953).

91. *Vtoroi vsesoiuznyi s"ezd sovetskikh pisatelei. Stenograficheskii otchet* (Moscow: Sovetskii pisatel', 1956), 254, 258, 260–261, 267.

92. A. Leites, "Perevod kak iavlenie rodnoi literatury," in *Voprosy khudozhestvennogo perevoda* (Moscow: Sovetskii pisatel', 1955), 97–119. Earlier critiques: Vl. Rossel's, "O peredache natsional'noi formy v khudozhestvennom perevode (Zametki perevodchika)," *DN* 6 (1953): 257–278; N. I. Fel'dman's review in *Voprosy iazykoznaniia* 2 (1954): 117–227, here 122, 126–127; Toper, "Traditsii realizma," 239–240, 244n3; Maksim Ryl'skii, "Iz razmyshlenii perevodchika," *NM* 9 (1954): 227–233, here 228; Karp and Tomashevskii, "Vysokoe masterstvo," 234; Mark Shekhter, "Vzyskatel'nost' i dobrozhelatel'nost'," *LG*, November 23, 1954.

93. RGALI f. 2854, op. 1, d. 125, l. 50 (quotation); ibid., d. 130, l. 28.

94. Vl. Rossel's, "Za eti gody (obzor)," *Masterstvo-59*, 208–243, here 224; Abdulla Kakhkhar, "Zaboty desiatoi muzy," *LG*, May 17, 1962.

95. Leites, "Vvedenie," 261; Rossel's, "Za eti gody," 231, italics added. This was what the 1951 All-Union Congress on Translation and the 1954 Writers' Congress had called for: *Vtoroi vsesoiuznyi s"ezd*, 266, 365, 461; P. Toper, "O malom vnimanii k bol'shomu delu," *LG*, August 19, 1954; Vs. Rozhdestvenskii, "Nereshennye voprosy," *LG*, November 20, 1954.

96. RGALI f. 2854, op. 1, d. 125, l. 27; RGALI f. 2464, op. 2, d. 15, l. 20; Kundzich, "Perevod i literaturnyi iazyk," 11; Azov, *Poverzhennye bukvalisty*, 96–106; Sherry, *Discourses of Regulation and Resistance*, 29.

97. I. Kashkin, "V bor'be za realisticheskii perevod," in *Voprosy khudozhestvennogo perevoda*, 120–154; L. Sobolev, "O perevode obraza obrazom," in ibid., 259–309.

98. RGALI f. 2854, op. 1, d. 125, l. 82.

99. Ibid., ll. 26–27; E. Etkind, "Voprosy khudozhestvennogo perevoda," *Zvezda* 5 (1957): 196–200, esp. 197–199 (quotation: 198); Azov, *Poverzhennye bukvalisty*, 106–111.

100. "Vystuplenie P. Antokol'skogo," *Masterstvo-63*, 444–446 (quotation: 445); "hypnosis of the original": S. Markish and M. Zand, "Voprosy i otvety," *Masterstvo-69*, 284–293, here 285; *Vtoroi vsesoiuznyi s"ezd*, 255–256.

101. RGALI f. 2854, op. 1, d. 125, l. 92; Chukovskii, "Marshak," 225; Toper, "Predislovie," 9.

102. Metaphors of marriage, betrayal, and love-hate relationship: Barbara Johnson, "Taking Fidelity Philosophically," in *Difference in Translation*, ed. Joseph F. Graham (Ithaca, NY: Cornell University Press, 1985), 142–148, here 142–144.

Comparisons between Soviet and Western understandings of translation: K. Naumov, "Problemy perevoda," *NM* 5 (1958): 222–228.

103. The importance of translators trained in the 1930s: RGALI f. 2854, op. 1, d. 359, l. 71.

104. Liubov' Kachan, "Ee velichestvo perevodchik! Rita Rait," Proza.ru, February 29, 2012, http://www.proza.ru/2012/02/29/434.

105. Azov, *Poverzhennye bukvalisty*, 94–95.

106. Nora Gal', "Pomniu," in *Slovo zhivoe i mertvoe* (Moscow: Izdatel'skii dom "Sofiia," 2003), 352–358.

107. RGALI f. 1573, op. 1, d. 105, ll. 6–7, 58.

108. RGALI f. 1204, op. 2, d. 2643, l. 105.

109. Aivar Valeev, "Prazdnik, kotoryi u nas eshche budet," *Cheliabinskii rabochii*, July 21, 1999, http://www.chelpress.ru/newspapers/chelrab/archive/21-07-1999/3/A8746.DOC.shtml.

110. Example: an editor of a local youth newspaper gives an assignment to a novice author with these words: "Hemingway, write down the address." Oleg Filippov, *Khronika chastnoi zhizni, 1957–1969* (Tomsk: Vodolei Publishers, 2004), 89.

111. Petr Vail' and Aleksandr Genis, *60-e: Mir sovetskogo cheloveka* (Moscow: Novoe literaturnoe obozrenie, 2001), 65–66.

112. Gal', *Slovo zhivoe i mertvoe*, 252–253, 348; Raisa Orlova and Lev Kopelev, *My zhili v Moskve, 1956–1980* (Moscow: Kniga, 1990), 122–123; Safiullina, "Window to the West," 133, 136, 138–140, 145–146, 149, 159.

113. "Khudozhnik, pedagog, uchenyi. Pamiati Ivana Kashkina (1899–1963)," *Masterstvo-63*, 447–450, here 448.

114. Gal', *Slovo zhivoe i mertvoe*, 269, 272, 276; Raisa Orlova, *Kheminguei v Rossii: Roman dlinoiu v polstoletiia* (Ann Arbor, MI: Ardis, 1985), 11, 66.

115. Orlova, *Kheminguei v Rossii*, 29.

116. V. A. Nevezhin, "Sovetskaia politika i kul'turnye sviazi s Germaniei, 1939–1941 gg," *Otechestvennaia istoriia* 1 (1993): 18–34; Safiullina, "Window to the West," 132.

117. Yuri Trifonov, "Ob amerikanskoi literature," in *Kak slovo nashe otzovetsia . . .* (Moscow: Sovetskaia Rossiia, 1985), 127–128; Orlova, *Kheminguei v Rossii*, 68; Orlova and Kopelev, *My zhili v Moskve*, 123; libraries: Revekka Frumkina, *Vnutri istorii. Esse. Stat'i. Memuarnye ocherki* (Moscow: Novoe literaturnoe obozrenie, 2002), 291.

118. Viktor Nekrasov, *Zapiski zevaki* (Moscow: Vagrius, 2003), 556; Trifonov, "Ob amerikanskoi," 127–128.

119. Matei Calinescu, *Rereading* (New Haven, CT: Yale University Press, 1993), 55, 77.

120. Vail' and Genis, *60-e*, 64–69.

121. Aleksandr Zholkovskii, *Erosiped i drugie vin'etki* (Moscow: Vodolei, 2003), 111–114; Frumkina, *Vnutri istorii*, 291.

122. Calinescu, *Rereading*, 31–39, 53–56.

123. RGALI f. 2854, op. 1, d. 359, l. 74.

124. Scott Donaldson, "Introduction: Hemingway and Fame," in *The Cambridge Companion to Ernest Hemingway* (Cambridge: Cambridge University Press, 1996), 1–15. Wilson cited in Kenneth S. Lynn, *Hemingway* (Cambridge, MA: Harvard University Press, 1995), 336–337.

125. Ivan Kashkin, "Perechityvaia Khemingueia," *IL* 4 (1956): 194–206.

126. Orlova, *Kheminguei v Rossii*, 38.

127. Ivan Kashkin, "Pomni o . . . ," *LG*, October 18, 1934.

128. Ivan Kashkeen, "Ernest Hemingway: The Tragedy of Craftsmanship," *International Literature* 5 (May 1935): 72–90; Hemingway's letters: Kashkin, *Dlia chitatelia-sovremennika*, 55–63; *Ernest Hemingway: Selected Letters, 1917–1961*, ed. Carlos Baker (New York: Scribner's Sons, 1981), 417–420, 429–432, 480–481; their correspondence: Carlos Baker, *Ernest Hemingway: A Life Story* (New York: Scribner's Sons, 1969), 276–277.

129. Cited in Baker, *Ernest Hemingway*, 277.

130. Ia. Zundelovich, "Zametki chitatelia na poliakh knigi rasskazov E. Khemingueia," *Krasnaia nov'* 5 (May 1935): 232–234, here 233.

131. Iu. Olesha, "'Fiesta' Khemingueia," *Literaturnoe obozrenie* 1 (1936): 29–31; N. Novoselov, "'Proshchai oruzhie!'" ibid., 8–12; T. Sil'man, "'Proshchai, oruzhie' Khemingueia," *Zvezda* 11 (1936): 171–178, here 172–174.

132. Zundelovich, "Zametki chitatelia," 233; Novoselov, "'Proshchai oruzhie!'" 10.

133. Ernest Hemingway, "Cat in the Rain," in *The Short Stories of Ernest Hemingway* (New York: Scribner's Sons, 1953), 167–170; Zundelovich, "Zametki chitatelia," 233; N. Eishiskina, "Khudozhnik 'poteriannogo pokoleniia,'" *Khudozhestvennaia literatura* 4 (1935): 38–40, here 39.

134. *Ernest Kheminguei (1899–1961). Metodicheskie materialy k vecheru, posviashchennomu 70-letiiu so dnia rozhdeniia* (Moscow: Vsesoiuznaia gosudarstvennaia biblioteka inostrannoi literatury, 1969), 8, 27–30.

135. The following is based on Ivan Kashkin, "Perechityvaia Khemingueia" and "Soderzhanie-forma-soderzhanie," in *Dlia chitatelia-sovremennika*, 17–49 and 64–93.

136. Svetlana Boym, *Common Places: Mythologies of Everyday Life in Russia* (Cambridge, MA: Harvard University Press, 1994), 284.

137. Kashkin, "Perechityvaia Khemingueia," in *Dlia chitatelia-sovremennika*, 44–47.

138. Ernest Hemingway, *A Farewell to Arms* (New York: Simon & Schuster, 1995), 249.

139. Italics added. Russian: *Kogda liudi stol'ko muzhestva prinosiat v etot mir, mir dolzhen ubit' ikh, chtoby slomit', i poetomu on ikh i ubivaet.*

140. In this passage, Hemingway's hurried prose is streamlined with abundant commas, but the translation compensates for this lyrical deficit by introducing repetition and cadence in the last sentence. ("If you are none of these" is rendered as *"A esli ty ni to, ni drugoe, ni tret'e,"* corresponding to the previous *"On ubivaet samykh dobrykh, i samykh nezhnykh, i samykh khrabrykh."*)

141. All Russian citations are from Ernest Kheminguei [Ernest Hemingway], *Proshchai, oruzhie!* in *Izbrannye proizvedeniia v dvukh tomakh* (Moscow: Gosudarstvennoe izdatel'stvo khudozhestvennoi literatury, 1959), 1: 355.

142. Ark. El'iashevich, "Cheloveka nel'zia pobedit' (zametki o tvorchestve Ernesta Khemingueia)," *VL* 1 (1964): 107–127, here 111.

143. Aleksandr Lebedev, *Chaadaev* (Moscow: Molodaia gvardiia, 1965).

144. Kornilov on Hemingway's place in his life: Orlova, *Kheminguei v Rossii*, 35; Vladimir Kornilov, "Starik (Kheminguei)," in *Pristan': Kniga stikhov* (Moscow: Sovetskii pisatel', 1964), 77–78.

145. Kornilov, "Lermontov," in *Pristan'*, 8–9.

146. Orlova, *Kheminguei v Rossii*, 8–9. Comparisons of Hemingway and Lord Byron in non-Soviet context: J. Donald Abrams, "Speaking of Books," *New York Times*, July 16, 1961; Harold Bloom, "Introduction," in *Ernest Hemingway* (Philadelphia: Chelsea House Publishers, 2005), 5.

147. RGALI f. 2464, op. 21, d. 775, ll. 125–126.

148. Samizdat readings: Aleksandr Solzhenitsyn, *Bodalsia telenok s dubom. Ocherki literaturnoi zhizni* (Moscow: "Soglasie," 1996), 22. Rereading the book in print after the first, samizdat reading: Iulii Daniel', *"Ia vse sbivaius' na literaturu . . ."* *Pis'ma iz zakliucheniia. Stikhi* (Moscow: Izdatel'stvo "Zven'ia," 2000), 417, 814; Orlova and Kopelev, *My zhizli v Moskve*, 131; Julius Telesin, "For Whom the Scissors Cut: How to Improve Hemingway (Moscow style)," *Encounter* 46: 6 (June 1976): 81–86.

149. Tamara Motyleva, *Inostrannaia literatura i sovremennost': Stat'i* (Moscow: Sovetskii pisatel', 1961), 190n1; Ivan Kashkin, "Ispaniia v rasskazakh Khemingueia," *IL* 2 (February 1964): 216–226; El'iashevich, "Cheloveka nel'zia pobedit'," 107–127.

150. "Proizvedeniia zarubezhnykh pisatelei," *LG*, April 23, 1955; "Podarki knigoliubam," *LG*, August 17, 1963; Raisa Orlova, "O revoliutsii i liubvi, o zhizni i smerti: K vykhodu russkogo izdaniia romana Khemingueia 'Po kom zvonit kolokol,'" *Zvezda* 1 (1964): 206–213; Orlova, *Kheminguei v Rossii*, 52–57; "Iz istorii izdanii v SSSR romana E. Khemingueia *Po kom zvonit kolokol*," *VL* 2 (1993): 240–253, here 240–244.

151. RGANI f. 5, op. 17, d. 539, ll. 110–112, 115.

152. Ibid., ll. 105–109, 113–114; Baker, *Ernest*, 310, 347, 356–357; "Protest uchastnikov brigady Linkol'na protiv knigi Khemingueia," *Internatsional'naia literatura* 11–12 (1940): 364; M[ike]. Gold, "V boiakh za peredovuiu literaturu SShA,"

Internatsional'naia literatura 6 (1941): 142–157, here 153–156; "Iz istorii izdanii," 241, 251–253.

153. Kashkin, "Perechityvaia Khemingueia," in *Dlia chitatelia-sovremennika*, 28–29, 30 (quotations); idem, "Soderzhanie-forma-soderzhanie," in ibid., 93 (quotation); idem, "Ispaniia v rasskazakh," 221.

154. "Iz istorii izdaniia," 244–245. Quotations about Marty: Ernest Hemingway, *For Whom the Bell Tolls* (New York: Charles Scribner's Sons, 1940), 417–419, 422–423, the showdown with Karkov: 424–426; Orlova, "O revoliutsii i liubvi," 213; idem, *Kheminguei v Rossii*, 43, 58, 63.

155. Solzhenitsyn, *Bodalsia telenok*, 22.

156. Lynn, *Hemingway*, 9, 82–85, 91–92, 262–263, 370, 391–393, 402, 509–514, 525–527, 545–553, 559–560.

157. Ivan Kashkin, "O samom glavnom. Proza Ernesta Khemingueia," *Oktiabr'* 3 (March 1960): 215–223 (quotation: 216).

158. RGALI f. 2854, op. 1, d. 133, ll. 9, 14, 22; photograph: *Ogonek* (April 14, 1960): 26.

159. RGALI f. 2854, op. 1, d. 133, l. 1; Zubok, *Zhivago's Children*, 174.

160. Orlova and Kopelev, *My zhili v Moskve*, 131.

161. Yuri Paporov, *Kheminguei na Kube: Ocherki* (Moscow: Sovetskii pisatel', 1982), 15, 42, 44, 55–56, 74–75; some of this material was published in the 1960s.

162. Vail' and Genis, *60-e*, 64–74.

163. R. Orlova, "Posle smerti Khemingueia (po stranitsam zarubezhnoi pressy)," *NM* 9 (1961): 173–178; Sergo Mikoian, "Nashedshii dorogu k serdtsam," *Moskva* 8 (1961): 200–201; idem, "Slovo o cheloveke," *Izvestiia*, October 13, 1964; Genrikh Borovik, "U Ernesta Khemingueia," *Ogonek* (April 14, 1960): 26–29; idem, "Muzhestvennyi talant. Pamiati Ernesta Khemingueia," *LG*, July 4, 1961; idem, "Serdtse Khemingueia," *Ogonek* 28 (July 9, 1961): 29; idem, "Kto skazhet, chto on mertv?" *LG*, May 12, 1966.

164. Boris Gribanov, *Kheminguei* (Moscow: Molodaia gvardiia, 1970).

165. RGALI f. 2854, op. 1, d. 133, l. 28.

166. Vasilii Aksenov, *Amerikanskaia kirillitsa: Proza i stikhi* (Moscow: Novoe literaturnoe obozrenie, 2004), 76.

167. V. L. Lidin, "Pamiati Khemingueia," in *Doroga zhuravlei: Rasskazy, 1959–1961* (Moscow: Sovetskii pisatel', 1962), 375–378.

168. Gennadii Shpalikov, *Ia zhil kak zhil: Stikhi, proza, dramaturgiia, dnevniki, pis'ma* (Moscow: Izdatel'skii dom "Podkova," 1998), 313–316; "Smert' Khemingueia," *Pravda*, July 3, 1961.

169. Kashkin, "Soderzhanie-forma-soderzhanie," in *Dlia chitatelia-sovremennika*, 93; Shpalikov, *Ia zhil kak zhil*, 314–315.

170. Erikh Mariia Remark [Erich Maria Remarque], *Na zapadnom fronte bez peremen. Vozvrashchenie. Tri tovarishcha* (Leningrad: Lenizdat, 1959).

171. RGALI f. 613, op. 8, d. 1654, l. 5.

172. Mikhail German, *Slozhnoe proshedshee (Passé composé)* (St. Petersburg: Iskusstvo–SPb, 2000), 320.

173. Andrei Bitov, "Kak chitali 30 let nazad," in *Piatoe izmerenie: Na granitse vremeni i prostranstva* (Moscow: Izdatel'stvo Nezavisimaia gazeta, 2002), 34–41, here 34; RGALI, f. 1573, op. 1, d. 162, l. 33.

174. Bitov, "Kak chitali 30 let nazad," 39.

175. RGALI f. 613, op. 8, d. 1654, ll. 6–10.

176. Ibid., ll. 18–19.

177. Lev Kopelev, "Predislovie," in Erikh Mariia Remark [Erich Maria Remarque], *Tri tovarishcha* (repr. Tashkent: Gosudarstvennoe izdatel'stvo khudozhestvennoi literatury Uzbekskoi SSR, 1960), 5, 8, 10.

178. RGALI f. 613, op. 8, d. 1654, l. 4.

179. Ibid., ll. 5–6, 10.

180. RGALI f. 2464, op. 1, d. 702, ll. 49–54; "Hemingway-like" novel: L. Lazarev, "Vremia zhit'," *NM* 11 (1958): 253–258, here 255, 257.

181. RGALI f. 613, op. 8, d. 1654, ll. 26–28.

182. B. Suchkov, "Kniga, kotoraia sudit (Erikh-Maria Remark 'Vremia zhit' i vremia umirat')," *IL* 4 (1955): 201–208; G. Gerasimov, "Ser'eznoe napominanie," *Novoe vremia* 41: 6 (October 1955): 27–29; E. Etkind, "Vremia zhit' i vremia umirat'," *Neva* 1 (1957): 205–206; V. Zalesskii, "Vremia zhit', vremia borot'sia," *Oktiabr'* 6 (June 1957): 203–210.

183. Zalesskii, "Vremia zhit'," 205–206.

184. Etkind, "Vremia zhit' i vremia umirat'," 205–206; Viktor Pankov, "Vremia zhit' i vremia borot'sia," *Znamia* 2 (February 1957): 211–214.

185. A. M. Gorbunov and M. I. Davydova, *Zarubezhnaia literatura* (1958). *Rekomendatel'nyi ukazatel'* (Moscow: Gosudarstvennaia biblioteka SSSR im. V. I. Lenina, 1959), 44–45, 179–182.

186. Orlova and Kopelev, *My zhili v Moskve*, 127.

187. RGALI f. 1573, op. 5, d. 242, l. 57.

188. Ibid., op. 3, d. 70, l. 54; ibid., d. 134, l. 13.

189. Bitov, "Kak chitali 30 let nazad," 36–37.

190. RGALI f. 613, op. 8, d. 73, l. 20.

191. Bitov, "Kak chitali 30 let nazad," 37.

192. Bella Ezerskaia, "Tri tovarishcha. Neobiazatel'nye razmyshleniia po povodu gastrolei teatra 'Sovremennik' v kazino 'Foksvud,'" *Chaika/Seagull Magazine*, November 19, 2004.

193. RGALI f. 1573, op. 1, d. 187, l. 112ob.

194. RGALI f. 1204, op. 2, d. 2615, l. 50b.

195. First trope: N. Kartseva, "Iz dvukh zol—oba . . . ," *KP*, May 22, 1960; S. Bol'shakova, "'Kogda u vas nachalas' liubov'? . . .'" *KP*, December 10, 1960; O.

Kuchkina, "'Zanimalis' tem, chto . . . tselovalis'," *KP*, January 18, 1961. Second trope: S. Bol'shakova, "Chelovek v bede . . . ," *KP*, March 6, 1957; I. Shatunovskii, "O driani," *KP*, September 7, 1958; V. Benderova, "Liudi i liudishki," *KP*, January 14, 1960; E. Bruskova, "Po zakonam besserdechnykh," *KP*, January 4, 1962; K. Kozhevnikova, "Solntse v pautine," *KP*, March 16, 1963; "Slushaetsia delo o pari," *KP*, March 21, 1963. Advice on love: A. Sukontseva, "Tolia plius Sveta," *KP*, July 23, 1960; "Dvoe vykhodiat v zhizn'," *KP*, November 13, 1960; Sergei L'vov, "Oskorblenie khanzhestvom," *KP*, December 19, 1962; N. Rudenko, "U poroga liubvi," *KP*, October 19, 1963.

196. A. Protopopova, "Logika serdtsa," *KP*, July 7, 1963; R. Fraerman, "Poeziia iunoi zhizni," *KP*, February 19, 1963.

197. A. Elkin, "Otdavat' nel'zia," *KP*, December 1, 1960.

198. Viktor Rozov, "Schastlivoi liubvi!" *KP*, August 12, 1964. On attempts to write about love: A. Iakovlev, "Itak, liubov' . . ." *MG* 6 (1961): 216–222.

199. Orlova and Kopelev, *My zhili v Moskve*, 128–129; Raisa Orlova, *Vospominaniia o neproshedshem vremeni: Moskva, 1961–1981 gg.* (Ann Arbor: Ardis, 1983), 217.

200. Elkin, "Otdavat' nel'zia"; Rozov, "Schastlivoi liubvi."

201. RGALI f. 1573, op. 3, d. 70, ll. 81–85 (quotation: 83).

202. Elkin, "Otdavat' nel'zia"; I. Prelovskaia, "Krushenie 'nigilista,'" *KP*, July 25, 1962; I. Ziuziukin, "Ot sebia ne uiti," *KP*, March 7, 1963; "Kogda tebe vosemnadtsat' . . . ," *KP*, May 17, 1964; RGANI f. 72, op. 1, d. 16, l. 52.

203. I. Ovchinnikova, "Net, ne zapretnaia tema," *KP*, December 1, 1963.

204. RGALI f. 634, op. 4, d. 2519, l. 35.

205. Viktor Sukhorukov, "Erikh Maria Remark—kak predposlednii romantik," *Priazovskii rabochii* 41 (2004).

206. German, *Slozhnoe proshedshee*, 320–321.

207. Il'ia Fradkin, "Remark i spory o nem," *VL* 1 (January 1963): 92–119, here 97–98.

208. Bitov, "Kak chitali 30 let nazad," 35; Yurchak, *Everything Was Forever*, 190–198.

209. Shpalikov, *Ia zhil kak zhil*, 313.

210. Bitov, "Kak chitali 30 let nazad," 35–36.

211. Etkind, "Vremia zhit' i vremia umirat'," 206.

212. Zalesskii, "Vremia zhit'," 209.

213. Aleksandra Borisenko, "Nostal'gicheskoe chtenie," *Russkii zhurnal*, July 28, 2000, http://old.russ.ru/krug/razbor/20000728.html; Sergei Schepotiev, "Erich Maria Remarque's Conception of Goodness and Its Perception in Russia Today," in *Erich Maria Remarque: Leben, Werk und weltweite Wirkung*, ed. Thomas F. Schneider (Osnabrück: Universitätsverlag Rasch, 1998), 455.

214. Tamara Motyleva, "Remark i sovetskie chitateli," *LG*, March 1, 1960. See also A. Dmitriev, "Gumanizm bez very v buduiushchee," *MG* 9 (February 1960): 215–222.

215. RGALI f. 634, op. 4, d. 2519, ll. 35–36.
216. Fradkin, "Remark i spory o nem," 96–97. See also Lazarev, "Vremia zhit'," 257.
217. Lazarev, "Vremia zhit'," 257.
218. RGALI f. 1573, op. 3, d. 134, l. 13.
219. Ibid., d. 188, l. 15.
220. Plaschevsky to Remarque, December 22, 1966, Remarque Papers, series 3, box B, Folder 28. Remarque as psychologist: Schepotiev, "Erich Maria Remarque's Conception of Goodness," 453–454.
221. RGALI f. 1573, op. 3, d. 134, l. 76; ibid., d. 135, ll. 56–58; ibid., d. 70, l. 9; ibid., d. 71, l. 3.
222. Ibid., d. 70, l. 46; ibid., d. 188, l. 15 (quotation).
223. Ibid., d. 71, ll. 39–400b.
224. Ibid., d. 135, l. 54.
225. Ibid., d. 134, ll. 23, 76; ibid., d. 188, ll. 48, 76; ibid., op. 1, d. 188, ll. 71, 73.
226. Shimon Markish, "O perevode," *Ierusalimskii zhurnal* 18 (2004), http://www.antho.net/jr/18.2004/22.php.
227. Orlova and Kopelev, *My zhili v Moskve*, 127.
228. V. Kirpotin, "Bez putevodnoi zvezdy. O romanakh E. M. Remarka," *Izvestiia*, November 18, 1959. For a similar position, see R. Samarin, "Nastoiashchee i fal'shivoe," *Molodoi kommunist* 5 (May 1960): 112–117. In defense of Remarque: Fradkin, "Remark i spory o nem," 97–99.
229. RGALI f. 631, op. 26, d. 75, l. 64.
230. RGALI f. 1573, op. 5, d. 242, l. 4; ibid., op. 1, d. 162, ll. 32–33, 38; ibid., op. 3, d. 92, ll. 23–29.
231. *Ideologicheskie komissii*, 230–235; *Apparat TsK KPSS i kul'tura, 1958–1964: Dokumenty* (Moscow: ROSSPEN, 2005), 334.
232. "Dokumenty svidetel'stvuiut . . . ," *VL* 5 (1993): 271–338, here 303; Orlova, *Vospominaniia o neproshedshem vremeni*, 217. See also: RGALI f. 1573, op. 5, d. 407, ll. 4–5.
233. *Apparat TsK KPSS i kul'tura*, 721; Erikh Maria Remark [Erich Maria Remarque], "Vozliubi blizhnego svoego," *Sever* 6 (1966), 1 (1967).
234. Erikh Maria Remark [Erich Maria Remarque], "Noch' v Lissabone," *Prostor* 12 (1965).
235. The rules were laid down in the famous polemic between Maksim Gorky and Fedor Panferov on the uses of colloquial and substandard speech in literature. Panferov's literary sins included peasant and regional patois and depictions of the body. Gorky campaigned for accessible, sanitized, "pure," and proper Russian. Gorham, *Speaking in Soviet Tongues*, 134–137; Clark, *Petersburg*, 284–288; D. E. Rozental', *Kul'tura rechi* (Moscow: Izdatel'stvo Moskovskogo universiteta, 1964), 20–21, M. Golubkov, *Utrachennye al'ternativy: Formirovanie monicheskoi kontseptsii sovetskoi literatury, 20–30-e gody* (Moscow: Nasledie,

1992), 56–64; N. Primochkina, *Pisatel' i vlast'*: M. Gor'kii v literaturnom dvizhenii 20-kh godov (Moscow: ROSSPEN, 1996), 138–145.

236. This discussion is based on: V. G. Kostomarov, *Kul'tura rechi i stil'* (Moscow: Izdatel'stvo VPSh i AON pri TsK KPSS, 1960), 10, 42; *Pravil'nost' russkoi rechi. Slovar'-spravochnik*, ed. S. I. Ozhegov, L. P. Krysin, L. I. Skvortsov (Moscow: Nauka, 1965), 4–5; E. A. Bakhmutova, *Kul'tura rechi. Orfoepoiia. Leksicheskie normy. Uchebnoe posobie* (Kazan': Izdatel'stvo Kazanskogo universiteta, 1960), 5; Chukovskii, *Zhivoi kak zhizn'*, 3–12, 22–24.

237. Boris Timofeev, "O zhargone i modnykh slovechkakh . . . ," *Neva* 9 (1960): 200–203; I. Kotova, "Tol'ko li shkola?" *LiZh*, August 30, 1961.

238. Juliane Fürst, *Stalin's Last Generation: Soviet Post-War Youth and the Emergence of Mature Socialism* (Oxford: Oxford University Press, 2010), 221–222.

239. Jan Plamper, "Abolishing Ambiguity: Soviet Censorship Practices in the 1930s," *Russian Review* 60: 4 (October 2001): 526–544.

240. N. Aleksandrova and L. Pochivalov, "Otstupnik—tak on i nazyvaetsia," *KP*, July 9, 1958.

241. L. I. Skvortsov, "Ob otsenkakh iazyka molodezhi (zhargon i iazykovaia politika)," *Voprosy kul'tury rechi* 5 (Moscow: Nauka, 1964), 45–70; idem, "Literaturnyi iazyk, prostorechie i zhargony v ikh vzaimodeistvii," in *Literaturnaia norma i prostorechie* (Moscow: Nauka, 1977), 29–57, esp. 54; E. G. Borisova-Lukashanets, "O leksike sovremennogo molodezhnogo zhargona (Angloiazychnye zaimstvovaniia v studencheskom slenge 60–70-kh godov)," in *Literaturnaia norma v leksike i frazeologii* (Moscow: Nauka, 1983), 104–120.

242. Lorie, "O redakture khudozhestvennogo proizvedeniia," 99; Liubimov, "Perevod—iskusstvo," 241. See also: Even-Zohar, "The Position of Translated Literature," 166; Gideon Toury, "The Nature and Role of Norms in Translation," in *The Translation Studies Reader*, 168–181, here 174.

243. Vl. Rossel's, *Estafeta slova: Iskusstvo khudozhestvennogo perevoda* (Moscow: Znanie, 1972), 17.

244. Peter Vail' in conversation with Ivan Tolstoi, "Dzherom Devid Selindzher," Radio Svoboda, July 16, 2001, http://www.svoboda.org/archive/ll_man/0701/ll.071601-1.asp.

245. Rait-Kovaleva, "Nit' Ariadny," 7.

246. Vail' and Tolstoi, "Dzherom Devid Selindzher."

247. RGALI f. 1573, op. 5, d. 307, ll. 3–20 (quotations: ll. 4, 6, 8, 14, 15).

248. Ibid., ll. 4, 6, 8, 10–12, 14.

249. L. S. Kustova, "Roman Selindzhera 'Nad propast'iu vo rzhi' i ego perevod na russkii iazyk," *Vestnik Moskovskogo universiteta* 7: 1 (1964): 68–81.

250. Anya Motalygo Kroth, "V. Aksenov i Dzh. D. Selindzher: Sravnitel'nyi analiz" (MA thesis, Florida State University, 1969). Kroth was a physics student at

Moscow State in the 1960s. I treat this thesis as both a reader's reflections and a work of scholarship.

251. Vasilii Aksenov, "Zvezdnyi bilet," in *Apel'siny iz Morokko* (Moscow: Izograf and EKSMO-Press, 2000).

252. RGALI f. 2924, op. 2, d. 69, ll. 15–150b; ibid., d. 28, l. 17 (quotation).

253. Ibid., l. 72.

254. Kotova, "Tol'ko" and "Stroki iz pisem," *LiZh*, August 30, 1961; I. Astakhov, "Ne po-gor'kovski!" and I. Motsarev, "Nikakogo opravdaniia: pis'mo v redaktsiiu," *LiZh*, August 23, 1961; V. Pankov, "Pravo na zvezdnyi bilet," *LiZh*, August 25, 1961; K. Pozdniaev, "'Zvezdnyi bilet'—kuda?" *Oktiabr'* 10 (October 1961): 210–213; N. Dolinina, "Legkii sposob sporit'," *LG*, August 26, 1961; "Lish' by posporit' . . . ," *LG*, August 31, 1961; Chukovskii, *Dnevnik*, 2: 360–361; Kornei Chukovskii and Lidiia Chukovskaia, *Perepiska, 1912–1969* (Moscow: Novoe literaturnoe obozrenie, 2003), 383–384n2–n6.

255. Pozdniaev, "Zvezdnyi bilet'—kuda?" 211–213 (quotation: 213); Larisa Kriachko, "Geroi ne khochet vzroslet' . . . ," *LG*, March 19, 1963.

256. Kornei Chukovskii, "Nechto o labude," *LG*, August 12, 1961; idem, *Zhivoi*, 99–109; idem, "Kantseliarit," *LG*, September 9, 1961 and September 16, 1961.

257. Idem., "Bednyi slovar'—i bogatyi," *LG*, July 20, 1963; idem., *Dnevnik*, 2: 347.

258. RGALI f. 2924, op. 2, d. 69, ll. 18–180b.

259. Ibid., d. 28, ll. 9, 26.

260. RGALI f. 1204, op. 2, d. 2647, l. 128.

261. RGALI f. 2924, op. 2, d. 28, l. 27.

262. Ibid., d. 69, ll. 15–150b, 200b.

263. Ibid., ll. 1–4. Sincerity and opposition: Rutten, *Sincerity After Communism*, 40–41.

264. RGALI f. 1573, op. 3, d. 71, l. 123.

265. Vail' and Tolstoi, "Dzherom Devid Selindzher."

266. G. Vladimov, "Tri dnia iz zhini Kholdena," *NM* 2 (1961): 254–256.

267. Rossel's, *Estafeta slova*, 17.

268. Respectively: lomat'/batsat', khiliat'/proshvyrnut'sia, labat', dudochki, lepen', makasy/shuzy, babki/titi-miti, tusovka/seishen, motor, gerla/chuvikha/kadra/baton/mochalka.

269. Rozental', *Kul'tura rechi*, 20–21.

270. The phrase "artificial vernacular" is from Laura Routti, "Norms and Storms: Pentti Saarikoski's Translation of J. D. Salinger's *The Catcher in the Rye*," *Helsinki English Studies: The Electronic Journal of the Department of English at the University of Helsinki* 1 (2001), http://www.eng.helsinki.fi/hes/Translation /catcher_in_the_rye.htm; Warren French, "The Artist as a Very Nervous

Young Man," in *Holden Caulfield*, ed. Harold Bloom (Philadelphia: Chelsea House Publishers, 2005), 51–75; Walter Riedel, "Some German Ripples of Holden Caulfield's Goddam Autobiography: On Translating and Adapting J. D. Salinger's *The Catcher in the Rye*," *Canadian Review of Comparative Literature* 7: 2 (Spring 1980): 196–205; Siegfriend Mandel, "Salinger in Continental Jeans: The Liberation of Böll and Other Germans," in *Critical Essays on Salinger's The Catcher in the Rye*, ed. Joel Salzberg (Boston: G. K. Hall, 1990), 214–226; John Robert Schmitz, "Suppression of References to Sex and Body Functions in the Brazilian and Portuguese Translations of J. D. Salinger's *The Catcher in the Rye*," *Meta: Journal des traducteurs* 43: 2 (1998): 242–253.

271. Kustova, "Roman Selindzhera." A different reading of Rait-Kovaleva's choice of words: Sherry, *Discourses of Regulation and Resistance*, 129.

272. Donald P. Costello, "The Language of *The Catcher in the Rye*," in *Critical Essays on Salinger's* The Catcher in the Rye, 44–53 (quotation: 45–46). The looseness of thought is achieved with "and all," "or something," "or anything" at the end of sentences. The Russian translation eliminated such endings.

273. Rait-Kovaleva, "Nit' Ariadny," 7; Rait-Kovaleva, "Predislovie," 7.

274. Kustova, "Roman Selindzhera," 80–81.

275. Another way to translate the title is *Lovets vo rzhi*, but that would alter Rait-Kovaleva's understanding of Holden. Not everybody was comfortable with her vision: some critics writing on American literature at the time consistently used *Lovets vo rzhi* and retranslated Holden's fantasy to include only "the cliff," dispensing with "the abyss." I. Levidova, "Neprikaiannye dushi (Geroi knig Dzheka Keruaka, Dzheimsa Selindzhera, Trumena Kepota i Ivena Konnella)," *VL* 10 (October 1960): 108–131. Criticism of Rait-Kovaleva's title and imagery: Kustova, "Roman Selindzhera."

276. French, "The Artist as a Very Nervous Young Man," 71.

277. R. Rait-Kovaleva, *Robert Berns* (Moscow: Molodaia gvardiia, 1959), 5.

278. Rait-Kovaleva, "Nit' Ariadny," 5; Rait-Kovaleva, *Robert Berns*, dedication. The relationship between Rait-Kovaleva and Marshak: "Nadpisi na knigakh," in *Ia dumal, chuvstvoval, ia zhil. Vospominaniia o S. Ia. Marshake* (Moscow: Sovetskii pisatel', 1971), 259–271. Marshak inspired her to write the biography in the first place.

279. "Ob avtore knigi," in Rait-Kovaleva, *Robert Berns*; Rait-Kovaleva, "Nadpisi," 263; B. Galanov, *S. Ia. Marshak: zhizn' i tvorchestvo* (Moscow: Detskaia literatura, 1965), 258–274.

280. *Esli kto-to zval kogo-to . . . vecherom vo rzhi*. Marshak's poetic distortions of Burns: Yang De-you, "On Marshak's Russian Translation of Robert Burns," *Studies in Scottish Literature* 22 (1987): 10–29; Karp and Tomashevskii, "Vysokoe masterstvo," 235–236, 239–240.

281. This interpretation of the mistake in the English original is based on Luther S. Luedtke, "Robert Burns's Poem 'Comin' Thro' the Rye' and *Catcher*," in *Readings on The Catcher in the Rye*, ed. Steven Engel (San Diego: Greenhaven Press, 1998), 63–67. Another interpretation, "catch a body" as signifying death and "meet a body" as signifying love: Duane Edwards, "Holden Caulfield: 'Don't Ever Tell Anybody Anything,'" in *Critical Essays on Salinger's* The Catcher in the Rye, 148–158, here 149.

282. E. Knipovich, "Liudi nad propast'iu," *Znamia* 6 (June 1961): 215–224, here 219; Levidova, "Neprikaiannye dushi," 121 (quotation); I. Anastas'ev, "Miry Dzheroma Selindzhera," *MG* 2 (February 1965): 292–302.

283. Levidova, "Neprikaiannye dushi," 124.

284. R. Orlova, *Potomki Gekl'berri Finna: Ocherki sovremennoi amerikanskoi literatury* (Moscow: Sovetskii pisatel', 1964), 197–198.

285. "Chuma na vashi oba doma?" *LG*, July 2, 1961; Knipovich, "Liudi nad propast'iu," 218, 220.

286. Levidova, "Neprikaiannye dushi ," 112 (quotation), 123; Nora Gal', "Nad propast'iu," *KP*, December 13, 1960; Anastas'ev, "Miry Dzheroma Selindzhera," 294; Orlova, "Chto znachit zhit'," 233.

287. Orlova, *Potomki Gekl'berri Finna*, 195–196.

288. Vera Smirnova, "Deti Ameriki," in *Sovremennyi portret: Stat'i* (Moscow: Sovetskii pisatel', 1964), 160–180, here 177–178; Gal', "Nad propast'iu."

289. Vladimov, "Tri dnia iz zhini Kholdena," 254.

290. Maiia Kaganskaia, "Vnebrachnaia noch' ili semidesiatye gody," *Vremia i my* 20 (1977): 123–134, here 123–124.

291. Peter Burke, "The Renaissance Translator as Go-Between," in *Renaissance Go-Betweens: Cultural Exchange in Early Modern Europe*, ed. Andreas Höfele and Werner von Koppenfels (New York: Walter de Gruyter, 2005), 17–31.

292. Translations as a distinct literary system within a larger cultural context: Even-Zohar, "The Position of Translated Literature," 162–163.

293. George Steiner, *After Babel: Aspects of Language and Translation* (Oxford: Oxford University Press, 1998), 76.

294. Ibid., 22.

295. On immobility: Chapter 6. Physical mobility as an important feature of translators' profile: Burke, "The Renaissance Translator," 21–24.

296. André Lefevre, *Translation, Rewriting, and the Manipulation of Literary Fame* (London: Routledge, 1992), 5–7; Stephen Greenblat, *Marvelous Possessions: The Wonder of the New World* (Chicago: University of Chicago Press, 1991), 122.

297. Interview with Liudmila Maksovna Kipnis, Moscow, August 15, 2004. Also: *Tsenzura v tsarskoi Rossii i Sovetskom Soiuze*, 22.

298. These statements belong to different people, cited in Orlova, *Kheminguei v Rossii*, 8, 36, 63–64, 67; Bitov, "Kak chitali 30 let nazad," 38.

4. Cinema without an Accent

1. RGALI f. 2329, op. 15, d. 19, l. 98.
2. RGALI f. 2918, op. 5, d. 283, l. 40.
3. RGANI f. 5, op. 36, d. 153, l. 64.
4. See Chapter 1.
5. RGALI f. 2329, op. 15, d. 19, ll. 109–110.
6. RGANI f. 5, op. 36, d. 82, ll. 146, 159; ibid., d. 129, ll. 132–136, 142–150; ibid., d. 138, ll. 63–67, 140–152, 221–225.
7. RGALI f. 2918, op. 5, d. 283, l. 40.
8. Ibid., d. 61, ll. 74, 76, 208; ibid., d. 226, ll. 7–11; RGANI f. 5, op. 36, d. 82, ll. 85–90, 127–132; ibid., d. 129, ll. 204–209; ibid., d. 138, ll. 149–153.
9. RGALI f. 2918, op. 5, d. 61, ll. 9, 61, 71, 149; ibid., d. 226, ll. 108, 123.
10. Ibid., d. 61, ll. 14, 19, 69.
11. Ibid., ll. 130–131.
12. RGALI f. 2923, op. 1, d. 1038, ll. 26–27.
13. Ibid., l. 13; RGALI f. 2329, op. 15, d. 10, ll. 145–146.
14. On Soviet-American media diplomacy in the late 1940s, see: Sergei Kapterev, "Illusionary Spoils: Soviet Attitudes toward American Cinema during the Early Cold War," *Kritika: Explorations in Russian and Eurasian History* 10:4 (Fall 2009): 779–807.
15. "Meeting of Subcommittee on Film Exchange," November 13, 1957, folder October talks–General, lot 59D127, box 19, RG 59, NARA.
16. "Meeting with Mr Harry S. Woodbridge," May 11, 1956, Bureau of European Affairs Country Director for the Soviet Union Records Relating to Soviet-US Relations 1945–1966, folder Todd-films 1640-22, Entry 5287, box 9, ibid.; RGANI f. 5, op. 30, d. 119, passim; ibid., op. 36, d. 8, ll. 100–103; ibid., d. 30, ll. 105–108.
17. "Department of State Instruction. Sale of commercial films in Eastern Europe," September 17, 1956, Miscellaneous Records of the Bureau of Public Affairs, 1944–1962, folder 1953–1957 Films, lot 60D605, box 58, RG 59, NARA; "Confidential memorandum," October 8, 1956, ibid.
18. "Cannes film festival," February 12, 1957, folder JJ1957 Cannes Film Festival, box 58, lot 60D605, ibid.
19. RGALI f. 2918, op. 1, d. 78, ll. 5, 9.
20. Thomas Doherty, *Hollywood's Censor: Joseph I. Breen & the Production Code Administration* (New York: Columbia University Press, 2007), 275.
21. RGALI f. 2329, op. 15, d. 10, ll. 196–197; ibid., f. 2918, op. 1, d. 78, l. 7.
22. RGALI f. 2918, op. 4, d. 279, l. 5. Artkino distributed films in the Western Hemisphere, in countries with which the Soviet Union did not have trade agreements: RGANI f. 5, op. 17, d. 502, ll. 22–23.

23. RGANI, f. 5, op. 36, d. 154, ll. 215–216; RGASPI f. 17, op. 132, d. 251, l. 56;
   RGALI f. 2918, op. 5, d. 283, ll. 64–67; GARF f. 9576, op. 2, d. 129, l. 197; Bert
   Hogenkamp, *Film, Television and the Left in Britain, 1950 to 1970* (London:
   Lawrence & Wishart, 2000), 4–5, 7–14.

24. RGALI f. 2918, op. 5, d. 283, l. 64.

25. Michael Leach, *I Know It When I See It: Pornography, Violence, and Public
   Sensitivity* (Philadelphia: Westminster Press, 1975), 29–32.

26. RGALI f. 2329, op. 15, d. 10, ll. 196–197; ibid., f. 2918, op. 1, d. 78, l. 7; ibid., op.
   5, d. 169, l. 142; ibid., f. 2923, op. 1, d. 1038, ll. 11, 24, 27.

27. RGALI f. 2918, op. 4, d. 28, l. 19; ibid., d. 284, l. 3; "Sovetskie fil'my v SShA," *IK*
   10 (October 1956): 111.

28. RGALI f. 2918, op. 1, d. 78, ll. 9, 16, 19; Andrei Kozovoi, "A Foot in the Door:
   The Lacy-Zarubin Agreement and Soviet-American Film Diplomacy during
   the Khrushchev Era, 1953–1963," *Historical Journal of Film, Radio and
   Television* 36:1 (2016): 21–39.

29. RGANI f. 5, op. 36, d. 82, ll. 61–65; RGALI f. 2918, op. 1, d. 80, ll. 16–17 (new
   pagination); ibid., d. 78, l. 8.

30. RGANI f. 5, op. 36, d. 82, ll. 115–116 (quotation: 116), 118–120; RGALI f. 2918,
   op. 1, d. 80, l. 88.

31. RGALI f. 2918, op. 1, d. 78, ll. 5–7, 9.

32. Ibid., l. 62.

33. Ibid., op. 4, d. 279, l. 2.

34. A point made in recent scholarship: Kate Brown, *Plutopia: Nuclear Families,
   Atomic Cities, and the Great Soviet and American Plutonium Disasters* (Oxford:
   Oxford University Press, 2015).

35. Jean Jerolaman, "Memo: Motion picture consideration of manner and control
   of sale of films to Eastern European countries," August 21, 1956, Miscellaneous
   Records of the Bureau of Public Affairs, 1944–1962, folder 1953–1957 Films, lot
   60D605, box 58, RG 59, NARA.

36. Streibert to Fox, January 20, 1956, ibid.; "Memo for Mr Lightner, Mr Burris
   from Jean Jerolaman," October 25, 1956, folder 1957 Films, lot 60D605, box
   58, RG 59, NARA. Psychological warfare: Walter Hixson, *Parting the Curtain:
   Propaganda, Culture, and the Cold War, 1945–1961* (New York: St. Martin's
   Press, 1998).

37. RGANI f. 5, op. 36, d. 86, ll. 158–160; RGALI f. 2918, op. 1, d. 80, ll. 74–76;
   ibid., op. 4, d. 279, l. 3; Moscow to State, Telegram no. 1375, November 10,
   1959, 511.615 / 11–1059, box 2176, RG 59, NARA; Moscow to State, Airgram no.
   G-190, November 17, 1959, 511.61 / 11–1759, ibid.

38. RGALI f. 2918, op. 4, d. 284, l. 2.

39. Ibid., op. 4, d. 28, ll. 1a, 2–3, 7, 18.

40. Ibid., op. 5, d. 61, ll. 167–168; Kozovoi, "A Foot in the Door," 8–12; David Caute, *The Dancer Defects: The Struggle for Cultural Supremacy During the Cold War* (Oxford: Oxford University Press, 2003), 231.

41. RGALI f. 2329, op. 15, d. 19, ll. 101–102.

42. RGALI f. 2329, op. 13, d. 80, ll. 14, 17–19.

43. Ibid., ll. 3, 13; RGANI f. 5, op. 36, d. 4, ll. 1–2; *Frantsuzskie kinofil'my v SSSR* (Moscow: Iskusstvo, 1955); *EK 1955* (Moscow: Iskusstvo, 1956), 109–117.

44. RGALI f. 2329, op. 13, d. 80, ll. 5, 11–12.

45. "V neskol'ko strok," *IK* 7 (July 1956): 115–117, here 115; "Vo imia mira i sozidaniia," *IK* 1(January 1956): 3–5, here 4; *Zherar Filip: Vospominaniia, sobrannye Ann Filip* (Leningrad: Iskusstvo, 1962).

46. RGALI f. 2329, op. 13, d. 80, ll. 2, 4.

47. Ibid., ll. 3, 7; ibid., f. 2918, op. 5, d. 5, ll. 119–120.

48. M. L. Zhezhelenko, *Russkie fil'my na mezhdunarodnom ekrane* (St. Petersburg: Rossiiskii institut istorii iskusstv, 1992), 17–22; "Iz istorii Moskovskogo kinofestivalia," June 21, 2007, http://tvkultura.ru/article/show/article_id/43301.

49. Benjamin Martin, *The Nazi-Fascist New Order for European Culture* (Cambridge, MA: Harvard University Press, 2016), 44–73; Marijke de Valck, *Film Festivals: History and Theory of a European Phenomenon That Became a Global Network* (Amsterdam: University of Amsterdam, 2006), 59–60.

50. Heide Fehrenbach, *Cinema in Democratizing Germany: Reconstructing National Identity after Hitler* (Chapel Hill: University of North Carolina Press, 1995), 236–239, 251–252; de Valck, *Film Festivals*, 64–65.

51. RGANI f. 5, op. 36, d. 114, ll. 4–6.

52. Fehrenbach, *Cinema in Democratizing Germany*, 251–252.

53. Ibid., 236, 245–246; Thomas Elsaesser, *European Cinema: Face to Face with Hollywood* (Amsterdam: Amsterdam University Press, 2005), 82–107.

54. Cannes excluded Germany, Spain, and Japan in 1946.

55. Vanessa Schwartz, *It's So French! Hollywood, Paris, and the Making of Cosmopolitan Film Culture* (Chicago: University of Chicago Press, 2007), 57–58, 62–63; Kieron Corless and Chris Drake, *Cannes: Inside the World's Premier Film Festival* (London: Faber & Faber, 2007). Cf.: Victoria de Grazia, *Irresistible Empire: America's Advance through Twentieth-Century Europe* (Cambridge, MA: Harvard University Press, 2005), 284–335.

56. RGALI f. 2923, op. 1, d. 1000, ll. 27–29; Zhezhelenko, *Russkie fil'my*, 41–54.

57. RGALI f. 2329, op. 15, d. 23, ll. 22–23.

58. RGANI f. 5, op. 36, d. 81, l. 29.

59. Sergei Urusevskii, *S kinokameroi i za mol'bertom* (Moscow: Algoritm, 2002), 67–69 (quotation: 69), 71, 73.

60. Neia Zorkaia, "Kann, 1960," *Teatr* 10 (October 1960): 176–183, here 176–177.

61. Grigorii Chukhrai, *Moe kino* (Moscow: Algoritm, 2002), 117–118; L. Pogozheva, "Kann, 1957," *IK* 6 (June 1957): 139–145, here 142.

62. RGALI f. 2923, op. 1, d. 1000, l. 27.

63. Ibid., ll. 26 (quotation), 33.

64. Pogozheva, "Kann," 139; Zorkaia, "Kann," 177.

65. RGALI f. 2923, op. 1, d. 1000, l. 26; Chukhrai, *Moe kino*, 119–120, 135.

66. Chukhrai, *Moe kino*, 135.

67. Chukhrai, *Moe kino*, 135; A. Kalashnikov, "Kann, 1956," *IK* 8 (August 1956): 100–105, here 100, 102; Pogozheva, "Kann," 142; RGALI f. 2923, op. 1, d. 904, l. 11; ibid., d. 783, ll. 19–20.

68. Also: Nikolai Cherkasov, "Segodniashnie volneniia," *IK* 7 (July 1960): 13–20, here 13.

69. Kalashnikov, "Kann," 102. So new and real that Americans noticed: "Communist Bloc Participation at International Film Festivals," December 5, 1960, USIA Office of Research and Analysis, R–82–60, box 3, RG 306, NARA; "The Communist Bloc in International Film Festivals of 1961: A Repeat Performance," March 27, 1962, USIA Office of Research and Analysis, R–27–62, box 7, ibid.; "Communist Bloc Has Another Successful Year in International Film Festivals (1962)," USIA, Research and Reference Service, R–90–63 (C), box 15, ibid.

70. RGALI f. 2923, op. 1, d. 804, ll. 4–6, 17–18.

71. Kalashnikov, "Kann," 103–104.

72. RGALI f. 2923, op. 1, d. 912, ll. 31–35.

73. RGALI f. 2936, op. 1, d. 1324, ll. 90, 96, 1300b, 152, 1820b–184.

74. Ibid., ll. 2, 173.

75. Ibid., l. 19; ibid., d. 1498, ll. 23–24, 28; ibid., d. 1732, ll. 14–16.

76. Some of the last documents on film at the Youth Festival were filed with some of the earliest papers about the Moscow Film Festival: RGALI f. 2329, op. 15, d. 16, ll. 6–7, 70.

77. RGANI f. 5, op. 55, d. 113, l. 125; *Mezhdunarodnyi kinofestival' v Moskve* (Moscow: Iskusstvo, 1959), 13–14; RGALI f. 2936, op. 1, d. 1324, l. 25.

78. RGANI f. 5, op. 36, d. 138, l. 4; RGALI f. 2936, op. 1, d. 1324, l. 9 (quotations).

79. RGALI f. 2936, op. 1, d. 1324, ll. 16, 18–20; ibid., d. 1498, nonpaginated; ibid., d. 1502, l. 4. Lists of participating countries in 1959: ibid., op. 1, d. 1324, ll. 68–71, 86–87; in 1965: RGANI f. 5, op. 36, d. 154, l. 52.

80. Elsaesser, *European Cinema*, 82–107; de Valck, *Film Festivals*, 17–18, 30–31, 36, 70–73, 99–106, 118–131.

81. Sergei Gerasimov, "Neravnodushie khudozhnika," *IK* 10 (October 1959): 10–15; RGANI f. 5, op. 36, d. 154, ll. 54–55, 58; ibid., op. 58, d. 49, ll. 69–70; Kristin Roth-Ey, *Moscow Prime Time: How the Soviet Union Built the Media Empire that Lost the Cultural Cold War* (Ithaca, NY: Cornell University Press, 2011), 26–27.

82. Elsaesser, *European Cinema*, 92–98, 103; de Valck, *Film Festivals*, 16, 27, 34–35, 38–45, 84–88.
83. RGALI f. 2936, op. 1, d. 1502, ll. 2, 4.
84. Prior agreement on allocation of prizes: RGANI f. 5, op. 30, d. 431, l. 108.
85. Chukhrai, *Moe kino*, 149–157.
86. RGALI f. 2936, op. 1, d. 1733, ll. 7–9, 26–33, 49.
87. Ibid., l. 76.
88. Ibid., ll. 64, 73, 79.
89. Ibid., ll. 74–75, 119.
90. Pogozheva, "Kann," 141–142; L. Vagarshian, *Kinopanorama mira: Zametki o Moskovskom mezhdunarodnom kinofestivale* (Erevan: Armgosizdat, 1961), 28–32, esp. 31–32; RGALI f. 2923, op. 1, d. 1000, ll. 5–9.
91. RGALI f. 2936, op. 1, d. 1733, ll. 120–121.
92. Ibid., ll. 78, 80, 82–85, 123–128, 131, 137. Prizes for Kramer: RGALI f. 2944, op. 13, d. 11, ll. 47–48.
93. RGALI f. 2936, op. 1, d. 1733, ll. 148–149.
94. Ibid., l. 161.
95. Ibid., l. 164. A different account of the film festival and the situation around 8½: Caute, *The Dancer Defects*, 235–238.
96. RGALI f. 2936, op. 1, d. 1733, ll. 124–126, 145; rumors: Valerii Rubinchik in "Ia vspominaiu . . . ," *IK* 3 (March 1994): 87–105, here 92.
97. RGALI f. 2944, op. 13, d. 11, l. 46; Chukhrai, *Moe kino*, 156; RGALI f. 2936, op. 1, d. 1747, l. 63.
98. Filmmakers and critics, however, discussed the film in print repeatedly: *Vashe slovo, tovarishch avtor* (Moscow: Iskusstvo, 1965), 49–50, 247–248, 250.
99. RGANI f. 5, op. 36, d. 154, l. 42.
100. Ibid.
101. Ibid., ll. 43–45, 50.
102. RGALI f. 2936, op. 1, d. 1502, l. 39; ibid., d. 1747, ll. 77–78.
103. RGALI f. 2329, op. 15, d. 39, l. 13; ibid., d. 47, ll. 1–2, 6; RGALI f. 2918, op. 4, d. 288, l. 15; ibid., op. 5, d. 61, l. 126; RGALI f. 2936, op. 1, d. 1318, l. 44; ibid., d. 1502, l. 28.
104. RGALI f. 2936, op. 1, d. 1747, l. 4; ibid., d. 1502, l. 6; RGALI f. 2918, op. 4, d. 288, ll. 15, 17–18, 26–38; ibid., d. 28, l. 22; RGANI f. 5, op. 36, d. 154, l. 56.
105. Abé Markus Nornes, *Cinema Babel: Translating Global Cinema* (Minneapolis: University of Minnesota Press, 2007); Antje Ascheid, "Speaking Tongues: Voice Dubbing in the Cinema as Cultural Ventriloquism," *The Velvet Light Trap* 40 (Fall 1997): 32–41; Martine Danan, "Dubbing as an Expression of Nationalism," *Meta* 36:4 (1991): 606–614; Thomas Herbst, "Dubbing and the Dubbed Text—Style and Cohesion: Textual Characteristics of a Special Form of Translation," in *Text Typology and Translation*, ed. Anna Trosborg (Am-

sterdam: John Benjamins Publishing Company, 1997), 291–308. On another option, simultaneous translation at festivals and special screenings: Elena Razlogova, "Listening to the Inaudible Foreign: Simultaneous Translators and Soviet Experience of Foreign Cinema," in *Sound, Speech, Music in Soviet and Post-Soviet Cinema*, ed. Lilya Kaganovsky and Masha Salazkina (Bloomington: Indiana University Press, 2014), 162–178; Idem, "The Politics of Translation at Soviet Film Festivals during the Cold War," *SubStance* 44:2 (2015): 66–87.

106. Ginette Vincendeau, "Hollywood Babel: The Coming of Sound and the Multiple-Language Version," in *"Film Europe" and "Film America": Cinema, Commerce and Cultural Exchange, 1920–1939*, ed. Andrew Higson and Richard Maltby (Exeter: University of Exeter Press, 1999), 207–224; Joseph Garncarz, "Made in Germany: Multiple-Language Versions and the Early German Sound Cinema," in ibid., 249–273; Richard Maltby and Ruth Vasey, "The International Language Problem: European Reactions to Hollywood's Conversion to Sound," in *Hollywood in Europe: Experiences of a Cultural Hegemony*, ed. David Ellwood and Rob Kroes (Amsterdam: VU University Press, 1994), 68–93; Nornes, *Cinema Babel*, 208–209, 227. Varieties of dubbing (including parody and preservation of original soundtrack): ibid., 192–198.

107. *Subtitles: On the Foreignness of Film*, ed. Atom Egoyan and Ian Balfour (Cambridge, MA: MIT Press, 2004); Nornes, *Cinema Babel*, 219–221; Ali Hajmohammadi, "The Viewer as the Focus of Subtitling: Towards a Viewer-oriented Approach," http://translationjournal.net/journal/30subtitling.htm.

108. RGALI f. 2936, op. 1, d. 397, l. 15 (quotation); ibid., d. 452, l. 14; S. Shaikevich, "Zapiski 'aeta,'" *Masterstvo perevoda* 7 (Moscow: Sovetskii pisatel', 1970), 121–149, here 123; G. Zargar'ian, "Iskusstvo perevoda fil'ma," *Masterstvo perevoda* 12 (Moscow: Sovetskii pisatel', 1981), 109–153, here 112–113. Accessibility as infantilization: Nornes, *Cinema Babel*, 189.

109. RGALI f. 2936, op. 1, d. 397, ll. 15–16, 57; ibid., d. 452, l. 14.

110. Ibid., d. 397, ll. 10–12.

111. Ibid., ll. 8, 12, 53; ibid., d. 452, l. 11 (quotation).

112. Ella Shochat and Robert Stam, "The Cinema after Babel: Language, Difference, Power," *Screen* 26:3–4 (1985): 35–58.

113. RGALI f. 2936, op. 1, d. 398, ll. 4–6; RGANI f. 5, op. 36, d. 81, ll. 22–23; Ascheid, "Speaking Tongues," 34.

114. RGALI f. 2329, op. 13, d. 7, l. 90.

115. Example (Scano Boa, dir. Renato Dall'Ara, 1961): RGANI f. 5, op. 36, d. 147, ll. 41–46; RGALI f. 2918, op. 5, d. 113, l. 47.

116. RGANI f. 5, op. 36, d. 129, ll. 145, 204; ibid., d. 82, l. 159; ibid., d. 138, l. 149.

117. Ibid., op. 36, d. 30, l. 181.

118. RGALI f. 2936, op. 1, d. 397, l. 14. Dubbing as monstrosity: Robert Stam, *Subversive Pleasures: Bakhtin, Cultural Criticism and Film* (Baltimore: Johns

Hopkins University Press, 1989), 76; Shochat and Stam, "The Cinema after Babel," 52.

119. A. Andrievskii, *Postroenie tonfil'ma* (Moscow: Gosudarstvennoe izdatel'stvo khudozhestvennoi literatury, 1931), 13, 32. For a different perspective—Soviet filmmakers' discomfort with the illusion of naturalness and their experiments with prioritizing sounds over images—see: Lilya Kaganovsky, *The Voice of Technology: Soviet Cinema's Transition to Sound, 1928–1935* (Bloomington: Indiana University Press, 2018).

120. RGALI f. 2494, op. 1, d. 306, ll. 1a0b–4; Grigorii Aleksandrov, *Epokha i kino* (Moscow: Izdatel'stvo politicheskoi literatury, 1983), 127; Ian Christie, "Making Sense of Early Soviet Sound," in *Inside the Film Factory: New Approaches to Russian and Soviet Cinema*, ed. Richard Taylor and Ian Christie (New York: Routledge, 1991), 178–192.

121. RGALI f. 2494, op. 1, d. 306, ll. 1a0b, 3–4. See also: Natalie Ryabchikova, "ARRK and the Soviet Transition to Sound," in *Sound, Speech, Music*, 81–99, here 90.

122. RGALI f. 2494, op. 1, d. 256, ll. 1a–1a0b, 50b–60b (quotation: 50b).

123. RGALI f. 2936, op. 1, d. 397, ll. 32, 72–73, 75.

124. Ibid., ll. 31–32.

125. Shaikevich, "Zapiski," 130–131, 141. Also: Zoë Pettit, "The Audio-Visual Text: Subtitling and Dubbing Different Genres," *Meta* 49:1 (2004): 25–38; Nornes, *Cinema Babel*, 214–215.

126. RGALI f. 2936, op. 1, d. 397, ll. 28–30; Shaikevich, "Zapiski," 127, 129–130, 137, 139. Also: Herbst, "Dubbing and the Dubbed Text," 292–293; István Fodor, *Film Dubbing: Phonetic, Semiotic, Esthetic and Psychological Aspects* (Hamburg: Helmut Buske, 1976), 11–21; Nornes, *Cinema Babel*, 204.

127. Viktoriia Chaeva, "Menia sogrevaiut vospominaniia," *SE* 25 (June 2004): 6–7 (quotation: 6); Interview with Viktoriia Leonidovna Chaeva, Moscow, August 7, 2004.

128. Shaikevich, "Zapiski," 127; RGALI f. 2936, op. 1, d. 452, l. 16; ibid., d. 397, l. 85; Chaeva interview. Further discussion of the dubbing process: Nornes, *Cinema Babel*, 201–207.

129. RGALI f. 2936, op. 1, d. 453, ll. 13–15.

130. Ibid., ll. 11–12, 36, 56 (quotation); ibid., d. 397, ll. 25–26, 32, 34; ibid., d. 398, l. 38.

131. Ibid., d. 397, l. 4; Evgenii Vesnik, *Dariu, chto pomniu* (Moscow: Vagrius, 1995), 88–89, 203.

132. RGALI f. 2936, op. 1, d. 453, l. 11.

133. Ibid., d. 397, ll. 32, 34–35; ibid., d. 452, l. 37; ibid., d. 398, l. 25 (quotation); Vladimir Troshin, *Moi gody—rossyp' samotsvetov* (Moscow: Veche, 2007), 206. On dubbers' obscurity and prestige: Nornes, *Cinema Babel*, 199–201.

134. RGALI f. 2936, op. 1, d. 397, ll. 22, 53 (quotation); ibid., d. 452, l. 36; ibid., d. 474, l. 10.

135. Ibid., d. 452, ll. 19, 35; ibid., d. 397, l. 65.

136. Ibid., d. 397, ll. 19–20, 74, 76; ibid., d. 398, l. 25; ibid., d. 474, l. 4; *EK* 1958 (Moscow: Iskusstvo, 1960), 310–341.

137. Matvei Geizer, *Zinovii Gerdt* (Moscow: Molodaia gvardiia, 2012), 72–74, 89 (quotation).

138. Geizer, *Zinovii Gerdt*, 89–90; *Ziama—eto zhe Gerdt* (Nizhnii Novgorod: Dekom, 2006), 22–23, 126.

139. Rick Altman, "Moving Lips: Cinema as Ventriloquism," *Yale French Studies* 60 (1980): 67–79; Nornes, *Cinema Babel*, 209. On a puppeteer's intimate relationship with his puppet: N. I. Smirnova, *Teatr Sergeia Obraztsova* (Moscow: Nauka, 1971), 201, 204; Gerdt's treatment of puppets: *Ziama*, 86–87.

140. Smirnova, *Teatr Sergeia Obraztsova*, 266–267.

141. Geizer, *Zinovii Gerdt*, 191–192.

142. *Ziama*, 128–129.

143. *Ziama*, 103.

144. Chaeva interview.

145. Gerdt's poetry reading: Geizer, *Zinovii Gerdt*, 103.

146. Entry under ment52, discussion forum, "V Rossii ee liubili sil'nee, chem v Argentine," http://ngasanova.livejournal.com/534604.html.

147. "V pamiat' o Lolite Torres," http://www.purtov45.narod.ru/.

148. RGALI f. 2936, op. 1, d. 397, ll. 23, 54; ibid., d. 452, l. 35; Troshin, *Moi gody*, 210.

149. RGALI f. 2936, op. 1, d. 397, ll. 21–24, 26–27. On simultaneous translators' claims to artistry: Razlogova, "Listening to the Inaudible Foreign," 163.

150. RGALI f. 2936, op. 1, d. 397, l. 42; Shaikevich, "Zapiski," 125; Chaeva interview.

151. RGALI f. 2936, op. 1, d. 397, l. 21.

152. Ibid., d. 398, l. 23.

153. Ibid., d. 397, l. 27.

154. Ibid., ll. 26, 31, 87; ibid., d. 398, l. 62; Shaikevich, "Zapiski," 126, 135–136.

155. Lawrence Venuti, *The Translator's Invisibility: A History of Translation* (New York: Routledge, 1995).

156. On intimate, unprofessional voice in Soviet cinema and in international context: Oksana Bulgakowa, "Vocal Changes: Marlon Brando, Innokenty Smoktunovsky, and the Sound of the 1950s," in *Sound, Speech, Music*, 145–161.

157. AKG op. 9, d. 36, l. 32; ibid., sv. 223, d. 1901, ll. 95, 113; ibid., sv. 224, d. 1903, l. 60; ibid., d. 1905, ll. 2, 5, 15, 30; ibid., sv. 223a, part II, 4 / 1/ 1958–8 / 29 / 1958, ll. 37, 53; ibid., sv. 223a, 6 / 1957–12 / 15 / 1957, ll. 91, 103; ibid., sv. 223a, d. 6, ll. 3, 6; ibid., d. 5, ll. 34, 39, 47, 63, 75, 78, 83; ibid., d. 4, l. 37.

158. *Global Neorealism: The Transnational History of a Film Style*, ed. Saverio Giovacchini and Robert Sklar (Jackson: University Press of Mississippi, 2012); Inna Solov'eva, *Kino Italii, 1945–1960: Ocherki* (Moscow: Iskusstvo, 1961).

159. R. Khlodovskii, "Problema 'neorealizma,'" *IK* 5 (May 1956): 86–93; P'ero Nelli, "Beseda s Dzavattini," *IK* 2 (February 1958): 149–151; Rentso Rentsi, "Armiia 's'agapo,'" *IK* 5 (May 1959): 125–130; Rodol'fo Sonego, "Prikliucheniia mula i pushki," ibid., 132–138.

160. Korrado Vadiani, "Budet li zhit' ital'ianskoe progressivnoe kino?" *IK* 6 (June 1955): 104–105.

161. "Vechera ital'ianskoi kinematografii," *IK* 1 (January 1954): 123–126, here 124; Khlodovskii, "Problema," 90; "Beseda s Eduardo de Filippo," *IK* 6 (June 1958): 141–142; "Vpechatleniia i plany," ibid., 143. The connection between the Soviet avant-garde and Italian neorealism: Masha Salazkina, "Soviet-Italian Cinematic Exchanges, 1920s–1950s: From Early Soviet Film Theory to Neorealism," in *Global Neorealism*, 37–51.

162. Iu. Glizer and M. Shtraukh, "O tom, chto nam dorogo," *IK* 1 (January 1957): 140–142; A. Chernov, "Interes v Italii k sovetskomu kinoiskusstvu," *IK* 2 (February 1955): 104–105; *Mezhdunarodnyi kinofestival'*, 45; Vagarshian, *Kinopanorama mira*, 9; RGALI f. 2923, op. 1, d. 854, l. 20; Andrei Shemiakin, "Chuzhaia rodnia," in *Kinematograf ottepeli: kniga pervaia* (Moscow: Materik, 1996), 238–261, here 242–243.

163. B. Galanov, "Ital'ianskie fil'my," *LG*, December 12, 1953; A. Room, "Realizm v ital'ianskom iskusstve," *IK* 2 (February 1954): 85–95; A. Gurvich, "Znamenie vremeni (Mysli o finalakh ital'ianskikh fil'mov)," *IK* 4 (April 1955): 101–113; G. D. Bogemskii, *Vittorio de Sika* (Moscow: Iskusstvo, 1963), 42–43, 47, 74–75.

164. Gurvich, "Znamenie vremeni," 104; *Rim, 11 chasov* (Moscow: Iskusstvo, 1958).

165. Roth-Ey, *Moscow Prime Time*, 25–83.

166. Maria Belodubrovskaya, *Not According to Plan: Filmmaking under Stalin* (Ithaca, NY: Cornell University Press, 2017), 23–26, 34–43, 47–51, 114–115.

167. Ibid., 228. Slightly different numbers: M. Romm, "Pered shirokim razvorotom kinoiskusstva i kinoindustrii," *IK* 9 (September 1954): 11–21; A. Dovzhenko, "Pisatel' v kino v svete trebovanii sovremennosti," *IK* 2 (February 1955): 7–14, here 12. See also: Peter Kenez, *Cinema and Soviet Society: From the Revolution to the Death of Stalin* (London: I. B. Tauris, 2001), 187–221.

168. "Rezko uvelichit' vypusk novykh fil'mov!" *IK* 8 (August 1954): 3–6; "Tematicheskii plan proizvodstva khudozhestvennykh fil'mov," *IK* 8 (August 1955): 3–8; "V Ministerstve kul'tury SSSR," ibid., 112–113; I. Rachuk, "Khudozhestvennaia kinematografiia v 1956 godu," *IK* 1 (January 1956): 6–14; "Uvelichenie proizvodstva fil'mov—vazhnaia gosudarstvennaia zadacha," *IK* 2 (February 1956): 3–5; Roth-Ey, *Moscow Prime Time*, 29; Joshua First, *Ukrainian Cinema: Belonging and Identity during the Soviet Thaw* (London: I. B. Tauris, 2015), 21, 46–52, 61.

169. T. Trifonova, "Protiv stilisticheskogo raznoboia," *IK* 9 (September 1956): 3–16, here 16.

170. Belodubrovskaya, *Not According to Plan*, 93–94.

171. Romm, "Pered shirokim razvorotom," 11–12.

172. Pierre Sorlin, *Italian National Cinema, 1896–1996* (London: Routledge, 1996), 69–92; Salazkina, "Soviet-Italian Cinematic Exchanges," 38–46. The issue was discussed in translated essays by Italians: Lorentso Kval'etti, "Obshchii istochnik," *IK* 7 (July 1957): 130–135; Solov'eva, *Kino Italii*, 12.

173. B. Zingerman, "Krugozor neorealizma," *IK* 4 (April 1958): 152–168, here 152.

174. Salazkina, "Soviet-Italian Cinematic Exchanges," 48; First, *Ukrainian Cinema*, 26–27.

175. Romm, "Pered shirokim razvorotom," 13–14 (quotation); Dovzhenko, "Pisatel' v kino," 11–12 (quotation: 11); S. Gerasimov, "Sovetskaia kinodramaturgiia," *IK* 1 (January 1955): 3–31, here 13–15; Yu. Khaniutin, "Tragediia, kotoraia ne rasskazana," *IK* 9 (September 1956): 17–28, here 27–28.

176. Gerasimov, "Sovetskaia kinodramaturgiia," 14; A. Groshev, "Lichnoe i obshchestvennoe," *IK* 9 (September 1954): 27–32, here 28; "Istochnik vdokhno-veniia," *IK* 3 (March 1956): 3–6, here 5; N. Klado, "Chelovekovedenie— glavnaia zadacha iskusstva," *IK* 12 (December 1955): 16–33, here 22; First, *Ukrainian Cinema*, 23–24.

177. Romm, "Pered shirokim razvorotom," 12 (quotation); Dovzhenko, "Pisatel' v kino," 13; M. Papava, "O pisatel'skoi individual'nosti v kino," *IK* 2 (February 1955): 15–20, here 18; M. Biliavskii, "O serosti i posredstvennosti," *IK* 8 (August 1955): 35–45; K. Piotrovskii, "O spetsifike predmeta kino," *IK* 8 (August 1956): 73–86; M. Iof'ev, "Obrazy trebuiut siuzhetov," *IK* 2 (February 1956): 54–58, here 56; Vladimir Semerchuk, "Slova velikie i prostye: kinematograf ottepeli v zerkale kritiki," in *Kinematograf ottepeli: kniga vtoraia* (Moscow: Materik, 2002), 60–84, here 67.

178. Romm, "Pered shirokim razvorotom," 15–16.

179. Klado, "Chelovekovedenie," 18; Iof'ev, "Obrazy trebuiut," 56; I. Vaisfel'd, "Rasstavanie s oshibkami," *IK* 10 (October 1956): 3–16, here 11–12. Love in Stalinist cinema: Oksana Bulgakova, *Sovetskii slukhoglaz: Kino i ego organy chuvstv* (Moscow: Novoe literaturnoe obozrenie, 2010), 174–188, 202; Tat'iana Dashkova, "Liubov' i byt v kinofil'makh 1930-kh—nachala 1950-kh godov," in *Istoriia strany—istoriia kino*, ed. S. Sekirinskii (Moscow: Znak, 2004), 218–234, here 225–229, 232.

180. Dovzhenko, "Pisatel' v kino," 13–14; V. Razumnyi, "Eticheskoe i esteticheskoe," *IK* 4 (April 1959): 125–133.

181. Vitalii Troianovskii, "Chelovek ottepeli (50-e gody)," in *Kinematograf ottepeli: kniga pervaia*, 5–76, here 17–31.

182. Semerchuk, "Slova velikie i prostye," 68.

183. Gerasimov, "Sovetskaia kinodramaturgiia," 20–21, 24; E. Gabrilovich, "Ob elementakh prozy v kinostsenarii," *IK* 5 (May, 1955): 69–80, here 71, 74; idem,

"Rabota nad epizodom," *IK* 1 (January 1956): 93–102, here 98–99; M. Baskin, "Za izuchenie spetsifiki kinoiskusstva," *IK* 2 (February 1955): 66–77, here 72 (referring to the *Encyclopedia*).

184. Gerasimov, "Sovetskaia kinodramaturgiia," 26; Baskin, "Za izuchenie," 72–75; Gabrilovich, "Ob elementakh prozy," 71.

185. An. Vartanov, "K voprosu o spetsifike kino," *IK* 6 (June 1956): 76–88.

186. Gerasimov, "Sovetskaia kinodramaturgiia," 10, 21. On the status of the screenplay as "an independent work of literature," see: Belodubrovskaya, *Not According to Plan*, 155–156, 160–163.

187. Dovzhenko, "Pisatel' v kino," 12 (quotation); Baskin, "Za izuchenie," 72–73 (quotation, citing Dovzhenko: 73); Vartanov, "K voprosu," 85–86; idem, "O prirode kinostsenariia," *IK* 2 (February 1959): 39–56; First, *Ukrainian Cinema*, 41–42.

188. L. Kozlov, "O sintetichnosti kinoiskusstva," *IK* 11 (November 1956): 82–90, here 89 (quotation); M. Smirnova, "Blagorodnaia zadacha stsenarista," *IK* 2 (February 1956): 69–73, here 72.

189. Vartanov, "K voprosu," 85–86; Piotrovskii, "O spetsifike," 83, 85–86; Trifonova, "Protiv stilisticheskogo," 4.

190. Solov'eva, *Kino Italii*, 6.

191. V. Ognev, "O sovremennosti," *IK* 7 (July 1956): 10–20, here 18; Marietta Shaginian, "Neskol'ko angliiskikh fil'mov," *IK* 7 (July 1957): 73–87, here 74, 78.

192. A. Gastev, "Zaplanirovannoe ubi'stvo," *IK* 9 (September 1956): 82–88, here 82–83.

193. Room, "Realizm," 91.

194. Vartanov, "O prirode," 53.

195. Solov'eva, *Kino Italii*, 5; G. Monglovskaia, "Krysha (Novyi fil'm De Sika)," *IK* 2 (February 1956): 101–102; Kalashnikov, "Kann," 102–103; *EK–1958*, 172–173; Bogemskii, *Vittorio de Sika*, 48. Visconti's language: P. Adams Sitney, *Vital Crises in Italian Cinema: Iconography, Stylistics, Politics* (Oxford: Oxford University Press, 2013), 58–61.

196. Vartanov, "O prirode," 53.

197. Gabrilovich, "Rabota," 97.

198. Gastev, "Zaplanirovannoe," 83 (quotation), 87.

199. André Bazin, "In Italy," in *André Bazin and Italian Neorealism*, ed. Bert Cardullo (New York: Continuum, 2013), 117–141. Exception: Mira Liehm, *Passion and Defiance: Film in Italy from 1942 to the Present* (Berkeley: University of California Press, 1984), 60, 64, 78.

200. Semerchuk, "Slova velikie i prostye," 69, 71–72; Shemiakin, "Chuzhaia rodnia," 241.

201. Zingerman, "Krugozor," 155.

202. Solov'eva, *Kino Italii*, 7, 16, 19–20, passim; also: Bogemskii, *Vittorio de Sika*, 48.

203. Zingerman, "Krugozor," 155–156; Solov'eva, *Kino Italii*, 5, 7, 16, 22. Critical discourse on neorealism as a "coded polemic" about Soviet cinema: Salazkina, "Soviet–Italian Cinematic Exchanges," 47.

204. I. Kokoreva, "Po dorogam voiny i mira," *IK* 1 (January 1960): 8–10, here 9.

205. F. Khodzhaev, "My ishchem geroiia," *IK* 1 (January 1959): 56–73, here 58.

206. Josephine Woll, *Real Images: Soviet Cinema and the Thaw* (London: I. B. Tauris, 2000), 79–82.

207. K. Paramonova, "O pravde zhizni nastoiashchei i mnimoi," *IK* 3 (March 1956): 7–22, here 10.

208. "Programma deistvii sovetskogo kinoiskusstva," *IK* 11 (November 1957): 1–14, here 5–6; "O khudozhestvennykh printsipakh, vzgliadakh, vkusakh," *IK* 10 (October 1959): 41–46; Ia. Varshavskii, "Nado razobrat'sia," *IK* 5 (May 1959): 61–65.

209. I. Kokoreva, "Geroi i personazhi," *IK* 11 (November 1957): 53–62, here 54, 56–57 (quotation: 57); D. Pisarevskii, "Izmenit' mir k luchshemu," *IK* 12 (December 1957): 66–77, here 69–71.

210. Aleksandr Zarkhi, "Flazhok Nikolaia Pasechnika," *IK* 6 (June 1957): 70–78, here 72.

211. A. Levada, "O nekotorykh problemakh ukrainskoi kinodramaturgii," *IK* 6 (June 1959): 97–107, here 105; Sergei Vasil'ev, "Pered pod"emom," *IK* 11 (1957): 63–69, here 68; A. Speshnev, "Tvorchestvo kinodramaturga i sovremennost'," *IK* 2 (February 1959): 32–56, here 37; Paramonova, "O pravde," 10 (quotation).

212. So much so that by the early in 1960s, in auteur classics like Marlen Khutsiev's *July Rain* or Georgii Daneliia's *Walking the Streets of Moscow* (*I Walk around Moscow*), narrative ceded to poetry.

213. I. Kokoreva, "Geroi," 53–54, 56–60; N. A. Mikhailov, "Nekotorye voprosy razvitiia sovetskogo kinoiskusstva," *IK* 2 (February 1958): 1–15, here 7; Speshnev, "Tvorchestvo," 34, 37–38; Varshavskii, "Nado razobrat'sia," 65; "O khudozhestvennykh," 45.

214. Solov'eva, *Kino Italii*, 107–109; G. Kozintsev, "Glubokii ekran," *IK* 2 (February 1959): 138–143 (quotations: 141).

215. Zarkhi, "Flazhok," 72–73; Mikhailov, "Nekotorye," 7, 10.

216. Solov'eva, *Kino Italii*, 52; G. Bogemskii, "Planeta Dzavattini," in *Chezare Dzavattini*, ed. idem (Moscow: Iskusstvo, 1982), 5–32, here 13–15.

217. Viktor Demin, *Fil'm bez intrigi* (Moscow: Iskusstvo, 1966). Fellini's subversion of neorealism: Georgii Bogemskii, "V poiskakh cheloveka," in *Federiko Fellini*, ed. idem (Moscow: Iskusstvo, 1968), 9–38, here 11–13. The emergence of "difficult films": First, *Ukrainian Cinema*, 182–186. "Chekhovian" theme: Semerchuk, "Slova velikie i prostye," 66, 70, 77–81.

218. RGALI f. 2923, op. 1, d. 863, ll. 6–9, 26–32, 46.

219. Ibid., d. 786, ll. 19, 23, 25, 27, 30–31; ibid., d. 791, ll. 3, 5, 7–8; ibid., d. 858, ll. 5–7; ibid., d. 859, ll.18–19, 21; ibid., d. 870, passim; ibid., d. 900, passim; ibid., d. 907, passim; ibid., d. 908, passim. Other venues of closed screenings: Donald J. Raleigh, *Soviet Baby Boomers: An Oral History of Russia's Cold War Generation* (Oxford: Oxford University Press, 2012), 159, 191, 210; Razlogova, "Listening to the Inaudible Foreign."

220. RGALI f. 2923, op. 1, d. 786, l. 152; ibid., op. 2, d. 22, l. 12.

221. Ibid., op. 2, d. 4, ll. 26–27.

222. RGALI f. 2329, op. 13, d. 80, l. 31; RGALI f. 2936, op. 1, d. 1747, ll. 56–57.

223. RGALI f. 2923, op. 2, d. 4, ll. 26–27. Also see: Razlogova, "Listening to the Inaudible Foreign," 166, 173.

224. RGALI f. 2923, op. 1, d. 790, l. 9; ibid., op. 2, d. 20, l. 36; ibid., op. 2, d. 22, ll. 6–7, 11–12, 31–33 (quotation: 32); ibid., d. 17, ll. 3–4, 10.

225. Ibid., op. 1, d. 786, ll. 43, 68–69; ibid., d. 792, ll. 20–24; ibid., op. 2, d. 4, ll. 18, 23, 26, 28–30; ibid., d. 9, l. 49; ibid., d. 20, ll. 22, 28, 36; ibid., d. 22, ll. 6–7, 11–12, 32–33.

226. I. Rumanov, "Eshche o reklame," *Kinomekhanik* (November 1955): 8–10; V. Bessonov, "Nekotorye voprosy reklamirovaniia kinofil'mov," *Kinomekhanik* (May 1955): 8–13.

227. Postcard. Dzhina Lollobridzhida (Rostov-na-Donu: Izdanie biuro propagandy soiuza rabotnikov kinematografii SSSR, 1960). See biographies and photographs: *Aktery zarubezhnogo kino* 1 (Moscow: Iskusstvo, 1965); *Aktery zarubezhnogo kino* 2 (Moscow: Iskusstvo, 1965); *Aktery zarubezhnogo kino* 3 (Moscow: Iskusstvo, 1966). Postcard fan culture: Roth-Ey, *Moscow Prime Time*, 111–112.

228. N. Fedukhin, "Na poberezh'e Belogo moria," *Kinomekhanik* (July 1955): 9; A. Zasukha, "Riadovoi kul'turnogo fronta," *Kinomekhanik* (April 1957): 7–8; L. Kishinovskii, "Po taezhnym dorogam," *Kinomekhanik* (February 1957): 8–9; V. Saltykov, "Cherez tundru na sobakakh . . . ," *Kinomekhanik* (February 1957): 10; F. Peshchanskaia, "Po sel'skim dorogam," *Kinomekhanik* (July 1958): 8–10; E. Kapustin, "S kinoperedvizhkoi na mototsikle," ibid., 10; I. Ivanov, "Ee ne ispugali trudnosti," *Kinomekhanik* (September 1959): 4–5.

229. E. Stepanian, "Kol'tsevoe fil'mosnabzhenie v Azerbaidzhanskoi SSR," *Kinomekhanik* (March 1953): 18; "Vyshe uroven' raboty kinoseti," *Kinomekhanik* (February 1953): 1–4, here 2; A. Shaginian, "Za obraztsovoe obsluzhivanie naseleniia," *Kinomekhanik* (December 1958): 15–18, here 17; "Khronika," *Kinomekhanik* (October 1953): 13; "Uluchshim rabotu kinoseti Kirgizii," *Kinomekhanik* (September 1953): 5–7; "Dorozhit' doveriem zritelia," *Kinomekhanik* (November 1955): 1–2; K. Davletdurdyev, "Izzhit' nedostatki v rabote kinoseti Turkmenii," *Kinomekhanik* (March 1957): 15–16; Roth-Ey, *Moscow Prime Time*, 78.

230. M. Shmatko, "Bol'she initsiativy i nastoichivosti," *Kinomekhanik* (September 1953): 14–15; "Sel'skuiu kinoset'—na vysshuiu stupen'," *Kinomekhanik* (August 1953): 1–3; "K novym uspekham kinofikatsii RSFSR," *Kinomekhanik* (April 1958): 10–11.

231. "S chest'iu vypolnit' ukazanie partii!" *Kinomekhanik* (November 1953): 1–3, here 3; "Dorozhit' doveriem"; A. Mikhailov, "Chto im meshaet khorosho rabotat'," *Kinomekhanik* (October 1955): 13–14.

232. V. Poltavtsev, "Strogo reglamentirovat' rabotu sel'skikh kinoustanovok," *Kinomekhanik* (April 1957): 10–11.

233. N. Gontsov, "Novosely blagodariat kinomekhanika," *Kinomekhanik* (October 1955): 3–5.

234. *Kinomekhanik* (June 1959): cover.

235. RGANI f. 5, op. 55, d. 112, ll. 72, 103; ibid., op. 58, d. 49, ll. 1–2.

236. Ibid., op. 55, d. 112, ll. 14, 18–20, 29–30, 51, 55, 102–104, 110; also: ibid., op. 36, d. 146, l. 58; P. Maskin, "Rabotat' po starinke nel'zia," *Kinomekhanik* (August 1959): 13–15; Roth-Ey, *Moscow Prime Time*, 90–91. The origins of this problem: Belodubrovskaya, *Not According to Plan*, 20, 39.

237. RGANI f. 5, op. 55, d. 112, ll. 30, 33, 35; Roth-Ey, *Moscow Prime Time*, 44–45.

238. RGALI f. 2329, op. 12, d. 99, l. 98.

239. See also Roth-Ey, *Moscow Prime Time*, 79–81. My approach assumes the importance of material conditions under which movies were seen and is indebted to: Richard Maltby, "How Can Cinema History Matter More," http://tlweb.latrobe.edu.au/humanities/screeningthepast/22/board-richard-maltby.html; idem, "New Cinema Histories," in *Explorations in New Cinema History: Approaches and Case Studies*, ed. Richard Maltby, Daniel Biltereyst, and Philippe Meers (Chichester, West Sussex: Wiley-Blackwell, 2011), 3–40; Ian Christie, "Introduction: In Search of Audiences," in *Audiences*, ed. idem (Amsterdam: Amsterdam University Press, 2012), 11–21, here 13, 17, 21; Nicholas Hiley, "'At the Picture Palace': the British Cinema Audience, 1895–1920," ibid., 25–34, here 32–33; Martin Baker, "Crossing Out the Audience," ibid., 187–205.

240. RGALI f. 2329, op. 12, d. 48, l. 1310b; ibid., d. 120, l. 10.

241. Ibid., d. 48, l. 1310b; ibid., d. 108, l. 99.

242. Ibid., d. 98, ll. 131–1310b.

243. Ibid., d. 109, l. 410b; ibid., d. 99, l. 1030b; ibid., d. 75, l. 880b.

244. Ibid., d. 48, l. 13.

245. Ibid., d. 63, l. 750b.

246. Ibid., d. 48, l. 1880b.

247. Ibid., ll. 13–130b; Bulgakowa, *Sovetskii slukhoglaz*, 284n439.

248. RGANI f. 5, op. 55, d. 112, l. 106.

249. Ibid., l. 119; Maskin, "Rabotat' po starinke," 13–15.

250. RGALI f. 2329, op. 12, d. 75, l. 1210b; RGANI f. 5, op. 55, d. 112, l. 119; Ia. Rogozhnikov, "Kak ia organizuiu kinoseansy," *Kinomekhanik* (July 1955): 7; "Bol'she zaboty o sel'skikh zriteliakh," *Kinomekhanik* (December 1960): 2–3.

251. RGALI f. 2329, op. 12, d. 120, l. 15 (quotation); ibid., d. 48, l. 190 (quotation); d. 98, ll. 108–1080b; ibid., d. 63, ll. 750b–760b.

252. Ibid., d. 99, l. 150 (quotation); ibid., d. 120, l. 53 (mother of a twelve-year-old boy, writing about teenagers "speaking of love, jealousy, kissing, and not only speaking. To a large degree, cinema is to blame").

253. Ibid., d. 98, l. 7.

254. Ibid., d. 63, l. 76; ibid., d. 120, l. 10; ibid., d. 75, l. 158.

255. Ibid., d. 63, l. 78.

256. Linda Williams, *Screening Sex* (Durham, NC: Duke University Press, 2008), 30–40, 49, 83–84, 87, 113.

257. RGALI f. 2329, op. 12, d. 48, l. 136 (quotation); ibid., d. 108, l. 94; ibid., d. 120, ll. 9–10, 98–99. Also: Williams, *Screening Sex*, 30, 56–57, 126.

258. RGALI f. 2329, op. 12, d. 48, l. 134; ibid., d. 98, l. 131.

259. Bulgakowa, *Sovetskii slukhoglaz*, 174, 185–186; Dashkova, "Liubov' i byt," 227–228, 232; Igor' Kon, *Seksual'naia kul'tura v Rossii: Klubnichka na berezke* (Moscow: OGI, 1997), 145–146, 150–151, 164–165.

260. RGALI f. 2329, op. 12, d. 108, l. 36.

261. Ibid., d. 98, ll. 7, 1080b, 131.

262. "Kinozritel' o fil'makh," *IK* 12 (December 1956): 95–99, here 95.

263. RGALI f. 2329, op. 12, d. 48, l. 135. Cinema as an illusion of voyeurism: Laura Mulvey, "Visual Pleasure and Narrative Cinema," in idem, *Visual and Other Pleasures* (Bloomington: Indiana University Press, 1989), 16–17.

264. "Chuzhaia manera," *Izvestiia*, July 30, 1960.

265. RGALI f. 2329, op. 12, d. 99, ll. 96, 98.

266. Ibid., d. 98, ll. 1080b, 131–1310b.

267. Ibid., d. 48, ll. 13–130b (quotations), 131–1310b; ibid., d. 98, l. 1080b.

268. Ibid., d. 48, l. 190 (quotation); ibid., d. 98, l. 131; ibid., d. 75, ll. 88–880b.

269. Ibid., d. 63, ll. 4 (quotation), 76; ibid., d. 48, l. 69. French comparisons: ibid., d. 109, l. 410b. Education vs commerce: ibid., d. 75, l. 1210b.

270. Ibid., d. 75, ll. 119–122.

271. Ibid., d. 121, l. 18.

272. Ibid., d. 48, ll. 188–1880b; ibid., d. 121, l. 18.

273. RGALI f. 2732, op. 1, d. 1066, ll. 53–550b.

274. Ibid., d. 1070, ll. 51–520b; ibid., d. 1125, ll. 20–200b (quotations).

275. RGALI f. 2329, op. 12, d. 75, ll. 121, 122.

276. Ibid., d. 98, ll. 108–1080b; "foreign shots": ibid., d. 48, l. 130b.

277. Ibid., d. 120, l. 10.

278. Ibid., d. 75, l. 88; ibid., d. 63, ll.750b–760b, 86–87.

279. Leach, *I Know It When I See It*, 15–26, 33.

280. A similar, but more essentializing argument: Semen Golod, "Karnaval'nost' liubvi i orgiinost' seksa," *Rubezh (al'manakh sotsial'nykh issledovanii)* 5 (1994): 142–158, here 149–150.

281. Alexander Prokhorov, *Unasledovannyi diskurs: Paradigmy stalinskoi kul'tury v literature i kinematografe "ottepeli"* (St. Petersburg: Akademicheskii proekt Izdatel'stvo DNK, 2007).

282. Kon, *Seksual'naia kul'tura*, 146–147, 171–201.

283. Williams, *Screening Sex*; Leach, *I Know It When I See It*, 116 (quotation); Barry Forshaw, *Sex and Film: The Erotic in British, American, and World Cinema* (New York: Palgrave Macmillan, 2015), 15–25, 98–100, passim; Doherty, *Hollywood's Censor*, 282; Jon Lewis, *Hollywood v. Hard Core: How the Struggle over Censorship Saved the Modern Film Industry* (New York: New York University Press, 2000), 105–127; Stephen Tropiano, *Obscene, Indecent, Immoral, and Offensive: 100+ Years of Censored, Banned, and Controversial Films* (New York: Limelight Editions, 2009), 90–96.

284. Williams, *Screening Sex*, 68–69, 73 (quotation), 89; Doherty, *Hollywood's Censor*, 271–277; Forshaw, *Sex and Film*, 19–21, 62–70; Leach, *I Know It When I See It*, 37–38; Geoffrey Nowell-Smith, *Making Waves: New Cinemas of the 1960s* (New York: Bloomsbury Academics, 2013), 60, 62.

285. Doherty, *Hollywood's Censor*, 275–276 (quotation: 276), 282; Leach, *I Know It When I See It*, 34, 40, 103–104; Lewis, *Hollywood v. Hard Core*, 98–102.

286. Forshaw, *Sex and Film*, 86–87; Williams, *Screening Sex*, 114; Leach, *I Know It When I See It*, 116–117; Lewis, *Hollywood v. Hard Core*, 90–91, 129–133, 241–243; Tropiano, *Obscene, Indecent*, 204–205. For release in Britain, *The Lovers* was excised: Nowell-Smith, *Making Waves*, 60.

287. Williams, *Screening Sex*, 73, 158.

288. The pill: Natal'ia Lebina, *Muzhchina i zhenshchina: Telo, moda, kul'tura. SSSR—ottepel'.* (Moscow: Novoe literaturnoe obozrenie, 2017), 78–79.

5. Barbarians in the Temple of Art

1. Jan Plamper, "Abolishing Ambiguity: Soviet Censorship Practices in the 1930s," *Russian Review* 60:4 (October 2001): 526–544.

2. Susan E. Reid, "Destalinization and the Remodernization of Soviet Art: The Search for a Contemporary Realism, 1953–1963." (PhD diss., University of Pennsylvania, 1996), 34–38, 43, 75, 109–110, 130–132, 168–169, 223–224, 231–232.

3. Also: Susan E. Reid, "Toward a New (Socialist) Realism: the Re-engagement with Western Modernism in the Khrushchev Thaw," in *Russian Art and the West: A Century of Dialogue in Painting, Architecture, and the Decorative Arts*, ed. Susan E. Reid and Rosalind P. Blakesley (DeKalb: Northern Illinois University Press, 2007), 217–235; Stephen Bittner, *The Many Lives of*

Khrushchev's Thaw: Experience and Memory in Moscow's Arbat (Ithaca, NY: Cornell University Press, 2008), 3, passim.

4. James Elkins, *Pictures & Tears: A History of People Who Have Cried in Front of Paintings* (New York: Routledge, 2001).

5. On this source, see Appendix.

6. Molly Brunson, *Russian Realisms: Literature and Painting, 1840–1890* (DeKalb: Northern Illinois University Press, 2016), 2–25, 32–57, 128–145.

7. Boris Groys, *The Total Art of Stalinism: Avant-garde, Aesthetic Dictatorship, and Beyond* (Princeton, NJ: Princeton University Press, 1992).

8. A. I. Morozov, *Konets utopii. Iz istorii iskusstva v SSSR 1930-kh godov* (Moscow: GALART, 1995).

9. Nataliia Semenova, *Moskovskie kollektsionery* (Moscow: Molodaia gvardiia, 2010), 29–34, 47–52, 68–72, 81–103, 163–165, 204–208, 218–220.

10. N. V. Iavorskaia, *Istoriia gosudarstvennogo muzeia novogo zapadnogo iskusstva. Moskva, 1918–1948* (Moscow: GMII im. A. S. Pushkina, 2012), 23–141; Al'bert Kostenevich, "Russkie sobirateli frantsuzskoi zhivopisi," in *Morozov i Shchukin—russkie kollektsionery. Ot Mone do Pikasso* (Cologne: DuMont, 1993); Semenova, *Moskovskie kollektsionery*, 126–128, 130, 225–230.

11. Iavorskaia, *Istoriia gosudarstvennogo muzeia*, 163–254, 333–371.

12. Ibid., 422–426.

13. RGALI f. 652, op. 13, d. 1020, ll. 1–8.

14. AGMII f. 5, op. 3, d. 269, ll. 23, 24 (quotation); ibid., d. 224, l. 1; RGALI f. 2329, op. 4, d. 1406, l. 30 (quotation); ibid., f. 2458, op. 2, d. 1339, ll. 12, 44, 45, 46 (quotation).

15. RGALI f. 2458, op. 2, d. 1344, l. 81; ibid., d. 1336, l. 120.

16. AGMII f. 5, op. 3, d. 224, l. 10b.

17. Elkins, *Pictures & Tears*, 15–19; AGMII f. 5, op. 3, d. 306, ll. 28, 95, 103.

18. RGALI f. 2458, op. 2, d. 1336, l. 97 (quotation); ibid., d. 1339, ll. 46, 146 (quotation); ibid., d. 1341, ll. 160, 167; ibid., d. 1344, ll. 32, 52.

19. AGMII f. 5, op. 3, d. 216, ll. 380b–39.

20. Ibid., ll. 100b (quotation), 12, 14, 37–370b (quotation); ibid., d. 239, l. 4 (quotation); ibid., d. 219, l. 21.

21. Susan E. Reid, "The Exhibition Art of Socialist Countries, Moscow 1958–9, and the Contemporary Style of Painting," in *Style and Socialism: Modernity and Material Culture in Post-War Eastern Europe*, eds. Susan E. Reid and David Crowley (Oxford: Berg, 2000), 101–132, here 117; idem, "In the Name of the People: The Manège Affair Revisited," *Kritika: Explorations in Russian and Eurasian History* 6:4 (2005): 673–716, here 670, 708.

22. RGALI f. 2458, op. 2, d. 1336, l. 48 (quotation); ibid., d. 1339, l. 145 (quotation); ibid., d. 1341, ll. 181, 189; ibid., d. 1359, l. 1; AGMII f. 5, op. 3, d. 227, ll. 170b–18, 340b.

23. RGALI f. 1204, op. 2, d. 2608, l. 1260b; ibid., d. 2614, l. 61; ibid., d. 2615, l. 114; ibid., d. 2616, l. 89.

24. RGALI f. 2458, op. 2, d. 521, l. 21; ibid., d. 1336, l. 113; ibid., d. 1337, l. 37; AGMII f. 5, op. 3, d. 227, l. 13. Also: Reid, "Destalinization and the Remodernization of Soviet Art," 265–266.

25. V. N. Lazarev, "Protiv fal'sifikatsii istorii kul'tury Vozrozhdeniia"; M. V. Alpatov, "V zashchitu Vozrozhdeniia (Protiv teorii burzhuaznogo iskusstvoznaniia)"; V. S. Kemenov, "Protiv reaktsionnogo burzhuaznogo iskusstva i iskusstvoznaniia," all in *Protiv burzhuaznogo iskusstva i iskusstvoznaniia. Sbornik statei*, ed. I. E. Grabar' and V. S. Kemenov (Moscow: Izdatel'stvo Akademii nauk SSSR, 1951). The politics of Renaissance scholarship and "the battle for the Renaissance": M. A. Gukovskii, "Rozhdenie i gibel' ital'ianskogo Vozrozhdeniia (o novoi literature po voprosu o sushchnosti i khronologicheskikh ramkakh Vozrozhdeniia)," in *Zapadnoevropeiskoe iskusstvo. Trudy Gosudarstvennogo Ermitazha* (Leningrad: Sovetskii khudozhnik, 1964), 8: 5–22.

26. AGMII f. 5, op. 3, d. 216, l. 190b; ibid., d. 227, ll. 13, 24–25; ibid., d. 260, l. 490b; RGALI f. 1204, op. 2, d. 2616, ll. 50b–70b.

27. RGALI f. 2458, op. 2, d. 1341, l. 53; ibid., d. 1339, ll. 28, 35, 102; AGMII f. 5, op. 3, d. 227, ll. 6, 190b; ibid., d. 260, l. 490b; ibid., d. 306, l. 3.

28. RGALI f. 2458, op. 2, d. 1344, l. 21; ibid., d. 1359, l. 11.

29. Ibid., d. 1341, ll. 51, 154, 162; ibid., d. 1339, ll. 32, 96, 102; ibid., d. 1359, l. 40b.

30. AGMII f. 5, op. 3, d. 227, ll. 30b, 5 (quotation); ibid., d. 306, ll. 93, 94 (quotation).

31. Ibid., d. 224, ll. 3–30b (quotation); RGALI f. 2458, op. 2, d. 1341, ll. 75 (quotation), 82, 84; ibid., d. 1339, ll. 27, 31–32, 35–36, 38, 141; ibid., d. 1344, ll. 23–24, 35, 56; ibid., f. 2329, op. 4, d. 1406, l. 11.

32. Harry Freeman, "Dzhekson i Dzhek," *Izvestiia*, January 26, 1963; F. P. Reshetnikov, *Tainy abstraktsionizma. Risunki avtora* (Moscow: Izdatel'stvo Akademii khudozhestv SSSR, 1963).

33. RGALI f. 2458, op. 2, d. 1336, ll. 31, 35.

34. Ibid., d. 1341, l. 188.

35. Ibid., ll. 42, 175; ibid., d. 1339, ll. 48, 102, 131, 138; RGALI f. 1204, op. 2, d. 2645, l. 103; RGALI f. 2329, op. 4, d. 1406, l. 27.

36. For the understanding of art as craftsmanship in other contexts, see: Dario Gamboni, *The Destruction of Art: Iconoclasm and Vandalism since the French Revolution* (London: Reaktion Books, 1997), 173–175.

37. Also: Elkins, *Pictures & Tears*, 66–69.

38. RGALI f. 2458, op. 2, d. 1339, ll. 30 (quotation), 34–36, 139–140.

39. Ibid., ll. 29, 134; ibid., d. 1341, ll. 54, 170; ibid., d. 1344, ll. 22, 37; AGMII f. 5, op. 3, d. 269, l. 300b; ibid., d. 306, ll. 26, 430b.

40. RGALI f. 2458, op. 2, d. 1341, ll. 52, 70, 80 (quotation), 155; ibid., d. 1339, ll. 97, 131 (quotation); ibid., d. 1337, ll. 13, 33; ibid., d. 1344, l. 69. Compare: Elkins, *Pictures & Tears*, 42–46.

41. RGALI f. 2458, op. 2, d. 1341, ll. 84, 152, 162, 164, 174; ibid., d. 1339, ll. 29, 32, 102, 130, 138 (quotation); ibid., d. 1344, ll. 14, 27, 44, 65, 72, 77; ibid., d. 1337, ll. 14, 17, 31; ibid., f. 2329, op. 4, d. 1406, ll. 8, 29.

42. RGALI f. 2458, op. 2, d. 1336, ll. 21, 75, 95, 110; ibid., d. 1344, ll. 31, 57, 73.

43. AGMII f. 5, op. 3, d. 269, nonpaginated insert after l. 300b; ibid., d. 278, l. 41; RGALI f. 2458, op. 2, d. 1336, ll. 71, 85, 115; ibid., d. 1339, ll. 35, 145; ibid., d. 1344, ll. 61, 71.

44. RGALI f. 2458, op. 2, d. 1336, ll. 41 (quotation), 96.

45. Reid, "In the Name of the People," 687–688, 690, 708. Viewers' explanations: AGMII f. 5, op. 3, d. 224, l. 7; ibid., d. 227, ll. 4, 7, 140b, 22, 300b–31; ibid., d. 278, l. 390b; ibid., d. 306, ll. 101–102; RGALI f. 1204, op. 2, d. 2603, l. 46; ibid., d. 2604, ll. 1860b–187; ibid., d. 2616, ll. 40b–5; ibid., f. 2329, op. 4, d. 1406, ll. 10b, 15.

46. Belinda Thomson, *Impressionism: Origins, Practice, Reception* (London: Thames & Hudson, 2000), 59, 124–129; George Heard Hamilton, *Manet and His Critics* (New York: W. W. Norton, 1969), 38–48, 67, 72–75, 125, 131–132, 139.

47. Olaf Peters, "From Nordau to Hitler: 'Degeneration' and Anti-Modernism between the Fin-de-siècle and the National Socialist Takeover of Power," in *Degenerate Art: The Attack on Modern Art in Nazi Germany, 1937*, ed. Olaf Peters (Munich: Prestel, 2014), 16–35.

48. On Cold War antimodernism, specifically among US government officials and congressmen: Jane de Hart Mathews, "Art and Politics in Cold War America," *American Historical Review* 81: 4 (October 1976): 762–787; Gamboni, *The Destruction of Art*, 135–137, 144–146, 173–179, 184–192, 207–211.

49. Sovietness and *kul'turnost'*: Sheila Fitzpatrick, "Becoming Cultured: Socialist Realism and the Representation of Privilege and Taste," in *The Cultural Front: Power and Culture in Revolutionary Russia* (Ithaca, NY: Cornell University Press, 1992), 216–237.

50. RGALI f. 2458, op. 2, d. 1336, ll. 27, 47, 91; ibid., d. 1337, ll. 15, 18; ibid., d. 1341, l. 179; AGMII f. 5, op. 3, d. 239, ll. 20b, 160b; ibid., d. 260, l. 50.

51. Svetlana Boym, *Common Places: Mythologies of Everyday Life in Russia* (Cambridge, MA: Harvard University Press, 1994), 29–103.

52. RGALI f. 2329, op. 4, d. 1406, l. 21; ibid., f. 2458, op. 2, d. 521, l. 99; ibid., d. 1336, l. 111; ibid., d. 1339, ll. 23, 30; ibid., d. 1341, ll. 51–52, 155; ibid., d. 1344, l. 56; ibid., d. 1364, l. 90b.

53. "Temple der Kunst": Kenneth Hudson, *Museums of Influence* (Cambridge: Cambridge University Press, 1987), 43–47; Stephen Weil, *A Cabinet of Curiosities: Inquiries into Museums and Their Prospects* (Washington, DC: Smithsonian Institution Press, 1995), 3–17, here 7.

54. Michael Levin, *The Modern Museum: Temple or Showroom* (Jerusalem: Dvir Publishing House, 1983), 33–41; James Sheehan, *Museums in the German Art World: From the End of the Old Regime to the Rise of Modernism* (Oxford: Oxford University Press, 2000), 98–137; Ingrid Steffensen-Bruce, *Marble Palaces, Temples of Art: Art Museums, Architecture, and American Culture, 1890–1930* (Lewisburg, PA: Bucknell University Press, 1998), 16–46.

55. Bénédicte Savoy and Sabine Skott, "A European Museum-Cocktail around 1900: The Pushkin State Museum of Fine Arts in Moscow," in *The Museum is Open: Towards a Transnational History of Museums, 1750–1940*, ed. Bénédicte Savoy and Andrea Meyer (Berlin: De Gruyter, 2014), 77–88.

56. Museum and worship: Colleen Denney, *At the Temple of Art: The Grosvenor Gallery, 1877–1890* (Madison, NJ: Fairleigh Dickinson University Press, 2000).

57. RGALI f. 2458, op. 2, d. 1359, l. 17; ibid., d. 1344, l. 36; AGMII f. 5, op. 3, d. 260, ll. unpaginated between 13 and 12 (*sic*), 48 (quotation); ibid., d. 227, ll. 6, 32 (quotation); ibid., d. 306, l. 12 (quotation).

58. RGALI f. 2458, op. 2, d. 1339, ll. 26, 48, 51, 137; ibid., d. 1359, l. 110b; AGMII f. 5, op. 3, d. 227, l. 32; ibid., d. 260, l. 48; ibid., d. 321, ll. 14–140b; ibid., d. 306, ll. 12, 58, 66, 71, 74, 78–79.

59. RGALI f. 2458, op. 2, d. 1336, ll. 51, 57 (quotation), 65, 92; ibid., d. 1341, l. 157; Vladislav Zubok, *Zhivago's Children: The Last Russian Intelligentsia* (Cambridge, MA: Harvard University Press, 2011), 95–96.

60. An analysis of the social composition of comment writers (1955–1966) does not reveal a strong correlation between aesthetic preferences and education or occupation. For a different view: Reid, "In the Name of the People," 692, 701, 715.

61. RGALI f. 2458, op. 2, d. 1336, ll. 4, 35, 42, 84, 111; ibid., d. 1341, ll. 156, 173; ibid., d. 1339, ll. 49, 129; ibid., d. 1344, ll. 29, 46; ibid., d. 1359, l. 11.

62. Ibid., d. 1336, ll. 48, 50, 90; ibid., d. 1339, l. 56; AGMII f. 5, op. 3, d. 278, l. 390b.

63. RGALI f. 2329, op. 4, d. 1406, l. 12; ibid., f. 2458, op. 2, d. 1336, ll. 51, 68, 88; ibid., d. 1337, ll. 32, 36, 61; AGMII f. 5, op. 3, d. 306, l. 42.

64. RGALI f. 2329, op. 4, d. 1406, l. 90b; ibid., f. 2458, op. 2, d. 1336, ll. 2, 3, 17, 59, 76, 79, 87; ibid., d. 1337, ll. 33, 36; ibid., d. 1339, ll. 28, 132; ibid., d. 1341, ll. 172, 174, 175; ibid., d. 1344, ll. 16, 33, 45, 56.

65. Besides Russian realist paintings, Tretyakov sought out portraits of great Russian artists and writers, creating a gallery that embodied Russian culture. I. S. Nenarokomova, *Pavel Tret'iakov i ego galereia* (Moscow: "Galart," 1994), 31–32, 83–96; "P. M. Tret'iakov i ego sobiratel'skaia deiatel'nost'," in *Gosudarst vennaia Tret'iakovskaia galereia. Ocherki istorii, 1856–1917* (Leningrad: Khudozhnik RSFSR, 1981), 67–68, 101–102; Anna Fedorets, *Tret'iakov* (Moscow: Veche, 2011), 227, 229, 231, 242, 245–254, 275–281, 303–306, 309–316.

66. RGALI f. 2458, op. 2, d. 1336, l. 26 (1st quotation); ibid., d. 1341, l. 170 (2nd quotation).

67. Brunson, *Russian Realisms*, 21–25.

68. "Sumbur vmesto muzyki," *Pravda*, January 23, 1936; Leonid Maksimenkov, *Sumbur vmesto muzyki. Stalinskaia kul'turnaia revoliutsiia, 1936–1938* (Moscow: Iuridicheskaia kniga, 1997), 223–231; Leonid Heller, "A World of Prettiness: Socialist Realism and Its Aesthetic Categories," in *Socialist Realism without Shores*, ed. Thomas Lahusen and Evgeny Dobrenko (Durham, NC: Duke University Press, 1997), 51–75; Reid, "Destalinization and the Remodernization of Soviet Art," 80–83, 94–97.

69. Morozov, *Konets utopii*, 39–47.

70. N. V. Iavorskaia, "Problema impressionizma v sovetskom iskusstvoznanii i khudozhestvennoi kritike poslednikh desiatiletii," in *Iz istorii sovetskogo iskusstvoznaniia: o frantsuzskom iskusstve XIX–XX vekov* (Moscow: Sovetskii khudozhnik, 1987), 65.

71. A. Zotov, "Za preodolenie perezhitkov impressionizma," *Iskusstvo* 1 (January–February, 1950): 75–80, here 77, 90–91; idem, "Impressionizm kak reaktsionnoe napravlenie v burzhuaznom iskusstve," *Iskusstvo* 1 (January–February, 1949): 86–91, here 90; B. Ioganson, "Zametki o masterstve," *Iskusstvo* 1 (1949): 39–43. Plein air in socialist realism: Alison Hilton, "Holiday on the Kolkhoz: Socialist Realism's Dialogue with Impressionism," in *Russian Art and the West*, 205–208.

72. Zotov, "Za preodolenie"; N. Sokolova, "Za boevuiu partiinuiu kritiku," *Iskusstvo* 6 (1948): 75–78, here 76.

73. P. Sysoev, "Bor'ba za sotsialisticheskii realizm v sovetskom izobrazitel'nom iskusstve," *Iskusstvo* 1 (January–February 1949): 5–28; Zotov, "Impressionizm."

74. *Zhivopis' impressionistov. K 100-letiiu pervoi vystavki 1874 goda* (Leningrad: Avrora, 1974), 6.

75. *Frantsuzskaia zhivopis' kontsa XIX–nachala XX veka v sobranii Gosudarstvennogo muzeia izobrazitel'nykh iskusstv imeni A. S. Pushkina* (Leningrad: Avrora, 1970).

76. A. Pavlov, "Novaia ekspozitsiia Muzeia izobrazitel'nykh iskusstv imeni A. S. Pushkina," *Iskusstvo* 3 (May–June 1954): 70–76.

77. Soviet exhibition: November 14, 1955 to March 4, 1956; exhibition on loan from French museums: August 18, 1956 to September 25, 1956 in Moscow; October 12, 1956 to November 15, 1956 in Leningrad. *Vystavka frantsuzskogo iskusstva, XV–XX vv. Katalog* (Moscow: Iskusstvo, 1955), 15–16 (quotation).

78. RGALI f. 2329, op. 8, d. 364, ll. 139, 141.

79. AGMII f. 5, op. 3, d. 219, ll. 1–7.

80. RGALI f. 652, op. 13, d. 1002, ll. 1–7.

81. Ilya Ehrenburg, "Impressionisty," in *Sobranie sochinenii* (hereafter *Ss*) (Moscow: Khudozhestvennaia literatura, 1996), 6: 151–180.

82. Idem, *Liudi, gody, zhizn'* (hereafter LGZh), in *Ss*, 6: 397–401. Inventories and literary impressionism: Jessica Haigney, *Walt Whitman and the French*

Impressionists: A Study of Analogies (Lewiston, NY: Edwin Mellen Press, 1990), 37–38, 40, 67.

83. Ilya Ehrenburg, "Pablo Pikasso," in *Ss*, 6: 181–192, here 187.

84. Idem., *Frantsuzskie tetradi: zametki i perevody* (Moscow: Sovetskii pisatel', 1958, 1959); idem, "Impressionisty," 151.

85. Idem, "Impressionisty," 154, 180.

86. Ibid., 163, 165.

87. Ibid., 164–165.

88. Ibid., 174–176.

89. Offense: Nikolai Vladimirovich Eremchenko interview recording, March 13, 2003, tape no. 5, TsAADM; *Pochta Il'i Erenburga: Ia slyshu vse . . . 1916–1967* (Moscow: AGRAF, 2006), 618.

90. Ehrenburg, "Impressionisty," 177.

91. Ibid., 155, 168.

92. GARF f. 6903, op. 15, chast' 3, d. 329 (March 19–21, 1960).

93. RGALI f. 1204, op. 2, d. 2614, l. 62.

94. Ibid., d. 2616, ll. 105, 114, 131.

95. Ibid., l. 111.

96. Ibid., ll. 106–107 (quotation), 127–127ob; ibid., d. 2617, ll. 95–97.

97. Ibid., d. 2616, ll. 124, 135ob, 145; ibid., d. 2617, ll. 17, 38, 101, 110; ibid., d. 2610, l. 125ob; ibid., d. 2611, l. 26.

98. Ibid., d. 2616, l. 135.

99. Ibid., d. 2617, ll. 116–116ob (quotation); ibid., d. 2601, l. 105; ibid., d. 2617, l. 2. According to contemporary sociological research, among the five factors of gender, age, profession, education, and place of residence, the latter made for the greatest difference in patterns of museum visitation. B. A. Grushin, *Chetyre zhizni Rossii v zerkale oprosov obshchestvennogo mneniia. Epokha Khrushcheva* (Moscow: Progress-Traditsiia, 2001), 455, 480–481.

100. RGALI f. 2329, op. 18, d. 168, ll. 40–41; RGALI f. 1204, op. 2, d. 2614, ll. 100–100ob.

101. RGALI f. 1204, op. 2, d. 2645, ll. 59ob–60.

102. Ibid., d. 2617, l. 2 (quotation); ibid., d. 2616, l. 128.

103. Benjamin Tromly, *Making the Soviet Intelligentsia: Universities and Intellectual Life under Stalin and Khrushchev* (Cambridge: Cambridge University Press, 2014), 53–76, 159–186.

104. RGALI f. 1204, op. 2, d. 2610, l. 96 (quotation); ibid., d. 2614, l. 167.

105. Ibid., d. 2616, l. 137 (quotation); ibid., d. 2650, l. 113; ibid., d. 2643, l. 106.

106. Ibid., d. 2617, l. 20; ibid., d. 2614, l. 163; ibid., d. 2616, l. 116.

107. Ibid., d. 2617, l. 6.

108. Venturi was published in Russian in 1958; John Rewald in 1959: RGALI f. 652, op. 12, d. 37, ll. 5–7.

109. RGALI f. 1204, op. 2, d. 2616, ll. 89–89ob.

110. Ibid., ll. 111–1120b.

111. Ibid., d. 2617, l. 98.

112. See Chapter 1.

113. RGALI f. 1204, op. 2, d. 2643, ll. 42–420b.

114. Jonathan Crary, *Techniques of the Observer: On Vision and Modernity in the Nineteenth Century* (Cambridge, MA: MIT Press, 1992), 3–4, 9, 14, 19–20, 24, 50–74, 91–92, 95; idem, *Suspensions of Perception: Attention, Spectacle, and Modern Culture* (Cambridge, MA: MIT Press, 2001), 83–88, 94–97; Haigney, *Walt Whitman and the French Impressionists*, 96–98.

115. Kent Papers, reel 5242, frames 41–43.

116. Kent to the Jones, October 1, 1960, ibid., reel 5185, frames 1119–1120; Kent to Paul [Bjarnason?], October 17, 1960, ibid., frames 1131–1132; Kent to Lawson, October 5, 1959, ibid., reel 5207, frame 275.

117. Sybil Gordon Kantor, *Alfred H. Barr, Jr. and the Intellectual Origins of the Museum of Modern Art* (Cambridge, MA: MIT Press, 2002), 6.

118. Moscow to State, Telegram 2661, May 26, 1956, 511.613 / 5–2656, box 2179, RG 59, NARA; Moscow to State, Telegram 2715, June 2, 1956, 511.613 / 6–256, ibid.

119. RGALI f. 2329, op 8, d. 567, ll. 65–82.

120. Ibid., d. 327, l. 99; RGALI f. 2458, op. 2, d. 654, l. 8; ibid., d. 663, l. 12.

121. RGALI f. 2329, op. 8, d. 567, ll. 66, 82–86.

122. Merrill to White, December 19, 1956, Museum of Modern Art 1233.8, Bureau of European Affairs, entry 5287, RG 59, NARA. The State Department was in the midst of its own negotiations for exchange of exhibitions; these were suspended when Soviet troops entered Budapest. Suspension of exchanges: Moscow to State, Telegram 1076, November 5, 1956, 861.191-MO / 11–556, box 4725, 1955–1959 CDF, RG 59, NARA; State to Moscow, Telegram 573, November 9, 1956, 861.191-MO / 11–556, ibid.; Memorandum, November 20, 1956, 861.191-MO / 11–2056, ibid. Temporary nature of suspension: State to Moscow, Telegram 1245, May 24, 1957, 861.191-MO / 5–2457, ibid.; Moscow to State, Telegram 2600, May 25, 1957, 861.191-MO / 5–2557, ibid.

123. RGALI f. 2329, op. 8, d. 564, ll. 58–62.

124. Ibid., ll. 60–61. Also: "Meeting of Soviet and US Art Experts at the Museum of Modern Art," November 3, 1956, Museum of Modern Art 1233.8, Bureau of European Affairs, entry 5287, RG 59, NARA.

125. Moscow to State, Telegram 745, "Embassy Recommendations for US Exhibition in Moscow, 1959," October 3, 1958, 861.191-MO/10-358, box 4725, RG 59, NARA (quotation); Thompson to Herter, January 19, 1959, 511.612/1-1959, box 2178, ibid.; "Policy Guidance for the US Exhibit in Moscow in 1959," 511.61/9-1558, box 2175, ibid.; Soviet loss of control: GARF f. 9518, op. 1, d.621, l. 140.

126. "Meeting of Soviet and US Art Experts."

127. Bingham to Roderick, June 30, 1959, Moscow Show Correspondence, G-1098, box 62, RU321, SIA (quotations); "Excerpts from an Address by George V. Allen," August 13, 1959, Bureau of Cultural Affairs, box 24, RG 59, NARA. Also: Marilyn Kushner, "Exhibiting Art at the American National Exhibition in Moscow, 1959," *Journal of Cold War Studies* 4:1 (2002): 6–26; Greg Barnhisel, *Cold War Modernists: Art, Literature, and American Cultural Diplomacy* (New York: Columbia University Press, 2015), 86–91.

128. Helen M. Franc, "The Early Years of the International Program and Council," in *The Museum of Modern Art at Mid-Century, At Home and Abroad*, ed. John Elderfield (New York: The Museum of Modern Art, 1994), 109–149, here 118–120, 125–127, 129; Barnhisel, *Cold War Modernists*, 25–28, 39–42, 47, 53, 57–58, 80–82; Nancy Jachec, *The Philosophy and Politics of Abstract Expressionism, 1940–1960* (Cambridge: Cambridge University Press, 2000), 165; Andrew James Wulf, *U.S. International Exhibitions during the Cold War: Winning Hearts and Minds through Cultural Diplomacy* (Lanham, MD: Rowman & Littlefield, 2015). On antimodernism in the USIA: Mathews, "Art and Politics," 778.

129. Franc, "The Early Years," 116–117; Mathews, "Art and Politics," 778, 780; Jachec, *The Philosophy and Politics*, 166–167, 197.

130. Franc, "The Early Years," 116; d'Harnoncourt quoted in Jachec, *The Philosophy and Politics*, 166.

131. Zubok, *Zhivago's Children*, 114–115.

132. "Policy Guidance for the U.S. Exhibit in Moscow in 1959"; Lightner to Tuckermann, "Comments on Script for Gorki Park Exhibit," October 13, 1958, 511.61/10–1358, ibid.; "U.S. National Exhibit, Gorki Park, Moscow, 1959," ibid.; "Some Notes Concerning the U.S. Exhibit in Moscow," Records Relating to the American National Exhibition, Moscow, 1957–1959, box 7, RG 306, NARA. See also: Jachec, *The Philosophy and Politics*, 165, 175–178, 184–187, 190.

133. State to Moscow, Instruction 1896, February 20, 1959, 861.191-MO/10-358, RG 59, NARA (quotation); *Amerikanskaia zhivopis' i skul'ptura* (Detroit, 1959), MacLanathan Papers, box 8.

134. Susan E. Reid, "Who Will Beat Whom?: Soviet Popular Reception of the American National Exhibition in Moscow, 1959," *Kritika: Explorations in Russian and Eurasian History* 9:4 (2008): 855–904.

135. Comment Books (Moscow Fair), G-1098 E&F, box 62, RU321, SIA. Further analysis of these comments: Reid, "Who Will Beat Whom?"

136. Mamedova to Kent, March 11, 1957, Kent Papers, reel 5177, frames 1445–1446; Kent to McIntyre, May 8, 1957, ibid., frame 1459. Another hint, connecting the disappointed MoMA project and the Kent exhibition: Chugunov to Roberts, February 12, 1957, ibid., reel 5156, frame 395.

137. Mamedova to Kent, May 25, 1957, ibid., frames 1480–1481.

138. "Suggestions for Ambassador's Letter," ibid., reel 5177, frame 1447.

139. Richard V. West, "Rockwell Kent: After the Odyssey," in *Distant Shores: The Odyssey of Rockwell Kent*, ed. Constance Martin (Berkeley: University of California Press, 2000), 113–121.

140. Kent to VOKS, May 2, 1957, Kent Papers, reel 5177, frame 1458.

141. Kent to Balken, March 11, 1958, ibid., reel 5160, frame 654.

142. "Moscow to See Modern U.S. Art," *New York Times*, May 31, 1959.

143. David Traxel, *An American Saga: The Life and Times of Rockwell Kent* (New York: Harper & Row, 1980).

144. Seymour Topping, "Moscow Gets Art of Rockwell Kent," Kent Papers, reel 5242, frame 364.

145. Kent to Popova, May 24, 1960, ibid., reel 5242, frame 366–367.

146. Kent to Balken, March 11, 1958, Kent Papers, reel 5160, frame 654; Kent to Gropper, April 6, 1959, ibid., reel 5188, frame 142.

147. Kent to Young Guard Publisher, November 23, 1961, ibid., reel 5183, frame 1033; Kent to Jimmie [Rosenberg?], October 6, 1960, ibid., reel 5185, frame 1112.

148. Kent to Jessica [Smith?], October 3, 1960, ibid., reel 5185, frame 1111; Kent to Paul [Bjarnason?], October 17, 1960, ibid., frame 1131.

149. Rockwell Kent, "Art Belongs to People," in *Rockwell Kent: An Anthology of His Works*, ed. Fridolf Johnson (London: Collins, 1982). Graphics were divided equally between the Hermitage and the Pushkin Museum; each also received 22 paintings, while museums in Riga, Erevan, Odessa, and Kiev acquired nine paintings each: RGALI f. 2329, op. 4, d. 1301, ll. 3–4.

150. RGALI f. 2329, op. 4, d. 1201, l. 1.

151. Kent Papers, reel 5242, frames 362–363; ibid., reel 5199, frames 157–158, 174, 180; RGALI f. 2458, op. 4, d. 372, ll. 43, 50.

152. Katerina Clark, *The Soviet Novel: History as Ritual* (Bloomington: Indiana University Press, 2000), 225–230; Yuri Slezkine, *Arctic Mirrors: Russia and the Small Peoples of the North* (Ithaca, NY: Cornell University Press, 1994), 358–364.

153. Yuri Vizbor, "Karel'skii val's," in *Ne ver' razlukam, starina. Stikhi i pesni raznykh let* (Moscow: Eksmo, 2004), 17.

154. Aleksandr Gorodnitskii, *I zhit' eshche nadezhde . . .* (Moscow: Vagrius, 2001), 64–65.

155. Ada Iakusheva, *Pesnia—liubov' moia* (Moscow: "Lokid-Press," 2001), 134.

156. Traxel, *An American Saga*, 20–23, 150; Constance Martin, "Rockwell Kent: the Odyssey," in *Distant Shores*,17–47, here 19.

157. *Rockwell Kent*, 56.

158. RGALI f. 2458, op. 4, d. 372, l. 190b.

159. Kent Papers, reel 5185, frame 1277; ibid., reel 5199, frame 166, 174.

160. RGALI f. 2458, op. 4, d. 372, ll. 47–470b; Kent Papers, reel 5185, frame 1269.

161. RGALI f. 2458, op. 4, d. 372, l. 8.

162. Ibid., ll. 180b, 32.

163. Ibid., ll. 28, 210b.

164. Ibid., l. 9.

165. Ibid., ll. 240b, 270b, 650b.

166. Kent Papers, reel 5185, frame 1257.

167. RGALI f. 2458, op. 4, d. 372, ll. 140b, 190b.

168. Kent Papers, reel 5185, frames 1277, 1279; ibid., reel 5199, frame 180.

169. Ibid., reel 5185, frame 1275; RGALI f. 2458, op. 4, d. 372, l. 8. Also: Elkins, *Pictures & Tears*, 174–184.

170. RGALI f. 2458, op. 4, d. 372, ll. 80b, 15, 53, 69.

171. Martin, "Rockwell Kent: The Odyssey," 36; RGALI f. 2458, op. 4, d. 372, ll. 400b, 48, 540b–55, 560b, 580b, 680b.

172. RGALI f. 2458, op. 4, d. 372, ll. 5 (quotation), 8 (quotation), 100b, 22, 34, 680b.

173. Ibid., ll. 160b, 39, 440b, 500b–51, 61, 660b.

174. Kent Papers, reel 5185, frame 1261.

175. RGALI f. 2458, op. 4, d. 372, ll. 2, 31.

176. Ibid., ll. 80b (quotation), 17, 32.

177. Ibid., ll. 200b–21.

178. Ibid., l. 31.

179. For a more detailed analysis of these paintings: Reid, "Destalinization and the Remodernization of Soviet Art," 442–473.

180. Ibid., 333–522, 572–587; idem, "Toward a New (Socialist) Realism," 232–234; idem, "Modernizing Socialist Realism in the Khrushchev Thaw: the Struggle for a 'Contemporary Style' in Soviet Art," in *The Dilemmas of De-Stalinization: Negotiating Cultural and Social Change in the Khrushchev Era*, ed. Polly Jones (New York: Routledge, 2006), 209–230; A. Bobrikov, "Surovyi stil': mobilizat-siia i kul'turnaia revoliutsiia," *Khudozhestvennyi zhurnal* 51–52 (2003): 25–29; Nonna Stepanian, *Iskusstvo Rossii XX veka: Vzgliad iz 90-kh* (Moscow: EKSMO-Press, 1999), 202–205.

181. Pascale Casanova, *The World Republic of Letters* (Cambridge, MA: Harvard University Press, 2004), 22–23.

182. Viktor Pivovarov, *Serye tetradi* (Moscow: Novoe literaturnoe obozrenie, 2002), 24; V. Slavkin, *Pamiatnik neizvestnomu stiliage* (Moscow: Artist, Rezhisser, Teatr, 1996), 51; Dmitrii Bobyshev, *Ia zdes' (Chelovekotekst)* (Moscow: Vagrius, 2003), 135; Eremchenko interview; Reid, "Toward a New (Socialist) Realism," 222.

183. Slavkin, *Pamiatnik neizvestnomu stiliage*, 51; Eremchenko interview.

184. Mikhail German, *Slozhnoe proshedshee (Passé composé)* (Saint Petersburg: Iskusstvo-SPb, 2000), 395; Ilya Ehrenburg, *LGZh*, 6: 552; idem, *LGZh in Ss* (Moscow: Khudozhestvennaia literatura, 2000), 8: 462; Evgenii Shvarts, *Zhivu bespokoino . . . Iz dnevnikov* (Leningrad: Sovetskii pisatel', 1990), 635; Valerii

Val'ran, *Leningradskii andergraund: Zhivopis', fotografiia, rok-muzyka* (Saint Petersburg: Izdatel'stvo imeni N. I. Novikova, 2003), 58.

185. Pivovarov, *Serye tetradi*, 24; Slavkin, *Pamiatnik neizvestnomu stiliage*, 51; Bobyshev, *Ia zdes'*, 135; Eremchenko interview.

186. Anatolii Lunacharskii, "Putevye ocherki," in *Ob izobrazitel'nom iskusstve* (Moscow: Sovetskii khudozhnik, 1967), 1: 324–327, 331, 337, 353; *Iz istorii khudozhestvennoi zhizni SSSR. Internatsional'nye sviazi v oblasti izobrazitel'nogo iskusstva, 1917–1940* (Moscow: Iskusstvo, 1987), 69–70, 75, 114, 127, 132–142, 196–197, 207–208, 256.

187. "K rastsvetu sovetskogo izobrazitel'nogo iskusstva!" *Pravda*, August 11, 1947; Vladimir Kemenov, "Aspects of Two Cultures," *VOKS Bulletin* 52 (1947): 20–36; B. Ioganson, "Korni zla," *Iskusstvo* 2 (1948): 7–8, here 7; L. Reingardt, "Po tu storonu zdravogo smysla (Formalizm na sluzhbe reaktsii)," *Iskusstvo* 5 (1949): 77–87, here 84; V. N. Vakidin, *Stranitsy iz dnevnika* (Moscow: Sovetskii khudozhnik, 1991), 165–166, 169; Antoine Baudin, "'Why Is Soviet Painting Hidden from Us?' Zhdanov Art and Its International Relations and Fallout, 1947–53," in *Socialist Realism without Shores*, 227–256; Gertje R. Utley, *Picasso: The Communist Years* (New Haven, CT: Yale University Press, 2000); Pierre Daix, *Picasso: Life and Art* (New York: Icon Editions, 1993), 277–283, 295–301, 304–319.

188. Ehrenburg, *LGZh*, 6: 397–401, 427–434, 458–461, 478–495; B. Ia. Frezinskii, "Il'ia Erenburg i Pablo Pikasso," *Pamiatniki kul'tury: Novye otkrytiia. Ezhegodnik* (Moscow: Nauka, 1998), 67, 70, 72, 80.

189. RGANI f. 5, op. 36, d. 27, l. 80.

190. RGANI f. 5, op. 17, d. 499, l. 93.

191. Ibid., ll. 206–207; ibid., op. 36, d. 25, ll. 77–78; ibid., d. 14, l. 104; *Apparat TsK i kul'tura, 1953–1957. Dokumenty* (Moscow: ROSSPEN, 2001), 198–201.

192. RGANI f. 5, op. 17, d. 543, ll. 101–104; ibid., d. 498, ll. 95–101, reprinted in *Apparat TsK i kul'tura*, 258–261; ibid., d. 534, ll. 9–16; ibid., op. 36, d. 25, ll. 77–78.

193. RGANI f. 5, op. 36, d. 25, ll. 24–25; ibid., d. 48, l. 16; ibid., d. 47, l. 106.

194. L. Liulchanov, "O 'literaturnosti' v zhivopisi," *Tvorchestvo* 1 (1957): 11–12; "Vernyi put'," *Iskusstvo* 1 (1957): 3–7; D. T. Shepilov, "Za dal'neishii rastsvet sovetskogo khudozhestvennogo tvorchestva," *Iskusstvo* 1 (1957): 6–13; "Traditsii i novatorstvo (Tvorcheskaia diskussiia v Moskovskom soiuze sovetskikh khudozhnikov)," *Iskusstvo* 2 (1956): 17–22; A. Lebedev, "Slovo s preds"ezdovskoi tribuny," *Iskusstvo* 6 (1956): 7–10; G. Manizer, "Mesto i rol' siuzheta v kartine," *Iskusstvo* 7 (1956): 3–8; A. Kamenskii, "Nekotorye osobennosti siuzheta v zhivopisi," *Iskusstvo* 8 (1956): 20–27; Reid, "Destalinization and the Remodernization of Soviet Art," 161–169, 201–204, 213–237, 249–280.

195. RGANI f. 5, op. 36, d. 27, ll. 80–81; GARF f. 9576, op. 1, d. 1, t. 1, l. 36; ibid., op. 2, d. 7, l. 114.

196. AGMII f. 5, op. 1, d. 2025, ll. 2, 98, 119–120, passim.

197. Ibid., op. 3, d. 222, ll. 7–8, 21 (quotation); AGE f. 1, op. 11, d. 815, l. 45. (Thanks to Denis Kozlov for providing this document.)

198. AGMII f. 5, op. 1, d. 2025, l. 2; ibid., d. 2034.

199. Zhorzh Marten and Vol'f Sedykh, *Moskva-Parizh: Velenie serdtsa i razuma* (Moscow: Mezhdunarodnye otnosheniia, 1998), 67; Vladimir Erofeev, *Diplomat: Kniga vospominanii* (Moscow: Zebra E, 2005), 320–326.

200. AGE f. 1, op. 11, d. 775, ll. 27–28.

201. RGANI f. 5, op. 30, d. 172, l. 170; ibid., op. 36, d. 27, ll. 80–82.

202. M. Gukovskii, "Vremennye vystavki khudozhestvennykh proizvedenii iz stran zapadnoi Evropy v 1956 g.," *Soobshcheniia Gosudarstvennogo Ermitazha* (Leningrad: Iskusstvo, 1958), 13: 15.

203. AGE f. 1, op. 11, d. 775, l. 27; Saint Petersburg television interview with L. A. Dukel'skaia, ASB-6, tape 149 (I thank Peter Bagrov for making the transcript of the interview available to me). Curators and enthusiasts: Kostenevich, "Russkie sobirateli," 137n172; Elena Kumpan, "Vspominaia Lidiiu Iakovlevnu," *Zvezda* 3 (2002): 135–167, here 138. Since each museum drew primarily on its own collection, the Pushkin exhibition was smaller and included *Young Acrobat on a Ball, Family of Saltimbanques, Head of an Old Man in Tiara, Still Life with Violin, Bowl of Fruit with Bunch of Grapes and Sliced Pear.* (Anatoly Podoksik, *Picasso: The Artist's Works in Soviet Museums* [Leningrad: Aurora Art Publishers, 1989], 179.)

204. AGMII f. 5, op. 3, d. 222, ll. 26–27; Dukel'skaia interview.

205. AGMII f. 5, op. 3, d. 222, ll. 7, 13.

206. Ibid., l. 20.

207. Ibid., ll. 16–18, 20; RGALI f. 1204, op. 2, d. 2648, l. 590b.

208. For a different perspective: Reid, "The Exhibition Art of Socialist Countries," 118; idem, "In the Name of the People," 703.

209. AGMII f. 5, op. 3, d. 222, l. 19.

210. Ilya Ehrenburg, "K risunkam Pablo Pikasso," *IL* 10 (1956): 243–253; idem, "Pablo Pikasso," 183, 186–187, 189, 190 (quotation).

211. RGALI f. 1204, op. 2, d. 2603, l. 19.

212. Ehrenburg, "Pablo Pikasso," 182, 186, 191 (quotation); idem, *LGZh*, 6: 551.

213. Ehrenburg, "K risunkam"; idem, "Pablo Pikasso," 181.

214. RGALI f. 1204, op. 2, d. 2616, ll. 1110b–1120b.

215. Ibid., d. 2644, l. 47.

216. Ibid., d. 2616, ll. 50–54; ibid., d. 2644, ll. 1600b–161; AGMII f. 5, op. 3, d. 222, ll. 2, 5 (quotations).

217. AGMII f. 5, op. 3, d. 222, l. 5; Ehrenburg, *LGZh*, 6: 552.

218. RGALI f. 1204, op. 2, d. 2641, l. 117.

219. Ibid., d. 2643, l. 50.

220. Ibid., d. 2605, ll. 68–690b (quotations); ibid., d. 2614, ll. 140–1400b.
221. AGMII f. 5, op. 2, d. 222, l. 2. This comment was written in English; original syntax has been preserved.
222. Ibid., ll. 6, 8 (quotations); ibid., op. 1, d. 2025, ll. 119–120. Viewers also got to see Matisse: in 1957, Jean Vercors brought to the Soviet Union an exhibition of reprints and illustrations, which included several Matisses. For devotees, a volume of critical articles was published in 1959. (Vakidin, *Stranitsy iz dnevnika*, 205; RGALI f. 2458, op. 2, dd. 1363, 1364; *Matiss: Sbornik statei o tvorchestve* [Moscow: Izdatel'stvo inostrannoi literatury, 1959].)
223. The institutes included the Stroganov Art School, the Architecture Institute, the Theatre Institute, and the Institute of Cinematography. Upheaval in universities: Zubok, *Zhivago's Children*, 68–69; Bittner, *The Many Lives of Khrushchev's Thaw*, 40–74; Kathleen Smith, *Moscow 1956: The Silenced Spring* (Cambridge, MA: Harvard University Press, 2017), 139–168; O. G. Gerasimova, *"Ottepel'," "zamorozki" i studenty Moskovskogo universiteta* (Moscow: AIRO-XXI, 2015), 73–116; Robert Hornsby, *Protest, Reform and Repression in Khrushchev's Soviet Union* (Cambridge: Cambridge University Press, 2013), 34–41, 66–68, 257–261.
224. RGANI f. 5, op. 36, d. 27, ll. 102–105; GARF f. 8131, op. 31, d. 76945, l. 4; B. B. Vail', *Osobo opasnyi* (London: Overseas Publications Interchange, 1980), 136–145. Another version of events: Mikhail Trofimenkov, "Pablo Pikasso—vozhd' russkoi revoliutsii," *Kommersant"* (Saint Petersburg), December 14, 2001; *Kul'turnyi sloi: Detonator—Pikasso* (TRK, St. Petersburg, Russia, 2004) (Thanks to Peter Bagrov for a tape of this program).
225. RGANI f. 5, op. 36, d. 27, ll. 102–105.
226. Ibid., d. 25, ll. 106–108, 110–112; ibid., d. 47, ll. 58, 94–95; ibid., d. 48, ll. 16–24.
227. Dukel'skaia interview.
228. Naiman and Gordin in *Kul'turnyi sloi*.
229. GARF f. 8131, op. 31, d. 76945, ll. 2–4. Krasovskaia was released shortly thereafter for lack of evidence of anti-Soviet activity. Also: Smith, *Moscow 1956*, 301–303.
230. Vail', *Osobo opasnyi*, 144.
231. TsAOPIM f. 1007, op. 2, d. 122, l. 98.
232. Evgenii Evtushenko, "Nigilist," *Iunost'* 12 (1960): 7.
233. RGASPI f. M-1, op. 46, dd. 190, 192, 199; TsAOPIM f. 4, op. 113, d. 21; ibid., d. 41, ll. 1–14, 135–141; ibid., f. 3991, op. 1, d. 6, ll. 222–223; ibid., d. 7, ll. 89–90, 92; TsMAM f. 1609, op. 2, d. 410, ll. 22–24; ibid., d. 415, ll. 82–84; Vail', *Osobo opasnyi*, 137; Revol't Pimenov, *Vospominaniia* (Moscow: Informatsionno-ekspertnaia gruppa "Panorama," 1996), 1: 33–47, 75–78. Student discussions in 1956: Juliane Fürst, "The Arrival of Spring? Changes and Continuities in

Soviet Youth Culture and Policy Between Stalin and Khrushchev," in *The Dilemmas of De-Stalinization*, 135–153.

234. TsAOPIM f. 4, op. 113, d. 42, ll. 5–6 (quotation), 110.

235. RGASPI f. M-1, op. 46, d. 199, ll. 169–171.

236. Ibid., ll. 99–101, 117–119, 127–128, 170; ibid., d. 192, ll. 196–201.

237. TsAOPIM f. 4, op. 113, d. 42, l. 110.

238. Revekka Frumkina, "Spichechnyi korobok i sinee ukho," http://azbuka.gif.ru /critics/box-ear.

239. Evgenii Evtushenko, "Nasledniki Stalina," *Pravda*, October 21, 1962.

240. Eunice Lipton, *Picasso Criticism, 1901–1939: The Making of an Artist-Hero* (New York: Garland, 1976), 346–347.

241. Sergei Iutkevich, "Pikasso bez tain," *IK* 3 (1957): 150–154, here 153; Ehrenburg, *LGZh*, 6: 548, 551.

242. "Pablo Pikasso," Gosteleradiofond no. B-019657; Iutkevich, "Pikasso," 152.

243. Iutkevich, "Pikasso," 152–153.

244. V. Prokof'ev, "Pikasso," *Ogonek* 44 (1966): 8–9; Gosteleradiofond no. B-019657.

245. Dm. Moldavskii, "O Pablo Pikasso," *Neva* 12 (1962): 193–200, here 195–196, 199–200.

246. Idem, *Sneg i vremia: Zapiski literatora* (Leningrad: Sovetskii pisatel', 1989), 185, 224–226, 257; idem, *S Maiakovskim v teatre i kino: Kniga o Sergee Iutkeviche* (Moscow: VTO, 1975), 301–302.

247. Valentin Kataev, "Khudozhnik mira," *Iunost'* 8 (1962): 80–81.

248. Moldavskii, "O Pablo," 196–197; Prokof'ev, "Pikasso," 8.

249. Moldavskii, "O Pablo," 196; Andrei Voznesenskii, *Proraby dukha* (Moscow: Sovetskii pisatel', 1984), 357.

250. Prokof'ev, "Pikasso"; Moldavskii, "O Pablo," 196; Igor' Golomshtok and Andrei Siniavskii, *Pikasso* (Moscow: Izdatel'stvo "Znanie," 1960), 17, 39; G. Nedoshivin, "Pablo Pikasso," *Tvorchestvo* 10 (1966): 20–22, here 22; *Zapadnoevropeiskaia zhivopis' i skul'ptura. Al'bom* (Moscow: Sovetskii khudozhnik, 1966), nos. 112–114.

251. Golomshtok and Siniavskii, *Pikasso*, 38–41.

252. Interview with I. N. Golomshtok, London, September 2, 2004; Golomshtok and Siniavskii, *Pikasso*, 17, 18, 20, 22, 24–28, 30, 42–45, 51–52. On the book's writing and reception: Igor' Golomshtok, *Zaniatie dlia starogo gorodovogo: Memuary pessimista* (Moscow: AST, 2015), 99–101, 105.

253. Ilya Ehrenburg, "Iz vospominanii o Pablo Pikasso," in Golomshtok and Siniavskii, *Pikasso*.

254. Ehrenburg, *LGZh*, 6: 495–560.

255. Pavel Antokol'skii, "Pikasso," in *Chetvertoe izmerenie: Stikhi, 1962–1963* (Moscow: Sovetskii pisatel', 1964), 41–60.

256. *Vospominaniia o Pavle Antokol'skom: Sbornik* (Moscow: Sovetskii pisatel', 1987), 31, 47, 55, 59, 90, 92, 179, 180, 326–327, 342; Pavel Antokol'skii, *Dnevnik, 1964–1968* (St. Petersburg: Izdatel'stvo "Pushkinskogo fonda," 2002), 79, 136–137, 148.

257. Vladimir Mayakovsky, "Semidnevnyi smotr frantsuzskoi zhivopisi," in *Polnoe sobranie sochinenii v trinadtsati tomakh* (Moscow: Gosudarstvennoe izdatel'stvo khudozhestvennoi literatury, 1957), 4: 242, 245–246. Mayakovsky's statements on Picasso were more complex and ambiguous than the 1960s critics presented (ibid., 237, 244, 249–250, 252). N. V. Reformatskaia, "Frantsuzskie khudozhniki i Maiakovskii," *IL* 3 (1961): 249–251.

258. Golomshtok and Siniavskii, *Pikasso*, 37; Moldavskii, "O Pablo"; Nedoshivin, "Pablo Pikasso," 21.

259. Liudmila Polikovskaia, *My predchuvstvie . . . predtecha . . . Ploshchad' Maiakovskogo, 1958–1965* (Moscow: Zven'ia, 1997), 27–29, 40–42, 51–52, 102–103, 130, 143–145, 328–329.

260. Vladimir Al'fonsov, *Slova i kraski: Ocherki iz istorii tvorcheskikh sviazei poetov i khudozhnikov* (Moscow: Sovetskii pisatel', 1966), 91–174.

261. V. Gaevskii, "Na vystavke Pikasso," *Teatr* 3 (1967): 86–88, here 88; Nedoshivin, "Pablo Pikasso," 22; Moldavskii, "O Pablo."

262. *Grafika Pikasso* (Moscow: Iskusstvo, 1967), 19–30; I. Karetnikova, "Keramika Pikasso," *Dekorativnoe iskusstvo SSSR* 8 (1967): 28–30.

263. *Pablo Pikasso. Grafika—keramika. Vystavka iz galerei Luizy Leris v Parizhe i moskovskikh kollektsii* (Moscow: Sovetskii khudozhnik, 1966).

264. *Pablo Pikasso. Grafika*; N. Dmitrieva, "Vystavka rabot Pikasso v Moskve," *Sovetskaia kul'tura*, December 29, 1966. This discourse—child, devil, genius, hero, and poet—was not particular to Soviet authors: Carsten-Peter Warncke, *Pablo Picasso, 1881–1973* (Köln: Taschen, 1995), 1: 9–15, 2: 673, 676–678.

265. Zhorzh [Georges] Leon, "Frantsiia chestvuet Pikasso," *LG*, October 27, 1966; Iu. Ponomarev, "V chest' Pikasso," *Sovetskaia kul'tura*, October 27, 1966 (quotation); B. Kotov, "Pablo Pikasso—85 let," *Pravda*, October 25, 1966; reprint B. Kotov, "Bol'shaia zhizn' Pablo Pikasso," *Pravda*, October 26, 1966, provincial edition.

266. AGMII f. 5, op. 3, d. 365, ll. 214ob, 282–283.

267. Ibid., ll. 45–45ob, 47, 58, 61ob, 99–99ob, 210, 263.

268. Ibid., ll. 50, 176 (quotation).

269. Ibid., ll. 27–27ob, 99.

270. Ibid., ll. 108–108ob, 112, 137–137ob, 203.

271. Ibid., l. 50; RGALI f. 1204, op. 2, d. 2679, l. 350b; Aleksandr Gitovich, "Pikasso," in *Stikhotvoreniia* (Leningrad: Khudozhestvennaia literatura, 1982), 176–180.

272. Golomshtok and Siniavskii, *Pikasso*, 29; Kataev, "Khudozhnik mira"; Prokof'ev, "Pikasso"; *Gosudarstvennyi muzei izobrazitel'nykh iskusstv im. A. S.*

Pushkina. Zapadnoevropeiskaia zhivopis' (Moscow: Gosudarstvennoe izdatel'stvo izobrazitel'nogo iskusstva, 1962), no. 48; *Zapadnoevropeiskaia zhivopis' i skul'ptura*, nos. 112–114; *Ot Mane do Pikasso: Frantsuzskaia zhivopis' vtoroi poloviny XIX–XX veka v Gosudarstvennom muzee izobrazitel'nykh iskusstv im. A. S. Pushkina* (Moscow: Izobrazitel'noe iskusstvo, 1974), nos. 86–92. Until the mid-to-late 1960s, Soviet guidebooks and albums usually reproduced the same several paintings of the Blue and Rose periods.

273. AGMII f. 5, op. 3, d. 365, ll. 201, 218.

274. Ibid., ll. 68, 232, 235; RGALI f. 1204, op. 2, d. 3208, l. 16. The most obvious social fault-line is generational: none of the pensioners, but 74 percent of all "young people," those who identified themselves as students or their age as under thirty, welcomed this exhibition. Also: Reid, "The Exhibition Art of Socialist Countries," 118, 122.

275. AGMII f. 5, op. 3, d. 365, ll. 84, 86, 93; RGALI f. 2926, op. 2, d. 148, l. 15.

276. AGMII f. 5, op. 3, d. 365, ll. 21 (quotation), 79.

277. Ibid., ll. 68, 80, 229.

278. Ehrenburg, *LGZh*, 6: 552.

279. AGMII f. 5, op. 3, d. 365, l. 165.

280. RGAKFD no. 1–24173; TsAADM photographs nos. 0-10527, 1-7208, 0-10523.

281. Truth / revelation—three comments (1%); freedom—two comments (0.8%); discussion—three comments (1%); youth—no comments. AGMII f. 5, op. 3, d. 365, ll. 44, 75, 960b, 147, 157, 2360b, 256.

282. Eugene Chen Eoyang, *The Transparent Eye: Reflections on Translation, Chinese Literature, and Comparative Poetics* (Honolulu: University of Hawaii Press, 1993), 48–49.

283. RGALI f. 2458, op. 2, d. 1336, l. 97; ibid., d. 1339, l. 54; ibid., d. 1359, l. 50b.

284. Ibid., d. 1339, ll. 37, 96, 132, 136; ibid., d. 1341, l. 185; ibid., d. 1336, ll. 22, 73; ibid., d. 1359, ll. 12–14; ibid., op. 4, d. 145, ll. 22, 280b; RGALI f. 2926, op. 2, d. 148, ll. 17, 18; AGMII f. 5, op. 3, d. 239, l. 40b; ibid., d. 278, ll. 39–390b.

285. Differentiation of audiences: Reid, "The Exhibition Art of Socialist Countries," 124.

286. Ludmila E. Gaav and Marina V. Potapova, "New Audiences for New Art: The Public at the Avant-garde Exhibitions at the State Russian Museum," *Poetics* 24 (1996): 131–159, here 148–149, 155.

6. Books and Borders

1. Maiia Ganina, "Lino ulybaetsia," in *Den' priezda, den' ot"ezda—odin den': Putevoi ocherk* (Moscow: Sovetskii pisatel', 1965), 62. Travel to Europe as a literary pilgrimage: Yuri Lotman and Boris Uspenskii, "'Pis'ma russkogo puteshestvennika' Karamzina i ikh mesto v razvitii russkoi kul'tury," in Yuri Lotman, *Karamzin* (Saint-Petersburg: Iskusstvo-SPb, 1997).

2. Ilya Ehrenburg, "Angliia (glavy iz knigi)," in *Sovetskie pisateli ob Anglii* (Leningrad: Lenizdat, 1984), 52.

3. Iakov Khelemskii, "Sto pervaia Venetsiia," in *Den' priezda*, 33.

4. David Espey, "Childhood and Travel Literature," in *Travel Culture: Essays on What Makes Us Go*, ed. Carol Williams (Westport, CT: Praeger, 1998), 52–53.

5. Ganina, "Lino ulybaetsia," 63.

6. Lotman and Uspenskii, "'Pis'ma russkogo puteshestvennika,'" 531.

7. Espey, "Childhood and Travel Literature," 52–53, 57.

8. Mobility as a natural condition versus sessility as a historical condition: Eric J. Leed, *The Mind of the Traveler: From Gilgamesh to Global Tourism* (New York: Basic Books, 1991), 4. Soviet travel restrictions: Violetta Gudkova, "Neputeshestvie kak literaturnyi fakt: obrazy Frantsii v proizvedeniiakh rossiiskikh pisatelei 1920–1930-kh godov," in *Rossiia i Frantsiia: XVIII–XX vv. Lotmanovskie chteniia* (Moscow: RGGU, 2013), 310–334.

9. David Bellos, *Is That a Fish in Your Ear? Translation and the Meaning of Everything* (New York: Faber and Faber, 2011), 116–130.

10. Marina Balina, "Literatura puteshestvii," in *Sotsrealisticheskii kanon*, ed. Hans Günther and Evgeny Dobrenko (St. Petersburg: Akademicheskii proekt, 2000), 896–910.

11. Anne Gorsuch, *All This Is Your World: Soviet Tourism at Home and Abroad after Stalin* (Oxford: Oxford University Press, 2011), 1, 10–14.

12. GARF f. 9612, op. 1, d. 359, l. 11.

13. Ibid., d. 369, l. 32; RGANI f. 5, op. 30, d. 113, l. 32.

14. Timothy Johnston, "Peace or Pacifism? The Soviet 'Struggle for Peace in All the World,' 1948–54," *Slavonic and East European Review* 86:2 (April 2008): 259–282; Shawn Salmon, "To the Land of the Future: A History of Intourist and Travel to the Soviet Union, 1929–1991" (PhD diss., University of California, Berkeley, 2008), 108–110.

15. GARF f. 9612, op. 1, d. 388. Intourist in the 1930s: Salmon, "To the Land of the Future"; Michael David-Fox, *Showcasing the Great Experiment: Cultural Diplomacy and Western Visitors to the Soviet Union, 1921–1941* (Oxford: Oxford University Press, 2012), 176–183.

16. GARF f. 9401, op. 2, d. 498, l. 37; GARF f. 9612, op. 1, d. 369, l. 20.

17. GARF f. 9612, op. 1, d. 442, l. 100.

18. Ibid., d. 515, l. 35; ibid., d. 369, ll. 9, 52–53, 65, 149–150; GARF f. 9576, op. 2, d. 82, l. 131.

19. GARF f. 9612, op. 1, d. 369, ll. 55–56, 145, 147.

20. Ibid., ll. 27–30.

21. Ibid., ll. 68ob–69.

22. Ibid., ll. 30, 41–44, 61–63, 90–91; ibid., d. 86.

23. GARF f. 9576, op. 2, d. 82, l. 81; ibid., d. 86, l. 10 (quotation).

24. Ibid., d. 9, l. 232 (new pagination).

25. Ibid., op. 1, d. 7, l. 46; RGASPI f. M-1, op. 4, d. 2504, l. 117 (quotation).

26. GARF f. 9576, op. 2, d. 9, l. 232 (new pagination).

27. GARF f. 9612, op. 1, d. 515, ll. 35, 47–48; ibid., d. 516, ll. 12–13; ibid., d. 442, l. 27; TsAOPIM f. 4, op. 139, d. 54, l. 27; Gorsuch, *All This Is Your World*, 113–115.

28. GARF f. 9612, op. 1, d. 442, ll. 91–92, 96; ibid., d. 516, l. 15.

29. TsAOPIM f. 4, op. 139, d. 52, ll. 4–5, 12 (quotation).

30. RGANI f. 89, per. 46, dok. 15, ll. 1–2; ibid., dok. 18, l. 2; TsAOPIM f. 4, op. 139, d. 53, ll. 24–25.

31. GARF f. 9612, op. 1, d. 515, ll. 27, 35, 49, 70; GARF f. 9576, op. 2, d. 9, l. 295.

32. TsAOPIM f. 4, op. 139, d. 54, l. 30.

33. GARF f. 9576, op. 2, d. 9, ll. 296–297, 322; ibid., d. 82, l. 130.

34. GARF f. 9518, op. 1, d. 34, l. 63.

35. RGANI f. 5, op. 30, d. 113, ll. 32–35; GARF f. 9612, op. 1, d. 359, l. 36.

36. RGANI f. 5, op. 30, d. 172, ll. 35–38.

37. GARF f. 9612, op. 1, d. 357, l. 15; Gorsuch, *All This Is Your World*, 81.

38. GARF f. 9612, op. 1, d. 387, l. 1.

39. GARF f. 9401, op. 2, d. 498, l. 37. Travel to Eastern Europe: Donald J. Raleigh, *Soviet Baby Boomers: An Oral History of Russia's Cold War Generation* (Oxford: Oxford University Press, 2012), 211–213; Gorsuch, *All This Is Your World*, 79–105.

40. GARF f. 9612, op. 1, d. 387, ll. 28–29, 38–39; RGANI f. 5, op. 30, d. 172, ll. 35–36; Gorsuch, *All This Is Your World*, 81–84; Kathleen Smith, *Moscow 1956: The Silenced Spring* (Cambridge, MA: Harvard University Press, 2017), 242; Vladislav Zubok, *Zhivago's Children: The Last Russian Intelligentsia* (Cambridge, MA: Harvard University Press, 2011), 91–92; Raleigh, *Soviet Baby Boomers*, 211.

41. GARF f. 9612, op. 1, d. 369, l. 36.

42. RGANI f. 5, op. 36, d. 20, ll. 113–117.

43. Ibid., op. 30, d. 172, l. 35.

44. GARF f. 9576, op. 2, d. 9, l. 175 (new pagination); ibid., d. 4, l. 134.

45. RGANI f. 5, op. 30, d. 172, l. 35; Smith, *Moscow 1956*, 228–229; Gorsuch, *All This Is Your World*, 108–110.

46. TsAOPIM f. 4, op. 139, d. 54, l. 25; GARF f. 9612, op. 1, d. 369, l. 37.

47. TsAOPIM f. 4, op. 139, d. 52, l. 13; GARF f. 9612, op. 1, d. 369, l. 36; ibid., d. 442, l. 68.

48. GARF f. 9612, op. 1, d. 369, l. 38.

49. Ibid., l. 142; Gorsuch, *All This Is Your World*, 117–118.

50. TsAOPIM f. 4, op. 139, d. 54, l. 26.

51. GARF f. 9612, op. 1, d. 369, l. 36.

52. Ibid., l. 35; ibid., d. 442, l. 69.

53. Gorsuch, *All This Is Your World*, 119–122; Smith, *Moscow 1956*, 247; Raleigh, *Soviet Baby Boomers*, 216.

54. GARF f. 9612, op. 1, d. 385, ll. 23–24.

55. GARF f. 9576, op. 2, d. 9, l. 246.

56. Ibid., op. 1, d. 34, l. 53.

57. GARF f. 9518, op. 1, d. 14, ll. 100–1000b.

58. GARF f. 9576, op. 1, d. 34, l. 7.

59. Ibid., ll. 12–120b.

60. Ibid., op. 2, d. 75, l. 11.

61. Ibid., d. 120, l. 41; GARF f. 9612, op. 1, d. 369, l. 142; Gorsuch, *All This Is Your World*, 85.

62. Smith, *Moscow 1956*, 240–243; Gorsuch, *All This Is Your World*, 112; Gudkova, "Neputeshestvie kak literaturnyi fakt," 312.

63. Ekaterina Sheveleva, *Zhil na svete chelovek . . . Dnevniki, dokumental'nye novelly, stikhi* (St. Petersburg: Neva, 1996), 45, 97, 86–91.

64. RGANI f. 5, op. 36, d. 65, ll. 77–78.

65. Ibid., d. 111, ll. 28–29.

66. Ibid., d. 65, ll. 77–78.

67. Ibid., d. 128, l. 79.

68. GARF f. 9576, op. 17, d. 130, l. 168; ibid. op. 2, d. 128, l. 36; RGALI f. 2458, op. 2, d. 858, entire; RGALI f. 2732, op. 1, d. 1066, l. 30.

69. RGALI f. 1204, op. 2, d. 2603, l. 190b; ibid., d. 2617, l. 130b; GARF f. 9518, op. 1, d. 34, l. 120.

70. Y. Neprintsev, "Desiat' dnei v Parizhe," *Khudozhnik* 4 (1961): 41–43, here 41; Ilya Konstantinovskii, "Okean Parizha," in *Sovetskie pisateli o Frantsii* (Leningrad: Lenizdat, 1985), 356; Viktor Sytin, *Parizh—gorod raznyi* (Moscow: Sovetskii pisatel', 1973), 25–26.

71. S. Shurtakov, *Frantsiia vblizi* (Moscow: Molodaia gvardiia, 1962), 8; E. Levinson and G. Polikarpov, "Piat'desiat dnei v Parizhe," *Neva* 7 (1965): 203–211, here 206.

72. Viktor Nekrasov, *Pervoe znakomstvo: Iz zarubezhnykh vpechatlenii* (Moscow: Sovetskii pisatel', 1960), 20, 30.

73. Konstantin Paustovsky, "Mimoletnii Parizh," *Oktiabr'* 3 (March 1960): 184–202.

74. Sytin, *Parizh*, 27–28.

75. Shurtakov, *Frantsiia vblizi*, 5.

76. Sytin, *Parizh*, 26; Levinson and Polikarpov, "Piat'desiat dnei," 206.

77. Irina Freidlin, "Polgoda v Parizhe," *Zvezda* 9 (September 1966): 156–170, here 162–163.

78. A. L. Kursanov, *Po Frantsii i Zapadnoi Afrike* (Moscow: Gosudarstvennoe izdatel'stvo geograficheskoi literatury, 1956), 82, 104; Rudol'f Bershadskii, *Poltorasta stranits o Frantsii* (Moscow: Sovetskaia Rossiia, 1972), 6–7.

79. Bershadskii, *Poltorasta stranits*, 18–22; Aleksandr Zhitomirskii, "Parizh," *Neva* 1 (1969): 166–172, here 172; Valentin Kataev, "Malen'kaia zheleznaia dver' v stene," in *Sovetskie pisateli o Frantsii*, 31–32; Viktor Sytin, *Sovsem nemnogo Parizha: Ocherki* (Moscow: Sovetskii pisatel', 1962), 37–40; Shurtakov, *Frantsiia vblizi*, 19.

80. Sytin, *Parizh*, 98, 100–101.

81. Ibid., 94–95, 104–105.

82. Ibid., 96.

83. Nekrasov, *Pervoe znakomstvo*, 33–34.

84. Sytin, *Sovsem nemnogo*, 17–18; Sytin, *Parizh*, 179; Kursanov, *Po Frantsii*, 50; Gorsuch, *All This Is Your World*, 149–150.

85. Kursanov, *Po Frantsii*, 50; Sytin, *Parizh*, 46; Yuri Nagibin, "Vorobei," in *Sovetskie pisateli o Frantsii*, 292.

86. Sytin, *Parizh*, 74.

87. Konstantinovskii, "Okean Parizha," 352–353; Lev Sheinin, "Parizh—Veve," *Oktiabr'* 8 (August 1961): 173–185, here 175.

88. Kursanov, *Po Frantsii*, 50; Sheinin, "Parizh—Veve," 174.

89. Zhitomirskii, "Parizh," 168, 170; voyeurism: Gorsuch, *All This Is Your World*, 150.

90. Sytin, *Parizh*, 76.

91. Ibid., 78–79; Sytin, *Sovsem nemnogo*, 10.

92. Daniil Granin, "Ploshchad' Pigal'," in *Sovetskie pisateli o Frantsii*, 263–266.

93. Sytin, *Sovsem nemnogo*, 12, 17 (quotations); Levinson and Polikarpov, "Piat'desiat dnei," 211.

94. Shurtakov, *Frantsiia vblizi*, 16; Sheinin, "Parizh—Veve," 174–175; Zhitomirskii, "Parizh," 169.

95. Sytin, *Sovsem nemnogo*, 12.

96. Ibid., 40; Sytin, *Parizh*, 83.

97. Sytin, *Sovsem nemnogo*, 12; Sytin, *Parizh*, 79, 83–84.

98. Zhitomirskii, "Parizh," 169; Sheinin, "Parizh—Veve," 176.

99. Also: Gorsuch, *All This Is Your World*, 152–155.

100. Sytin, *Parizh*, 201.

101. Ibid., 208.

102. Shurtakov, *Frantsiia vblizi*, 94–96.

103. Kataev, "Malen'kaia zheleznaia dver'," 18; Sheinin, "Parizh—Veve," 173.

104. Sytin, *Parizh*, 10.

105. Zhitomorskii, "Parizh," 167; Sytin, *Sovsem nemnogo*, 20–21, 76, 144–145.

106. Zhitomirskii, "Parizh," 169; Sytin, *Parizh*, 171, 245; Kursanov, *Po Frantsii*, 39.

107. Sytin, *Sovsem nemnogo*, 50; Nagibin, "Vorobei," 280–281.

108. Zhitomirskii, "Parizh," 168.

109. Neprintsev, "Desiat' dnei," 41.

110. For example: Kursanov, *Po Frantsii*, 50.

111. On the ideological campaign, see Chapter 1.

112. English translation: Ilya Ehrenburg, *The Storm* (New York: Gaer Associates, 1949), 11; Mikhail German, *V poiskakh Parizha, ili, Vechnoe vozvrashchenie* (St. Petersburg: Soiuz pisatelei Sankt-Peterburga, 2013), 46.

113. RGALI f. 1204, op. 2, d. 2645, ll. 139–139ob; Ehrenburg, *The Storm*, 11.

114. RGALI f. 1204, op. 2, d. 2606, ll. 92–92ob (quotations); ibid., d. 2614, ll. 114–116ob.

115. Ibid., d. 2600, ll. 150–161ob; An invented West: Alexei Yurchak, *Everything Was Forever, Until It Was No More: The Last Soviet Generation* (Princeton, NJ: Princeton University Press, 2006), 158–206.

116. GARF f. 9576, op. 17, d. 123, ll. 5–7.

117. Ibid., d. 124, ll. 7ob, 12–12ob.

118. Ibid., l. 2ob.

119. Ibid., ll. 12ob (quotation), 16.

120. Ibid., ll. 1, 2 (quotation).

121. Ibid., l. 4ob.

122. Ibid., l. 2.

123. Ibid., ll. 2ob, 8, 10, 16ob.

124. Ibid., ll. 4ob, 8, 13–13ob.

125. Ibid., ll. 16, 17. Original spelling has been preserved.

126. Ibid., ll. 7ob, nonpaginated after 14ob, 15, 17ob (quotation).

127. Ibid., ll. 1, 4.

128. Ibid., l. 18ob.

129. Ibid., l. 3.

130. Ibid., l. 9.

131. Ibid., l. 15ob.

132. RGALI f. 1204, op. 2, d. 2600, l. 115ob.

133. Ibid., d. 2606, l. 58ob.

134. Ibid., d. 2615, ll. 15–16.

135. Ibid., d. 2601, ll. 107–108ob.

136. Ibid., d. 2614, l. 61 (quotation); ibid., d. 2600, ll. 151–151ob.

137. Mikhail German, *Dom'e* (Moscow: Molodaia gvardiia, 1962), 5–6.

138. Idem, *Slozhnoe proshedshee (Passé compose)* (St. Petersburg: Iskusstvo–SPb, 2000), 82–87, 90.

139. Ibid., 95–99.

140. Ibid., 358.

141. Idem, *Dom'e*, 11.

142. Idem, *Slozhnoe proshedshee*, 385.

143. Idem, *V poiskakh Parizha*, 65.

144. Idem, *Dom'e*, 21–22, 42–43.

145. Ibid., 55, 67, 75, 137.

146. German, *Slozhnoe proshedshee*, 385, 416.

147. Ibid., 427–429. Other examples of this sentiment: Raleigh, *Soviet Baby Boomers*, 62–63.

148. German, *Slozhnoe proshedshee*, 432, 441, 443–444.

149. German, *V poiskakh Parizha*, 120.

150. Idem, *Slozhnoe proshedshee*, 438.

151. Ibid., 519.

152. Ibid., 438.

153. Ibid., 432–434.

154. Ibid., 439–440; another reading: Gorsuch, *All This Is Your World*, 165.

155. German, *Slozhnoe proshedshee*, 500–516, 521 (quotation).

156. Ibid., 514–515, 524–525.

157. Ibid., 534–536.

158. R. I. Khlodovskii, *Italiia i khudozhestvennaia klassika Rossii* (Moscow: IMLI RAN, 2008); Pavel Muratov, *Obrazy Italii* [1911–1912], which, by the late 1960s, Soviet authors already had discovered. http://az.lib.ru/m/muratow_p_p/text_0010.shtml.

159. James Buzard, *The Beaten Track: European Tourism, Literature, and the Ways to Culture, 1800–1918* (Oxford: Clarendon Press, 1993), 104–106, 120–121, 158–160, 165–185, 203–207. Romanticism in Soviet culture of the 1930s: Katerina Clark, *Moscow, the Fourth Rome: Stalinism, Cosmopolitanism, and the Evolution of Soviet Culture, 1931–1941* (Cambridge, MA: Harvard University Press, 2011), 245–251, 277–303, 325–340; Anatoly Pinsky, "The Origins of Post-Stalin Individuality: Aleksandr Tvardovskii and the Evolution of the 1930s Soviet Romanticism," *Russian Review* 76:3 (July 2017): 458–483.

160. Sergei Smirnov, *V Italii* (Moscow: Molodaia gvardiia, 1961), 12.

161. Grigorii Boiadzhiev, *Ital'ianskie tetradi* (Moscow: Iskusstvo, 1968), 5–7; Buzard, *The Beaten Track*, 164–165, 169.

162. Sergei Gerasimov, "Nabliudeniia i zapisi," in *Ital'ianskie vpechatleniia* (Moscow: Sovetskii khudozhnik, 1958), 6.

163. G. Nedoshivin, "XXVIII Biennale," in *Ital'ianskie vpechatleniia*, 130.

164. Boiadzhiev, *Ital'ianskie tetradi*, 24.

165. Smirnov, *V Italii*, 30–33.

166. Georgii Bogemskii, *Po gorodam Italii* (Moscow: Gosudarstvennoe izdatel'stvo geograficheskoi literatury, 1955), 87, 91, 148, 151 (quotation), 161–163, 166.

167. Bogemskii also included city maps: Ibid., 8, 141, 161, 200.

168. Semen Chuikov, *Ital'ianskii dnevnik* (Moscow: Sovetskii khudozhnik, 1966), 9; Y. Pimenov, *God puteshestvii* (Moscow: Sovetskii khudozhnik, 1960), 8.

169. Yuri Kolpinskii, *Po Gretsii i Italii* (Moscow: Izdatel'stvo Akademii khudozhestv SSSR, 1960), 102–103, 105. Similar descriptions: Valerii Prokof'ev, *Po Italii* (Moscow: Iskusstvo, 1971), 235.

170. Nedoshivin, "XXVIII Biennale," 132; Kolpinskii, *Po Gretsii i Italii*, 123. Painting analogies: Prokof'ev, *Po Italii*, 335.

171. Kolpinskii, *Po Gretsii i Italii*, 108.

172. Chuikov, *Ital'ianskii dnevnik*, 9.

173. Konstantin Paustovsky, "Ital'ianskie zapisi," in *Sovetskie pisateli ob Italii* (Leningrad: Lenizdat, 1986), 233.

174. Kolpinskii, *Po Gretsii i Italii*, 161, 182.

175. Ibid., 106, 115.

176. Ibid., 120, 149.

177. Prokof'ev, *Po Italii*, 48 (quotation), 50 (quotation), 76, passim.

178. Ibid., 18 (example), 51, 131.

179. Ibid., 12 (example), 24, 65, 68, 281, 298–299, 311.

180. Ibid., 159, 210–214, 327.

181. Ibid., 154, 156.

182. A. Laptev, "Chetyre dnia v Venetsii," in *Ital'ianskie vpechatleniia*, 127–128; Prokof'ev, *Po Italii*, 332; Boris Evgen'ev, *Iz Avzonii v Italiiu* (Moscow: Sovetskii pisatel', 1967), 294–299.

183. Prokof'ev, *Po Italii*. 332; Yu. D. Kolpinskii, "Vstrechi i vpechatleniia," in *Ital'ianskie vpechatleniia*, 74.

184. Gerasimov, "Nabliudeniia," 14–15; E. Kibrik, "Venetsiia—Florentsiia—Rim—Milan," in *Ital'ianskie vpechatleniia*, 29; Prokof'ev, *Po Italii*, 91, 101; Boiadzhiev, *Ital'ianskie tetradi*, 11.

185. Gerasimov, "Nabliudeniia," 15; Kolpinskii, "Vstrechi," 71–72, 82–85; Laptev, "Chetyre dnia," 120; Prokof'ev, *Po Italii*, 326–328; Boiadzhiev, *Ital'ianskie tetradi*, 31.

186. Smirnov, *V Italii*, 100.

187. Chuikov, *Ital'ianskii dnevnik*, 96, 100; Nekrasov, *Pervoe znakomstvo*, 77.

188. Pimenov, *God puteshestvii*, 50.

189. Aleksandr Krivitskii, "Prekrasnaia Elena," in *Sovetskie pisateli ob Italii*, 269.

190. Valeriia Gerasimova, "Malen'kie znamena," in *Den' priezda*, 71.

191. Chuikov, *Ital'ianskii dnevnik*, 35; Evgen'ev, *Iz Avzonii*, 42–43.

192. Bogemskii, *Po gorodam*, 71, 73, 217 (quotation).

193. Nekrasov, *Pervoe znakomstvo*, 124, 127.

194. Gerasimov, "Nabliudeniia," 25; A. V. Kokorin, "12 dnei v Venetsii," in *Ital'ianskie vpechatleniia*, 58–59; Nedoshivin, "XXVIII Biennale," 132; Kolpinskii, *Po Gretsii i Italii*, 108–109; Smirnov, *V Italii*, 38; Prokof'ev, *Po Italii*, 333–335; Bogemskii, *Po gorodam*, 11–12; Nekrasov, *Pervoe znakomstvo*, 79–80, 93.

195. Chuikov, *Ital'ianskii dnevnik*, 39.

196. Gerasimov, "Nabliudeniia," 25; Petr Pavlenko, "Ital'ianskie vpechatleniia," in *Sovetskie pisateli ob Italii*, 173.

197. Kokorin, "12 dnei," 58–59.

198. Smirnov, *V Italii*, 39–41.

199. Bogemskii, *Po gorodam*, 12.

200. Ibid., 60–61, 97, 129, 131, 139, 145–146, 157.

201. Krivitskii, "Prekrasnaia Elena," 278, 281.

202. Buzard, *The Beaten Track*, 132–138.

203. Evgen'ev, *Iz Avzonii*, 22–23.

204. Ibid., 8.

205. Ibid., 17–19.

206. Ibid., 41, 251.

207. Ibid., 49–56.

208. Prokof'ev, *Po Italii*, 210.

209. Chuikov, *Ital'ianskii dnevnik*, 40, 65, 73.

210. Prokof'ev, *Po Italii*, 271 (with citations from Goethe), 316.

211. Bogemskii, *Po gorodam*, 163 (quotation), 173–175.

212. Chuikov, *Ital'ianskii dnevnik*, 139.

213. These were long-standing stereotypes, which appeared in the mid-nineteenth century, as Americans began to travel to the Continent: Buzard, *The Beaten Track*, 217–219.

214. Boris Polevoi, *Amerikanskie dnevniki* (Moscow: Sovetskii pisatel', 1956), 97, 125, 131–133, 149, 151 (quotation), 157–162.

215. Polevoi, *Amerikanskie*, 69.

216. Ibid., 142.

217. Ibid., 183.

218. The journalists were: Boris Polevoi, Aleksei Adzhubei, Valentin Berezhkov, Nikolai Gribachev, Boris Izakov, Viktor Poltoratskii, and Anatolii Sofronov.

219. Rósa Magnúsdóttir, "Keeping Up Appearances: How the Soviet State Failed to Control Popular Attitudes Toward the United States of America, 1945–1959" (PhD diss., University of North Carolina at Chapel Hill, 2006), 162–165 (agricultural delegation), 167–171, 178 (journalists).

220. RGANI f. 5, op. 16, d. 734, ll. 134–135; Magnúsdóttir, "Keeping Up Appearances," 166, 176–178.

221. Polevoi, *Amerikanskie*, 59, 188, 262, 330, 348.

222. Ibid., 342, 381.

223. Ilya Il'f and Evgenii Petrov, "Odnoetazhnaia Amerika," in *Sobranie sochinenii v piati tomakh* 4 (Moscow: Khudozhestvennaia literatura, 1996). The book's significance in shaping perceptions of America: Clark, *Moscow, the Fourth Rome*, 188; the book's significance in literature and cinema of the 1930s: Anne Nesbet, "Skyscrapers, Consular Territory, and Hell: What Bulgakov and Eizenshtein Learned about Space from Il'f and Petrov's America," *Slavic Review* 69:2 (Summer 2010): 377–397.

224. Further discussion: Milla Fedorova, *Yankees in Petrograd, Bolsheviks in New York: America and Americans in Russian Literary Perception* (DeKalb: Northern Illinois University Press, 2013), 85–87.

225. Polevoi, *Amerikanskie*, 98.

226. Ibid., 99–106, 141, 157, 185, 211–215, 217, 289; Fedorova, *Yankees in Petrograd*, 135–137.

227. Polevoi, *Amerikanskie*, 179, 191–193.

228. Polevoi's intention to write his travelogue in "the spirit of Geneva": RGANI f. 5, op. 16, d. 734, l. 137. Il'f and Petrov's style: Aleksandr Etkind, *Tolkovanie puteshestvii: Rossiia i Amerika v travelogakh i intertekstakh* (Moscow: Novoe literaturnoe obozrenie, 2001), 162–163.

229. Il'f and Petrov as pioneers of the "ordinary people" perspective: Clark, *Moscow, the Fourth Rome*, 188. "Ordinary people" as a journalistic trope: Dina Fainberg, "Ordinary Russians and Average Americans: Cold War International Correspondents Describe 'Regular People' on the Other Side of the Iron Curtain," in *The Soviet Union and the United States. Rivals of the Twentieth Century: Coexistence and Competition*, ed. Eva-Maria Stolberg (Frankfurt am Main: Peter Lang, 2013), 115–138; Thomas Wolfe, *Governing Soviet Journalism: The Press and the Socialist Person after Stalin* (Bloomington: Indiana University Press, 2005), 48–65.

230. Polevoi, *Amerikanskie*, 109–110.

231. Ibid., 188, 317.

232. Ibid., 119–122.

233. Ibid., 223 (quotation), 225–227.

234. Ibid., 124, 278–282.

235. Ibid., 82 (quotation), 107 (quotation), 382.

236. Ibid., 181, 382.

237. Ibid., 205, 258–259, 359.

238. Originally published: Viktor Nekrasov, "Po obe storony okeana," *NM* 11 (1962): 112–148; 12 (1962): 110–152. Citations from: Viktor Nekrasov, "Po obe storony okeana," in *Sobranie sochinenii v trekh knigakh* 2 (Moscow: Izograf", 2005).

239. Nekrasov, "Po obe," 597.

240. Ibid., 569, 571.

241. Ibid., 583.

242. Ibid., 580, 582.

243. Polevoi, *Amerikanskie*, 5–7.

244. Ibid., 9–10.

245. Ibid., 80–82.

246. Ibid., 82, 123–124 (quotation: 124), 381, 385 (quotation).

247. Nekrasov, "Po obe," 628–631.

248. Ibid., 631–632.

249. Ibid., 631.

250. Maksim Gorky, *Gorod zheltogo d'iavola* (Moscow: Khudozhestvennaia literatura, 1972).

251. Polevoi, *Amerikanskie*, 61.

252. Ibid., 80 (quotations).

253. Nekrasov, "Po obe," 574; Gorky's metaphors: Fedorova, *Yankees in Petrograd*, 40–47, 87.

254. *V Amerike. Risunki i tekst Oresta Vereiskogo* (Moscow: Sovetskii khudozhnik, 1965), 21, 29, 62, 64.

255. Polevoi, *Amerikanskie*, 348–351 (quotation: 348).

256. Ibid., 61, 85.

257. Nekrasov, "Po obe," 614. For all of Nekrasov's claims to an account free of the influence of stereotypes, such statements echo Il'f and Petrov, who wrote about the uniformity of American cities.

258. Nekrasov, "Po obe," 573, 613.

259. Ibid., 613.

260. Ibid., 614–615.

261. Ibid., 612–613.

262. Ibid, 575–577.

263. "Turist s trostochkoi," *Izvestiia*, January 19, 1963.

264. RGANI f. 5, op. 36, d. 138, ll. 78–93.

265. *Apparat TsK KPSS i kul'tura, 1958–1964. Dokumenty* (Moscow: ROSSPEN, 2005), 637; "Travlia Nekrasova V. P. so storony vlastei razvorachivaetsia, 1963," in *Viktor Nekrasov v raznykh izmereniiakh*, http://www.famhist.ru/famhist /klasson/0040ef5e.htm; "Nekrasov V. P. na partsobranii Ukrainskogo Soiuza Pisatelei," in ibid., http://www.famhist.ru/famhist/klasson/0033b81b.htm; "Soveshchanie aktiva tvorcheskoi intelligentsii Ukrainy skloniaet V. P. Nekra-sova," in ibid., http://www.famhist.ru/famhist/klasson/003f1732.htm.

266. "Marksizm-leninizm—nashe znamia, nashe boevoe oruzhie," *Pravda*, June 29, 1963; Viktor Nekrasov, "Vzgliad i nechto," in *Zapiski zevaki* (Moscow: Vagrius, 2003), 247–249.

267. *Apparat TsK KPSS*, 784–785; "Nekrasov V. P. na partsobranii Ukrainskogo Soiuza Pisatelei," in *Viktor Nekrasov v raznykh izmereniiakh*, http://www .famhist.ru/famhist/klasson/0033b81b.htm.

268. "'Po obe storony okeana' Nekrasova V. P. ne ponravilis' N. S. Khrushchevu," in *Viktor Nekrasov v raznykh izmereniiakh*, http://www.famhist.ru/famhist/klasson /0000b2fo.htm.

269. RGALI f. 1702, op. 10, d. 72, ll. 35, 48.

270. Ibid., l. 77.

271. Ibid., l. 67. Nekrasov's exposé of such stereotypes: Nekrasov, "Po obe," 597–598.

272. RGALI f. 1702, op. 10, d. 72, ll. 61, 67, 77, 83.

273. Ibid., ll. 35, 42, 45–45ob, 70.

274. Ibid., l. 76.

275. Ibid., ll. 70–71.

276. Ibid., ll. 45ob, 70.

277. Ibid., ll. 22ob, 70–71 (quotation).

278. Ibid., l. 45; Nekrasov, "Po obe," 571–573.

279. Readers wrote to Ehrenburg about Nekrasov's travelogue: RGALI f. 1204, op. 2, d. 2644, ll. 166, 198–2000b.

280. Denis Kozlov, *The Readers of Novyi mir: Coming to Terms with the Stalinist Past* (Cambridge, MA: Harvard University Press, 2013), 187–201.

281. RGALI f. 1702, op. 10, d. 72, ll. 32–33ob.

282. Ibid., ll. 36, 39, 41 (quotation).

283. Ibid., l. 77.

284. Ibid., l. 49.

285. Melor Sturua, *Desiat' iz tridtsati: Zarubezhnye ocherki* (Tbilisi: Merani, 1978).

286. Ibid., 373–374.

287. Ibid., 381–386, 390, 394–397, 415–422.

288. Ibid., 381, 398.

289. Ibid., 425–426, 461–484 (quotation: 425).

290. Ibid., 510–590.

291. Ibid., 427–431.

292. Ibid., 434.

293. RGALI f. 1204, op. 2, d. 2617, ll. 113–117.

294. Ibid., d. 2610, ll. 18–22ob.

Epilogue

1. "Emigratsiia iz SSSR prekrashchena," *Strana i mir* 12 (1985): 25; "Ispytanie svobodoi," *Tribuna* 1 (March 1983): 14–19, here 15; "Skol'ko russkikh za rubezhom," *SD*, March 2, 1984.

2. "Istoriia rasskazchika," *SD*, October 5, 1984, 33–40.

3. Ibid., 39; Petr Vail' and Aleksandr Genis, "Tret'ia volna: Podvodia itogi. Zametki starozhilov," *SD*, July 6, 1984, 9–13, here 9; idem, "Russkii, evrei, amerikanets . . . /nuzhnoe podcherknut'/," *SD*, January 13, 1984, 37–38; Aleksandr Batchan, "Buridanov osel v 'Blumingsdeile,'" *SD*, January 6, 1984, 6–9, here 7; Aleksandr Lazarev, "Istsaidskaia istoriia," *SD*, January 20, 1984, 9–12.

4. O. Biriukov, "Zagublennaia iunost'," *Veche* 24 (1986): 55–67.

5. Natal'ia Sharymova, "Plavanie Fellini," *SD*, November 4, 1983, 38–40; Iu. Avgustinskii, "Velikii obzhora Fellini," *SD*, June 1, 1984, 37–38.

6. Vail' and Genis, "Tret'ia volna."

7. P. Vail' and A. Genis, forward to Dzh. D. Selindzher [J. D. Salinger], "I eti guby, i glaza zelenye . . . ," *SD*, July 6, 1984, 46–51, here 46.

8. "'Chrevo Parizha', Mikhaila Shemiakina," *Tret'ia volna* 2 (1977): 76–79.

9. Ksana Mechik, "Zimnie vpechatleniia ob uiutnoi strane," *SD*, February 24, 1984, 32–33.

10. Mechik, "Zimnie vpechatleniia," 32–33; Igor' Flore, "Amerika—u rodnika," *SD*, November 9, 1984, 32–36, here 32; "Beseda s Dmitriem Plavinskim," *Slovo* 33 (2002): 73–81, here 77.

11. Petr Vail' and Aleksandr Genis, "Dorogi, kotorye nas vybiraiut," *SD*, August 17, 1984, 12–19.

12. Ibid., *SD*, August 31, 1984, 16–21. English quotation: Alexandre Dumas, *The Three Musketeers* (New York: Peter Fenelon Collier, 1893), 14.

13. Petr Vail' and Aleksandr Genis, *Poteriannyi rai: Emigratsiia, popytka avtoportreta* (1983), https://www.litmir.me/br/?b=99601&p=1, here https://www.litmir.me/br/?b=99601&p=31.

14. Sergei Dovlatov, "From USA with Love," *SD*, July 20, 1984, 6–8; "Zametki redaktora," *Svobodnyi mir* 5 (1987): 3–10, here 4.

15. Alexei Yurchak, *Everything Was Forever, Until It Was No More: The Last Soviet Generation* (Princeton, NJ: Princeton University Press, 2006), 205–206.

16. Y. M. Lotman, "K postroeniiu teorii vzaimodeistviia kul'tur," in *Semiosfera* (St. Petersburg: Iskusstvo-SPb, 2000), 603–614, here 611.

17. B. Shneider, "Letnaia pogoda (vospominaniia)," *SD*, November 30, 1984, 12.

18. Mikhail Korol', "Iz tsikla 'molodye liudi,'" 22 72 (July–August 1990): 8–13, here 13.

19. Valerii Skorov, "Garbich," *SD*, December 23, 1983, 16.

20. Eduard Limonov, *Eto ia, Edichka* (Moscow: Nezavisimyi al'manakh "Konets veka," 1992). All quotations are from Edward Limonov, *It's Me, Eddie: A Fictional Memoir* (New York: Grove Press, 1983), 42.

21. Limonov, *It's Me, Eddie*, 1, 6–9, 11–13, 18–19.

22. Dmitrii Savitskii, *Niotkuda s liubov'iu*, http://modernlib.net/books/savickiy_dmitriy/niotkuda_s_lyubovyu/read/.

23. Savitskii, *Niotkuda s liubov'iu*.

24. Savitskii, *Niotkuda s liubov'iu*.

25. Savitskii, *Niotkuda s liubov'iu*.

26. Aleksandr Batchan, "Pesn' o Braitone," *SD*, February 10, 1984, 24–25.

27. Petr Vail' and Aleksandr Genis, "Roundtrip: Istoriia Neschastii, Vozvysheniia i Okonchatel'nogo Padeniia Grishi Rabinovicha, Cheloveka s Braiton-Bich," *SD*, November 25, 1983, 45–48; Petr Vail' and Aleksandr Genis, "Roundtrip. Kinopovest'," *SD*, December 2, 1983, 25–28.

28. Savitskii, *Niotkuda s liubov'iu*.

29. Petr Vail' and Aleksandr Genis, "Tret'ia volna," *SD*, July 13, 1984, 10–15, here 15.

30. S. Zapol'skaia, "Prazdnik, kotoryi vsegda s toboi: Seks i supruzhestvo," *SD*, May 4, 1984, 36–38, here 37; Petr Vail' and Aleksandr Genis, "Tret'ia volna: Podvodia itogi. Zametki starozhilov," *SD*, June 29, 1984, 7–11.

31. "Muzhchiny o zhenshchinakh," *SD*, March 23, 1984, 30–33, here 32–33.

32. Vail' and Genis, "Roundtrip."

33. Limonov, *It's Me, Eddie*, 5, 11.

34. Ibid., 5–6, 27.

35. Ibid., 25, 260.

36. Ibid., 5, 19–20.

37. Zapol'skaia, "Prazdnik, kotoryi vsegda s toboi," 37; "Fenomen striptiza: Ot Afrodity do Sofi Loren," *SD*, June 29, 1984; Petr Vail' and Aleksandr Genis, "Detiam do 16: Reportazh s 42-I," *SD*, March 16, 1984, 32–36; L. Arkadin, "Puteshestvie v mir seksa," *SD*, November 18, 1983, 19–20, and November 25, 1983, 50–53.

38. Zapol'skaia, "Prazdnik, kotoryi vsegda s toboi," 37.

39. Arkadin, "Puteshestvie," 20.

40. "Proshchaias' s ezhemesiachnikom 'Strelets,'" *Strelets* 61:1 (1989): 218–232.

41. Mariia Shneerson, "2×2=22," *SD*, January 20, 1984, 42–45.

42. Tat'iana Menaker, "Grekh razvedchika—Dmitrii Bykov o russkoi emigratsii," September 28, 2016, http://kstati.net/greh-razvedchika-dmitrij-bykov-o-russkoj-emigratsii.

43. "Zametki redaktora," *Svobodnyi mir* 12 (1991): 3–8.

44. E. Korman, "Odin iz nas," *SD*, December 16, 1983, 6–7.

45. Editorial, "Pobeditelei ne sudiat," *SD*, February 3, 1984, 4–5.

46. Aleksandr Batchan and Natal'ia Sharymova, "'Mosfil'm' na Gudzone," *SD*, April 20, 1984, 24–29; Lazarev, "Istsaidskaia istoriia," 9; Petr Vail' and Aleksandr Genis, "Tret'ia volna," *SD*, July 6, 1984, 9–13.

47. Igor' Flore, "Ser'eznoe poniatie—status," *SD*, March 9, 1984, 26–29, here 26; A. D., "Gospodi, russkie davno uzhe zdes' . . . ," *SD*, August 17, 1984, 6–7.

48. Ksana Mechik, "Zhenskii vopros," *SD*, January 13, 1984, 13–15; Petr Vail' and Aleksandr Genis, "Arkhipelag Gudlak," *SD*, June 8, 1984, 6–12.

49. Petr Vail' and Alekandr Genis, "Vid na zhitel'stvo," *SD*, April 27, 1984, 7–13, here 7; Savitskii, *Niotkuda s liubov'iu*.

50. The controversy around the film had an afterlife: the film was shown in the Soviet Union, with a companion piece, a Soviet anti-emigration documentary, profiling interviews with immigrants who had applied to return to the Soviet Union.

51. Aleksandr Batchan, "Kto boitsia Ofru Bikel'?" *SD*, November 4, 1983, 3–11, here 4.

52. Ibid., 9.

53. Petr Vail' and Aleksandr Genis, "Tret'ia volna," *SD*, June 22, 1984, 7–10.

54. A. D., "Gospodi," 7.

55. Svetlana Aleksievich, *Vremia sekond khend*, https://e-libra.ru/read/368093
-vremya-sekond-hend.html.

56. Olga Shevchenko, *Crisis and Everyday Life in Postsocialist Moscow* (Bloom-
ington: Indiana University Press, 2009); Michelle Parsons, *Dying Unneeded:
The Cultural Context of the Russian Mortality Crisis* (Nashville: Vanderbilt
University Press, 2014), 79–88, 98–116, passim; Serguei Oushakine, *The
Patriotism of Despair: Nation, War, and Loss in Russia* (Ithaca, NY: Cornell
University Press, 2009); Tova Höjdestrand, *Needed by Nobody: Homelessness
and Humanness in Post-Socialist Russia* (Ithaca, NY: Cornell University
Press, 2000), 3–4; Nancy Ries, *Russian Talk: Culture & Conversation during
Perestroika* (Ithaca, NY: Cornell University Press, 1997), 15–19, 42–62,
97–102.

57. Aleksievich, *Vremia sekond khend*.

58. Parsons, *Dying Unneeded*, 101–123; Oushakine, *The Patriotism of Despair*,
24–26, 34–35; Ries, *Russian Talk*, 174–176; Roy Medvedev, *Post-Soviet Russia: A
Journey through the Yeltsin Era* (New York: Columbia University Press, 2000),
14–45, 67–76, 136–153.

59. Medvedev, *Post-Soviet Russia*, 270; Aleksievich, *Vremia sekond khend*; Aleksandr Ilichevskii, *Matiss: Roman* (Moscow: Vremia, 2008), 330.

60. Höjdestrand, *Needed by Nobody*, 32–38, 112–122; Caroline Humphrey, *The
Unmaking of Soviet Life: Everyday Economies after Socialism* (Ithaca, NY:
Cornell University Press, 2002), 20–39.

61. Höjdestrand, *Needed by Nobody*, 40–42, 47–48, 57–60, 64–65, 75, 77–79,
84–94, 166–181 (quotation: 4).

62. Ilichevskii, *Matiss*, 12, 103, 123, 161–162, 188, 210, 223–224, 250, 299–300,
308–309, 322–323, 337–338.

63. Parsons, *Dying Unneeded*, 2–5, 9–13, 86–90, 98–100, 121–159.

64. Eliot Borenstein, *Overkill: Sex and Violence in Contemporary Russian Popular
Culture* (Ithaca, NY: Cornell University Press, 2008).

65. Medvedev, *Post-Soviet Russia*, 170–200, esp. 187–188; Parsons, *Dying Unneeded*, 91–93; Humphrey, *The Unmaking of Soviet Life*, 58–62, 175–201.

66. Oushakine, *The Patriotism of Despair*, 15–20; Höjdestrand, *Needed by Nobody*,
80, 109–111; Stephen Bittner, *The Many Lives of Khrushchev's Thaw: Experience and Memory in Moscow's Arbat* (Ithaca, NY: Cornell University Press,
2008), 27–28.

67. Michael Gorham, *After Newspeak: Language Culture and Politics in Russia
from Gorbachev to Putin* (Ithaca, NY: Cornell University Press, 2014), 88–93;
Sheila Fitzpatrick, *Tear Off the Masks! Identity and Imposture in Twentieth-
Century Russia* (Princeton, NJ: Princeton University Press, 2005), 304–307.

68. Humphrey, *The Unmaking of Soviet Life*, 45, 55.

69. Gorham, *After Newspeak*, 93–102, 107, 110, 116–130; Fitzpatrick, *Tear Off the Masks!*, 313.

70. Gorham, *After Newspeak*, 75–87, 110–112, 134–138.

71. Borenstein, *Overkill: Sex and Violence*, 11–75; Fitzpatrick, *Tear Off the Masks!*, 310–312.

72. Ilichevskii, *Matiss*, 104.

73. David Bellos, *Is That a Fish in Your Ear: Translation and the Meaning of Everything* (New York: Faber and Faber, 2011), 202–205.

74. Interview with Viktoriia Chaeva, Moscow, August 7, 2004; Viktor Golyshev and Aleksandr Livergant in "50-letie zhurnala *Inostrannaia literatura*," Radio Svoboda, October 14, 2005, http://trauberg.com/chats/50-letie-zhurnala -inostrannaya-literatura/; "Perevodchik Viktor Golyshev: K 70-letiiu so dnia rozhdeniia," Radio Svoboda, April 23, 2007, http://www.svoboda.org/a/389271 .html; Aleksandr Livergant, "Inkognito prokliatoe, ili Delo nashe veseloe," *IL* 5 (2012), http://magazines.russ.ru/inostran/2012/5/l9.html.

75. Aleksandr Liusyi, *Nashestvie kachestv: Rossiia kak avtoperevod* (Moscow: Tovarishchestvo nauchnykh izdanii KMK, 2008), 14.

76. Judith Butler and Athena Athanasiou, *Dispossession: The Performative in the Political* (Cambridge: Polity Press, 2013), 2–4, 10–11, 24–27, 31–32, 36; Dawn Chatty, *Displacement and Dispossession in the Modern Middle East* (New York: Cambridge University Press, 2010). In post-Soviet context: Humphrey, *The Unmaking of Soviet Life*, 21–39; Joma Nazpary, *Post-Soviet Chaos: Violence and Dispossession in Kazakhstan* (London: Pluto Press, 2002).

77. Grigorii Zaslavskii, "Staromodnaia tragediia," *Nezavisimaia gazeta*, October 5, 1999, http://www.ng.ru/culture/1999-10-05/tragedy.html; Alena Zlobina, "Pochem nynche muzhskaia druzhba?" *Znamia* 1 (2000), http://magazines.russ .ru/znamia/2000/1/zlobina.html; Marina Raikina, "Rostok na pomoike," *Moskovskii komsomolets*, October 2, 1999; Larisa Iusipova, "Tovarishchi grazhdane," *Vedomosti*, October 5, 1999; Marina Davydova, "Stolp i utverzh- denie shestidesiatnichestva," *Vremia MN*, October 4, 1999; Elena D'iakova, "Pro to, chto ne prodaetsia," *Novaia gazeta*, http://www.smotr.ru/pressa/rec /sovr.htm#%D0%9D%D0%BE%D0%B2%D0%B0%D1%8F; "Erikh Mariia Remark. Tri tovarishcha. Kratkie otzyvy pressy na spektakl'," http://old .sovremennik.ru/play/abouteac4.html?article=3&id=12.

Acknowledgments

This book began as an undergraduate paper at the University of Chicago; there can be no better place for finishing it.

My engagement with the discipline of history has its origins in the department I now call home. In my sophomore year, I met Sheila Fitzpatrick, and, for better or for worse, she made me want to be a historian. Our conversations and her books taught me how to be one. Her readings of my chapters were most astute, her questions most challenging, and her ability to retain a sense of surprise provided matchless lessons for me.

I am deeply grateful to my Chicago colleagues for the generous spirit with which they welcomed me to the Department of History. My department chairs, Bruce Cumings, Kenneth Pomeranz, and Emilio Kourí, offered meticulous and discerning advice and created opportunities for me at every step of the way. Leora Auslander, Ken Pomeranz, and Jonathan Hall have mentored me with wisdom and empathy. A special thank you to Tara Zahra for engaging with my work and for cheering me toward its completion. For candid counsel about writing, teaching, publishing, and U of C life, my heartfelt thanks to Fredrik Albritton Jonsson, Robert Bird, Mark Bradley, Paul Cheney, Michael Geyer, Faith Hillis, Jonathan Levy, William Nickell, Emily Osborn, Ada Palmer, Michael Rossi, James Sparrow, and Amy Dru Stanley.

While I started and finished this book at Chicago, it is also very much a Berkeley project. It emerged from my dissertation written at the University of California at Berkeley and was inspired by my teachers there. Classes with Thomas Laqueur and Randolph Starn presented model cultural histories and spurred me to write one of my own. Margaret Lavinia Anderson brought a Europeanist's perspective to my topic and gave unwavering moral and intellectual support, which I could not have done without. Olga Matich opened up the world of Soviet bohemia and Soviet literature for me and led me to think about connections between Western imports and late Soviet emigration. Several cohorts of Berkeley peers read my work at our Russian history *kruzhok* and responded with trenchant questions that forced me to think harder and rewrite.

Yuri Slezkine oversaw the conceptual design of this work, guided my exploration of evidence and arguments, and tirelessly read each chapter again and again. In the worst of times, he was a dependable confidant, helping me to untangle situations that seemed desperate. In the best of times, he was there to celebrate every discovery. From our first meeting until the present day, he has remained my most inspiring interlocutor. For all he has done for me words cannot do justice—but then again, he understands half-words.

Two dear teachers did not live to see this book. Richard Hellie's stoicism, hard-to-earn praise, and touching care left a deep mark on my personal and professional outlook. Of Reggie Zelnik, I can only repeat what countless students and colleagues have said about him. His ethical stance, dedication to students, and personal warmth were inimitable exemplars for me. I know this book would have been much better had it had the benefit of Richard's and Reggie's insights. I miss you both and wish you were here.

Over the years, my research and writing were sustained by the goodwill and encouragement of colleagues. Laurent Coumel, Mark Edele, Marc Elie, Olga Gerasimova, Rosa Magnusdottir, Mie Nakachi, Nordica Nettleton, and Larisa Zakharova shared ideas and pastimes in Moscow. I spent two productive years in Toronto, largely because Lynne Viola took me into her circle of students and looked out for me in numerous ways. Thomas Lahusen's analysis of Soviet reading practices was an early inspiration, and, many years later, his comments on a penultimate draft of chapter 4 pushed me to tighten the text, while introducing new literature. Conversations with Stephen Bittner, Christine Evans, Victoria Smolkin, and Amir Weiner enriched my thinking. In the last stages of this project, David Shneer and Jan Plamper gave invaluable advice. Peter Bagrov, an unsurpassed reservoir of knowledge about Soviet and world cinema, helped in countless ways on every occasion. My home department provided resources to organize a book manuscript workshop. I appreciate the feedback I received at the workshop from Leora Auslander, Faith Hillis, Jan Goldstein, Adam Green, James Ketelaar, Bill Nickell, Ethan Pollock, and Tara Zahra. The anonymous readers chosen by the press offered critique and reassurance in equal measure. A special thank you to one of the readers for suggestions about the ending. In the last trying months, Michael Coates was an exceptionally gifted research assistant.

Among the archivists, I am especially grateful to Galina Mikhailovna Tokareva of the Komsomol archive, without whose open-mindedness chapter 2 would have looked very different; to Natal'ia Georgievna Tomilina of the Russian State Archive of Contemporary History, who approved endless requests for photocopies; and to Natal'ia Borisovna Volkova and Tat'iana Mikhailovna Goriaeva, successive directors of the Russian State Archive for Literature and the Arts. Elena Evgen'evna Chugunova, head of the reading room at RGALI, assured that every day of my time there went smoothly. Boris Yakovlevich Frezinskii gave permission to work with Ilya Ehrenburg's personal collection. This book, and my understanding of Soviet culture, would have been much poorer without those materials.

Securing permissions for illustrations is always a tedious, even distressing, process, but I nonetheless found it rewarding, because it introduced me to some extraordinary people. Feliks Aronovich Bukh accompanied me to the Moscow Artists' Union. Aleksei Alekseevich Savinov, curator of personal collections at the Pushkin Museum, moved mountains for me. Anna Orestovna Khmeleva and Ivan Semenovich Chuikov responded to my requests with graciousness. A miserable evening schlep through Moscow's snow mounds brought me to the loveliest, funniest, and most irreverent people in the world, Liubov' Fedorovna Reshetnikova and Grigorii Grigor'evich Tsikunov.

I thank the Moscow city archive, TASS, RIA-Novosti, the Russian Authors' Society, Gosfil'mofond, and the Tretyakov Gallery for assisting in my hunt for permissions. Every effort has been made to identify copyright holders and obtain permission for the use of copyrighted material. Notification of any additions or corrections that should be incorporated in future reprints or editions of this book would be greatly appreciated. Chapters 1 and 2 expand on the concepts presented in "The Revival of Soviet Internationalism in the Mid to Late 1950s," published in *The Thaw: Soviet Society and Culture during the 1950s and 1960s*, edited by Denis Kozlov and Eleonory Gilburd (Toronto: University of Toronto Press, 2013). Chapter 5 builds on ideas published as "Picasso in Thaw Culture," *Cahiers du monde russe*, vol. 47, n. 1-2 (2006). I am grateful to the *Cahiers* and the University of Toronto Press for giving me a chance to introduce this research.

I appreciate Joyce Seltzer's interest in this project and Deborah Grahame-Smith's composure, kindness, and patience as she oversaw this book's production.

The many organizations that supported my work over the years gave me peace of mind and a vote of confidence—in addition to much-appreciated funding. Thanks to the Fulbright-Hays Program of the Department of Education for awarding me a dissertation fellowship. An International Dissertation Research Fellowship from the Social Science Research Council allowed me to stay in Russia for another year. Fellowships from the American Councils for International Education's Title VIII program, the University of California's Institute for Global Conflict and Cooperation, Western Association of Women Historians, and the Berkeley Program in Soviet and Post-Soviet Studies made possible several summers of additional archival research. A Short-Term Research Grant from the Kennan Institute brought me to archival repositories in the District of Columbia area. The years of reading and writing were made financially feasible by fellowships from UC Berkeley's Graduate Division, the Phi Beta Kappa, the University of California's Institute for Global Conflict and Cooperation, Berkeley's Institute of International Studies, the Mabelle McLeod Lewis Memorial Fund, and the Social Science Research Council. Fellowships from the National Endowment for the Humanities and the National Council for Eurasian and East European Research were crucial in bringing this project to completion. My first trip to the Russian archives was funded by the University of Chicago's International Traveling Research Fellowship for undergraduates. In the final stretch, the University of Chicago's Division of Social Sciences and the Department of History helped to pay for permissions, illustrations, and indexing.

For emotional, intellectual, and editorial support, my gratitude to my friends is boundless. Svetlana Orekhova in New York and Anna Taranenko in Chicago took my mind off work. Maya Raber made me believe in miracles: she wields a magic wand. Our college-dorm conversations with Ann Livschiz in no small measure set us both on this path. Charles Hachten appeared and reappeared in my life to offer that proverbial shoulder at just the right time. Johanna Ransmeier set an example of perseverance and refused to entertain my insecurities. Elizabeth McGuire stood behind me through it all, always with the keenest of insights into the nature of texts, people, and situations. She prodded me in times of doubt, rejoiced with me in successes, taught me much about writing, and put her own schedule on hold to edit several chapters. Tamara Chapman read the text many times, shared with me her incisive vision and gift for language in smoothing my prose, and responded to my incessant questions with uncommon grace and compassion.

Julia and Andy checked in every day, waited patiently, modeled positivity, and loved unconditionally. My grandparents kept faith in this project until the very end.

For lighting up my world, I owe immeasurable gratitude:

To Denis, who has lived with these pages for years, set an impossibly exacting standard with his own work, listened to every argument here, read drafts while I slept, and, when the muses slept, pulled up a chair to sit next to me. His reading of the entire manuscript resulted in dramatic revisions and is responsible for its present shape.

To my parents, who crossed with me the first and most decisive border in my life and later allowed me to return, suggested the Thaw as a subject of exploration, flew great distances on short notice for me, stayed up with me through the nights, took me back as if I had never left, and have cared for us beyond any measure.

And to Anthony, my favorite officemate and guardian angel.

Index

Note: Pages in *italics* refer to illustrative matter.